Business Emergence and Growth

Custom Publication

Business Emergence and Growth: From opportunity recognition to global competition

Custom Publication

University of Newcastle

palgrave
macmillan

First published 2011 by
PALGRAVE MACMILLAN

Entrepreneurship and Small Business © Paul Burns 2001, 2007, 2011
Entrepreneurship © David Rae 2007
Understanding Enterprise © Simon Bridge, Ken O'Neill and Frank Martin 1998, 2003, 2009
Corporate Entrepreneurship © Paul Burns 2005, 2008
Business Strategy © David Campbell, David Edgar and George Stonehouse 2011
Social Enterprise © Frank Martin and Marcus Thompson 2010

Palgrave Macmillan in the UK is an imprint of Macmillan Publishers Limited, registered in England, company number 785998, of Houndmills, Basingstoke, Hampshire RG21 6XS.

Palgrave Macmillan in the US is a division of St Martin's Press LLC, 175 Fifth Avenue, New York, NY 10010.

Palgrave Macmillan is the global academic imprint of the above companies and has companies and representatives throughout the world.

Palgrave® and Macmillan® are registered trademarks in the United States, the United Kingdom, Europe and other countries

ISBN 978–0–230–35883–6

This book is printed on paper suitable for recycling and made from fully managed and sustained forest sources. Logging, pulping and manufacturing processes are expected to conform to the environmental regulations of the country of origin.

A catalogue record for this book is available from the British Library.

A catalog record for this book is available from the Library of Congress.

10 9 8 7 6 5 4 3 2 1
20 19 18 17 16 15 14 13 12 11

Printed and bound in Great Britain by
CPI Antony Rowe, Chippenham and Eastbourne

To my Mentor Dr. James C. Hayton
The David Goldman Professor of Innovation and Enterprise
&
To my students at the Newcastle University Business School

Contents

List of Figures

[handwritten margin note: page 222 on Internet, good for exam question.]

Photos

List of Tables

Preface

Business, as part and parcel of the economic institution of human society, is undoubtedly as old as society itself. From the primeval business exchange of a barter economy in a local setting to the contemporary digitalized transactions of goods, services and money on a global scale individuals and groups have dramatized specific roles and exhibited special skills in creating and expanding various business activities.

Successful business owners and entrepreneurs from antiquity to the 20th century were considered to be gifted personalities with inborn psychological characteristics such as risk taking behavior, talent and capacity for identifying opportunities and profits where others failed to see them, courage to venture in uncertain environments, self-fulfillment and self-actualization from their endeavors.

Social and behavioral sciences research efforts during the second half of the 20th century established the fact that the propensity and ability for management and business venturing is not the exclusive domain of a small fraction of humanity but that each and every individual, without limitations of gender, ethnicity, race or creed could potentially possess the basic ingredients necessary to become a successful manager, business owner and/or entrepreneur. What of course is needed is to provide such aspiring individuals with the necessary knowledge, skills and competencies through appropriate learning, which combines theoretical education and apprenticeship in practical exercises.

Research by Handy et al[1] (1988) on UK's businesses and business education suggested that part of the decline on UK's economic performance in the 1980s could be attributed to the way managers are educated. Although the general principles of management offered in any traditional business and management degree program are essential for any business related career and can be applied to any organization and of any size there are fundamental differences between principles and practices that are applied to new business/entrepreneurial start-ups and to established large enterprises. In response to this, in the last two decades we have witnessed, in addition to classical management and business administration courses a proliferation of specially designed courses dealing with the various aspects of enterprise and entrepreneurship in almost each and every business school existing not only in UK but worldwide.

Business schools shifted their focus from a narrow, too specialized, too quantitative and theoretical educational model towards educating students to the day-to-day realities of the business world and the real links between theory and practice.

---

1 Handy, C.B., Gordon, C., Gow, I. and Randlesome, C. 1988. *The Making of Managers*. Oxford: Pitman.

Business schools awaken the thought processes so as to encourage and stimulate the entrepreneurial imagination. The nature of the business schools' curricula changed with the introduction of new approaches and methodologies focusing on small businesses, entrepreneurship, creativity and innovation.

These new foci of educational activities, as one could have logically expected, created a parallel growth in the publishing business of university/college textbooks. In addition, and in order to satisfy the lay public's quest for "do it yourself" guides for aspiring business owners and entrepreneurs, national and international publishers brought forth a significant volume of relevant 'popular' books laying on the periphery of the demands of scientific writing.

Scanning, even with a quick glimpse, the bibliography pertaining to published books on various business and entrepreneurship subjects will verify that there exists a plethora of textbooks that can be useful for the business student in a university setting. Examining such established texts currently circulating in advanced editions as well as newer appearances in the market the careful reader will easily diagnose the strengths and limitations of each individual book written by one or co-authored by more than one expert in the various special fields under the general subject matter of business education.

Searching for an appropriate textbook to be used as the essential reference for a pioneering one year long module entitled *Business Emergence and Growth* which is taught to the undergraduate students of the Newcastle University Business School in the UK I came to the realization that a textbook which could satisfy my students needs simply does not exist.

The module *Business Emergence and Growth* explores the concepts of entrepreneurs and owner-managers, opportunity recognition and exploration, creativity and business ideas, types of organizations (start ups, spin-offs, small and medium enterprises, large enterprises, multinational enterprises and social enterprises), personality, gender and ethnicity in entrepreneurship/management, business growth strategies, competitive advantages, corporate entrepreneurship, internationalization and the web. The course will inform students and provide them with an opportunity to develop an understanding and a critical awareness of current theories and approaches relevant to recognizing a business opportunity, establishing a new business, being creative, growing the business, innovating and competing globally. The course is designed to introduce students, through lectures, case studies and small group learning activities, to the different kinds of businesses and entrepreneurship and equip them with the knowledge and skills necessary for the next stages of their management and entrepreneurial education.

Examining a variety of published texts I came to the conclusion that if I could selectively choose and bring together in one volume specific chapters from various texts creating in essence an "anthology" I could have the first edition of a textbook that could be useful to my students and, understandably, to students in other business schools in other institutions of higher learning in the UK and elsewhere.

I shared my thoughts and explained my aims to Martin Drewe (Publisher Editor – Business & Finance) and Rebecca Levene (North of England representative) of the Palgrave Macmillan publishing company and I was pleasantly surprised to find that they not only understood my concerns and my aims but they encouraged me to proceed with the creation of this edited book to which I gave the title: "Business Emergence and Growth: from opportunity recognition to global competition"

The book

This edited book, as stated earlier, came into existence as a result of my concern in providing my undergraduate students with a rich and yet concise textbook bringing together state-of-the-art theoretical and practical business and entrepreneurial knowledge. However, given the breath and depth of the contents of the 15 chapters that comprise it, I feel that it could also serve as a useful contemporary textbook for postgraduate students in business related courses of study. I furthermore believe that business practitioners as well as members of the lay public interested in acquiring further current knowledge on the various aspects of business emergence, sustenance and growth could find this edited book useful especially in view of the fact that it is a selected compilation of material appearing in several best-selling textbooks published by Palgrave Macmillan publishing company.

The Editor

Dr. Panos G. Piperopoulos joined Newcastle University Business School in September 2010 as a Lecturer in Enterprise and Creativity. Formerly he was a Lecturer in Management, Entrepreneurship and Innovation in the Department of Marketing and Operations Management of the University of Macedonia in Greece. He also taught in the Department of Business Administration of the Hellenic Open University. Prior to entering academia Dr. Piperopoulos was a Business Consultant and a mentor to several successful start-up companies. He has contributed on a regular basis to Greece's leading financial newspapers and blogs and was a frequent guest on radio and television programs. He is a member of the British Academy of Management, of the Institute of Small Business and Entrepreneurship, of the Hellenic Economic Chamber of Commerce and holds a professional license as a business consultant.

Acknowledgements

This custom publication for the University of Newcastle draws on chapters from the following books:

Burns, (2011) *Entrepreneurship and Small Business 3rd Edition*, Basingstoke: Palgrave Macmillan

Burns (2008) *Corporate Entrepreneurship 2nd Edition*, Basingstoke: Palgrave Macmillan

Bridge, Martin and O'Neill (2009) *Understanding Enterprise 3rd Edition*, Basingstoke: Palgrave Macmillan

Campbell, Edgar and Stonehouse (2011) *Business Strategy 3rd Edition*, Basingstoke: Palgrave Macmillan

Martin and Thompson (2010) *Social Enterprise*, Basingstoke: Palgrave Macmillan

Rae (2007) *Entrepreneurship*, Basingstoke: Palgrave Macmillan

Every effort has been made to trace all copyright holders, but if any have been inadvertently overlooked the publishers will be pleased to make the necessary arrangements at the first opportunity.

CHAPTER 1
Entrepreneurs and owner-managers

CONTENTS

- Start-up influences
- Personal character traits
- Character traits of owner-managers
- Character traits of entrepreneurs
- Antecedent influences
- Ethnicity and immigration
- Gender
- Growth businesses
- National culture
- Situational factors
- Summary

CASE INSIGHTS

- Steve Hulme
- Simon Woodroffe and YO! Sushi
- Market traders
- Kenyan Asians
- Elizabeth Gooch and EG Solutions
- Will King and King of Shaves

CASES WITH QUESTIONS

- Duncan Bannatyne, Dragon
- Hilary Andrews and Mankind

LEARNING OUTCOMES

By the end of this chapter you should be able to:
- Explain the factors that influence the start-up decision;
- Describe the character traits of owner-managers;
- Describe the character traits of entrepreneurs;
- Explain the methodological problems associated with trying to measure character traits and the linkages with growth businesses;
- Describe the antecedent influences that are likely to influence owner-managers and entrepreneurs;
- Recognise the importance of national culture in influencing entrepreneurship;
- Explain what constitutes an entrepreneurial culture and how it might be measured;
- Recognise the importance of female and ethnic minority entrepreneurs;
- Explain the situational factors influencing start-ups and how blocks to start-up might be overcome.

Start-up influences

Why does anybody want to take the risk of starting up their own business? It is hard work without guaranteed results. But millions do so every year around the world. The start-up is the bedrock of modern-day commercial wealth, the foundation of free-market economics upon which competition is based. So can economists shed light on the process?

Economists would tell us that new entrants into an industry can be expected when there is a rise in expected post-entry profitability for them. In other words, new entrants expect to make extra profits. Economists tell us that the rate of entry is related to the growth of that industry. They also tell us that entry is deterred by barriers such as high capital requirements, the existence of economies of scale, product differentiation, restricted access to necessary inputs and so on. What is more, the rate of entry is lower in industries with high degrees of concentration where it may be assumed that firms combine to deter entry. However, research also tells us that, whereas the rate of small firm start-up in these concentrated industries is lower, the rate of start-up for large firms is higher (Acs and Audretsch, 1989).

These seem useful, but perhaps obvious, statements about start-ups. But do they really explain what happens and why? Somehow economists fail to explain convincingly the rationale for, and the process of, start-up. They seem to assume that there is a continuous flow of entrants into an industry just waiting for the possibility of extra profits. But people are not like that. They need to earn money to live; they have families who depend on them. Leaving a secure job to start up a business, for example, needs more of a rationale than just 'extra profits'. Certainly the personal characteristics of owner-managers and entrepreneurs and their antecedents – their history and the environment they grow up in – are factors that economists are both unfamiliar and uncomfortable with. Economists are not really interested in individuals who are likely to set up their own firms, or their personal motivations for doing so. Economists are just interested in explaining how many might consider doing so and into which sectors they might be expected to go. What is more, economists are generally not altogether happy with the idea that the number of start-ups can be influenced by non-economic factors like personal situation, character traits and the antecedent influences on it like family and national culture; but most people believe they are.

Many people talk about business ideas but don't get on and do them. Starting up a business is like taking part in an amateur boxing match. You don't know how good either guy is – but unless you get in there and have a go, you never will.

Gary Redman, founder of Now Recruitment
Sunday Times 8 August 2004

Figure 1.1 shows all these start-up influences. The model proposes that owner-managers and entrepreneurs are in fact both born and made. We are all born with certain personal character traits. Research indicates that owner-managers have a certain identifiable set and entrepreneurs – who want to set up growth firms – have a somewhat different set. Entrepreneurs share the character traits of owner-managers but they have certain additional, almost magical, qualities that the average owner-manager does not possess. However, these character traits are also shaped by

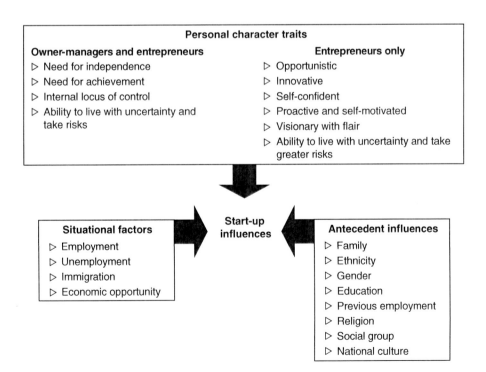

Figure 1.1 Start-up influences

Case insight   Steve Hulme

Steve Hulme retired from teaching on health grounds in 1997. For two-and-a-half years he and his wife got by on his pension and her salary. However, he became restless and decided to become self-employed. He had previously written a textbook for teenagers about problem-solving and lateral thinking, and based on this experience, he wanted to run courses for the young unemployed to introduce them to the kind of 'joined up' thinking skills he believed industry wanted. Aged 52, he set up his training business with the help of the Prince's Initiative for Mature Enterprise (Prime). Prime was set up in 1999 to provide advice, support and loans for over-45s who are jobless.

antecedent influences – your history and experience of life and the environment they grow up in. This includes their family, ethnic origins, gender, education, previous employment, religion and social group. The national culture of the country that they grow up in also seems to be an important influence. The GEM studies show that entrepreneurial activity varies significantly from country to country. Finally there are situational factors that influence the decision to start up your own business. As well as the positive economic influences – the opportunities that may attract, or 'pull', people into self-employment – there may also be the negative ones such as unemployment or immigration that 'push' them into it.

All these factors influence the decisions on whether to start up a business and whether to grow it. If all the factors are favourable the volume of start-ups should increase, as should the number of businesses that grow. Indeed, both antecedent influences and the dominant culture of the society will almost certainly influence the personal character traits of individuals as they develop over time and vice versa – over time entrepreneurial characters will start to shape society and influence those they come in contact with. These three factors are inter-related.

Therefore, if owner-managers are the heroes of this book, then entrepreneurs must be the super-heroes. Were it not for those who have a vested interest in identifying our super-heroes at an early stage in their business development, it is unlikely that economists, sociologists and psychologists would have paid this area so much attention. Because of this it remains an area of heated academic debate and constant development, not least over the question as to whether entrepreneurs are born rather than made.

Personal character traits

The issue of linking the character traits of an individual to the success of a business – picking winners – needs to be approached with caution. Even if it is possible to identify the personal characteristics of owner-managers and entrepreneurs, it is not always possible to link them directly with a particular sort of business. So far we have considered three types of managers and implicitly linked them to three types of small firm:

	Type of manager	Type of business
1.	Owner-manager	Lifestyle firm. Often trade- or craft-based. Will not grow to any size.
2.	Entrepreneur	Growth firm. Pursuit of growth and personal wealth important.
3.	Manager	Manages a business belonging to someone else. Will build an organisation by putting in appropriate controls, similar to a large firm. May be entrepreneurial.

These were broad generalisations. The linkages are not that simple or direct all of the time. For example, an entrepreneur might manage a business belonging to someone else, at least for a time. Similarly, an owner-manager may find himself with a growth business, either by accident or design. Success or failure in business, as we shall see later, comes from a mix of many different things. The character traits of the manager are just one factor in the equation. What is more, it takes time for entrepreneurs to prove that the business they manage is in fact a growth business. So do you measure aspirations or reality?

A further difficulty is that much of the research often fails to distinguish between owner-managers and entrepreneurs, assuming anyone who starts their own business is an entrepreneur. However, research into the character traits of owner-managers of growth businesses, who should mainly be entrepreneurs, does allow us to come to some broad conclusions and to paint a picture of the different characters of owner-managers compared to entrepreneurs.

There are also a number of methodological problems associated with attempting to measure personality characteristics (Deakins, 1996):

- They are not stable and change over time.
- They require subjective judgements.
- Measures tend to ignore cultural and environmental influences.
- The role of education, learning, and training is often overlooked.
- Issues such as age, sex, race, social class and education can be ignored.

The last three issues we shall address in looking at the antecedent influences on entrepreneurship, but they go to the heart of the question of whether entrepreneurs are born or made. The area, therefore, is an academic minefield. Notwithstanding this, many researchers do believe that, collectively, owner-managers have certain typical character traits, although the mix and emphasis of these characteristics will inevitably be different for each individual. Whether a clearly definable set of entrepreneurial characteristics exists is more controversial. Furthermore, many so-called 'entrepreneurial' character traits are similar to those found in other successful people such as politicians or athletes (Chell et al., 1991). Perhaps, the argument goes, it just happens that the individual has chosen an entrepreneurial activity as a means of self-satisfaction. Certainly, even if you believe the character traits can be identified,

Owner-managers	Entrepreneurs
Need for independence	Opportunistic
Need for achievement	Innovative
Internal locus of control	Self-confident
Ability to live with uncertainty	Proactive and self-motivated
and take measured risks	Visionary with flair
	Willing to take greater risks and live
	with even greater uncertainty

Figure 1.2 Character traits of owner-managers and entrepreneurs

Sources: Aldrich and Martinez, 2003; Andersson et al., 2004; Baty, 1990; Bell et al., 1992; Blanchflower and Meyer, 1991; Brockhaus and Horwitz, 1986; Brush, 1992; Buttner and More, 1997; Caird, 1990; Chell et al., 1991; Cuba et al., 1983; de Bono, 1985; Hirsch and Brush, 1987; Kanter, 1983; Kirzner, 1973, 1979, 1997, 1999; McClelland, 1961; Pinchot, 1985; Rosa et al., 1994; Schein et al., 1996; Schumpeter, 1996; Schwartz, 1997; Shapero, 1985; Shaver and Scott, 1992; Storey and Sykes, 1996.

they do not explain why the individual chose to apply them in an entrepreneurial context.

Notwithstanding these issues, most researchers believe that, collectively, owner-manager entrepreneurs have certain typical character traits, although, as for non-entrepreneurial owner-managers, the mix and emphasis of these characteristics will differ between individuals. The character traits of the owner-manager might be characterised as an instinct for survival – most owner-managed businesses never grow to any size – and those of the entrepreneur might be characterised as an instinct for growth. Figure 1.2 summarises these character traits, accumulated from numerous research studies. Those associated with owner-managers are also present in entrepreneurs, but those associated with entrepreneurs are not necessarily present in owner-managers – particularly if they run a lifestyle business.

Character traits of owner-managers

Need for independence

Owner-managers have a high need for independence. This is most often seen as 'the need to be your own boss' and is the trait that is most often cited, and supported, by researchers and advisors alike. However, independence means different things to different people, such as controlling your own destiny, doing things differently or being in a situation where you can fulfil your potential. It has often been said that once you have run your own firm you cannot work for anybody else.

> *Entrepreneurs don't like working for other people ... I was once made redundant by the Manchester Evening News. I had a wife who had given up a promising career for me, and a baby. I stood in Deansgate with £5 in my pocket and I swore I would never work for anyone else again.*

> Eddy Shah, founder of Messenger Group
> *The Times*, 16 March 2002

Need for achievement

Owner-managers typically have a high need for achievement, a driving force that is even stronger for entrepreneurs. Achievement for individual owners means different things depending on what type of person they are; for example, the satisfaction of producing a beautiful work of art, employing their hundredth person, or making the magic one million pounds. Often money is just a badge of achievement to the successful entrepreneur. It is not an end in itself.

> *You have to enjoy what you do and have a passion for it, otherwise you're bound to fail. But of course the financial rewards are important and apart from anything else reflect how successful your company is.*
>
> Martyn Dawes, founder of Coffee Nation
> Startups: www.startups.co.uk

> *Money doesn't motivate me. But it's not to say I don't drive a Bentley Continental T2.*
>
> Stephen Waring, founder of Green Thumb
> *Sunday Times* 2 October 2005

> *As a child I never felt that I was noticed. I never felt that I achieved anything or that there was any expectation of me achieving anything. So proving myself is something that is important to me and so is establishing respect for what I have achieved.*
>
> Chey Garland, founder of Garlands Call Centres
> *Sunday Times* 27 June 2004

Public recognition of achievement can be important to some owner-managers and entrepreneurs. And this can lead to certain negative behaviours or unwise decisions. For example, overspending on the trappings of corporate life – the office, the company car and so on (often called the corporate flagpole syndrome) – or the 'big project' that is very risky but the entrepreneur 'knows' they can do. These can lead to cash flow problems that put at risk the very existence of the business.

Internal locus of control

If you believe that you can exercise control over your environment and ultimately your destiny, you have an internal locus of control. If, however, you believe in fate, you have an external locus of control and you are less likely to take the risk of starting a business. Owner-managers typically have a strong internal locus of control, which is the same for many senior managers in large firms.

> *Most of the pleasure is not the cash. It is the sense of achievement at having taken something from nothing to where it is now.*
>
> Charles Muirhead, founder of Orchestream,
> acquired by MetaSolv in 2003 for £8 million
> *Sunday Times* 19 September 1999

> *We don't feel like millionaires at all. Money doesn't come into it. It's not really why you do it, it really isn't.*
>
> Brent Hoberman, co-founder of Lastminute.com
> *Sunday Times* 19 September 1999

I want to take control of my life and achieve something.

Jonathan Elvidge, founder of Gadget Shop
Sunday Times 17 March 2002

In extreme cases this trait can also lead to certain negative behaviours. In particular, it can show itself as a desire to maintain personal control over every aspect of the business. That can lead to a preoccupation with detail, overwork and stress. It also leads to an inability or unwillingness to delegate as the business grows. Again, in extreme cases it might show itself as a mistrust of subordinates. Kets de Vries (1985) thinks that these behaviours lead to subordinates becoming 'infantilised'. They are expected to behave as incompetent idiots, and that is the way they act. They tend to do very little, make no decisions and circulate very little information. The better ones do not stay long.

This need for control also shows itself in the unwillingness of many owner-managers to part with shares in their company. They just do not want to lose control, at any price.

Ability to live with uncertainty and take measured risks

Human beings, typically, do not like uncertainty and one of the biggest uncertainties of all is not having a regular pay cheque coming in. That is not to say owner-managers like it. Uncertainty about income can be a major cause of stress. The

Owner managers must be willing to take measured risks

possibility of missing out on some piece of business that might affect their income is one reason why they are so loath to take holidays.

There are also other commercial aspects of uncertainty that owner-managers have to cope with. Often they cannot influence many aspects of the market in which they operate, for example, price. They must therefore react to changes in the market that others might bring about. If a local supermarket has a special price promotion on certain goods it may well affect sales of similar goods in a local corner shop. A business with a high level of borrowing must find a way of paying interest charges but has no direct influence over changes in interest rates. Many small firms also have a limited customer or product base and this can bring further uncertainty. If, for whatever reason, one large customer ceases buying it can have an enormous impact on a small firm.

Hand in hand with owner-managers' ability to live with uncertainty is their willingness to take measured risks. Most people are risk averse. They try to avoid risks and insure against them. Setting up your own business is risky and owner-managers are willing to take more risks with their own resources than most people. They might also risk their reputation and personal standing if they fail. However, they do not like it and try always to minimise their exposure, hence their preference to risk other peoples' money and borrow, sometimes too heavily, from the bank. Another example of this is the way they often 'compartmentalise' various aspects of their business. For example, an owner-manager might open a second restaurant but set it up as a separate limited company just in case it fails and endangers the other. In this way they sometimes develop a portfolio of individually small businesses and their growth and success is measured not just in the performance of a single one but rather by the growth of the portfolio.

When I was made redundant self-employment was my only option and the work with the Business Link made it possible. The money was good, but I don't like the uncertainty – where the money for next month is coming from. It did not help to have three young boys to support. Eventually I went back into teaching.

Jean Young, self-employed 1998–99

You have to be prepared to lose everything and remember that the biggest risk is not taking any risk at all.

Jonathan Elvidge, founder of Gadget Shop
Sunday Times 17 March 2002

One important characteristic of owner-managers is their approach to dealing with uncertainty and risk is the short-term view they take on all business decisions. It really is a case of not being certain that the business will survive until tomorrow. Therefore decision-making is short-term and incremental. Strategies often evolve on a step-by-step basis. If one step works then the second is taken. At the same time owner-managers will keep as many options open as possible because they realise the outcome of their actions is very uncertain. Prudent entrepreneurs also seek to keep their investment and fixed costs as low as possible, trying to minimise the risk they face. We discuss ways to do this later in the book. Owner-managers also see assets as a liability, limiting the flexibility that they need, which is just as well since finding the resources to start a business is usually a problem.

Taking a chance, a risk or a gamble is what unites entrepreneurs. Without risk there is no reward. You won't discover America if you never set sail.

Jonathan Elvidge, founder of Gadget Shop
The Times 6 July 2002

Character traits of entrepreneurs

Entrepreneurs share the characteristics of owner-managers. However, they have certain additional traits. Nevertheless, owner-managers can be entrepreneurial in some of their actions and the boundaries between the two are not always clear. Consequently, many of these traits are present in owner-managers, but to a far lesser extent.

Opportunistic

By definition, entrepreneurs exploit change for profit. In other words, they seek out opportunities to make money. Often entrepreneurs see opportunities where others see problems. Whereas ordinary mortals dislike the uncertainty brought about by change, entrepreneurs love it because they see opportunity and they do not mind the uncertainty.

I have always lived my life by thriving on opportunity and adventure. Some of the best ideas come out of the blue, and you have to keep an open mind to see their virtue.

Richard Branson quoted by Anderson (1995)

With many entrepreneurs the problem is getting them to focus on just one opportunity, or at least one opportunity at a time. They see opportunity everywhere and have problems following through on any one before becoming distracted by another. This is one reason why some entrepreneurs are not able to grow their business beyond a certain size. They get bored by the routines and controls; they see other market opportunities and yearn for the excitement of another start-up. They probably would be well advised to sell up and do just that. However, others recognise this element of their character and become serial entrepreneurs, moving to set up and sell on one business after another. You see this very often in the restaurant business where an entrepreneurial restaurateur launches a new restaurant and makes it successful, then sells it on so as to move onto another new venture. They make money by creating a business with capital value, not necessarily income, for themselves.

Case insight   Simon Woodroffe and YO! Sushi

Simon Woodroffe, founder of YO! Sushi, took a while to home in on his final business idea. His first idea was to drive a van on the hippy trail to India, charging passengers to accompany him, but he did not have enough money to buy a van and his father declined to invest. Soon after this he started producing belts. He put together £100, bought an old sewing machine, some buckles and snakeskin trimmings. The belts sold well. Later he intended to make indoor rock climbing popular – another idea he never got round to pursuing. Then a Japanese man over a sushi lunch suggested what he really needed to do was open a conveyor-belt sushi bar with girls dressed in black PVC mini skirts. The idea stuck. Two years later, in 1997, he opened his first YO! Sushi bar in London – but without the girls in mini skirts. Simon sold his majority shareholding to Primary Capital in 2003, who in turn sold it to Quilvest and the company's management team in 2008.

Innovative

The ability to spot opportunities and to innovate are the most important distinguishing features of entrepreneurs. Innovation is the prime tool entrepreneurs use to create or exploit opportunity. These characteristics set entrepreneurs apart from owner-managers. Entrepreneurs link innovation to the market place so as to exploit an opportunity and make their business grow. Although innovation is difficult to define and can take many forms, entrepreneurs are always, in some way, innovative.

> *True innovation is rarely about creating something new. It's pretty hard to recreate the wheel or discover gravity; innovation is more often about seeing new opportunities for old designs.*
>
> Neil Kelly, owner and managing director of PAV
> *Sunday Times* 9 December 2001

Self-confident

Facing uncertainty, you have to be confident in your own judgement and ability to start up your own business. Many start-up training programmes recognise this and try to build confidence by developing a business plan that addresses the issue of future uncertainty. As well as a useful management tool, the plan can become a symbol of certainty for the owner-manager in an otherwise uncertain world and some even keep it with them at all times, using it almost like a bible, to reassure them of what the future will hold when the business is successful.

> *My mother gave me a massive self-belief. I will always try things – there is nothing to lose.*
> Richard Thompson, founder and chairman of EMS,
> quoted in Steiner (1999)

Entrepreneurs, therefore, need self-confidence aplenty to grow their business given the extreme uncertainty they face. If they do not believe in the future of the business, how can they expect others to do so? However, the self-confidence can be overdone and turn to an exaggerated opinion of their own competence, and even arrogance.

Some researchers believe entrepreneurs are actually 'delusional'. In an interesting piece of research, two American academics tested the decision-making process of 124 entrepreneurs (defined as people who started their own firm) and 95 managers of big companies in two ways (Busenitz and Barney, 1997). Firstly, they asked five factual questions, each of which had two possible answers. They asked respondents to rate their confidence in their answer (50 per cent, a guess; 100 per cent, perfect confidence). Entrepreneurs turned out to be much more confident about their answers than managers, especially those who gave wrong answers. Secondly, they were given a business decision. They were told they must replace a broken foreign-made machine and they had two alternatives. The first was an American-made machine, which a friend had recently bought and had not yet broken down, and the second a foreign-built machine, which was statistically less likely to break down than the other; 50 per cent of the entrepreneurs opted for the American machine but 90 per cent of the managers opted for the foreign one. The researchers concluded that the entrepreneurs were more prone to both delusion and opportunism than normal managers. So the question is raised, is entrepreneurial self-confidence so strong as to make them delusional, blinding them to the reality of a situation?

An entrepreneur is unfailingly enthusiastic, never pessimistic, usually brave, and certainly stubborn. Vision and timing are crucial. You have to be something of a workaholic, too. You have to be convinced that what you are doing is right. If not you have to recognise this and be able to change direction swiftly – sometimes leaving your staff breathless – and start off again with equal enthusiasm.

Chris Ingram founder of Tempus
Sunday Times 17 March 2002

Proactive and self-motivated

Entrepreneurs tend to be proactive rather than reactive and more decisive than other people. They are proactive in the sense that they seek out opportunities, they do not just rely on luck. They act quickly and decisively to make the most of the opportunity before somebody else does.

Entrepreneurs have drive and determination. They are often seen as restless and easily bored. They can easily be diverted by the most recent market opportunity and often seem to do things at twice the pace of others, unwilling or unable to wait for them to complete tasks. Patience is certainly not a virtue many entrepreneurs possess. They seem to work 24 hours a day and their work becomes their life with little separating the two. It is little wonder that it places family relationships under strain. One important result of this characteristic is that entrepreneurs tend to learn by doing. They act first and then learn from the outcomes of the action. It is part of their incremental approach to decision-making, each small action and its outcomes contribute to the learning process.

Neither my grandfather nor my father would be surprised if they could see me now. My success didn't just happen As a young boy, I was always working. My parents and my brothers and sisters all had high energy.

Tom Farmer, founder of Kwik-Fit
Daily Mail 11 May 1999

Enthusiasm is my strength And good health, and energy and endeavour. I love what I do. It's just so interesting, it is new every day, exciting every day. I work 364 days a year. The only day I don't work is Christmas Day, because it's my wife's birthday.

Bob Worcester, founder of MORI
Financial Times 7 April 2002

I have never had anything to do in my life that provides so many challenges – and there are so many things I still want to do.

Martha Lane Fox, co-founder of Lastminute.com
Sunday Times 19 September 1999

Entrepreneurs' drive and determination comes from being highly self-motivated, amounting almost to an irresistible urge to succeed in their economic goals. This intrinsic motivation is, in turn, driven by their exceptionally strong inner need for achievement, far stronger than with the average owner-manager. Running your own business is a lonely affair, without anyone to motivate and encourage you. You work long hours, sometimes for little reward. You, therefore, need to be self-motivated, committed and determined to succeed.

I am motivated by my success not money. But success is partly measured by money.

Wing Yip, founder of W. Wing Yip & Brothers
Sunday Times 2 January 2000

Be incredibly focused on what you're trying to achieve. You can't do everything well, because you spread your attention, talents and money, thinly, but you can do things you focus on well, if you really focus properly.

Martyn Dawes, founder of Coffee Nation
Startups: www.startups.co.uk

Fun is at the core of the way I like to do business and has informed everything I've done from the outset. More than any other element, fun is the secret of Virgin's success.

Richard Branson

This strong inner drive – what psychologists call type 'A' behaviour – is quite unique and can be seen as almost compulsive behaviour. This is not to say that entrepreneurs are not motivated by other things as well, such as money. But often money is just a badge of their success that allows them to measure their achievement. What drives them is their exceptionally high need to achieve. 'A' types tend to be goal-focused, wanting to get the job done quickly. However, they also tend to be highly reactive, focusing on the future and often not in control of the present.

An important part of this self-motivation comes from enjoyment – enjoyment in the challenges of being entrepreneurial. Entrepreneurs do what they do because they enjoy doing it, not because they are forced in any way. The entrepreneur will actually enjoy their work, often to the exclusion of things that are important in other people's lives – such as spouse and family. The long hours worked by entrepreneurs have often been known to break marriages. But ultimately the entrepreneur will always regard their business as 'fun', and this is one reason they can be so passionate about it. It provides an intrinsic motivation and, generally, people with an intrinsic motivation outperform those who undertake tasks because of extrinsic motivation – doing something because of an external influence or simply because they 'have to'.

Visionary with flair

In order to succeed, entrepreneurs need to have a clear vision of what they want to achieve. That is part of the fabric of their motivation. It also helps them to bring others with them, both employees and customers. The flair comes with the ability to be in the right place at the right time. Timing is everything. Innovation that is before its time can lead to business failure. Innovation that is late results in copy-cat products or services that are unlikely to be outstanding successes. A question constantly asked about successful entrepreneurs is whether their success was due to good luck or good judgement? The honest answer in most cases is probably a bit of both. But, as we shall see, real entrepreneurs can help to make their own luck.

> *My strength and my weakness is that I am very focused. Some people would describe me as obsessive ... The secret is to have vision and then build a plan and follow it. I think you have to do that, otherwise you just flounder about ... You change your game plan on the way, as long as you are going somewhere with a purpose ... I wouldn't say it was at the cost of everything else, but when I am at work, I work hard and do long hours – and when I am not at work my mind still tends to be there anyway.*
> Mike Peters, founder of Universal Laboratories
> *Sunday Times* 11 July 2004

Willingness to take greater risks and live with even greater uncertainty

It is worth stressing that, whilst all owner-managers are willing to take risks and live with uncertainty, true entrepreneurs are willing to take far greater risks and live with far greater uncertainty. Often they are willing to put their own home on the line and risk all, so strong is their belief in their business idea.

> *You have to have nerves of steel and be prepared to take risks. You have to be able to put it all on the line knowing you could lose everything.*
> Anne Notley, co-founder of The Iron Bed Company
> *Sunday Times* 28 January 2001

What is more, growth businesses face rapid change. Even with careful management they are extremely risky. Growth businesses require large amounts of capital and entrepreneurs are, if necessary, willing to risk all they own for the prospect of success. Faced with such extreme uncertainty a high degree of self-confidence is essential.

Antecedent influences

Whilst inherent character traits are important, there are other influences at work and there are other approaches to trying to explain the complicated process of entrepreneurship. Cognitive theory shifts the emphasis from the individual towards the situations that lead to entrepreneurial behaviour. Research has identified certain 'antecedent influences' – the entrepreneur's history and experience of life (Carter and Cachon, 1988). We are all born with certain character traits. However, we are also influenced by the social environment that we find ourselves in, for example, our family, ethnic group, education and so on. They influence our values, attitudes and even our behaviours. These are also antecedent influences.

In many ways the academic research in this area is even more confusing, and sometimes contradictory, than with personal character traits. There are a myriad of claimed influences that are difficult to prove or, indeed, disprove. There are simply too many variables to control. A further confusion is the one noted before; differentiating between owner-managers and entrepreneurs. Most of the research is about influences on start-ups. But start-ups comprise both owner-managers and entrepreneurs. However, there is a body of research on antecedent influences on managers of growth businesses which can apply, in the main, to entrepreneurs. The problem here is that some of the influences that seem to influence growth are not those that can be proved to influence start-ups. The only really safe conclusion is that, except for a handful of influences, the research is inconclusive.

One influence that comes through on many studies for both start-up and growth is educational attainment. Clearly there are problems with measuring educational attainment consistently over studies. However, particularly in the USA, research consistently shows a positive association between the probability of starting up in business and increasing educational attainment (Evans and Leighton, 1990). Similar research in other countries tends to support this result, albeit less strongly and not consistently. However, what is altogether stronger is the relationship between educational attainment and business growth. Storey (1994) reviewed seventeen multivariate studies of antecedent influences and found that educational attainment was a positive influence in eight. This led him to conclude that there was 'fairly consistent support for the view that educated entrepreneurs are more likely to establish faster-growing firms'. The GEM studies suggest that people with higher incomes and better education are more likely to be entrepreneurs.

This is not a widely acknowledged result and perhaps one that is more true of the USA than Britain. It is the stuff of folk lore that the entrepreneur comes from a poor, deprived background and has little formal education. In fact, some writers go further and claim that 'anecdotal evidence' suggests that too much education can discourage entrepreneurship (Bolton and Thompson, 2000). But times are changing and if you ask venture capitalists why they think certain firms will grow rather than others, they will tell you that they are looking for background and track record in

Case insight   Market traders

Notwithstanding the research, there are a number of millionaire entrepreneurs in the UK who started out as stall-holders in a market. They learnt their trade the hard way and they learnt the need for hard work. Indeed, the giant shop-chains of Marks & Spencer (M&S) and Morrison both started out as market stalls. Here are just seven entrepreneurs that featured in the *Sunday Times* Rich List in 2010.

Sir Ken Morrison, boss of the 375-store Morrison supermarket chain is estimated to be worth £1.4 billion. He started out by joining the family market stall in Bradford.

Lord Alan Sugar, these days better known for his appearances on *The Apprentice* TV show, set up Amstrad and Viglen. He began by boiling beetroot to sell from market stalls in London's East End.

Julian Dunkerton launched his clothing firm on a market stall in Cheltenham in 1984. His fashion business, Supergroup, owns the Superdry label favoured by many celebrities and he realised £200 million in a stock market float in 2010.

John Hargreaves founded the Matalan clothing chain which he sold to a private equity firm for £1.5 billion in 2009. A docker's son who left school at 14, he started out with a market stall in Liverpool selling M&S seconds.

David Whelan, founder of JJB Sport and owner of Wigan Athletic football club, started by selling toiletries from a market stall after being told by his mother to get a 'real job'.

Peter Simon, chairman of the Monsoon fashion chain started by selling knitted coats from a stall in London's Portobello Road.

Bill Adderley started selling curtains in Leicester market but went on to set up the Dunelm Mill homeware chain.

the firm's management, and education counts. It is also particularly true of the new generation of entrepreneurs pursuing technology-based opportunities.

The rationale for the relationship might be two-fold. Firstly, educational attainment might provide the basis for better learning through life, enabling entrepreneurs to deal better with business problems and giving them a greater openness and more outward orientation. Secondly, it might give them higher earning expectations that can only be attained by growing the business. What is more, it might also give them greater confidence in dealing with customers and other business professionals.

Other influences on start-ups have been cited, many supported by univariate research (linking the characteristic on its own with start-ups), for example the influence of family. In a survey of 600 respondents, Stanworth et al. (1989) found that between 30 per cent and 47 per cent of individuals either considering, about to start, or in business had a parent who had been in business. However, Storey (1994) in his review of antecedent influences concluded that there is little support from multivariate studies (linking more than one characteristic) for the impact of family, family circumstances, cultural or ethnic influences on self-employment decisions. He could not prove the following factors had any influence on start-up propensity:

- Marital status;
- Dependants (children);
- Previous wage level;
- Length of experience;
- Age;
- Gender;

- Ethnicity;
- Social class;
- School type;
- Personality;
- Being a manager in a previous job.

One interesting perspective on entrepreneurship is provided by Kets de Vries (1997) who believes that entrepreneurs often come from unhappy family backgrounds. This makes them unwilling to accept authority or to work closely with others. He paints the picture of a social deviant or misfit who is both hostile to others and tormented in himself:

> A prominent pattern among entrepreneurs appears to be a sense of impulsivity, a persistent feeling of dissatisfaction, rejection and pointlessness, forces which contribute to an impairment and depreciation of his sense of self-esteem and affect cognitive processes. The entrepreneur is a man under great stress, continuously badgered by his past, a past which is experienced and re-experienced in fantasies, daydreams and dreams. These dreams and fantasies often have a threatening content due to the recurrence of feelings of anxiety and guilt which mainly revolve around hostile wishes against parental figures, or more generally, all individuals in a position of authority.

In reality there is little support for this extreme view.

A further strand of cognitive theory is worthy of note because it reinforces at least two elements of trait theory. Chen et al. (1998) set out the idea that successful entrepreneurs possess high levels of 'self-efficacy'. Self-efficacy is 'the strength of an individual's belief that he or she is capable of successfully performing the roles and tasks of an entrepreneur'. Clearly this is part of the self-confidence of entrepreneurs described in the last section, but it is also created by their internal locus of control and rooted firmly in their need for achievement and, therefore, it is more than just self-confidence. Chen et al. argue that it is self-efficacy that motivates entrepreneurs and gives them the dogged determination to persist in the face of adversity when others just give in. With this characteristic entrepreneurs become more objective and analytical and attribute failure to insufficient effort or poor knowledge. They argue that self-efficacy is affected by a person's previous experiences – success breeds success.

Ethnicity and immigration

Despite Storey's conclusion, immigration is often cited as a positive influence on the propensity to start up a business. In fact, self-employment rates in the UK for ethnic minorities are not uniform. Those for Asians (Indian, Pakistani, Bangladeshi and so on) and Chinese are higher than those for white males, whilst those for black Africans and black Caribbeans are lower (Annual Population Survey, 2004). There are some 200 000 Asian-owned businesses in the UK, collectively punching above their weight in their contribution to the economy. Asians are recognised as the most likely ethnic minority group in the UK to become entrepreneurs. They are represented across all sectors of business. The case insight on Kenyan Asians gives some examples of these successes.

One reason for the high self-employment rate for Asians compared to black Africans and black Caribbeans appears to be family background and expectations. Traditionally Asian families have valued the independence of self-employment. This seems to be changing, with second generation Asians in the UK being encouraged to enter more traditional professions. However, one of the problems with looking for a pattern is that these ethnic groups are no longer homogenous and there is a complex set of family, community and societal influences at play. There is also some evidence of different financing patterns for ethnic businesses.

> It's an Asian way of working. We are all focused on what we are doing and we are working for succession. It's all in the family. We are not growing the business for an exit route. We all had one thing in common – we came to a country where we had to make it and our families supported us. My wife didn't mind me working 14 hours a day on the business and not being home to read the children bedtime stories. But we had, and still have, a good relationship. We have no regrets.'
>
> Bharat Shah, founder of Sigma Pharmaceuticals
> Kenyan Jewels, www.alusainc.wordpress.com

Case insight   Kenyan Asians

It is an astonishing fact that six of the most successful wholesale companies supplying drugs and medicines to Britain's retail pharmacies and hospitals were founded by Kenyan Asians who are now in their fifties. All left poverty in Kenya to come to Britain in the late 1960s and early 1970s where they went to college to achieve pharmacy qualifications, generally supporting themselves with menial part-time jobs. Then they set up their own retail pharmacies before building their much bigger wholesale businesses. All are now multimillionaires.

Bharat Shah has built up the family firm of **Sigma Pharmaceuticals**. It sells some 100 generic medicines and also deals in parallel imports – whereby drugs are bought in a country where wholesale prices are much lower and repackaged for a country where the price is higher. Two of his brothers work in the business – Manish is an accountant and Kamal works in operations – and his son Halul runs retail pharmacies.

Bharat and **Ketan Mehta** founded **Necessity Supplies** in 1986. It also sells generic drugs and deals in parallel imports.

→

Vijay and **Bikhu Patel** have built up **Waymade Healthcare** into a business with 700 employees. They have ambitions to turn the company into a 'mini-Glaxo' and in 2003 launched Amdipham to develop medicines that are too small for the big pharmaceuticals.

Ravi Karia founded **Chemilines** in 1986. It claims to be one of Britain's fastest growing companies.

Naresh Shah founded **Jumbogate** with his wife Shweta in 1982. Whilst still involved in retailing the business is predominantly wholesale.

Navin Engineer came to London with only £75 in his pocket in 1969 at the age of 16 to live with his aunt. He worked in a Wimpy burger restaurant in Oxford Street in the evenings to support himself through sixth form and then the London School of Pharmacy. On graduation he took a job with Boots, the retail chemist. Eventually he opened his own pharmacy in Chertsey, Surrey, working long hours to make money to buy other pharmacies. By 1999 he had 14 such shops and, when the German group GEHE offered him £12 million for the retail chain, he decided to take it. He invested most of the proceeds in his much smaller wholesale business. He bought a range of small turnover branded pharmaceuticals from bigger companies, switched production to established factories in Eastern Europe and the Far East, and realised cost savings as profit. He then went into generic medicines – copies of branded drugs produced after the expiry of their patent. This involves checking patents and making certain the drug can be developed without infringing the patent. At the same time regulatory authorities have t o be satisfied. His company, **Chemidex**, is now a wholesaler of both branded and generic medicines including treatments for gout, depression and an antibiotic for anthrax.

It has to be admitted that Storey's cold analytical approach to the immigrant issue does not stand the test of observation. As Harper (1985) observed:

> The Indians in East Africa, the Armenians in Egypt, the Lebanese in West Africa, the Kikuyu in Masailand, the Mahajans all over India except in their desert homeland of Rajasthan, the Tamils in Sri Lanka, the Palestinians in Arabia and the British almost everywhere except in Britain; all have shown that dislocation and hardship can lead to enterprise. The very experience of living in a difficult environment, and of planning, financing and executing a move and then surviving in a new and often hostile environment requires the qualities of self-restraint, abstinence, hard work and voluntary postponement of gratification which are normally far more severe than those demanded by the lifestyle of those who remain at home, or of the indigenous people of the place in which these refugees relocate.

Starting and running your own business is not easy and immigrants often have the motivation to work the long hours. Often with few options open to them, they have little to lose from failure and much to gain from success.

Gender

In the UK, and in most of the rest of the world, women are less likely to start up a business than men. Self-employment rates in the UK for women are almost half those for men (7 per cent compared to 13 per cent (Annual Population Survey, 2004)). As Gordon Brown observed when he was Chancellor of the Exchequer: 'If the UK could achieve the same levels of female entrepreneurship as the US, Britain would gain three quarters of a million more businesses' (Advancing Enterprise Conference, 4 February 2005).

More recent data from the Global Entrepreneurship Monitor in 2008 (GEM, 2009) show that:

- In most high income countries, men are about twice as likely to be entrepreneurially active as women.
- In the UK female early-stage entrepreneurial activity was about 49 per cent that of men – a figure that has held for some years: 3.6 per cent compared to 7.4 per cent. This compares to about 70 per cent in the USA, up from 60 per cent in 2007.
- In the UK female entrepreneurs of established businesses were just 40 per cent that of males: 3.4 per cent of the population compared to 8.6 per cent. This compares to about 62 per cent in the USA.

What is more, a consistent research finding is that women-owned businesses are likely to perform less well than male-owned businesses, however measured – turnover, profit or job creation (Kalleberg and Leicht, 1991; Rosa et al. 1996; Cliff, 1998). There are also differences in business and industry choice. For example, whilst male-owned businesses are represented across all industries, female-owned businesses are concentrated in the retail and service sectors (Carter and Shaw, 2006). There are also differences in financing strategies and governance structures. Since a major factor appears to be start-up capital, defined in its broadest sense.

Notwithstanding these issues, women-owned businesses are among the fastest growing entrepreneurial populations in the world and make significant contributions to innovation, employment and wealth creation in all economies. They can be a force to be reckoned with. The Center for Women's Business Research (2008) showed that there were over 1 million women-owned businesses in the USA, employing 13 million people and generating almost $2 trillion in sales annually.

Case insight   Elizabeth Gooch and EG Solutions

Elizabeth Gooch was named as the seventh most successful female entrepreneur in the UK by *Management Today* in 2006. About 25 per cent of the top 100 entrepreneurs in the list are female. Elizabeth is founder and CEO of EG Solutions, a company selling operations management software that helps clients to generate improvements in operational performance. EG prides itself on implementing its programmes on a fixed cost, fixed timescale basis. It is the only company that guarantees return on investment and its sales receipts are based on the results delivered. Typically implementation will pay for itself within six months.

Elizabeth started work for HSBC aged 18 but left after only 12 months to work for a consultancy that helped large firms find better ways to use their staff. Eight years later she started her own business, EG Consulting, aged 26, financed by £1000 borrowed from family and friends and a credit card. EG Consulting initially offered consultancy and training on operations management to financial services companies. In its first year turnover reached £600000. However,

→

the complexity of collecting the information needed to advise on improving efficiency led Elizabeth to develop software to help in the task. In 1993 the software, called Operational Intelligence, was launched as a product in its own right. It allowed data to be collected in real time, enabling all departments of a company to monitor the production process. At that point the business had six employees, several contract workers and a turnover of £1 million.

It was not until Elizabeth met Rodney Baker-Bates, then CEO of Prudential Financial Services, that things changed dramatically. He believed she was not making enough of the business and said she should focus on the software rather than the consultancy work. The company changed its name to EG Solutions and he became Chairman, engaging the services of a strategic planning consultant to help them develop the business in a focused way. The strategy worked, increasing turnover by 28% a year until 2005. At this point turnover was £4.2 million and the business needed more capital to meet some ambitious growth targets. Elizabeth decided to float the company on the Alternative Investment Market (AIM) rather than going for venture capital because she did not want to lose control.

> 'We had two options really – venture capital or floatation. I liked the float model where you had several institutional investors with a range of views and advice rather than a venture capital investor with a large stake in the business.'

The float was successful, but the problem with the stock market is that it expects the company to deliver good results year after year. Unfortunately in 2006 EG Solutions failed to make its sales targets by £700 000. Worse still, in 2007 it posted loses of £800 000. The analysts and shareholders were damning.

> 'I had really personal attacks from analysts and shareholders alike. They told me they had never seen anything so bad and that the business would never recover. I took it all very personally.'

Elizabeth's reaction was to cut costs by £1.2 million, returning the business to profit by 2008, admitting that she took her eye off the UK market as she looked overseas for business opportunities that would help her achieve her ambitious growth targets.

> 'Floatation gives a public face to your business and access to finance that is so often key to development. But there needs to be a lot more attention to strategy.
>
> Persevere and never see anything as failure. Look at what you can learn from something that does not go the way you want. It's all about attitude. I do not believe in failure. I have needed sheer determination – although my shareholders would probably describe it as stubbornness.'

> *Sunday Times* 23 November 2008

By 2009 the company was back on track. Cutting costs ahead of the recession stood them in good stead, and the recession was actually helping the recovery because companies were looking to improve their efficiency. Elizabeth's objectives in 2009 involved growing the business and then exiting via a trade sale within the next two or three years.

Asked for the best advice she would give to prospective entrepreneurs, she gave six tips:

- 'When the going gets tough – pitch in and keep working. Nothing comes easy so you should expect it to get tough and to have to work hard.
- Cash is king – everybody says that, but fulfilling orders so you can raise invoices and collect the cash are the most important things you can do.
- Focus – have a clear strategy and don't get side tracked by activities that don't enable you to achieve this. Review your strategy constantly to ensure you are meeting market demands.

→

- Think big, act small. Reach for the stars and you will get there (or at least close). Aim low and you'll get there too. But always retain the fit, fast and flexible culture of a small business.
- Agility is a major strength that big businesses would die for.
- Starting your own business doesn't mean doing everything yourself, that's a recipe for staying small. Delegation is an important skill to learn.'

Launch Lab (www.launchlab.co.uk) 13 January 2009

Visit the EG Solutions website: www.eguk.co.uk

Growth businesses

Storey's review of the research (op. cit.) concludes that there are three further factors that are positively correlated with growth companies:

1. Growth companies are more likely to be set up by groups rather than individuals. This proves the venture capitalists' view that they invest in a management team not in a business, and explains why they are so willing to invest in management buy-outs and buy-ins. Managing growth needs a range of different skills with managers able to work as a team. Attracting a strong management team can be a problem for a start-up. How do you tempt successful managers to leave secure jobs and face the risks associated with a start-up? The answer is that you offer them a share in the business. In that way they share in the success of the business as well as the risks that it faces.
2. Middle-aged owners are more likely to be associated with growth companies. Middle age does have some advantages. It brings experience, credibility and financial resources. With the family possibly grown up, middle-aged entrepreneurs can devote more time and resources to the business.

   However, as with all research these results must be treated with caution. Findings like these come from looking at what has happened in the past and if situations change, the past may not be a good indication of what might happen in the future. Opportunities in the new technologies, most lately the internet, have often been grasped by very young entrepreneurs, many of whom have become millionaires as a consequence.
3. Owners with previous managerial experience are more likely to be associated with growth companies. This is likely to be the case because they bring with them both managerial and, probably, market experience. They also know their previous worth, which may create salary expectations that can only be satisfied by a growth business.

The factors that Storey could not prove influenced growth were:

- Gender (see previous section);
- Prior firm size experience;
- Prior sector experience;
- Training;
- Social marginality;
- Ethnicity (see previous section);
- Family history;
- Prior self-employment.

However, he also concluded that the picture was 'fuzzy' and that what the entrepreneur has done prior to establishing the business 'only has a modest influence on the success of the business'. One frequently debated factor is entrepreneurs' experience of prior business failure. Whether or not this is a positive experience is still to be adequately researched. Until then no conclusion can be drawn.

One curious conclusion is that the influence of training cannot be proved. If you believe that entrepreneurs are both born and made, then you must accept that they can be influenced. Just like an athlete or a musician, if they have the basic ingredients, then training should improve their performance. There are at least two major problems related to this variable. Firstly, there is the question of what constitutes training. Smaller firms are notoriously poor at undertaking formal training but that does not necessarily mean they do not undertake informal training. Secondly, those small firms that do seek out formal training are also likely to seek out other sources of help and so the influence of the formal training becomes more difficult to measure.

These studies of growth businesses allow us to draw an, albeit tentative, identikit picture of the antecedent influences on an entrepreneur which are most likely to result in them successfully growing their business. Founders of growth businesses are likely to be:

- Middle-aged (or very young?);
- White, Asian or Chinese male;
- Well educated;
- Leaving a managerial job;
- Willing to share ownership.

Remember, however, that these are generalisations. Whilst broadly supportable because of the samples on which they are based, they do not apply to every individual. Just like small firms, entrepreneurs are not homogeneous. The results are also based on ex-post research, that is, analysis based on the past. Circumstances change and the past is not always a good predictor of the future. What is more, if picking winners were really that easy there would be an awful lot of rich people around.

National culture

The final element in the jigsaw puzzle is culture. In his seminal work on the subject, Hofstede (1980) defined culture as the 'collective programming of the mind which distinguishes one group of people from another'. It is a pattern of taken-for-granted assumptions. Different groups have different cultures and most people operate in groups that have different subcultures – family, ethnic groups, religious groups, companies and so on. However the over-riding culture of the nation in which we live is a significant over-arching influence. An entrepreneurial culture is one that fosters positive social attitudes towards entrepreneurship. Cultures can change over time, albeit slowly. So, most people would argue that Britain has developed a more entrepreneurial culture from the 1970s through to today. Similarly the subcultures within which we live will be more or less entrepreneurial and also may have changed over time.

It has been argued that there is no such thing as one identifiable entrepreneurial culture; what is needed is a favourable environment which combines social, political and educational attributes (Timmons, 1994). However, many would consider the culture in the USA to be the most entrepreneurial in the world. It is an achievement-orientated society that values individualism and material wealth. According to Welsch (1998):

> Entrepreneurship is ingrained in the fabric of North American culture. It is discussed at the family dinner table among intergenerational members, practised by pre-school children with their lemonade stands, and promoted every day through personal success human interest stories in the media. Furthermore, entrepreneurship is taught in school from kindergarten through to the twelfth grade, it has been integrated into college and university curricula, and is taught and promoted through various outreach and training programmes including government Small Business Development Centres in every state of the nation. Consequently, through one's life as an American citizen, entrepreneurship as a career option is espoused early and reinforced regularly.

Americans are said to have a 'frontier culture', always seeking something new. They are restless, constantly on the move. They have a strong preference for freedom of choice for the individual. The individual is always free to compete against established institutions. Rebellious, non-conformist youth is the accepted norm. If there is an 'American dream' it is that the humblest of individuals can become the greatest of people, usually measured in monetary terms. Achievement is prized and lauded throughout society. Individuals believe they control their destiny. Americans think big. Nothing is impossible. They prefer the new, or at least the improved. They worship innovation. Time is their most precious commodity. They are tolerant of those who make mistakes as long as they learn from them. Things need to get done quickly rather than always get done perfectly.

Measuring the dimensions of culture in a scientific way is extremely difficult. The most widely used dimensions are those developed by Hofstede (1981) who undertook an extensive cross-cultural study, using questionnaire data from some 80 000 IBM employees in 66 countries across seven occupations. From his research he established four dimensions (Figure 1.3):

1. *Individualism vs collectivism* This is the degree to which people prefer to act as individuals rather than groups. Individualistic societies are loosely knit social frameworks in which people primarily operate as individuals or in immediate families. Collectivist societies are composed of tight networks in which people operate as members of ingroups and outgroups, expecting to look after, and be looked after by, other members of their ingroup. In the individualist culture the task prevails over personal relationships. The atmosphere is competitive. In the collectivist culture the opposite is true. 'Anglo' countries (USA, Britain, Australia, Canada and New Zealand) are the highest scoring individualist cultures, together with the Netherlands. France and Germany just make it into the upper quartile of individualist cultures. South American countries are the most collectivist cultures, together with Pakistan.

2. *Power distance* This is the degree of inequality among people that the community is willing to accept. Low power distance countries endorse egalitarianism, relations are open and informal, information flows are functional and unrestricted and organisations tend to have flat structures. They are more empowered cultures. High power distance cultures endorse hierarchies, relations are

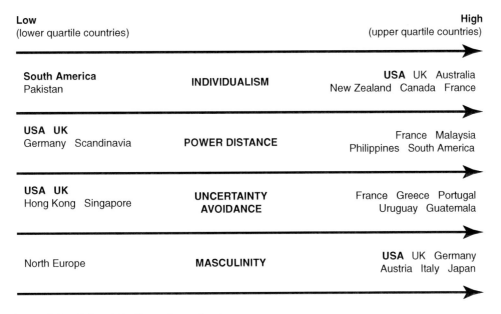

Figure 1.3 Hofstede's dimensions of culture

more formal, information flows are formalised and restricted and organisations tend to be rigid and hierarchical. Austria, Ireland, Israel, New Zealand and the four Scandinavian countries tend to be low power distance countries. The USA, Britain and Germany also make it into the lower quartile. High power distance countries are Malaysia, the Philippines and four South American countries, with France also making it into the upper quartile.

3. *Uncertainty avoidance* This is the degree to which people prefer to avoid ambiguity, resolve uncertainty and favour structured rather than unstructured situations. Low uncertainty avoidance cultures tolerate greater ambiguity, prefer flexibility, stress personal choice and decision-making, reward initiative, risk-taking and team-play and stress the development of analytical skills. High uncertainty avoidance cultures prefer rules and procedures, stress compliance, punish error and reward compliance, loyalty and attention to detail. The lowest uncertainty avoidance countries are Hong Kong, Ireland, Jamaica, Singapore and two Scandinavian countries. The USA and Britain are in the lowest quartile group. The highest uncertainty avoidance countries are Greece, Portugal, Guatemala and Uruguay, with France also in the highest quartile group. Germany is about halfway.

4. *Masculinity vs femininity* This defines quality of life issues. Masculine virtues are those of assertiveness, competition and success. Masculine cultures reward financial and material achievement with social prestige and status. Feminine virtues are those such as modesty, compromise and cooperation. In feminine cultures, issues such as quality of life, warmth in personal relationships, service and so on are important, and in some societies having a high standard of living is thought to be a matter of birth, luck or destiny (external locus of control). The most masculine countries are Japan, Austria, Venezuela, Italy and Switzerland. The USA, Britain and Germany all fall into the highest quartile. Four North

European countries are the highest scoring feminine countries. France is about halfway.

Hofstede and Bond (1991) have added a fifth dimension – short/long-term orientation. A short-term orientation focuses on past and present and therefore values respect for the status quo, including, for example, an unqualified respect for tradition and for social and status obligations. A long-term orientation focuses on the future and therefore the values associated with this are more dynamic. For example, they include the adaptation of traditions to contemporary conditions and promote only qualified respect for social and status obligations.

Using Hofstede's dimensions, therefore, the USA, our role model for entrepreneurial culture, emerges as a highly individualistic, masculine culture, with low power distance and uncertainty avoidance. It is a culture that tolerates risk and ambiguity, has a preference for flexibility and it is an empowered culture that rewards personal initiative. It is a highly individualistic and egalitarian culture, one that is fiercely competitive and the home of the 'free-market economy'. Assertiveness and competition are central to the 'American dream'. If there is a key virtue in the USA it is achievement, and achievement receives its monetary reward. It is an informal culture. According to the Declaration of Independence, all men are created equal, but they also have the freedom to accumulate sufficient wealth to become very unequal. The USA is the original 'frontier culture'. It actually seems to like change and uncertainty and certainly rewards initiative and risk-taking.

The American Dream proposes that every individual can become successful

This, then, is the anatomy of an enterprise culture: one that encourages enterprise and entrepreneurship, one where the probability of an entrepreneur being made, rather than just born, is highest. This is the sort of culture that many other countries have been trying to promote and develop because it seems to encourage the characteristics that are needed for successful management. This culture, combined with the other antecedent influences, is said to be likely to develop the largest number of that most valuable resource – entrepreneurs.

However, notice one thing from Figure 1.3. Alongside the USA, at the extreme ends of these dimensions, is the UK and that country can hardly have been held to be the epitome of an enterprise culture at the time these studies were conducted. The explanation may lay in the timing of the study. In the 1970s, in both the UK and USA, political interest focused on enterprise as a means of rescuing their stagnant economies (O'Connor, 1973). It was argued that structural change was needed to achieve an 'enteprise culture' (Morris, 1991; Carr, 2000) and this would have to be accompanied by cultural change at the level of the individual, so much so that it would bring about a revolution that was moral, economic and enduring. And in the UK it was, arguably, the Thatcher government that brought about that change at the end of the 1970s.

It is also possible, however, that the dimensions measured by Hofstede are just not relevant to entrepreneurship. Perhaps there are other equally relevant, important but uncharted dimensions. After all, his work was based upon IBM employees and they can hardly be described as the most entrepreneurial in the world, particularly at the time when Microsoft was setting out in business. Whilst other countries try to emulate the enterprise culture of the USA, the jury is out on how precisely the dimensions of their enterprise culture are to be measured.

Notwithstanding this serious reservation about measurement, we know that deep cultures take time to change, if indeed they can be changed. There is little evidence, as yet, of different cultures around the world converging. What is more, we do not understand how best to go about changing national cultures, even if we believe it desirable. Rather than trying to change a nation's culture perhaps it would be best just to ensure that, at the very least, it does not inhibit entrepreneurship.

Culture is, however, something that can be influenced and shaped in an organisational context.

Situational factors

Most people, at some time in their life, have an idea that could form the basis for establishing their own business. But few people choose to do so. What is needed is a trigger to spur them into action, to turn the idea into reality. These triggers can take the form of 'push' or 'pull' factors. Push factors are those that push you into self-employment – unemployment or forced redundancy, disagreement with your boss, being a 'misfit' and not feeling comfortable in an organisation for some reason, or simply having no alternative because, for example, you have a physical disability or illness. These are very strong motivations for self-employment, but not necessarily to grow your business. Pull factors – the need for independence, achievement and recognition, personal development and wealth – are positive reasons for setting up a business. Sometimes the factors combine and an entrepreneur emerges with a positive motivation, for example, to make a success of an innovative idea, having felt a 'misfit' in their old organisation.

> *We got the inspiration (for Lush) because we were broke. The previous business had gone bust. We had three mortgages, three children and no money. So – make a living!*
>
> Mark Constantine, founder of Lush
> *RealBusiness* interview 26 May 2009

All too often these triggers are blocked by other factors – the need for regular income, a family to support, no capital or a doubt about your own ability. These all boil down to two things – insufficient self-confidence and an inability to cope with

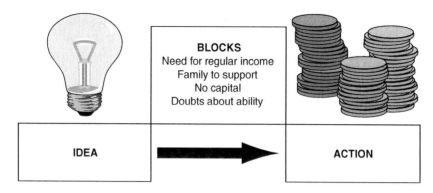

BLOCKS
Need for regular income
Family to support
No capital
Doubts about ability

IDEA → ACTION

TRIGGER

PUSH FACTORS	PULL FACTORS
Unemployment	Independence
Disagreement with management	Achievement/Recognition
Does not 'fit in' to company	Personal development
No other alternatives	Personal wealth

Figure 1.4   Reasons for setting up in business

high risk and uncertainty. Without these key ingredients the business will not get past the ideas stage. Figure 1.4 summarises these influences.

It is no coincidence that many people try to start up their own businesses either at an early age or in their late thirties and forties. At those ages, the blocks are fewer. This is particularly the case later in life when children will probably have grown up and left home and there might be some capital in savings that can be used in the start-up. At the same time the prospective entrepreneur will have gained experience and confidence and, very possibly, be seeking new challenges for self-development.

Storey's (1994) review of antecedent literature also came to some important conclusions regarding the influence of employment and unemployment. Reviewing three multivariate studies, he found two had statistically significant relationships between

Case insight   Will King and King of Shaves

Will King has sensitive skin and had started mixing his own shaving oils. However, when he was made redundant in 1992 he decided to try to make this into a business. He mixed the oils in his kitchen and spent two weeks hand filling 9600 bottles with his girlfriend's help. He managed to sell the shaving oil to Harrods using the brand name King of Shaves. Today KMI, Will's toiletries and fragrance business, employs 50 people and has a turnover in excess of £42 million. His products are now sold in Harrods, Bentalls, Boots, Tesco and Sainsbury. What is more, his new Azor razor, has overtaken Wilkinson Sword in the UK market and is second only to Gillette.

Up-to-date information on King of Shaves can be found on their website: www.shave.com

unemployment and the probability of starting up in business. However, when he came to look at growth, four out of eight studies showed a negative relationship and the other four showed no relationship at all. What is more, four out of seven studies found a positive relationship between positive motives for setting up the business (for example, market opportunity, making money) and subsequent growth. This led Storey to conclude that 'if the founder is unemployed prior to starting a business, that firm is unlikely to grow as rapidly as where the founder is employed'.

It would seem that unemployment gives people a strong push into self-employment. They possibly have limited options open to them. However, they may not have the skills needed to grow the business and may have lower aspirations than those who leave employment to start their own business. It would seem that what is needed to make the firm grow is positive motivation – a real desire, an ambition, almost a need to achieve certain internally generated goals or pursue some market opportunity. Growth does not happen (often) by chance. The entrepreneur must want it.

Measuring Entrepreneurial Personality

The **General Enterprise Tendency (GET)** test has been developed by staff at Durham University Business School over several years to measure a number of personal 'tendencies' commonly associated with the enterprising person. The test aims to measure 'tendency' rather than traits and was developed following research into a variety of dimensions used to measure entrepreneurship and enterprise. It was validated with a number of different groups of people and amended accordingly. It is a 54-question instrument that measures entrepreneurial personality traits in five dimensions:

- Need for achievement – 12 questions.
- Autonomy – 6 questions.
- Drive and determination – 12 questions.
- Risk-taking – 12 questions.
- Creativity and potential to innovate – 6 questions.

It is relatively quick and simple to administer – with either agree or disagree questions – and score. Each dimension receives a score of up to 12 points (Autonomy six points) and the final composite score measures inherent entrepreneurial character traits on a scale of 0–54.

Stormer et al. (1999) applied the test to 128 owners of new (75) and successful (53) small firms. They concluded that the test was acceptable for research purposes, particularly for identifying owner-managers. It was poor at predicting small business success. They concluded that either the test scales needed to be refined for this purpose or that the test did not include sufficient indicators of success such as situational influences on the individual or other factors related to the business rather than the individual setting it up. It would seem that, while entrepreneurs are both born and made, success requires more than an ounce of commercial expertise … oh yes … and a little luck!

An electronic version of the tool is available online at the website accompanying this book (www.palgrave. com/business/burns). Why not try it and see whether you are entrepreneurial?

Research in France also casts doubt on the long-term viability of start-ups generated by unemployed people (Abdesselam et al., 1999). They found that firms with the shortest life-spans were set up by the young (under 30) and unemployed. They also found that there was a high probability that the fledgling business people would be female and the business would be in the retail or wholesale sector. These results cast worrying doubt on the wisdom of any government policy to encourage the unemployed to start up their own business – one aspect of policy option 1.

Motivations can be difficult to disentangle and, although growth businesses are more likely to be set up as a result of pull factors, often people face a combination of push and pull factors. What is more, size of business may not feature in their vision at start-up. Indeed motivations change over time. Many owner-managers may start out with no wish to grow their company to be a future Microsoft or Virgin. However, if a business shows potential for being successful, few owners will hinder growth until their personal resources are really stretched. At this point the owner reaches a watershed.

Case with questions   Duncan Bannatyne, Dragon

Duncan Bannatyne is probably the best known entrepreneur in the UK because of his appearances on the BBC TV series *Dragons' Den* rather than his achievements as a serial entrepreneur. His life has, however, been a colourful one. He was born in 1949 into a relatively poor family in the town of Clydebank, Scotland. The second of seven children, his father was a foundry-man at the local ship yard. When told that the family could not afford to buy him a bicycle Duncan tried to get a job delivering newspapers for the local newsagents, only to be set the challenge of finding 100 people who wanted a newspaper to be delivered. By knocking on doors he collected the names, got his newspaper round and eventually was able to buy his bicycle.

Duncan left school at 15 to serve in the Royal Navy. He served for five years before receiving a dishonourable discharge – after 9 months detention – for threatening to throw an officer off a jetty. He spent his twenties moving from job to job around the UK, including taxi driving and selling ice creams, ending up in Stockton-on-Tees. It was here, in his early 30s, that Duncan's entrepreneurial career started when, using his personal savings, he bought an ice cream van for £450. He built this business into a fleet of vans selling 'Duncan's Super Ices'. Even here he showed entrepreneurial flair. He was innovative – he started using a scoop that speeded up serving and made a shape like a smile in the ice cream, which the children loved. He was good at spotting opportunities – he bought one pitch in a local park for £2000 which gave him profits of £18000 in one summer. He eventually sold the business for £28000, but not before he had spotted another opportunity. In the 1980s the government started helping unemployed people by paying their rent. Duncan used his profits from the ice cream business to buy and convert houses into bedsits for rent. He rented to the unemployed, so the rents were guaranteed by the government.

Duncan used the proceeds from the sale of the ice cream business – and almost everything else he owned – to move into residential care homes with a business partner. He took out a bank loan, re-mortgaged his own home and started building up credit card debt. The building costs of the care home were to be financed by a 70 per cent mortgage, but this would only be released when building work was complete and the home was available for occupation.

➡

When building costs for the first home spiralled out of control and no more funds were available, he, his partner, friends and family decided to finish the work themselves. The total costs for the care home came to £360 000, and nearly bankrupted Duncan. But the bank then valued the finished home at £600 000, giving a mortgage of £420 000. This meant that Duncan could recover his costs, pay off his debts and still have equity to put into the next care home. Using a mix of retained profits and borrowings, and by offering shares in the company, he expanded the number of homes.

'When I opened my first nursing home, I had considered newsagents and bed and breakfast establishments but then Margaret Thatcher started to revolutionise care for the elderly ... I spotted an opportunity. I came to the conclusion that landlords who owned nursing homes could make a lot of money from the scheme. I took advantage and bought a plot of land with a bank loan and set up my first nursing home in Darlington as soon as I could. When that was full, I paid off all my debts, bought another plot and repeated the process until the portfolio included 45 homes.'

The company was called Quality Care Homes and it was eventually floated on the Stock Exchange. Duncan also went into children's nurseries with the Just Learning chain. In 1996 he sold Quality Care Homes for £26 million and Just Learning for £22 million. By now, however he had expanded into health clubs with the popular Bannatyne's chain.

'I remember while I was working in the nursing home industry, I injured my knee and used to travel 30 minutes to a local gym in the North East for exercise and physiotherapy. While working out my knee, I also tried to work out the gym's business plan. I knew the membership fees and the number of members and I calculated approximately how much the building cost because I sat and counted the number of tiles on the ceiling and equated them to square footage in my nursing homes. I did the necessary sums and worked out that, if I opened my own health club, I would make a 35%–40% return on capital. It was a no-brainer.'

Daily Telegraph 30 July 2009

By buying plots of land next to the health club sites Duncan expanded into the hotel business. He worked out that by sharing staffing, reception and other facilities he could save costs and offer hotel residents use of the health club facilities during their stay. So Bannatyne Hotels was born. Duncan has since acquired 26 health clubs from Hilton Hotels making it the largest independent chain of health clubs in the UK. He has also launched Bar Bannatyne and, in October 2008, opened Bannatyne Spa Hotel in Hastings.

Duncan's wealth is estimated by the *Sunday Times* 2009 Rich List at £320 million, which places him as the 167th richest person in the UK. He is also by far the wealthiest of the Dragons in the Den.

Question

What entrepreneurial character traits can you spot in Duncan?

Case with questions   Hilary Andrews and Mankind

Hilary Andrews comes from a family of entrepreneurs. Her father ran a building and landscaping company and her sister ran a public relations company. Hilary wanted to be a beauty therapist so she left sixth form college to go to a private college ahead of going to work in a beauty salon. However it was not too long before she opened her own salon in Woking, in 1983. But Hilary got bored and felt unhappy with the insecurity of self-employment, so in 1990 she took a teacher training course and then a degree in education, going on to teach beauty and holistic therapy in Farnborough. She then got a job in a company distributing products to the spa industry, working in their mail order department. It was here that she came upon the idea for her business. Men kept asking for advice on products to use on their skin, so she decided to research the emerging market for men's skin care products. She quickly decided there was a real business opportunity in setting up a mail order company selling just men's cosmetics. The market for male grooming products was growing rapidly but, more importantly for her idea, many men preferred not to visit shops.

However, Hilary was by now 38 years old and she found the prospect of setting up on her own daunting. Luckily she was able to find a business partner, Paul Jamieson, through a mutual friend. She enthused him with her business idea and he decided he was willing to back her. But more money was needed and the banks and private investors were not convinced. They thought the idea untried and untested and did not believe men would buy grooming products in this way. Not to be put off, Hilary remortgaged her house, raising £10 000 and

→

Paul put in £20 000 of his own money. Hilary managed to borrow a further £20 000 from two family members and two friends. With £50 000 of capital, Mankind was launched in 2000.

First Hilary secured the products she wished to sell by entering into distributor agreements for a range of selected products. Then she bought mailing lists and printed some 100 000 catalogues. Friends and family helped stuff the catalogues into envelopes and mail them out. Sufficient sales came from this first mailshot to establish the business and it quickly developed its own mailing list. But it was through developing a website and exploiting the internet market that the business really took off. This was a key decision that allowed it to grow, just as online shopping was becoming popular.

'We knew there were guys who wanted these products but didn't want the hassle of going to a shop and speaking to a consultant. The internet has made it easy to buy products that were previously difficult to get and enabled us to give people a lot of information about them. About 99 per cent of our sales are through the internet now. We have watched things develop very quickly in both the male grooming and the internet market. But we have tried to control the growth so we don't try to run before we can walk. I'm a cautious person who looks at the downside of things.

It's about being really focused on what you do ... You have to watch the bottom line constantly. Its not about starting a business and getting yourself a nice car; its about starting a business and having a really solid model that works ... What motivates me is being successful in an industry I love. It's a rewarding thing to give people confidence.'

Sunday Times 9 October 2005

By 2005 Mankind's turnover had grown to almost £3 million – and despite the hard work Hilary had still found time to marry and have a son.

Up-to-date information on Mankind can be found on their website: www.mankind.co.uk

Questions

1. Which of the character traits of the entrepreneur does Hilary exhibit?
2. What other influences can you detect?
3. How much of the success of this venture is down to the right idea at the right time?

Summary

▨ The decision to start your own business is influenced by your own character traits, antecedent influences and the situation you face at any point in time. You can assess your character traits using the GET test.

▨ Owner-managers and entrepreneurs have certain personal character traits that they are born with but that can be developed over time. These character traits are summarised in Figure 1.2. Entrepreneurs like **Simon Woodroffe, Richard Thompson, Duncan Bannatyne** and **Hilary Andrews** exhibit many of these traits.

However, the issue of linking the character traits of an individual to the success of a business – picking winners – needs to be approached with caution. Success or failure in business comes from a mix of many different things. The character traits of the manager are just one factor in the equation. What is more, there are a number of methodological problems associated with trying to measure personality traits:

- Traits are not stable and change over time.
- They require subjective judgements.
- Antecedent influences can be overlooked or ignored:
  - cultural and environmental influences;
  - education, learning and training;
  - age, sex, race and social class.

■ Women are generally less likely to start up a business than men and, even when they do, that business is likely to perform less well than male-owned businesses, however measured. There are, however, many exceptions to this, such as **Elizabeth Gooch**.

■ By way of contrast, self-employment rates in the UK for ethnic minorities are not uniform and many ethnic minority-owned businesses exhibit above-average performance. Asian-owned businesses perform particularly well – as was the case with the **Kenyan Asians**.

■ Education is an important antecedent influence on start-ups but more particularly entrepreneurial growth businesses. Whilst unemployment is a strong push into self-employment, entrepreneurial growth businesses are more likely to be set up for more positive motives. Growth companies are also more likely to be set up by groups than individuals, often sharing ownership to attract experienced managers. They are more likely to be set up by middle-aged owners with previous managerial experience who leave their job for the start-up.

■ National culture – 'the software of the mind' – also influences the decision whether to set up one's own firm and whether to grow it. Culture can be measured in four dimensions: individualism vs collectivism; power distance; uncertainty avoidance; and masculinity vs femininity. The USA is probably the role model for an entrepreneurial culture. It emerges as a highly individualistic, masculine culture, with low power distance and low uncertainty avoidance. Whether or not you accept these dimensions of culture as saying anything about entrepreneurship, what is true is that entrepreneurship is ingrained into the fabric of culture in the USA, part of the 'American dream'.

■ Situational factors also influence the start-up decision. Many people have business ideas but few have the confidence to start up their own business. The blocks to doing so include the need for regular income to support a family, the lack of capital and self-doubt. What is needed is a trigger. This can be a push factor such as unemployment – as in the case of **Will King** – or immigration – as was the case with the **Kenyan Asians**. It can also be a pull factor such as a desire to make money through an economic opportunity. As we saw with **Steve Hulme** and **Duncan Bannatyne**, it can be a combination of these factors. Generally businesses set up for positive motives or pull factors are most likely to grow.

Further resources are available at www.palgrave.com/business/burns

Essays and discussion topics

1. Are entrepreneurs born or made?
2. Do you think you have what it takes to be an owner-manager or entrepreneur?
3. Which character traits of owner-managers and entrepreneurs might have negative effects on a business?
4. What factors do you think affect the success or otherwise of a business venture?
5. Can you 'pick winners'?
6. How do entrepreneurs cope with risk and uncertainty?
7. What are the defining characteristics of an entrepreneur?
8. Are immigrants more entrepreneurial?
9. Why are women less entrepreneurial than men?
10. Can training help develop entrepreneurship?
11. Has your education, so far, encouraged you to be entrepreneurial? If so, how? If not, how could it be changed?
12. Does this course encourage entrepreneurship?
13. Is entrepreneurship really just for the middle-aged?
14. Are there advantages to setting up your own business when you are young?
15. What are the blocks you personally face in starting your own business? Against each block consider the changes that would be needed for it to be removed.
16. Why might so many dot.com entrepreneurs be young and well educated?
17. Is it really better to set up in business with other individuals?
18. Does previous business failure mean that you are more likely to succeed in the future?
19. Have attitudes to entrepreneurs changed in this country over the last twenty years?
20. Does this country have an enterprise culture?
21. How can enterprise culture be encouraged?
22. Why is the USA considered to be the most entrepreneurial culture in the world?
23. Which other countries would you consider to have an entrepreneurial culture?
24. Are there any other dimensions along which an enterprise culture could be measured?

Exercises and assignments

1. Write a mini case study on the motivations and other influences on an entrepreneur you know who set up their own business.

   List the questions you would ask an owner-manager or entrepreneur in trying to assess their character traits.

   Use the list of questions to conduct an interview with an owner-manager of a local small firm. Once you have done this get them to complete the GET test. Summarise the most important observation and insights you have gained from the interview. Make sure you justify your conclusions about their character with evidence from the interview and the GET test.

2. Find out all you can about a well known entrepreneur and write an essay or report describing their character. Give examples of their actions that lead you to make your conclusions.

3. Using the GET test and the questions developed in exercise 1 as a basis, evaluate your own entrepreneurial character. Write a report describing your character. Give examples of actions or behaviours that support these conclusions.

References

Abdesselam, R., Bonnet, J. and Le Pape, N. (1999) 'An Explanation of the Life Span of New Firms: An Empirical Analysis of French Data', *Entrepreneurship: Building for the Future*, Euro PME 2nd International Conference, Rennes.

Acs, Z. and Audretsch, D.B. (1989) 'Births and Firm Size', *Southern Economic Journal*, 55.

Aldrich, H.E. and Martinez, M. (2003) 'Entrepreneurship as a Social Construction: A Multi-Level Evolutionary Approach', in Z.J. Acs and D.B. Audretsch (eds), *Handbook of Entrepreneurship Research: A Multidisciplinary Survey and Introduction*, Boston, MA: Kluwer Academic Publishers.

Anderson, J. (1995) Local Heroes, Scottish Enterprise, Glasgow.

Andersson, S., Gabrielsson, J. and Wictor, I. (2004) 'International Activities in Small Firms – Examining Factors Influencing the Internationalisation and Export Growth of Small Firms', *Canadian Journal of Administrative Science*, 21(1).

Annual Population Survey (2004) *Annual Population Survey, January–December, 2004*, London: Office for National Statistics.

Baty, G. (1990) *Entrepreneurship in the Nineties*, Englewood Cliffs, NJ: Prentice Hall.

Bell, J., Murray, M. and Madden, K. (1992) 'Developing Expertise: An Irish Perspective', *International Small Business Journal*, 10(2).

Blanchflower, D.G. and Meyer, B.D. (1991) 'Longitudinal Analysis of Young Entrepreneurs in Australia and the United States', National Bureau of Economic Research, Working Paper no. 3746, Cambridge, MA.

Bolton, B. and Thompson, J. (2000) *Entrepreneurs: Talent, Temperament, Technique*, Oxford: Butterworth-Heinemann.

Brockhaus, R. and Horwitz, P. (1986) 'The Psychology of the Entrepreneur', in D. Sexton and R. Smilor (eds), *The Art and Science of Entrepreneurship*, Cambridge, MA: Ballinger Publishing Co.

Brush, C.G. (1992) 'Research on Women Business Owners: Past Trends, A New Perspective and Future Directions', *Entrepreneurship: Theory and Practice*, 16(4).

Busenitz, L. and Barney, J. (1997) 'Differences between Entrepreneurs and Managers in Large Organisations: Biases and Heuristics in Strategic Decision Making', *Journal of Business Venturing*, 12.

Buttner, E. and More, D. (1997) 'Women's Organisational Exodus to Entrepreneurship: Self-Reported Motivations and Correlates with Success', *Journal of Small Business Management*, 35(1).

Caird, S. (1990) 'What Does it Mean to be Enterprising?', *British Journal of Management*, 1(3).

Carr, P. (2000) *The Age of Enterprise: The Emergence and Evolution of Entrepreneurial Management*, Dublin: Blackwell.

Carter, S. and Cachon, J. (1988) *The Sociology of Entrepreneurship*, Stirling: University of Stirling Press.

Carter, S. and Shaw, E. (2006) *Women's Business Ownership: Recent Research and Policy Developments*, Report to the Small Business Service, London: DTI.

Center for Women's Business Research (2008), *Key Facts*, Center for Women's Business Research, Washington, DC, www.nfwbo.org/facts/index.php.

Chell, E., Haworth, J. and Brearley, S. (1991) *The Entrepreneurial Personality*, London: Routledge.

Chen, P.C., Greene, P.G. and Crick, A. (1998) 'Does Entrepreneurial Self Efficacy Distinguish Entrepreneurs from Managers?', *Journal of Business Venturing*, 13.

Cliff, J. (1998), 'Does One Size Fit All? Exploring the Relationship Between Attitudes Towards Growth, Gender and Business Size', *Journal of Business Venturing*, 13(6).

Cuba, R., Decenzo, D. and Anish, A. (1983) 'Management Practises of Successful Female Business Owners', *American Journal of Small Business*, 8(2).

Deakins, D. (1996) *Entrepreneurs and Small Firms*, London: McGraw-Hill.

de Bono, E. (1985) *Six Thinking Hats*, Boston: Little Brown & Company.

Evans, D.S. and Leighton, L.S. (1990) 'Small Business Formation by Unemployed and Employed Workers', *Small Business Economics*, 2(4).

Harper, M. (1985) 'Hardship, Discipline and Entrepreneurship', Cranfield School of Management, Working Paper no. 85.1.

Hirsch, R.D. and Brush, C.G. (1987) 'Women Entrepreneurs: A Longitudinal Study', *Frontiers in Entrepreneurship Research*, Wellesley, MA: Babson College.

Hofstede, G. (1980) *Culture's Consequences: International Differences in Work-related Values*, Beverly Hills, CA: Sage.

Hofstede, G. (1981) *Cultures and Organisations: Software of the Mind*, London: HarperCollins.

Hofstede, G. and Bond, M.H. (1991) 'The Confucian Connection: From Cultural Roots to Economic Performance', Organisational Dynamics, Spring.

Kalleberg, A.L. and Leicht, K.T. (1991), 'Gender and Organisation Performance: Determinants of Small Business Survival and Success', *Academy of Management Journal*, 34(1).

Kanter, R.M. (1983) *The Change Masters*, New York: Simon & Schuster.

Kets de Vries, M.F.R. (1985) 'The Dark Side of Entrepreneurship', *Harvard Business Review*, November–December.

Kets de Vries, M.F.R. (1997) 'The Entrepreneurial Personality: A Person at the Crossroads', *Journal of Management Studies*, February.

Kirzner, I.M. (1973) *Competition and Entrepreneurship*, Chicago: University of Chicago.

Kirzner, I.M. (1979) *Perception, Opportunity and Profit: Studies in the Theory of Entrepreneurship*, Chicago: University of Chicago.

Kirzner, I.M. (1997) 'Entrepreneurial Discovery and Competitive Market Processes: An Austrian Approach', *Journal of Economic Literature*, 35.

Kirzner, I.M. (1999) 'Creativity and/or Alertness: A Reconsideration of Schumpeterian Entrepreneur', *Review of Austrian Economics*, 11.

McClelland, D. C. (1961) *The Achieving Society*, Princeton, NJ: Van Nostrand.

Morris, P. (1991) 'Freeing the Spirit of Enterprise: The Genesis and Development of the Concept of Enterprise Culture', in R. Keat and N. Abercrombie (eds), *Enterprise Culture*, London: Routledge.

O'Connor, J. (1973) *The Fiscal Crisis of the State*, New York: St. Martin's Press.

Pinchot, G. (1985) *Intrapreneuring*, New York: Harper & Row.

Rosa, P., Hamilton, S., Carter, S. and Burns, H. (1994) 'The Impact of Gender on Small Business Management: Preliminary Findings of a British Study', *International Small Business Journal*, 12(3).

Rosa, P., Carter, S. and Hamilton. D. (1996). 'Gender as a Determinant of Small Business Performance: Insights from a British Study', *Small Business Economics*, 8.

Schein, V., Mueller, R., Lituchy, T. and Liu, J. (1996) 'Thinking Manager – Think Male: A Global Phenomenon?', *Journal of Organisational Behaviour*, 17.

Schumpeter, J.A. (1983/1996) *The Theory of Economic Development*, New Brunswick, NJ: Transaction Publishers.

Schwartz, E.B. (1997) 'Entrepreneurship: A New Female Frontier', *Journal of Contemporary Business*, Winter.

Shapero, A. (1985) *Managing Professional People – Understanding Creative Performance*, New York: Free Press.

Shaver, K. and Scott, L. (1992) 'Person, Processes and Choice: The Psychology of New Venture Creation', *Entrepreneurship Theory and Practice*, 16(2).

Stanworth, J., Blythe, S., Granger, B. and Stanworth, C. (1989) 'Who Becomes an Entrepreneur?', *International Small Business Journal*, 8(1).

Steiner, R. (1999) *My First Break: How Entrepreneurs Get Started*, Sunday Times Books.

Storey, D.J. (1994) *Understanding the Small Business Sector*, London: International Thomson Business Press.

Storey, D. and Sykes, N. (1996) 'Uncertainty, Innovation and Management', in P. Burns and J. Dewhurst (eds), *Small Business and Entrepreneurship*, London: Macmillan – now Basingstoke: Palgrave Macmillan.

Stormer, R., Kilne, T. and Goldberg, S. (1999) 'Measuring Entrepreneurship with the General Enterprise Tendency (GET) Test: Criterion-Related Validity and Reliability', *Human Systems Management*, 18(1).

Timmons, J. (1994) *New Venture Creation*, Boston, MA: Irwin.

Welsch, H. (1998) 'America: North', in A. Morrison (ed.), *Entrepreneurship: An International Perspective*, Oxford: Butterworth Heinemann.

CHAPTER 2

Personal enterprise: connecting opportunities and personal goals

CONTENTS

- Introduction
- Key ideas on entrepreneurial learning
- A model of entrepreneurial learning
- Assessing the fit between ideas and personal goals
- Personal orientation to risk and uncertainty
- Entrepreneurial personality, roles, skills and capabilities
- Being a leader: forming and leading entrepreneurial teams
- Networking, influencing and selling: vital skills in seeding opportunities
- Review

Introduction

The purpose of this chapter is to explore personal enterprise: the human aspects of the entrepreneurial process. It explores how people learn to work in entrepreneurial ways and become entrepreneurs, why they select the opportunities they do, and the connections between learning and selecting opportunities. It asks you to relate these ideas to your own development.

The chapter explains the important concept of entrepreneurial learning and key elements which relate to this. A model of entrepreneurial learning is introduced to help you to reflect on your own personal experience and development. There is a series of exercises to help you map your personal learning to date and identify areas and needs for development. These involve reflection and self-assessment of your personal values, goals, motivations, self-confidence and capabilities.

The learning goals of this chapter are intended to enable you to:

- relate your own learning experiences to a framework for entrepreneurial learning
- identify and reflect on your values, goals and motivations to help develop your confidence to take entrepreneurial actions

- assess your entrepreneurial capabilities and skills
- develop a learning map to summarise and plan your entrepreneurial development.

The outcome of the chapter is to develop a map of your entrepreneurial learning at a personal and social level, and to show how this connects with the types of opportunity which you can select. This chapter covers the first quadrant of Opportunity-Centred Entrepreneur-ship, which focuses on personal enterprise and includes the questions shown in Figure 2.1. Activities in the chapter encourage you to reflect on the importance of self-confidence, motivation and achievement in entrepreneurial working. The chapter explores personal goals, motivations, and ways of assessing the 'fit' between these and ideas. Personal skills and capabilities are assessed in relation to changes in roles and skills at different stages of the entrepreneurial venture. You will be asked to consider your preferred role in forming and leading entrepreneurial teams. The social skills required in entrepreneurial working to seed opportunities through networking, influencing and selling are explored.

Key ideas on entrepreneurial learning

If we accept that people can learn to work in entrepreneurial ways, the question is: how? This chapter is based on research which explored how people learn to work in entrepreneurial ways and identified the significant processes and experiences in their learning (Rae, 2005b). This is used to develop the entrepreneurial learning model included in the chapter.

We know that entrepreneurship consists of the interrelated processes of creating, recognising and acting on opportunities, by combining innovating, decision making and enaction. Learning is an emergent, sensemaking process in which people develop the ability to act differently. Learning comprises knowing, doing, and understanding why (Mumford, 1995). Through learning, people construct meaning through experience in a context of social interaction, and create new reality,

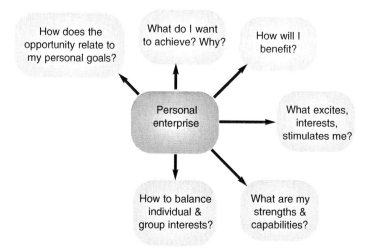

Figure 2.1 Relating opportunity to personal goals

or sensemaking as Weick (1995) termed this process. Both entrepreneurship and learning are behavioural and social processes, so they are not just about 'knowing' but also acting, and they are not simply individual, but constantly involve interaction with other people as an inescapable part of the learning process. The term 'entrepreneurial learning' means learning to recognise and act on opportunities, for example by working socially and by initiating, organising and managing ventures in social and behavioural ways.

If entrepreneurship can be learned, can it be taught? If you are reading this book as part of an entrepreneurship course, then either you or your tutor probably assumes that it can. However the extensive research into entrepreneurship education suggests that while education can provide cultural and personal support, knowledge and skill development about and for entrepreneurship, the 'art' of entrepreneurial practice is learned from experience rather than the educational environment alone. So learning must take place through action in the 'real world', rather than being a purely educational and theoretical process. Gaining practical experiences and 'learning by doing' is a key part of the entrepreneurial learning process.

Increasingly entrepreneurship is viewed as 'plural not singular' – that is to say, entrepreneurial effectiveness depends on several people working effectively together rather than just on the 'lone entrepreneur'. So a business is often the product of an entrepreneurial team, in which people must learn to work effectively together. Therefore it is essential to develop skills of leadership and teamworking for a venture to grow, and for individuals to appreciate the distinctive contribution they can make.

A model of entrepreneurial learning

Figure 2.2 introduces a model of entrepreneurial learning. This is a social learning model, which connects individuals with their social context (Wenger, 1998). It centres on people's *lifeworlds* as they develop their entrepreneurial identity and

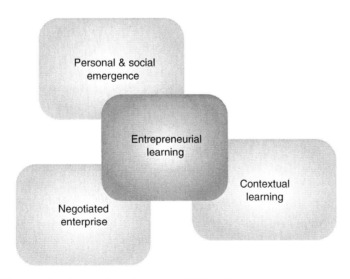

Figure 2.2   Three major themes in entrepreneurial learning

capability through social learning (Berger and Luckman, 1967). The model includes the three major themes of:

- *Personal and social emergence*: becoming an entrepreneur.
- *Contextual learning*: how people use their experience to find and work on opportunities.
- *The negotiated enterprise*: how entrepreneurs interact with others to create ventures.

Opposite is a short example which illustrates all three major themes.

Each of the three themes is developed at a detailed level by specific sub-themes. There are 11 sub-themes added, and these are shown in Figure 2.3 (overleaf). A set of reflective questions is integrated into the model to help you to develop your personal awareness of entrepreneurial and business practice.

Personal and social emergence: becoming an entrepreneur

Creating an entrepreneurial identity, or 'becoming an entrepreneur', is an outcome of personal and social emergence, including:

- narrative construction of identity – our changing story of who we are
- identity as practice – how what we do shapes our identity

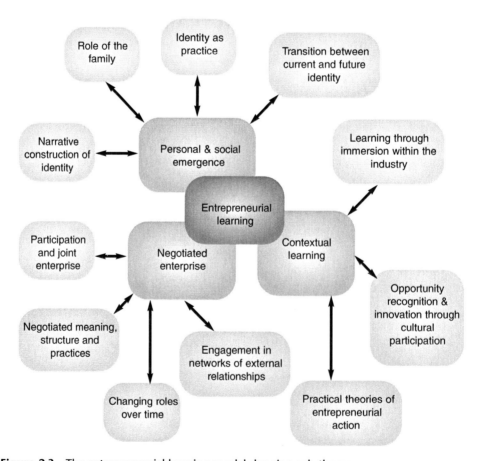

Figure 2.3 The entrepreneurial learning model showing sub-themes

- the role of the family – how family relationships influence us
- tension between current and future identity – how dissatisfaction can lead to entrepreneurship.

EXAMPLE

Mike: Shires FM

Mike, the founder of Shires FM, an independent radio broadcaster, describes his personal emergence from employee to entrepreneur, and the development of his own commercial radio station as a negotiated enterprise that began after he recognised the opportunity through his contextual learning within the industry.

Personal and social emergence
'I grew up around here, there was no commercial radio station. I went to work for another radio station where I was successful in building audiences and advertising, but became increasingly fed up with the way it was being managed.'

   'I decided I couldn't stand the contradiction with what I knew worked any longer, so I agreed to end my contract with them. I took a huge risk, it was a really dangerous thing to do because any sensible person would have stuck in there until they'd got another job.'

Negotiated enterprise
'I applied for the licence for this station when the Radio Authority offered it, along with one of the directors from my old station as a backer. There were five applicants for it and we were the outsiders, but we won and that's how I got to be running it. I found the shareholders and I persuaded them to invest £500,000 in the operation.'

   'In radio you have to start big time, because you spend a huge amount of money winning an audience before you get a single penny in revenue. You're winning customers who don't pay you a penny to listen, and it only comes when you can turn round to advertisers to say 'Hey, all these people can listen to you if you advertise with us.''

Contextual learning
'This station, down to the last dot of the 'i' in the prospectus, was mine. It was my opportunity to run the station from scratch in the way I knew it would work. I hadn't enjoyed having to do things in a radically different way from what I believed was right, I had been successful and I believed the way I wanted to set up the organisation would work.'

   'You couldn't start it like a small business. Even when we started we weren't the smallest radio station, we were employing 22 or 23 people, so it's not a small start-up situation, it's straight in there.'

Opportunity recognition arising from contextual learning.

Recognising and acting on opportunities is an outcome of contextual learning, which includes:

- learning through immersion within an environment such as career or work experience within an industry or community
- opportunity recognition and innovation through participation – developing ideas from experience
- practical theories of entrepreneurial action – finding out 'what works for me'.

Negotiated enterprise

Starting and growing a business venture over time is an outcome of processes of negotiated enterprise, which include:

- participation and joint enterprise – working with others on the venture
- negotiating meaning, structures and practices – developing shared beliefs about the venture
- engaging in networks of external relationships – building and managing relationships with people around the venture
- changing roles over time – roles growing with the venture.

Personal learning and entrepreneurial working

We will use each of the three themes of the entrepreneurial learning model in turn to explore personal understanding of entrepreneurial working. Figure 2.3 is a diagram of the full entrepreneurial learning model, showing the three major themes and 11 sub-themes.

How to use the entrepreneurial learning model

The purpose of the entrepreneurial learning model is to stimulate deeper personal awareness and reflection on your journey of entrepreneurial learning. It is not a simplistic 'Am I an entrepreneur?' questionnaire. This section explains the model and provides a set of questions on each of the sub-themes. It aims to help you to reflect on your entrepreneurial development, either individually or in a small group discussion with other people.

Read through each of the three themes and clusters of sub-themes to gain an overall understanding, then return to the first theme, personal and social emergence.

Not every sub-theme will be relevant to your experience at present, unless you have been involved in a venture of some kind. Focus first on those which make sense to you. Those where you may not yet have had experience, for example in the 'negotiated enterprise' theme, may be where you can aim to gain experience through the practical activities as part of your development.

Start to take notes as you go through it, which will help make sense of your own learning. You can do this by using the opportunity mapping approach to map your learning so far and ideas for your development, taking each sub-theme as a branch and making notes of your thoughts on each of the questions as you go along.

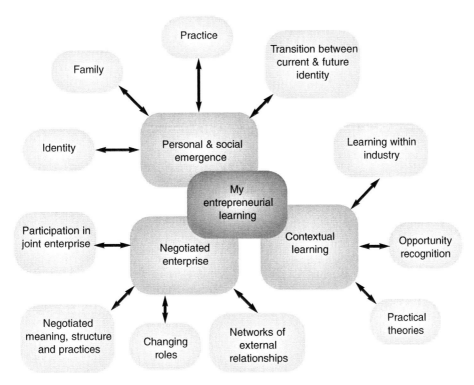

Figure 2.4 Entrepreneurial learning map

An example is shown in Figure 2.4 to help you to get started. In this way, you can build up your personal map of your entrepreneurial learning.

Allow several periods of time for this, to reflect on each theme in turn.

Personal and social emergence

Personal and social emergence is the development of *entrepreneurial identity* expressed through a person's narrative or life story. We all tell stories to explain our biography. Emergence is the story of the person you are becoming, as you move through transitional life experiences, being influenced by early life and family experiences, education and career formation, and social relationships. Forming an entrepreneurial identity means becoming and behaving as an entrepreneurial person.

Through personal and social emergence, people develop an identity which expresses their sense of who they are, their self and future aspirations. Becoming an entrepreneurial person often involves people renegotiating and changing personal and social identity which expresses who they are, who they want to be, and how they prefer to be recognised within their social world.

Questions in each of the four sub-themes aim to help you reflect on your personal and social emergence:

- Narrative construction of identity.
- Role of the family.

- Identity as practice.
- Tension between current and future identity.

Narrative construction of identity

We relate our lives and identities to other people through the stories we tell about ourselves. Personal and social identity develops over time, shaped by life experiences of change and learning. This identity is negotiated with others through self and social perceptions, and as we renegotiate or 're-invent' ourselves, we can develop an entrepreneurial identity through our life story, as if we are the lead actor within a self-narrated entrepreneurial drama. Think of when you meet someone new at a business networking event: how would you describe being an entrepreneur?

- How would you tell the story of your life? Reflect on your past, your present, and how you expect your future to be.
- How do you feature in your story? Think of examples of when you have acted as an enterprising person who seeks out and takes advantage of opportunities, or as an innovator who experiments with new ideas.
- How do you want your identity to change as your life story unfolds?

Role of the family

Families are often significant in shaping people's identities and actions. Families in which parents have started or run businesses often encourage their children's entrepreneurial behaviour as role models. Entrepreneurial stories are constructed with reference to personal relationships with spouses, parents and children. In turn, relationships with family members and expectations are renegotiated through entrepreneurship. This is especially the case within the 'family business', where traditional gender and cultural roles such as husband and wife, father and mother, can play an important part in the construction of identity, as Kal described. These can constrain people's development through an assumption that they will conform to stereotyped roles, for example the role of women in certain communities, unless they are able to renegotiate their roles by changing social perceptions.

- What are your roles in your family? What does your family expect of you?
- Has the experience of family members in business influenced your aspirations?
- How do your family's expectations affect your life, career and entrepreneurial aspirations?
- How do you feel about these family expectations?
- How would you wish to change your family's expectations of you?
- What consequences for your own relationships and future family could result from your becoming an entrepreneur?

Identity as practice

People also develop their identity from their activities, practices and roles in social interactions. They discover from experience what they are good at, through education, hobbies or interests, through finding and gaining confidence in natural talents and abilities, and learning how these can be applied and be of value within networks of social relationships and situations. Identity and capabilities developed in education and early employment are often applied in the core activity of a new enterprise.

EXAMPLE

Kal: Sawari Culture

Kal explains why she wanted to start her business, called Sawari Culture, and demonstrates the creation of entrepreneurial identity through personal and social emergence. See if you can recognise in her story the four sub-themes of narrative construction of identity, the role of the family, identity as practice, and tension between current and future identity.

> I was working in my husband's print business, doing the accounts and I realised I wanted something more than that. The industry is male dominated, most of our clients were men who thought that 'she just does the book-keeping'. At the time I accepted that. I'm not like that any more, I do challenge it.
>
> It was a major thing for my husband to realise that I wanted to start my own business because we'd come from a very orthodox upbringing. I started to do computer design work which I enjoyed, and found my talent for creative design. But there came a point when I didn't want to be seen as only a wife and a mother. I wanted recognition as a person in my own right. Something inside me said, 'I can do a lot more than this.'
>
> That made me realise that I wanted my own business: you have an idea for something you want to do and you develop it. I want to achieve something for myself. It's not that I want to say 'I've done all this myself, created a business of my own', because you need to have support from other people. But I've always had this energy and belief that I want to achieve something.

- What are you good at doing and what do you enjoy doing?
- How can you best apply your skills, talents and abilities?
- How can you find the situations, opportunities and people where you can make best use of your capabilities?

Tension between current and future identity

There is often a significant point at which an enterprising person becomes dissatisfied with his or her existing reality and identity, and seeks to change this by starting a new venture. For example, employees may feel increasingly at odds with work roles and practices that are defined by others and just 'don't feel right' for them. Some of these people may seek to change their reality through a new business venture, enabling them to work in harmony with their personal values and practices. This may lead to a change in identity by becoming an entrepreneur.

- What do you want to achieve from your life at work or in education?
- Does your existing work or educational environment give you the space and opportunity you need to achieve this?
- What might cause you to move on from your current role? Would you start your own business?

- Is there a 'future reality' you want to create which is different from the present? What could this be?
- Do you believe you can make this happen? How can you start to do this?

The entrepreneurial act is imagining the possibility of 'what could be' and acting to make it happen. Entrepreneurial people create their new reality, taking responsibility for shaping future events. They move from assuming an identity defined by others, through work and family roles, into creating, changing and renegotiating a new identity as the author of an entrepreneurial drama. They will experience emotional uncertainties, and need to draw on resources of personal confidence and self-belief that it 'feels right' and they are able to make it happen.

Self-belief and motivation in entrepreneurial working

Self-belief and self-efficacy, our confidence in our ability to accomplish a task, are fundamental in entrepreneurial behaviour and performance. Self-confidence is a way of thinking and behaving in which individuals see the interrelationships between themselves, the world and other people around them as being one that they can change if they wish to do so. Self-efficacy is the belief that they can accomplish what is important to them. People can demonstrate the ability to change the world around them through the way they think, speak and act. Self-confidence grows and develops through successful experience, social learning from others, positive feedback and reinforcement, and personal maturity. People who work in entrepreneurial ways are less likely to accept 'given' conditions, and to act to change things around them in order to get things done. If they decide to do something, they will often set out to accomplish it, 'no matter what'.

Look at the following list of behavioural characteristics which often mark out entrepreneurial people:

- ambition to be successful
- motivation to achieve and accomplish difficult tasks
- pursuit of opportunities
- creative, unconventional thinking
- innovating, experimenting, causing change and pioneering new activities
- resilience in learning from failure and setbacks
- desire to be independent and in control of their lives and businesses
- desire to make a difference, for themselves and frequently for others.

What would you say are your dominant behavioural characteristics? Which ones are similar and which ones are different from those listed above? What could be the disadvantages or limitations of each of these behaviours?

These are questions to reflect on, which may help your personal emergence into an entrepreneurial way of living and working, if that is what you want.

Not all entrepreneurs display all of these characteristics, and most of them are displayed by many 'high achieving' people we would not categorise as entrepreneurs. Athletes, performers and scientists, for example, might well display similar characteristics. So these characteristics might be seen as behaviours practised by achieving people who wish to be successful in their given field. They may be inherent aspects of personality, but equally they may be developed through experience.

Personal and social emergence: review

Creating personal goals involves learning through self-discovery and social emergence. Forming and agreeing goals, and deciding how to assess their success are important processes in considering the wider impact and outcomes we aim to achieve. This exercise on personal and social emergence encourages you to reflect on your intentions. What do you seek to achieve in your life and career, and why do you feel this is important? What are your emotional, social, material and achievement needs? The development of self-belief and social confidence is essential for entrepreneurial attainment.

What do I want and why? Personal values, goals and motivations

- What personal values are most important to you? Values are the enduring beliefs which always guide our direction and decision making.
- What factors motivate you? What would you say you want out of life?
- What excites, interests and stimulates you?
- What does 'success' mean for you? Think of what success means in each of these life dimensions:
  - business
  - career or employment
  - financial and material terms
  - social success as judged by you and others
  - self-fulfilment
  - emotional success.
- What are your goals? What do you want to achieve, and why?
- What gives you confidence in your ability to achieve these goals? Would you describe yourself as a naturally confident person, or is your self-belief affected by what other people say?

Contextual learning

Our learning is shaped by the context, the environment or situation within which it takes place. In entrepreneurship, this often happens in the workplace and through social participation in social, cultural, industry and other networks. This learning is interpersonal and shared, occurring through people relating and comparing their individual experiences, at work and in other arenas. Through these social relationships and contextual experiences, people create shared meaning, learn intuitively and can develop the ability to recognise opportunities and generate the ideas for innovation.

Contextual learning connects people's personal emergence with the negotiated enterprise, as they learn in their social world 'who they can become' and 'how to work with others to achieve their goals' as well as the realism of 'what can and cannot be'. But contextual learning can be limiting and discouraging, for if the social context does not encourage innovative or entrepreneurial activity, or is poor in opportunities, people may learn that they have to change their context by leaving it and moving to a different environment.

Questions to help you reflect on your contextual learning are given in each of the three sub-themes:

- learning through immersion within the industry or community
- opportunity recognition and innovation through participation
- practical theories of entrepreneurial action.

Learning through immersion within the industry

People develop skills, expert knowledge and social contacts from their work, often as employees gaining experience, understanding and know-how in an industry. This learning is gained from discovery and experience, and socially by interpersonal participation. It is often functional, technical and problem solving in nature, finding out how things are done, developing intuitive practices and skills which work in given situations and which people can go on to use in creating their own businesses.

- What are the most useful skills and expertise you have developed? In what situations could you apply these?
- What intuitive, tacit abilities and skills have you developed, which you use without needing to think about them?
- What social, industry and professional relationships, contacts and networks have you formed? Who do you know within these networks?
- How might you use these contacts to your advantage in creating a new venture?

Opportunity recognition and innovation through participation

Opportunities are apparent to those who are alert and learn to recognise them, using knowledge, experience and behaviour. By being active within social and industry networks, paying attention to what people say, noticing what goes on, you can recognise and imagine future possibilities in that environment. If you identify an opportunity to create a new venture within a familiar context, you can find out how things are done and who to talk to.

Contextual learning also aids innovation: you can use your knowledge of what exists now, and combine this with imagination to create future reality. Thinking

---

EXAMPLE

Opportunity recognition: Cryosolve

'I'd worked in the engineering industry for many years, I'd started and run a business and like so many we found it was always a struggle to make a profit. Then a couple of years ago I was in the States and noticed the way that cryogenics – using very low temperature treatment of materials and components – was expanding. I thought there must be an opportunity to make that work in the UK – there are lots of applications in engineering and no-one here was offering a good service, so we decided to do it.'

Derek, Cryosolve UK

prospectively is envisaging the future and imagining how an opportunity can be created, before all the necessary knowledge or circumstances exist. This creative and associative learning brings together ideas, opportunities, technologies and resources in innovative ways. Such resources may include people and their expertise, finance, technology, information and physical resources, and acting ahead of others.

- What needs and problems do you recognise in your everyday life or career?
- Which of these could provide possible opportunities for you?
- How can your experience and contacts help you to create new opportunities?
- What ideas can you think of for future creative and business possibilities?
- How could you combine existing knowledge, technology and ideas to create new possibilities or innovations?

Practical theories of entrepreneurial action

People develop rules, routines and ways of working which work for them in getting things done successfully. This is knowledge of 'what works', why, how and with whom, gained from contextual experience, intuition and sensemaking. These are practical theories which enable people to reduce risk through experience because they 'know what they are doing'.

- What 'works' for you, in developing new ideas and making them happen?
- How do you make this work, and why? Which people does it work with?
- What are your 'practical theories' and how could you apply these in a business venture?

Contextual learning: review

Contextual learning connects personal goals and opportunities. The reasons why people select particular opportunities are various, and not necessarily or exclusively rational. Self-learning about the relationships between personal goals and motivations, shared interests between people, and the decision to focus on a specific opportunity is important. Our interests and experiences are likely to be significant in the commitment and ability to act on an opportunity successfully.

- What experiences and interests do you have which could be useful to you in finding and selecting entrepreneurial opportunities?
- How would you relate these opportunities to your personal goals?
- How could you use your contextual learning and life experiences from work and community to select and develop opportunities?
- How do you assess 'risk' and uncertainty? How could you use previous learning and experience to manage or reduce risk in acting on opportunities?

The negotiated enterprise

The concept of the negotiated enterprise is that a business venture is dependent on negotiated relationships between people, and is not enacted by one person alone. As Wenger (1998) noted, 'the enterprise is joint ... in that it is communally negotiated'. The ideas and aspirations of individuals are realised through interactive processes of negotiation and exchange with others in and around the enterprise, including customers, investors and co-actors such as employees or partners. The negotiated enterprise includes four sub-themes:

- participation and joint enterprise
- negotiated meaning, structures and practices
- engagement in networks of external relationships
- changing roles over time.

The negotiated enterprise is a process which doesn't happen until you start developing a venture with other people. So some of the questions related to the sub-themes below can only be answered from experience of working with others, for example in a business or organisation. If you are a student, you may not yet have gained this experience. If you work on a business idea as a project with one or more other people as a venture team, this will give you experience of negotiated enterprise. 'Young enterprise' company projects at school or college can also provide useful experience of team venturing.

Participation and joint enterprise

People act together to create enterprises which they could not achieve individually. Entre-preneurship is often plural, not singular. Even the sole founder of an enterprise is dependent on successful interactions with others to become an entrepreneur. A vital aspect of the entrepreneurial learning process is the ability to engage and work constructively with others towards the goal of venture creation. It is necessary for the entrepreneur to create shared belief in the potential of the venture to exist and succeed. Participative action is required to create this new reality, and to realise personal dreams and aspirations. Co-participants must put the collective identity of the enterprise as a project of shared significance before their individual identity. This is accompanied by social learning in which people learn to work together. Shared interests or goals, such as wealth creation, economic survival or the desire to enact a particular activity, are necessary for joint enterprise.

- How effectively do you work with others in agreeing shared goals and working towards them?
- Do you know what your preferred role and strengths would be in a team venture? What are you best at?

EXAMPLE

Negotiated enterprise: Blue Fish, a creative marketing business

'Three of us started Blue Fish. After a few years we took time out for each of us to write down what we wanted for this business, when we wanted to sell it, and what tone of voice we wanted to present to the market. We wrote down four words between us: creative, effective, fun, and integrity. Those words summarised the business and became our values.'

Tony, Blue Fish

- Are you more of an individualist or a team player? How well are you able to put a team's shared interests ahead of your own?
- How do you recognise and employ the abilities of others – even when you disagree with their methods?
- Can you trust people you work closely with, and do they trust you?

Negotiated meaning, structures and practices

In an enterprise, people develop practical theories of 'what works' as individuals and these become a shared repertoire of practices and routines within the business, often described as 'the way we do things round here – what works for us'. This produces a distinctive culture within a business, where what is known and done does not belong to any single person, but rather is shared amongst the members.

An enterprise depends on these negotiated ways of working, which often reflect the founders' style, language, values, ambitions and ways of working, and those of the employees. Tom Kirby, CEO of Games Workshop, asserts that organisations have a 'spiritual life' with which people engage – or not. The lives, interests and aspirations of people within the business must be recognised by the founders who hold formal power and ownership of the business, which is of limited value without the employees' participation. Conflict and disagreement are inevitable from time to time and form an integral aspect of this negotiation.

In many enterprises, there is a strong emotional engagement between the people and the business, in which the culture is expressed through the style, language, behaviours, and feeling between people. For many people, this is why they enjoy coming to work. The 'buzz', the emotional and spiritual life and energy of the enterprise, comes from people expressing themselves, their identities and their abilities in their work, and in sharing this with their customers.

- What works for you and others within a shared project? How do you share goals, values, ways of working?
- How do you stimulate and sustain the emotional life of the venture: the passion, buzz, excitement and fun?
- How do you turn individual learning into shared learning?
- How can you manage conflict and disagreement to positive effect?

Engagement in networks of external relationships

The enterprise depends on relationships being developed and maintained with key individuals and networks. These may include customers, suppliers, investors, lenders, and others such as technology experts, resource holders and opinion formers. This starts as soon as you start to talk to people about a possible venture. Social capital ('who you know') is vital in affording access to resources and expertise. Entrepreneurs are selective in developing social networks, seeking to influence certain groups whilst choosing not to participate in others.

Similarly, customers need to be engaged as active participants who identify culturally with the enterprise, not simply as passive consumers; more than economic value is then generated in the interchange. Relationships and 'rapport' with some customers and suppliers may be more productive than with others.

The cultural identity of the enterprise is formed and enacted through the interactions between it and these external groups. The skills of listening, understanding the other party's position, negotiating and storytelling are essential in maintaining effective relationships. The enterprise depends on its identity, practices and the credibility of its message – its story – being accepted and understood within its chosen networks.

- What are the most important external relationships for an enterprise? With whom, and why?
- What would your expectations be of them, and theirs of the business? Are these realistic and can they be met or, if not, renegotiated?
- How can the customer be engaged in the life of the business?
- Are there gaps in the external relationships with key groups and individuals, and what actions are needed to fill these?

Changing roles over time

A business evolves through a process of ongoing learning and negotiation. If this is successful, the business tends to grow, becoming larger and more complex in operation and structure, and employs more people. This clearly applies to existing businesses, though you may not yet have experienced it. It is a series of transitions from informal to formal roles, relationships and structures. Significant changes in the roles of founders and others are inevitable as the business develops. Growth occurs through changes in human and social behaviour and relationships, and productive interpersonal negotiations around the enterprise. Different capabilities are required to manage the enterprise at different stages of its development, and people who do not grow with the business may be best advised to leave it.

This negotiated change in roles means that self-sustaining capability can be developed gradually, through people other than the founders taking responsibility for managing the business. Developing entrepreneurial and work teams, competent managers and functional experts is integral to the growth process and depends on managing relationships effectively, changing past expectations, sharing practices, and resolving interpersonal tension and conflict effectively. As new people are employed by the business, a mark of its cultural effectiveness is how well they learn to integrate and identify with it, adopting its cultural values of participation, behaviour and language.

- Can you accept that your role and others roles will change as an enterprise grows?
- How easily can you 'learn to let go' and entrust important roles to others?
- How well can you integrate new people into a team or business?
- How would you deal with people whom you have worked with from the start but who have not grown with the business, and whose skills no longer fit?

Negotiated enterprise – review

These questions focus on an opportunity and potential new venture you may be considering:

- What skills, capabilities and expertise do you think your opportunity will require, which you do not possess yourself?
- How could you identify people with those characteristics through using networks of contacts?
- How could you engage compatible people with the venture?

- What would be the basis for negotiation? What are the prospective benefits for them, and what input would be required?
- How can your individual interests be balanced with bringing other people into the business?

Assessing the fit between ideas and personal goals

Why do people choose the opportunities that they do? The relationship between entrepreneurs and the opportunities that they choose to work on is not well understood. People perceive different opportunities, even when the same information is available to them, because of their differing past experiences, learning and individual perspectives. Here are some of the factors which are often significant in connecting ideas, opportunities and personal goals:

- family background
- personal interest or hobby
- previous career experience
- education, training and professional development
- social and community network and connection.

Family background may be significant where there is a family history of starting and running businesses in a particular trade, industry or profession. There are many examples; the Forte family ran hotels and restaurants, and Rocco Forte launched his own hotel chain; Stelmar tankers was the first business started by Stelios Haji-Ioannou, whose father also ran a shipping business. Experience within the family may be influential, but there are also many cases of sons and daughters deciding not to follow in the 'family footsteps', for example rural people moving away from family farming businesses, or second-generation Indian and Chinese young people in the UK deciding not to join the retail or food businesses started by their parents. Gender can also be a factor: for example, women entrepreneurs often recognise opportunities and start businesses in ways which are qualitatively different from men.

Personal interests or hobbies can provide a means of learning about a particular activity and starting a business, either early in working life or, as is increasingly common, after a career in employment. The numbers of mid-career and 'third-age' entrepreneurs is growing, as people leave corporate careers and seek self-fulfilment and additional income rather than retirement. Often these businesses can be termed 'lifestyle', turning a leisure interest into a source of income; if the numbers of hobby-based businesses were counted they would be very large indeed. At one extreme is someone like Mike, who in his teenage years is fascinated by independent radio, and persistently works his way into hospital radio, progressing to running a radio station as his first job and then founding the business that he builds into a chain of commercial radio stations. At the other is a lady such as Rosa, who participated in a business start-up programme and after a career in financial services started a niche business selling bird-seed to garden birdwatchers, having spotted an unmet need in her own hobby. It is of course vital for the market opportunity to be thoroughly understood and for such a business to be run on strictly commercial principles, not as an extension of the hobby.

Previous career experience often provides the starting point for a business. Employment in an industry enables 'niche' opportunities to be identified, networks of contacts to be built up and skills developed, as demonstrated in the contextual learning theme of the entrepreneurial learning model. People develop distinctive expertise which they can use in their own business. The commercial and technical or professional skills and insights or 'practical theories' provide a knowledge base and reduce risk. However the move from employment to self-employment or entrepreneurship is not always simple, and many who have done this have found that they needed to learn the additional skills of running a business, for which their previous career had not prepared them. These are covered in the section on 'personal skills and readiness' later in this chapter.

Education, training and professional development often provide the knowledge, the realisation that entrepreneurship is possible and some of the contacts necessary to start a business. There are more graduates in certain subject areas, such as art, design, fashion and computer gaming, than there are career opportunities, and self-employment is a necessity for an increasing number of them. Unfortunately this can produce too many small creative businesses struggling to make a living, and business skills may not have been developed at college to the same extent as creative skills. Practice and experience in the industry provides a major advantage over education alone, and whilst graduate enterprise is to be commended, it may not be an ideal initial career choice.

Social and community networks and connections provide many experienced entrepreneurs with subsequent business opportunities; through their networks, they become aware of opportunities and are able to use these to develop business ventures. The community can also be a resource and stimulus for social enterprise. Social and economic problems in communities, such as unemployment, lack of amenities such as leisure facilities, a shop or childcare, have been the spur for many social entrepreneurs to get started. One advantage of social enterprise is that there is an almost inexhaustible supply of needs which can be translated into opportunities, as social problems and needs change with demographics. So needs such as community dentistry, teenage literacy, and English language learning for asylum-seekers constantly present themselves, together with the considerable challenges of how to create a viable and sustainable business model which avoids grant-dependency, and developing the skills and confidence people need to make the business happen.

These are the main reasons why people select the type of opportunities they do. As suggested in the section on contextual learning, the prior experience, knowledge and social connections which people develop play a significant part in forming their choices and enabling them to recognise opportunities which others would not. Sometimes, this prior learning may blinker people and prevent them from seeing better, more rewarding opportunities. However, prior experience and learning reduce risk, and the track record of people pursuing business opportunity completely outside their previous experience shows it is considerably more risky. An example is the chairman of a successful furniture retailing business who, after achieving a merger and flotation of the business, was invited to chair an engineering business. Having spent his career in furniture retailing, and despite very highly developed managerial skills, he did not have the experience to understand the very different context of the engineering business, which came close to failure as a result. Contextual learning is therefore extremely important in entrepreneurial learning and opportunity selection.

ACTIVITY

Consider these factors in the selection of entrepreneurial opportunities:

- family background
- personal interest or hobby
- previous career experience
- education, training and professional development
- social and community network and connections.

Are there any other factors you would add to these from your own experience? Which factors are most influential in the types of opportunities you look for?

Personal orientation to risk and uncertainty

People have markedly different orientations to risk-taking in business. We should not accept the popular stereotype of 'entrepreneur as risk-taker' without exploring the issue of risk in opportunity selection more carefully. Contextual learning can be seen as a means of reducing risk. Mike, for example, took what others saw as a big risk in leaving his job to start a radio station but his career experience had provided him with the confidence to know 'what worked' in building a successful commercial radio business. The negotiated enterprise also plays a role in risk reduction, as in many ventures the entrepreneur or entrepreneurial team do not carry the entire risk, as other investors or partners share the exposure to the business success or failure. However that still leaves the issue of personal exposure to risk.

These are some of the factors involved in considering risk

- *Self-confidence* and the personal belief in the ability to make a new venture or innovation work is an important factor. Personal dynamism, and intense and sustained effort to achieve change are required, but are not sufficient on their own.
- The ability to *manage emotional tension* and arousal connected with risk is significant, in that people who are prone to become anxious and fearful are better off not taking such risks.
- *Negotiated risk sharing,* by engaging investors, partners and others in the venture to share risk is a sensible strategy, and is necessary in any venture where the entrepreneur does not wish or is not able to fully self-finance a venture which is an attractive investment.
- *Iterative,* step-by-step working, can break apparently big risks down into smaller, limited ones where the exposure at each stage to failure is reduced. An example is checking that each stage of an innovation works before going on to the next,

and that each decision has been evaluated to determine its impact before the next is made. However, time pressure can reduce the scope for this form of risk management.

EXAMPLE

Entrepreneurs often calculate the percentage chances of success in their decision making as one form of reducing risk. Here Tony, in the marketing business Blue Fish, describes how they learned to evaluate their prospects for success in competing for new clients:

> A lot hangs on whether we think we have a chance of getting a job. With one client, we had lots of background in the business, so we had a good chance of winning it. We're up against four other agencies. We managed to find out a little about the others: one we dismissed straight away, it was down to three others, so 25 per cent chance. It was worth a quarter of a million, and it was a bigger job to go for with lots of ongoing work. We've drawn up a set of criteria now on which we act. It has to be the start of an ongoing relationship; if it's a one-off job it's not worth it. If the next job after that is going to be a pitch, then we don't even go for the first one.

This demonstrates the use of 'practical theory' in decision making and in this case evaluating the chances of success against the risk of wasting time on an unproductive business development. Entrepreneurs also assess the 'downside', the worst possible outcome from the decision, and their ability to accept this.

Entrepreneurial personality, roles, skills and capabilities

This section summarises the skills which are needed to develop entrepreneurial ventures. The focus is on skills and capabilities to complete given tasks, because skills are behavioural and can be learned, although each individual has differing degrees of innate ability and readiness to learn them. They are not dependent on personality, which is individually variable, although personality does influence the readiness and personal style we bring to learning and practising the skill. This emphasis on skills also helps in understanding the issue of roles in the entrepreneurial venture.

Personality

There is little firm evidence of a correlation between one's personality type and entrepreneurial success. However, by being self-aware, you can behave in ways which are more effective. An understanding of personality is important to entrepreneurship because it facilitates self-knowledge and of course the interrelationships between ourselves and others. If we know and are comfortable with 'who we are', our self-confidence, rapport and relationships with others in their roles as customers, investors and employees are more likely to be productive and profitable.

Roles

In developing an opportunity and creating and subsequently managing a business venture, a number of roles may be assumed by an individual. A role can be seen as a socially defined identity which comprises certain functions, attributes and types of behaviours used in accomplishing the tasks which normally accompany the role. Here are some of the roles which the creator of an entrepreneurial business may play, or be expected by others to play:

Inventor: creates a new product.
Innovator: applies a new technology.
Entrepreneur: starts a business to exploit a future opportunity.
Manager: builds and runs a business organisation.
Marketeer: creates a market for a new product or service.
Leader: leads and inspires people to achieve business goals.

The difficulty with viewing entrepreneurial work as a series of roles is that they are static, whereas entrepreneurship is a dynamic process which will involve some or all of these roles being played during the first few years of a business. It should not be assumed that the founder of the business can or will play all of them, or that he or she has the personality preferences or capabilities to excel in a particular role. A venture often requires multiple contributions, and roles will be taken on by others within a team in which flexibility is important.

If we consider Trevor Bayliss as an example, he is best known for developing the clockwork radio, and has a long history of inventing new products which tend to use existing technologies and materials in new ways. Trevor describes himself as an inventor. The business which he founded, Freeplay, has required all of the other roles to be played at various stages, but this has been accomplished by other people and the business has its own professional management team. It is more helpful to identify the skills and capabilities which may be required by a business at particular points and periods in its development, than to be over-concerned with individual roles, which often overlap and change. The concept of entrepreneurial teams has become influential, and in the development of an enterprise the range of capabilities needed in the team should be considered (Shepherd and Krueger, 2002).

Capability

We can identify a number of capabilities, or clusters of skills and behaviours which are required in entrepreneurial activity, and these do change at different points and stages of the development of a business. These clusters are shown in Figure 2.5 and grouped in Table 2.1 under the broad headings of entrepreneurial capabilities and management capabilities. Entrepreneurship is concerned with the creation and exploitation of the opportunity, connecting innovation with market need, whereas management is concerned with the organisation of the business venture. Both are needed to establish and then to grow and develop a successful and sustainable enterprise.

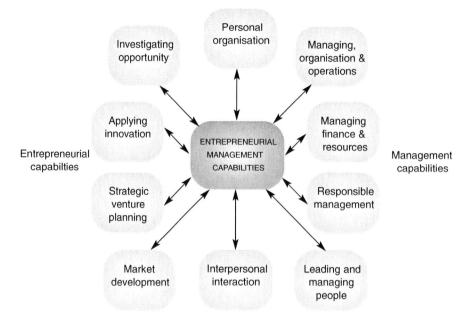

Figure 2.5 Entrepreneurial management capabilities

Table 2.1 Entrepreneurial and management capabilities

Entrepreneurial capabilities	Management capabilities
Personal organisation*	Leading and managing people
Interpersonal interaction*	Managing organisation and operations
Investigating opportunity	Managing finance and resources
Applying innovation	Responsible management – social, legal,
Strategic venture planning	environmental and ethical responsibility
Market development	

*These are both entrepreneurial and managerial capabilities

ACTIVITY

The toolkit includes a section which enables you to assess yourself in terms of the personal, entrepreneurial and managerial capabilities which are generally required for the development of a new business venture. Work through this now to help you to assess your own preferred approach to entrepreneurial work. Include the capability of leading and managing people.

Individuals operating in both areas need skills of personal organisation and interpersonal interaction, as well as technical capabilities relevant to the business activities. The combination of the entrepreneurial and management skill-sets can be defined as entrepreneurial management, or an entrepreneurial way of running an organisation. Entrepreneurial management is a capability-based approach which identifies and develops or finds the skills needed for an organisation at that stage in its development. A range of skills are required, contributed by different people, which change and evolve over time. This takes the emphasis off one particular role – and the person who is seen to be in that role, such as innovator, entrepreneur or leader – which may be emphasised at one stage in the life of a business.

Being a leader: forming and leading entrepreneurial teams

An important application of your entrepreneurial capabilities is in considering what contribution you can make to an entrepreneurial team. An entrepreneurial team is a group who have come together to exploit an opportunity, usually by setting up a new venture. The ideal entrepreneurial team is likely to have:

- complementary skills and expertise
- compatible goals and motivation – people want to achieve the same things
- compatible personalities and working styles
- trust, honesty with each other and mutual respect
- effective leadership.

The map of entrepreneurial management capabilities in Figure 2.5 includes 'leading and managing people', and effective leadership capability is needed in any business. There are many different approaches to defining leadership, and these have some parallels with the development of an understanding of entrepreneurship, for there has been considerable reliance on defining personality traits and what might be classified as 'the *great man* school of leadership'. However, more helpful approaches have started to emerge, including distributed leadership, where the cultural norm is that everyone in an organisation can demonstrate leadership, an approach that is of value in the flat, non-hierarchical entrepreneurial organisation. One such approach originates from the Sloan School of Management at Massachusetts Institute of Technology, where entrepreneurial leadership is taught. The model of leadership developed at Sloan includes five core leadership capabilities (Ancona, 2005):

- *Visioning*: fostering individual and collective aspiration towards a shared vision.
- *Analysing*: sensemaking and strategic planning in complex and conflictual settings.
- *Relating*: building relationships and negotiating change across multiple stakeholders.
- *Inventing*: inventing new ways of working together – social and technical systems.
- *Enabling*: ensuring the tools and resources to implement and sustain the shared-visions.

These capabilities can be compared to the model of entrepreneurial and managerial capabilities shown in Figure 2.5 to identify points of connection. The model includes leading and managing people. Additionally, visioning and analysing connect with strategic venture planning; relating connects with interpersonal interaction; and inventing connects with applying innovation.

ACTIVITY

Leadership and entrepreneurial teamwork

From your self-assessment of entrepreneurial and management capabilities in the toolbox:

- What are the top two or three capabilities you bring to an entrepreneurial team?
- Looking at the Sloan leadership capabilities, do you think you can demonstrate leadership, or would you prefer to support someone else in a leadership role by being a team member?
- What aspects of personality, roles, capabilities and expertise would you look for in others to complement your own?

Networking, influencing and selling: vital skills in seeding opportunities

As discussed in the negotiated enterprise theme, the interpersonal skills of networking are highly important in finding, exploring and resourcing opportunities. You may find it helpful to look back at your answers to the questions in the sub-theme of 'Engagement in networks of external relationships' and your self-assessment in the capability cluster of 'Interpersonal interaction'.

Entrepreneurial effectiveness does depend to a significant extent on being able to develop and utilise networks of contacts. This is not about simply having a world-class collection of business cards or e-mail addresses, or sending hundreds of Christmas cards, or even being a compulsive attender of business breakfast meetings, networking events or parties, although some of these may be useful in generating and maintaining contacts. Effective networking is constructing and participating in a world of social connections to create new opportunities and enable existing opportunities to be taken forward. Even reserved people, who may not feel comfortable in social gatherings, can do this.

Effective entrepreneurial networking depends on a number of behaviours which are outlined below.

- Create a distinctive and confident identity. People need to now who you are, what you are about, and what is interesting and memorable about you (personal and social emergence).
- Be strategic, purposive and focused in your choice of networks and investment of time in them. Which ones are useful and which are not?
- Work towards getting to know the decision makers, resource holders, experts, influencers and most useful people in your chosen networks.
- Practise conversational skills of listening and asking questions, finding out about people's needs, interests and their networks (interpersonal interaction).
- Manage contacts. Keep a contact file, database or business card folder up to date, and categorise groups of contacts, e.g. all the news media people you know, as they will be useful when you want to get media coverage.

Remember that human relationships depend on trust and reciprocity, so be prepared to do favours for people and to keep your promises. This builds up 'favours in the goodwill bank'. Successful entrepreneurs often 'give without the expectation of receiving in return' and find that goodwill consistently repays them. Renew and keep warm the contacts you value and want to maintain, but be selective. By participating in separate networks, covering a range of industries, and expert-professional, interest, cultural, even international domains, you will be the point of convergence and be able to introduce people from one network to contacts in another. When you need information, advice or access to a resource, then use your network – once you have developed it.

Networking activity

This is an action-learning approach which can help you to develop further your skills and confidence in entrepreneurial networking.

- Identify a need, opportunity or question you want to explore.
- Use your contacts or other research (e.g. Internet search, Chamber of Commerce) to identify a network where you can find out more about the opportunity. This should not be a network in which you have previously participated. It may be an expert, professional, trade, industry or interest group. Internet groups can be used to locate networks, but face-to-face contact is vital.
- Negotiate your way into the group and attend the next possible meeting.
- Talk to at least ten people you have not met before to find out about their areas of interest, points of connection with your own interests, and who they know who could help you further.
- Review your success in starting a new network and exploring your opportunity.
- Keep your promises to your new contacts.

One important reason for participating in networks in this way is to represent your business, and to make sure both that people are aware of you and that you can find opportunities for influencing, finding prospective new clients, and other forms of relationship development. It is not about selling, because social contacts generally find it embarrassing to receive unsolicited sales pitches at parties, and few people are good at delivering them. The aim is to identify prospective clients who may be interested in what your business can do, to create a relationship of rapport and trust with them, and to obtain their details, promising to contact them later. The next day, you can contact them and suggest a meeting or, if this is not possible, ask questions to find out about their needs, listen attentively, and only open a selling conversation if that is appropriate. The effective entrepreneur is always alert to the possible sales opportunity!

Review

Look back over your work in this chapter, including your learning map following the entrepreneurial learning model, your self-assessment of entrepreneurial capabilities, the leadership and entrepreneurial team exercise, and your development of networking skills.

Use the following questions to update your entrepreneurial learning map, to reflect on your learning so far, and to plan your continuing development.

- What are your personal values, goals and motivations?
- How would you select the best opportunities for you, and how would you make use of your contextual learning in doing this?
- What are your most developed entrepreneurial capabilities, and how could you apply these to your best advantage?
- Which capabilities do you most need to develop, and how could you achieve this?
- Do you see yourself as an entrepreneurial leader, and if so how can you develop in this role?
- What complementary expertise, personality and capabilities would you look for in other people as team members?
- How will you develop the networks you need for your opportunities and business?

Further reading

Bolton, B. and Thompson, J. (2000) *Entrepreneurs: Talent, Temperament, Technique.* Butterworth-Heinemann.

Fletcher, D. (2002) *Understanding the Small Family Business.* Routledge, London.

Kaplan, J. (2003) *Patterns of Entrepreneurship.* Wiley, Hoboken, N.J.

References

Ancona, D. (2005) *Leadership in an Age of Uncertainty.* MIT Leadership Center Research Brief, MIT, Cambridge, Mass.

Berger, P. and Luckmann, T. (1967) *The Social Construction of Reality.* Allen Lane, London.

Mumford, A. (1995). *Effective Learning.* Institute of Personnel and Development, London.

Rae, D. (2005b) Entrepreneurial Learning: A Narrative-based Conceptual Model. *Journal of Small Business and Enterprise Development,* **12**(2), pp. 323–35.

Shepherd, D. and Krueger, N. (2002) An Intentions-based Model of Entrepreneurial Teams' Social Cognition. *Entrepreneurship Theory and Practice,* **27**(2), p. 167.

Weick, K. (1995) *Sensemaking in Organizations.* Sage, Thousand Oaks, Calif.

Wenger, E. (1998) *Communities of Practice: Learning, Meaning and Identity.* Cambridge University Press, Cambridge.

CHAPTER 3

Opportunity exploration

CONTENTS

- Introduction
- Creativity and innovation in entrepreneurship
- The innovation journey
- Recognising opportunities in the external environment
- Creative problem solving
- Opportunity and problem mapping
- Creative thinking to generate innovation
- Innovation function analysis
- Innovation and solution development
- Opportunity building: matching needs and resources
- Current and future scenarios for opportunity creation
- Exploring opportunities: market and related investigation and research
- Idea-banking: opportunities as a knowledge resource
- Intellectual property: protecting ideas
- Critical questions to consider from this chapter

Introduction

This chapter focuses on how to create and explore opportunities. The purpose is to demonstrate how entrepreneurial opportunities can be created, identified and developed through a process of opportunity exploration. This chapter takes a creative approach to finding opportunities. This chapters provide a detailed exposition of the questions in the second theme of Opportunity-Centred Entrepreneurship, creating and exploring opportunities, which is shown in Figure 3.1.

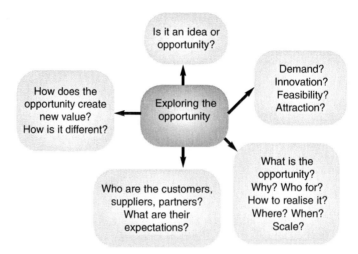

Figure 3.1 Exploring the opportunity

The learning goals for this chapter will enable you to:

- identify and define problems as potential opportunities
- generate ideas and solutions to problems using creative thinking techniques
- use mapping techniques to explore problems, opportunities and resources
- define and follow a structured process of creativity from idea to innovation.

The chapter explores the roles of creative thinking and innovation in generating ideas and building on them to form opportunities through associative thinking. Gaps, needs and problems can be identified and analysed as a starting point for creative problem solving and opportunity recognition in the external environment. Opportunity, problem and resource mapping are introduced as core techniques. The use of future scenarios and time perspectives in opportunity recognition and innovation is explored. Models and methods for exploring opportunities through market and related investigation and research are covered in detail. Finally, idea-banking of opportunities as a knowledge resource, and protecting intellectual property rights in the entrepreneurial process are summarised. Use is made of practical business examples and 'cameo' mini-cases to illustrate the concepts. The chapter is activity based, and you will be asked to identify potential opportunities to explore and work on.

The outcome of the chapter is for you to develop an idea into an opportunity by using mapping techniques, and then to plan how to undertake detailed market investigation of the opportunity. As a result you will be able to use this information to assess and evaluate the potential of the opportunity.

Creativity and innovation in entrepreneurship

Entrepreneurial opportunities require both creativity and innovation to progress from idea to solution. Creativity and innovation are often associated, but the terms are not synonymous and their respective meanings are important. The creative act can be defined as 'bisociation', or combining two unrelated pieces of information to form a new third idea (Koestler, 1964). Creativity is the association of ideas, information or materials to form new concepts – or as Schumpeter described, 'new combinations'. Creativity sees the world in new ways, through free expression, by developing new and original ideas and concepts. This involves divergent, associative and non-linear thinking which may appear illogical to others. Creative art, for example, is judged by aesthetic criteria and subjective perception, so creative activity does not require practical or financial value.

Creativity has several important roles in the entrepreneurial process. It enables people to develop completely new ideas and to envision possibilities of 'new reality'. Imagining a business or a product which does not yet exist is a creative act. Creativity enables people to imagine the future and to construct future scenarios for business ventures. This is strategic creativity, by imagining and then enacting a new reality. However there are at least two other significant roles for creativity. One can be described as tactical creativity; it involves thinking and acting in creative ways to exploit opportunities or to manage and develop the business, often dealing with problems of limited time, expertise or resource. Entrepreneurial working is applied creativity, and entrepreneurial people are frequently creative in practical ways, in devising new product ideas, routes to market and solutions to problems, and it is certainly worth developing and using skills of creative thinking and working.

The other aspect is the application of creative skill within the business, for example in designing or producing creative media, products or experiences.

ACTIVITY

Creative thinking using the 'Idea Space'

The purpose of this activity is to introduce a method for stimulating creative thinking by associating ideas, to show how this can assist innovation.

The Idea Space has four boxes (see Figure 3.2), headed 'resource', 'information', 'attributes' and 'environment', which feed into the Idea Space. All the factors listed in these boxes can be changed, depending on the specific details of the idea you are working on.

1. Select a 'resource'; this may be a product, technology, material or process which is easily available to you.
2. Select from the list of 'attributes' those which apply to this resource, e.g. purpose, shape, colour, structure, texture.
3. Select the 'information' which is available from the list about the resource, e.g. knowledge of a problem, opportunity, demand, 'what works' or does not work, 'what-if' idea for improvement.

4. Select the 'environment' factors which affect the conditions in which the resource is used, e.g. people, place, posture, language, close or remote.

5. How can the resource, attributes, information and environment factors be combined in new ways? Experiment with making different connections.

6. Think of how each of the attributes can be changed in turn to see what ideas this produces.

7. List the new combinations from stages 5 and 6 in the Idea Space in the centre.

8. Harvest the best, most feasible or interesting ideas from the list.

The Idea Space is based on a simple concept of making information explicit and then connecting this information in new ways to create new ideas. Associating or combining information in new ways can help us to imagine new possibilities by shifting our perceptions of reality, even if no practical use or innovation results from the creative insights. If we 'flip-flop' by looking at different perspectives, such as seeing a problem through the customer's eyes rather than the organisation's, or starting from the end of a process rather than the beginning, and working back, creative insights begin to emerge.

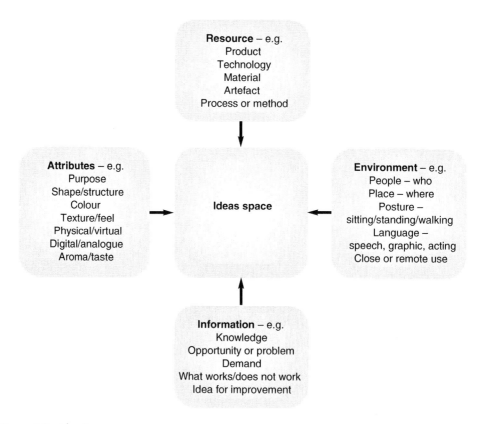

Figure 3.2 Idea Space

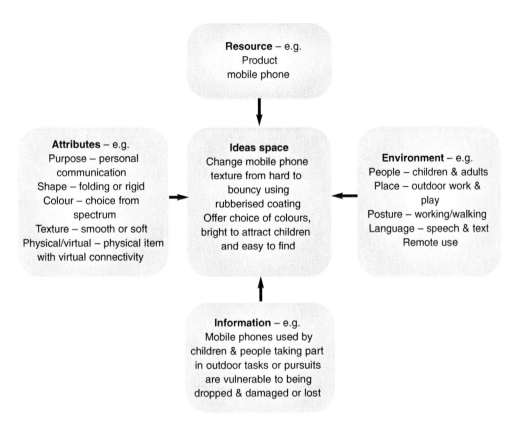

Figure 3.3 Idea Space example – bouncy mobile phone

The relationship between creativity and innovation is shown simply in Figure 3.4. Creative thinking is divergent, often intuitive and unstructured, opening up new ideas, connections and possibilities. Innovative working is convergent, focusing on combining a limited number of ideas on a workable application or solution to a problem. Think of pouring water into a funnel: the mouth is broad and contains splashes and turbulence, but the spout is narrow and produces an easily directed and consistent flow of water.

Divergent thinking is valuable in generating ideas for an opportunity or project. It includes these activities:

- identifying and defining the opportunity, need or problem
- researching – gathering and analysing information
- exploring – open-ended quest for new information
- investigating – focused search for specific information.

Convergent thinking focuses on moving from many ideas and rich data to concluding, developing and implementing an opportunity or project. Convergent activities are structured and focused on completion – making decisions and choices, taking action, getting results, and 'making things happen':

- deciding the possible solutions
- planning what to do

Divergent thinking generates new associations and possibilities

Creativity: generating ideas

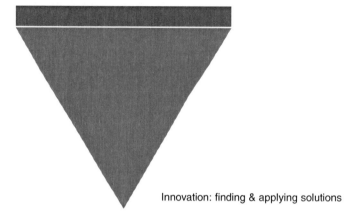

Innovation: finding & applying solutions

Convergent thinking enables selection between alternatives

Figure 3.4 Divergent and convergent thinking

- developing and implementing the innovation (e.g. a product or service)
- communicating the idea to stimulate demand
- monitoring progress, measuring and reviewing the results.

Creativity involves imagining a new reality, and innovation is required to make it work. Innovation is developing ideas into applications and solutions. Innovation introduces new products, methods or technologies through convergent thinking, by moving from opening-up many options to selecting between alternatives. Innovation integrates knowledge to solve problems and meet needs in new ways, by applying ideas, technology and resources to create new solutions. Innovation is an iterative process, driven by the search for 'what works'. It is assessed by the utilitarian criteria of meeting a need successfully, and producing applications which work and are economically viable.

Innovation is integral to the entrepreneurial process. New ideas are of little value without the ability to apply and harness them as value-creating products, services or processes. It includes research and new product development, and applying science, knowledge or technology in new ways to create new methods, processes, and applications. It can take many forms, from technology, science or engineering-based activities to simple forms of 'doing something new'. However it is best considered as a logical process, often iterative, going back repeatedly, by trial and error, to find the best approach.

The ability to innovate can provide vital advantages for an entrepreneurial organisation. Being able to think creatively and identify new applications and markets for ideas, products and technologies, working quickly and flexibly, is essential. Innovative companies have higher rates of new or improved product introduction, and are faster or first to market compared with competitors. They are more flexible, better able to attract external finance, and experience more positive impact on company performance, turnover, profitability and return on investment than the norm. However innovation is inherently uncertain because it involves risk and is resource-hungry, so effective project management is vital for successful innovation. Moving effectively between divergent and convergent activity is one means of achieving this.

Innovation vanguard firms show the way to beating the downturn

Robert Tucker (2002) suggested five points as strategies for creating new value through innovation-led growth in corporate organisations, including BMW, Herman Miller and Whirlpool. Innovation must:

- be approached as a discipline
- be approached comprehensively
- include an organised, systematic and continual search for new opportunities
- involve everyone in the organisation
- be customer-centred.
  (Source: www.innovationresource.com)

The innovation journey

During this chapter we will go through a journey from generating ideas to establishing innovative solutions as business opportunities. The process of developing and implementing innovation is described as a journey rather than a conceptual model because, as on a journey, you can have different starting and finishing points, you may well go backwards as well as forwards, and diverge to explore interesting avenues, possibly becoming lost or side-tracked at times. That is what the innovation experience is like in practice, because it often involves trial and error, experimentation and even luck.

The journey is shown as a diagram in Figure 3.5. The steps along the journey are the main stages to work through, showing the techniques and activities included in the book which can be used at each step. So whilst there is no one 'correct way' of innovating, it does need to be seen as a process in which knowledge is generated and used, and different skill-sets and methods are required to develop and manage innovation at each stage of the journey.

EXAMPLE

Kelly was an art and design student, skilled in designing fashion accessories. One night, whilst ironing clothes on the floor of her flat, she accidentally welded an item to the carpet. Investigating the damage, she found that the unintentional heat-treatment had turned the carpet into a different material. She decided to experiment further, and found that this new material could be easily shaped and formed in three dimensions.

Being environmentally aware, she found out that huge quantities of both new carpet offcuts and old carpets were dumped as landfill each year, and this presented two opportunities: a limitless source of recyclable material, and a way of reducing waste.

Kelly experimented for months with different methods of heating and forming carpet, finally perfecting a simple process which resulted in a malleable material. Raising money from the Prince's Trust, she applied for and eventually secured a patent to protect her rights to this process and started her business, Carpet-burns.

Kelly progressed from being a design student into becoming a designer-maker of fashion accessories, and then into an innovator and young entrepreneur. She had to overcome disadvantages of being young, having little money and no business skills or experience to persuade people to take her seriously. Initially, she designed and made small batches of products such as mobile phone cases and handbags, which gained attention and won awards and sponsorship.

However she realised that these products alone would not provide a viable base from which to grow her business. Being involved in business networks and working with others, she identified that by producing sheets of heat-treated carpet, this material could be made available for a range of industrial uses such as packaging and re-manufacturing into shaped products. Five years on, she repositioned the business to focus on this opportunity.

The Carpet-burns story demonstrates that opportunities and innovations can occur through serendipity or by chance, but that major investment of focused time, energy and resources is then required to develop, protect and exploit the innovation. Also, the individual's initial view of the market and application for the innovation may not be the most promising. To be successful, people have to develop their personal skills, especially in finance, marketing and team-working to engage others with complementary skills to help to grow the business.

Recognising opportunities in the external environment

An opportunity was defined as: 'the potential for change, improvement or advantage arising from our action'. The opportunity may be an existing one which we can identify now, or it may be a future one for which we recognise the potential. This chapter deals with the following types of opportunity:

- 'gaps in the market' or a mismatch between supply and demand
- current and future opportunities
- the solving of a problem, e.g. developing and applying a solution
- a new product, service or experience people would find useful.

Is an idea the same as an opportunity? This is a simple but important question. An idea is a creative connection between two or more pieces of information. An opportunity can exist where there is a need, problem, and either actual or potential demand for a product, service or experience. It may be that an idea includes the demand – but again it may not. There have been many ideas for new products where the demand did not exist and could not be created.

It is also possible to identify needs and to think creatively about them without being able to solve the problem or to fulfil the demand. If the idea is not technically

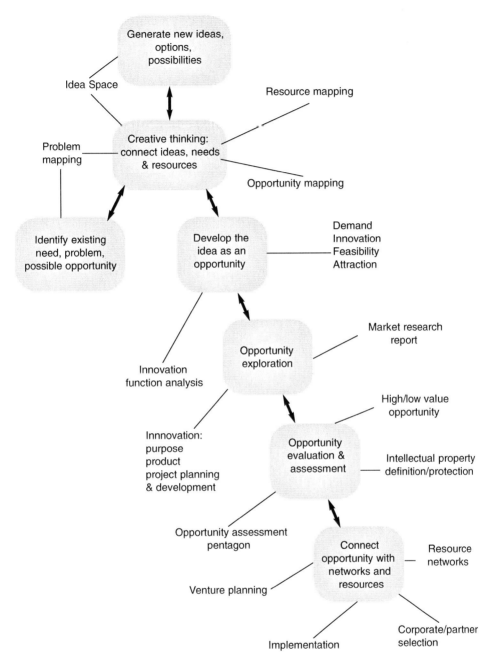

Figure 3.5 The innovation journey

or otherwise feasible it is not a real opportunity. These considerations help to define three of the four essential features of an opportunity:

Demand: there is a need, problem or potential demand to be satisfied.
Innovation: there is an idea for the product, service or experience to be provided.
Feasibility: the idea is technologically feasible.

These can be investigated objectively, but we need to add a fourth, based on more subjective judgement, which in practice often makes the vital difference between opportunities which are exploited and those which are not:

Attractiveness: the potential reward and the level of interest to the entrepreneur.

Together these produce the DIFA (Demand, Innovation, Feasibility, Attractiveness) method of defining whether an opportunity actually exists.

The factors which give rise to opportunities can be divided between, on the one hand, 'supply-side' or 'push' factors, which arise from the availability of technology, resources, economic and policy changes which provide the ability to create new opportunities, and on the other, 'demand-side' or 'pull' factors which arise from market need. In both cases, changes in these factors over time can create the space for new opportunities.

Supply-side or push factors

- technological advance, new possibilities and innovations
- new products or processes becoming available
- legislation, compliance and standardisation
- increase or decrease in cost and availability of resources
- increase or decrease in transaction and process costs
- supplier and distributor capabilities
- availability of skilled people.

Demand-side market and customer needs, or 'pull' factors

- demand for innovation or novelty
- social and consumer trends, e.g. rising expectations, increasing disposable income, less free time
- demand for value for money
- the effects of competition, e.g. rising or falling prices
- potential advantages, e.g. saving of time or cost, convenience,
- demand from supplier and distributor chains
- reduction in risk, uncertainty or variability.

These lists are not exhaustive, but they indicate the range of factors which affect and give rise to opportunities, and provide an initial framework for opportunity analysis. As shown in Figure 3.6, the entrepreneur operates in the space where supply and demand converge, connecting supply-side resources with market opportunities to create new value.

EXAMPLE

EasyJet and the low-cost airline industry in the UK

Supply side
The EU 'open skies' legislation provided the deregulation which gave rise to the possibility of timetabled cheap flights from the UK to continental Europe.

The Southwest Airlines business model in the United States demonstrated that a low-cost model based on minimising transaction costs and service levels combined with maximising aircraft and staff utilisation was viable and more profitable than the industry norm. Aircraft and air crews could be hired, ground services provided by sub-contractors, and takeoff and landing slots provided at less congested secondary airports.

Demand side

Air travel had been maintained at high fare levels through an industry cartel. Rising income levels, growing demand for European travel, and congested roads and expensive rail travel created the potential demand. Offering low fares would stimulate people to travel and gain value for money, for short breaks or on business, especially if it was made easy to book. There was an opportunity to create a completely new market for air travel.

The demand (the potential market) could be created; the innovation (the business model) was based on the Southwest Airlines pioneer; and the feasibility came about through deregulation and the ability to lease or sub-contract the services and assets required. For easyJet founder Stelios Haji-Ioannou, the attraction was to be the disruptive innovator, breaking into an established industry with a new business model and using limited assets to build a business with potentially high profits and asset value.

Creative problem solving

Business opportunities can be based on devising a solution to a problem which affects enough people to make the solution viable, following the old maxim of 'find a need and fill it'. This activity leads you through a systematic approach to defining the problem before starting to look for solutions.

Opportunity and problem mapping

We will apply a technique called 'opportunity mapping' in several different ways. This is a variation of mind-mapping, developed by Tony Buzan (2003), and is used as a means of defining problems, exploring opportunities, establishing resources, planning and developing an opportunity. The next activity could easily be done using a problem map.

Opportunity mapping, like mind mapping, is a creative way of connecting ideas together by association rather than by step-by-step logical thinking. It can be used with pictures as well as words, and gives great flexibility in the way information is expressed and processed. Opportunity mapping works by enabling us to generate thoughts quickly, creatively and intuitively, by 'free association' rather than sticking to a logical process. It can be used by one person, or more productively by a small group – for example to sort the results from a brainstorming session where a group of people 'freewheel' to come up with as many ideas as possible.

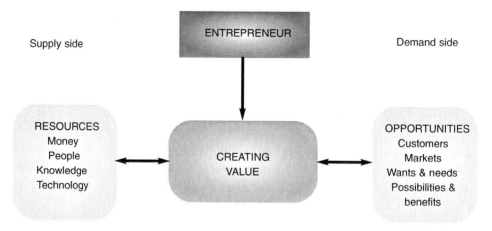

Figure 3.6 The entrepreneur: creating new value by connecting supply and demand

Opportunity mapping has a range of applications in entrepreneurial working, including:

- reviewing and making connections between ideas, experiences and resources
- creating and developing new concepts
- developing ideas, strategies and plans for projects and business ventures.

ACTIVITY

Seeing existing needs as creative opportunities

Think of a problem which continually recurs, or a repetitive unmet need. It could be something you have noticed, which affects or annoys you.

If you cannot think of anything, choose one of these real problem-based opportunities:

- how to find part-time jobs in term-time for students
- how to use resources such as old CDs, personal computers, textbooks or supermarket food which has reached its use-by date
- how to reduce the number of solo-occupied cars in city rush hours.

Now go through the following stages to define the problem by answering as many of the questions as you can; guess or estimate to fill in the gaps.

- What is the problem you have identified?
- What are its results or effects? What is the scale or measure (e.g. numbers of people affected)?
- Why is it a problem? Why does it happen? What factors cause it?
- Who is causing, and who is affected by, the problem? How do those causing the problem benefit from it?
- Where, when, and how does it happen?

- What are the costs – financial, time, resources – that are incurred?
- What are the potential gains from solving it?

At this point you can review the problem and consider:

- Is the problem capable of being solved? Is a solution feasible?
- Does solving it offer a big opportunity? What benefits or value could be created?
- Is the problem interesting and useful to solve?
- Is this an isolated, individual problem or a recurring one which affects many people?
- Could resources potentially be found to solve the problem?

  Asking questions like these can screen out problems on which it may not be worth investing further time.

Figure 3.7 Starting point for a problem or opportunity map

Here is how to draw a problem or opportunity map. The starting point is shown in Figure 3.7.

1. Write or draw the topic, such as the problem or opportunity, in a bubble in the centre of a piece of paper, flipchart or whiteboard.
2. Draw branches out from the centre, label each of these 'who, what, why, when, where, how', or use other labels if they are more relevant.
3. Print the ideas/pieces of information on lines going outwards from each branch.
4. Use different colours or simple pictures if this helps.
5. Make connections between associated ideas on different branches.
6. Review the map to remove any irrelevant ideas.

The result is a map which connects the key ideas and information associated with each branch or sub-topic. This can then be used to develop the opportunity further.

The important stage is in moving from 'implicit' understanding (information in people's heads) to explicit information on paper where different pieces of information become connected, leading to fresh ideas, insights and possibilities.

Creative thinking to generate innovation

Creativity generates new ideas by bringing existing knowledge together in new ways, opening the door to innovation. Opportunity mapping can be a useful way of associating information visually to produce new ideas, as we will see in the next section. A new concept only needs two or three elements, which may already exist separately. So a customer need and a technology can be combined to create a new product innovation. If we think of creative resources that we can use, these can include knowledge, technology, materials, skills, production and distribution capacity and many others. There are numerous examples; think of the increasing applications being found for Broadband technology, for radio frequency identification devices (RFID), and so on.

Creativity can result from 'breakthrough' thinking: taking something out of its existing context and applying it in a new situation. Most innovations are adaptive – small-scale incremental improvements on existing products, such as the latest model of the VW Golf for example. Radical or 'disruptive' innovations, which create entirely new concepts and which can transform their industry, are much rarer, and generally higher risk. However any successful innovation requires other ingredients, which include a clear focus on the customers: how will the innovation benefit the customers' life or business, what will it do for them and what will they value? It makes sense to involve customers in the creative process, to find out about their needs, problems and desires, and what innovation they would value. Another ingredient, good design, can make the difference between an ordinary and outstanding innovation. The principles of design can be applied to any innovation, from a physical product such as a digital camera, an Internet or computer gaming virtual application, or a service such as a travel tour organiser. Good design makes the customer's experience 'natural' and enjoyable, whilst also being functional, robust and economical and conveying the distinctive identity of the product. Finally, the innovation must function effectively and provide the benefits the customer expects. This means that all aspects from design, production, delivery, customer information and support must be provided and managed effectively. All these aspects can form part of the creative process of originating the innovation.

EXAMPLE

Time wasted by missed appointments

Every year, many working hours are wasted by people failing to turn up for appointments with professionals whose time is at a premium and costed by the hour. This especially affects doctors in the UK National Health Service, where it is estimated to cost £162m a year, but it is also experienced in other professions such as law, accounting, and consultancy. The map in Figure 3.8 (overleaf) defines the problem by presenting information on the causes, effects, costs and other factors.

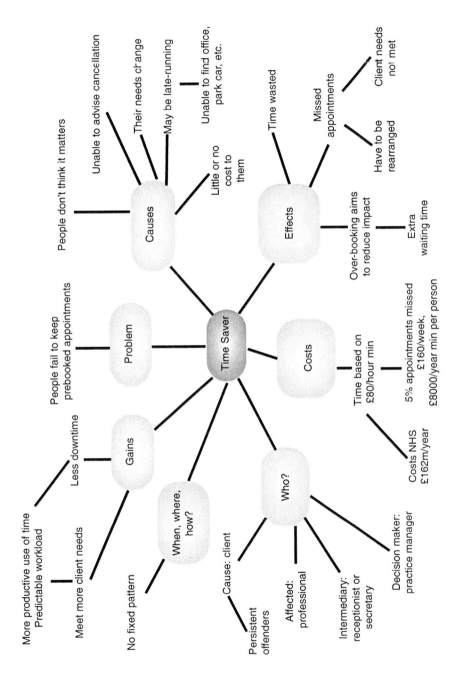

Figure 3.8 Mapping 'time saver' problem as opportunity

Innovation function analysis

The purpose of this technique is to assess the detailed requirement for an innovation by establishing the design and performance parameters which it needs to achieve. It can be used for a more detailed investigation once the existence or potential of an opportunity has been identified, and helps the innovation journey to move from 'idea' to 'opportunity'.

The method is to identify, analyse and specify systematically the job, task or function which has to be performed. This can be applied to any situation, from a personal service or product, such as a digital entertainment device, to new business models and industrial and public service applications. The technique is to identify customers, users or 'performers' of the function, and gather information by interviewing and observing them in order to analyse the function. The aim is to specify the job the innovation must perform by collecting as much of the following information as is applicable:

- What is the job, task or function which has to be completed?
- What is the value produced as an outcome or result of this function?
- What are the success criteria of this function for the user? And for the customer of the end result (if different)? These success criteria should include:
  - value-added
  - cost/value for money
  - speed
  - consistency of performance
  - how the quality of the outcome is assessed.
- What inputs are used to complete the task (materials, information, human effort, energy, money)?
- What is the cost of these each time the function is performed?
- How is this task or function performed at present? What is the process?
- What problems, deficiencies or frustrations arise at present (e.g. what costs, time, effort, inconsistent performance or quality occur?)
- What desire or scope for improvement can the user or customer suggest?

As well as the function being specified in this way, the scale of adoption of the task also needs to be assessed or estimated as far as is feasible:

- How many users of this function can be identified? Are they increasing or decreasing in number?
- What is the cost of this activity (number of users x frequency of use x cost per use)?
- Which products and organisations benefit from the function being performed at present?
- What would be the costs to the user of changing to a new system?

Once the function and its scale has been specified in this way, it can be assessed whether this is a 'problem worth solving'. If it is a widespread task in which users experience variable performance and frustration, and if there may be scope for enhancing quality of outcome and performance, or reducing cost, then further

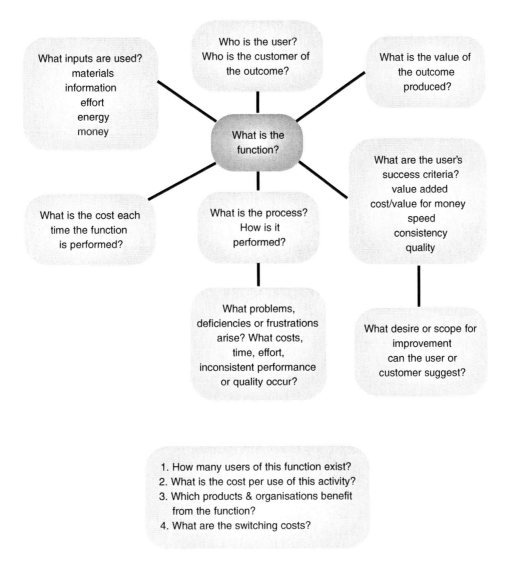

Figure 3.9 Innovation function analysis

investigation is worthwhile. If so, the specification which has resulted from the function analysis is the starting point for creative thinking and problem solving to develop an innovation which is capable of meeting it.

Figure 3.9 (overleaf) shows the innovation function analysis as a diagram. This format can be used as a problem map to gather the information.

Innovation and solution development

We can now move from defining the problem to thinking creatively and developing ideas about potential solutions. Just defining the problem may have started to trigger ideas. Start to write these down, either on Post-it notes or on a piece of paper. Rather than using a checklist, which may not be helpful to creative thinking, some of the following questions can be used to stimulate analysis of the problem, and result in generating ideas of how to work on the opportunity:

- Consider each of the branches and how it relates to the problem.
- What are the causes, and how could these be prevented or minimised?
- What would people affected by the problem see as the ideal solution?
- What factors need to change for the problem to be solved? These may include:
  - changing people's *behaviour* (e.g. that of people who cause the problem)
  - changing or introducing a *system* as a formal way of doing things
  - changing or introducing *technology*
  - changing *awareness* by educating or making information available
  - changing or influencing *environmental* factors.
- What resources are available? How can you combine these resources in new ways to solve the problem?
- Resources could include:
  - information
  - skills and know-how
  - technology
  - social, supplier and distributor networks
  - capacity, land, finance.
- How have similar problems been solved by others? What can be learned from them?

Once you have identified one or two possible ideas to work on, start to draw an opportunity map of how these might work.

For the 'time saver' problem introduced earlier, the result is shown in the opportunity map in Figure 3.10. The underlying cause and the 'change' to be worked on was the behaviour of the people making the appointment. Various options to achieve this change were identified, including:

- introducing or raising charges for missed appointments
- confirming appointments by e-mail or text message
- downgrading or dropping clients who missed more than two appointments
- informing clients about the negative effects of their missed appointments.

A way to change clients' behaviour was identified; this used an automated system to remind them of appointments by sending e-mail or text messages which they had to respond to in order to confirm the appointment. This could become a commercial software product which could be sold to medical practices, consultancies and other professional businesses. This is shown in the opportunity map in Figure 3.10, which now represents the 'flip-side' of the problem. It starts to show how a technology-based product could be developed to solve the problem and to provide a more widely applicable opportunity from this solution.

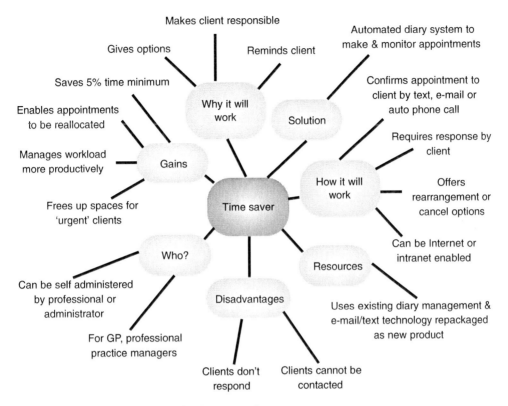

Figure 3.10 Opportunity map for 'time saver'

Opportunity building: matching needs and resources

ACTIVITY

Use the approaches shown so far in this chapter – of analysing the problem, thinking creatively, and opportunity mapping – to develop a potential solution to the problem you identified earlier.

Review whether it includes the four key features of an opportunity in the DIFA model:

- *Demand*: what is the need, problem or demand to be satisfied?
- *Innovation*: what is the product, service, process or experience?
- *Feasibility*: is it technologically feasible?
- *Attraction*: is it worth doing? Why?

There are three important points here, each connected with how we recognise opportunities.

We perceive, recognise or create opportunities in our subjective consciousness. This is part of our learning process. Ideas are not the same as opportunities, since an idea is simply a creative thought, which may not be practical or viable in any sense.

However an opportunity is something which can be acted on and made to happen. So turning a business idea into a business opportunity involves demonstrating that it is feasible, viable and worthwhile. The same opportunities are not apparent to everyone, and some people will perceive the same opportunity more quickly than others through imagination and foresight. Opportunities start off as individual, unique perceptions, even if different people who are quite unconnected coincidentally recognise the same opportunity at around the same time.

The second point is that time is an important dimension in recognising and working on opportunities. Opportunities are transient and temporary, occurring through combinations of such forces as technological change, social and market trends, or even the weather. The 'opportunist' trader at the seaside will sell ice-cream on sunny days but switch to waterproofs and umbrellas when it rains. So opportunities are time-limited, and if we recognise one then the decision to work on it or not should be made quickly, since others may already have noticed it or will become aware of it. Inevitably this leads to competition where the first or best comes to dominate. Future-based rather than current opportunities give greater scope for strategic innovation and developing something new in a 'white space', unoccupied future market niche, rather than an intensively competitive existing market.

Third, just because we recognise an opportunity that does not mean it is a 'good' opportunity for us. We live in an opportunity-rich society. Being opportunistic and pursuing every opportunity will quickly exhaust personal resources of money and energy. 'Good' opportunities, those which we should select and develop, are likely to be ones where we already have some relevant skills, knowledge, experience and understanding, where we have an interest or fascination which excites us, and where the opportunity is in harmony with, or at least compatible with, our personal and business or career goals. And it is only an opportunity we can exploit if we can gain access to and harness the necessary resources – of finance, information, technology and people – to do so.

So here are some basic questions to use in assessing and filtering an opportunity you have identified:

- Is it an idea or an opportunity?
- Is it a current or future opportunity?
- Has anyone else already noticed or seized the opportunity?
- Is the opportunity distinctive and different from existing approaches?
- Is the opportunity compatible with my goals, interests, and experience?
- Where are the resources which would be needed?

One important process in developing an opportunity is to match the need, problem or demand with the resources needed to make it happen. That does not mean the entrepreneur needs to own or control the resources, but is rather able to find them and connect them with the project in a negotiated way, for example by offering the resource owners the opportunity to participate as investors or partners in the venture. The resources which may be required to exploit an opportunity could include:

- knowledge – skills, expertise, specialist know-how and information
- technology – existing technical capability or capacity
- physical equipment and plant or materials and components
- finance – investment capital and start-up capital
- human – skills, expertise and capability which is required in the venture
- access – permission, licences, distribution networks
- intellectual property – patents, brands, trademarks, design rights, copyright
- capacity – facilities which need to be bought-in or sub-contracted.

Opportunity mapping can be used to create a resource map of the resources and capabilities needed to develop the opportunity. An example of a resource map for the 'time saver' product is shown in Figure 3.11.

This leads to the conclusion that because of the type of knowledge-based resources required in this case, the opportunity could best be developed through seeking a partnership with an existing IT services provider which possessed some of the technology-based expertise and distribution and marketing capability, but which would be unlikely to develop this niche-market product independently.

Figure 3.11 Resource map of the opportunity

ACTIVITY

- Draw a resource map for the opportunity you have identified, using the categories of knowledge, finance, technology, materials, access, intellectual property and any others which apply.
- Review it to identify where these resources currently exist and could be located.

Current and future scenarios for opportunity creation

Acting at the right time is a critical factor in opportunity recognition.

Current opportunities are those where customer demand already exists and the innovation is feasible now; the idea may be a new one, an adaptation of an existing one, or a simple replication. Generally, current opportunities are less innovative than future opportunities, or may not be innovative at all. The opportunity may result from the market growth being greater than existing businesses can fully exploit, making competition possible, or exploitation of a defined market niche feasible. A new market does not have to be created. Current market opportunities involve less uncertainty, but it is certain that increased competition with possible price-cutting will result. The technology already exists and is known, and the risks and costs can be defined with greater certainty.

However if one new firm is able to enter the market, then it is likely that others will also do so, potentially leading to price-cutting and over-supply. Competition is almost inevitable with existing opportunities, although introducing an innovation which gives a clear cost or customer advantage into an existing market, especially one which is growing, can be a viable strategy.

Opportunities have an optimum period in time at which they can be exploited, when the need can be created or is self-generating, the resources and technology can be brought together, and the potential return is greatest. We can use creative thinking about the future to imagine opportunities which do not yet exist, but which are possible or emergent, because the resources required to make them happen are or will become available. Future thinking is inherently innovative, yet risky, demanding confidence and the availability of significant resources into the future.

Potential market opportunities arise where the demand may not yet exist but can be stimulated, where the technology either already exists or will become available in the foreseeable future, and where the innovation, or idea, has not yet been applied. Future opportunities require prediction of future market, customer and other trends. The further into the future, the higher the degree of uncertainty or risk in implementing the opportunity. Significant investment may well be needed and it may be difficult to quantify how much is required. However the entrepreneur may also have the potential to gain a much higher return from being first to exploit the opportunity, to gain a market lead, and possibly to secure intellectual property rights on the innovation.

EXAMPLE

Fascia Mania Ltd – 'rooflines Britain looks up to'

Fascia Mania Ltd was started by two brothers in the UK East Midlands during the early 1990s. The family business was in building and carpentry, and they identified the replacement of uPVC fascia and soffit boards to domestic property rooflines as an emerging market with strong prospects for growth. There were no specialist firms, whilst poor installation, product and service standards were being offered by double-glazing and general building firms. The brothers set out to offer a well-operated, reliable and professional roofline replacement service.

The firm showed early promise and the brothers learned important lessons about marketing, developing and training installation teams, planning business finance and managing the business effectively. They became established as the market leaders in the regional market and were able to attract investment capital which funded a marketing-led growth strategy, including showrooms, local radio advertising, additional installation teams and movement into the housing refurbishment contracting market. They expanded to cover the Midlands region, aiming to become the UK's most trusted name in the industry.

However, their early success was noticed by people who started 'copycat' businesses based on the same business idea; names such as Familiar Fascias, Fascia World, and numerous small imitators sprang up, aiming to undercut Fascia Mania on price. In this type of business there is little intellectual property to protect other than the brand name, and Fascia Mania's strategy was to use their reputation for quality and superior buying power to defend their market presence, reinforced by their effective sales capability.

Amazon.com in Internet-based book and cultural media retailing, and Sky in satellite pay-TV are two examples of future opportunities which were exploited successfully. In both cases the potential was identified by the founders significantly in advance of their competitors. Substantial investment was made in establishing the technological, market and product bases for the businesses. Establishing a controlling position in a new industry which they created was the goal, rather than short-term return or profitability. When the businesses were launched they provided a unique service which was impossible for rivals to copy quickly. The founders continued to invest substantially in the businesses to build up market dominance over a period of several years, this being considered more important than short-term profitability. Both businesses developed a market, product and technological dominance which competitors who entered the market later with similar offers have not been able to rival.

These, like easyJet, are examples of successful future opportunity exploitation. However, future opportunities can have significant disadvantages, in particular the uncertainties giving rise to risk, the uncertain time period before implementation and break-even or profitability, and the uncertainty over the investment needed to support this. There are many cases of unsuccessful attempts to create and exploit future opportunities, and the reasons for failure are important to learn from.

ITV Digital TV

This satellite service was launched in the UK in 1998 and failed in 2002. The reasons for its failure provide an interesting comparison with the success of Sky TV:

- The technology did not work effectively or consistently in all areas.
- The service was not sufficiently differentiated from those already available, with too few new benefits for customers.
- The service did not meet a clear market need and was not adopted widely enough.
- The investment required to fully develop the service was too high and could not be financed.
- The pricing was too high to be competitive.
- It depended on an alliance between two terrestrial TV companies which both had to provide short-term returns to investors.

Exploring opportunities: market and related investigation and research

This section explores the market-related aspects of the opportunity in increasing depth. This will provide information for the opportunity assessment and evaluation. Exploring the market is a key learning process for any opportunity, especially if it is in a sector which is new or unfamiliar to the entrepreneur. The market focus funnel in Figure 3.12 visualises the market exploration as a progression where we move

ACTIVITY

Future thinking

Assess the opportunity you have identified in relation to time perspectives.

- Is the opportunity current, or one which will exist in the future?
- If it is in the future, how many years ahead will this be?
- Is it currently being explored or exploited by others?
- Do all the conditions exist for it to be exploited? Which do not?
- Are you bringing a significant innovation or advantage to exploit the opportunity?
- What assumptions about future conditions are you making? (e.g. demand, innovation, technology, resource availability, social trends etc)
- What factors could change to affect these assumptions?
- What are the most significant risk factors in the opportunity? How could these be reduced?

- Identify potential markets.
- Market characteristics:
  - total value, growth, accessibility.
- Decide on target market.
- Identify customer segments within market.
- Identify segment characteristics:
  - total value, growth, accessibility.
- Decide on target segment(s).
- Identify customer needs, preferences.
- Decision-making factors, pricing.
- Identify media, promotional and sales channels.
- Develop marketing plan.

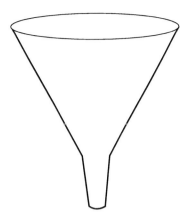

Figure 3.12   The market focus funnel

from an overview to detailed and specific probing. You may recognise this as an example of moving from divergent to convergent thinking.

To use this model we need information at several different levels: the overall markets available, the target market, the customer segments available, and the target segment. We may already have assumed that there is a given market and target group of customers. However in developing an opportunity, it may become apparent that the initial target market is not the most attractive or rewarding. Therefore even if a single potential market has been identified, it is worth moving back up the funnel to ask 'What are all the markets available for the product?' or, as one entrepreneur challenged his team, 'What is the *sales universe* for this product?'

If you are unfamiliar with marketing theory, the definition we are using of a market is the demand for a product or service within a given geographical, social or industry boundary. Segments are defined as the discrete customer groups within the market, using a number of characteristics that enable different segments to be identified at increasing levels of precision.

Questions to use in conducting market research

The following questions are intended for use within the market focus funnel, in order to gauge the size and value of the market and to move from the 'big picture' of the potential markets to the characteristics of the target customer segment in the chosen market.

EXAMPLE

Recorded music

The market for recorded music in the UK is one of a number of major world markets for the product. This market can be segmented by using the following characteristics:

- Type of music: classic, jazz, pop, rock, punk, R'n'B, urban, dance, easy listening etc.
- Format: Internet download, I-tune, CD, DVD, audio tape, MP3, LP.

- Preferred mode of purchase: online MP3 or iPod, mail order, multiple store, independent store, club, file-swapping, other.
- Average monthly spend: less than £5, £5–£10, £10–20, £20–30, £30–40, £40+.
- Age group: under 10, 10–15, 15–20, 20–30, 30–40, 40–55, 55+.
- Media channels most used – terrestrial TV; satellite or digital TV; BBC radio; independent radio; magazines, newspapers, Internet sites.
- Gender: male or female.
- Ethnic group: white, Afro-Caribbean, Indian, Chinese, Arab, other.

From these characteristics the target segment for a new online music magazine and catalogue business could be defined as:

Male/female aged 15–30, listening to R'n'B, urban and dance in CD and MP3 format, currently buying increasingly by online download, spending £30+ per month, listening to independent radio, in any ethnic group.

Detailed consumer research could then take place with this group to identify their likes, dislikes, dissatisfaction with existing channels and their buying criteria for the new product.

Potential markets
- What are all the potential markets for the opportunity?
- What is the size of each market: global, national, regional, local?
- What is the total value of each market in sales per year?
- Is each market growing, static or declining?
- What is the intensity of the competition in each market?
- What percentage share of each market could be achieved within (say) two years?
- Which is the most attractive market to enter?

Target market
- How many customers are in the target market?
- What is the anticipated lifetime of the market in years?
- What are the key factors which drive demand and price in the market?
- Who are the dominant sellers in the market?
- What are their market shares by per cent, their competitive strengths and weaknesses?

Customer segments
- How can the market be segmented, for example by geography, industry sector (business/institutional), socio-economic group, age range, occupation, interests (consumers), average spend and media consumption?
- What are the customer segments?
- Which of these are most attractive in terms of under-met needs or aspirations, growth in size/spend and affinity with product?

Target segment

- Who are the target customers?
- What is the average spend per customer per transaction and per year on this product?
- What percentage of the annual spend by this segment can the business secure?
- What is known about these customers?
- What do they want or need? What do they like and dislike?
- Why do they want or need the product? What benefits do they gain from it?
- How far are these wants and needs met at present? How well are they met?
- What problems or dissatisfaction do the customers experience?
- What are their buying criteria: what, how and from whom to buy?
- What factors do they see as 'value for money' and 'quality'?
- What are their 'affinity habits' – what related purchases do they make, what are their listening, viewing, Internet-browsing, reading, visiting habits?

Gathering this information is a process of market research. At the top three levels of the funnel this is mainly secondary research. This can be done through the Internet and by using information normally held in university and business libraries. The Small Business Service, official publications and statistics, Mintel and other reports can be used. The references section in the appendices lists useful sources. At the bottom level of the funnel, secondary information will only provide limited intelligence, so primary, direct research will be needed to generate the very specific information needed to really build up detailed understanding about the segment characteristics, to get to know the customer, and to be able to make informed decisions. A market research project that targets individuals or groups of people in the segment will be required. Corporate and well-resourced entrepreneurs may commission market research specialists to undertake this, whilst students, startup entrepreneurs and smaller firms can normally do it themselves, which takes time but facilitates direct learning from the customer.

The methods available for direct market research can include:

- direct one-to-one interviews
- focus group meetings
- informal conversations at trade shows, network events etc.
- telephone interviews
- e-mail survey questionnaires
- postal survey questionnaires.

Direct, personal contact requires the greatest investment of time, but also yields a higher level of qualitative knowledge about the customers and the opportunity than is achieved through remote questionnaires. Also, an initial list of prospective customers can be developed by retaining customer details.

From the research process, a detailed picture of the market, the segment and the customers can be built up. This can be used to start developing the opportunity as a business model and provide vital information for the venture plan. Here are some of the important questions to be considered in analysing the market research information and developing the business opportunity. Not all questions are applicable to every opportunity, and even if they were, not all the information will be available.

However the important point is for the entrepreneur to be posing the important questions for the business, trying to find the best information, and deciding at what point there is enough information on which to make decisions.

Analysing the industry

- What is the structure of the industry at present: globally, nationally, regionally, locally? What is the chain from supplier to end user?
- Who are the dominant firms which supply the market? How do they exercise control over the market?
- What is the strength of competition in the market? Who are the existing suppliers which the new venture will be competing with?
- What are their strengths and weaknesses?
- How will the new venture be differentiated from existing suppliers?
- How are competitors likely to respond to a new entrant to the market?
- Who else is known or likely to be working on a comparable opportunity? How far advanced are they? What advantages and disadvantages do they have? How fast can others replicate it?

The customer and the new venture

- What percentage of the annual spend by this segment can the business aim to secure?
- What advantages over competitors can the business offer customers?
- How will customers be persuaded of this?
- What is the added value to customers?
- How much is this worth to them?
- How will the product be priced?
- What selling and distribution channels will be used to reach the target customer segment?
- What are the costs of gaining and selling to a new customer?
- Is the customer relationship loyalty-based or (one–off) transaction-based?
- Is the product unique, desirable, essential or a discretionary commodity?
- What factors will affect customer retention, repeat and added-value purchases?

ACTIVITY

This activity asks you to consider how you would use the market focus funnel as a research tool, and to apply it to a specific opportunity as described in this section. The objective is to gather as much relevant data as you can, which can be used to evaluate the opportunity and to reduce uncertainty. You may have limited time and access to information, so you will need to be selective and focused in your research.

- How would you go about applying the market focus funnel to a real market opportunity?
- How would you gather the primary market research information?

- If you are working on a specific opportunity, then decide on the most relevant questions to investigate that opportunity. There are 44 questions of which you should aim to answer at least 30.
- Then conduct initial research using the funnel approach, and go down the funnel gathering data on as many of these questions as you are able. If you cannot find the information go on to the next question. Some of the questions in the final section on 'the customer and the new venture' ask you to start making initial decisions on the business in relation to customers.
- Keep the information you gather in the headings of the potential and target market, customer segment, industry analysis. This information will be used to assess the opportunity.

Idea-banking: opportunities as a knowledge resource

The purpose of idea-banking is to build up a resource bank of ideas which have not yet been used and are potentially applicable at the right time, combined with a market opportunity and other resources. An idea-bank is an information resource or library for organisations or groups to use. Some idea-banks are maintained by companies, universities and research institutes and have restricted access, with a 'stock' of creative and technology ideas and innovations on which they hold intellectual property. Unexploited patents which are held by companies, research institutes or universities can be a source of opportunities. It is possible to conduct patent searches to determine what has been patented in a particular field and by whom, and to explore the potential of these. However it would then be necessary to contact and open discussions with the patent holder to find out if they are prepared to negotiate a licence for another party to exploit it. Other idea-banks offer open access to subscribing groups, researchers or even to everyone. An example is in the social enterprise arena, where some groups openly share ideas developed in one context so that they can be copied, adapted and put to work in other situations. References to idea-bank and social enterprise websites can be found in the resources section.

To work, an idea-bank needs ideas to be held in a common format for cataloguing and access. So for example, each idea can be submitted and held as an opportunity map with defined branches. Alternatively, the same information categories can be used to hold the idea on a database. The information required to idea-bank an opportunity normally includes:

- what the idea is, what it does
- why – the purpose and rationale
- how it works
- any actual and potential applications
- innovation and unique features
- drawings, design or technical information and 'prior art'
- research or development work carried out, such as trials or proof

- limitations and disadvantages
- resources and conditions needed for use
- who could benefit from and use the idea
- originator and ownership with details of intellectual property ownership
- keywords to enable database searching.

Intellectual property: protecting ideas

A vital area to consider in exploring opportunities is whether the ownership of the idea can be protected. The area of idea ownership is termed intellectual property (IP), and relates to the following forms of intellectual property rights (IPR):

- patents
- trademarks
- design protection, including registered design and design right
- copyright
- trade secrets.

Full details of intellectual property in the UK can be found on the Patent Office website (see the list of websites at the end of the book) and this organisation also publishes excellent guidance booklets. In summary:

- *Patents* protect original discoveries and inventions, such as processes and products, which must be new, inventive and capable of industrial application. An application is filed and a full patent may be granted after a search and examination has been carried out by the Patent Office. Once published, the patent gives the holder exclusive rights to use or licence the innovation for up to 20 years. It is vital not to disclose the invention to a third party, or to use it, before the patent is applied for, and the application must include full disclosure of all details since nothing can be added subsequently. The patent process is complex, and the use of an expert such as a Patent Agent or lawyer on a confidential basis is likely to be necessary. UK patents only provide protection in the UK or, by extension, within 23 European states, and beyond these areas other national patents have to be taken out. If a patent is infringed the holder needs to defend it, although insurance cover may be taken out against the costs of this. The process of securing, renewing and defending patents is complex and costly, especially for the solo inventor, but it is vital if the rights to a valuable invention are to be protected. Imagine how you would feel if you invented something and another organisation patented it, preventing you from using it; this has happened.
- *Trademarks* are signs, such as words, logos and pictures, which distinguish the products and services of one organisation from another. They include product and organisation brands such as Virgin, McDonald's and Orange. Registering a trademark prevents others from using the same mark in relation to the types of products and services for which it is registered. International registration can also be applied for.
- *Design protection* includes *Registered Design*, which is the total right of ownership to use the design. It covers the appearance of a product or part of a product, which must be novel, individual and not generic. It can be granted on

submission of photos or drawings of the design with an application and fee, and lasts for five years with extensions to 25 years. *Design right* also exists as intellectual property when the design is unregistered, but provides less cover. It provides an exclusive cover against copying for up to five years, but only within the UK.

- *Copyright* is similar to *design right,* giving creators of all creative works the right to control use and publication for between 25 and 70 years, depending on the type of work. In both copyright and design right, it is up to the creators to record and retain proof of their origination of the work and the date this took place, so that they can subsequently defend their right to the work.

All these categories of IPR can be sold, licensed or given by the owner to another party; needless to say, the future potential value of the rights should be considered carefully before taking such a step, and professional advice obtained from a legally qualified IP expert in cases where there is substantive potential value. Just think that J.R.R. Tolkein, author of *The Lord of the Rings,* sold the film rights for a tiny proportion of the eventual value of his creative work, and many songwriters, authors and designers have never received more than a nominal payment from the exploitation of their work.

Trade secrets are unregistered intellectual property, which include confidential processes, techniques and recipes – for example, the secret ingredients of Coca-Cola. They can be protected by confidentiality agreements or by being handed down verbally from one family generation to another, effectively depending on trust. But once the secret is disclosed it is impossible to assert ownership, protect the product or prevent copying.

It is important for innovators to assess what unique intellectual property they are creating, and how their rights to its ownership can be protected most effectively. The future value of the opportunity and the ability to exploit it nationally or internationally may well depend on the strength of intellectual property. Also, it is not enough simply to register the patent, design or trademark. If it is infringed it is necessary to defend ownership, which is inevitably costly, especially on an international basis. However in a number of countries, intellectual property rights are almost impossible to assert or defend, since international trade agreements are not enforced, and copying and counterfeiting of products are widespread. China, India and a number of other developing countries are territories in which it is very difficult to enforce intellectual property rights.

ACTIVITY

- What intellectual property could your idea potentially produce?
- In which category or categories of IPR would this fall?
- How would you go about securing your IPR?

Critical questions to consider from this chapter

- What are the four essential features which distinguish an opportunity from an idea?
- What factors are most important in creating an opportunity?

- What methods would you use to investigate an opportunity to explore its potential? What use would you make of opportunity mapping and innovation function analysis? Develop your skills by using these techniques on the problems or opportunities you identify from working through this chapter.
- How can you translate a need or problem into an opportunity through creative thinking and the application of innovation?
- How are creativity and innovation different? In what ways do they relate to the entrepreneurial process?
- What have you learned from applying the market focus funnel to researching the market for an opportunity?

Further reading

Buzan, T. and B. (2003) *The Mind Map Book.* BBC Books, London.

Lumsdaine, E. and Binks, M. (2005). *Entrepreneurship, Creativity, and Effective Problem Solving: Keep on Moving!* E&M Lumsdaine Solar Consultants, Hancock, Mich.

Southern, M. and West, C. (2002) *The Beermat Entrepreneur: Turn Your Good Idea Into a Great Business.* Pearson Prentice Hall, London.

Drucker, P. (1985) *Innovation and Entrepreneurship.* Heinemann, London.

Morgan, G. (1993) *Imaginization: The Art of Creative Management.* Sage, Thousand Oaks, Calif.

References

Buzan, T and B. (2003) *The Mind Map Book.* BBC Books, London.

Koestler, A. (1964). *The Act of Creation.* Hutchinson, London.

Tucker, R. (2002) *Driving Growth Through Innovation: How Leading Firms Are Transforming Their Futures.* Berrett-Koehler, San Francisco, Calif.

CHAPTER 4
Small business: definitions, characteristics and needs

CONTENTS

- Introduction
- Definitions
- Some UK SME statistics
- The entrepreneur or the business
  - Novice and habitual entrepreneurs, serial and portfolio entrepreneurs
  - Owners' motivation
- Distinctive characteristics of small businesses
- The implications of being small
  - Culture
  - Influence
  - Resources
  - Ambition
- The varieties of small businesses
  - Industry sector
  - Legal structure
  - Family businesses
  - Women-owned businesses
  - Ethnic businesses
  - Other categorisations of small business
- Small businesses and job creation
- Conclusions

KEY CONCEPTS

This chapter covers:
- The definitions of a small business.
- The different perspectives provided by taking the entrepreneur and the business as the core unit of study.

- The key areas of difference between small and big business.
- Other variations in small businesses, including family firms, and the different issues relevant to them.
- The implications of being small.
- The statistics on job creation by small businesses.

LEARNING OBJECTIVES

By the end of this chapter the reader should:
- Know the main definitions of a small business.
- Be aware of the major changes in SME numbers and employment in the UK.
- Understand the different perspectives produced by taking either the business or the entrepreneur as the unit of study.
- Appreciate the differences in types of small business.
- Understand other variations in the types of small businesses and the different issues relevant to them.
- Understand some of the problems in interpreting statistics on the role of small businesses in job creation.

Introduction

This chapter seeks to explore further what is meant by the term 'small business'. Small businesses are not just small versions of big businesses. They have a number of distinctive features which are not always obvious to the untutored observer. Nevertheless they are, in many other respects, heterogeneous rather than homogeneous. This chapter therefore considers some of the many different definitions of a small business. It considers small businesses at different stages of their development, in different sectors and under different types of ownership. It seeks to establish what they have in common, as well as the range of their diversity. It also looks at their job creation potential, as this is of interest to many people.

Definitions

ILLUSTRATION 4.1
Some official definitions of a small business

United Kingdom

In the UK, for statistical purposes, the Department for Business, Enterprise and Regulatory Reform (BERR), and the Department for Trade and Industry (DTI) before it, have used the following definitions (at the time of writing, November 2007):

- micro-firm: up to nine employees

- small firm: up to 49 employees (includes micro)
- medium firm: 50–249 employees
- large firm: 250 employees and over.

Companies Act

Section 249 of the Companies Act of 1985 states that a company is 'small' if it satisfies at least two of the following criteria:

- a turnover of not more than £2.8 million
- a balance sheet total of not more than £1.4 million
- not more than 50 employees.

A medium-sized company must satisfy at least two of the following criteria:

- a turnover of not more than £11.2 million
- a balance sheet total of not more than £5.6 million
- not more than 250 employees.

Value added tax

In the UK the VAT registration threshold is a turnover of £67,000 and the deregistration limit is a turnover of £65,000.

Small Firms Loan Guarantee Scheme

The Small Firms Loan Guarantee scheme applies to businesses with fewer than 200 employees and with a turnover of not more than £5.6 million. The lending limit to all SMEs is now £250,000 and the scheme covers 75 per cent of the loan.

Corporation tax

The Small Companies Rate of corporation tax applies to businesses with taxable profits of up to £300,000 and a marginal rate applied to profits between £300,000 and £1,500,000. Over that the full rate applies. The SME tax rate is 19 per cent and the full rate is 30 per cent.

British Bankers' Association (BBA)

For BBA statistical purposes, small businesses are defined as those having an annual debit account turnover of up to £1 million per year.

European Commission

In 1996 the European Commission adopted the following definitions of SMEs:

Maximum	Micro-enterprise	Small	Medium-sized
Number of employees	10	50	250
Turnover (€ million)	N/a	7	40
Balance sheet total (€ million)	N/a	5	27
Independence criterion*	N/a	25%	25%

* The independence criterion refers to the maximum percentage that may be owned by one, or jointly owned by several, enterprises not satisfying the same criteria.

> To qualify as an SME both the number of employees and the independence criteria must be met, and either of the turnover or the balance sheet total criteria.

The Bolton Report in 1971 was very significant in developing the understanding of small businesses in the UK. It defined a small business by reference to an ideal type:

> First, in economic terms, a small firm is one that has a relatively small share of its market. Secondly an essential characteristic of a small firm is that it is managed by its owners or part-owners in a personalised way, and not through the medium of a formalised management structure. Thirdly, it is also independent in the sense that it does not form part of a larger enterprise and that the owner-managers should be free from outside control in taking their principal decisions.[1]

This summary of definitions indicates that, although small businesses have been the subject of considerable interest since the Bolton Report, today there is still no single, clear, precise and widely accepted definition of what is a small business. Different definitions exist, often for different purposes such as the application of support policy, taxation or legislation. Many people, however, feel that they know what is meant by a 'small business'. It is one that has few employees, a low turnover, little or no formal structure and is usually managed by one person, who is also the business owner. It is these characteristics that make a small business behave in the way it does, and many feel that the key point at which a growing business ceases to be small is when it has to change its organisational and control system, from the loose and informal to the structured and formal, if it is to continue to be effective. However, most definitions use the size of the business as its distinguishing feature, presumably because that is easier to measure. Definitions vary widely in the way they measure the size of a small business. Some use turnover, which can change over time with inflation, but most go for employment, which, as already indicated, also happens to be the benefit which very often provides the rationale for small business support. Even when employment is used there are different definitions. The EU definition of an SME* used to be one that had fewer than 500 employees, but the limit is now 250. (See Illustration 4.1.) The US Small Business Administration uses 500 as the limit for its remit. Elsewhere the limit is often set at 200, which many take as being closer to the size that forces a change in organisational structure. Some use 100 as the limit, and there are some small business agencies which use 50.

The above definitions are almost entirely quantitative, but there are qualitative ones. Small businesses tend to share a number of qualities. They are generally businesses that serve only local customers and have only a very limited share of the available market; that are owned by one person, or by a small group of people; and are managed by their owners, who deal with all management issues, usually with little other help; and they are independent businesses, not parts of, or owned by, larger companies.

---

* The term 'small business' is, on occasion, used to embrace medium-sized businesses also. To avoid confusion, however, the now ubiquitous term 'SME' (small and/or medium-sized enterprise) has entered the language, particularly that of policy-makers.

A definition based on only one of these qualities would be in danger of excluding some businesses that others would regard as small. A number of qualitative characteristics should therefore be included. One attempt to do so has been to define a small business as one which possesses at least two of the following four characteristics:

- Management of the business is independent. Usually the managers are also the owners.
- Capital and ownership are provided by an individual or a small group.
- The areas of operation are mainly local, with the workers and owners living in one home community. However the market need not be local.
- The relative size of the business within its industry must be small when compared with the biggest units in the field. This measure can be in terms of sales volume, number of employees or other significant comparisons.[2]

Most of the definitions of a small business given above are, however, in effect only attempts to provide a proxy for what is the essence of 'smallness' in business units. Smallness is about being autonomous yet having limited resources of manpower, time, skills, expertise and finance, and therefore having to be dependent on external support. It is about having to cope with greater uncertainty and about carrying greater risk while having few opportunities for risk spreading. It is also about:

- the influence of ownership on entrepreneurial behaviour
- having greater individual authority
- managing a total activity and carrying total responsibility; being closer to customers, and being potentially more flexible and adaptable; managing networks of suppliers, customers, and financiers
- paying greater attention to business opportunities
- taking a strategic approach while also having close and informal control structures and communication channels
- embracing a 'can-do' culture.

These are the things that being small means and that present challenges and opportunities different from those in larger businesses.

Some UK SME statistics

Table 4.1 provides a statistical profile of business enterprises in the UK at the start of 2006. The importance of SMEs can be seen from the figures that indicate that SMEs together (0–249 employees) accounted for nearly half of the employment (47.6 per cent) and turnover (49.4 per cent) in the UK economy. Small enterprises alone (0 to 49 employees) accounted for 37.4 per cent of employment and 35.2 per cent of turnover. Small businesses are clearly important to the economy but so too are larger businesses.

The change in some of the statistics over the previous years is of interest. In 2000 the number of 'all enterprises' was about 3.8 million. In 2003 it was just over 4 million and, as shown above, for 2006 it has increased to over 4.5 million, a 20 per cent increase in six years. The number of businesses with no employees was 2.6 million

Table 4.1 A recent statistical profile of business enterprises in the UK

Number of enterprises, employment and turnover in the whole economy by number of employees, UK, start 2006

	Number				Percent			
	Enterprises	*Employment (/1,000)*	*Employees (/1,000)*	*Turnover (/£ million)*	*Enterprises*	*Employment*	*Employees*	*Turnover*
All enterprises	4,550,930	29,331	25,460	2,820,025	100.0	100.0	100.0	100.0
With no employees	3,270,105	3,570	440	207,617	71.9	12.2	1.7	7.4
All employers	1,280,830	25,761	25,020	2,612,408	28.1	87.8	98.3	92.6
1–4	845,375	2,376	1,845	232,507	18.6	8.1	7.2	8.2
5–9	218,795	1,530	1,429	161,726	4.8	5.2	5.6	5.7
10–19	118,120	1,638	1,584	173,370	2.6	5.6	6.2	6.1
20–49	60,575	1,874	1,840	217,197	1.3	6.4	7.2	7.7
50–99	18,925	1,316	1,308	164,223	0.4	4.5	5.1	5.8
100–199	9,120	1,271	1,267	170,404	0.2	4.3	5.0	6.0
200–249	1,810	404	403	66,932	0.0	1.4	1.6	2.4
250–499	3,700	1,287	1,285	211,081	0.1	4.4	5.0	7.5
500 or more	4,415	14,065	14,058	1,214,967	0.1	48.0	55.2	43.1

Source: BERR Enterprise Directorate Analytical Unit.

in 2000 but had increased to nearly 3.3 million in 2006: an increase of 25 per cent. These were the highest levels of 'all enterprises', and incidentally of businesses with no employees (self-employed people), since the time series began in 1994. The increase in the numbers of self-employed people is in the context of a growing labour market which might imply that people are being pulled into entrepreneurship rather than being pushed.

(NB: In the statistics shown in Table 4.1 the 'employment' figures given include every person employed by the business, including the business owner-manager(s), and the 'employees' figures do not include the owner-manager(s). A full review of UK business statistics, including survival rates, is available on the BERR web site: www.berr.gov.uk.)

The entrepreneur or the business

The previous section gives some definitions of a small business and information on the number of small businesses in the UK. However, before going on to explore other aspects of the concept of a small business, another issue should be highlighted. So far the emphasis has been on the firm, on the enterprise or business created, and that tends to imply that it is that entity which is the primary unit of analysis. It is easy to see why there should be such a focus. It is the business which can be seen to start or to end, it is the business which has the turnover or employment which can be measured, and it is the business which delivers things people want such as jobs and economic growth.

This existence of the business as a potential subject for consideration is clearest when the business is a separate legal entity, such as a limited company, and is least clear when the business is the activity of an individual operating as a 'sole trader'. The assumption may have been that the sole trader should be seen as an embryonic limited company which has not yet made it, but nevertheless the lack of a clear distinction between a sole trader and his or her business points to an important consideration. The business is not only the creation of the person but is also the expression of the person, even when the business is legally separate from that person. A person may start up and close down a business but the person will still continue to exist. The closure of the business is not therefore the end of the matter. It might, as in the case of a 'habitual entrepreneur' (see below), be followed by the start-up of another business and the reason for the closure may lie with the entrepreneur rather than with the business. To make sense of the totality of the entrepreneurial process it is therefore necessary to take the entrepreneur as the focus and unit of investigation, not the business.

Analysing the small business process from this different perspective also reveals another potentially useful focus: that of the group, or cluster, of businesses linked together in some way through common ownership and management by an entrepreneur or entrepreneurial team.[3] Measured on the performance of their latest venture, habitual entrepreneurs may seem to perform no better than novice entrepreneurs, whereas if the performance is measured across the cluster it has been found to be considerably better. Indeed is it quite likely that new firm formation within a cluster is a growth mechanism and therefore that, while individual firms in a cluster may not grow, the cluster does.[4] It may also be relevant to realise that the individual businesses in such a cluster may not, at least under the EU definition, be considered to be SMEs because they do not satisfy the ownership criterion.

Another relatively common form of very small business is the part-time business. Here, looked at from the perspective of the business, a part-time business may seem to indicate a lack of seriousness, but from the point of view of the person it may be a very sensible arrangement. Therefore, in exploring many aspects of the subject of business development, the fundamental unit should be the entrepreneur, not the firm.

Novice and habitual entrepreneurs, serial and portfolio entrepreneurs

There are entrepreneurs who start just one business and those who start more than one. The term 'habitual entrepreneur' was coined to describe a person who is not satisfied with starting just one business but who goes on to start others also, either in sequence or simultaneously. He or she was considered to be a special type of entrepreneur, different from the supposedly more common 'novice entrepreneur'. Research, for instance by Scott and Rosa, has indicated that multiple business ownership is more common than had been suspected and has more variety.[5] Habitual entrepreneurs have been subdivided therefore into 'serial entrepreneurs', who start a succession of businesses but only manage one at a time, and 'portfolio entrepreneurs', who start a succession of businesses and keep some or all of them going at the same time.[6]

Scott and Rosa have studied the process of multiple business ownership, considering it to be 'fundamental to understanding the process of capital accumulation in a free enterprise capitalist economy'.[7] Their work on the diversity of business foundations revealed many differences between entrepreneurs as regards the kind of ventures they started, the strategies they followed and the management practices they adopted which, due to the considerable heterogeneity of individual entrepreneurs, could only be categorised on very broad criteria (see Table 4.2).

Once it is recognised and looked for, habitual entrepreneurship appears to be very common. Rosa and Scott looked at the extent of habitual entrepreneurship in Scotland and found that up to 40 per cent of new limited companies had multiple-ownership and/or cross-linkages with other firms.[8] Others have explored the implications this has for the businesses concerned. Research by Westhead et al. into habitual entrepreneurs in Scotland, yielded information on business performance in 2001 which indicated that the average sales revenues reported by portfolio entrepreneurs were higher than those reported by serial entrepreneurs by a factor of three times, and higher than those reported by novice entrepreneurs by a factor of five times.[9] Marked differences in employment patterns were also detected. In 2001, in terms of total employment, portfolio entrepreneur firms were on average about three times larger than serial entrepreneur firms and about four times larger than novice entrepreneur firms. The authors of the study suggested that such findings highlighted the need for policy-makers and practitioners to target policies towards the varying needs of each type of entrepreneur rather than provide broad 'blanket' policies to all types of entrepreneur.

In contrast, however, a study of the changing nature of entrepreneurship over a 30-year period (the 1970s, 1980s and 1990s) in the 'low' enterprise area of Teesside found that 'portfolio entrepreneurs performed no better than others who did not own another business' and that 'the performance of serial entrepreneurs was even

Table 4.2 Three dimensions of habitual entrepreneurship

Dimension 1: The background and nature of the habitual entrepreneur
- Multiple venture founders from corporate backgrounds, who tended to be more deliberate in their formation of business clusters and who used more formal management practices in their new ventures
- Multiple venture founders from financial and consultancy backgrounds, who tended to start their careers as management consultants or financial advisers, as well as high-technology engineers founding new firms with limited managerial experience
- Multiple venture founders from non-corporate backgrounds (mostly associated with traditional family businesses), who were especially creative in reacting to new opportunities but who often lacked the resources or capability to take full advantage of them
- Non-entrepreneurial habitual founders, who were involved in several businesses but as a partner of the true driving entrepreneur

Dimension 2: The nature of ventures founded
- Related diversifications: by far the most common form of new venture
- New types of mainstream venture: a complete change of direction (rare)
- Pilot businesses: 'suck-it-and-see' experimental businesses
- Phantom businesses: non-trading ventures set up to trade but which never got off the ground
- Financial management businesses: businesses set up to manage the funds flowing from other businesses
- Buyouts, mergers and acquisitions
- Holding companies

Dimension 3: The strategies used to create and manage ventures
- Competitive efficiency: many new ventures did appear to some respondents to have resulted in some operational advantage
- Serendipity: entrepreneurial opportunism can appear to be an unplanned and serendipitous process
- Strategic accommodation of serendipity: small business owners can have a high degree of strategic awareness
- Strategic management of adversity: the tendency of most entrepreneurs when faced with recession or financial difficulty is to 'pull in their horns' and reduce or eliminate the formation of new ventures

---

Source: Based on P. Rosa, 'Entrepreneurial Process of Business Cluster Formation and Growth by "Habitual Entrepreneurs"', *Entrepreneurship Theory and Practice* (1998), 22, pp.48–51. Reprinted with the permission of Baylor University, the publisher of *Entrepreneurship Theory and Practice*.

worse.'[10] The apparent difference between these findings and those of Westhead et al. may be due to the nature of the sample used. Teesside is associated with a decline in heavy manufacturing and subsequent rates of high unemployment whereas the Scottish study relates to a larger area of the country with a more diverse economic performance and used a different array of research methods. Nevertheless the different findings do suggest that local factors may be important and that the conclusions of such studies might therefore have limited application outside areas studied.

The importance of location is further supported in a study of rural farmers in a specific area of England (East Anglia) which had, at the time of the study, the fastest growing population of any region of the UK, the lowest levels of unemployment and the highest levels of self-employment.[11] The study demonstrated that there is a core of farmers who have multiple business interests and that these additional business activities made a substantial contribution to both the number of enterprises and employment creation. In presenting these conclusions, Carter commented that within small business studies the conventional use of the firm as the sole unit of analysis appears to have obscured not only the range of activities of individual entrepreneurs, but also their wider economic contribution.[12]

Owners' motivation

As Elizabeth Chell and her colleagues reported there are different types of entrepreneur with different clusters of traits and behaviours. Different types will have different motivations and these can affect their businesses. There will be a lot of difference between a business developed by a sole owner who wants enough income to support his or her lifestyle and a business currently of the same size developed by a group of investors with a view to maximising its future value.

Owners' motivations have been divided into three broad categories:

- *Lifestyle*: This is the description often given to a business run by an individual because it not only facilitates, but is also part of, the lifestyle that individual wants to have. Examples of lifestyle businesses are frequently to be found in art or craft businesses where the owner lives to practise that craft rather than only practising that craft in order to live.
- *Comfort-zone*: A comfort-zone business is typically one that provides its owner with sufficient returns for the level of comfort he or she wants in life. Unlike in the case of the lifestyle business, the basis of the business is less important than the level of benefit it can provide in return for a reasonable amount of effort. In some places the comfort-zone business has been characterised as the 'BMW syndrome'. This is where the level of comfort desired includes the possession of recognised symbols of success. Once that level of comfort is reached, however, there is little incentive to build the business further.
- *Growth*: The 'growth' business is the one that approaches closest to what to many is the ideal business, namely one where the owner wishes to manage the business to maximise its earning potential, especially for the future.

It is the influence of the owner, in whatever category his or her motivations may fall, that is a major determinant of how a business behaves, and the particular ways in which small businesses behave.

Distinctive characteristics of small businesses

The section above highlighted the importance of recognising the influence of the entrepreneur behind the business. Nevertheless the more traditional approach to considering small businesses, and the one used in most research and writing about enterprise, has been to take the business as the key unit of analysis. Both approaches can have their uses but this chapter is primarily concerned with businesses and so the remaining sections generally take the business-centred approach.

The differences in the administrative structure of the very small and the very large firms are so great that in many ways it is hard to see that the two species are of the same genus. ... We cannot define a caterpillar and then use the same definition for a butterfly.

Dame Edith Penrose[13]

Many commentators, including Gibb, have identified differences between the behaviour of small and big businesses, differences manifest in a range of characteristics.[14] Where the meaning of 'enterprise' was explored. Others significant differences include those discussed below.

An absence of functional managers

Often the management of a small business resides with one person. The advantage of this can be that an overall view of management, including production, finance and marketing, is taken instead of there being a conflict between the different functions. On the other hand, knowledge of such functions may not be evenly developed and in some areas may be severely lacking.

On-the-job learning

Many small business owner-managers have acquired most of their business knowledge on the job. They will often have been in the job a long time and may therefore have a deep experience, but not necessarily a broad one or an objective and informed view. The business systems employed are likely to be of their own devising, based on experience, and are unlikely to be changed unless experience also suggests it is necessary.

Investment and resources

Money invested in the business is often personal money, not that of impersonal investors. There can therefore be a reluctance to spend this money on anything except the bare essentials, for short-term obvious returns. More formal investment appraisal methods are not seen as being as useful as a 'feel' for what is right. Similarly, the time needed for formal 'training' or review is seen as both an unaffordable distraction from the real work of the business and as earning a return that is more theoretical than practical. Change, where it occurs, is likely to be the response to short-term need rather than the result of long-term strategy.

Discontinuities

There are thresholds and discontinuities in a small business that do not occur in a bigger one. In a bigger business, for instance, increasing capacity by 10 per cent in a key department to cope with a 10 per cent increase in turnover may be relatively straightforward. In a small business however there may be only two people in the department, who are already fully loaded. Extra capacity is still needed, but taking on an extra person would be a 50 per cent increase and may not be justified by the likely extra return. This is also true of getting a second machine when one is only just unable to cope.

Informal systems and procedures

Many businesses start with one person, for whom formal systems and procedures will seem unnecessary. They will grow by taking on new employees in ones and twos and, again, it would seem strange to introduce formal systems for just a few people, who will learn what is going on quickly enough through their direct involvement in the small team. In any case the owner-manager is probably too busy to introduce more formal systems for running the business. This state of affairs is likely to continue until a crisis arises because the business has grown too big to be run informally. As many small businesses never get to that stage, informality in systems and procedures is a characteristic that they share.

Control and organisation in small businesses
Top-down

In a small business the dominant position of the entrepreneur can create a person-centred culture. Consequently the strategy, or absence of one, of the business will correspond to that of the entrepreneur. This top-down approach can be attractive in a stable environment, if the entrepreneur articulates a vision that motivates others. Increasingly, however, even in small businesses, it is often the intelligent employees, more than the entrepreneur, who are in touch with the latest technological, economic and sociological developments. Considerable decision-making discretion, even at the strategic level, may have to be delegated to these individuals, but entrepreneurs are notoriously reluctant to share their power. In a world of discontinuous change that is a drawback.[15]

Decision making

In general, the decision-making process in small businesses will be less formal and more personalised than in larger ventures. In a rational approach, objectives are set, alternatives are investigated and economic evaluations are made of alternatives. In a large business the distance from top to bottom, and the consequent number of layers and communication steps, may mean that the message and the rationale behind it can be distorted. In small businesses the omnipresence of the owners can mean that everyone in the business can hear a clear articulation of the goals and objectives. However, the smallness of the business, and the lack of managerial skills of its owner, can also mean that goals are not articulated at all. Clear objectives facilitate rationality, but rational economic decisions often depend on having access to large amounts of information and the employment of sophisticated quantitative techniques to make sense of it. The lack of resource in small businesses, and their heavy reliance on information gleaned from personal contacts, are unlikely to encourage rational evaluations of alternatives. The information available to decision makers in small businesses will be even more inaccurate, incomplete and time-bounded than in other organisations.[16] In the same way, time horizons for planning, whether formal or informal, will tend to be much shorter than in larger businesses. Moreover, decisions are much more likely to be influenced by an owner-manager's emotions and personal interests than by objective analysis.

Organisational structures

Most work in large organisations is highly specialised, and much of the brainwork is removed from operational tasks. However, an extensive division of tasks, especially at management level, only makes sense when there is a large volume of work; it is no use employing experts if they are underemployed. By definition, a small business does not have a large volume of output and the work must often be done by generalists. Furthermore, organisations tend to perpetuate the fruits of their learning and standardise regularly recurring activities; however, this is sensible only when environmental conditions are stable. In the turbulent environment so characteristic of the small business, change is the order of the day and problem solving is a higher requirement of organisations than efficiency.[17] As a result of these factors, small firms tend to have simple, flexible, non-differentiated structures and flexible work practices, to possess general-purpose rather than specialised machines, and to exhibit few of the features so characteristic of bureaucracies. The general nature of employee skills and flexible production capabilities means that much more of the creative aspects of production can be easily delegated to operators. Faced with an order from a customer, operators and their managers are more likely to plan operations jointly.

Control

If the all-pervasive control mechanisms of large organisations are absent, how do managers in small businesses exercise control? Decision making can be considered to take place at three levels: strategic, administrative and operational. In the bigger business these will each happen at different levels of the organisation and involve different people. In small businesses they are, as often as not, all done by the same person with no formal or recognised boundaries or hierarchical split amongst them. There is therefore a lack of clarity about the type of decision being taken, with little distinction in thought between strategic and tactical decisions. Once a decision is taken, control through standardisation, performance measurement and bureaucratic structures is often absent in small businesses. Instead the presence of the owners, or their representatives, will mean that control is exercised by direct supervision. These individuals are never far away, and the numerous work-related discussions that take place will confirm the position of managers in an overseeing role. Yet this often leads to much speedier decision making and shorter reaction times, which in turn can mean an improved competitive edge.[18]

A lack of objectivity

Another key feature of small businesses is the inability, or unwillingness, of their owners to be objective about them. Instead they frequently identify closely with their businesses, seeing them almost as extensions of themselves. This, and its implications, are considered in more detail later in the chapter.

The implications of being small

Small businesses have assumed an importance in many people's minds, largely, it would seem because of their employment creation and innovation potential. They are classified as small by their size, whether that is measured in terms of their worth, their turnover or their employment. There are, however, many differences amongst the businesses in those size categories, and there are many aspects, apart from just their size, that small businesses tend to have in common and where they differ from big businesses. It is for these reasons that they often need to be treated differently.

Some aspects of small businesses that require particular insight if misunderstandings are not to occur. It is, nevertheless, relevant to consider here some of the aspects of small businesses that make them different. These differences can be grouped under the headings of culture, influence, resources and ambition. They encompass some of the crucial differences between small and big businesses for which distinctions by size are only a proxy. They are the reason for a separate analysis and consideration of small businesses as a category distinct from big business.

Culture

The culture of a small business is tied in with the needs, desires and abilities of its owner. He or she tends to focus on independence; flexibility, both from preference and necessity; closeness to the customer and supplier; individual and personal, rather than system, control; working with networks of contractors; tolerating uncertainty;

and the shorter-term view rather than the longer one. There can be different types of owner with different needs and desires.

For many people however the culture of a small business epitomises enterprise. It can, nevertheless, be argued that, while starting a small business may be enterprising, running it need not be. In the case, for instance, of an inherited family business, running it may be what the person concerned has been expecting and preparing to do, possibly from a young age, and involves little that is new or innovatory. Nevertheless, businesses, and particularly small businesses, are frequently referred to as enterprises, which emphasises this aspect of their culture.

Influence

Small businesses have very little influence over their environments or their markets. Their small size may enable them to respond more quickly to changes in those environments or markets but, unlike their bigger counterparts, they have little influence on these changes. Their job creation potential, especially when combined with groupings to promote combined lobbying, may give them some political influence, but it is unrealistic to assume that they will individually be able to change their markets in the ways they might wish.

As well as their final markets, the intermediate markets or distribution channels of small businesses are also beyond their control. Again, bigger businesses may be able to dictate terms to distributors, or may be able to acquire their own distribution channels through 'vertical integration'. But not the small businesses: they are at the mercy of their distributors, and also their suppliers, to a very considerable extent.

Resources

It is almost invariably the case that small businesses lack sufficient resources. Most of them are started on a financial shoestring and few get cash-rich subsequently. Most therefore do not have easy access to the financial reserves necessary to carry them through a lean period or to utilise a sudden opportunity for expansion.

But it is not just finance which they lack. They are usually short of both management time and management skills. As has already been mentioned, there is often only one person, the owner, in a management role, and this role will embrace all aspects of managing the business. This means both that the amount of management time that can be focused on a problem is very limited and that aspects of management expertise are also likely to be missing, because the single manager is unlikely to be fully conversant with marketing, production, financial, technical, legal and human resource aspects of business.

In the business world, therefore, small may mean poor, but not always. There are examples of small businesses that do make very large profits, and others that, if not wealthy in themselves, have, by virtue of their technology, markets or other intangible assets, been very attractive propositions for prospective investors.

Ambition

In terms of their behaviour, however, the biggest difference between small and big businesses is likely to be that which results from the ambition and goals of their owners and managers. As indicated above, the larger the business, the more likely it is to be run by a professional management trying to maximise its financial value. The converse is that the smaller the business, the more likely it is that it will be run by an owner-manager with an aim based on personal values.

The varieties of small businesses

The stage of development of the business may be the consideration most used for distinguishing different types of business, but there are many others that, although sometimes bewildering in their variety, can help to define the distinctions between different types of businesses and their characteristics.

Industry sector

The average size of businesses can differ widely in different industry sectors. Where the purpose of classifying a business as small or large is in relation to its place in its industry and the influence it might have on that industry, it is important to pick a definition that recognises the average size of businesses in the relevant sector. For instance, in relation to other businesses in the same sector, a ten-person window cleaning business would be very large, while a 100-person car manufacturer would be very small. Examples from Europe show some of the ranges: thus in 1995 the average employment in a coalmining business was 924, in a railway business 996, and in a communications business 376; but in a travel agency 12, in a retail business four and in an estate agency two.[19]

Legal structure

In the UK a number of terms are encountered describing possible forms of business structure:

- *Sole trader*: Operating as a sole trader is the simplest form of business. An individual can start a business in this way with the minimum of fuss. In this situation, however, there is no legal distinction between the assets of the business and those of its owner. Such people are 'self-employed' and subject to income tax.
- *Partnership*: A business can be established as a partnership of a group of individuals doing business together. However, the business does not have a separate legal identity, and each partner is jointly and severally liable for any liability incurred by the partners acting for the business. The liability of the partners is unlimited, except in the case of the less common (in the UK) 'limited partnership'.
- *Company*: A business can be established as a company. The company then has its own separate legal existence independent of that of its owners. If it is a limited company, this limits the liability of its owners. This limit can be achieved by shares, in which case the business has shareholders who together own the business and can receive dividends from its profits in proportion to the number and type of shares they hold, or the limit can be by guarantee. A business limited by guarantee is controlled by its members, who each agree to guarantee its liabilities up to an agreed amount (often £1 each) but who cannot benefit from the

distribution of the profits of the business. A company limited by shares can be a public or a private company depending on whether the invitation to subscribe for the shares is open to the public or restricted in certain ways.

- *Co-operative*: Co-operative businesses are governed by different legislation from companies. They have to be registered as co-operatives and they have the benefit of limited liability. A co-operative is owned and controlled by its members, who may for instance be a group of workers or people living in a local community, who want to use the business for the benefit of themselves and/or the community. This can be reflected in the memorandum and articles of association of the business. A workers' co-operative is a business owned and controlled by the people working in it, an approach which can lead to greater involvement and responsibility.
- *Social enterprise*: A form of business also sometimes encountered is the social enterprise or community business. This, however, is not a distinct legal form of business but an intention of the owners of the business to use the returns from the business for the benefit of the community in which the business operates. Many co-operatives are social enterprises.

There were an estimated 2.8 million sole proprietorships in the UK at the start of 2006, of which just 11 per cent had employees. In that year there were also an estimated 500,000 partnerships of which 37 per cent had employees and about 1.1 million companies of which 60 per cent had employees.

Family businesses

One distinct type of business that is often small is the family business. In the days when craft businesses and farms were virtually the only businesses in existence, it was almost the universal practice for them to be passed on through generations of the same family. It is now widely accepted that family businesses still make a major contribution to many economies and their particular characteristics are therefore worth considering.[20] Recent research suggests that in the United States one household in ten has a family business.[21] Of the 22 million firms in America, between 4 million and 20 million of them (depending on the definition used and the survey carried out) are said to be family businesses, making a contribution to GDP of between 12 and 49 per cent.[22] Most of them are small, with more than 90 per cent of them employing fewer than 20 people; they operate mainly in the service, retail, construction and agricultural sectors; 55 per cent had a turnover of less than $100,000, and three-quarters are run by men. One of the early studies of family businesses in the UK found that, of its sample, 52 per cent operated in the service sector, 44 per cent employed 100 or fewer people, 83 per cent had a turnover in the range £2 million to £50 million, and only 25 per cent of family firms achieved growth rates exceeding 20 per cent per annum.[23] In general, family businesses are smaller and less likely to grow than non-family businesses. However, the UK study was based on the top 6000 UK private companies and all 2000 companies quoted on the London Stock Exchange, and consequently it represents the larger and more prosperous stock of UK family firms. A more realistic representation of the typical British family business is presented by Cromie et al.[24] They found that approximately 45 per cent of their sample traded in the service sector and a similar proportion in manufacturing; that 31 per cent had fewer than ten full-time employees and

Table 4.3 Different criteria by which family businesses have been defined

Ownership and management	Family involvement in the business	Generational transfer
Ownership and control by a family unit	Transactions and interaction between two systems: the business and the family	The actual transfer of ownership and control from one generation to another
One family member has to own and manage the business	Interactions involve lots of family members	The intentions to continue transfers between generations
Two or more family members must own and manage the business	Specific family involvement in business decisions and actions	

Source: Based on R. K. Z. Heck and E. Scannell-Trent, 'The Prevalence of Family Businesses from a Household Sample', *Family Business Review* (1999), 12, pp. 210–11.

81 per cent had fewer than 50; that annual turnover was less than £1 million for half of the sample and less than £5 million for almost 90 per cent. These businesses were therefore typically small; but there are some very large firms amongst them.

One of the problems of identifying and describing family businesses is the variety of definitions. One researcher identified more than 20 different definitions[25] but there are a number of common themes. Table 4.3 is an attempt to summarise a recent review of definitions used in US research on the matter which shows that ownership and control by family members, the degree of family involvement in a business, and the intention or practice of transferring ownership and/or control from generation to generation are for many people the key issues in characterising family businesses.[26]

Some of the confusion arises because there are various types of family business.[27] It is unlikely, for example, that a micro-business run just by a husband and wife, on the one hand, and on the other the Ahlstrom Corporation in Finland, which has 200 family members, will display similar characteristics of ownership, control, family-to-business interaction and intergenerational transfers. Issues of age, size and numbers of founders and whether family involvement is increasing, stable or declining will influence the business and they way it behaves.

Broader definitions allow for a developmental, flexible approach to family businesses, but most family business research seems to have focused on the firm and to have considered that family matters are merely an adjunct to that.[28] In line with the suggestion above that often a focus on the entrepreneur provides a better perspective on business development, it has been argued that for family businesses the focus of interest should be on households and that the two-way interaction between business and family dynamics has been neglected in family business research.[29]

Much of the traditional research into the family firm, however, has often been based on a frame of reference in which the family business was regarded as the core system and the family itself was viewed 'only as a component of the business environment'.[30] Other models however recognise that businesses and families are independent systems with each having resources, processes and goals. In a family business context there are interactions between these systems but 'family issues are seen as disabling the effective working of the (business) system'.[31] As a result it is often argued that it is good practice to keep family and business affairs separate. Family business researchers have often used a model of family businesses which sees them as rational units which pursue economic goals. The assumption is then made that family feelings, values and dynamics have a detrimental influence on the business.[32]

This line of reasoning leads to conclusions that family businesses are less efficient than non-family business. Nevertheless, family businesses are reported to be relatively long-lived, with 60 per cent of the family firms in one survey[33] having been established for over 30 years, compared with only 35 per cent of their non-family counterparts. And their managements had longer tenure: over two-thirds of the family businesses had been under the same management for eight years compared with only one-third of non-family businesses.

The problems of family firms

Cromie et al. found that families are very keen to control the issue of shares and are not keen on selling shares to raise finance for growth, that family members dominate boards and senior management positions, and that families are not keen on using outside advisers. In addition conflicts often arise between parents and their offspring, between siblings and between family and non-family personnel. Furthermore, managerial succession is fraught with difficulties with the result that, while there is an impression of stable, conservative, family-dominated institutions, they are often riddled with conflict. The stereotypical image of the family firm is of a rather dismal working environment which offers little opportunity to non-family personnel and which 'becomes sterile and eventually fails'.[34]

The pre-eminence of the controlling family, centralised decision making and long-standing management teams can also result in static thinking. It can make it less likely that new ideas which are essential for long-term development will emerge, and family businesses are often reluctant to use outside advisers, preferring instead the counsel of the family when exploring business matters.

Another difficulty in family businesses can be the conflict that often emerges between family members, in particular founders and their children. The founders often recognise that they have to let go of the reins and develop their successor, but the business is such an important feature of their lives that they fear that the 'loss' of it will damage their self-image and bring their competency into question. Such behaviour can be resented, and tension can build as a result.

Rivalry between siblings is another common source of difficulties. This conflict can reach such a level of seriousness that it has an impact on 'every management decision and magnifies the jockeying for power that goes on in all organisations'.[35] Where multiple family members have an interest in the business they may all expect equal treatment but, in the nature of things, this is rarely possible. Also, they may have different expectations such as short-term riches or long-term growth. As a consequence, various family members may set about gaining power and influence by means of internecine warfare that is often to the detriment of the business.

Conflict is inevitable in organisations, and it must be managed, but its management presents special problems for family-run businesses. Because the conflict can be intense, and because it is transposed from the business to the personal or family arena, it is often suppressed and not resolved. Therefore open discussion and the challenge of ideas, which can help progress in a changing world, may be avoided. In addition, when disputes do occur, the anger and resentment that occurs may also be transferred to family life, and this makes it difficult for family members to break out of a self-defeating cycle of conflict. All this can make rational business decision making exceedingly difficult. In family businesses there are often family concerns that over-ride business sensibilities. Incompetent family members may be retained in post as a favour to shore up deteriorating family relationships, and promotion for otherwise eligible non-family managers may be blocked as a result. Business logic and rationale may thus take a back seat in favour of family preference. There is some evidence that this is especially likely in second-generation family businesses. Attempts to improve the business by recruiting professional managers bring other problems: such managers may find that they can never achieve the measure of recognition, such as promotion to the board, and control that their expertise and contribution merit.

Managing the transition of power and control can often be a difficulty in family businesses, especially the transition from one chief executive to another. There is evidence that this is rarely planned in family firms, and that the transition is, as a result, frequently traumatic. This may contribute to the failure of many family businesses to survive to the second or third generation. This seemingly unprofessional behaviour can come about because owners:

- will not face up to their limited lifespan
- may unconsciously care little about what happens when they are gone
- may resent their successor
- may have an aversion to planning.[36]

Many of the difficulties found in family businesses can be attributed to non-rational behaviour and this view is supported by the traditional approach to family business research. However it has been pointed out that values and perceptions play a key part in the succession process and that concepts from behavioural economics can offer insights into the process. The 'endowment effect' can mean that the person handing over control in a family firm's transition 'is likely to place greater value on the business than is the new leader'.[37] This may well explain why succeeding generations sometimes take risks with or dispose of a business they inherit, and not much can be done about it. However, drawing on notions of 'sunk costs' and 'windfall gains', it is suggested that the more it costs a successor in terms of money, time and effort to buy into a new business, the more highly he or she will value the business and the more likely he or she is to behave in a conservative manner.

It is argued that when people gain assets easily they will not value them highly and will be prepared to gamble with them. In a family business context if a successor is required to display superior performance before succeeding to a position of control, the business will be highly valued and will be treated with discernment. If the succession process is structured in a way which requires successors to invest money and time in the business and to prove themselves before they are handed the reins, they will assume that the business is worth having. Decision making is influenced by rational considerations but values also play an important part.

Advantages of family businesses

There may be drawbacks to family businesses but there are advantages too. When a family group strongly influences management and control, a permanent, solid atmosphere and an esprit de corps can develop. This can often encourage both a closeness among staff and long-lasting relationships with customers, suppliers and other contacts. Family businesses can as a result often build a reputation for dependability and for excellent service.

Staff in family businesses can have a sense of belonging and strong commitment to the goals of the organisation. When the owning family are justly proud of their venture, their enthusiasm and commitment can enthuse non-family staff. This sense of togetherness is a powerful asset in that it can focus the energies of all involved on customers and on the need to serve them.

This commitment can produce a flexibility in terms of working practices, working hours and remuneration. Family members do what is necessary to get a job done. There is little demarcation of duties, and many family members are reluctant to take money out of the business. Some of this flexibility rubs off on non-family members, and this can allow the family business to respond rapidly to changing technological, sociological and economic conditions.

Family businesses are normally free from stock market pressure to produce quick results, since they are not quoted on the market and have no institutional shareholders. They can, as a result, often take a longer-term view. They are not forced to vacillate, and can pursue a consistent long-term strategy. This long view is reinforced by the permanent nature of their management teams. Permanence of management tends to allow behavioural norms to emerge and a recognised way of doing things to develop.

Family businesses therefore have both advantages and disadvantages, and these are summarised by Kets de Vries in Table 4.4

Family business performance

The result of this combination of advantages and disadvantages can be a business that has staying potential, but which does not usually last beyond the tenure of the founder. For instance, UK data suggest that:[38]

- Fewer than 14 per cent of established family businesses will last until the third generation.
- Fewer than 24 per cent will make it to the second generation.
- The majority of businesses will fail in the first five years.

There is however no conclusive evidence about the performance of family versus non-family businesses. Barbara Dunn, drawing on work in the UK and in the United States, argued that publicly quoted family firms were more profitable than non-family businesses in the 1970s and 1980s.[39] Anecdotal evidence from Finland supports this point of view, where it has been suggested that the $3.3 billion Ahlstrom Corporation prospered by combining the benefits of family involvement with the pursuit of sound business principles.[40] However other British researchers have reported no differences 'in the performance and effectiveness of family and non-family firms'.[41] Inconclusive results can emerge for many reasons but problems with definitions have been alluded to. Definitions are sometimes the product of the working model employed by researchers, and it is noted above that some alternatives to the traditional approach have been proposed recently.

Family business models

It has been suggested that traditional models play down the role of the family in family businesses because they consider family interpersonal and intergenerational

Table 4.4 Advantages and disadvantages of family-controlled businesses

Advantages	Disadvantages

• Long-term orientation
• Greater independence of action
  – less (or no) pressure from stock market
  – less (or no) takeover risk
• Family culture as a source of pride
  – stability
  – strong identification/commitment/motivation
  – continuity in leadership
• Greater resilience in hard times
  – willing to plough back profits
• Less bureaucratic and impersonal
  – greater flexibility
  – quicker decision-making
• Financial benefits
  – possibility of great success
• Knowing the business
  – early training for family members
	• Less access to capital markets may curtail growth
	• Confusing organisation
	  – Messy structure
	   No clear division of tasks
	• Nepotism
	  – tolerance of inept family members as managers
	  – inequitable reward systems
	  – greater difficulties in attracting professional management
	• Spoiled kid syndrome
	• Internecine strife
	  – family disputes overflow into business
	• Paternalistic/autocratic rule
	  – resistance to change
	  – secrecy
	  – attraction of dependent personalities
	• Financial strain
	  – family members milking the business
	  – disequilibrium between contribution and compensation
	• Succession dramas

Source: Reprinted from M. F. R. Kets de Vries, 'The Dynamics of Family Controlled Firms: The Good News and the Bad News', *Organisational Dynamics* (1993), 21, p.69. © 1993 With permission from Elsevier Science.

relations and processes to be an aspect of the business environment, not of the business. In contrast, Stafford et al. combine a model of family functioning with one of business prosperity to 'yield a model of family business sustainability'.[42] The latter is the product of family and business attainments, together with transactions between the two entities. In this model the family is afforded much more prominence than formerly. It is regarded as a goal-directed system which utilises resources and manages constraints in making transactions which contribute towards desirable goals. If goals are attained a strong sense of achievement results. The achievements can be objective and include such variables as the standard of living. They can also be subjective as represented by such outcomes as satisfaction and successful socialisation. Family resources include physical capital such as property and money, and human capital such as knowledge and effective co-operation. Constraints include such variables as the law, economic realities and societal norms. Families use and combine resources by means of various transactions to achieve desirable goals. Like businesses, families structure their relationships and tasks in various ways to attain their goals.

Stafford et al. present a similar model for businesses. Systems models of organisations are quite common and that of Stafford et al. contains many commonly reported elements but they do point out that the criteria by which success is measured include both objective matters and more subjective issues such as providing a way of life for the family. Business transactions include both resource and

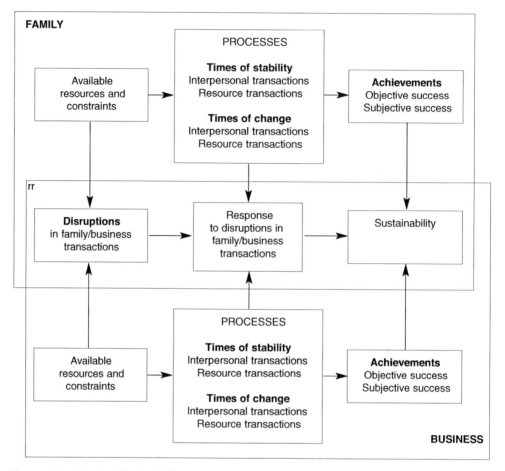

Figure 4.1 Sustainable family business model

Source: K. Stafford, K. A. Duncan, S. Dane and M. Winter, 'A Research Model of Sustainable Family Business', *Family Business Review* (1999), 12, pp.197–208. Reprinted with permission from the Family Firm Institute Inc. All rights reserved.

interpersonal transformations to reflect both the task-related and emotional transactions in a business.

In a family business there will be regular transactions from family to business and vice versa. Family labour and money might be used by the business, business decisions will reflect the needs of the family, business resources and assets may be used by the family in the pursuit of their objectives, and business managers might allocate time to family needs while at work. In addition to the normal transactions the model includes responses and adjustments by both the family and the business to major changes within either system. In the model, which is reproduced in Figure 4.1, the business and family systems overlap and a sustainable family business is one in which consideration is given to 'the ability of the family and business to co-operate in responding to disruptions in a way that does not impede the success of both'.[43]

The model supports the view that there are different kinds of family business. In some cases the overlap between the systems will be small, and business and family issues will be kept separate. In others there will be a large overlap with lots of transactions and responses between the two systems. An important feature of the model is the attention it devotes to the family, the interaction between family and business, and the introduction of the issue of family firm sustainability and its adaptability. It is suggested that the family business is a continuous concept with completely separate and completely embroiled systems only to be found at the extremities of a continuum. However, even where the spheres are kept separate, the family still exerts an influence on the business. The family element makes family businesses unique. To accommodate this reality some American researchers advocate using a household sampling frame rather than a sample composed of firms and they have produced some interesting work on the adjustments that families and businesses make in turbulent times. Both make adjustments but the family accommodates the business more often than conversely.

Women-owned businesses

Another aspect of business ownership which might be expected to have an influence on the business is the gender of the owner. In the UK, there are approximately 1 million self-employed women (7.6 per cent of women in employment) in comparison to 2.7 million self-employed men (17.4 per cent of men in employment). Carter and Shaw point out that there are three main socio-economic issues that influence women's abilities and prospects as business owners:[44] firstly the gender pay-gap; secondly occupational segregation and unequal employment opportunities; and finally work-life balance issues. It is their view that one of the key differences between male and female start-ups is the lower levels of capital that are available to female entrepreneurs. For example, women working in a full-time capacity in the UK earn 17 per cent less than men. This reduced ability to accumulate capital both restricts the type of business that women can start and can restrict future business growth and development. Businesses in fields with low barriers to entry may often have poor growth potential; this restricts the performance of these businesses and could be a factor in the reported incidence of a faster rate of female business exit. As Carter and Shaw (2000) point out, this does not mean that female-owned businesses perform any less well than male businesses; they simply lack the initial resources. This lack of resources is a clear characteristic of female-owned businesses.

Cromie however examined the problems experienced by male and female-owned young businesses and discovered that the problems experienced did not really vary by gender.[45] His sample faced a diverse set of personal problems, including lack of time, having to perform a myriad of duties, working too hard, selling oneself, being too conservative, lacking interpersonal skills, and not being taken seriously. Men and women both experienced personal problems but women recorded more difficulties. This is especially true with respect to a lack of self-confidence and not being taken seriously which, when applied by providers of funds, has led to the under-capitalisation of their businesses. However, women respondents did say that once it was clear that they were committed to making a success of their businesses these problems disappeared.

Carter argues that certain problems were perceived by women to be gender related. These include the 'late payment of bills; a tendency to undercharge; getting business and finding clients; and... the effect of proprietorship upon personal and domestic circumstances'.[46]

Access to business finance

In Britain, Carter reviewed recent work on the financing of women-owned firms and suggested that there have been four recurring problems:[47]

- They have difficulty in obtaining start-up finance.
- They are required to provide guarantees when seeking external finance and they are sometimes unable to provide the requisite collateral.
- They find it more difficult to obtain ongoing finance.
- Bankers tend to have negative stereotypes of women entrepreneurs and discriminate against them.

Results from a study by Carter and Rosa indicate that there is support for some of these propositions but that some differences are accounted for by factors such as firm size and industrial sector.[48] Women do have less start-up finance than men but they use the same sources: personal money, overdrafts and bank loans. There are also gender differences in the use of ongoing finance: women are more likely to use loans while men are more likely to use overdrafts and supplier credit. Carter and Rosa found no support for the propositions about the need for guarantees nor the supposed negative stereotypical images of women among bankers. In general there appears to be little evidence of deliberate discrimination against women.

Ethnic businesses

Another type of small business ownership with distinctive features is the ethnic or minority community-owned business. Immigrants come to their adopted country for a number of reasons. In Britain after the Second World War, immigrants came from the Caribbean, South Asia and other areas to work in various industries which were short of labour, but their intention was often to earn money to send back home and eventually to return home themselves. However, in 1962 entry to the UK from the British Commonwealth was severely restricted and immigrant workers already in Britain's urban areas decided to remain and to bring their families there as well. This led to the development of large ethnic enclaves in inner city areas where, it has been suggested, due to the decline in large-scale industrial employment, to the racism and discrimination they faced in the labour market, and to the revival of the SME sector in the 1980s, people were encouraged to create their own firms.[49]

Ethnic entrepreneurs, but what, if anything, distinguishes an ethnic business from a small business which happens to be run by someone from an immigrant community? Among the answers suggested are the following:

- A business which draws heavily on a group 'that is socially distinguished (by others or itself) by characteristics of cultural or national origin' for tangible and intangible resources, markets and support constitutes a special kind of small business.[50] Ethnic businesses also develop 'connections and regular patterns of interaction' among people from particular cultural backgrounds.[51] Such ethnic enterprises are commonplace in many parts of the world, but problems with definitions and the sheer diversity of these ventures present difficulties for those who try to quantify the phenomenon.
- Ethnic entrepreneurs in different countries may be from different backgrounds. In Britain Pakistanis, Indian Sikhs, Nigerians, West Indians and East African

refugees are common, whereas in the United States, Koreans, Mexicans and Vietnamese are found in large numbers. Nevertheless there is some uniformity in their choice of business activity. For example in North America studies have revealed that ethnic businesses predominate in the wholesale, retail and service sectors, with some presence in light manufacturing.[52] a recent study in Britain of 82 ethnic minority businesses supports the American finding.[53] However, there were variations amongst the different groups of ethnic business and these can be explained partly by the cultural backgrounds of the respondents, their educational backgrounds and the length of time they have been in the country.

- Educational attainment is another factor in the rate of ethnic enterprise and in the nature of the businesses operated. Li identified that amongst the most poorly qualified (with little formal qualifications) it was the Chinese men (34 per cent) and Chinese women (21 per cent) who were most likely to be self-employed, whereas amongst the best qualified, namely those with a first degree or above, it was the Indian and Pakistani/Bangladeshi men who were the most likely to be self-employed.[54] The Chinese tend to operate predominately micro-businesses whereas the Indian and Pakistani sample tended to operate small to medium-sized enterprises. It was also noted by Li that Black Africans tended to feature amongst the most qualified but showed the lowest incidence of entrepreneurship. Yet this same group, when they did start a business, tended to be amongst the biggest employers, with 25 per cent of Black African businesses employing more than 25 people.

- Two aspects of business in which ethnic businesses rely particularly heavily on others from the same ethnic group are in finding customers and in obtaining labour. Successful businesses must find customers and it is sometimes argued that firms which fully understand the special needs of ethnic groups, and can thus deliver more appropriate benefits, have a competitive advantage. In addition, co-ethnic customers may patronise a particular firm because of a sense of ethnic solidarity with the owner. These factors may confer initial competitive advantage, but it has been argued that sustained competitive advantage will only arise when a business has a strategy which no other business is following and when other businesses cannot duplicate the benefits on offer. However, for ethnic businesses located in service and retail areas where barriers to entry are low, there are many competitors who can follow the same strategy and offer similar benefits. In Britain, therefore, the outcome is increasingly 'a mass of ethnic small business owners trapped in a hostile trading milieu'.[55]

- Labour requirements for small ethnic businesses also come largely from co-ethnics in the community and from the extended family. At start-up, having a supply of part-time labour allows firms to adjust to the ebb and flow of initial workloads and in a way that is cheap and easy to organise. Many of the jobs on offer in the start-up phase are offered to co-ethnics on an informal basis. Indeed, the most noticeable feature of the labour force amongst ethnic businesses is the widespread use of family labour. It is argued that family labour seems attractive in that it helps avoid obstacles to recruitment in the open market, it is flexible and cheap, and problems with the supervision of staff can be avoided.[56] Family members can be loyal and committed to the firm and consequently confer advantages on the firm. There is, however, another side to the employment of family members which is more contentious. In many ethnic businesses women manage the production processes as well as attending to the administrative and financial aspects of the business. Men tend to handle external relationships whilst women manage the workflow. This division of labour by gender could be a source of competitive advantage but there is often an exploitative element in the hiring of women. Women manage the work processes and domestic affairs but get little financial or social reward for their endeavours. Men are the official managers, even though women often play 'critical *de facto* managerial roles in running the business'.[57] The domestic subordination of women is reinforced in the workplace in many ethnic businesses.

The lack of prestige afforded to women who manage ethnic family businesses could well have a detrimental effect on economic performance. Another feature of family involvement which is also problematic is the reluctance, also found in non-ethnic family businesses, to recruit non-family managers even when incumbent family managers are less than competent. Family members can be important to ethnic businesses as a means of overcoming the disadvantages of racism and of providing a flexible source of labour, but their over-reliance on the family can also be a source of disadvantage.

Other categorisations of small business

In a population as heterogeneous as that of small businesses there will be many different ways in which firms can be categorised, and it is neither practicable nor appropriate to try to list them all here. However there are some which get quite frequent mention, even if only by policy-makers seeking to target assistance appropriately. Among them are the following.

High-tech/low-tech

High-tech is a category of businesses often favoured by those promoting small business because of an assumption that high-tech businesses contribute most to an economy. This depends however on what is meant by a high-tech business. Often the definition seems to be that of a business based on a new and relatively hard-to-acquire technology and which is, as a consequence, likely to be less vulnerable to competition and therefore able to earn more, to export more and to survive longer than businesses based on older technologies. However there is more to business success than the technology on which it is based and therefore, while high-tech businesses may have the newness of their technology in common, there is no guarantee that they share the same level of profitability, of exports or of success. They are studied nevertheless as a category because of issues that they are perceived to have in common, such as longer lead times to market, greater difficulty in communicating their potential to other people and needing greater financial resources in order to get started.

Urban/rural

In places like England and Wales, where only 7 per cent of the population live in completely rural areas, it might be expected that the urban business is the norm. Yet there is evidence that in recent years many people have left the city and moved to the country, sometimes to start small businesses. Those businesses are often set up in rural areas for environmental and lifestyle reasons and they would be classed as rural businesses because they are located in a rural area.[58] However that is often in practice the only rural thing about them: they benefit from cheaper property costs and overheads and they have greater distances to go to market, but in other aspects they are just urban businesses which happen to be in a rural setting. Businesses which would have better claims to be rural would be farms and farm diversifications, other primary food producers and rural tourism initiatives.

A distinction is sometimes made between 'accessible' and 'remote' rural areas. Storey points out that 'accessible' rural areas have generally been amongst the most prosperous parts of the United Kingdom and quotes research showing that many businesses there are arts and craft-based and are started by relatively highly educated individuals who are in-migrants to the area seeking a higher quality of life.[59] It is businesses in the 'accessible' areas that outperform comparable firms in urban areas, whereas firms set up in 'remote' rural areas do not appear to perform as well.

Apart from these distinctions there seems to be little evidence that rural businesses are in general significantly distinct from urban businesses, although some research has indicated that a few differences may be discernible. Storey reports a finding that owners of rural businesses are more reluctant to move out of their existing town or village than urban owners and have a commitment to a particular location, even though the opportunities for expansion there might be limited.[60] Another survey in England which was conducted in 1991 found that:[61]

- Rural and small-town firms were younger than conurbation firms and that southern firms were frequently young new enterprises set up in the 1980s.
- There were differences in workforce skill composition between northern and rural firms on the one hand, and southern and conurbation firms on the other. The former employed significantly higher proportions of semi-skilled, unskilled and skilled manual workers, while the latter had higher proportions of clerical and administrative staff, higher professionals and technologists, and managers.
- Urban/rural differences in innovation activity were striking, with higher innovation rates in rural firms compared with conurbation firms.
- There is also a consistent urban/rural gradient in employment growth, with the most rapid employment expansion reported in rural firms and the least rapid in conurbation firms.

'Third age' businesses

Age distributions of self-employed people generally show that self-employment becomes increasingly common as middle age approaches and that it does not cease at the normal retirement age. The reasons given for these features are that middle age may be a time when capital or knowledge assets have been accumulated, and commitments may be reducing, so a start-up can be attempted. Alternatively it might be a time when people are particularly vulnerable to redundancy or attracted by early retirement offers. Self-employment may persist into the sixties and longer because of a reluctance to let go, although hours can be adjusted to allow for age, and there is no statutory retirement age for the self-employed. Alternatively it may continue because some of those in self-employment may not have adequate pension arrangements.[62]

Craft businesses

A further classification often used to distinguish among categories of business is that of craft, manufacture, service, technology or agricultural. However, while these categories are in common use, there are no fixed definitions of them. Confusion can therefore arise in their use. For instance the distinction between 'craft' and 'manufacturing' is not clear, and there would appear to be some overlap. Indeed in mainland Europe the category 'craft business' depends more on size and ownership than on the type of handcrafted manufacturing associated with the concept of a UK craft business.

Small businesses and job creation

One aspect of small businesses in which there has been considerable interest in recent years has been their role in job creation. Two questions in particular have been raised: first, what is the extent of the overall contribution of small businesses to job creation; and second, does this contribution come, in the main, from all small businesses or from only a few of them? The questions are very relevant to the targeting of government intervention to promote employment, but the answers are not always clear. The first is about the validity of Birch's work and its application to other countries such as the UK, and the second is about which small businesses create most jobs. Exploring issues such as these highlights a number of problems in small business statistics, which may require some insight if they are to be interpreted properly.

A note of caution

Before looking at these questions in more detail it is important to emphasise that a key problem in studying entrepreneurship and small businesses quantitatively is the availability of appropriate data. There is often a distinct difference between the data which are desired and those that are available. Frequently therefore the data used are borrowed from other sources. For instance, in order to explore the issue of entrepreneurship in the UK, many people would like to know how many small businesses there are and the rate at which new ones are started and others terminate. However the data source often used to indicate this is that of business VAT registrations and many businesses do not register for VAT because their turnover is below the threshold; and many businesses de-register, not because they are terminating, but because their turnover has fallen below the threshold. VAT statistics do not provide good small business data because they cover neither only small businesses nor every small business. Nevertheless they are used because they are the best that are available. Another problem is that the data borrowed may record the right subject but use a different definition in a different context. For instance when researching the characteristics of fast-growth small business, which is a popular area for intervention, making comparisons between different studies is often problematic because of significant variations in the definitions of 'fast growth'. The terms 'small businesses', 'start-ups', 'self-employment', 'owner-managers', 'entrepreneurs' and 'SMEs' are all frequently used, often apparently interchangeably, but they are not the same and to explore each fully would require different datasets in each case. Often however these are not readily available and therefore in many cases the distinction is lost in those data which are used.

The validity of Birch

Birch first indicated in 1979 the significant role that small businesses play in the creation of employment. His original work concluded that 81.5 per cent of all net new jobs formed in the United States between 1969 and 1976 were formed by firms with fewer than 100 employees. Armington and Odle, on the other hand, subsequently looked at job creation results for 1978–80 using a database specially created by the US Small Business Administration (SBA) and found that less than 40 per cent of net new jobs were created by businesses with fewer than 100 employees.[63] They had no explanation for the difference as against Birch's figures, but speculated that Birch may have made errors. Subsequently, Armington and Odle have been cited as experts who found Birch to be in error but, according to Kirchhoff, what is less commented on is that their subsequent research validated Birch and showed that percentages calculated in their way were cyclical.[64]

Sixteen years after Birch, Kirchhoff stated that 'It seems safe to say that, on average, firms with less than 100 employees create the majority of net new jobs in the US economy'.[65] Others however still disagree. Davis et al., in their book *Job Creation and Destruction,* based on the Longitudinal Research Database constructed by the US Census Bureau, state that they 'found no strong, systematic relationship between employer size and net job growth rates'.[66] There is therefore no single agreed verdict on the validity of Birch, who was in any case only looking at the situation in the United States. Nevertheless, right or not, his work was, to a very large extent, the trigger for much current interest in small businesses. Subsequent careful work in both improving and examining the SBA's database appears to have shown that fluctuations in the economy of the United States reveal themselves mainly through job changes in larger firms and that small businesses are consistent net creators of jobs. Taking the period 1976–88 as a whole, it is now estimated that businesses with fewer than 20 employees provided 19.4 per cent of total employment, but about 37 per cent of net new jobs. In the UK a similar analysis has been carried out with broadly similar results. One analysis indicated 'that during the 1987–9 period, 54 per cent of the increase in employment was in firms with fewer than 20 workers'.[67] In the UK, however, all components of employment change are of lower magnitude than in the United States, and job change in the latter is more strongly influenced by births and deaths, especially of large businesses, whereas in the UK job change 'is more influenced by expansions and contractions'.[68] Nevertheless in both countries there are arguments that small businesses do indeed make a disproportionately large contribution to net job creation. Studies of European, Japanese and Australian businesses, as well as American ones, have also found that firms with fewer than 100 employees are net contributors to employment growth, contributing as much as 75 per cent of new jobs.[69]

Which small businesses create jobs?

If small businesses do create significant proportions of net new jobs then governments and others trying to increase employment will be particularly interested in them. However, there are very many small businesses, and support would be spread thinly if it went to all of them. Indications that within the small business population it is a relatively small proportion of each year's cohort of businesses that create a disproportionate share of the jobs over time have had a particular appeal. In the UK, Storey has asserted that 'out of every 100 small firms, the fastest growing four firms will create 50 per cent of the jobs in the group over a decade.'[70] The implication of this was that, if support could be focused on those four businesses, or on the few businesses that had the potential for such growth, it would be applied much more effectively than if all 100 businesses were to be supported. These high-growth businesses are the sort of businesses that Birch called 'gazelles'.

Storey's statement needs to be examined with some care, however. He himself points out that the data it is based on are rather old, but he does indicate that other data, in particular from Northern Ireland, produce fairly similar results. He also acknowledges that the data refer only to manufacturing businesses and then only to new ones.

There is also another issue. Despite the way it is sometimes interpreted, Storey's statement does not mean that 4 per cent of small businesses create 50 per cent of the jobs. What Storey says is that if 100 businesses are started in year t, in the year t + 10 only 40 of those businesses may have survived and just four of those surviving businesses will between them employ as many people as are employed by all the other survivors put together. However, that also means that half of the employment in the survivors will not be in those four businesses, nor will the employment during the intervening ten years in the 60 businesses that did not survive to the end of the period. Storey's own table indicates that all of the four high-growth businesses at the end of ten years employ more than 25 people (one employs 25 to 49, two employ 50 to 99, and one employs over 100);[71] yet he also indicates that businesses with fewer than 20 employees created 'between 78 per cent (1985–7) and 85 per cent of total new employment' from small businesses.[72] It is very hard to compare these figures directly with the ten-year cohort figures and to say how many of them are due to the early stages of growth of the 4 per cent of high-growth businesses. For instance in any one year there will be the following:

Jobs in Storey's 4 per cent of the businesses which started ten years earlier

plus

An equal number of jobs in the other surviving businesses which started ten years earlier

plus

Jobs in businesses which started fewer than ten years earlier (not all of which will survive the ten years but are nevertheless employing people in the interim)

plus

Jobs in businesses started more than ten years ago (some of which will be the 4 per cent of businesses from the earlier cohorts but some of which will also be the other businesses which are nevertheless growing).

Without comparable figures for all these groups, comparisons cannot be made. It would be expected from a Pareto analysis that a relatively small proportion of small businesses that grow significantly would have a disproportionate share of the total employment over time. Nevertheless, the major part of the employment in small businesses appears to come from the other small businesses employing fewer than 20 people, not from the fastest-growing 4 per cent.

Recent analysis has also confirmed a link between small business start-up rates and employment. A model produced by van Stel et al. using data for the period 1980 to 1998 shows that in Britain business start-up activity in the late 1980s had a direct positive effect on subsequent employment change, whereas in the early 1980s start-up activity contributed to growth only after a number of years.[73]

A further factor in small business employment which should not be ignored is that most small businesses are in the service sector, which is labour intensive and for which output can often only be increased by taking on new staff. These staff frequently come from the secondary labour market and may be prepared to work for relatively low wages. Expansion of these businesses will therefore increase employment, and consequently reduce unemployment payments, without causing inflation. This is very attractive to governments.

Dynamic versus static analysis

One of the reasons why Birch's original findings were surprising was that they were contrary to previous research and thinking on job creation. They were also based on a dynamic analysis, while the previous research was carried out using static analysis. Such static analysis is carried out using classified data in the form published by government statistics agencies. Those publications will, for instance, list the number of businesses in given size ranges and the number of jobs in them at the end of each period. However, for a given business size range, the difference between the number of jobs at the end of one period and the number at the end of the previous period does not give the number of jobs created in that period by businesses in that size range. The reason may be illustrated by considering a business employing 70 people which over a period grows by 50 per cent and therefore at the end employs 105 people. At the beginning it would have been classified in the 1–100-employee size range, but at the end it is in the 100-plus size range. The effect is thus to reduce by 70 the number of jobs in businesses in the 1–100 size range, and increase by 105 the number of jobs in businesses in the higher size range. The static statistics will therefore show a reduction of jobs in businesses in the lower size range and an increase in the higher size range. The reality however is that the net increase came from a business that was in the lower size range. In the reverse situation, however, the shrinkage of a business initially in a higher size range will appear at the end of the period as a reduction in that size range, because either the business will still be in the size range but with fewer jobs or it will have left the size range and all its jobs will appear to have gone. A lower size range will then correspondingly appear to have grown. Static analysis assumes implicitly that the net inter-class movement of businesses is negligible, which may not be the case.

Cohort analysis

Cohort, or dynamic, analysis, in which a class of subjects is tracked as it changes over time, will avoid the problem of static research analysis. It will also reveal other interesting features of growth. Dynamic analysis of US small businesses has, for instance, indicated that survival rates of businesses improve exponentially with, for a group founded at the same time, a smaller proportion of the original number terminating in each successive year. It has also shown that less than half of the surviving businesses show any growth in the first six years, but that at between six and eight years of age the number of businesses that show growth leaps increases significantly: a result that confirms suggestions of the 'seven lean years' of business development and indicates that observing business survival and growth over a lesser period may be misleading. In taking only new business starts and looking at their employment after ten years, Storey may therefore be missing from his 'high-growth' business those businesses that do not start to grow until after seven years or more.

Another factor which might usefully be taken into consideration when looking for growth is highlighted in the work of Rosa and Scott. They suggest that if the unit of analysis is the business, which it often is, then this will not provide a full picture. Instead they suggest that the unit of analysis should be the entrepreneur, or team of entrepreneurs, who may start several businesses. They talk of clusters of businesses with linked ownership in which 'diversifying into additional businesses may not only be common but may also be associated with positive growth strategies.'[74] This means that growth from an entrepreneur already in business can occur through new business creation rather than through the growth of already established businesses, and that would not be picked up by an analysis with a business unit focus.

Summary

It would appear that there is now clear evidence that small businesses do create a disproportionate amount of new employment. However, different researchers vary in their estimates of how much, and there do appear to be variations over time and across countries. It is not yet clear whether this employment is mainly due to only a small proportion of that small business population or to all of it. This lack of clarity may be due to different researchers measuring different things and to their findings being misinterpreted or misrepresented, but overall it would appear that most of those new jobs at a particular point in time come from the very small businesses in the smallest size ranges and not from Birch's 'gazelles'. The impact of the 'gazelles' is seen when following the job creation activity of a cohort of businesses over time. It is also important to be aware that, while on average net new jobs may come from small businesses, the performance of the large firms sector and the fluctuations in its employment will also have a significant impact on the overall employment position.

Conclusions

Although their size distinguishes small businesses from their larger counterparts, there are other features which many of them have in common. Nevertheless small businesses are very diverse, and this chapter has looked not only at their common features but also at their variety by examining them under a number of different classifications. There is no one best way of classifying the different types of small business. Which is most appropriate in a particular circumstance will depend on what form of analysis or prescription one is engaged in.

THE KEY POINTS OF CHAPTER 4

- There is no single definition of what is a small business. Most definitions use the size of the business as the distinguishing feature, as indicated by either asset value or turnover, or, more commonly, by employment. The upper limit in employment terms can however vary from 50 people to, in the case of American SMEs, 500. It is, however, important to remember that 'small' is often used as a relative term, and what is relatively small in one industry may be relatively large in another.

- In examining small businesses the focus of the analysis has often been the business. However, if the primary unit of analysis is instead taken as the entrepreneur, a different perspective often emerges, which can explain many features of small businesses and which throws light on the process of capital accumulation and entrepreneurship.

- The variety of small businesses is not just due to their different stages of development. Different industry sectors and different legal structures, family ownership and other considerations can all make a difference.

- There is also variety between entrepreneurs, who can, for instance, be categorised as novice or habitual and, if habitual, as serial or portfolio.

- Nevertheless, despite the many differences between different types, stages or ownership of small businesses, they do have a number of key aspects in common, and many of these aspects distinguish them from big businesses. These aspects include issues of culture, influence, resources and ambition. For many commentators it is these aspects that represent the crucial difference associated with size, and even the description 'small' is only a convenient distinction to serve as a proxy for these real differences.

- One other aspect of small businesses which is of considerable interest to many people is their contribution to job creation. The statistics on this need to be interpreted with some care but they do indicate that significant numbers of jobs are created by small businesses, but not by all small businesses.

QUESTIONS, ESSAY AND DISCUSSION TOPICS

- Are definitions based on size meaningful when there is such a variety of small businesses?
- In the absence of a single universally accepted definition how would you summarise the essence of a small business?
- Is the entrepreneur or the business the more enlightening unit of study in seeking to understand business development and wealth creation?
- In what ways do family businesses differ from non-family businesses?

- What are the implications of studying family businesses from the perspective of the family instead of focusing just on the business?

- Apart from a lack of accumulated capital is there really any real argument for saying female businesses are any different from male businesses and should be treated differently?

- How important is formal education in the development of a successful business enterprise?

- Do small businesses create the majority of jobs in your area?

Suggestions for further reading and information

P. Burns, *Entrepreneurship and Small Business*, 2nd edn (Basingstoke: Palgrave Macmillan, 2007).

The BDO Stoy Hayward Centre for Family Business: The Family Business Management Series: Succession management in family companies (2007) www.bdo.co.uk.

Global Entrepreneurship Monitor: www.entreworld.org.

References

1. *The Report of the Committee of Enquiry on Small Firms* (The Bolton Report) (London: HMSO, 1971).
2. D. Carson and S. Cromie, 'Marketing Planning in Small Enterprises: A Model and Some Empirical Evidence', *Journal of Marketing Management*, 5 (1989), pp. 33–50.
3. P. Rosa and M. Scott, 'Entrepreneurial Diversification, Business-Cluster Formation, and Growth', *Government and Policy*, 17 (1999), pp. 527–47, p. 530.
4. P. Rosa and M. Scott, 'The Prevalence of Multiple Owners and Directors in the SME Sector: Implications For Our Understanding of Start-Up and Growth', *Entrepreneurship and Regional Development*, 11 (1999), pp. 21–37, at p. 34.
5. M. Scott and P. Rosa, 'Has Firm Level Analysis Reached its Limits? Time for a Rethink', *International Small Business Journal*, 14 (1996), pp. 81–9.
6. P. Westhead and M. Wright, 'Novice, Portfolio and Serial Founders: Are They Different?' *Journal of Business Venturing*, 13 (1998), pp. 173–204.
7. Scott and Rosa, op.cit, p. 81.
8. Rosa and Scott (1999), op. cit., p. 21.
9. P. Westhead, D. Ucbasaran, M. Wright and F. Martin, *Habitual Entrepreneurs in Scotland* (Scottish Enterprise, 2003).
10. F. J. Greene, K. F. Mole, and D. J. Storey, *Three Decades of Enterprise Culture* (Basingstoke: Palgrave, 2008) p. 238.
11. S. Carter, 'The Economic Potential of Portfolio Entrepreneurship: Enterprise and Employment Contributions of Multiple Business Ownership', *Journal of Small Business and Enterprise Development*, 5(4) (1998), pp. 297–307.
12. Carter, op. cit., p. 297.
13. E. T. Penrose, *The Theory of the Growth of the Firm* (Oxford: Basil Blackwell, 1959).
14. A. A. Gibb, 'Towards the Building of Entrepreneurial Models of Support for Small Business', The 11th (UK) National Small Firms Policy and Research Conference (Cardiff, 1988), pp. 12–15.
15. C. Handy, *The Age of Unreason* (London: Arrow Books, 1990).
16. See A. Minkes, *The Entrepreneurial Manager* (Harmondsworth: Penguin, 1987) for a discussion of entrepreneurial decision-making.
17. H. Mintzberg, *The Structuring of Organisations* (Englewood Cliffs, NJ: Prentice-Hall, 1979), pp. 305–13.

18. R. Goffee and R. Scase, 'Proprietorial Control In Family Firms', *Journal of Management Studies*, 22 (1985), pp. 53–68.
19. *The Third Annual Report of the European Observatory for SMEs* (Zoetermeer, the Netherlands: EIM Small Business Research and Consultancy, 1995), pp. 50–1.
20. Stoy Hayward, *The Stoy Hayward/BBC Family Business Index* (London: Stoy Hayward, 1992).
21. R. K. Z. Heck and E. Scannell-Trent, 'The Prevalence of Family Business From a Household Sample', *Family Business Review*, 12 (1999), pp. 209–24.
22. M. C. Shanker and J. H. Astrachan, 'Myths and Realities: Family Business Contributions to the US Economy: A Framework for Assessing Family Business Statistics', *Family Business Review*, 9 (1996), pp. 107–23.
23. Stoy Hayward, *Managing the Family Business in the UK* (London: Stoy Hayward, 1990).
24. S. Cromie, B. Stephenson and D. Monteith, 'Managing Family Firms: An Empirical Investigation', *International Small Business Journal*, 13 (1995), pp. 11–34.
25. M. S. Wortman, 'Critical Issues in Family Business: An International Perspective of Practice and Research', Proceedings of the ICSB 40th World Conference (1995), pp. 53–76.
26. Heck and Scannell-Trent, op. cit, pp. 209–20, base their model of family firms definitions on W. C. Handler, 'Methodological Issues and Considerations in Studying Family Businesses,' *Family Business Review*, 2 (1989), pp. 257–76.
27. D. Fletcher, 'Family and Enterprise' in *Enterprise and Small Business*, edited by S. Carter and D. Jones-Evans, (London: Financial Times/Prentice-Hall, 2000), pp. 155–65.
28. K. Stafford, K. A. Duncan, S. Dane and M. Winter, 'A Research Model of Sustainable Family Business', *Family Business Review*, 12 (1999), pp. 197–208.
29. Heck and Scannell-Trent, op. cit., p. 212.
30. Stafford et al., op. cit.: 203.
31. Fletcher, op. cit., p. 160.
32. S. Birley, D. Ng and A. Godfrey, 'The Family and the Business', *Long Range Planning*, 32 (1999), pp. 598–608.
33. Stoy Hayward (1990), op. cit.
34. Birley et al., op. cit., p. 598.
35. H. Levinson, 'Conflicts That Plague the Family Business', *Harvard Business Review*, March-April (1971), pp. 53–62.
36. H. Levinson, 'Don't Choose Your Own Successor', *Harvard Business Review*, November-December (1974), pp. 53–62.
37. A. Shepherd and A. Zacharakis, 'Structuring Family Business Succession: An Analysis of the Future Leader's Decision Making', *Entrepreneurship Theory and Practice*, 25 (2000), pp. 25–39.
38. BDO Stoy Hayward, *Across the Generations: Insights from 100 Year Old Family Businesses* (2004).
39. B. Dunn, 'Success Themes in Scottish Family Enterprises: Philosophies and Practices Through the Generations', *Family Business Review*, 8 (1995), pp. 8: 17–28.
40. J. Magretta, 'Governing the Family-Owned Enterprise: An Interview With Finland's Krister Ahlstrom', *Harvard Business Review*, January-February (1998), pp. 113–23.
41. Fletcher, op. cit., p. 157
42. Stafford et al, op. cit.: 203.
43. Ibid.: 205.
44. S. Carter and E. Shaw, 'Women's Business Ownership: Recent Research and Policy Developments', Report to the Small Business Service, November 2000.
45. S. Cromie, 'The Problems Experienced by Young Firms', *International Small Business Journal*, 9 (1991), pp. 43–67.
46. S. Carter, 'Gender and Enterprise', in *Enterprise and Small Business*, edited by S. Carter and D. Jones-Evans (Harlow: Pearson Education, 2000), p. 172.
47. Ibid., p. 167.
48. S. Carter and P. Rosa, 'The Financing of Male- and Female-Owned Businesses', *Entrepreneurship and Regional Development*, 10 (1998), pp. 225–41.
49. A. Phizacklea and M. Ram, 'Ethnic Entrepreneurship In Comparative Perspective', *International Journal of Entrepreneurial Behaviour and Research*, 1 (1995), pp. 48–58.
50. L. M. Dyer and C. A. Ross, 'Ethnic Enterprises and their Clientele', *Journal of Small Business Management*, 38 (2000), pp. 48–60.
51. R. Waldinger, H. E. Aldrich and R. Ward, *Ethnic Entrepreneurs: Immigrant Businesses in Industrial Societies* (Newbury Park, Calif.: Sage, 1990), p. 33.

52. V. C. Vincent, 'Decision-Making Policies Among Mexican-American Small Business Entrepreneurs', *Journal of Small Business Management,* 34 (1996), pp. 1–13; Dyer and Ross, op.cit.; P. G. Greene, 'A Resource Based Approach to Ethnic Business Sponsorship: A Consideration of Ismaili-Pakistani Immigrants', *Journal of Small Business Management,* 35 (1997), pp. 57–71.

53. A. Fadahunsi, D. Smallbone and S. Supri, 'Networking and Ethnic Minority Enterprise Development: Insights From a North London Study', *Journal of Small Business and Enterprise Development,* 7 (2000), pp. 228–40.

54. Y. Li, 'Assessing data needs and gaps for studying ethnic entrepreneurship in Britain: A review paper', ESRC (URN 07/1052), March 2007.

55. D. Storey, *Understanding the Small Business Sector* (London: Routledge, 1994), pp. 272–3.

56. M. Ram, 'Unravelling Social Networks In Ethnic Minority Firms', *International Small Business Journal,* 12(3) (1994), pp. 42–53, at p. 44.

57. Ibid., p. 51.

58. Economic and Social Research Council, *Characteristics of the Founders of Small Rural Businesses* (Swindon: The Council, 1989).

59. D. Storey, *Understanding the Small Business Sector* (London: Routledge, 1994), pp. 272–3.

60. Storey, op.cit, p. 273, quoting D. Smallbone, D. North and R. Leigh, 'The Use of External Assistance by Mature SMEs in the UK: Some Policy Implications', *Entrepreneurship and Regional Development,* 5 (1993), pp. 279–95.

61. Economic and Social Research Council, *The State of British Enterprise* (Swindon: The Council, 1992).

62. D. Brooksbank, 'Self-Employment and Small Firms', in *Enterprise and Small Business,* edited by S. Carter and D. Jones-Evans, (London: Financial Times/Prentice-Hall, 2000), pp. 15–16.

63. C. Armington and M. Odle, 'Small Businesses - How Many Jobs?' *Brookings Review* 20, Winter 1982.

64. B. Kirchhoff, 'Twenty Years of Job Creation Research: What Have We Learned?' The 40th Conference of the International Council for Small Business, 1995, pp. 201–2.

65. Ibid., p. 202.

66. S. J. Davis, J. C. Haltiwanger and S. Schuh, *Job Creation and Destruction* (Cambridge, Mass.: MIT Press, 1996), p. 170.

67. Storey, op.cit., p. 165.

68. Ibid., p. 168.

69. OECD, *Globalisation and Small and Medium Enterprises, Synthesis Report, Vol. 1* (Paris: OECD, 1997), p. 122.

70. Ibid., p. 113.

71. Ibid., p. 114.

72. Ibid., p. 168.

73. A. van Stel, S. Dielbandhoesing, W. van den Heuvel and D. Storey, 'Entrepreneurial Growth in Great Britain: British Regions In the Period 1980–1998', personal correspondence relating to a not yet published paper.

74. P. Rosa and M. Scott, 'Entrepreneurial Diversification, Business-Cluster Formation and Growth', *Government and Policy,* 17 (1999), pp. 527–47, at p. 527.

CHAPTER 5
Entrepreneur super-hero

CONTENTS

- Personal character traits
- The survival instinct
- The growth instinct
- Antecedent influences
- Implications for entrepreneurial management
- Summary

LEARNING OUTCOMES

By the end of this chapter you should be able to:

- Describe the character traits of owner-managers and entrepreneurs and explain how they affect their approach to management;
- Explain the methodological problems associated with trying to measure character traits and, in particular, the linkages with growth businesses;
- Explain the influence of cognitive theory;
- Describe and give examples of the antecedent influences on successful entrepreneurs;
- Assess the implications of all these factors for corporate entrepreneurship.

Personal character traits

In order to understand the nature of corporate entrepreneurship we need to understand the entrepreneurs themselves – their personal characteristics, their personality and how they go about business. They shape the organization they start up. They dominate it to the extent that it takes on many of their characteristics. They are its strengths and can be its weaknesses.

Entrepreneurs are both born and made. They have certain personal character traits that they are born with, but they also shaped by their background, history and experience of life – called antecedent influences – as well as the culture of the different groups of society in which they operate. Some cultures encourage entrepreneurial activity, others discourage it. Figure 5.1 summarizes the effects of these influences.

Despite the limitations of this research, a focus on research into the character traits of owner-managers of growth businesses – who should mainly be entrepreneurs – does allow us to come to some broad conclusions and to paint a picture of the different character traits of both owner-managers and entrepreneurs. Figure 5.2 summarizes these traits. Of course, by definition, owner-manager entrepreneurs share the character traits of owner-managers, since these influenced their decision to start their own business in the first place. The character traits of owner-manager entrepreneurs therefore comprise two parts perhaps generating two instincts. The first relates to survival

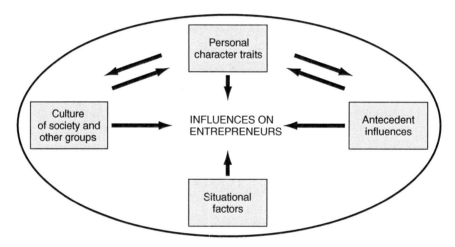

Figure 5.1   Influences on entrepreneurs

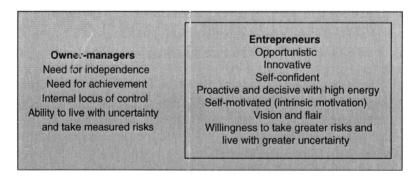

Figure 5.2   Character traits of owner-managers and entrepreneurs

Sources: Based on Aldrich and Martinez, 2003; Andersson *et al.,* 2004; Baty, 1990; Bell *et al.,* 1992; Blanchflower and Meyer, 1991; Brockhaus and Horwitz, 1986; Brush, 1992; Buttner and More, 1997; Caird, 1990; Chell, Haworth and Brearley, 1991; Cuba *et al.,* 1983; de Bono, 1985; Hirsch and Brush, 1987; Kanter, 1983; Kirzner, 1973, 1979, 1997, 1999; McClelland, 1961; Pinchot, 1985; Rosa *et al.,* 1994; Schein *et al.,* 1996; Schumpeter, 1996; Schwartz, 1997; Shapero, 1985; Shaver and Scott, 1992; Storey and Sykes, 1996.

and its traits are found in the owner-manager. The second relates to growth and its traits are found in the entrepreneur.

The problem of linking the personal character traits of any individual to the success of a business needs to be approached with caution and can be an academic minefield. As we have seen, success or failure in business, comes from a mix of many different things and the character of the entrepreneur is just one factor in the equation. We have no way of knowing how important the different ingredients are at any point of time. What is more, it takes time for the owner-manager entrepreneur to prove that the business he or she manages is in fact a successful growth business. So, do you measure aspirations or reality, and over what time scale? We have held up Michael Dell and Richard Branson as successful entrepreneurs, but will their companies eventually fail and their reputations become tarnished? And, if so, what part will their personalities play in this? Furthermore, many of the character traits that have been found significant in entrepreneurs are similar to those found in other successful people such as politicians or athletes (Chell, Haworth and Brearley, 1991). Perhaps, the argument goes, it just happens that the individual has chosen an entrepreneurial activity as a means of self-satisfaction.

There are also a number of methodological problems associated with attempting to measure personality characteristics which are worth bearing in mind when interpreting these results (Deakins, 1996):

- The traits are not stable and change over time.
- They require subjective judgements.
- Measures tend to ignore cultural and environmental influences.
- The role of education, learning, training is often overlooked.
- Issues such as age, sex, race, social class and education may also be ignored.

Notwithstanding these issues, most researchers believe that, collectively, owner-manager entrepreneurs have certain typical character traits, although the mix and emphasis of these characteristics will inevitably be different for each individual. These character traits and their implications for the entrepreneurial organization need to be explored in more detail. We shall characterize those of the owner-manager as an instinct for survival – since most owner-managed businesses never grow to any size -and those of the entrepreneur as an instinct for growth.

The survival instinct

Need for independence

'Entrepreneurs don't like working for other people ... I was once made redundant by the Manchester Evening News. I had a wife who had given up a promising career for me, and a baby. I stood on Deansgate with £5 in my pocket and I swore I would never work for anyone else again.'

Eddy Shah
founder of Messenger Group
The Times, 16 March 2002

Owner-managers and entrepreneurs have a high need for independence. This is most often seen as the need to 'be your own boss' and is the trait that is most often cited, and supported, by researchers and advisors alike. However, independence means different things to different people, such as controlling your own destiny, doing things differently or being in a situation where you can fulfil your potential. It has often been said that, once you run your own firm, you cannot work for anybody else.

Implications for the entrepreneurial organization:

- *Issues for management style.* If individual members of the organization are entrepreneurial they will need to be managed with a 'light touch' and given independence of decision making.

- *Issues for culture.* Will entrepreneurial members of the organization naturally want to leave, often to set up in competition? If so, can they be tied into the organization by sharing in its success through share ownership etc.? Can other psychological needs be met so as to compensate for this need for independence? They need to feel they belong to and even 'own' the organization.

- *Issues for structure* Staff will need to feel independent to some extent but will an entrepreneurial unit or division have to be separate from the rest of the organization in order to satisfy the aspirations of its members? Can the separate identity be recognized in any way other than by structure?

Need for achievement

'Most of the pleasure is not the cash. It is the sense of achievement at having taken something from nothing to where it is now.'

Charles Muirhead founder of **Orchestream**
Sunday Times, 17 September 1999

Owner-managers and entrepreneurs typically have a high need for achievement, a driving force that is particularly strong for entrepreneurs. Achievement for individuals means different things depending on the type of person they are: for example, the satisfaction of producing a beautiful work of art, employing their hundredth person, or making the magic one million pounds. Often money is just a badge of achievement to the successful entrepreneur. It is not an end in itself.

'We don't feel like millionaires at all. Money doesn't come into it. It's not really why you do it, it really isn't.'

Brent Hoberman co-founder of **Lastminute.com**
Sunday Times, 17 September 1999

Public recognition of achievement can be important to some owner-managers and entrepreneurs. And this can lead to certain negative behaviours or unwise decisions: for example, overspending on the trappings of corporate life – the office, the company car and so on (often called the corporate flag-pole syndrome) – or the 'big project' that is very risky but the entrepreneur 'knows' it is achievable. These can lead to cash flow problems that put at risk the very existence of the business.

> ### Implications for the entrepreneurial organization:
>
> * *Issues for culture.* An achievement-orientated culture needs to be created. Goals need to be set and achievement encouraged, publicly acknowledged and rewarded.

Internal locus of control

If you believe that you can exercise control over your environment and ultimately your destiny, you have an internal locus of control. If, however, you believe in fate, you have an external locus of control and you are less likely to take the risk of starting a business. Owner-managers typically have a strong internal locus of control, which is the same for many senior managers in large firms.

'I want to take control of my life and achieve something.'

Jonathan Elvidge
founder of **Gadget Shop**
Sunday Times, 17 March 2002

In extreme cases this trait can also lead to certain negative behaviours. In particular, it can show itself as a desire to maintain personal control over every aspect of the business. That can lead to a preoccupation with detail, over-work and stress. It also leads to an inability or unwillingness to delegate as the business grows. Again, in extreme cases it might show itself as a mistrust of subordinates. Kets de Vries (1985) thinks these behaviours can lead to the danger of subordinates becoming 'infantilized'. They are expected to behave as incompetent idiots, and that is the way they behave. They tend to do very little, make no decisions and circulate very little information. The better ones do not stay long. For an entrepreneurial manager this needs to be avoided.

This need for control can also show itself in the unwillingness of many owner-managers to part with shares in their company. They just do not want to lose control, at any price. This also needs to be avoided because, as we shall see later, sharing ownership can be a very positive motivation for staff that encourages an entrepreneurial culture.

> **Implications for the entrepreneurial organization:**
>
> - *Issues for culture.* Create a 'can-do' culture.
> - *Issues for management style.* If individual members of the organization are entrepreneurial they need to be managed with a 'light touch' so that they believe they can control their own destiny. There is therefore likely to be a high degree of delegation.

Ability to live with uncertainty and take measured risks

Whilst all owner-managers are willing to take risks and live with uncertainty, true entrepreneurs are willing to take far greater risks and live with far greater uncertainty. Often they are willing to put their own home on the line and risk all, so strong is their belief in their business idea, despite the uncertainties surrounding it.

> 'You have to be prepared to lose everything and remember that the biggest risk is not taking any risk at all.'
>
> **Jonathan Elvidge**
> founder of **Gadget Shop**
> *Sunday Times,* 17 March 2002

Human beings, typically, do not like uncertainty and one of the biggest uncertainties of all is not having a regular pay cheque coming in – particularly when you have a family to support. That is not to say owner-managers or entrepreneurs like this aspect of risk and uncertainty. Uncertainty about income can be a major cause of stress. The possibility of missing out on some piece of business that might affect their income is one reason why they are so loath to take holidays. However, true entrepreneurs thrive on uncertainty and risk. They love pitching their judgement against the odds, although they believe they will win. This is one reason why so many grow tired of a business after a while and sell it on or bring in professional managers to free them from day-to-day involvement.

> 'You have to have nerves of steel and be prepared to take risks. You have to be able to put it all on the line knowing you could lose everything.'
>
> **Anne Notley**
> co-founder of **The Iron Bed Company**
> *Sunday Times,* 28 January 2001

There are other commercial aspects of uncertainty that owner-managers or entrepreneurs have to cope with. Often they cannot influence many aspects of the market in which they operate, for example, price. They must therefore react to changes in the market that others might bring about. If a local supermarket has a special price promotion on certain goods it may well affect sales of similar goods in a local corner shop. A business with a high level of borrowing must find a way of paying interest charges but has no direct influence over changes in interest rates. Many small firms also have a limited customer or product base and this can bring further uncertainty. If, for whatever reason, one large customer ceases buying, it can have an enormous impact on a small firm.

> 'People ask me now, "Were you scared?" Sure. Nearly everyone's motivated by fear in some form. I was afraid that I wouldn't do a good enough job, that the business would be a complete failure. However, in my case the downside was limited.'
>
> **Michael Dell**

Hand in hand with the ability to live with uncertainty is the willingness to take measured risks. Most people are risk averse. They try to avoid risks and insure against them. Setting up your own business is risky and owner-managers are willing to take more risks with their own resources than most people.

> 'Taking a chance, a risk or a gamble is what unites entrepreneurs. Without risk there is no reward. You won't discover America if you never set sail.'
>
> **Jonathan Elvidge**
> founder of **Gadget Shop**
> *The Times*, 6 July 2002

Owner-managers and entrepreneurs might risk their reputation and personal standing if they fail. However, they do not like this risk and try always to minimize their exposure; hence their preference to risk other people's money and borrow, sometimes too heavily, from the bank. Another example of this is the way they often 'compartmentalize' various aspects of their business. For example, an entrepreneur might open a second and third restaurant but set each one up as a separate limited company just in case any should fail and endanger the others. In this way they sometimes develop a portfolio of individually small businesses and their growth and success is measured not just in the performance of a single one but rather by the growth of the portfolio.

> 'Don't worry about failure: if you lose because of market conditions then another time someone will say "Hey, this guy can make things happen. I'll back him".'
>
> **Gururaj Deshpande**
> serial entrepreneur and founder of
> **Sycamore Networks**
> *The Financial Times*, 21 February 2000

> **Implications for the entrepreneurial organization:**
>
> - *Issues for management style.* If the organization faces uncertainty, management need to engender a 'positive' attitude, one that builds self-confidence and self-efficacy.
> - *Issues for culture.* Measured risk taking needs to be encouraged rather than penalized.

The growth instinct

Opportunistic

This is the first of the two prime distinguishing features of entrepreneurs. By definition, entrepreneurs exploit change for profit. In other words they seek out opportunities to make money. Often entrepreneurs see opportunities where others see problems. Whereas ordinary mortals dislike the uncertainty brought about by change, entrepreneurs love it because they see opportunity and they do not mind the uncertainty.

For many entrepreneurs the problem is focusing on just one opportunity, or at least one opportunity at a time, and then exploiting it systematically. They see opportunity everywhere and have problems following through on any one before becoming distracted by another. This is one reason why some entrepreneurs are not able to grow their business beyond a certain size. They get bored by the routines and controls, they see other market opportunities and yearn for the excitement of another start-up. Many would probably be well advised to sell up and do just that, but go on to try to manage a company they have really lost interest in. And the result can be disastrous.

> 'I have always lived my life by thriving on opportunity and adventure. Some of the best ideas come out of the blue, and you have to keep an open mind to see their virtue.'
>
> **Richard Branson**

However, some entrepreneurs do appreciate this element of their character and play to it, becoming serial entrepreneurs, moving to set up and sell on one business after another. You see this very often in the restaurant business where entrepreneurial restaurateurs launch one new restaurant and make it successful, then sell it on so as to move onto another new venture. They make money by creating a business with capital value, not necessarily income for themselves.

> 'Hundreds of computer stores were popping up in Houston. And dealers would pay $2000 for an IBM PC and sell it for $3000, making $1000 profit. They also offered little or no support to the customer. Yet they were making lots of money because people really wanted computers. At this point, I was already buying the

exact same components that were used in these machines, and I was upgrading my machines selling them to people I knew. I realized that if I could sell even more of them, I could actually compete with the computer stores – and not just on price but on quality. I could also earn a nice little profit and get all the things your typical high school kid would want. But beyond that, I thought, "Wow, there's a lot of opportunity here." '

Michael Dell

Implications for the entrepreneurial organization:

- *Issues for culture.* Change should be endemic, seen as the norm and not something to be avoided. Opportunity perception, through closeness to customers, needs to be encouraged.

- *Issues for structure.* Systems for sharing information and knowledge – including opportunity perception – need to be in place. However, the challenge is to pursue only those opportunities where the organization has distinctive capabilities upon which it can capitalize.

Innovative

The ability to innovate is the second most important distinguishing feature of entrepreneurs. Innovation is the prime tool they use to create or exploit opportunity. Entrepreneurs link innovation to the market place so as to exploit an opportunity and make their business grow. Although innovation is difficult to define and can take many forms, entrepreneurs are always, in some way, innovative.

'True innovation is rarely about creating something new. Its pretty hard to recreate the wheel or discover gravity; innovation is more often about seeing new opportunities for old designs.'

Neil Kelly
owner and managing director of **PAV**
Sunday Times, 9 December 2001

Implications for the entrepreneurial organization:

- *Issues for culture.* Innovation needs to be encouraged, never penalized. The process of innovation needs to be understood. Continuous improvement is seen as the regular part of the innovation process.

- *Issues for structure.* Systems and structures that encourage creativity and innovation need to be in place.

Self-confident

> 'My mother gave me a massive self-belief. I will always try things – there is nothing to lose.'
>
> **Richard Thompson**
> founder and chairman of **EMS**
> Rupert Steiner; *My First Break: How Entrepreneurs Get Started,*
> Sunday Times Books, 1999

Facing uncertainty, you have to be confident in your own judgement and ability to start up your own business. Many training programmes for start-ups recognize this by trying to build personal self-confidence through developing a business plan that addresses the issue of future uncertainty. As well as being a useful management tool, the plan can become a symbol of certainty for the owner-manager in an otherwise uncertain world. Some can keep it with them at all times, using it almost like a bible, to reassure them of what the future will hold when the business eventually becomes successful. Entrepreneurs, therefore, need self-confidence aplenty to grow their business, given the extreme uncertainty they face. If they do not believe in the future of the business, how can they expect others to do so? However, the self-confidence can be overdone and turn to an exaggerated opinion of their own competence and even arrogance.

> 'An entrepreneur is unfailingly enthusiastic, never pessimistic, usually brave, and certainly stubborn. Vision and timing are crucial. You have to be something of a workaholic, too. You have to be convinced that what you are doing is right. If not you have to recognise this and be able to change direction swiftly -sometimes leaving your staff breathless - and start off again with equal enthusiasm.'
>
> **Chris Ingram**
> founder of **Tempus**
> *Sunday Times,* 17 March 2002

Some researchers believe entrepreneurs are actually 'delusional'. In an interesting piece of research, two American academics tested the decision-making process of 124 entrepreneurs (defined as people who started their own firm) and 95 managers of big companies in two ways (Busenitz and Barney, 1997). Firstly, they asked five factual questions each of which had two possible answers. They asked respondents to rate their confidence in their answer (50%, a guess; 100%, perfect confidence). Entrepreneurs turned out to be much more confident about their answers than managers, especially those who gave wrong answers. Secondly, they were given a business decision. They were told they must replace a broken foreign-made machine and they had two alternatives. The first was an American-made machine, which a friend had recently bought and had not yet broken down, and the second a foreign-built machine, which was statistically less likely to break down than the other. 50% of the entrepreneurs opted for the American machine whilst only 10% of the managers opted for it. The researchers concluded that the entrepreneurs were more prone to both delusion and opportunism than normal managers, who were seen as more rational. So the question is raised, is entrepreneurial self-confidence so strong as to make them delusional, blinding them to the reality of a situation?

Implications for the entrepreneurial organization:

- *Issues for culture.* Need to build a self-confident organization by celebrating achievement in the face of uncertainty. However, this self-confidence needs to be grounded in reality – a realistic understanding of the organization's capabilities and achievements.

Proactive and decisive with high energy

'Neither my grandfather nor my father would be surprised if they could see me now. My success didn't just happen As a young boy, I was always working. My parents and my brothers and sisters all had high energy.'

Tom Farmer
founder of **Kwik-Fit**
Daily Mail, 11 May1999

Entrepreneurs tend to be proactive rather than reactive and more decisive than other people. They are proactive in the sense that they seek out opportunities, they do not just rely on luck – this is part of their nature. They act quickly and decisively to make the most of the opportunity before somebody else does – this is the only way to achieve success.

Entrepreneurs are often seen as restless and easily bored. They can easily be diverted by the most recent market opportunity and often seem to do things at twice the pace of others, unwilling or unable to wait for others to complete tasks. Patience is certainly not a virtue many possess. Many entrepreneurs seem to work twenty-four hours a day and their work becomes their life with little separating the two. It is little wonder that it places family relationships under strain.

'Enthusiasm is my strength. And good health, and energy and endeavour. I love what I do. It's just so interesting, it is new every day, exciting every day. I work 364 days a year. The only day I don't work is Christmas Day, because its my wife's birthday.'

Bob Worcester
founder of **MORI**
The Financial Times, 7 April 2002

> 'Never sit back and admire what you've achieved, never think you have a divine right to succeed. What you have already done is just the starting point – it's all about the future, about the ability to push the boundaries out as far as they will go and create concepts and answers that don't yet exist.'
>
> **Derrick Collin**
> founder of **Brulines Ltd**
> *The Times,* 10 October 2002

One important result of this characteristic is that entrepreneurs act first and then learn from the outcomes of the action. They tend to learn by doing. This is logical since time is important in pursuing opportunity. Extensive analysis of a market opportunity is likely to mean that the entrepreneur will not be first to market. It is part of their incremental approach to decision making, each small action and its outcomes take them closer to the market opportunity and contribute to the learning process which mitigates the risks they face.

> **Implications for the entrepreneurial organization:**
>
> - *Issues for culture.* Need to develop a 'can-do', achievement-orientated culture which generates enthusiasm, commitment and a willingness and ability to act quickly. Need to build learning into the culture – 'learn' from all aspects of the business and disseminate knowledge.

Self-motivated

Entrepreneurs are highly self-motivated, amounting almost to a driving urge to succeed in their economic goals. This is driven by their exceptionally strong inner need for achievement, far stronger than with the average owner-manager. Running your own business is a lonely affair, without anyone to motivate and encourage you. You work long hours, sometimes for little reward. You therefore need to be self-motivated, committed and determined to succeed.

> 'I have never had anything to do in my life that provides so many challenges - and there are so many things I still want to do.'
>
> **Martha Lane Fox**
> co-founder of **Lastminute.com**
> *Sunday Times,* 17 September 1999

This strong inner drive – what psychologists call type 'A' behaviour – is quite unique and can be seen as almost compulsive behaviour. This is not to say that entrepreneurs are not motivated by other things as well, such as money. But often money is just a badge of their success that allows them to measure their achievement.

What drives them is their exceptionally high need to achieve. 'A' types tend to be goal-focused, wanting to get the job done quickly. However, they also focus mainly on the future and are often not in control of the present, appearing highly reactive – entrepreneurs are notorious for their unwillingness to focus on issues of detailed financial control.

> 'I am motivated by my success not money. But success is partly measured by money.'
>
> **Wing Yip**
> founder of **W Wing Yip & Brothers**
> *Sunday Times*, 2 January 2000

An important aspect of this self-motivation is the enjoyment of doing it – enjoyment in the challenges of being entrepreneurial. They do what they do because they enjoy doing it, not because they are forced to in any way. Entrepreneurs actually enjoy their work – often to the exclusion of other things in more ordinary people's lives such as spouse and family. The long hours worked by entrepreneurs have often been known to break marriages. But ultimately entrepreneurs will always regard their business as 'fun', and this is one reason they can be so passionate about it. This provides for them an intrinsic motivation and generally people with an intrinsic motivation outperform those who undertake tasks because of extrinsic motivation – doing something because of an external influence or simply because they 'have to'.

> 'Fun is at the core of the way I like to do business and has informed everything I've done from the outset. More than any other element fun is the secret of Virgin's success.'
>
> **Richard Branson**

Implications for the entrepreneurial organization:

- *Issues for culture.* Need to develop a 'can-do', achievement-orientated culture which generates enthusiasm and commitment. Need to build 'fun' and learning into the culture – 'learn' from all aspects of the business and disseminate knowledge.

Vision and flair

To succeed, entrepreneurs need to have a clear vision of what they want to achieve – a vision that stays with them giving them direction when all around is uncertainty. That is part of the fabric of their motivation. It motivates them and also helps bring others with them, both employees and customers. It is the cornerstone of their motivation and self-confidence.

'You must have a vision of what you want to achieve and be very single minded in achieving it. Do not be deflected. Never say die.'

Terry Saddler
founder of **Bioglan Pharma**
The Times, 10 October 2001

The flair comes with the ability to be in the right place at the right time. Timing is everything. Innovation that is before its time can lead to business failure. Innovation that is late results in copycat products or services that are unlikely to be outstanding successes. A question constantly asked about successful entrepreneurs is whether their success was due to good luck or good judgement? The honest answer in most cases is probably a bit of both.

'You have to have passion, a clear goal and the drive to see it through.'

Jonathan Elvidge
founder of **Gadget Shop**
Sunday Times, 17 March 2002

Implications for the entrepreneurial organization:

- *Issues for management.* Vision is vital. It also needs to be communicated effectively. Timing is crucial, but only easily judged with the benefit of hindsight.

Antecedent influences

Whilst inherent character traits are important, there are other influences at work and there are other approaches to trying to explain the complicated process of entrepreneurship. Cognitive theory shifts the emphasis from the individual towards the situations that lead to entrepreneurial behaviour. Research has started to distinguish a certain 'antecedent influence' – the entrepreneur's history and experience of life (Carter and Cachon, 1988). However, whilst these may be interesting observations – part of the literature on picking entrepreneurial 'winners' – they are of little use in constructing an entrepreneurial organization as they cannot be influenced *ex-post*. The most important of these is education which is an important antecedent influence for start-up but more particularly for entrepreneurial growth (Evans and Leighton, 1990; Storey, 1994). Success seems to be associated with a better education – particularly in the USA. This perhaps mirrors the generally accepted importance of education and training as an important strategic tool in the development of the organization. Continual learning is an important characteristic of the entrepreneurial organization.

Burns' (2007) summary of the important antecedent influences on the owner-manager of a growth business – an entrepreneur – does have implications for an entrepreneurial organization. He concludes that the true entrepreneur is more likely to be:

- Better educated.
- Leaving a managerial job to start the business.
- Middle-aged and experienced. (There are, however, a small but significant and growing number of very young entrepreneurs with little or no business experience, who are usually successful because of their innovative business ideas.)
- Starting the business because of positive motivations such as a need for independence, achievement or recognition, personal development or simply a desire to make money.
- Willing to share ownership of the business.

Implications for the entrepreneurial organization:

- *Issues for structure and culture.* Continual learning from experience is important.
- *Issues for culture.* Positive motivation – rather than compulsion – is the most important motivation for staff.

One further strand of cognitive theory is worthy of note because it reinforces at least two elements of trait theory. Chen *et al.* (1998) set out the idea that successful entrepreneurs possess high levels of 'self-efficacy'. Self-efficacy is 'the strength of an individual's belief that he or she is capable of successfully performing the roles and tasks of an entrepreneur'. Clearly this is part of the self-confidence of entrepreneurs referred to in the last section, but it is also created by their internal locus of control and rooted firmly in their need for achievement and therefore more than just self-confidence. Chen *et al.* argue that it is self-efficacy that motivates entrepreneurs and gives them the dogged determination to persist in the face of adversity when others just give in. With this characteristic entrepreneurs become more objective and analytical and attribute failure to insufficient effort or poor knowledge. They argue that self-efficacy is affected by a person's previous experiences – success breeds success.

Implications for the entrepreneurial organization:

- *Issues for culture.* Building organizational self-confidence and creating organizational self-efficacy is important. Celebrate achievement. Nothing breeds success like previous success.

There are other influences, most of which have few implications for the entrepreneurial organization. Self-employment normally needs a trigger. Unemployment is a strong push into self-employment but entrepreneurial growth businesses are more likely to set up for more positive motives such as the need for independence, achievement etc. (Abdesselam, Bonnet and Le Pape, 1999; Storey, 1994). It is possible that having a parent who was previously self-employed is more likely to lead a person to set up his or her own firm (Stanworth *et al.*, 1989) and observation tells us that immigration to a foreign country is another influence (Harper, 1985).

Cognitive theory underlines the fact that entrepreneurs are both born (with character traits) and, more importantly, made – shaped by their environment and experiences. In other words, it acknowledges that an entrepreneurial organization *can* be created, with individuals within it shaped by the environment it creates and the experiences it faces – part culture, part structure. However, it also implies that the organization itself must deal with the environmental context in which it is placed – commercial, political, national and economic. It also underlines the complexity of the influences on individuals, many of which are outside the control of the organization – family, race, religion, nationality. Developing the entrepreneurial organization is an imprecise science.

Implications for the entrepreneurial organization:

- Entrepreneurial organizations can be constructed through culture and structure, but this is a complex process and there are many influences outside the control of the organization.

Implications for entrepreneurial management

This chapter has looked at the personal characteristics of entrepreneurs. Most of these characteristics need to be replicated either in the management, structure or, most importantly, through the culture of the entrepreneurial organization – entrepreneurship is primarily a frame of mind, a set of beliefs, a way of thinking and approaching life. Figure 5.3 summarizes many of the words that would be used to describe this entrepreneurial culture, insofar as they are derived from the character of the entrepreneur.

The two most important personal characteristics of the entrepreneur that any organization must ensure are replicated are, of course, the ability to spot opportunities and innovate. However, there are others. The entrepreneurial culture must:

- Spot opportunities;
- Value creativity and innovation;

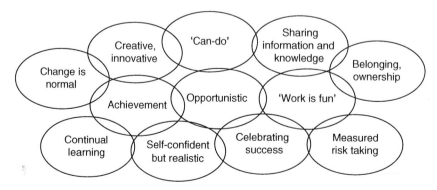

Figure 5.3 Entrepreneurial culture

- Recognize the importance of balanced risk taking and not unnecessarily penalize failure;
- Recognize change as endemic, the norm, not something to be avoided;
- Motivate people to achieve – goals set, achievement encouraged, publicly acknowledged and rewarded.
- Be a 'can-do' and 'work-is-fun' culture;
- Encourage organizational self-confidence and self-efficacy by celebrating achievement and success, but not at the expense of recognizing reality;
- Share information, knowledge and learning;
- Encourage people to belong to and 'own' the organization.

Many of these cultural characteristics are reinforced by the way entrepreneurs do business and manage the organization. There are also further implications for entrepreneurial culture that derive from how they do business and manage people as the firm grows as well as some pitfalls to be avoided.

There are additional implications for organizational structure that derive from the personal characteristics of entrepreneurs. As we look at how entrepreneurs do business. Structures must facilitate by:

- Encouraging opportunity spotting, creativity and innovation;
- Sharing information, knowledge and learning, so as to react quickly to environmental changes and capitalize on opportunities;
- Encouraging a sense of belonging and 'ownership', ensuring remuneration is adequate and other psychological needs met, so that staff are motivated not to leave the organization;
- Delegating and decentralizing. Does the entrepreneurial unit or division have to be small and separate from the rest of the organization? Is size a limiting factor?

Finally, there are some direct implications for management of the entrepreneurial organization:

- Strong vision is essential;
- Effective communication is vital;
- Timing is crucial, but difficult to manage;
- Management with a 'light touch' and a high degree of autonomy and delegation required;
- 'Positive' attitude required to encourage organizational self-confidence and self-efficacy.

As we look at how the entrepreneur does business and manages the organization as it grows.

Summary

Entrepreneurs are both born and made. They have certain personal character traits that they are born with and are shaped by their history and experience of life – their background – as well as the culture of the society they are born into.

The issue of linking the character traits of an individual to the success of a business needs to be approached with caution because it is not always possible to link the individual and his or her traits solely to the success or failure of the venture. The character of the manager is just one factor in the equation. Success or failure in business comes from a mix of many different things including the history and experience of the entrepreneur – entrepreneurs are both born and made. However it also comes out of the commercial decisions the business makes in relation to its strengths and weaknesses and the environment it faces.

Notwithstanding these issues, researchers generally agree that entrepreneurs have the following 'survival' character traits:

- A need for independence; evidenced by the comments of **Eddy Shah**.
- A need for achievement; evidenced by the comments of **Brent Hoberman** and **Charles Muirhead**.
- An internal locus of control, that is a belief that they can control their own destiny; evidenced by the comments of **Jonathan Elvidge**. In extremes this can lead to a desire to maintain personal control over every aspect of the business.
- Ability to live with uncertainty and take measured risks; evidenced by the comments of **Jonathan Elvidge** and **Anne Notley**. However, uncertainty is a major cause of stress and entrepreneurs will always try to minimize their own downside risk; evidenced by the comments of **Michael Dell**.

In addition, entrepreneurs have the following 'growth' character traits:

- Opportunistic, creating or exploiting change for profit; evidenced by the comments of **Richard Branson** and **Michael Dell**.
- Innovative, using innovation as their prime tool to create or exploit opportunity; evidenced by the comments of **Neil Kelly**.
- Self-confident; evidenced by the comments of **Richard Thompson** and **Chris Ingram**.
- Proactive and decisive with high energy; evidenced by the comments of **Tom Farmer** and **Derrick Collin**.
- Self-motivated, enjoying what they do; evidenced by the comments of **Martha Lane Fox**, **Wing Yip** and **Richard Branson**. Self-efficacy is a stronger, deeper version of this and is built on previous experience.
- Vision and flair; evidenced by the comments of **Terry Saddler** and **Jonathan Elvidge**.

Growth companies are more likely to be set up by groups of better educated, middle-aged managers with previous experience, often sharing ownership to attract other experienced managers, rather than individuals. They leave their jobs for positive motivations, such as the need for independence, achievement or recognition. There are, however, a small but significant number of very young entrepreneurs with little or no business experience, who are usually successful because of their innovative business ideas.

Entrepreneurship is also influenced by its environment. In other words, entrepreneurial organizations can be constructed but they and the individuals that work in them are in turn influenced by the complex environment they find themselves in.

Deriving from the entrepreneurs' character are certain words and phrases that describe their beliefs and the way they think. These start to describe the entrepreneurial culture. They include: change is normal, achievement, creative, innovative, opportunistic, continual learning, self-confident but realistic, 'can-do', sharing information and knowledge, belonging, ownership, 'work is fun', celebrating success, measured risk taking.

There are also implications for the appropriate organizational structure and the style and approach to management in an entrepreneurial organization.

Measuring Entrepreneurial Personality

The **General Enterprising Tendency (GET)** test has been developed by staff at Durham University Business School over a number of years. It is a 54-question instrument that measures entrepreneurial personality traits in five dimensions:

- Need for achievement – 12 questions.
- Autonomy – 6 questions.
- Drive and determination – 12 questions.
- Risk taking – 12 questions.
- Creativity and potential to innovate – 6 questions.

It is relatively quick and simple to administer – with either agree or disagree questions – and score. Each dimension receives a score of up to 12 points (Autonomy 6 points) and the final composite score measures inherent entrepreneurial character traits on a scale of 0–54. The test is available free of charge from Durham University Business School.

Stormer *et al.* (1999) applied the test to 128 owners of new (75) and successful (53) small firms. They concluded that the test was acceptable for research purposes, particularly for identifying owner-managers, it was poor at predicting small business success. They concluded that either the test scales need to be refined for this purpose or that the test did not include sufficient indicators of success such as situational influences on the individual (see next section) or other factors related to the business rather than the individual setting it up. It would seem that, while entrepreneurs are both born and made, success requires more than an ounce of commercial expertise ... oh yes ... and a little luck!

An electronic version of the tool is available online at the website accompanying this book (www.palgrave.com/business/burns). Why not answer the questions and see if you are entrepreneurial? It will take about 10 minutes.

Essays and discussion topics

1. Are entrepreneurs born or made? Which factors are most important and why?
2. Do you think you have what it takes to be an owner-manager or entrepreneur, or both?
3. How do you think a manager of an entrepreneurial organization might differ from an entrepreneur?
4. What are the defining characteristics of an entrepreneur?
5. What character traits do you think affect the success or otherwise of a business venture?

6. What are the possible negative consequences of the entrepreneur's strong internal locus of control?
7. Do you think it is possible to 'pick winners'?
8. Is entrepreneurship really just for the middle-aged?
9. Why might so many e-commerce entrepreneurs be young and well educated?
10. Does previous business failure mean that you are more likely to succeed in the future?
11. Is entrepreneurship just a set of beliefs, a way of thinking and an approach to life?
12. How much control does the CEO or MD of an organisation have over its culture?
13. Can training help develop entrepreneurship?
14. Has your education, so far, encouraged you to be entrepreneurial? If so, how? If not, how could it be changed?
15. Does this course encourage entrepreneurship?

Exercises and assignments

1. Answer the GET test and write a report analyzing whether or not you are entrepreneurial. When agreeing or disagreeing with the results of the test, be sure to give concrete examples of your past behaviour that support your analysis.
2. List any additional questions you would ask an owner-manager or entrepreneur in trying to assess their character traits.
3. Use the GET test and exercise 2 to conduct an interview with an owner-manager of a local firm. Analyze their responses and write a report supporting your view as to whether they are entrepreneurial or not. Make sure you justify your conclusions with evidence from the interview or other objective information.

References

Abdesselam, R., Bonnet, J. and Le Pape, N. (1999) 'An Explanation of the Life Span of New Firms: An Empirical Analysis of French Data', *Entrepreneurship: Building for the Future*, Euro PME 2nd International Conference, Rennes.

Aldrich, H. E. and Martinez, M. (2003) 'Entrepreneurship as a Social Construction: A Multi-Level Evolutionary Approach', in Z. J. Acs and D. B. Audretsch (eds), *Handbook of Entrepreneurship Research: A Multidisciplinary Survey and Introduction*, Boston, Mass: Kluwer Academic Publishers.

Andersson, S., Gabrielsson, J. and Wictor, I. (2004) 'International Activities in Small Firms – Examining Factors Influencing the Internationalisation and Export Growth of Small Firms', *Canadian Journal of Administrative Science*, 21(1).

Baty, G. (1990) *Entrepreneurship for the Nineties*, New Jersey: Prentice Hall.

Bell, J., Murray, M. and Madden, K. (1992) 'Developing Expertise: An Irish Perspective', *International Small Business Journal*, 10(2).

Blanchflower, D. G. and Meyer, B. D. (1991) 'Longitudinal Analysis of Young Entrepreneurs in Australia and the United States', *National Bureau of Economic Research*, Working Paper 3746, Cambridge, MA.

Brockhaus, R. and Horwitz, P. (1986) 'The Psychology of the Entrepreneur' in Sexton, D. and Smilor, R. (eds), *The Art and Science of Entrepreneurship*, Cambridge: Ballinger Publishing Company.

Brush, C. G. (1992) 'Research on Women Business Owners: Past Trends, A New Perspective and Future Directions', *Entrepreneurship: Theory and Practice*, 16(4).

Burns, P. (2007) *Entrepreneurship and Small Business*, 2nd edn, Basingstoke: Palgrave Macmillan.

Busenitz, L. and Barney, J. (1997) 'Differences between Entrepreneurs and Managers in Large Organisations: Biases and Heuristics in Strategic Decision Making', *Journal of Business Venturing*, 12.

Buttner, E. and More, D. (1997) 'Women's Organisational Exodus to Entrepreneurship: Self-Reported Motivations and Correlates with Success', *Journal of Small Business Management*, 35(1).

Caird, S. (1990) 'What does it Mean to be Enterprising?', *British Journal of Management*, 1(3).

Carter, S. and Cachon, J. (1988) *The Sociology of Entrepreneurship*, Stirling: University of Stirling.

Chell, E., Haworth, J. and Brearley, S. (1991) *The Entrepreneurial Personality*, London: Routledge.

Chen, P. C., Greene, P. G. and Crick, A. (1998) 'Does Entrepreneurial Self Efficacy Distinguish Entrepreneurs from Managers?', *Journal of Business Venturing*, 13.

Cuba, R., Decenzo, D. and Anish, A. (1983) 'Management Practises of Successful Female Business Owners', *American Journal of Small Business*, 8(2).

Deakins, D. (1996) *Entrepreneurs and Small Firms*, London: McGraw-Hill.

de Bono, E. (1985) *Six Thinking Hats*, Boston: Little Brown & Company.

Evans, D. S. and Leighton, L. S. (1990) 'Small Business Formation by Unemployed and Employed Workers', *Small Business Economics*, 2(4).

Harper, M. (1985) 'Hardship, Discipline and Entrepreneurship', *Cranfield School of Management*, Working Paper 85(1).

Hirsch, R. D. and Brush, C. G. (1987) 'Women Entrepreneurs: A Longitudinal Study', *Frontiers in Entrepreneurship Research*, Wellesley, Mass: Babson College.

Kanter, R. M. (1983) *The Change Masters*, New York: Simon & Schuster.

Kets de Vries, M. F. R. (1985) 'The Dark Side of Entrepreneurship', *Harvard Business Review*, November/ December.

Kirzner, I. M. (1973) *Competition and Entrepreneurship*, Chicago: University of Chicago.

Kirzner, I. M. (1979) *Perception, Opportunity and Profit: Studies in the Theory of Entrepreneurship*, Chicago: University of Chicago.

Kirzner, I. M. (1997) 'Entrepreneurial Discovery and Competitive Market Processes: An Austrian Approach', *Journal of Economic Literature*, 35.

Kirzner, I. M. (1999) 'Creativity and/or Alertness: A Reconsideration of the Schumpeterian Entrepreneur', *Review of Austrian Economics*, 11.

McClelland, D. C. (1961) *The Achieving Society*, Princeton, NJ: Van Nostrand.

Pinchot, G. (1985) *Intrapreneuring*, New York: Harper & Row.

Rosa, P., Hamilton, S., Carter, S. and Burns, H. (1994) 'The Impact of Gender on Small Business Management: Preliminary Findings of a British Study', *International Small Business Journal*, 12(3).

Schein, V., Mueller, R., Lituchy, T. and Liu, J. (1996) 'Thinking Manager – Think Male: A Global Phenomenon?', *Journal of Organisational Behaviour*, 17.

Schumpeter, J. A. ([1983] 1996) *The Theory of Economic Development*, New Jersey: Transaction Publishers.

Schwartz, E. B. (1997) 'Entrepreneurship: A New Female Frontier', *Journal of Contemporary Business*, Winter.

Shapero, A. (1985) *Managing Professional People – Understanding Creative Performance*, New York: Free Press.

Shaver, K. and Scott, L. (1992) 'Person, Processes and Choice: The Psychology of New Venture Creation', *Entrepreneurship Theory and Practice*, 16(2).

Stanworth, J., Blythe, S., Granger, B. and Stanworth, C. (1989) 'Who Becomes an Entrepreneur?', *International Small Business Journal*, 8(1).

Storey, D. J. (1994) *Understanding the Small Business Sector*, London: International Thomson Business Press.

Storey, D. and Sykes, N. (1996) 'Uncertainty, Innovation and Management' in P. Burns and J. Dewhurst (eds), *Small Business and Entrepreneurship*, Basingstoke: Macmillan – now Palgrave Macmillan.

Stormer, R., Kline, T. and Goldberg, S. (1999) 'Measuring Entrepreneurship with the General Enterprise Tendency (GET) Test: Criterion-related Validity and Reliability', *Human Systems Management*, 18(1).

CHAPTER 6

The process of business formation

CONTENTS

KEY CONCEPTS

This chapter covers:
- Models of the possible stages of the development of a business.
- The process of business start-up and the supply of entrepreneurs.
- The connection between the business idea and the business opportunity.
- The role and importance of a business plan.

- The nature of start-up finance.
- The many facets of entrepreneurship in relation to types of business start-up.

LEARNING OBJECTIVES

By the end of this chapter the reader should:

- Be aware of the possible development paths for a business.
- Have an understanding of the process of moving from idea to opportunity, and the nature of opportunity development and evaluation.
- Have an appreciation of the relevance of the business plan.
- Have an understanding of the different sources of start-up finance.
- Have an understanding of what constitutes small business success and failure.
- Be aware of the many varied reasons and attitudes behind different types of business start-up.

Introduction

Small business by looking at how they are sometimes defined and by exploring some of their distinctive features. This chapter looks at how they are formed and developed through the entrepreneurial process. In a general sense the emphasis in business development, and in writing about enterprise, has been to look primarily at the business but, it can be more helpful to take the entrepreneur as the fundamental unit of analysis. This chapter therefore looks at aspects of business development and start-up and, in particular, at the role in this played by the entrepreneur. It also considers a number of aspects of small business entrepreneurship.

The stages of business development

It is customary to see business formation as consisting of one or more stages in the development of businesses. However, it is important to recognise that the use of the term 'stage' in relation to the business development process does not mean that businesses develop in discrete phases with clear boundaries between them. Separating the development process into stages is rather like dividing the spectrum of visible light into colours. Traditionally there are said to be seven, but in reality there are not seven distinct colours but a continuing gradation through the colours. We can say that one area is green compared with another area which is yellow, but we cannot say precisely where one changes to the other. Dividing the business development process into stages is helpful, in that there are issues at the heart of each stage that differ from the issues central to other stages; but, while we can indicate broadly the stage of development of a business, we cannot say precisely when it moves from one stage to another.

Like the number of colours in the spectrum, the number of areas ascribed to the process is a matter of interpretation. However, unlike the colour spectrum, the order of the areas is not necessarily fixed. While a 'pre-start' stage cannot follow 'start-up', and 'termination' has to be the end, businesses do not have to progress through every possible stage between; they can be static, they can grow and they can decline in any order, they can do these things more than once, and they can reverse their steps. There are many models of the different stages and the sequence in which they occur, but the reality is that very few businesses actually follow the models. Many of the models, in the way they are presented, imply steady growth, for instance by presenting a steadily rising line on a plot with axes of size and time. Growth, however, is not the norm, and where there is growth it is generally achieved through a number of discrete steps rather than by a steady, even progression. It is also important to recognise that these models do not explain what is happening inside a business; they only describe its situation, and they present symptoms not causes. Therefore they do not help in predicting what will happen next to a business.

Nevertheless some models are presented here to provide a context in which to consider different aspects of business formation. One of the simplest, and one of the most used, models has been that of Churchill and Lewis which suggests that there can be five stages from early business existence to eventual maturity (see Table 6.1).

Other models, however, have additional stages that come either before or after the Churchill and Lewis stages, or show additional features in a progression through the stages. While stages which come before the formation of a business are not strictly stages in the development of that particular business, they are nevertheless relevant to the development of the entrepreneur and to an understanding of the inception of the business. These prior-to-business-start stages can include the following.

- *Culture*: People are more likely to think of starting a business, and that business is more likely to survive, if the underlying culture is one that will help to nurture awareness and interest as well as ideas and embryonic businesses.
- *The idea*: Before they can proceed to start-up, people need to have both the notion they can start a business and a product or service idea around which the business can be formed. This is the stage where they are not only aware that business start is possible, but must feel that it might be appropriate for them and that they can do it.
- *The pre-start phase*: This is the process whereby those thinking of starting a business progress from the business idea to the stage of actually starting the business.

Table 6.1 The five stages of business growth

- Existence: staying alive by finding products or services and customers
- Survival: establishing the customer base, demonstrating viability
- Success: confidence in its market position, options for further growth
- Take-off: opting to go for growth
- Maturity: the characteristics of a larger, stable company

Source: N. C. Churchill and V. L. Lewis, 'Growing Concerns: The Five Stages of Small Firm Growth', *Harvard Business Review* (1983) May–June, pp.31, 32, 34, 40.

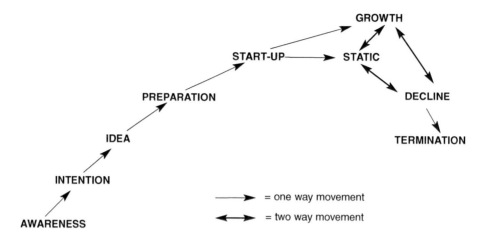

Figure 6.1 Small business paths from conception to death

There are also stages at the end of a businesses life when it declines and terminates. A fuller list of stages might therefore include the following sequence (which is also presented diagrammatically in Figure 6.1):

- culture and awareness
- intention – the notion and intention to start a business
- idea – a product/service idea for the business
- pre-start/preparation
- start-up/inception
- growth and expansion
- static – including survival, consolidation, comfort and maturity
- decline
- termination.

As well as showing both pre-start and termination phases, this model also recognises the dynamics of business development. Despite the straight lines of most models, businesses very rarely progress steadily onwards and upwards. Figure 6.2 recognises this by showing possible paths for a business, not only in steady growth, but also in a phase of growth reversal, in stability with possible oscillation, in a merger with another business and in early failure. This model therefore suggests that there can be problems to be faced by a business as it grows which are elaborated further in Greiner's model in Figure 6.3. These models therefore, in effect, present the precursors or stimulators of change, rather than the change itself. These precursors or stimulators are, however, very hard to measure compared with qualities such as turnover or numbers of employees, and are therefore much harder in practice to use to describe the extent of the development of a business. Nevertheless, their presentation can provide useful insights.

While the stage model approach may have its drawbacks, it helps nevertheless to divide small businesses into different categories to make them easier to examine.

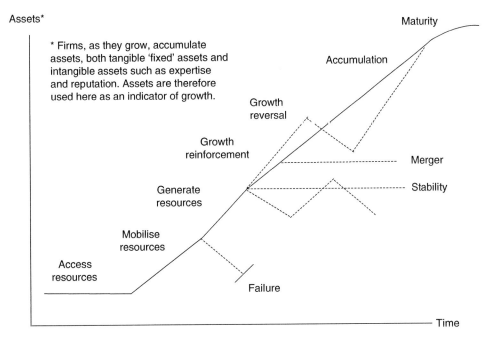

Figure 6.2 Growth process as reflected in possible growth paths

Source: E. Garnsey, 'A New Theory of the Growth of the Firm', Paper presented to the ICSB 41 st World Conference, Stockholm, June 1996, p.4.

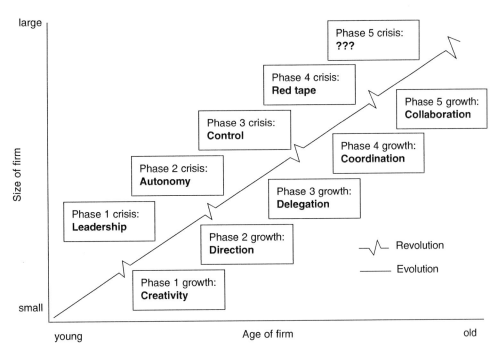

Figure 6.3 The Greiner growth model

Source: L. E. Greiner, 'Evolution and Revolution as Organisations Grow', *Harvard Business Review,* July/August 1972 quoted in P. Burns, *Entrepreneurship and Small Business,* (Basingstoke: Palgrave, 2007) p. 211.

Preparing for business start-up

The entrepreneur and the opportunity

Shane has suggested that the components needed for entrepreneurial outcomes are individuals and opportunities:

> The entrepreneurial process begins with the perception of the existence of opportunities or situations in which resources can be recombined for a potential profit. Alert individuals, called entrepreneurs, discover these opportunities, and develop ideas for how to pursue them, including the development of a product or service that will be provided to customers. These individuals then obtain resources, design organisations or other modes of opportunity exploitation or develop a strategy to exploit the opportunity.[1]

The supply of entrepreneurs: the culture stage

What all the listed stages of business development, apart from culture and awareness, have in common is that they are all concerned with people who might be or already are in business. To use a horticultural analogy, they all deal with plants: with sowing the seeds of plants, with growing plants, with pruning plants, with plants flowering and even with plants dying. The culture and awareness stage, however, deals with the preparation of the ground: the preparation of a medium which will encourage, feed and support the seeds and growing plants. The surrounding human society or culture is important for business growth, just as the condition and type of the soil are important for plants.

The influences on new firm formation can be many and varied. Krueger's model of entrepreneurial potential, and other cognitive approaches, illustrate some of the antecedent influences on enterprise. An alternative presentation, which represents the same framework but also highlights some of the specific factors that may be influential in a business context, is shown in Figure 6.4.

This approach illustrates the variety of possible antecedent factors that may be relevant to the 'culture' or 'awareness' stage. This stage can be sub-divided to show the progression from no particular interest in enterprise, through awareness and potential interest, to actual new business formation.

The supply of opportunities

A distinction has been made between a small business opportunity and an entrepreneurial business opportunity. As Bolton and Thompson indicate, small business people typically spot an opportunity to do something they can do, but which does not necessarily have any real growth potential.[2] Entrepreneurial opportunities however are opportunities that offer something new and different to the market: where there is a degree of innovation and therefore growth potential.

In a World Bank study, Klapper et al. indicated that there is a clear split between the industrialised countries and the developing countries in the sectors on which entrepreneurs typically tend to focus their efforts.[3] Entrepreneurs in developing countries tend to focus their start-up intentions in the retail trade sector because

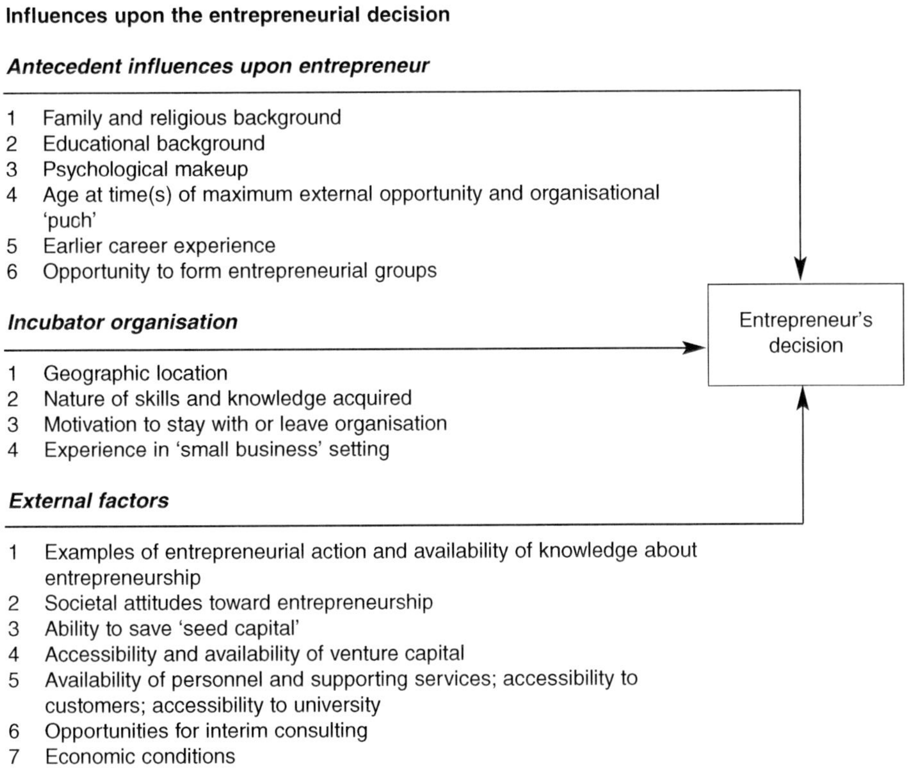

Influences upon the entrepreneurial decision

Antecedent influences upon entrepreneur

1   Family and religious background
2   Educational background
3   Psychological makeup
4   Age at time(s) of maximum external opportunity and organisational
    'puch'
5   Earlier career experience
6   Opportunity to form entrepreneurial groups

Incubator organisation

1   Geographic location
2   Nature of skills and knowledge acquired
3   Motivation to stay with or leave organisation
4   Experience in 'small business' setting

External factors

1   Examples of entrepreneurial action and availability of knowledge about
    entrepreneurship
2   Societal attitudes toward entrepreneurship
3   Ability to save 'seed capital'
4   Accessibility and availability of venture capital
5   Availability of personnel and supporting services; accessibility to
    customers; accessibility to university
6   Opportunities for interim consulting
7   Economic conditions

Entrepreneur's decision

Figure 6.4   Model of new enterprise formation

Source: Arnold C. Cooper, 'Technical Entrepreneurship', *R & D Management,* vol. 3 (1973) pp.59–64.

of the lower requirements of investment, human resources, knowledge and capital; whereas in the industrialised nations it is the services and industry sectors that dominate.

According to Wickham[4] a business opportunity is a gap in the market which presents the possibility of new value being created, and according to Bolton and Thompson[5] opportunities are ideas that have commercial potential and can be realised. The assertion here is that opportunities are ideas that exploit unmet, and sometimes unrealised, customer needs. Drucker suggests that change often provides the opportunity for the new and the different.[6] Therefore, given the rapid pace of change in, amongst other things, consumer tastes and technology, these are areas where there should be business opportunities to exploit. Table 6.2 provides examples of the quickening pace of change in the introduction of new technology but, as well as opportunity, new technology also involves risk. Many businesses described as being based on 'cutting-edge' (i.e. does not yet work!) technology are often found to be based on under-developed technology that runs away with resources and leads to high failure rates. Illustration 6.1, however, provides an example of a technology which offered the potential for a business opportunity and of a business which has capitalised on that potential.

Table 6.2   New technology adoption rate

The time it has taken for new technology to reach 25 per cent of the US population. For example household electricity was first made available in 1873 and it took 46 years for 25 per cent of the US population to get electricity.

The Technology	Time in Years
Household electricity (1873)	46
Telephone (1875)	35
Automobile (1885)	55
Airplane travel	54
Radio (1906)	22
Television (1925)	26
Video recorder (1952)	34
Personal computer (1975)	15
Cellular phone	13
www (1991)	Less than 10 (estimate)

Source: Wall Street Journal, June 1997 in B. Bygrave, 'Building an Entrepreneurial Economy: Lessons from the United States', *Business Strategy Review* (1998), 9(2), p.11.

ILLUSTRATION 6.1
Business opportunities in technology

The technology: text messaging in the UK

In the UK, text messaging reached 4 billion messages a month for the first time in December 2006, according to figures announced by the Mobile Data Association (MDA). December's remarkable total of 4.3 billion took the overall figure for 2006 to 41.8 billion, surpassing the MDA's prediction of 40 billion and giving a daily average for the year of 114 million.

Person-to-person texts sent across the UK GSM network operators throughout the last month of the year showed a growth of 38 per cent on the December 2005 figure of 3.1 billion, representing an average of 138 million messages per day. On Christmas Day this leapt to 205 million texts, an average of 8 million per hour, with the figure for New Year's Day 2007 even higher, reaching a record breaking 214 million, the highest daily total ever recorded by the MDA.

When compared to the mere 42 million messages sent per day five years ago throughout December 2001, it becomes clear just how far the nation has come in embracing text messaging technology which has emerged from a popular craze to becoming an essential communication tool, inclusive to all age groups. The number of mobile phone users accessing the Internet on their handsets is also rising. According to figures announced today by the Mobile Data Association (MDA), a total of 40.7 million users were recorded as having used their phones for downloads and browsing the mobile Internet in the UK during the third quarter of 2006. The total number of users recorded in July 2006 was 13 million, which had increased to 14 million by September.

Source: Mobile Data Association, January 2007.

The opportunity: an SMS reminder service

The growth in text messaging in the UK described above represents an opportunity, and one of the first text messaging business ideas has been used by the National Health Service.

In December 2005 an innovative NHS appointment text messaging service was rolled out to six London-based primary care trusts. The messaging service uses software that is designed to access NHS patient databases and send reminders of appointments. Patients can also be contacted if they are deemed to be 'at risk', and can send confirmation back by SMS.

Toby Gockel, business development manager for iPlato, which supplies the software the messaging service uses, said:

> We extract the relevant information – the mobile phone number, the date and time of the appointment – from each client's site.
>
> Clients could be hospital trusts, surgeries, any independent unit that arranges appointments. We then send the information via a TCP/IP encrypted connection from our server, which enables automatic text messaging. The server generates an appointment reminder message, which is sent via the Orange SMS gateway to every mobile phone.

Source: www.silicon.com (19 December 2005).

Pre-start preparation

Businesses do not arise fully fledged from even the most positive of enterprise cultures. A time of preparation is still needed first. The preparation may include identifying a suitable opportunity (stemming from the idea), acquiring the necessary knowledge and skills, and locating the contacts who will help. Continuing the horticultural analogy, it is the stage of planting and germination of seeds. The growing medium is important, but seeds are also needed to produce plants and those seeds have to have the ability to take root and to put out leaves. In business terms, negotiating this stage requires both a willingness to start it and some ideas about what might best be done in it.

Krueger has argued that a willingness to start comes from the credibility gained for the proposed action because of its perceived desirability and perceived feasibility; in other words from a recognition that there are rewards that can be gained from starting a business and a desire for those rewards, together with a belief that the rewards (not necessarily financial) can be achieved. It may also be relevant to add that this presupposes that the possibility of engaging in the action in question has already occurred to the person concerned.

If these conditions are met and there is a desire to proceed then it is important to know how to do so. Various suggestions have been made about the key components of the ideal pre-start process. The formula produced by Peterson and Rondstadt (Figure 6.5) summarises some of the key components that are needed for start-up success, components that by implication might then be assembled in the pre-start stage.[7] It is also important to recognise that the pre-start process can be very long.

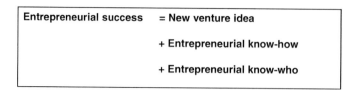

Figure 6.5 Entrepreneurial success

Source: R. Peterson and R. Rondstadt, 'A Silent Strength: Entrepreneurial KnowWho', *The 16th ESBS/EFMD/IMD Report*, 86(4), p.11.

The pre-start stage can be defined as ending when a business starts, and beginning when there is an intention at some time to prepare for that eventuality.

A traditional view of enterprise has been based on the assumption that some individuals are inherently more enterprising than others. Because of that predisposition towards enterprise, it was assumed that, given the right stimulus, such individuals were more likely to try starting a business. There could then be virtually no pre-start stage in the sense defined above. Another view of enterprise, and of enterprising behaviour. It is based on the attributes and resources that individuals may possess, or may believe they possess. Attributes may include self-confidence, diligence, perseverance, interpersonal skills and innovative behaviour. Resources may include finance, experience, knowledge, skills, a network and a track record. It is suggested then that it is the interaction amongst these factors that produces a rational response, on the basis of available information, when the possibility occurs of a business start-up. Illustration 6.2 brings this situation together under a Six Phases of Start-up model.

It is acknowledged that there is inertia in individual behaviour and that it may take a discontinuity in work or in life to trigger a review of an individual's situation. Whether this review will lead to individuals trying to start their own enterprise will then depend on the attributes and resources they have accumulated and their perception of the opportunity and of environmental factors such as the availability of grants. The acquisition of those attributes and resources, if it is done with a view to a possible business start, is the pre-start stage. It is generally perceived as a stage of individual, or small team, preparation.

An individual, or a team, can be helped to acquire the components for a start-up. There are many ways in which this can be done, but the following paragraphs illustrate some of the possibilities.

The idea

The 'idea' can cover both the idea of starting a business and the product or service idea for a particular business. The idea of starting a business comes from the issues just explored and particular business ideas come from the opportunities considered earlier, which may come from a number of sources but usually from the entrepreneur's own experience or from a personal desire. Table 6.3 looks at the self-employment business idea spectrum common in small businesses.

Finding an idea can be done either by deliberate search or by unforeseen coincidence. In the deliberate search mode the would-be entrepreneur is deliberately

---

ILLUSTRATION 6.2
Starting a business

There are lots of things that it is necessary to do in starting a business. The following list divides them into six phases:

- *Acquiring motivation*: Finding the stimulus and commitment to the notion of starting a business.

- *Finding an idea*: Getting a idea for further investigation. This may involve considering different ways of getting into business, such as franchising or buying a business.

- *Validating the idea*: Testing the proposed product/service, both for technical and functional efficiency and for market acceptance. Also protecting the idea.

- *Identifying the resources needed*: Planning the scale of business entry. Identifying in detail the resources required, the timing, and the other support needed.

- *Negotiating to get into business*: Applying the plan, negotiating for finance, premises and contracts, deciding the type of business (such as limited company, partnership or sole-trader) and registering it.

- *Systems and linkages*: Developing the ongoing business system. Coping with statutory requirements. Establishing ties with customers and suppliers. Developing the workforce.

Table 6.3 The self-employment spectrum

Form or approach	Platform	Springboard
Turning a hobby into a business	Long-standing passion	Personal connections
Becoming a professional consultant/trainer	Specialised knowledge	Professional contacts
Acquiring an existing business	Managerial and marketing skills	Financial resources
Taking on a franchise	Organisational ability	Financial and marketing resources
Creating a business of your own	Enterprising spirit	Marketplace
Matching personal and market potential	Personal knowledge and potential	Knowledge and potential of yourself and others
Developing your vision	Personal charisma and inspiration	Economic and social need/potential

Source: Reprinted by permission of Sage Publications Ltd from R. Lessem, 'Getting Into Self-Employment', *Management Education and Development* (1984), Spring, p.31.

trying to start a business and is actively looking for an idea. This may involve attending business meetings and events of all kinds or getting together with other like-minded individuals to brainstorm ideas. Alternatively, again in deliberate search mode, the entrepreneur, whilst in employment, is looking for a business opportunity which is perhaps not being taken up by his/her present employer. In the unforeseen coincidence mode, however, the idea may actually find the would-be entrepreneur. Often business ideas develop because people find they cannot purchase a product or

Table 6.4   The four dimensions of management development

Functional knowledge and skills The technical knowledge and abilities appropriate to the business. The main know-how typically of 'the butcher, the baker and the candlestick maker'	*Generic management knowledge and skills* Planning, organising, managing time, negotiating, coordinating resources, solving problems (not functionally specific)
Business and strategic awareness Understanding the bigger picture, conceptual skills, analysis, synthesis, creativity, opportunity-spotting	*Personal competencies* Results orientation, initiative, interpersonal skills, enthusiasm, perseverance, commitment, leadership

Source: Based on R. E. Boyatzis, *The Competent Manager: A Model for Effective Performance* (New York: Wiley, 1982).

service and decide to start a business to supply the product or service they could not obtain. Here daily observations are important, as are perhaps hobbies, networking and prior business experience.

Know-how

Know-how covers a number of areas of knowledge and skill, all of which may be needed by the owner-manager of a small business if that business is to be successful. This know-how has been shown to have (at least) four dimensions (see Table 6.4).

Small business training is often the means offered for increasing small business know-how. Despite the plethora of courses sometimes offered, it is important to recognise the potential barriers that can make small business owners averse to conventional forms of training, and some of the possible counterbalancing incentives (see Table 6.5).

One skill often overlooked is communication: the ability to relate to and exchange appropriate information with the people who matter to the business, including staff, suppliers, customers, investors and advisers. It has been suggested that the traditional components of pre-start training, namely finance, accounting/bookkeeping, marketing/selling and so forth are secondary skills and that the core skill is communication. Communication is necessary in all aspects of small business development and is of particular relevance in building up and using an appropriate personal network of contacts.

Know-who

The expressions, 'it's not what you know, but whom you know' and 'the old-boy network' reflect a sometimes popular, but essentially negative, perception of certain social networks. Yet those who have examined small firm networking are convinced of its importance for the success of enterprise.

Credibility is established through personal contact and knowledge of the skills, motivation and past performance of the individual - the bankers call this the 'track record'. Since for an embryonic business there is no trading track record, investors must look to their previous relationship with the individual, whether it be commercial or personal. Thus, for example, a previous employer may agree to be the first customer, a friend may allow use of spare office space, or a relative may be prepared to lend money with little real hope of a return in the short or even the medium term.[8]

Table 6.5   Barriers and incentives to training

Barriers	Incentives
Cost implications • Time is the most valuable and precious resource and time spent on training is considered to be a cost not an investment • Time training is time not working • Much training is not relevant • Much training is not effective	*Value* • Courses of real current relevance that require minimal time off the job, and have identified early benefits *Funding available* • Grant assistance available to help with the cost
Attitudes • Bad experiences of formal training, e.g. at school • Failure to perceive the need and the potential benefits • A belief that the benefits will not last	*Content* • Trainers with business credibility • Training itself promotes further training • Process counselling will be accepted but not expert consultancy
Lack of relevance • No desire to improve or grow the business • Want solutions to yesterday's problems today • Not prepared to look ahead	*Promotion* • Peer business managers will be believed • Influences will be listened to, but not 'officials' • Mail shots don't work • 'It's about increasing profits' • Through networks of contacts
Promotion of training • The word 'training' is a turn-off • Suggestions of paternalism • Government initiatives are distrusted • Government initiatives are distrusted	
Apprehension • Too many courses on offer • Too many agencies • They may be sold something they don't need • It's an admission of defeat	

What used to be referred to as networking has clear links to, or is sometimes now referred to as social capital. Advice and guidance are often seen as the benefits of a network or part of social capital, and they may be the traditional base upon which many small firms' support agencies have been built. But while they may be important characteristics of an active network they are not the only ones:[9]

- *Information*: Entrepreneurs use their social networks to signal their intentions, and to gather information about potential opportunities.
- *Sponsorship and support*: Family and friends will not only provide introductions into appropriate networks, but will also offer emotional and tangible support.
- *Credibility*: Membership of the network gives added weight to the evaluation of skills. Family and friends can provide credibility in areas unfamiliar to the entrepreneur.
- *Control*: Membership of the network, and assistance from it, require certain standards of behaviour. Owner-managers who do not conduct their business in a way that is acceptable to the community will quickly find themselves and their businesses isolated.

- *Business*: There are market networks of customers, suppliers and partners as well as production networks of subcontractors, consultants and service suppliers. In addition, there are networks of firms that may work together on projects on a basis of collaboration. This structure can provide all the components necessary for a project without the need for 'vertical integration'.
- *Resources*: Friends and family can also be sources of resources for a new small business, and many businesses are assisted by the informal venture capital market that their owners access through their networks.

These networks are complex but relatively user friendly and informal systems for the exchange of information. They have been described as 'creative communication in the business milieu'. They are not rigidly bounded and exclusive, and individuals often belong to more than one network. In general they facilitate the economic co-operation that is a feature present to at least some extent in all markets.

Networks involving small firms have a number of particular features. They are usually based on personal contacts, not official links, they are informal and are not openly advertised. They are flexible, being built up and maintained specifically to suit the purposes of their members. It is often these networks that give their member entrepreneurs the potential to react quickly to new developments. Having 'know-who' competency, networking skills and social capital can therefore be essential for success in dynamic environments.

And the result

Possessing or acquiring some or all of the possible components of the pre-start stage does not guarantee that a business will be started. The decision still has to be made actually to do it, although this is often triggered by an external event. It has been suggested that the decision is essentially a choice about the balance of risk. While the chances of success increase as relevant attributes and resources are built up, the costs of failure can also increase as personal financial commitments accumulate. It has therefore been suggested that there is a window of opportunity when the balance between benefits and costs is at the optimum, typically when people are in their thirties or early forties.

Getting started

The typical small business start-up is a new business venture; in temporary, small or unusual premises; nearly always financed from within, plus bank borrowings and with little or no long-term borrowing; usually small in terms of employment, often with only family members involved.[10] Table 6.6 presents an analysis of such a business. The reasons for starting a business may vary, but the main values driving the firm will be those of the founder(s). The basic skills of the founder will also determine the functional emphasis of the business. Normally management will be by direct supervision. The main efforts will hinge around developing a commercially acceptable product or service and establishing a niche for it in the marketplace.

Table 6.6 Analysis of a start-up business

Aspect of the business	Description
Key issues	Obtaining customers
Economic production	
Top-management role	Direct supervision
Organisational structure	Unstructured
Product and market research	None
Systems and controls	Simple book-keeping
Eyeball contact	
Major sources of finance	Owner's savings
	Owner's friends and relatives
	Suppliers and leasing
Cash generation	Negative
Major investments	Premises, plant and equipment
Product/market	Single line, limited channels and market

Source: Reprinted from M. Scott and R. Bruce, 'Five Stages of Growth in Small Business', *Long Range Planning* (1987), 20(3), p.48. © 1987, with kind permission from Elsevier Science Ltd, The Boulevard, Langford Lane, Kidlington, OX5 1GB, UK.

The result will normally be one working unit, operating in a single market with limited channels of distribution. Sources of funds will be haphazard, and will place heavy demands on the founder, his/her partner(s) and friends and relatives. With the high level of uncertainty the level of forward planning is low.[11]

Needs
At the stage of starting up a business, the entrepreneur doing it and/or the business can have many needs. This is one list:

- capital
- family support
- customers
- suppliers
- employees
- premises
- company formation: a business name, stationery, management procedures
- infrastructure
- management skills: provided externally (consultants), or internally (training)
- information and advice
- confidence.[12]

Barriers
As well as facing the start-up needs of businesses, which are in the main an inevitable aspect of the process in which they are engaged, entrepreneurs can at this stage also face a number of distinct barriers:

- *The resource/credibility merry-go-round*: This refers to the problem of how to acquire credibility in order to get the resources necessary to prove what you can do (see Figure 6.6).

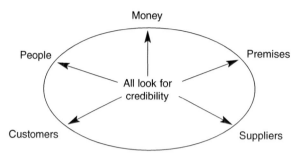

Figure 6.6   The resource/credibility merry-go-round
Source: S. Birley, personal communication (1987).

- *High entry or survival barriers*: The barriers to entry into business will depend on the amount of investment, technology and labour skills required, or on the availability of niches or of growing markets. Then, once started, the business may find that there may also be barriers to survival. High survival barriers occur when there is intense competition, saturated markets, excess capacity and changing technology or product quality requirements.
- *The burden of government bureaucracy*: Ignorance is no defence when dealing with the legal requirements of officialdom. There are penalties if forms are not returned or are returned incorrectly, but full and proper compliance can be costly, even if only in the time it requires, and this is proportionally more costly for small businesses than for large ones.
- *The business plan*: Business plans are often not appropriate. When asked for a plan, the new entrepreneur feels irritated because producing it takes him or her away from the real work, frightened because he or she is not sure what it means, and confused about how to plan at all when things change daily.[13]

Business regulation

As indicated above, it is often stated by many would-be entrepreneurs and those in business that 'red tape' is a prime cause of angst amongst business owners. The World Bank Entrepreneurship Survey 2007 provides a new set of indicators relating to the relationship between business creation, the investment climate and economic development.[14] In the World Bank study a total of 84 countries were included in the analysis, and whilst the researchers did reiterate the views of other researchers[15] on the positive correlation between economic expansion, renewed optimism and incidences of entrepreneurship, the researchers discovered that the barriers to starting a business were significantly and negatively correlated with business density and the entry rate. In essence the fewer the procedures required to start a business, the greater the number of registered firms - and the higher the entry rate.

In the UK this concern about the impact of business regulation is reflected in the title of the new government department concerned with the promotion of business and enterprise, which is the Department for Business, Enterprise and Regulatory Reform (BERR).

The business plan

> Before launching any new venture, the first step is to draw up a business plan.
> Introduction to a fact sheet on business plans.

Business plans are another area in which the appropriate approach for larger businesses is not necessarily also appropriate for small ones. The view that a business plan is essential for anyone starting a small business is, to some people, so obvious that it does not need to be proved. Others however believe that, at least for some businesses, a formal written business plan in the recommended format would not only be a waste of time but could even be a misleading distraction. To understand each point of view it is necessary to look more closely into the limitations of plans and what benefits business planning and plans can offer.

to BANK / INVESTORS

> I only did it for the bank, and a year later it was obvious that the bank had not looked at it.
> A successful businessman describing his first business plan.
>
> I had to present a business plan for my grant application and now, actually, I find it very useful. At the end of each week, if the sales are above the projected levels, I get a lot of comfort because it means that the business is actually succeeding. If I didn't have that reassurance I would have a lot of sleepless nights worrying whether the business was a good idea.
> Owner of a newly opened small shop.

→ SALES/ PROJECTED LEVELS

→ business is succeeding or not.

Owing, at least in part, to the way it has been presented, many people starting a business often see the business plan primarily as an obstacle - one that they have to address somehow, because it seems to be a compulsory part of the process. Professional advisers have told them that they should do it and may have indicated that its completion is a precondition for further help. The people thinking of starting a business may have been provided with some guidance on how to do it and given examples of suggested layouts. They may not, however, have been persuaded that it is anything but an unnecessary chore and they do not see it as a helpful tool for the venture they are about to undertake. This is especially so if all a potential investor appears to require in a plan, apart from a CV, are some financial projections (cash-flow, profit and loss, and balance sheet) and the entrepreneurs cannot see how they can possibly make meaningful forecasts of what they can achieve before they have the experience of actually being in business to guide them. Of course often what the investor really needs is the assumptions underlying the projected figures, but that is rarely apparent or disclosed to the entrepreneur.

Therefore, for the person starting a small business, the basic question to be answered in relation to the business plan is not how to do it, but why. Of what real use is a business plan to a small business? Only when this is understood may the question of 'how' be relevant.

If the question 'why' is honestly addressed, it will appear that there are some new business starts for which a formal written business plan may not actually be essential. To some advisers that is heresy, which may be why the concept of business plans can get a bad reputation. If the assumption is made that they are essential then there is a temptation to assume that others share this view, and so the reason for it does not have to be explained. Advisers then address the question of how to do it, while those being advised still do not see why. If there is no good reason why, the result is unlikely to be helpful. This is compounded when it is the possession of a business plan, rather than the process of its preparation, which is seen to be the key.

It is generally accepted that there are two ways in which the preparation of a good business plan can be of very real and direct help to a new business.

Funding the business

The simplest application of the business plan to understand may be its role in 'selling' the business, in other words, putting across its merits. Potential investors in the business often need to be persuaded of its worth. A business gets financial support because the providers of that support think that they will themselves benefit from its provision. Banks seek to get paid for an overdraft or loan (interest) and grant-givers seek a contribution to the achievement of their aims (often improvements in the economy). They do not have to help a business. It is like a supplier-customer relationship: both have to benefit for it to work. In this case, however, the funds have to be provided some time before the benefits can be delivered, and the investors have to be able to trust the recipients to do that. In such circumstances, the business plan can be an essential tool for persuading investors that if they provide the funds then the business will be able to deliver the benefits and will survive long enough to do so.

The business plan is in effect the sales document for the business, and an understanding of the benefits the funders seek can be helpful in its preparation, for the following reasons:

- Government agencies want a lasting contribution to the economy, by means such as increased business and exports and more jobs. They may use terms such as 'viability', 'additionality' and 'admissibility', so that is what the plan or sales document has to convey.
- Banks want interest on their capital, and eventually their capital back, so they will want to see how the business will be able to afford this.
- Business angels and venture capitalists want to see that their investment in the business will increase in value and can ultimately be realised.

Whilst most business start-ups are small in terms of the finance required to get them off the ground, a small but growing number of businesses may be funded in part from either business angel money or money from venture capitalists. These larger-scale investors will put money into a business in exchange for an equity stake, and they expect to see a business plan to indicate what returns might be expected.

It is important, therefore, for the entrepreneur to understand just what an investor wants to see from a business plan and in essence there are four main features:

- why the proposition is unique
- how it will make money (cash and profits)
- how it will be delivered effectively
- why it is a suitable investment vehicle.

The plan needs to be realistic and believable, understated rather than overstated, and grounded in hard facts. There are two crucial requirements. The plan must show how the management will deliver and what milestones are involved. The relationship between management and investors is crucial and should be one of mutual interest and trust.

Managing the venture

> The plan is nothing: planning is everything.
> Napoleon

Advice about business plans may vary, but it is generally agreed that one of the most important uses of a business plan - or rather of the process of preparing it - is that it can help the business owner to see that all relevant aspects of the potential business are addressed and allowed for. Further, the subsequent monitoring of events against the projections can show where action is needed, if any, to keep the business on course. Can someone, in a new business, in a venture and in a field that is to some extent new or novel, allow for everything without thinking it through, and probably putting it on paper? Is he or she prepared to invest savings in the business without analysing the risk? Can he or she do that without going through the analysis needed for a plan? The answer to these questions may be 'yes', but it may require some thought. The process of producing the plan can assist in focusing strategic thinking; and the plan, when completed, can provide a benchmark against which to measure subsequent performance.

When a business plan does not help

From the above it will appear that if someone starting a business does not need to raise funds, and understands what he or she is about to do and the process of doing it, then a written business plan may not be needed. That at least is the view of some small business commentators, although it may be a controversial one. They believe that strategy is often in the head of the small business owner, and he or she may see no need to write it down. All that is required is that the person starting a business has some idea of the goal and the route to be taken to it. In these circumstances, asking an aspiring entrepreneur for a formal business plan can actually be detrimental to the business. In deference to the apparent expertise, and therefore presumed superior knowledge, of the person making the request for the plan, the emerging entrepreneur may try to produce one in line with a prescribed format. If he or she does not understand what a business plan means, or the logic behind the format, then the plan may be a bad one and the time wasted on it may be considerable.

Demystifying the business plan

> Whereas anyone can make a plan it takes something quite out of the ordinary to carry it out.
>
> General Sir Frederick Morgan

It may help to understand what a plan is and what it is not:

- *What a plan is*: Planning is an essential part of the process of getting positive results. It is the working out of how those results can best be obtained. It is a means of communicating your thoughts on this to others. The emphasis is on the plan being a vehicle to communicate your idea to others.
- *What it is not*: A plan is not holy or magical. It is a forecast. It should not be a pious hope or fixed and absolute.

Professional help: a word of caution

Why don't businesses get someone else to prepare plans for them? Others can help, but they should not do it all - unless the sole reason is to get a grant. Getting someone else to prepare it will not give the entrepreneur an insight into the issues to watch for or an understanding of what will make the business work best. Apart from possibly securing a grant or a loan, a plan prepared by someone else, without the owner-manager's involvement, probably at best gives the business nothing and could actually do harm (see Illustration 6.3). Generally, the process of preparing the plan is much more valuable than the plan itself. What, however, if all the business wants is a grant or a loan? The business should invest the minimum of resources required to produce a plan with acceptable content.

Summary

Everyone plans in some way or other, but not always on paper. Properly used, a business plan is a help, not an obstacle. A lot of nonsense has been talked about it and it has in some cases been promoted as the answer to almost every business ill. A formal written plan is not the essential starting point for every successful business but

---

ILLUSTRATION 6.3
The failed plan

Sue and Mary were two partners who started a clothing design business with financial backing from their parents, who put up their houses as security. Because they were too busy setting up the business, an adviser prepared most of their business plan for them, including the financial projections. The business looked attractive and the bank supported them. Probably because of their personal appeal and enthusiasm, they even won a small business start-up award. Unfortunately, however, they had never understood cashflow forecasts and the adviser's business plan only served to disguise this. Almost inevitably they lost control of their cashflow, and the business collapsed. The parents of one of them lost their house as a result.

there have nevertheless been many businesses that suffered because they were not planned properly, and plans are often essential for securing the support of others.

For those who do want to prepare a business plan, or at least to know what that might involve, a brief guide to compiling one is provided at the end of this chapter.

Financing the start-up

To some extent small business financing issues vary from country to country. In many former communist countries in Central and Eastern Europe, the banking system has been very undeveloped and unreliable and, especially when this is combined with the need to charge very high interest rates in times of high inflation, the result had been that businesses there rarely used bank financing. Even in Western Europe the use of bank financing varies from country to country. This is shown by a survey that produced the results shown in Table 6.7. The majority of small businesses however rely on internally generated funds to finance new activities. According to one survey[16] between 70 and 80 per cent use retained profit and cashflow to fund activities and it has been reported that in the UK a third of small businesses do not borrow at all from banks, another third regularly move into and out of an overdraft, and a third are consistent borrowers.[17]

In many countries there are claims that small businesses are particularly disadvantaged because it is harder for them to find appropriate sources of funding than it is elsewhere. In almost every country there are claims of disadvantage because finding funding is harder for small businesses than it is for bigger ones. There is no doubt that the difficulty of financing small businesses is one of the most frequently heard complaints. The reasons why there is this difficulty include those shown in Table 6.7.

- Small businesses are not a good risk. Suppliers of business finance, when they exist, want something in return for their money. Usually this is a financial return, either interest or dividends, plus some way eventually of getting back the initial investment or a multiple of it. If the finance sought is a development grant then returning it may not be an issue, but there will nevertheless still be an expectation that some benefits will be delivered, such as job creation or other economic benefits. In all cases, if the money is to be provided in advance of the returns, which is inevitably the case, then there needs to be some indication that the return will come and that the business will survive to deliver it. Although the often quoted very high failure rates for young businesses are not always what

Table 6.7 Debt structure by country (percentage of total borrowings)

Type of facility	Britain	France	Germany	Italy	Spain	Overall
Overdraft	42	23	17	32	14	29
Short-term loans (under two years)	9	18	20	20	45	20
Medium-term loans (two to five years)	13	32	20	15	19	18
Long-term loans (over five years)	19	11	36	19	20	21
Leasing and hire purchase	17	14	7	13	3	12
Total	100	100	100	100	100	100

Source: P. Burns and O. Whitehouse, *Financing Enterprise in Europe 2*, (Milton Keynes: 3i Enterprise Centre, 1995).

they seem to be (see later in this chapter), a significant proportion of small businesses do fail soon after start-up. Small businesses are therefore more vulnerable than larger ones, and will need to provide potential investors with some evidence that in their particular cases they will not fail.

- New small businesses do not have a track record. It is said that business financiers generally assess a business on three aspects: the management, the management and the management. For a new business with no trading history, and often with untried management, it is very difficult to provide satisfactory evidence that it will not only survive but will also do well enough to provide investors with the returns they seek.

- It is not cost effective to provide small amounts of money. Any commercial source of funds will want to check the business, its backers and its proposals before investing, and will want to monitor its investment on a regular basis. This is sometimes known as 'due diligence'. The cost of these checks will have to be recouped from any eventual income from the investments made. It is therefore not cost effective to check requests for small amounts of money, because the cost of checking will not be significantly lower than for larger amounts yet there will be less interest out of which to recoup it. (However some steps can be taken to reduce the costs of small amounts of assistance. One example in the United States is the Wells Fargo Bank, which has stopped monitoring many of the small businesses to which it has advanced loans because the cost of monitoring was more than the bad debts it incurred.)

- Small businesses lack security for loans. Small businesses often lack the collateral needed to secure loans, having few or no significant realisable assets in the business.

- Small businesses can be equity-averse. There is evidence that many owners of small businesses can be averse to sharing the equity, and therefore the ownership, of the businesses with anyone else. Investors, however, often like to take some equity because it gives them some control over their investments and an opportunity to make greater returns.

- Grants produce dependency. Because of their potential contribution to economic development, grants are sometimes considered to assist small business development and in particular to fill the so-called funding gaps that are perceived. Without care in their use, however, grants can easily freeze out whatever other sources of funding there are and can build a culture of dependency on 'free' money.

The sources of finance that are generally used by small businesses, especially when they are very small and are in the early stages of development, are the owners' own savings or the resources of family and friends. The result is that a typical pattern of small business funding can be as depicted in Figure 6.7, which is based on American experience. In recent years significant amount of early-stage funding has also been found from credit card funding, often using multiple credit cards.[18]

In the UK many start-up businesses require finance of between £5000 and £25,000, and that is typically found from the famous 4Fs – founder, family, friends and foolish strangers. This money is often supplemented by a term-based bank loan and overdraft facility, and perhaps a small loan or grant from a public body.

The next level of funding can be anything between £25,000 and £250,000. This could come from a large bank loan secured on an asset and perhaps making use of

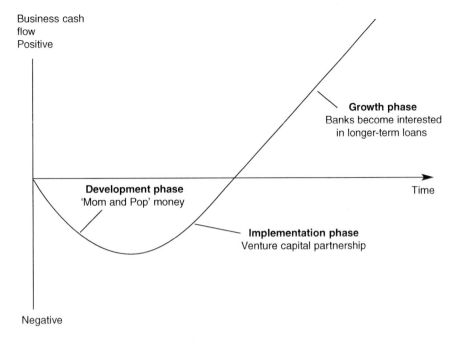

Figure 6.7 Early stage small business finance

Source: Based on author's personal contacts relaying US experience.

the Small Firms Loan Guarantee Scheme (SFLGS) to underwrite up to 75 per cent of the loan. Again an overdraft facility will most likely be provided. This could be supplemented by anything from £25,000 to £75,000 in the form of an equity stake from a business angel. It is however still the case that up to 80 per cent or more of funding at start-up does not involve an equity stake from an outside partner. The funding package still mainly remains personal funding and bank funding secured on an asset.

The third stage is the £250,000 to c.£1 million stage, where the funding is more likely to be of the package type, from a number of sources, perhaps combining personal, bank, public sector loans and grants and equity investment.

Beyond this stage is the use of large equity investment vehicles, often through a consortium of investors from different venture capital funds. In these cases the high risks of business failure are taken into account through the process of due diligence by investors seeking to manage risk.

The features of 'small' business entrepreneurs

In this chapter the point is made that in exploring the subject of enterprise the fundamental unit to consider should be the entrepreneur, not the firm. So far in this chapter, however, the process of business start-up has been perhaps related to the perspective of looking at the process and the generally held view of how that sequence should be considered. First, the idea, then the opportunity, followed by the business plan and the acquisition of the necessary resources manifests itself in small businesses. The process as outlined does need the entrepreneur and he or she can differ in his or her attitudes and actions from the owners and managers of larger businesses especially in the transition into entrepreneurship. Also the many different profiles of entrepreneurship need to be understood in terms of the distinctive elements in women-owned enterprises, ethnic businesses and social enterprise.

The transition out of employment

The pre-start-up stage of small business development has already been described, and it has its own particular issues to be understood. Despite the emphasis that has been put on the benefits of small business, the predictions of increasing numbers of people who will not have the option of lifetime employment, and the varieties of help available to ease the business start-up process, moving from employment to self-employment can be traumatic. Business planning can help to indicate the physical and financial provisions necessary to establish a business, but not the mental changes necessary.

Especially if the change is an enforced one, such as when it is occasioned by redundancy, the range of mental adjustments that have to be made can be considerable. One study identified six phases in the process of leaving employment in this way:[19]

Immobilisation	The change in status shocks and overwhelms to the extent that understanding, reasoning and planning are not possible.
Minimising change	The first reaction to change is to try to minimise it and to try to carry on as if it hadn't happened.
Depression	When the reality of change can no longer be avoided depression sets in; change has happened, but is neither desired nor understood.
Acceptance	Eventually however the reality of change is accepted, the turning point has been reached.
Testing	Previous attitudes and assumptions are relinquished; new concepts, methods and ways of coping are tested.
Meaning	As this progresses, stereotypes are abandoned, new possibilities emerge and success can be possible in the search for a new meaning.

If the process of leaving employment is continued into starting one's own business, then other changes have to be made. Lessem suggests that they include:[20]

Employee to employer	You become the giver, not just a receiver.
	You set the standards, not just adhere to them.
	You accept responsibility for other people's jobs.
	Money becomes important.
Salary to profit	You need to spend before you receive.
	Income becomes uncertain.
	Your family cannot be kept at arm's length.
Evaluator to decision-maker	You need to consider the options, evaluate them, and then make tough choices.

Specialist to generalist   You need to call on technical, marketing, financial,
                                administrative, people and management skills, and
                                possibly all of them from yourself.

Part-time businesses

Another category of small business with its own particular issues is the portfolio
or part-time business. This is not the same as portfolio entrepreneurship, in which
one entrepreneur simultaneously has a portfolio of businesses, each of which may
employ other people. Instead it is when one person engages in more than one activity, which may be a combination, or 'portfolio', of self-employment activities, or a
combination of part-time work and part-time self-employment.

Like other aspects of small business, portfolio or part-time businesses can seem
different when viewed from different perspectives. From the perspective of the business they can seem to be incomplete, and a less than whole-hearted dabbling in
business, which may be why business support agencies often refuse to support them.
Alternatively, from the point of view of the person concerned, they can be parts of
a complete life, and can both be complementary and together provide a balance
and diversity which might otherwise be lacking. Thus there are many artists who
teach part time and produce art part time, some of whom find that the combination of working with people and producing their own work is more rewarding than
doing either alone. Also, in rural areas, many people combine part-time farming
with another form of income generation, often a part-time business. Without the
part-time off-farm income they might have to give up farming completely, which
they do not want to do. Both these examples illustrate cases where small businesses
are part of the life of the owner, not the ends in themselves, and therefore need to
be understood from that perspective.

Identification with the business

Once the business has started, the founding entrepreneur is likely to identify with it
closely. No matter how dedicated he or she may be, a professional manager brought
in to run a business is unlikely to identify with that business to the extent many
business founders do. 'The business is the ego', as Gibb points out, 'and therefore
even objective criticism of the business is taken personally.'[21] The implications of
this include the facts that:

- A business 'consulting' approach, which attempts to analyse and list what is
  wrong with a business before suggesting corrective actions, will be rejected
  because it is perceived as a personal criticism. Instead, a 'counselling' approach,
  which seeks to help the owner to identify some of the issues, stands a better
  chance of being accepted and producing change.
- Perceived social status or acceptability may be linked to business success. Indications of business problems will therefore be played down, hidden or even denied,
  not just in public but also in private, in case they might have an impact on social
  status.

The values embodied in the business will often be those of the owner-founder and
can be revealed in the products or services supplied, growth orientation, quality

standards and employee relations. Where these values of the owner differ from those of business advisers, the input of the latter is likely to be rejected and, indeed, small business owners often lack the confidence to discuss problems with professionals. For these reasons, an owner's support network is likely to be based on personal friendships and contacts, rather than on the formal support network.

The influences on the small business owner

In seeking to understand the behaviour of a small business, what matters is often not so much the influences on the business as the influences on its owner. It is not always obvious however what these influences will be or what will be the interplay between the different influences. The relative strengths of the influences of different groups of people are indicated in a diagram produced by Gibb to indicate the layers of small business support networks (see Figure 6.8). One implication of this is that the closer, and more personal, layers may always have a much stronger influence than the outer, and more official, layers.

The totality of influences on a small business is often not appreciated. For instance, if assistance is made available to encourage small business development, it may be designed to add a positive influence, but it is unlikely to work if it does not outweigh other existing negative influences. If friends when consulted are negative in their advice then this will probably be far more influential than any positive input from government agencies. It can be helpful to portray the possible influences on a business as being of three types: those that may influence the business to be more competitive; those that may influence it to be less competitive; and those that may influence it to stay where it is. The latter can be the most powerful. Trying to make a business more competitive can be likened to trying to move a heavy weight uphill. Gravity may tend to drag it back, friction and inertia tend to keep it where it is, and only the push applied uphill will tend to move it in the desired direction.

It may also be relevant to compare the prime influences on, and sources of advice for, small businesses with those relating to big businesses. The most powerful influence in a small business often comes from the ownership. This is often one person

Figure 6.8 The layers of the small business support network

Source: A. A. Gibb, 'Towards the Building of Entrepreneurial Models of Support for Small Business', Paper presented at the 11th (UK) National Small Firms Policy and Research Conference, Cardiff, 1988, p.17.

or a small group who take an active role in the business. They are much more influential on the business than the shareholder owners of a bigger business who, because they are external and disparate, have less immediate impact. In contrast, however, suppliers and customers, although they are external, can have a much bigger influence on a small business than a big one. Some reasons for this are that a small business generally has less market influence in pricing or advertising than a big organisation, and is likely to have fewer customers and to work more closely with them. Other external influences on big businesses can include trades unions, public bodies and pressure groups. Small businesses, in contrast, are less likely to be unionised, are more likely to try to ignore regulations, and are a less rewarding target for campaigns.

Inside a small firm the owner-manager is often all-powerful. While in a big business the chief executive can be very powerful, he or she still has to answer to a chairman and board, and to work with professional senior managers who often have expert knowledge relevant to their particular functions. In big businesses a unionised workforce can have the influence of its combined strength exercised through the union structure. Also, in big businesses professional sources of advice are generally used. The small business owner-manager, in contrast, has fewer such sources of influence and will instead be more likely to listen to his or her own inclinations, to rely on his or her own experience and to seek advice, if necessary, from a network of personal contacts. The small business owner-manager, in comparison with the manager of a larger business, often has less general professionalism but more flexibility and knowledge of his or her particular niche.[22]

Women-owned businesses

A number of issues particular to women-owned small businesses, and are not therefore repeated here. It has however been suggested that, in general, because women's life experiences are very different from men's, they do business differently from men.[23] Men are said to aim for profit and growth whilst women focus on relationships and integrate business relationships into their lives. Others however do not feel that such conclusions can be drawn from the evidence.

The issue of whether or not female owned firms have different management styles from male-owned firms has moved the research focus on from broad descriptions of personal and business characteristics.[24] Additionally, as outlined by Carter and Shaw, recent research review papers have stressed very similar findings on the characteristics of female-owned enterprises.[25] These are:

- Women's experiences of business ownership are remarkably similar irrespective of international context.
- Women's businesses appear to take longer at the gestation stage.
- Female-owned businesses tend to be started by individuals rather than teams.
- They do not demonstrate the same level of business performance as businesses owned by men or co-owned by men and women.
- They exit at a faster rate.
- The presence of dependent children constrains entrepreneurial actions.
- Female-owned businesses use about one-third of the starting capital used by men.

The survival of female-owned businesses

There is, however, *prima facie* evidence that female-owned businesses do not survive as long as male-owned businesses, which might be because of the under-capitalisation of female firms at start-up. A recent British study investigated this issue but argued that research on the performance of women-owned firms is complicated by the different theoretical stances adopted by various authors; by the fact that only sole business owners are investigated; by assumptions that male and female entrepreneurs are homogeneous, and by conflicting ideas on whether biological differences between men and women cause them to adopt different socio-economic roles.[26] It was also pointed out that there were lots of contradictions in quantitative studies of the performance of male and female-owned firms and that some studies do not allow for the fact that women tend to set up businesses in sectors which traditionally have higher failure rates.

Ethnic businesses

Just as there are well-known and crucial questions relating to women-owned businesses, so too there can be particular issues in ethnic and minority community enterprise. The main theories concerning the basis of the disadvantage faced by the ethnic minority population fall under three main headings of human capital, social capital and economic capital. The human capital approach stresses the role of education, experience, job-related skills and training and language fluency.[27] The social capital approach emphasises the importance of networks and ties within the community, whereas economic capital explanations are based on the fact that many people in the ethnic minority community came from economically underdeveloped, war-torn, or former colonial countries. They did not arrive with much in the way of economic capital and have not really accumulated much after their arrival. However it has been argued that as time has gone by since the first arrival wave of ethnic minority immigrants into the UK, these groups have had the opportunity to some extent to accumulate both the human and economic capital to seek mainstream employment and possibly entrepreneurship (self-employment) as an effective form of upward social mobility.[28]

Academic spin-outs

The importance of knowledge transfer has been increasingly recognised by UK universities, particularly since the 1990s. The present interest in knowledge transfer has been linked to the enactment of the Bayh-Doyle Patent and Trademarks Amendment Act in the United States in 1980 which provided incentives for US universities to patent scientific breakthroughs with the help of Federal funding.[29] The desire to maximise the return on invention coming from universities is not a new one as the following comment from 1919 illustrates:

> the small band of British scientific men have made revolutionary discoveries in science yet the chief fruits of their work have been reaped by businesses in other countries, where industry and science have been in close touch with one another.[30]

The modern concern that the economic benefits of discoveries being made in the UK are only being felt in California has led various UK governments towards attempts to stimulate the commercialisation of university knowledge and technology. In 2001 the Government established the Higher Education Innovation Fund (HEIF) and this has continued into 2007, with the latest round of HEIF worth £238m over two years.[31]

The university knowledge transfer sector is commonly referred to as the 'third stream', following on from teaching and research. The 'third stream' agenda seeks to encourage four types of university activity:

- formation of university spin-out companies
- licensing of university technology to industry
- academic collaborations with industry and contract research
- knowledge-transfer activities including entrepreneurial teaching, student industry placements, encouragement of student start-up companies and university interaction with local SMEs.

The Sainsbury Report in 2007 found that there had been an impressive increase in the amount of knowledge transfer from British universities.[32] In 2005-6 over 1500 patent applications were filed and almost 2700 royalty licences executed, and 187 spin-out companies were formed by UK universities. There are currently over 9000 active patents held by UK higher education institutes, over half of which protect IP outside the UK.[33] Also in the three years from 2004 to 2007 a total of 25 UK university spin-outs were floated on the stock exchange and a further six university spin-outs, mostly from the biotechnology sector, had been acquired for £1.8 billion.[34] The Library House Report on university start-up companies found that UK start-ups are of similar quality to US university start-ups in terms of the venture investment they attract and their downstream durability.[35]

Spin-outs and the entrepreneur

In any potentially successful spin-out situation there are a number of key features that need to be in place or put in place if the venture is to succeed. These are:

- intellectual property and its evaluation
- management resources
- suitable capital structures.[36]

The majority of academic spin-outs are considered to be somewhat different from the typical small business start-up. In a spin-out, instead of just one entrepreneur, the management resources most frequently will comprise the founding scientist(s), a manager recruited to help at the initial stages and a representative from the university. Often the scientist will have little commercial acumen and will not be motivated primarily by any thoughts of financial return. The typical traits of the start-up entrepreneur (e.g. need for achievement, motivation, locus of control, risk taking) are not likely to be much in evidence. Instead the founder scientist will be product-driven, not business-driven. If it is to succeed however, a spin-out will need the focus of the research to be on commercial priorities rather than academic priorities: 'Most spin-outs, by definition, have unproven or immature business models, combined with inexperienced founders and incomplete management teams with little or no know-how from a commercial perspective.'[37]

If the spin-out is to work what usually has to happen is that an experienced CEO or chairperson needs to be brought in, usually by the investor(s). Here it is crucial that the scientist and the entrepreneur can understand each other's role in the development of the business and work together. This is the start of the build-up of the management team. Often the new CEO or chairperson will be by necessity someone with an extensive track record in several spin-outs. If the spin-out is to build to a major business then other common features will be introduced. They will take the form of the creation of a company board to act as a vehicle for stakeholders to provide guidance and expertise. Often this will mean one or two independent non-executive directors (NEDs) will be recruited alongside, if needed, an experienced marketing director and finance director.

Although easy to describe in terms of the process, this development of an executive team working alongside the scientist(s) and a board representing the interests of investors is not an easy situation and conflict of some kind is inevitable between the various stakeholders.

Business failure

According to Storey, the fundamental characteristic, other than size per se, which distinguishes small businesses from larger ones is their higher probability of ceasing to trade.[38] Ceasing to trade does not necessarily mean failure, but in at least some cases business are closed because they have failed to deliver the benefits their owners required. Why small businesses fail however is less easy to state with certainty, both because failure itself is not clearly defined and because the precise causes of it are hard to diagnose.

In theory post-mortems could be carried out on individual business failures but this is rarely done. What is more common is to ask small businesses which have not yet failed (and therefore still exist to be asked) to indicate what their problems are. This produces lists such as that in Table 6.8. But the problems are inevitably linked and it is hard to say which problems are causes and which are symptoms. For example, low turnover can mean it was a poor business opportunity, or poor selling skills.

Another approach is to look at the businesses which have failed and to try to establish correlations with other factors. Storey presents the following useful summary of factors which appear to influence the probability of failure of a business:[39]

- *Age*: As firms get older their chances of survival increase, and this is sometimes attributed to the liability of newness. There is a great deal to learn about running a business and expertise grows with time. Other researchers talk about the 'liability of adolescence'.[40] However most firms when they start have a stock of resources and energy, which sees them through their early months or years. When this stock is used up many firms will fail. Thereafter the usual liability of newness arguments apply.
- *Size*: Failure rates are inversely related to the size of the firm at start-up. It has been suggested that larger firms are less likely to fail because if a firm is relatively large at start-up then it will quickly benefit from economies of scale. Furthermore,

Table 6.8 Small business problems

Problems cited by a sample of 726 businesses	Proportion of all citings
Low turnover	31.8%
Regulation and paperwork	14.4%
Lack of skilled employees	10.9%
Cash flow/debtors	9.0%
Total tax burden	6.7%
Competition from big business	6.2%
Premises/rent/rates	2.9%
Internal management difficulties	1.9%
Access to finance	1.8%
High rates of pay	0.8%
Interest rates	0.4%
Shortage of supplies	0.4%
Inflation	0.1%
Other	11.0%
No response	1.8%
Total	100.0%

Source: Based on the Nat West/SBRT *Quarterly Survey of Small Business in Britain*, Vol. 17 (March 2001), p.20. Reproduced with permission from the Small Business Research Trust.

it will probably have sufficient financial resources to see it through its teething problems and it may also be in a good position to raise additional capital.

- *Sector*: Firms in different sectors of the economy exhibit different failure rates. In Britain, for example, the failure rates in manufacturing are greater than in various service sectors, although Storey notes that variations across sectors are not as great as economists would expect. Indeed, differences in failure rates within sectors are greater than across sectors.
- *Past performance*: Those firms which are able to grow are less likely to fail than those which maintain the status quo. Growth signifies development and learning, which are crucial ingredients for survival. Interestingly, survival rates are not linked to the rate of growth. Achieving some growth is the determining factor.

These are the more important factors connected with survival but there are others such as:

- *Ownership*: There is some evidence that the form of ownership can reverse the finding that, other things being equal, smaller firms have higher failure rates than larger firms. It has been argued that larger firms with less personal ownership will more readily leave an industry if demand is falling whilst smaller firms will struggle on. This might arise because larger firms have several plants and they may well close their non-economic ones promptly. In addition, larger firms may have multiple interests and they will divert their resources from an area of declining demand to more profitable sectors.
- *People/management*: It is likely that the kind of managers and non-managerial personnel who work in a firm will influence performance. At the very least there would seem to be a link between competence and success. Storey reviewed a number of studies which attempted to assess how work history with particular

reference to previous business ownership and management experience, education, family background and personal characteristics such as gender, age and ethnic background influenced business performance. He concluded that whilst there is much speculation on the impact of these variables, 'it is difficult to draw clear patterns from the results so far.'[41]

- *Location*: Research reveals that there are pro rata many more business failures in urban as opposed to rural areas in the United Kingdom. However, urban areas also have the greatest number of business formations, and since young firms are vulnerable it is not surprising that high start-up and failure rates are connected. Another finding in this area is that those locations which provide support for SMEs in the form of loans or business advice are likely to have lower failure rates than other areas. Support could be vital for success if crucial resources were being provided, but it might also be that the existence of support agencies is indicative of a supportive climate for business formation. Sometimes support is in essence a subsidy for the SME, and it is interesting to note that there is little association between subsidy and success. A subsidy is no substitute for a lack of ability or motivation.

- *Firm type*: The final issue investigated by Storey is the connection between the type of business and propensity to fail. Franchise businesses have been found to be less risky ventures than VAT-registered businesses in general, and limited companies are less risky than sole proprietorships or partnerships. Co-operatives however have similar failure rates to VAT-registered businesses in general.

- *Macro-economic conditions*: It would seem logical to expect that macro-economic conditions would have an influence on failure rates, and some studies have attempted to explore this. For instance the influence of interest rates, which might be thought to be a condition with a very direct influence, has been examined. In this case, however, the evidence seems to be inconclusive and it has been suggested that this may be because SMEs do not experience credit squeezes in the way that larger firms do. So too with other conditions and so, while there is some evidence that macro-economic conditions affect failure rates, overall it may not be as strong as might be expected.

An understanding of the connection between these factors and failures is very useful for economic planners, but few of the factors are amenable to manipulation by owner-managers. To identify things that owner-managers can do to minimise the chances of failure it is necessary to appreciate the everyday problems that they experience. An analysis carried out in Australia indicated that among those problems were:[42]

- Sales and marketing difficulties were the most common problems encountered. Owners had little appreciation of the marketing concept, had few marketing skills and considered that marketing was synonymous with public relations and advertising. More specifically they had considerable difficulty with market research and promotion. In view of the importance of developing markets for continued business success, interventions to increase marketing awareness and skill seem appropriate.

- The survey also found that the businesses were deficient in general management skills. They found it difficult to produce business plans and manage growth, but one particular area of concern at the time of the study was the need to have appropriate quality assurance systems. With respect to human resources the biggest problems by far concerned training and development, but recruitment and selection also created dilemmas. Some attempt was made to discover if this varied with the size of the firms but for all categories paying wages and benefits, obtaining good people and training were critical issues.

- Several firms were attempting to grow, and product development difficulties arose. A range of difficulties including pricing and promotion were raised but the biggest concern was over intellectual property protection. There is legislation in Australia for the protection of these rights but the high cost of the service means that many new product ideas are not exploited commercially. The firms also had difficulty in raising start-up finance and in managing cashflows.

Results from this study are largely in keeping with the findings from previous research in the UK and elsewhere, and provide a useful guideline for those whose aim is to support the owners and managers of small firms. It is possible to develop marketing, management, people and financial skills as well as the technical skills which are specific to a particular business enterprise, and improving competencies in these areas should improve business performance.

An understanding of the problems that small firms face and the environmental forces that put pressure on them is useful but problems can be overcome. Smallbone et al. argue that a key factor in survival is the adjustments that firms make to overcome their difficulties.[43] Adjustment requires diagnosis, decision making and action, and depends on effective change management. However, it can be argued that the very characteristics which are needed by entrepreneurs can prevent proper managerial adjustment. For example, high achievers can undertake high profile but unprofitable projects to feed their egos, independent entrepreneurs can reject the advice proffered by outsiders, and self-confidence can border on the delusional. These ingredients are present within many firms but failure does not always occur. However, small firms often do not have the financial resources to absorb environmental shocks, their owners and management teams are often deficient in managerial knowledge and skill, company structures are often weak, and the dominant position of the owner-manager means that any of his or her character flaws cannot easily be offset even by a strong management team. Consequently, any or all of these factors can prevent adjustment and trigger a decline and subsequent failure.

There is therefore no simple solution to the problem of failure. Enterprise does have an inherent element of risk, and failure might be reduced but will never be eliminated. The recipe for failure will vary from situation to situation but the ingredients for it are at least known. They are summarised by Burns in Figure 6.9.

Models of success and failure

Another factor which is only perceived when a business is considered from the point of view of its owner is that there can be different models of what constitutes business success or failure. When looking from a business perspective it might be thought that success or failure should be obvious, but a failure to appreciate the owner's perspective can lead to a misunderstanding of what is actually happening.

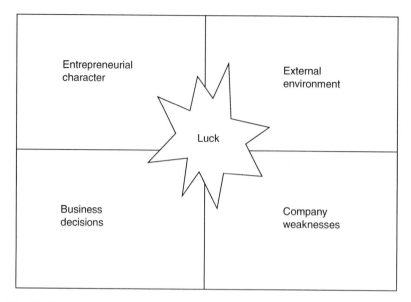

Figure 6.9 The ingredients of failure

Source: Slightly modified version of P. Burns, *Entrepreneurship and Small Business,* Second Edition, (Palgrave Macmillan, 2007), p. 329. Reproduced with the permission of Palgrave Macmillan.

What constitutes business success is an aspect of thinking about small business that has not been much commented upon, but which nevertheless probably affects many people's thinking on the subject. The model of success that people have in mind when they talk about small businesses and consider how well they are doing is likely to fall into one of two categories, depending on whether they are looking primarily at the business or at the person behind it:

- *The business professionals' model*: Many business professionals (which term could include the professional managers of larger businesses, as well as business commentators, advisers, institutional shareholders and academics) look primarily at the business and have as their model of the successful, or 'perfect', business one that is achieving its highest potential in terms of growth, market share, productivity, profitability, return on capital invested or other measures of the performance of the business itself. Professionals may not be conscious that they are adopting this model, because they may fail to see that there is an alternative but, whether it is consciously adopted or not, the result is that a business is often judged by how close it comes to what a 'perfect' business might do in particular circumstances. Small businesses often score badly in such comparisons.
- *The small business proprietors' model*: Many owner-managers of small businesses do not have the same model as the one just described. Their main concern is whether the business is supplying the benefits they want from it. These benefits are often associated with a lifestyle and an income level to maintain it. If, as already noted, that is achieved satisfactorily then there is no need to grow the business further. Business success for them is being able to reach a level of comfort ('satisficing') rather than achieving the business's maximum potential.

This difference of appreciation may be linked to the different ways in which persons making the appreciation are linked to the business concerned. Even if the 'professional' is employed as the chief executive of a business, he or she probably still sees the business simply as a business, and can compare it therefore with an ideal. It, and its success or failure, may be very important to such persons, but they can and do see those aspects of their life that are not involved with the business as being completely separate. For the small business owner, however, the business is such a crucial and integral part of his or her life that the business and non-business parts of life are not considered separately. Thus the business is seen in terms of life as a whole, including family life, and is subject to more than purely business considerations. The model of a 'perfect' business that the owner has is therefore one that best fits with desired personal goals and values. The stress of further business improvement may be too high a price to pay for a better business if it detracts from other aspects of life, and continuity of employment for well-known employees may be more important than increased efficiency.

The implications of having these two different models is that the professionals may see a business as under-performing in terms of its potential as a business, while the owner may see it as successful in terms of what he or she expects from it. In such cases the owners will not automatically share a professional's agenda of pursuing continued business improvement if that involves more effort but has no commensurate increase in benefits.[44]

That does not mean that there will not be scope for further improvement, but it will have to be improvement that also increases the returns desired by the owner from the business. Professionals advising small businesses will be puzzled and ineffective unless they understand this. There is room for their assistance, but they must look at the negative impact of business improvement on the owner's requirements as well as the positive impact, and ensure that the positive outweighs the negative. The professionals' business model assumes that growth in a business is almost always automatically positive in its effect; the owners' model may not share that assumption. This means that in the extreme case, which is not uncommon, it may be in the owner's perceived best interests to close the business completely, and that obviously does not lead to the business performing better. Such a closure is not a failure, but would be counted as such on the professionals' model.

One area where this lack of appreciation of two models is very significant is in business accounting. Traditional accounting focuses on money and therefore has a key place in businesses, because a lack of money is the final symptom of business failure. Thus it needs to be watched closely, and traditional accounting provides the methods of doing this. However, traditional accounting is often linked to business audits and then to reporting on business success or failure. Here the traditional approach is based on the professionals' model or at least on a similar way of thinking. It appraises a business in terms of its financial or other tangible returns and not on any other requirements a business owner may have. Provided that is realised and accepted by the appraisers no problems should emerge. Nevertheless, its very universality of usage means that the traditional method is usually taken as the whole picture, which leaves many business owners feeling that they may be perceived as having failed but not understanding why.

If this two-model concept is correct then it suggests that relatively low productivity in small businesses may sometimes be due, not to a failure of management, but to a different vision of management and of what management should be trying to achieve. The 'may' is because there is undoubtedly a considerable amount of management failure in small business, and by no means all of it is due just to differing agendas being pursued by the various stakeholders. It may be hard however initially to distinguish between 'satisficing' and a mere lack of competence.

Business survival rates

One of the main ways of estimating the success rates of new small business in the UK is the one-year and three-year survival rates based on Value Added Tax (VAT) registrations. The one-year survival rate in 2004 was 92 per cent, down slightly on the 2003 figure. The three-year survival rate was 71 per cent, also for 2004.[45] On this measure there has been a gradual increase in the one-year survival rates over the time period 1995-2004 and in the three-year rate since 1998.

Survival rates differ across the regions, with London having the lowest three-year survival rate at 67 per cent and Northern Ireland having the highest three-year survival rate at 79 per cent. The low survival rates in London and the high rates in Northern Ireland can be partly explained by differing start-up rates in both places. In London business start-up rates as a percentage of the population are high, leading to greater competition and making it more difficult for businesses to survive. In Northern Ireland business start-up rates are relatively low, leading to less competition and hence higher survival rates. Barclays Bank also produces small business survival rate surveys of its business customers, available online from the bank. The most recent survey for the second half of 2004 indicates increased levels of small business survival. The bank believes the improvement to be based on better use of business planning and better use of advice from business support organisations.

In the United States a study on survival and longevity in business covered some 212,182 new establishments tracked over the period March 1998 to March 2002.[46] The data collected across all sectors indicated the following survival rates:

81 per cent after one year
66 per cent after two years
56 per cent after three years
44 per cent after four years.

Interpreting closure

Statistics on registrations and de-registrations are considered to be the best official guide to the pattern of business start-ups and closures. They are an indicator of the level of entrepreneurship in the economy as manifested by actual business start-ups and of the health of the business population. As such they are used widely in regional and local economic planning. However they are based on VAT registrations and de-registrations. These do not necessarily represent business start-ups and terminations, and neither when a business terminates, is that necessarily a failure.

Just as caution is needed in evaluating the success of a small business, care must also be taken when considering so-called small business failures. Again the problem is one of interpretation and of a propensity to assume that a business closure and a business failure are the same thing.

Just as there are different models of what constitutes the success of a business, so too there are different models of what constitutes its failure. It may seem that the closure or termination of a business and its ceasing to exist as a trading entity is *prima facie* evidence that the business has failed, but that assumption presupposes that the purpose of the business could only be achieved if it continued to exist. That would be the case if the purpose of the business was to maximise the returns from its activities but would not necessarily be so if its owner had other aims in mind for it. If for instance a business is started to provide an income for someone until a pre-planned retirement, and if it does so and is then closed when that retirement time arrives, then the business will both have succeeded in its purpose and been closed. Alternatively, if a business is started as an investment and is then sold for a profit, but the new owner transfers the process to an existing business and closes down the bought business, then again the business has achieved its purpose despite being closed.

It is, however, relevant to point out here that instances of business closure are often wrongly described as business failure. Statistics on business failure should therefore be treated warily. The corollary of this is that there are some businesses that do fail, as least in terms of failing to meet their owner-founder's objectives for them, but which don't close. Such a business may still be kept in existence, for instance, either for possible revival in the future, or because it continues to fulfil at least some needs, or to deliver at least some benefit to its owner. The benefit may only be a sop to the owner's pride, but it may be enough to prevent the termination of the business's existence. In such cases, business failure may not lead automatically to business closure.

Conclusions

The process of starting a business is not a simple one-stage process. If the starting point is a culture which encourages, or at least tolerates entrepreneurship, then the successive stages variously involve an inclination to start a business, an opportunity and an idea, some assessment of feasibility, and a search for resources and/or the funding to pay for them. Only then can the business start, and success is not guaranteed. Starting a business is risky and businesses do fail, especially at an early stage. Much depends on the entrepreneur, but if the issues that he or she faces are understood, the risks can be minimised.

THE KEY POINTS OF CHAPTER 6

- Between its conception and its eventual termination a business can go through many stages, although there are no clear boundaries between the different stages.
- Among the first requirements for the development of a business are the sort of culture that encourages, or at least tolerates, business formation and then a source of business ideas.

- Another requirement is the entrepreneur who can both see an opportunity in an idea and is willing to try to turn it into reality.

- The start-up stage is where the business itself is formed. Often a business plan will be helpful either to help to plan to deal with likely funders or to persuade backers that the business is worthy of support, but sometimes a plan may not be needed. Finding sufficient funding is likely to be crucial.

- Just as it is wrong to assume that small businesses will behave and respond like big businesses, so too is it wrong to assume that all small businesses are alike. Small businesses in different sectors have their own particular characteristics, as do businesses of different ages and different sizes.

- The entrepreneurs behind small businesses can also differ in both their profile and their reasons for going into business. Also the influences on a small business are often much clearer if viewed with a focus on the owner rather than on the business.

- It is not always obvious, however, who or what will influence a small business or what the interplay will be between different influences. Often at an early stage close families and friends can have more influence than professional business advisers. As well as positive and negative influences on a business, there will also be influences that encourage a business not to change. A positive influence may therefore have no effect if there is a stronger contrary influence.

- In considering small business success there are two main models. Many business professionals have as their model of business success one that involves the business achieving its highest potential. On the other hand, many small business owners have as their main concern whether the business is supplying the benefits they want from it. Care must also be taken when considering business failures and closures because some failed businesses do not close and some businesses close which have not failed.

A BUSINESS PLAN

Why are you preparing a business plan? Normally there are two purposes which a business plan might serve:

- *To assess feasibility and/or aid control*: Are you checking to see whether your idea might work or how it might be made to work? A business plan can serve as your implementation plan, to help you prepare for and implement the process of creating a viable business. If you are considering feasibility and methods then there are two conflicting pieces of advice:
  - The military maxim that time spent on reconnaissance is seldom wasted.
  - The rock climbers' approach that studying a hard climb for too long before you climb may put you off. There comes a time when you must either start or go away.

into departments as well as targets.

- *To communicate*: Are you trying to communicate your idea to others? A plan can serve as a sales document, for instance to help to persuade a bank or other funder to support your venture. If so then you should try to ensure that it addresses any queries they might have and indicates how they should benefit from supporting your venture. Don't tell them that the plan has been written as a sales brochure just to persuade them, but make it persuasive nevertheless.

For either use a business plan is, in effect, the answers to a series of questions. Here are some of the usual ones:

The executive summary: What does the plan say?
This is the bit that people will read first to get an introduction to your venture. Some people may then read the rest of the plan and some may look at parts of the plan to get more detail on specific issues. Many however will not get past the executive summary, so make sure that it provides a good clear summary of the key points.

Write the summary last, so that it does reflect what is in the plan. Make sure that it highlights your aim and objectives and the key issues in realising them.

> Tip: If the plan is to communicate your vision, think about the gliding analogy. Why should someone think that you will be able to launch and then to fly your glider? Demonstrate that you should be able both to get your venture started and then to keep it going once it is launched. If you can't keep it going then it won't survive to deliver the benefits offered.

Introduction to the business: What is the business about?
- *Who is involved?* Give relevant information and stress anything which demonstrates your competence to run the business: in other words, establish your credentials. If other key persons are involved, give their details also.
- *What were the origins of the idea?* Describe how your business idea came about, for example from a hobby, previous work experience, replicated from elsewhere.
- *What is the basic proposal?* Describe clearly but briefly what the business is: that is, the product or service; manufacture, wholesale or retail; customer groups.
- *How was it developed?* What have you done to develop the idea to the stage where it might be a viable business proposal?
- *What form will the business take?* Indicate whether you will be a sole trader, partnership or limited company. Also indicate if there are any special features such as joint venture, franchise or licence arrangements. Give details.
- *What is the present position?* How far have you got in developing your idea?
- *What is your aim now?* What do you now want to do?

> Tip: A business is not an end in itself – but a means to an end. So why are you proposing to start or grow this business?

The product(s) or service(s): What do you propose to offer?

Expand upon the initial product/service description you provided in the introduction:

- What is the product or service which you propose to offer and what will be its key features? (If it is a technically complex product, confine details to an appendix and concentrate only on the main features.)
- How have you developed it and what have you done to test that it works? What is the present stage of development, e.g. R&D, prototype, production model?
- How will you produce or supply it? What you will manufacture, assemble or buy in?
- What future developments do you plan to ensure the longer-term viability of the business, such as new products or improvements?

The market: How will your offering be received?

The details given here form the basis of your expected sales and crucially affect the credibility of your business proposition. Do not assume, therefore, that your reader knows as much about the market as you do. Include the following:

- *What is the size and growth rate of the market?* If possible, indicate the value, volume, and number of customers for the product/service you offer and how the market is changing.
- *Where is the market?* Indicate the geographical areas where you intend to sell at first and in the future.
- *What is the customer profile?* Describe the typical person who will buy from you (age, sex, income group) or, if you are selling to an organisation (such as a manufacturer or wholesaler), is it to be large/small, high quality/low quality, specialist/general?
- *What is the competition?* Who will be competing against you?
- *What will be your competitive edge?* Explain why your product/service will be bought instead of your competitors' (for instance for its quality, design, packaging, after-sales service, price or your contacts). Have you got patent, copyright or trademark protection?
- *What is the evidence that there will be a demand for your offering?* Provide as much evidence as possible to indicate you will be able to sell your product/service (such as the findings of any market research or any invoices, orders or letters of intent). If you have carried out market research, put the finer details of method, questionnaires etc. into an appendix.

> Tip: While it is true that some new products create their own market (there was no significant demand for mobile phones until they were available), funders will like to see evidence that you should be able to sell what you propose to supply, and sell it at an acceptable price. Also remember that your competition may not be other suppliers of the same product or service but suppliers of other products or services which are after the same customer spend.

Costing, pricing and sales forecasts

Will you be able to sell enough?

- *Costing*: What will it cost you to provide your product/service?

  - Show how you have arrived at the estimates of material, labour and overhead costs for each of your products/services.
  - Indicate the level of sales (in value/volume) needed to break even.

- *Pricing*: What price are you going to put on your product or service?

  - Explain how you have arrived at the price for your product/service and relate the price to the cost of providing the product/service.
  - Indicate the expected mark-ups at each stage in the subsequent distribution chain so that the price to the final customer is known.

- *Sales forecast*: How much do you think you will sell?

Based on market and price analysis above, you may now be able to draw up forecasts of sales for each product/service you are supplying. These should usually be given monthly by value and volume where appropriate. (If you have difficulty in arriving at sales figures, it is sometimes useful to ask yourself: 'What sales do I need to achieve a break-even situation?' – and judge how much better or worse than that level you expect lo perform/achieve.)

Tip: Don't confuse cost and price. If you are buying something then the cost to you is the price you have to pay. If however you are selling something then the price is what you ask for it and the cost is what you have had to expend to provide it. If the price is more than the cost you make a profit, if it is less you make a loss and, if that continues, you go out of business.

Marketing plan

How will you get customers to buy your product or service?

- How you will you get your product to the final customer (for instance through wholesaler to retailer, direct to retailer, or mail order)?

- Who will do the selling and what promotional activity will be needed to support sales (for instance media advertising, introductory offers, mail shots and follow-up)?

- What will your promotion and distribution cost you?

Manufacturing plan

How will you produce your product/service?

The process: What is the process involved? Describe the production process in outline (if it is not obvious to a layman) and specify proposed quantities on a (monthly) forecast basis. Make clear whether:

- you will make to order only or for stock (if for stock, at what levels?)
- work will be subcontracted or bought in.

Capital equipment: What equipment will you need? List all the items of plant and machinery, fixtures and fittings, office equipment etc. that you need and include:

- description
- purpose
- cost (and whether purchased or leased), and

Premises: What space will you need? Include the following:

- location, size and layout
- build, purchase or rent
- lease arrangements
- circumstances as to planning permission/building control
- costs: start-up and continuing.

Organisation and staffing

What people do you need and how will the business be managed?
Organisation: How will the venture be run? How will it be:

- established
- owned
- directed
- advised
- organised
- managed?

Staffing: How will the venture be staffed?

- Show how many people you intend to employ, when, and how much you will pay them.
- Highlight any particular skills that are needed and how you intend to recruit them, whether management or operative.
- A salary and wages budget should also be prepared for the financial forecasts.

> Tip: You need to show that you have, or will be able to access or hire, the skills you need to launch the business and to keep it going once it is launched.

Financial forecasts: Will it fly?

You should now be in a position to put together the financial aspects of all this and to see if can both be launched and then keep going.

Launching the business

What resources will you need to launch the venture and how much will they cost? You might need:

- Premises, and fitting out
- equipment

- materials
- prototypes and testing
- promotion and advertising
- staff recruitment and training
- early operations until you break even.

And where will you get the money for this?

- your own investment?
- other investments?
- loans?
- overdraft?

Keeping the business going

Once it is launched will the venture generate enough income to cover its costs? What will your costs be?

Direct costs: Materials? Direct labour?	*Overhead costs*: Management? Administration? Office costs? Computers, phones, stationery etc? Advertising and selling? Cleaning and maintenance? Insurance? Rent and rates? Interest – the cost of borrowing money? Depreciation?

What will the business earn? You should assess this from your sales forecast.

Putting it all together

Support this analysis with financial projections to show the overall result:

- *Cash flow*: to see if you will run out of money.
- *Profit and loss*: to establish how much profit you should make.
- *Balance sheet*: to see what shape the business will be in.

> Tip: Financial projections may seem tiresome and boring – until you can't persuade someone to fund you or you find that the business has run out of money. Then you discover why they matter.

Other points

Although not always included in business plan formats, the following can also help to persuade people to support you.

Risk assessment: What are the risks? There will be risks associated with your business: so state what they are and what you will do to minimise them.

> Tip: Being honest about the risks will be much more convincing than trying to pretend there are no dangers ahead.

Projected benefits: What are the rewards that the business should deliver?

> Tip: Projected benefits don't often feature on official business plan formats, but this is where you try to persuade people to help you by indicating what is going to be in it for them.

QUESTIONS, ESSAY AND DISCUSSION TOPICS

- Why can the stage model not be used to predict what will happen next to a small business?
- What are the key features to examine when evaluating a business opportunity?
- Producing a business plan is the key to a small business's success. Discuss.
- Small businesses start-ups are so varied that it is not practical to have a small business policy. Discuss.
- What are the main sources of funding available to the business start-up? How can they be classified?
- What are the main categorisations of small business types? Are these categorisations useful?
- Are businesses owned by women or by individuals from ethnic minorities at a disadvantage compared with those owned by indigenous males, and what if any could be done to help them?
- Conduct research into business failure rate and survival rate statistics. What are the key variables that affect a small business's chances of surviving three years or more?

Suggestions for further reading

P. Burns, *Entrepreneurship and Small Business*, 2nd edn (Basingstoke: Palgrave, 2007).
S. Carter and D. Jones-Evans (eds), *Enterprise and Small Business*, 2nd edn (FT/Prentice Hall, 2006).
D. A. Kirby, *Entrepreneurship* (McGraw-Hill, 2003).
D. Rae, *Entrepreneurship from Opportunity to Action* (Basingstoke: Palgrave, 2007).
D. Storey, *Understanding the Small Business Sector* (London: Routledge, 1994).

References

1. S. Shane, *A General Theory of Entrepreneurship* (Cheltenham: Edward Elgar, 2003), pp. 10–11.
2. W. K. Bolton and J. L. Thompson, *Entrepreneurs: Talent, Temperament, Technique,* (Oxford: Butterworth Heinemann, 2000).
3. L. Klapper, R. Amit, M. Guillen, and J. Quesada 'Entrepreneurship and Firm Formation Across Countries', *World Bank Entrepreneurship Survey,* 2007. p. 16.
4. P. Wickham, *Strategic Entrepreneurship,* 4th edn (FT/Prentice Hall, 2006).
5. Bolton and Thompson, op. cit. (2000).
6. P. Drucker, *Innovation and Entrepreneurship* (London: Heinemann, 1985), p. 132.
7. HM Treasury News Release, 23 June 2000.
8. S. Birley, 'The Start-Up', in *Small Business and Entrepreneurship,* edited by P. Burns and J. Dewhurst (Basingstoke: Macmillan (now Palgrave Macmillan), 1989), p. 16.
9. S. Birley and S. Cromie, 'Social Networks and Entrepreneurship in Northern Ireland', Paper presented at the Enterprise in Action Conference, Belfast, September 1988.
10. Forum of Private Business, 'The Internal and External Problems That Face Small Businesses', Paper presented at the Sixteenth ISBC Annual Conference, October 1989, p. 6.
11. M. Scott and R. Bruce, 'Five Stages of Growth In Small Business', *Long Range Planning,* 20(3) (1987), pp. 45–52, at p. 49.
12. Forum of Private Business, op. cit, p. 6.
13. S. Birley, 'The Way Ahead for Local Enterprise Centres', Presentation at Enniskillen, Northern Ireland, January 1988.
14. L. Klapper, R. Amit, M. Guillen and J. M. Quesada, 'Entrepreneurship and Firm Formation Across Counties', World Bank Group Entrepreneurship Survey, 2007.
15. J. Brander, J. K. Hendricks, R. Amit and D. Whistler, 'The Engine of Growth Hypothesis: On the relationship between firm size and and employment growth.' Working Paper; University of British Columbia, 1998.
16. Bank of England, *Finance for Small Firms, Third Report,* January 1998.
17. P. Burns, *Entrepreneurship and Small Business* (Basingstoke: Palgrave, 2007).
18. T. Ashbrook, *The Leap: A Memoir of Love and Madness in the Internet Gold Rush* (Boston: Houghton and Mifflin, 2001).
19. J. Hayes and P. Nutman, *Understanding the Unemployed* (London: Tavistock, 1981).
20. R. Lessem, 'Getting into Self Employment', *Management Education and Development,* Spring (1984), pp. 44.
21. Gibb (1988), op. cit., p. 14.
22. For a discussion on the various sources of influence on organisations, see H. Mintzberg, *Power In and Around Organisations* (Englewood Cliffs, NJ: Prentice-Hall, 1983), pp. 32–46.
23. C. G. Brush, S. Marlow and A. Strange, 'Female Entrepreneurs: Success by Whose Standards?' in *Women in Management: A Developing Presence,* edited by M Taunton (London: Routledge, 1994).
24. S. Carter, S. Anderson, and E. Shaw, 'Women's Business Ownership: A Review of the Academic, Popular and Internet Literature', London: Small Business Service Research Report, RR002/01, 2001.
25. S. Carter and E. Shaw, 'Women's Business Ownership: Recent Research and Policy Developments' Report to the Small Business Service, November 2006. p. 5–8.
26. E. Chell and S. Baines, 'Does Gender Affect Business Performance? A Study of Microbusinesses In Business Services In the UK', *Entrepreneurship and Regional Development,* 10 (1998), pp. 117–35.
27. G. Borjas, 'Ethnicity, Neighbourhoods and Human Capital Externalities', *American Economic Review,* 85 (1995), pp. 365–90.
28. Y. Li., 'Assessing Data Needs and Gaps for Studying Ethnic Entrepreneurship in Britain', URN 07/152, ESRC/CRE/DTI/EMDA, 2007
29. E. M. Rogers, Y. Yin, and J. Hoffman, 'Assessing the Effectiveness of Technology Transfer Offices at U.S. Research Universities', *The Journal of the Association of University Technology Managers,* 12 (2000), p. 47–80.
30. A. Marshall (Economist) *Industry and Trade* (1919).
31. The Library House, *Spinning Out Quality: University Spin-out Companies in the UK* (London, 2007).
32. Lord Sainsbury of Turville, *The Race to the Top: A Review of the Government's Science and Innovation Policies* (HM Treasury, 2007).

33. Higher Education Funding Council for England (HEFCE), *Higher Education and Community Interaction Survey, 2007.*
34. Lord Sainsbury, op. cit.
35. The Library House, op.cit, p. 5.
36. Quester, 'A Quester Commentary' p. 6, October 2006 (www.quester.co.uk).
37. Ibid., p. 9.
38. D. Storey, *Understanding the Small Business Sector* (London: Routledge, 1994), p. 78.
39. Ibid., pp. 91–104.
40. T. Mahmood, 'Survival of Newly Founded Business: A Log-Logistic Model Approach, *Small Business Economics,* 14 (2000), pp. 223–37, at 313.
41. Storey, op. cit., p. 100.
42. X. Huang and A. Brown, 'An Analysis and Classification of Problems In Small Business', *International Small Business Journal,* 18 (1999), pp. 73–85.
43. D. Smallbone, D. North and R. Leigh, *Managing Change for Growth and Survival: A Study of Mature Manufacturing Firms in London During the 1980s,* Working paper No. 3 (London: Middlesex Polytechnic, Planning Research Centre, 1992).
44. For a discussion on the overlap between personal goals and business goals in SMEs, see R. Goffee and R. Scase, *Corporate Realities* (London: Routledge, 1995), pp. 1–21.
45. DTI 'Survival Rates of VAT-Registered Enterprises, 1995–2004: Key Results', URN 07/963.
46. A. E. Knaup, 'Survival and longevity in Business Employment Dynamics data', *Monthly Labour Review,* May (2005).

CONTENTS

CASE INSIGHTS

CASES WITH QUESTIONS

LEARNING OUTCOMES

By the end of this chapter you should be able to:
- Explain what makes an individual creative;

- Assess your own aptitude to be creative;
- Describe and recognise barriers to creativity;
- Describe the creative process;
- Use a range of techniques to help generate new ideas;
- Use a range of techniques to help spot commercial opportunities;
- Generate new business ideas based on these opportunities;
- Describe the business opportunities created by the internet;
- Safeguard new business ideas.

Creativity

Creativity is at the core of any true entrepreneur. Creativity is important in coming up with completely new ways of doing things, rather than looking for adaptive, incremental change. Parkhurst (1999) defined it as 'the ability or quality displayed when solving hitherto unsolved problems, when developing original and novel solutions to problems others have solved differently, or when developing original and novel (at least to its originator) products'. For the entrepreneur, the focus for their creativity is commercial opportunity leading to new products, services, processes or marketing approaches. It has been estimated that for every eleven ideas that enter the new product development process, only one new product will be successfully launched (Page, 1993). So new ideas are at a premium and it is a numbers game. The more you generate, the more are likely to see the light of day commercially. So how can you stimulate creativity?

> *When you don't have a lot of money you've got to be creative about how you go about things ... There's going to be a whole new range of 'clever companies' that set up because creativity is now king, not cash.*
>
> Will King, founder of King of Shaves,
> *RealBusiness* 1 July 2009

We are now starting to understand how the creative process works on an individual level. The brain has two sides that operate in quite different ways. The left side performs rational, logical functions. It tends to be verbal and analytic, operating in a linked, linear sequence (called logical or vertical thinking). The right side operates intuitive and non-rational modes of thought. It is non-verbal, linking images together to get a holistic perspective (called creative or lateral thinking). A person uses both sides, shifting naturally from one to the other. However, the right side is the creative side. Creative innovation is, therefore, primarily a right brain activity whilst adaptive innovation is a left brain activity.

Left brain thinkers tend to be rational, logical, analytical and sequential in their approach to problem-solving. Right brain thinkers are more intuitive, value-based and non-linear in their approach. The cognitive styles are also reflected in the preferred work styles with left brain thinkers preferring to work alone, learn about

Logical		**Creative**
Seeks answers		Seeks questions
Converges		Diverges
Asserts best or right view		Explores different views, seeks insights
Uses existing structure		Restructures
Says when an idea will not work		Seeks ways an idea might help
Uses logical steps		Welcomes discontinuous leaps
Concentrates on what is relevant		Welcomes chance intrusions
Closed		Open-ended

Figure 7.1 Dimensions of creative (lateral) vs logical (vertical) thinking

things rather than experience them and having the ability or preference to make quick decisions. By way of contrast, right brain thinkers prefer working in groups, experiencing things (for example, learning by doing) and generating lots of options in preference to focusing on making a speedy decision. People have a preference for one or other approach, but can and do switch between them for different tasks and in different contexts.

Normally the two halves of the brain complement each other, but many factors, not least our education, tend to encourage development of left brain activity – logic. Kirby (2003) speculates that this may well explain why so many successful entrepreneurs appear not to have succeeded in the formal education system. He argues that entrepreneurs are right brain dominant. But he goes even further by speculating that there may be a link between this and dyslexia, observing that many entrepreneurs are dyslexic and language skills are left brain activities. This is an interesting but unproved hypothesis.

However, the point is that most people need to encourage and develop right brain activity if they wish to be creative. And this is possible, with training. To overcome the habit of logic you need to deliberately set aside this ingrained way of thinking. Creative or lateral thinking is different in a number of dimensions to logical or vertical thinking. It is imaginative, emotional, and often results in more than one solution. Edward de Bono (1971) set out some of the dimensions of difference. Figure 7.1 is based on his work.

One important aspect of high level creativity is the ability to recognise relationships among objects, processes, cause and effect, people and so on that others do not see, searching for different, unorthodox relationships that can be replicated in a different context. These relationships can lead to new ideas, products or services. So, the inconvenience of mixing different drinks to form a cocktail led to the (obvious?) idea of selling them ready mixed. James Dyson was able to see that a cyclone system for separating paint particles could be used (less obviously?) to develop a better vacuum cleaner; doctors at Great Ormond Street Hospital were able to see that the efficiency of Formula 1 pit stops could help them to improve patient care. Most creativity skills can be practised and enhanced, but this particular skill is probably the most difficult to encourage. Majaro (1992) believes that, while stereotyping is to be avoided, creative types do exhibit some similar characteristics:

- *Conceptual fluency* They are able to produce many ideas.
- *Mental flexibility* They are adept at lateral thinking.
- *Originality* They produce atypical responses to problems.

- *Suspension of judgement* They do not analyse too quickly.
- *Impulsive* They act impulsively on an idea, expressing their 'gut-feel'.
- *Anti-authority* They are always willing to challenge authority.
- *Tolerance* They have a high tolerance threshold towards the ideas of others.

Creativity test

Find out how creative you are by going to www.creax.com/csa and answering the 40 questions in the creativity quiz. It is free and the analysis assesses you on eight dimensions against answers from others with similar backgrounds. The dimensions are:

- **Abstraction** – the ability to apply abstract concepts/ideas.
- **Connection** – the ability to make connections between things that do not appear connected.
- **Perspective** – the ability to shift one's perspective on a situation in terms of space, time and other people.
- **Curiosity** – the desire to change or improve things that others see as normal.
- **Boldness** – the confidence to push boundaries beyond accepted conventions. Also the ability to eliminate the fear of what others might think of you.
- **Paradox** – the ability to simultaneously accept and work with statements that are contradictory.
- **Complexity** – the ability to carry large quantities of information and the capacity to manipulate and manage the relationships between such information.
- **Persistence** – the ability to force oneself to keep trying to find more and stronger solutions even when good ones have already been generated.

Mintzberg (1976) makes the interesting suggestion that the very logical activity of planning is essentially a left brain activity whilst the implementation of the plan, that is the act of management, is a right brain activity. He bases this claim on the observation that managers split their attention between a number of different tasks, preferring to talk briefly to people rather than to write and reading non-verbal as well as verbal aspects of the interaction, take a holistic view of the situation and rely on intuition. He argues that truly effective managers are those that can harness both sides of the brain.

Barriers to creativity

People are inherently creative, but most of us stifle it because we find change threatening. We all create rituals and routines that we feel comfortable with and these normally mitigate against questioning the status quo. These routines help us through the day. Being creative often takes people outside of their 'comfort-zone'. They are uneasy with it. Sometimes blocks and barriers need to be attacked. Von Oech (1998) focuses on the blocks to individual creativity. He lists ten that are critical:

> *We learned the importance of ignoring conventional wisdom … It's fun to do things that people don't think are possible or likely. It's also exciting to achieve the unexpected.*
>
> Michael Dell (1999)

1. The fallacy that there is only one correct solution to a problem.
2. The fallacy that logic is important in creativity.
3. The tendency to be practical.
4. The tendency to follow established rules unquestioningly.
5. The tendency to avoid ambiguity in viewing a situation.
6. The tendency to assign blame for failure.
7. The unwillingness to recognise the creative power of play.
8. The tendency to think too narrowly and with too much focus.
9. The unwillingness to think unconventionally because of the fear of appearing foolish.
10. The lack of belief that you can be creative.

Realising these blocks may exist in yourself can be the first step to dismantling them. It is never easy to change an inherent tendency, but it can be done and the techniques in the next section can help.

The creative process

The creative process has four commonly agreed phases, shown in Figure 7.2. There is wide agreement on their general nature and the relationship between them, although they are referred to by a variety of names (de Bono, 1995).

Phase 1: Generating knowledge and awareness

A prerequisite to all creative processes is the generation of awareness of different ideas and ways of doing things through reading and travelling widely, talking with different people with different views about the world. You may, for example, see demands being met in one country that are not met in others. You may read about products made in one country that are not yet available in another. This is, of course, to be placed in the context of the issue being addressed. So, in these examples of demand and supply, the opportunities you have spotted in other countries are very relevant to your desire to set up your own business. It is not just about being aware of different approaches or perspectives on the problem, but also

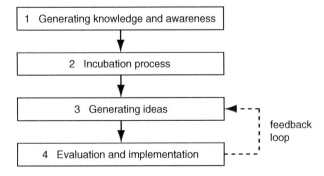

Figure 7.2 The creative process

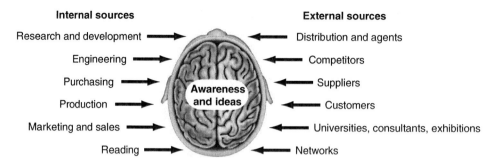

Figure 7.3   Sources of awareness and ideas

Travelling, reading and an open mind are of the utmost importance to the creative processes

about getting the brain to accept that there are different ways of doing things – developing both an open and an enquiring mind. Many people almost have to give themselves permission to be creative – to think the unthinkable. Carrying a notebook and recording ideas and information can be useful. So too can developing a small library. Look how far Lego, LG and Hallmark went in order to expose their staff to new ideas (p. 78). Some sources of commercial new ideas are shown in Figure 7.3.

Phase 2: Incubation process

People need time to mull over the tremendous amounts of information they generate in Phase 1. This incubation period happens when people are engaged in other activities (the best are those instinctive activities that do not require left brain dominance) and they can let their subconscious mind work on the problem. Interestingly, sleep happens when the left brain gets tired or bored and during this time the right brain has dominance. Incubation therefore often needs sleep. The old adage, 'sleep on the problem', has its origins in an understanding of how the brain works. It is little wonder that so many people have creative ideas when they are asleep – the problem is trying to remember them. Creativity, therefore, can take time and needs 'sleeping on'.

Ideas happen unexpectedly, even while you are asleep

Phase 3: Generating ideas

Ideas can come up unexpectedly during the incubation period, sometimes while you are asleep. However, often they need encouragement and there are a number of techniques that can help to encourage idea generation. Some of the more widely used ones are explained in the next section.

Phase 4: Evaluation and implementation

The next stage is to select which ideas are the most promising. This is the convergent stage of the process involving discussion and analysis, possibly voting. Some ideas generated in Phase 3 might be easy to discard because they are unrealistic but others might need to be worked up or modified before they can be properly evaluated. Sometimes a return to Phase 3 is required to do this.

Case insight   Martin Dix and Current Cost

The big idea came to Martin Dix, founder of Current Cost, on New Years Day 2004 but it was not until 2007 that he started selling it. The idea was a home electricity meter which showed the £ value of electricity being consumed at any point in time and was cheap enough for energy companies to give to customers. He started out by confirming that most people did not know the annual electricity running cost for ordinary household appliances. He then started to research the product, going to China to visit potential manufacturers and investigate logistics. Despite interest from UK government offices Martin was finding it impossible

➡

to get financial backing for the idea. Nevertheless he went back to China in 2005 to set up manufacturing partners. It was not until 2006 that he was able to find two partners, who put in £5000 each.

The business really took off in 2007 when OFGEM, Scottish and Southern Electricity gave Current Cost £250 000 to provide them with 5000 meters for a year-long trial. The results were so startlingly successful that four months later they started ordering more as part of one of their regular tariffs. A year later, in 2008 another electricity company, Eon, also started offering Current Cost meters. A new product had been developed for the international market and in the same year this started selling to the USA, France, Australia and New Zealand. December 2008 saw the launch of a second generation display for the UK.

By 2009 Current Cost had a turnover of £6 million and Chris still owned 50 per cent of the business.

Up-to-date information on Current Cost can be found on their website: www.currentcost.com

---

Roger von Oech (1986) has a slightly different view of the creative process, focusing on the changing role of the individual as it takes its course. He outlines four sequential roles:

1. The explorer – searching for new insights and perspectives by sifting through information, being curious, observing other fields, generating ideas, broadening perspectives, following unexpected leads, using difficulties and obstacles and constantly writing things down.
2. The artist – turning information and resources into new ideas by imagining, adapting, reversing, linking, parodying, evaluating and discarding.
3. The judge – evaluating and assessing the merits of a concept and incorporating ideas through objectivity and looking at assumptions, probabilities and timing.
4. The warrior – achieving organisational acceptance and implementation of ideas by being bold, courageous and persistent, developing plans, commanding resources, motivating stakeholders to commit themselves to the project.

In a start-up the entrepreneur may have to fulfil all four of these roles – a considerable achievement, not least because they require different types of left and right brain activity.

Some organisations have created environments designed to facilitate these stages of the creative process. The Royal Mail Group has its own 'Creativity Laboratory'. This is made up of a number of open areas – facilitating groups forming, breaking up and coming together again – all with very informal seating arrangements. Standing and walking are encouraged. There is background music as well as toys, drinks and other distractions for the left brain. All the walls are 'white walls' which can be written on with felt tip pens when ideas are in free flow. Pens are everywhere. There are computer systems that allow ideas to be posted and voted on anonymously. And records are kept of the whole process – even the white walls are photographed – so agreed actions and outcomes can be followed up back in the workplace.

Case insight Bruce Bratley and First Mile

The business idea developed slowly for Bruce Bratley. Having done a PhD in environmental science he was convinced there were commercial opportunities in waste recycling. He first got a job as commercial director in a start-up firm that recycled packaging materials but in 2002 left to start his own consultancy, advising waste businesses on their strategy. He became convinced that there was a gap in the market for a recycling company that could use internet technology to service business customers who found it expensive and difficult to dispose of their waste and who could not easily recycle. Initially he was looking around for a company to buy as a springboard for this idea, but that came to nothing.

FirstMile

Easy Recycling

It was not until 2007 that he found a business partner, Paul Ashworth, and they decided to set up their own business, each putting in £20000. First Mile was launched in 2007 on the back of a £95000 grant from Enhance, a support service for green enterprises in London. First Mile offers a unique kerbside collection service for waste collection and recycling. Customers buy prepaid sacks which they fill with non-recyclable waste or mixed recycling waste and place on the street for collection at a prearranged time. They can also dispose of confidential and other specialist waste. First Mile takes the waste to depots to be sorted and dealt with. To keep costs low all transactions are handled on the internet (there is a 0800 number for service enquiries). Customers can log on to their account, order sacks – delivered the next day – and payments are collected by direct debit, eliminating paperwork. There is no contract and First Mile guarantee to beat the local council price for waste disposal, so the service is particularly attractive to SMEs.

By 2009 First Mile had spread from London to Leeds, Birmingham and Bristol and had 5500 customers. Turnover was £4 million.

Up-to-date information on First Mile can be found on their website: www.firstmile.co.uk

Techniques for generating new ideas

There are many techniques designed to help encourage the generation of new ideas. Most are directed at generating a higher quality of idea rather than a greater volume. People with different thinking styles will respond differently to each of them. Here are just a few of the more widely used ones.

Brainstorming

This is one of the most widely used techniques. It is practised in a group. In the session you do not question or criticise ideas. You suspend disbelief. The aim is to encourage the free flow of ideas – divergent thinking – and as many ideas as possible. Everyone has thousands of good ideas within them just waiting to come out. But people inherently fear making mistakes or looking foolish in front of others. Here making 'mistakes' and putting forward ideas which don't work is not only acceptable, it is also encouraged.

You might start with a problem to be solved or an opportunity to be exploited. You encourage and write down ideas as they come by facilitating all the dimensions of creative thinking in Figure 7.1. There are no 'bad' ideas. All ideas are, at the very least, springboards for other ideas. You allow the right side of the brain full rein and only engage the left brain to analyse the ideas you come up with at a later date. It is often best undertaken with a multidisciplinary team so that the issue can be approached from many different perspectives, encouraging the cross-fertilisation of ideas.

Negative brainstorming, thinking about the negative aspects of a problem or situation, can often be used initially to unblock more creative and positive brainstorming. It is particularly useful in getting people to think about what might happen if they do not think more creatively and can be used to help change motivations and behaviour.

A seven-step guide to running a brainstorming session

1. Describe the outcome you are trying to achieve – the problem or opportunity – BUT NOT THE SOLUTION. This could be a broad area of investigation – new ideas and new markets can be discovered if you don't follow conventional paths.
2. Decide how you will run the session and who will take part. You need an impartial facilitator who will introduce things, keep to the rules and watch the time. This person will restate the creative process if it slows down. The group can number anything from 4 to 30. The larger the number the more diverse the inputs but the slower (and more frustrating) the process – so something around 12 is probably ideal.
3. Set out the room in a participative (i.e. circular) and informal style. Comfortable chairs are important. Refreshments should be available continuously. Make certain there are flip charts, coloured pens and so on or. If you want to be high tech, you can use some of the specialist software that is available (e.g. Brainstorming Toolbox). People should also have a note pad so they can write down ideas.
4. Relax participants as much as possible. The style is informal. The rules of engagement should be posted clearly for all to see and run through so that everybody understands:

   • Quantity counts, not quality – postpone judgement on all ideas;
   • Encourage wild, exaggerated ideas – all ideas are of equal value;
   • Build on ideas rather than demolish them.

5. Open the session by asking for as many ideas as possible. Get people to shout out. Write every idea down on the flip chart and post the sheets on the wall. Encourage and engage with people. Close down criticism. Try to create group engagement.
6. When the ideas have dried up – it might take a little time for it finally to do so – close the session, thanking participants and keeping the door open for them should they have any ideas later.
7. Analyse the ideas posted. Brainstorming helps generate ideas, not analyse them. What happens from here is up to you. Sometimes the people who generated the ideas can also help sort them, but remember to separate out the sessions clearly. Perhaps excellent ideas can be implemented immediately, but do not forget to investigate the interesting ones – no matter how 'off-the-wall'.

For more information on the technique visit www.brainstorming.co.uk.

A variant on brainstorming is called brainwriting, whereby ideas are written down anonymously and then communicated to the group (computer technologies, like those used in the Royal Mail's Creativity Centre, can help with this), thus avoiding the influence of dominant individuals.

Case with questions   Alex Tew and the Million Dollar Homepage

Alex Tew, a Nottingham Trent University student in the UK was only 21 years old when he had his big business idea in 2005. Within months he had set it up – his website that is – the Million Dollar Homepage, www.milliondollarhomepage.com. By January 2006 Alex was a millionaire.

The Million Dollar Homepage is a single web page that is divided into 10 000 boxes, each 100 pixels in size. Alex sold the space to advertisers at $1 for each pixel, with a minimum of 100 pixels. The result is a montage of company logos each with a hyperlink to the advertiser's website. The site features a web banner with 'a pixel counter displaying the number of pixels sold, a navigation bar containing nine small links to the site's internal web pages, and an empty square grid of 1 000 000 pixels divided into 10 000 blocks of 100 pixels. Alex promised customers that the site would remain online for five years – that is, until at least 26 August 2010.

The idea for the web page originated from brainstorming and came whilst Alex lay on his bed at home in August 2005:

> 'I have always been an ideas person and I have a brainstorming session every night before I go to bed and write things down on a note pad.'
>
> *Sunday Times* 18 December 2005

The site took just two days to set up and cost £50. Alex sold the first blocks of pixels to his brothers and some friends and used that money to advertise the site. The site address began appearing in internet blogs and chat rooms. Following a press release, a BBC technology programme ran a story on the page in September 2005. This was followed swiftly by articles in newspapers around the world, as well as features on national television. As the site caught on, more and more advertisers signed up – after all $100 was not a lot to pay. By January 2006 he had sold all 1 million pixels – the final 1000 pixels were sold by a 10-day auction on eBay – at which point he closed the site to new entrants and left it on the internet. Alex had become a celebrity millionaire ($1 037 100 to be precise) and the homepage had become a phenomenon, all within a year!

> 'From the outset I knew the idea had potential, but it was one of those things that could have gone either way. My thinking was I had nothing to lose, apart from the £50 or so it cost to register the domain and set up the hosting. I knew the idea was quirky enough to create interest ... The internet is a very powerful medium.
>
> The crucial thing in creating the media interest was the idea itself; it was unique and quirky enough to stand out. I only had to push the idea a bit in the first few days by sending out a press release which essentially acted as a catalyst. This interest coupled with traditional word-of-mouth created a buzz around the homepage, which in turn created more interest.'
>
> Ask the Expert: How to make a Million, FT.com 22 February 2006 (www.ft.com)

Visit the website on www.milliondollarhomepage.com

➡

Questions

1. In your opinion is this a 'one-off' business, or can it be replicated?
2. If you think it can, how would you set about it?
3. What lessons do you learn from Alex's success?

Analogy

This is a product-centred technique that attempts to join together apparently unconnected or unrelated combinations of features of a product or service and benefits to the customer to come up with innovative solutions to problems. Analogies are proposed once the initial problem has been stated. The analogies are then related to opportunities in the market place. Operated in a similar way to brainstorming, it is probably best explained with an example. Georges de Mestral noticed that burdock seed heads stuck to his clothing. On closer examination he discovered the seed heads carried tiny hooks. His analogy was to apply this principle to the problem of sticking and unsticking things and to develop what we recognise today as Velcro.

The first steps to building an analogy are to ask some basic questions:

- What does the situation or problem remind you of?
- What other areas of life or work experience similar situations?
- Who does these similar things and can the principles be adapted?

Often the analogy contains the words 'is like' So you might ask why one thing 'is like' another. For example, why is advertising like cooking? The answer is because there is so much preamble to eating. Anticipation from presentation and smell, even the ambience of the restaurant you eat in, are just as important as the taste and nutritional value of the food itself.

Attribute analysis

This is another product-centred technique which is designed to evolve product improvements and line extensions and is used as the product reaches the mature phase of its life cycle. It uses the basic marketing technique of looking at the features of a product or service which in turn perform a series of functions but, most importantly, deliver benefits to the customers. An existing product or service is stripped down to its component parts and the group then explores how these features might be altered but then focuses on whether those changes might bring valuable benefits to the customer.

For example, you might focus on a domestic lock. This secures a door from opening by an unwelcome intruder. The benefit is security and reduction/elimination of theft from the house. But you can lose keys or forget to lock doors and some locks are difficult or inconvenient to open from the inside. A potential solution is to have doors that sense people approaching from the outside and lock or unlock themselves depending on who is approaching. The exterior sensor could recognise 'friendly' people approaching the door because of sensors they carry in the form of 'credit cards' or keys. This technology is now being applied to car locks. You could even have a reverse sensor on the inside that unlocks the door when anyone approaches (which could be activated or deactivated centrally).

Gap analysis

This is a market-based approach that attempts to produce a 'map' of product/market attributes based on dimensions that are perceived as important to customers, analysing where competing products might lie and then spotting gaps where there is little or no competition. Because of the complexity involved, the attributes are normally shown in only two dimensions. There are a number of approaches to this task.

Perceptual mapping places the attributes of a product within specific categories. So for example, the dessert market might be characterised as hot vs cold and sophisticated vs unsophisticated. Various desserts would then be mapped onto these two dimensions. This could be shown graphically (see alongside). The issue is whether the 'gap' identified between one product and another is one that customers would value being filled – and means understanding whether they value the dimensions being measured. That is a question for market research to attempt to answer.

Non-metric mapping maps products in groups that customers find similar and then tries to explain why these groupings exist. A classic example would be the soft drinks market where products might be clustered and then described simply in terms of still vs carbonated and flavoured vs non-flavoured.

Unsophisticated

Hot ← → Cold

Sophisticated

The key here is also finding the appropriate dimensions that create opportunities for differentiating the product and creating competitive advantage. The mapping of soft drinks on the two dimensions above is unlikely to reveal any gaps in the market.

Repertory grid is a more systematic extension of this technique. Customers are asked to group similar and dissimilar products within a market, again normally in pairs. They are then asked to explain the similarities and dissimilarities. The sequence is repeated for all groups of similar and dissimilar products. The explanations are then used to derive 'constructs' which describe the way in which customers relate and evaluate the products. These constructs form a grid that can be used to map the products, applying the words used by the customers themselves.

Personal Construct Theory and the Repertory Grid

George Kelly was an American engineer who became a highly respected clinical psychologist, best known for the development in 1955 of his own theory of personality known as Personal Construct Theory and a tool to explore people's personalities in terms of the theory, called the Repertory Grid. Kelly believed that the personality theories of the day suffered from three things: an inherent observer bias, a lack of precision and prediction and an over-reliance on the expert.

Kelly believed that we all have our own 'constructs' – views of the world or biases – that help us navigate our way around the world quickly. Certain words will trigger certain preconceptions, be they logical or otherwise. When you open and walk through a door you do so without consciously thinking what you are doing but you are preconditioned to act in a way that has opened a similar door before. The fact that it is locked can often come as quite a sharp surprise. Construct systems influence our expectations and perceptions subconsciously –

→

and introduce bias. This means that one person's constructs are not those of another – and sometimes they can even be internally inconsistent because we never question them.

The Repertory Grid attempts to get rid of this bias. The technique identifies a small set of elements (objects, entities) and the user is asked to define some constructs (attributes, slots) which characterise those elements. All these terms are identified in terms of the user's own language. So, for example, 'good' can only exist in contrast to the concept of 'bad'. Any construct can reasonably be measured by answering the question 'compared to what?' Construct values are given for each element on a limited scale between extreme polar points. The process of taking three elements and asking for two of them to be paired in contrast with the third is the most effective way in which the poles of the construct can be discovered and articulated.

It is beyond this book to explain, in detail, how this technique should be deployed. However, one of the most accessible and short books on the topic is by Devi Jankovicz (2003). It really is 'The Easy Guide to Repertory Grids'.

Creativity resources

To find what must be the world largest resource of creativity and innovation resources go to www.creax.net. The website contains hyperlinks to almost 900 other sites around the world. These include: authors, articles, books, basic research, creative environments, creative thinking pioneers, design, e-learning and creativity, education, creativity tools, ideas factories, ideas markets, imagination tools, innovation tools, internet assisted creativity, mind mapping, online techniques, ideas management, tests and puzzles and many, many more.

All the techniques discussed here – and more – are covered in more detail somewhere on this website. There are also tools and resources to help you try them.

Recognising opportunity

Creativity on its own is not necessarily entrepreneurial. It is only entrepreneurial if it is applied to the process of innovation which leads to the development of new products or services that have a value in the market place. And the key to this is linking creativity and innovation to opportunities in the market place. The techniques outlined in the previous sections can be applied directly to commercial opportunity recognition in a systematic way.

When I started the Gadget Shop it was from frustration with the difficulties of finding gifts for the family and friends with a love of innovation and gadgets. There are lots of problems in life that could be solved with the right insight leading to a business opportunity: you just have to spot them. Some of the most successful ideas are actually simple.
Jonathan Elvidge, founder of Gadget Shop, *The Times* 6 July 2002

Valery (1999) believes that 'innovation has more to do with the pragmatic search for opportunity than the romantic ideas about serendipity or lonely pioneers pursuing their vision against all the odds.' Peter Drucker (1985) takes this further. He believes innovation can be practised systematically through a creative analysis of change in the environment and the opportunities this generates. It is not the result of 'happenstance'. Entrepreneurs can practise innovation systematically by using their creativity skills to search for change and then evaluate its potential for an economic or social return. Change provides the opportunity for innovation. Skills in creativity help identify these opportunities. And it is the actions of the entrepreneur that make this opportunity generate an economic return.

> *Our success is due, in part, to not just an ability but a willingness to look at things differently. I believe opportunity is part instinct and part immersion – in an industry, a subject, or an area of expertise ... You don't have to be a genius, or a visionary, or even a college graduate to think unconventionally. You just need a framework ... Seeing and seizing opportunities are skills that can be applied universally, if you have the curiosity and commitment.*
>
> Michael Dell

Drucker said 'innovation is the specific tool of entrepreneurs, the means by which they exploit change as an opportunity for a different business or a different service. It is capable of being presented as a discipline, capable of being learned and capable of being practised. Entrepreneurs need to search purposefully for the sources of innovation, the changes and their symptoms that indicate opportunities for successful innovation. And they need to know and to apply the principles of successful innovation'.

He lists seven sources of opportunity for firms in search of creative innovation. Four can be found within the firm itself or from the industry of which it is part and are therefore reasonably easy to spot. They are 'basic symptoms' – highly reliable indicators of changes that have already happened or can be made to happen with little effort. They are:

1. The *unexpected*, be it the unexpected success or failure or the unexpected event. Nobody can predict the future but an ability to react quickly to changes is a real commercial advantage, particularly in a rapidly changing environment. Information and knowledge are invaluable.
2. The *incongruity* between what actually happens and what was supposed to happen. Plans go wrong and unexpected outcomes produce opportunities for firms that are able to spot them.
3. The *inadequacy in underlying processes* that are taken for granted but can be improved or changed. This is essentially improving process engineering – especially important if the product or service is competing primarily on price and therefore costs need to be minimised.
4. The *changes in industry or market structure* that take everyone by surprise. Again, unexpected change, perhaps arising from technology, legislation or other outside events creates an opportunity for the entrepreneur and, as is often the case with all these sources of opportunity, first-mover advantage – making the most of the advantage before others do so – is usually worth striving for.

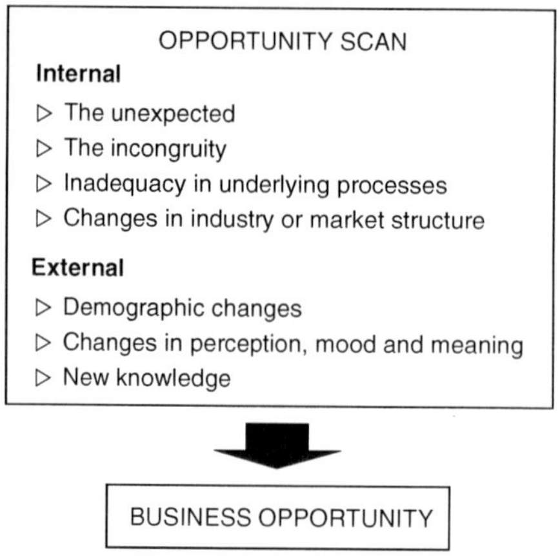

Figure 7.4 Generating a viable business idea

These changes produce sources of opportunity that need to be dissected and the underlying causes of change understood. The causes give clues about how innovation can be used to increase value added to the customer and economic return.

The other three factors come from the outside world:

5. *Demographic changes* – population changes caused by changes in birth rates, wars, medical improvements etc.
6. *Changes in perception, mood and meaning* that can be brought about by the ups and down of the economy, culture, fashion etc. In-depth interviews or focus groups can often give an insight into these changes.
7. *New knowledge*, both scientific and non-scientific.

Drucker lists the seven factors in what he sees as increasing order of difficulty, uncertainty and unreliability, which means that he believes that new knowledge including scientific knowledge, for all its visibility and glamour, is in fact the most difficult, least reliable and least predictable source of innovation. Paradoxically, this is the area to which government, academics and even entrepreneurial firms pay most attention. He argues that innovations arising from the systematic analysis of mundane and unglamorous unexpected successes or failures are far more likely to yield commercial innovations. They have the shortest lead times between start and yielding measurable results and carry fairly low risk and uncertainty.

Drucker's Opportunity Scanning process is summarised in Figure 7.4. It can be used with brainstorming and other techniques that encourage creativity to form the basis of a systematic business opportunity scanning process.

As Drucker's analysis makes clear, gaps in markets come from change. If you are looking for a business idea think of changes that are taking place – in markets, technology, society etc. – and the implications they may have. For example:

• Products or services that you have seen but are not available in your area can mean there are opportunities. Experience of overseas countries and markets is always valuable.

- Changes in customer demands or fashions can mean needs are not being met.
- Changes in markets can lead to opportunities; for example, the opening up of new retail outlets, shopping areas or sales channels such as the internet.
- Changes in legislation can create opportunities; for example, changes in Health and Safety regulations and Food Hygiene regulations have created opportunities in the past.

Case insight   Tom Mercer and mOma

Tom Mercer was a management consultant with Bain and Co. in London. Before going to work he would blend smoothies with oats for his breakfast in his flat in Waterloo. But it took time and he was often late for work. Then it suddenly struck him that his problem was actually a good business idea – pre-prepare the blend and then sell it to commuters from key points, like stations, around London. And so mOma was born in 2006.

Now you can see mOma's distinctively colourful carts around stations in London. They sell Oaties – smoothies and oats, Jumbles – oats soaked in apple juice and mingled with low-fat yoghurt and fruit, and Hodge-Podge – a layer of fruit cooked

with spices, yoghurt and a packet of granola. Tom spent five months developing his recipes. The first products were sold in used plastic water bottles with labels glued on. Now the breakfasts are prepared in Deptford, South East

London, then driven to central London to be sold from mOma's eight carts between 6.15 am and 10.45 am. In 2009 Tom had 25 people working for him, including 10 stall workers who are mainly students wanting to earn extra money. The driver picks up the stall workers and the leftovers at the end of the shift.

mOma products are also sold in Selfridges' food hall and served on Virgin Atlantic flights. Tom plans to open more stalls and extend the company beyond London by selling through Ocado, the internet grocer.

One technique for getting to the root cause of Drucker's 'unexpected events', 'incongruities' or 'inadequacies' is the 'Why? Why?' exercise. This is used to explore options related to the event. Figure 7.5 shows a 'Why? Why?' diagram exploring the reason for a fall in sales (Vyakarnham and Leppard, 1999). From it you can see there are several possible reasons, although the trails have not been taken to completion. The root cause will lie at the end of one of the 'why?' trails.

In the section on Attribute analysis, the 'why? why?' technique could have been used to question why the domestic lock was designed in a particular way, taking nothing for granted. In this way the technique should uncover the prime attributes that users are seeking. An alternative solution to the problem can then be constructed.

Even after start-up you must continue to work at opportunity spotting. Firms with a good track record for innovation practise it systematically. It does not happen by

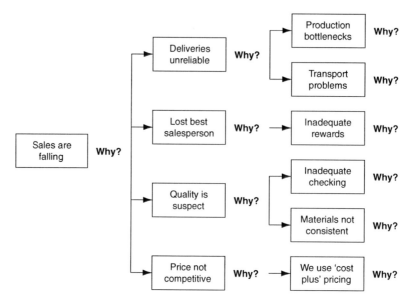

Figure 7.5 Why? Why? diagram

Source: Adapted from Vyarkarnham and Leppard (1999)

chance. They look for small changes that can be made to the way they do things. Indeed so systematic can the search for innovation be that some firms have been set up specifically to undertake it. Drucker (op. cit.) advocates a five-stage approach to purposeful, systematic innovation:

1. *Start with the analysis of opportunities, inside the firm and its industry and in the external environment.* Information and knowledge are invaluable – from as many sources as possible. Do not innovate for the future, innovate for now. Timing is everything. The right idea at the wrong time is worth nothing.
2. *Innovation is both conceptual and perceptual.* Therefore look at the financial implications but also talk to people, particularly customers, and analyse how to meet the opportunity.
3. *To be effective, an innovation must be simple and has to be 'focused'.* Keep it as simple as possible. Don't try to be too clever. Don't try to do too many things at once. The slightly-wrong-but-can-be-improved idea can always be developed and still earn a fortune.
4. *To be effective, start small.* Don't be grandiose. Take an incremental approach. Minimise the commitment of resources for as long as possible, thus maximising information and knowledge and minimising risk. This is called 'bootstrapping'.
5. *Aim at leadership and dominate the competition in the particular area of innovation as soon as possible.* This marketing strategy is called niche marketing it is the strategy that is most likely to lead to success.

How innovations, particularly technical innovations, see the light of commercial day is complex. Scientific discoveries do lead to commercial opportunities

Case insight   Adrian Wood and GTI

Adrian Wood set up GTI, a publishing company, in 1988 whilst at university. Adrian and two friends, Mark Blythe and Wayne Collins, were thinking about their futures and realised they did not know much about the jobs they were considering. The idea was to explain to students what was involved in various occupations. Adrian first thought of the idea in his second year studying economics at Reading University. He decided that he needed to 'sell' the idea to students – and more importantly to advertisers – by attracting some well known business names to contribute articles to the magazine. So he wrote to dozens of people and some, including Sir John Harvey-Jones, agreed to contribute.

Initially, Adrian and his two friends each put £200 into the business and used the university careers adviser as a consultant. Their first publication tackled quantity surveying and property. They took a week off studying and interviewed lecturers in different departments. They even got the backing of the head of education of the Royal Institute of Chartered Surveyors. About half of the publication was devoted to advertising and they personally delivered copies of it around the country. It made £6000 profit.

And so the company was born – 'to produce careers publications and an honest view of life'. The following year five magazines were published and sales came to £120 000. In 1990 GTI bought a barn in Wallingford, Oxfordshire and converted it into offices to accommodate its growing staff numbers.

Today GTI publishes over 100 careers products from offices in six countries. In the UK, their major brands are TARGETjobs, TARGETcourses and TARGETchances. In Ireland, GTI is the official careers publisher for all universities with their gradireland range of products. In Germany GTI operates as Staufenbiel – a highly respected name for graduate careers information. In 2008 GTI bought the UK and German graduate recruitment divisions of Hobsons, part of DMGI. GTI are also publishing partners for some 30 European universities through their Careers Service Guide range.

Up-to-date information on GTI can be found on their website: www.groupgti.com

which entrepreneurial firms can exploit. However, the linkages are not always as you would expect and they can involve a labyrinthine series of inter-relationships. William Shockley had to invent a theory of electrons and 'holes' in semiconductors to explain why the transistors that he and his colleagues at Bell Laboratories in the USA had invented in 1948 actually worked. Even then, in order for the transistor idea to see the light of day, he and his colleagues had to take it to Palo Alto in California and start a company that eventually became Intel.

The business idea

As we have seen, good business ideas can come from spotting good commercial opportunities – linked to market demand. Often the first attempt at putting that product or service together in a marketable way fails, so a series of trial-and-error iterations may be necesary. Howard Head, the inventor of the steel ski, made some 40 different metal skis before he finally made one that would work consistently. Most people base their business upon skills, experience or qualifications that they have already gained from a previous job or through a hobby. Often they think that their employer is not making the most of some opportunity. Sometimes they have an idea but cannot persuade their employer to take it up, so they decide to try it themselves. Often they have contacts in the industry they believe they can exploit to their own advantage.

As we saw in the previous section, you can create your own change and your own opportunity through innovation. This innovation could form the basis for a new business idea. For example, innovation could mean:

- *Invention*: Although, this is not necessarily the same thing as innovation. Often inventors are best advised to sell on their idea rather than to try to exploit it themselves.
- *Ways of doing things better or cheaper*: Better is good; cheaper, as we shall see, can lead to problems.
- *New developments in technology*: Computing, telephonics and the internet are at the forefront of technological change at the moment.
- *New ways of getting goods or services to markets*: Direct selling of certain types of goods or services firstly over the telephone and now the internet have created many millionaires in the last couple of decades.

However, there are many other sources of potential new business ideas. They come from an exposure to business and commerce around the world – an inquisitiveness and a constant searching for commercial opportunity. They come, not so much from asking the question 'why?', but rather from asking the question 'why not?'. And many of the techniques discussed in the previous section can be used to generate them. They could come from:

- Existing businesses around the world – either what they are offering or what they are not offering;
- Existing franchises not offered in certain countries;
- Innovations – your own or those belonging to other people;
- Patents and licences – your own or those belonging to others that are not yet fully exploited;
- Research institutes – where new products may have commercial potential;
- Industry and trade contacts yielding insights into gaps in markets;
- Industry and trade shows where new products and services are seeking new markets;
- Newspapers and trade journals – where new products, services or markets around the world are reviewed and, most importantly, gaps in markets might be exposed;
- Business networks and contacts – which might provide the blinding insight that a market opportunity exists;
- Television and radio.

One significant factor, of course, will be the sectors and markets in which small firms are currently growing most quickly. It is here that opportunities currently exist. But will you be able to capitalise on these developments as quickly as existing firms? And will those opportunities still exist in five years' time? A good business idea has a window of commercial opportunity. Too early or too late and it is unlikely to be successful. Cecil Duckworth set up his engineering firm to manufacture self-service petrol pumps, but when petrol in the UK was still being served by attendants. He did not sell a single one and the business nearly failed. However, within 18 months he started manufacturing central heating boilers and laid the foundations for the highly successful Worcester Engineering Group that he subsequently sold for over £30 million to the Bosch Group. It took another two or three years before self-service petrol pumps started to become popular and by then Worcester Engineering was no longer interested.

> *'I know everyone wants to think that it is like an act of God – that you sit down and have a brilliant idea. Well, when you start your own business it does not work like that. I remember walking through Littlehampton with the kids, one in a pushchair and one walking beside me. We went into the sweet shop, then into the greengrocer and then to Boots. In both the sweet shop and the greengrocers I had choice. I could buy as much, or as little, as I wanted. I could buy half a pound of gob-stoppers or a kilo of apples, the quantities were up to me. In Boots I suddenly thought "What a shame that I can't buy as little as I like here too. Why am I stuck with only big sizes to choose from? If I'm trying something out and don't like it, I am too intimidated to return it, so I'm stuck with it." That one thought, that single reaction, was me voicing a need, a disappointment with things as they were. But if that's a need I have, lots of other women must have the same need, I thought. Why can't we buy smaller sizes – like in the greengrocers?'*
>
> Anita Roddick, founder of Body Shop, Personal interview

Finally, Bolton and Thompson (2000) suggest that there are three basic approaches to innovation – in many ways taking a different perspective on Drucker's analysis. None of these approaches are mutually exclusive. They can all be used to generate new business ideas.

- *Identify a problem and seek a solution.* They cite as an example Edwin Land's invention of the Polaroid camera because his young daughter could not understand why she had to wait to have pictures of herself printed.
- *Identify a solution and seek a problem.* They cite 3M's Post-It notes as an example of a product with loosely-sticking qualities that was applied to the need to mark pages in a manuscript.
- *Identify a need and develop a solution.* The example they cite is James Dyson's dual cyclone cleaner that he developed because of his frustration with the inadequate suction provided by his existing vacuum cleaner when he was converting an old property.

Your creativity skills can be used in identifying the problem, solution or a need in Bolton and Thompson's approach. You can also use your creativity skills to identify the solution or even the problem. Put another way, you can use your creativity skills to spot an opportunity. You can also then use your creativity skills to develop a product or service to meet the opportunity. Either way creativity is the key to innovation. And innovation is the key to a successful business idea. If all else fails, try the internet for ideas (sites such as www.businessideas.net or www.entrepreneur. com/businessideas/index.php). They may not always be original but they get you to start thinking.

Start-up ideas from the USA

The USA is known for its entrepreneurship and here is a selection of some of the weirdest real start-up businesses in the USA. Some may have short life spans but it all goes to show that you can make money out of most things.

- **HappyBalls.com** of Cumming, Georgia, makes foam balls with colourful faces to be placed on top of car aerials. Do not mock – this is a million-dollar company.
- **Afterlife Telegrams** of New Athens, Illinois, offers to contact the dead. For a fee, they arrange for terminally ill patients to memorise a message that can be relayed to loved ones who have died when they themselves pass on.
- **eNthem** of San Francisco writes full length corporate theme songs.
- **Lucky Break Wishbone** of Seattle sells plastic wishbones so that all the family can have one despite the fact there is only really one in a chicken or turkey.
- **SomethingStore** of Huntington, New York, will, for a payment of $10, send you something, anything – but no telling what.
- **WeightNags** of Austin sends mildly abusive weekly messages to dieters, to encourage them to keep dieting.
- **Yelo** of New York City offers New Yorkers 20- or 40-minute naps in 'sleep pods'.
- **Throx** of San Francisco sells socks in packs of three – think about it.
- **Gaming-Lessons** of Jupiter, Florida offers video game lessons and coaching.
- **Cuddle Party** of New York City offers 'structured, safe workshops on boundaries, communication, intimacy and affection … A laboratory where you can experiment with what makes you feel safe and feel good.'
- **Neuticles** of Oak Grove, Missouri, offers testicular implants for dogs that have been neutered.

The internet

The internet was probably the most important innovation affecting business at the end of the twentieth century. It was a 'discontinuous innovation' that created major opportunities for new and small firms. The 'dot.com' boom in many ways resembled the 'railway mania' of the nineteenth century – another 'discontinuous innovation' – and the consequences were remarkably similar. The value of many of the internet's new companies became inflated and over-investment occurred. However, the new means of communication, just like the new means of transport in the nineteenth century, soon revolutionised many business functions and changed customers' buying habits by improving communications and lowering transaction and other costs, particularly for the service sector. Even the over-investment in the networks laid the basis for the broadband revolution, which made the internet faster and more powerful and itself laid the groundwork for the next phase of internet expansion.

The first start-up internet company to attract widespread stock market attention was Netscape, founded by Jim Clark and Marc Andreessen, who had originally developed a web browser called Mosaic. The company was featured in the first edition of this book. When Netscape went public in 1995, eighteen months after its launch, the founders became billionaires and the shares tripled in value on the first day of trading. Netscape soon disappeared as a rival browser, Microsoft's Internet Explorer, came to dominate the market. However, the internet boom continued, firstly with portals like Yahoo, Lycos, and AltaVista. They were set up, they were taken over and the market consolidated. Then came the telecommunications companies that provided the internet's hard-wired backbone, like MCI and WorldCom. Even companies that produced the switchgear, like Cisco Systems, experienced the boom. As customers learnt to shop online, the internet retailers like eToys and pets.com started to appear. The boom spread to the UK with firms like Lastminute.com, floating on the London stock market and a clothing start-up company called Boo.com raising millions of pounds before it had sold a single garment.

Many new and truly innovative businesses were set up to exploit the unique characteristics of the internet and the advantages it offered. Certainly the internet service providers came out of the boom. And firms with innovative business models like eBay – arguably the most successful of the internet business start-ups – prospered and grew (see Case insight). Community sites, bringing people with similar interests together from around the world, grew out of the new technology. Many were started in bedrooms and developed into valuable commercial enterprises.

This hectic dot.com boom probably came to a head with the disastrous merger of internet portal AOL and the entertainment or content-provider Time Warner in 2000. Between 1995 and 2000, the main US stock market index, the NASDAQ, rose five-fold. However, these share prices were over-inflated and in 2000 the stock prices of internet and other high-tech companies plummeted. The dot.com bubble had burst and reality was beginning to dawn. Firms with weak cash flow (like Boo.com) went into liquidation, others were forced into mergers. Generally the survivors consolidated their position and increased their market share of this growing market. Companies like Amazon, Yahoo, eBay and Google emerged as the dominant companies in their sector.

But the internet did more than just allow innovative businesses to be established. It allowed small firms to compete in a global market place on price, the differentiated qualities of the products or service or by being able to focus even more effectively on market segments – niche marketing. The internet's lasting legacy are the new routes to market that changed the balance of power in the small versus large firm equation of competition. Almost any market on the planet is now accessible by the smallest of firms. With barriers down, competition is likely to intensify.

Much of the cost-saving effect of the internet has happened quietly, inside departments of large companies. The internet encouraged the growth of outsourcing, which led to manufacturing companies moving much of their production to cheaper, overseas locations. It is business-to-business trading that has been the greatest success of the internet so far. Large companies such as Dell Computers showed the way forward for manufacturers. Dell's 'information partnership' and 'fully integrated value chain' link customers, Dell and their suppliers and allow stock to be delivered on a just-in-time basis, thereby minimising inventories and costs. Many back-office service functions, from data processing to personnel, also moved offshore, particularly to India. However, the increasingly symbiotic relationships between these large firms and their small firm suppliers carry many dangers for the supplier.

Business-to-consumer retailing has also expanded dramatically as broadband networks have expanded. There are many opportunities for small firms on the internet that allow them to tap large markets without the overheads associated with the high street. Firms like Amazon, Lastminute.com in the UK, Dangdang.com in China and NCsoft in Korea are all examples of this. For retailers the internet allows them to keep in stock items that would not be available offline – for example, the range of books available from Amazon. However, the big high-street names have now established themselves on the internet and they are capitalising on their established brand and their loyal customer base. And it has become second nature for many people to check out products, prices and availability online before buying – often using price comparison websites. The internet has also allowed markets to be established where none existed before, for example through the online auction house eBay. And the range of goods and services available online continues to expand, for example with digital music and video downloads and voice-over internet calls.

The internet has been a truly discontinuous innovation. However, whilst the internet has become mainstream in the sense that it now permeates all we do, we are unlikely yet to have seen its full potential. Many more entrepreneurial opportunities probably still remain, undiscovered, in the virtual world it has created.

Safeguarding your ideas

If you have an original business idea there are a number of ways you can help safeguard it. They come under the general heading of 'intellectual property' (IP), but they comprise a number of different approaches to giving you certain exclusive ownership rights to a variety of intangible assets broadly described as 'artistic and commercial creations of the mind'. Common types of IP include patents, trade marks, copyrights, industrial design rights and, in some countries, trade secrets.

The justification of these rights is that they encourage the creation of IP and pay for associated research and development. It is claimed that there are substantial benefits in terms of economic growth for countries that encourage IP protection, whether or not it is a form of monopoly. A report by Shapiro and Pham (2007) observes that, whilst economists trace 30 to 40 per cent of all US gains in productivity and growth over the course of the twentieth century to economic innovation in its various forms, today, some two-thirds of the value of America's large businesses can be traced to the intangible assets that embody ideas, especially the IP of patents and trade marks. They claim that 'IP-intensive industries produce 72% more value added per employee than non-IP-intensive industries and create jobs at a rate 140% higher than non-IP-intensive industries, excluding computers/electronics'. The authors go on to say that 'promoting and protecting new IP should be a high priority for US policymakers'.

However some critics characterise these rights as intellectual protectionism or monopoly and argue that public interest is harmed by protectionist legislation (Levine and Boldrin, 2008). Contrary to Shapiro and Pham's study, Dosi et al. (2006) observed that, despite the doubling of patent registrations and a tripling of related legal costs of enforcement in the USA in the 1990s, there was no observable

20 internet ideas from around the world

AUSTRALIA	**BestPlace Online** is a web design and hosting service that helps small firms to gain an effective web presence.
CZECH REPUBLIC	**Webnode** is an interactive real-time drag-and-drop website builder.
CANADA	**Octopz** helps creative professionals in fields like advertising, architecture, film, television and radio to work together in real time on a project online.
CHINA	**china-tomb.com** is an online mourning (tomb-sweeping) website.
FRANCE	**MyID.is** is a digital identity certification platform.
GERMANY	**StudiVZ** is a Facebook clone for the German market (many exist in other countries).
INDIA	**Vakow!** is a Web 2.0 subscription-based start-up that allows you to post and share SMS messages in Hindi, Tamil, Telgu or any other language.
IRELAND	**Cmypitch** is a website that enables aspiring start-ups to upload a video pitch which can be viewed by potential investors – a sort of 'Dragons' Den meets YouTube'.
KOREA	**Cmune** creates 3D multi-user social applications and games.
NETHERLANDS	**Myngle** is a global language e-learning market place where teachers and students come together to learn new languages and cultures.
NEW ZEALAND	**PocketSmith** is a web-based calendar that forecasts and allows you to manage your cash flow.
NIGERIA	**NaijaPulse** is Nigeria's version of Twitter.
RUSSIA	**WomanJournal** is a female-orientated online shopping site.
SINGAPORE	**RecordTV** allows users to download free-to-air TV programmes.
SOUTH AFRICA	**Amatomu** is an aggregator of South African blogs with a ranking system based on page views and inbound links with various widgets to facilitate its integration into other blogs.
SPAIN	**Bubok** is a service that allows you to upload your book, give it a professional image and offer it for sale.
SWEDEN	**Storytel** streams audiobooks to your mobile phone.
TUNISIA	**Ekree** (meaning 'rent' in Tunisian Arabic) is a portal for those who want to rent anything or put up anything for rent.
UK	**iSuki** is an online, subscription-based, social and dating agency.
USA	**MyMiniLife** is a new form of entertainment that allows people to design their own personal environment – a sort of virtual Lego Land.

step-change in the levels of innovation or profitability. From a managerial rather than a policy perspective, strong intellectual property rights (IPR) can also have some significant disadvantages. In particular, where systematic innovation requiring constant input of external knowledge is concerned, for example through various forms of networking, strong IPR gets in the way because it inhibits collaborative working. The argument is that by collaborative working the small firm may have a small part in a very much larger pie and is therefore better off. Indeed, one study

Case with questions eBay

Crucial to success for dot.com firms is the 'business model' – how income will be generated. Arguably the most successful model is that of the online auctioneer eBay. eBay was founded by Pierre M. Omidyar in 1995. The company has now expanded worldwide, claiming hundreds of millions of registered users, over 15 000 employees and revenues of almost $8 billion.

eBay's success comes from being nothing more than an intermediary – software running on a web server. Its customers, both buyers and sellers, do all the work. Sellers pay to set up their own auction, buyers use eBay's software to place their bids, shipping and payment are arranged between the seller and buyer and eBay takes between 7 and 18 per cent of the selling price as commission for letting them use its software. eBay is simply the trading platform. It holds no stocks and its involvement in the trade is minimal. After each transaction the buyer and seller rate each other. Next to each user's identification is a figure in brackets recording the number of positive comments – thus encouraging honesty and trust. It is a truly virtual business which also sells advertising space.

eBay developed a 'virtuous circle' in which more buyers attracted more sellers, which attracted yet more buyers and sellers – called 'network effects'. At the core of eBay's business is software rather than people. The company has bought software companies to gain exclusive use of their technologies and make the auction process more efficient. It therefore faces enormous economies of scale in attracting as many auction transactions as possible and, with that in mind, has moved into new areas such as used cars and hosting storefronts for small merchants where 'buy-it-now' goods are offered. It has also started to sell private-label versions of its service to companies, for a fee.

In 2002 eBay purchased iBazar, a similar European auction website. It also purchased PayPal, the dominant provider of internet payments in the USA. The two companies are complementary but depend on each other. Indeed, auctions account for almost two-thirds of PayPal's business. PayPal allows customers to register details of their credit card or bank account with it so that when they buy something on the internet they just enter an e-mail account and an amount. Like eBay, it is fully automated, relying on software rather than people. Like eBay, it also relies on 'network effects'.

Not all of eBay's new ventures have been successful. In 2005 it bought the internet phone company Skype, expecting to be able to use this medium as a platform for its main business. However it sold a 65 per cent share in 2009 to Netscape co-founder Marc Andreessen and a group of private equity firms, claiming Skype offered 'limited synergies'. In 2006, eBay opened its new eBay Express site, which was designed to work like a standard Internet shopping site for consumers with US addresses. It closed in 2008.

The company's business strategy involves achieving market dominance worldwide. It has already expanded into over two dozen countries including China and India. The only countries where expansion failed were Taiwan and Japan, where Yahoo! had a head start, and New Zealand, where TradeMe is still the dominant online auction site. Another element of its strategy is to leverage the relationship between it and PayPal. eBay's basic business model generates revenues from sellers. Driving buyers and sellers to use PayPal means eBay also turn buyers into clients. It also means that for each new PayPal registration it achieves via the eBay site, it also earns off-site revenues when the PayPal account is used in non-eBay transactions.

→

Questions

1. Why is eBay's business model so attractive?
2. How does PayPal enhance this business model?
3. Why does one element of eBay's strategy involve market dominance?

---

concluded that the use of IPR has a *negative* effect on a strategy of long-term value creation, the positive influences being lead time, secrecy and tacitness of knowledge (Hurmelinna-Laukkanen and Puumalainen, 2007). Tidd and Bessant (2009) conclude: 'Firms need to balance the desire to protect their knowledge with the need to share aspects of knowledge to promote innovation ... Theoretical arguments and empirical research suggest that from both a policy and management perspective, *only a limited level of IPR* is desirable to encourage risk taking and innovation.'

So, the message for an existing business is that you should not rely too much on IPR, and certainly do not let it get in the way of networking or collaborative working where external knowledge is an important part of your systematic innovation. Secrecy may be just as strong a tool as IPR. However, for a start-up the IP you have on your business idea may be one of the few real assets available to you and in seeking finance for your idea you will have to expose it to many people, some of whom may be less scrupulous than others. In this case you would be well advised to seek the maximum IPR you can find. Nevertheless being first to market is sometimes more effective in creating competitive advantage than IPR on an idea that has missed its window of commercial opportunity.

Modern use of the term IP goes back at least as far as 1888 with the founding in Berne of the Swiss Federal Office for Intellectual Property, but the origins of patents for invention go back even further. No one country can claim to have been the first in the field with a patent system, although Britain does have the longest continuous patent tradition in the world. Its origins date from the fifteenth century, when the Crown started making specific grants of privilege to manufacturers and traders. They were given open letters marked with the King's Great Seal called 'Letters Patent'. Henry VI granted the earliest known patent to Flemish-born John of Utynam in 1449, giving him a 20-year monopoly on a method of making stained glass.

IP law varies from country to country. It is complex and usually comprises a multiplicity of individual pieces of legislation generated over a number of years. With the exception of copyright, if you want to protect your IP in other countries you will generally need to apply for protection in that country. The World Intellectual Property Organisation, an agency of the United Nations, produces the *Guide to Intellectual Property Worldwide* (available at www.ipo.int). In the UK information on regulations and laws can be obtained from the Intellectual Property Office (IPO) (www.ipo.gov.uk). Detailed UK legislation can be viewed on this site, as well as practical help with searches and registering your IP. Generally, however, four fundamental methods of protection are offered in most countries: patents, trademarks, industrial design rights and copyright. A simplified guide to these is given below, but details may vary from country to country and professional help should always be sought over complex IP issues.

Patent

A patent is intended to protect new inventions. It covers how they work, what they do, how they do it, what they are made of and how they are made. It gives the owner the right to prevent others from copying, making, using, importing or selling the invention without permission. The existence of a patent may be enough on its own to prevent others from trying to exploit the invention. However should they persist in trying to do so, it gives you the right to take legal action to stop them exploiting your invention and to claim damages. And herein lies the problem for cash-strapped start-ups. Can they really afford the legal fees involved in pursuing such a claim? Nevertheless the patent allows you to sell the invention and all the IP rights, license it to someone else but retain all the IP rights or discuss the invention with others in order to set up a business based on the invention.

Intellectual property protection in the UK

The *Intellectual Property Office* (IPO), an executive agency of the Department of Business Innovation and Skills, became the operating arm of the *Patent Office* in 2007. The Patent Office was set up in 1852 to act as the sole office for the granting of patents, although its origins go back some 400 years. The *Design Registry* was set up in 1839 to protect industrial designs. Its responsibilities were transferred to the Patent Office in 1875. The registration of trade marks became a Patent Office function in 1876.

The IPO say that for the invention to be eligible for patenting it must be *new*, have an *inventive step* that is not obvious to someone with knowledge and experience in the subject and be capable of being *made* or *used* in some kind of industry. If a patent is granted, it lasts for 20 years but must in the UK be renewed every year after the fifth year. Patents are published after 18 months, which makes people aware of patents that they will eventually be able to use freely once the patent protection ceases. This also can be seen as a disadvantage and you should remember that there is no legal requirement for you to file a patent; you can always decide to keep your invention secret. This is undoubtedly cheaper but if the invention enters the public domain then you may lose your rights to it. However, in dealing with individuals you might approach regarding an unpatented invention you may ask them to sign a confidentiality agreement (also known as a non-disclosure agreement) to protect your rights.

The IPO lists some things for which a patent cannot be granted such as:

- a scientific or mathematical discovery, theory or method;
- a literary, dramatic, musical or artistic work;
- a way of performing a mental act, playing a game or doing business;
- the presentation of information, or some computer programs;
- an animal or plant variety;
- a method of medical treatment or diagnosis;
- anything that is against public policy or morality.

Trade mark ®,™

A trade mark is a sign – made up of words or a logo or both – which distinguishes goods and services from those of competitors. This is important as part of a strategy of differentiation, explained elsewhere. The IPO says that a trade mark must be *distinctive for the goods and services provided*. In other words it can be recognised as a sign that *differentiates* your goods or service from someone else's. Once registered, trade mark registration must be renewed every ten years.

Once registered a trade mark gives you the exclusive right to use your mark for the goods and/or services that it covers in the country in which you have registered it. You can put the ® or ™ symbol next to it to warn others against using it.

As with a patent, a registered trade mark may put people off using the trade mark without permission and allows you to take legal action against anyone who uses it without your permission. However, in the UK a trade mark also allows Trading Standards Officers or the Police to bring criminal charges against counterfeiters illegally using it. As with a patent, you can sell a trade mark, or let other people have a licence that allows them to use it. In the UK, even if you don't register your trade mark, you may still be able to take action if someone uses your mark without your permission, using the lengthier and onerous common law action of 'passing off'.

It is worth mentioning that, just because a company has its name registered with Companies House in the UK, it does not mean that that name is a registered trade mark – company law is different from trade mark law. Similarly, being the owner of a registered trade mark does not automatically entitle you to use that mark as an internet domain name, and vice versa. This is because the same trade mark can be registered for different goods or services and by different proprietors. Also, someone may have already registered the domain name, perhaps with its use being connected with unregistered goods or services. To search or register a domain name you should apply to an Accredited Registrar (available from the Internet Corporation for Assigned Names and Numbers, www.icann.org).

The IPO say that trade marks cannot be registered if they:

- describe goods or services or any characteristics of them, for example, marks which show the quality, quantity, purpose, value or geographical origin of the goods or services (e.g. Cheap Car Rentals or Quality Builders);
- have become customary in this line of trade;
- are not distinctive;
- are three dimensional shapes, if the shape is typical of the goods you are trading, has a function or adds value to the goods;
- are specially protected emblems;
- are offensive;
- are against the law (e.g. promoting illegal drugs);
- are deceptive.

Registered design

If you are creating products or articles, which are unique because they look different from anything else currently available, then you might want to protect the look by registering it as a design. A registered design is a legal right which protects the overall visual appearance of a product in the geographical area you register it. The registered design covers the things that give the product a unique appearance, such as the lines, contours, colours, shape, texture, materials and the ornamentation of the product (e.g. a pattern on a product or a stylised logo). It is a valuable asset that allows you to stop others from creating similar designs. It does not offer protection from what a product is made of or how it works.

Registering a design gives you exclusive rights for the look and appearance of your product. This may be enough on its own to stop anyone using your design, irrespective of whether they copied it or came up with the design independently. Once a design is registered you can sell or license it and sell or retain the IP rights.

The IPO say that to be able to register a design it must:

- be new – in the UK a design is considered new if no identical or similar design has been published or publicly disclosed in the UK or the European Economic Area;
- have individual character – this means that the appearance of the design (its impression) is different from the appearance of other already known designs.

In the UK, Design Right and Community Design Right may also give you automatic protection for the look of your product.

Copyright ©

Copyright allows you to protect your original material and stops others from using your work without permission. It can be used to protect any media:

- literary works such as computer programs, websites, song lyrics, novels, instruction manuals, newspaper articles and some types of database;
- dramatic works including dance or mime;
- musical works;
- artistic works such as technical drawings, paintings, photographs, sculptures, architecture, diagrams, maps and logos;
- layouts or typographical arrangements used to publish a work (e.g. for a book);
- sound or visual recordings of a work;
- broadcasts of a work.

Copyright does not protect ideas, only the 'published' manifestation of those ideas, for example in writing. This happens automatically in most countries, which means that you do not have to apply for it so long as it falls within one of the categories of media protected, but it also means there is no official copyright register. Although not essential, you should mark the material with the © symbol, the name of the copyright owner and the year in which the work was created. Copyright owners may also choose to use technical measures such as copy protection devices to protect their material. In the UK, in addition to or instead of copyright protection, a database may be protected by the 'database right'. Trade marks can be both registered designs (for the artwork) and copyright. You can only copy a work protected by copyright with the owner's permission, even when you cross media boundaries (e.g. crossing from the internet to print).

As copyright owner you have the right to authorise or prohibit any of the following actions in relation to your work:

- copying the work in any way (e.g. photocopying, reproducing a printed page by handwriting, typing or scanning into a computer, and taping live or recorded music);
- renting or lending copies of the work to the public, although in the UK some lending of copyright works falls within the Public Lending Rights Scheme and this does not infringe copyright;
- performing, showing or playing the work in public. (e.g. performing plays and music, playing sound recordings and showing films or videos in public);
- broadcasting the work or other communication to the public by electronic transmission, including transmission through the internet;
- making an adaptation of the work (e.g. by translating a literary or dramatic work, or transcribing a musical work or converting a computer program into a different computer language).

If you have copyright of a work you can sell or license it and sell or retain your ownership. You can also object if your work is distorted or mutilated. As with other forms of IP protection, the existence of copyright may be enough on its own to stop others from trying to copy your material. If it does not, you have the right to take legal action to stop them exploiting your copyright and to claim damages – that is if you can afford to go to court. Copyright infringement only occurs when a whole work or substantial part of it is copied without consent. However, what constitutes a substantial part is not defined and may therefore have to be decided by court action. Copyright is essentially a private right and therefore the cost of enforcing it falls to the individual.

Case with questions   Andrew Valentine and Streetcar

Andrew Valentine studied modern languages and anthropology at Durham University. Whilst there, he and a friend set up a student radio station, Purple FM. After graduating he joined the shipping company P&O and worked for them for six years, doing a part-time MBA. But in 2002 Andrew got itchy feet and decided he wanted to set up his own business, rather than work for other people. The problem was he did not have a business idea. So he and a friend, Brett Akker, became partners and set about searching systematically for the right business. They spent 18 months researching many ideas rom organic food to training courses, meeting twice a week, before coming up with the final idea.

> 'We looked at hundreds of ideas. We were basically trying to identify gaps, so we were looking at how society was changing and what was missing. Our business had to have potential, be capable of being scaled up and play to our strengths. We kept looking until we found something that matched our criteria.'

The final idea came from something Andrew read about in another country – a car sharing club. By 2009 Andrew and Brett's company, called Streetcar, had a turnover of £20 million and some 1300 cars based in six UK cities. The idea is that people in towns and cities can

➜

rent a car for as little as half an hour, replacing the need to buy. Cars are parked in residential streets and are ready to drive away using an electronic card to open the door and start up.

'I read about a similar business overseas and immediately thought, what an amazing idea. There were a couple of other companies already running this kind of service in Britain but they weren't doing it the way we imagined we would be able to do it. We thought we could be more effective.'

Once Andrew and Brett had the idea, they spent four months holding market research focus groups to test out the business model and developing financial projections to estimate the resources they would need.

'We were satisfying ourselves that not only would it work but that there was enough demand for it.'

Initially called Mystreetcar and based in Clapham, South London, the business was finally launched in 2004 on the back of their savings, £60000 of outside finance and £130000 of lease finance to purchase the first eight cars. Initially they did everything themselves, working almost a 24-hour day. They handed out leaflets at train and tube stations in the early mornings, eventually getting family and friends to help, they answered the phone and signed up members, meeting them to show how to use the cars. They even washed and maintained the cars themselves. They offered a 24-hour service to members so, to start with, one of them had to be near to a phone all day, every day. After three months they had 100 members, each having paid a membership deposit and joining fee, so they went out and leased 20 more cars at a cost of £300000.

The business model has changed slightly now. There is no deposit, just an annual membership fee and cars are rented by the hour, which includes 30 miles of petrol. In 2007 Andrew and Brett gave up 43 per cent of the business to Smedvig, a venture capital company, which invested £6.4 million in Streetcar.

'Brett and I share a healthy level of permanent dissatisfaction with the service. This means that we are constantly working at making it better and improving everything. I really enjoy the creativity of growing a business.'

Sunday Times 15 November 2009

Up-to-date information on Streetcar can be found on their website: www.streetcar.co.uk

Questions

1. How did Andrew and Brett go about getting their business idea?
2. How did they minimise their risks in setting up the business?

Summary

- Creativity is the soul of entrepreneurship. It underpins innovation.

- Creativity is a right brain activity that involves lateral as opposed to vertical thinking. It is intuitive, imaginative and rule-breaking. It requires interpersonal and emotional skills and is people-focused. Creative types do exhibit certain common characteristics and there are tests that purport to detect them.

■ The creative process involves four steps and, as with **Current Cost** and **First Mile**, can take time:

1. Generating knowledge and awareness.
2. Incubation.
3. Generating ideas.
4. Evaluation and implementation.

■ There are blocks to creativity. Realising they exist can be the first step to dismantling them. What is more, there are also techniques that can help in the process such as brainstorming (–the technique used by **Alex Tew** when he set up **The Million Dollar Homepage**), analogy, attribute analysis and gap analysis. A key element is the ability to spot relationships and then replicate them in a different context. Appropriate facilities and environments can help with the process.

■ You can use creativity skills to spot a commercial opportunity. You can also use them to develop a product or service to meet the opportunity.

■ Opportunities can be spotted from the systematic analysis of unexpected successes or failures, or the incongruities between what actually happens and what was supposed to happen. Opportunities also come from new knowledge, including scientific knowledge, but this is the most difficult form of opportunity to bring to market. The 'discontinuous innovation' of the internet created an enormous number of commercial opportunities and many companies went bust trying to pursue them. Those that survived consolidated their position, making their founders multimillionaires.

■ Alternatively, to help you spot opportunities you can adopt a three-stage process:

1. Identify a problem and seek a solution, like **Adrian Wood** and GTI;
2. Identify a solution and seek a problem;
3. Identify a need and develop a solution.

■ The thread that binds this all together is the entrepreneurial firm that links creativity and ideas to a commercial opportunity and, like **eBay**, offers an effective business model with good management that allows the idea to be exploited successfully. Entrepreneurs may have to be creative, but they also have to be good at business.

■ You can safeguard your business ideas through patents, trade marks, registered designs and copyright, depending on which mechanism is most appropriate. However, being the first to market is sometimes more effective in creating competitive advantage than IPR on an idea that has missed its window of commercial opportunity.

Further resources are available at www.palgrave.com/business/burns

Essays and discussion topics

1. Do you believe people can be trained to be more creative and generate business ideas?
2. What do you think is involved in being creative? Give examples.

3. Compare and contrast creative vs logical thinking.
4. Creativity is a more difficult skill than entrepreneurship to develop. Discuss.
5. Why is creativity the soul of entrepreneurship?
6. Can you think of an entrepreneur who was not creative?
7. Are you a left or a right brain person?
8. Are you comfortable being creative? If not, why?
9. Can one individual undertake the whole creative process without help?
10. Do you see yourself more as an explorer, artist, judge or warrior? Why?
11. Is creativity good in all individuals and organisations? Give examples to support your argument.
12. Can you make a living out of being creative without being entrepreneurial?
13. Over the last ten years what have been the major commercial opportunities that arose? How were they exploited? Were the developments technology-led or market-led? What were the consequences?
14. Over the next ten years, what do you think will be the main commercial opportunities that entrepreneurial firms might be best advised to exploit?
15. Have there been any disruptive events recently that have created commercial opportunities? What were they and what opportunities do they create
16. What makes a good internet business?
17. What lessons do you learn from the dot.com boom and bust?
18. Give some examples of new-to-the-world products that have been successful and some that have not. Why have they been successful or unsuccessful?
19. Why is 'time to market' important?
20. Do you have an idea for a new product or service? Explain why it might be successful.
21. How can government persuade more people to set up their own business? Should it do so?

Exercises and assignments

1. Try assessing your creative potential. You can find many resources by undertaking an internet search on 'creativity'. Tests can be found on:

   - www.creax.com/csa
   - www.angelfire.com/wi/2brains

2. List the barriers that you feel inhibit you from being creative at home and at your college or university. How might they be removed or circumvented?
3. List the sources for awareness and new ideas you have at your disposal. What do you need to do to capitalise on them in a systematic way?
4. Like Alex Tew, try applying brainstorming in a group to the generation of new ideas. Try thinking of a new product/service application. Define an area for review, for example by looking at a problem you face in your everyday life and trying to find a solution to it. If you have problems with the technique, go to wwww.brainstorming.co.uk for further explanation.
5. Trying to use analogy in a group to come up with innovative solutions to problems can be more difficult – even with a group of friends. Start with a problem

to be solved and find the way similar problems might be solved in a different context. Alternatively, find a natural solution to a problem and consider whether it can be applied to a different circumstance.

6. Try using attribute analysis in a group. Again, this can be difficult. Focus the group on an everyday product or service. Select one feature or aspect and ask 'why does it have to be that way – what benefit does it bring to the customer?' Try it a few times with different product/service features.

7. Try using gap analysis. Select an everyday product or service. Characterise the product or service in two dimensions and use perceptual mapping to plot where competing products lie on these dimensions. Is there a gap in the market? Repeat the exercise for another product/service.

8. Try applying some of the creativity techniques to generate new ideas. Try thinking of a new product/service application. Define an area for review, for example by looking at a problem you face in your everyday life and trying to find a solution to it.

References

Bolton, B. and Thompson, J. (2000) *Entrepreneurs: Talent, Temperament, Technique*, Oxford: Butterworth-Heinemann.

de Bono, E. (1971) *Lateral Thinking for Management*, Harmondsworth: Penguin.

de Bono, E. (1995) 'Serious Creativity', *Journal for Quality and Participation*, 18(5).

Dosi, G., Maengo, L. and Pasquali, C. (2006) 'How Much Should Society Fuel the Greed of Innovators? On the Relations Between Appropriability, Opportunities and Rates of Innovation', *Research Policy*, 35.

Drucker, P. (1985) *Innovation and Entrepreneurship*, London: Heinemann.

Hurmelinna-Laukkanen, P. and Puumalainen, K. (2007) 'Nature and Dynamics of Appropriability: Strategies for Appropriating Returns on Innovation', *R&D Management*, 37.

Jankowicz, D. (2003) The Easy Guide to Repertory Grids, New York: John Wiley & Sons.

Kirby, D. (2003) *Entrepreneurship*, London: McGraw Hill.

Levine. D. and Boldrin. M. (2008) *Against Intellectual Monopoly*, Cambridge: Cambridge University Press.

Majaro, S. (1992) 'Managing Ideas for Profit', *Journal of Marketing Management*, 8.

Mintzberg, H. (1976) 'Planning on the Left Side and Managing on the Right', *Harvard Business Review*, 54, July/August.

Page, A.L. (1993) 'Assessing New Product Development Practices and Performance: Establishing Crucial Norms', *Journal of Product Innovation* Management, 10.

Parkhurst, H.B. (1999), 'Confusion, Lack of Consensus and the Definition of Creativity as a Construct', *Journal of Creative Behaviour*, 33.

Shapiro. R. and Pham. N. (2007) *Economic Effects of Intellectual Property-Intensive Manufacturing in the United States*, World Growth, www.sonecon.com/docs/studies/0807_thevalueofip.pdf.

Tidd, J. and Bessant, J. (2009) *Managing Innovation: Integrating Technological, Market and Organizational Change*, Chichester: John Wiley.

Valery, N. (1999) 'Innovation in Industry', *Economist*, 5(28).

von Oech, R. (1986) *A Kick in the Seat of the Pants*, New York: Harper & Row.

von Oech, R. (1998) *A Whack on the Side of the Head*, New York: Warner Books.

Vyakarnham, S. and Leppard, J. (1999) *A Marketing Action Plan for the Growing Business*, 2nd edn, London: Kogan Page.

CHAPTER 8

Building an entrepreneurial structure

CONTENTS

- Size
- Traditional large firm structures
- Environmental change and task complexity
- Organic structures
- Networks and other new forms of organizing
- Strategic alliances
- Summary

LEARNING OUTCOMES

By the end of this chapter you should be able to:

- Explain and give examples of how size, structure and different organizational forms can encourage and contribute to the development of corporate entrepreneurship;
- Explain how this is related to the tasks being undertaken and the environment in which the organization finds itself;
- Explain why firms are increasingly exploring new forms of organizing;
- Describe different forms of networking and explain how and why they are built up.

Size

Structures create order in an organization. Although there is no one 'best' structure, different types of structure are good for particular types of task. The most appropriate structure depends on a number of factors: the nature of the organization, the strategies it is employing, the tasks to be undertaken, the environmental conditions under which the firm operates and the size of the firm.

Size does seem to matter. Large organizations are more complex than small and complexity impedes information flows, lengthens decision making and can kill initiative. To be entrepreneurial, a large organization needs to find ways of breaking itself down into a number of sub-organizations with varying degrees of autonomy. The span of control for management does seem to matter – 'walking the talk', a management approach advocated earlier, only seems possible up to a certain size. But large organizations can structure themselves so that they comprise smaller 'units'. Again there are no prescriptive 'correct' approaches. However, for some time large companies have been seeking to replicate the flexibility of the small firm and encourage entrepreneurial management by 'deconstructing' themselves – that is, breaking themselves down into smaller units. Peter Chemin, CEO of the Fox TV empire, believes that 'in the management of creativity, size is your enemy' (*Economist*, 4 December 1999). He has tried to break down the studio into small units, even at the risk of incurring higher costs.

Many companies believe that the initial stages of innovation – a particular form of task – require such a different culture that completely separate premises from the corporate offices need to be found. This leads them to set up separate 'research' establishments. But research is not the same as development and even then the innovation has to be exploited commercially. Having separate locations for many of these activities allows firms to maintain different cultures as well as different structures, staffing and remuneration.

Taking this idea further, big companies often 'spin off' new ventures, creating completely new, small companies that are lean and flexible and focused on getting their product to market. However, often the big company has to put in place mechanisms to make this happen, mini-organizations within the big company with the task of spotting innovative opportunities and facilitating their development. This can be the corporate venture capital firm – an autonomous company that underwrites and assists new product/service developments that meet formal venture capital criteria.

Amar Bhidé (2000) believes that, rather than trying to re-invent themselves, large firms should concentrate on projects with high costs and low uncertainty, leaving those with low costs and high uncertainty to small entrepreneurial firms – with entrepreneurial management. As ideas mature and risks and rewards become more quantifiable, large firms can adopt them. Even in capital-intensive businesses such as pharmaceuticals, entrepreneurs or smaller entrepreneurial organizations can conduct early-stage research, selling out to large firms when they reach the expensive, clinical trial stage. About a third of drug firms' revenue now comes from licensed-in technology. Many large companies, like General Electric and Cisco, have adopted the policy of buying up small firms who have developed new technology.

John Naisbitt (1994) also feels the future lies very much with small independent firms, whether owner-managed or 'deconstructed' from large firms. His book is based upon the apparent paradox that 'the bigger the world economy, the more powerful its smallest players'. He sees much of the growing importance of smaller firms, and with them entrepreneurs, coming from larger firms which will have to restyle themselves into 'networks of entrepreneurs' if they are to survive. In his view 'downsizing, re-engineering, the creative networking organization, or the latest virtual corporation, whatever it is called, it comes down to the same thing. Corporations have to dismantle bureaucracies to survive. Economies of scale are giving way to economies of scope, finding the right size for synergy, market flexibility, and above all, speed.' He observes that 'to survive, big companies today – ABB, AT&T, GE, Grand Metropolitan, Coca-Cola, Benetton, Johnson & Johnson, British Petroleum, Honda, Alcoa, Xerox – are all deconstructing themselves and creating new structures, many as networks of autonomous units. Deconstruction is now a fashion, because it is the best way to search for survival.'

The other side to this trend towards downsizing and deconstructing large firms is that the large firm will increasingly concentrate on its core activities, where they have competitive advantage, and sub-contracting of non-core activities will increase. This enables the large firm to reduce its fixed cost base and thus the risk it faces and flatten its organization structure thereby ensuring a quicker response time to changes in the market place. As with Dell, 'partnership sourcing' is likely to increase, whereby a close relationship is built between the bigger company and the smaller subcontractor, with one helping the other to grow. Entrepreneurial firms can take the lead in this. The development of e-commerce for supply chain management will just accelerate this trend.

The trend towards flattening organizational structures started in the USA in the 1980s and then came to Europe. In the UK, 1994 saw BT cut 5000 middle and senior managers in one year reducing its layers of management from twelve to six. WH Smith cut 600 store managers in the same year reducing its layers of management from four to two. In the following year Shell got rid of 1200 managers from its head office. In the late 1980s and early 1990s the entire UK banking industry saw over one-third of its managers leave the industry. This is not just about deconstructing, it is about changing the attitudes of the remaining managers about the security of their jobs as well as putting many middle-aged managers in the position of having few alternatives other than self-employment. No wonder self-employment blossomed over the same period. Charles Handy (1994) predicted that many larger firms will become 'shamrock organizations' – the three leaves being core staff, temporary staff to ease them over peaks and troughs in work and small organizations supplying specialist services, deeply embedded in, and dependent upon, the larger firm. Many of us will mix five kinds of work: wage work, fee work, home work, gift work and study work. This takes us back to entrepreneurial management and the architecture on which it is based.

Large firms are increasingly experimenting with different structures, organizational forms and processes. Pettigrew and Fenton (2000) noted the following trends:

- Decentralizing
- Delayering
- Outsourcing
- Downscoping
- Using project forms of organizing
- Developing strategic alliances
- Communicating horizontally as well as vertically
- Investing in information technology
- Practising new HRM techniques

One implication from all this experimentation is clear – size matters and small is, indeed, beautiful. The reason for this is to do with the need in entrepreneurial organizations for flatter structures which result in better communication, greater delegation of authority and faster decision making. The larger the unit of organization the more people and the broader the span of control, or number of people reporting to a given manager – which make it difficult to handle. Put another way, size, or the larger the number of people in the unit of organization, requires structures that involve hierarchies and these tend to rely on power to make decisions, and the exercise of power tends to be slow and inflexible.

The question is how to achieve the best of both worlds – the benefits in terms of resources of large scale and the benefits in terms of entrepreneurship of small scale. The answer is not straightforward, and, as already said, needs to be adapted to particular circumstances. However, part of the answer is in smaller sub-structures, which form part of a larger whole. These, as we shall see, can take many different forms. Each sub-structure may have its own sub-culture and, what is more important, smaller units can be more entrepreneurial. Within any structure there needs to be a hierarchy of some sort that gives managers confidence that they have the authority to manage. Generally, to encourage entrepreneurship levels or layers of management need to be kept to a minimum to ensure flexibility and responsiveness. To start with, it is worthwhile reflecting on how and why structures typically evolve as the organizations age and grow in size.

Traditional large firm structures

The classic work of Larry Greiner (1972) on organizational life cycles. For Greiner organizational structures evolve as the organization grows through a process of continuous change and development. He typified this as comprising a number of identifiable stages. First there is the 'spider's web' that is so typical of a newly formed entrepreneurial organization. Early on this can be a real advantage to the organization but, as the number of people reporting either formally or informally directly to the entrepreneur increases, it can become dysfunctional. As the organization grows more structure is put in place, often with a functional hierarchy and centralized control. Departmentalization – forming people into functional groups such as marketing, production and accounting – will occur. Figure 8.1A shows a classic hierarchical structure. Each level might represent a particular grouping or sub-grouping within the organization. A similar diagram could be drawn representing individuals within the organization.

'It doesn't make sense to stay true to a structure that makes it more difficult for your people to succeed. Your organizational structure must be flexible enough to evolve along with your people, rather than work against them. This is one of the biggest and most challenging cultural issues we face as a fast growing company.'

Michael Dell

Next comes greater decentralization either based on geographic or product groupings, built around profit centres. Again, each division or profit centre would be represented at a certain level in Figure 8.1A and would itself have a hierarchical structure. This is followed by a move towards merging product groups into strategic business units together with the development of a head office with centralized administrative and staff functions. Finally, to aid integrative working, matrix

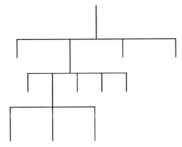

Figure 8.1a The hierarchical structure

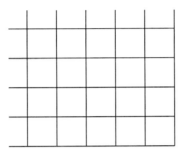

Figure 8.1b The matrix structure

structures and other cross-functional structures are adopted with head office staff reassigned to consultative teams. This form of organization is shown in Figure 8.1B.

The bureaucratic form of hierarchical structure (Figure 8.1A), with its universal organization structure, marks the earliest influential theory of organizational design. Based on the work of Weber (1947), it stresses rationality and functional efficiency. The literature was broadened by Chandler (1962), as technical and organizational complexity increased, by the inclusion divisions – a development that was seen as a rational solution to increasing scale and complexity. However, much of the later literature focuses on the dysfunctional consequences of this structure where people got in the way of rational efficiency (Pugh and Hickson, 1976).

It was the contingency theorists of the late 1950s and 1960s that concluded there was no single best way of organizing a business. That depends on the extent to which the structure furthers the objectives of the firm, but in particular it depends on:

- The environment it faces (Stinchcombe, 1959; Burns and Stalker, 1961; Emery and Trist, 1965; Haige and Aiken, 1967; Lawrence and Lorsch, 1967);
- The technology it uses (Woodward, 1965; Perrow, 1967);
- Its scale of operation (Pugh *et ah,* 1969; Blau, 1970);

In all cases, variations in structure can be rationalized in terms of task predictability and diversity. However, these approaches tend not to explain the underlying processes – how things happen.

The matrix structure (Figure 8.1B) came out of the contingency school. First posited by Galbraith (1973), it is based on the work of Lawrence and Lorsch *(op. cit.)* and is essentially an overlay on what is still a bureaucratic structure with hierarchical distributed power and decision making. It spawned the development of teams and task forces. Galbraith also observed how task complexity increased with task uncertainty and the amount of information that needs to be processed by the decision maker.

Environmental change and task complexity

A traditional hierarchical structure of the kind shown in Figure 8.1A is most suited to organizations that require security and stability. The matrix or task structure shown in Figure 8.1B is often seen in organizations undertaking project work, for example consultancies. But it can also be combined very effectively with the hierarchical structure so that individuals in different branches of the hierarchical structure come together as a team to undertake projects or tasks within the matrix structure. So, for example, the hierarchical structure might reflect functional areas such as design, production, marketing, sales and finance. Individuals from these areas, at appropriate levels in the hierarchy, might come together to form a matrix team to tackle a project such as new product development.

On its own, the traditional hierarchical structure shown in Figure 8.1A is mechanistic, bureaucratic and rigid. It has been called a 'machine bureaucracy' because it is most appropriate where the organization (or sub-organization) is tackling simple tasks with extensive standardization, in stable environments, and/or where security is important and where plans and programmes need to be followed carefully. Well developed information systems reporting on production/processing activity need to exist for it to be effective. Power is concentrated in the top executives. It is more concerned with production than marketing and is good at producing high volumes and achieving efficiency in production and distribution. As such, it is particularly appropriate when a product is at the mature phase of its life cycle and is being 'milked' as a 'cash cow'. It is the antithesis of an entrepreneurial structure and is designed to stifle individual initiative.

As the environment becomes more liable to change, standardization becomes less viable and responsibility for coping with unexpected changes needs to be pushed down the hierarchy. Complex tasks in stable environments mean that it becomes worthwhile developing standard skills to tackle the complexities. In both these cases the matrix organization can be an effective sub-structure within a more hierarchical organization. In a stable environment the matrix team can work on their complex tasks within set protocols – as they do, for example, in a surgical operation. In a changing environment the matrix team must have a high degree of discretion because established protocols may be inappropriate to the changing circumstances, even for the simple tasks they face. The implications of task complexity and environmental stability on organization structure are shown in Figure 8.2.

The main characteristic of the entrepreneurial environment is that it is one of change. In a changing environment where there is high task complexity an innovative, flexible, decentralized structure is needed, often involving structures within structures. Authority for decision making needs to be delegated and team working is likely to be the norm with matrix-type structures somehow built into the organization. Clear job definitions should never lead to a narrowing of responsibilities so that people ignore the new tasks that emerge. In many ways, far

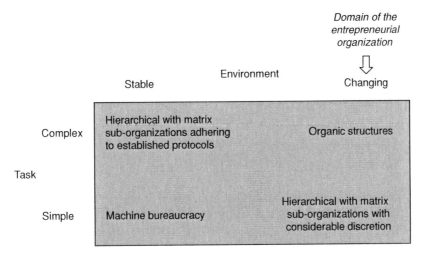

Figure 8.2 Organization structure based upon task complexity and environment

Source: Adapted from Burns, P. (2001) *Entrepreneurship and Small Business,* Basingstoke: Palgrave.

more important than the formal organization structure for a firm of this sort is the culture that tells people what needs to be done and motivates them to do it. This is often called an 'organic structure'.

Where there is low task complexity in a changing environment there is scope for greater centralization but the structure still needs to be responsive to change, probably through a degree of central direction and supervision. The structure, although hierarchical, should be relatively flat with few middle-management positions. However, culture is still important because the workforce still need to be motivated to make these frequent changes to their work practices. A business is a little like a house. If the organization structure is the plan and people are the bricks then culture is the cement that holds the whole thing together. Ignore any one element at your peril. Intrapreneurs and venture teams are examples of how hierarchical organizations can establish matrix teams to pursue entreprenurial opportunities.

Organic structures

Some authors (e.g. Morris and Kuratko, 2002) implicitly assume that all entrepreneurial organizations face complex tasks, based on the observation that the innovative process is complex. As they say, 'major innovations are most likely under structures that most closely mimic the organic structure.' But the complexity of innovation varies with the very nature of innovation and not all parts of the organization will be involved in 'cutting-edge' innovation. However, where this is the case, we are starting to define the nature of an effective entrepreneurial structure. Morris and Kuratko use Miller's (1986) definition of an organic structure saying it has 'limited hierarchy and highly flexible structure. Groups of trained specialists from different work areas collaborate to design and produce complex and rapidly changing products. Emphasis on extensive personal interaction and face-to-face communication, frequent meetings, use of committees and other liaison devices to ensure collaboration. Power is decentralized and authority is linked to expertise. Few bureaucratic rules or standard procedures exist. Sensitive information-gathering systems are in place for anticipating and monitoring the external environment.'

'Hyper-growth companies are quintessen-tially learn-by-doing organizations. Their survival depends on swift adaptation. Because resources and people are stretched, they most likely don't have excessive formal or overly structured systems in place. The key is to have enough structure in place that growth is not out of control -but not so much that the structure impedes your ability to adapt quickly ... Balancing the need for supporting infrastructure without building infrastructure too far ahead of growth is one of the more difficult and on going challenges any hyper-growth company will face.'

Michael Dell

So what will an organic structure look like? Unfortunately that is difficult to answer because, by its very definition, it is constantly forming and reforming to meet the changes it faces as it undertakes those complex tasks. Figure 8.3 is an example of one highly organic structure which comprises a series of spider's-web organizations within one large spider's web. There is no hierarchy. The organization is flat. In this organization the reporting lines between the smaller spider's webs are informal. Each operates almost autonomously and, in that sense, this may be seen more as a loose coalition of entrepreneurial teams, perhaps forming and reforming as opportunities appear. The danger is that each might operate with too much autonomy and too little direction, resulting in anarchy. In many organizations, particularly larger ones, more structure and hierarchy may therefore be needed.

Remember that it is unlikely that one organizational structure – even an organic one – will suit all situations. Greiner (*op. cit.*) emphasized how organizations naturally

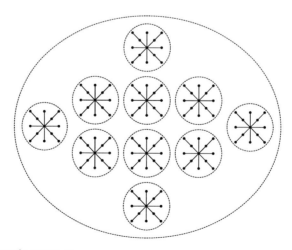

Figure 8.3 An organic structure

change and adapt and Galbraith (1995) underlines the importance of change and variety rather than rigidity and conformity: 'Organizational designs that facilitate variety, change, and speed are sources of competitive advantage. These designs are difficult to execute and copy because they are intricate blends of many different policies.' So flexibility and ability to change quickly are the key. Like the chameleon, the entrepreneurial organizational structure will adapt to best suit the environment it finds itself in.

The common themes are that the organic structure will be flexible, decentralized with a minimum of levels within the structures. It will be more horizontal than vertical. Authority will be based on expertise not on role and authority for decision making will be delegated and individuals empowered to make decisions. It will be informal rather than formal, with loose control but an emphasis on getting things done. Spans of control are likely to be broader. Team working is likely to be the norm. There will be structures within structures that encourage smaller units to develop, each with considerable autonomy, but there will be structures in place that encourage rapid, open, effective communication between and across these units and through any hierarchy. The success of these units will depend on the degree of fit with the mainstream organization requiring a high degree of awareness, commitment and connection between the two (Thornhill and Amit, 2001). What is more, with such a loose structure, strong entrepreneurial leadership and culture will be needed to keep the organization together and moving in the right direction.

CASE WITH QUESTIONS

Virgin

Virgin is one of the best known brands in Britain today, with 96% recognition, and it is well known world wide. It is strongly associated with its founder – 95% can name him. In 2004 Interbrand ranked it eighth in the global rankings for Brand of the Year. Research shows it is associated with value for money, quality, good service, innovation, fun and a sense of competitive advantage. But despite its high profile, Virgin is actually made up of lots of small companies – 20 umbrella companies with some 270 separate, semi-independent businesses, most set up in partnership with other companies. This mirrors a Japanese management structure called 'keiretsu', where different businesses act as a family under one brand, each empowered to run its own affairs independently, but offering help and support when needed. Richard Branson explains:

> 'Despite employing over 20,000 people, Virgin is not a big company – it's a big brand made up of lots of small companies. Our priorities are the opposite of our large competitors ... For us our employees matter most. It just seems common sense that if you have a happy, well motivated workforce, you're much more likely to have happy customers. And in due course the resulting profits will make your shareholders happy. Convention dictates that big is beautiful, but every time one of our ventures gets too big we divide it up into smaller units... Each time we do this, the people involved haven't had much more work to do, but necessarily they have a greater incentive to perform and a greater zest for their work.'

Virgin uses its brand as a capital asset in joint ventures. It is continually searching out opportunities where it can offer something 'better, fresher and more valuable'. Virgin contributes the brand and Richard Branson's PR profile, whilst the partner provides the operating capability and often the capital input – in some ways like a franchise operation. New firms are set up and sold off to finance Virgin's global expansion. In the three years to 2002 Virgin raised an estimated £1.3 billion in this way. Among these the biggest was the sale of 49% of Virgin Atlantic to Singapore Airlines for an estimated £600 million, followed in 2001 by a £75 million mortgage secured on his remaining stake. Virgin sold 50% of Virgin Blue, the Australian low-fare carrier to Patrick Corp. for £96 million. It also sold Virgin One to Royal Bank of Scotland for £45 million, the Virgin Active health clubs for £75 million and the French Megastore business to Lagardere for £92 million. Virgin has also raised smaller amounts by selling stakes in Raymond Blanc's restaurants.

The brand has been largely built through the personal PR efforts of its founder. According to Richard Branson:

'Brands must be built around reputation, quality and price ... People should not be asking "is this one product too far?" but rather, "what are the qualities of my company's name? How can I develop them?"'

According to Will Whitehorn, director of corporate affairs at Virgin Management:

'At Virgin, we know what the brand name means, and when we put our brand name on something, we're making a promise. It's a promise we've always kept and always will. It's harder work keeping promises than making them, but there is no secret formula. Virgin sticks to its principles and keeps its promises.'

Virgin defines its consumers as 'the public at large – anyone who will buy from us.' It defines its customers as 'people who are using Virgin products or services' and would like to extend its relationship with them, for example through Virgin Mobile. It believes its products and services are about making life easier – 'developing better value for money, a better service, challenging the status quo, and injecting an element of fun into what have traditionally been dreary marketplaces.' For example, in the airline industry it aims to offer excellent customer service and has consistently innovated in many ways like offering on-board messaging. In 2004 Virgin Atlantic was voted best long haul business airline by Business Travel and best transatlantic airline by Travel Weekly. Virgin Mobile offers one simple tariff with no extra charges rather than the complicated contracts offered by other mobile phone companies. In 2003 Mobile Choice Consumer placed it first for the best pre-pay package and best for customer service.

Service quality is at the core of many of the businesses and this is delivered by staff having the culture of 'going the extra mile'. Staff are seen as the company's most valuable asset. They give the company its personality, shape its culture and innovate. Staff training encourages empowerment and challenging of existing rules and reinforces the brand culture. There are numerous activities designed to promote team spirit and reinforce brand values, including Richard Branson's summer party for staff. All staff have annual appraisals and a continuous service policy allows them to move freely around the Virgin Group of companies. They enjoy a group-wide discount scheme. The Group conducts regular employee satisfaction surveys and focus groups. It has staff committees and makes use of ideas/suggestions boxes. The company encourages employees to 'go that extra mile' by schemes that reward this, such as Virgin Atlantic and Virgin Holidays' Heroes, Virgin Mobile Shout Scheme, Virgin Money's Academy Awards and the group-wide Star of the Year prize dinner. In 2003 Virgin was voted, by Business Superbrands, the brand that most values its employees.

Richard Branson now runs the Virgin empire from a large house in London's Holland Park. Although there does not appear to be a traditional head office structure, Virgin employs a large number of professional managers. It has a devolved structure and an informal culture. Employees are encouraged to come up with new ideas and development capital is available. Once a new venture reaches a certain size it is launched as an independent company within the Virgin Group and the intrapreneur takes an equity stake. Will Whitehorn, Branson's right hand man for the last 16 years, says of Richard: 'He doesn't believe that huge companies are the right way to go. He thinks small is beautiful... He's a one-person venture capital company, raising money from selling businesses and investing in new ones, and that's the way it will be in the future' (*The Guardian*, 30 April 2002). In 2007 Richard Branson announced that he would be taking a less active role in the day-to-day management of his companies.

Up-to-date information on Virgin and Richard Branson can be found on the company website: www.virgin.com

Questions

1. How would you describe the structure of the Virgin Group?
2. Do you agree that Virgin is now just a 'branded venture capital company'? Explain what this means.
3. What does the Virgin brand bring to a product or service? How far can the brand be stretched?
4. How dependent is the Virgin brand on its founder, Richard Branson?

Networks and other new forms of organizing

Over the last fifty years, firms have continued to organize based upon the enduring principles of Weber and Chandler. Whittington *et al.* (1999) noted that out of the top 500 companies in the three leading European economies the overwhelming majority used a multidivisional form of structure – 89% in the UK, 79% in Germany and 70% in France. However, Whittington *et al.* concede that their structural categories refer mainly to formal organizational characteristics and say little about the processes that go on under the surface – how managers actually behave. They also observe that the character of the divisional organization of the 1960s was not the same as in the 1990s. New technologies have emerged and continue to be a strong driver of organizational change, particularly in multinational companies. Management styles have altered and internal processes are different.

So what is going on under the surface? Over the last twenty years, there has been a proliferation of writing on new organization forms that broaden our concepts of organizational structures. In part this reflects the increasing complexity of organizations as they struggle and experiment with different organizational forms to maintain an effective global presence in a global economy where the pace of change is accelerating. In part it reflects the changing nature of society in terms of social norms and how computers and the internet make communication easier and quicker. In part it reflects the shift towards a knowledge economy with competitive advantage based upon the organization's ability to exploit knowledge quickly. Although this burgeoning literature seems to have no overarching perspective or theory it is fundamentally concerned with both structure and particularly process, but it has broadened to recognize the importance of relationships – which is at the core of entrepreneurial architecture. As Fenton and Pettigrew (2000) observe:

> 'It would seem that large organizations at the end of the twentieth century have the same structural characteristics as they did 50 years ago The evidence appears to be that formal hierarchical organization is still present as an institutional backdrop but not so crucial in determining organizational activities or capabilities. Instead "new" subtle coordination mechanisms stress the informal and social processes of the organization. There is also a move away from defining organizations purely in distributional terms toward more relational notions As firms add value via relationships and require ever greater internal and external interdependence to create, share and transfer knowledge, so the basis for organizational activity and configuration is centred on relationships and the wider social context within which firms are embedded.'

So the traditional hierarchical reporting structures mask important informal lateral relationships that add value to the firm through knowledge transfer. In looking at these new forms of organization Fenton and Pettigrew (*op. cit.*) identify three themes in the literature:

1. Networks and the socially embedded firm.
2. The knowledge firm in the knowledge economy.
3. The globalizing firm and its changing boundaries.

Networks and the socially embedded firm

One of the characteristics of entrepreneurs is their ability to command resources that they do not own and there are a number of organizational structures which can facilitate this characteristic. The network structure comprises either an internal or external network of independent members (individuals or organizations), unified by a common purpose and sharing in the benefits that stem from collaboration. An example of an internal network would be a large company organized around strategic business units (SBUs). An external network could take the form of a strategic alliances or joint ventures.

Networks are based on personal relationships and reciprocity, and all relationships are based on trust, self-interest and reputation (Dubini and Aldrich, 1991; Larson,

1992). Organizational networks develop based upon multiple networks of individuals. Each member of the network may have a different organization structure so relationships may be multi-level rather than flat, formed by clusters of coalitions at different hierarchical levels. The many links in these networks are strengthened by increased interaction and can be further strengthened by an entrepreneurial leader pulling the network together and giving it stability. These complex networks can facilitate many forms of organizational relationships. A network structure can be complex and difficult to chart – it could look very similar to Figure 8.3 – and it faces the same challenge of co-ordination as its size and complexity increases.

These networks create distinctive capabilities. In the case of strategic partnerships the relationships are usually designed to create value through synergy as partners achieve mutual gains that neither could gain individually (Teece, 1992). For example, since assets are owned by the constituent individuals or organizations, the financial resources needed and the risk associated with any joint venture are spread and flexibility increased. It has been shown that international networks are an important stimulant for international start-ups (McDougall *et al.*, 1994; Oviatt and McDougall, 1995; Johnson, 2004). Similarly alliances can create economic advantage by leveraging market presence (Ohmae, 1989; Lewis, 1990; Lorange and Roos, 1992). They can provide vertical integration and scale economies at a greatly reduced cost (Anderson and Weitz, 1992). There is growing evidence of the benefits of networking as a way of stimulating innovation and knowledge transfer. At a macro economic level strategic alliances and supplier networks are said to be crucial for the future success of US manufacturing (Goldhar and Lei, 1991).

A virtual structure is one that uses information technology – computers and the internet – to link many individuals or independent organizations, based in many different locations. It is frequently used to build supplier networks, as in the case of Dell. Virtual structures come together to exploit specific opportunities, forming and reforming in different groupings to exploit different opportunities. It is a structure that is best used to undertake specific tasks that do not need contact or the building of relationships. Because relationships are not built up it is likely to have a shorter life than a network structure. With this exception, it shares many of the advantages of the network structure. Handy (1996) described it as a 'box of contracts' and because of its lack of tangibility it has profound consequences for how we think of organizational forms.

Networks blur the boundaries of the firm extending them to a community of interest, rather than restricting them to a legal or economic unit. They mean that resources and risks can be shared across economic units so that networks of small firms can compete more effectively against large firms. They mean that organization relationships are not necessarily dictated by hierarchies and power structures, rather by trust, respect and mutual self-interest. And ultimately it is quite conceivable that these networks are more important than formal organizational structures.

The knowledge firm in the knowledge economy

Truly entrepreneurial organizations are learning organizations – organizations that add value in highly competitive, often technology-based, industries by sharing

knowledge and learning throughout their structure. Indeed 'sharing information and knowledge' is one of the high-level attributes in the cultural web of an
entrepreneurial organization whereby it becomes both a vehicle for knowledge access
and knowledge creation. And it is the ability to innovate, again and again, that creates sustainable competitive advantage.

The literature on knowledge management sees organizations as complex, without clear structure but with a high degree of integration brought about partly
by a strong culture. It explores how to achieve co-ordination and integration of
individuals' knowledge within an organization as greater complexity and hence
knowledge specialization occurs. The literature stresses the importance of tacit
knowledge (embedded in minds and activities), which is difficult to share, rather
than explicit knowledge (stated in verbal communications or documents), which
can be easily copied. For example, Grant (1996) assumes that knowledge creation
is primarily an individual activity and the primary role of the organization is
harnessing it for the production of goods or services. It is therefore logical that
the primary focus of the organization is to stimulate individual creativity and
learning and translate that into products and services that the market values.
In this context Grant proposes that: 'Once firms are viewed as institutions for
integrating knowledge, a major part of which is tacit and can be exercised only
by those who possess it, then hierarchical coordination fails.' Structures need to
be flat and non-hierarchical where knowledge must be shared but the boundaries of the organization can extend beyond formal lines where knowledge sharing
takes place. For knowledge firms new forms of organizing revolve around social
and relational dimensions (Nahapiet and Ghoshal, 1998). Networks can play an
important role.

The globalizing firm and its changing boundaries

This theme stresses the need to focus an organization on its core competencies to
add value in an increasingly global market place, whilst outsourcing other activities. It focuses on technology, in particular IT as a way of integrating the firm by
making knowledge transparent and developing global IT networks (Konstadt, 1990).
There is also a focus on managing business processes rather than departments which
has emphasized horizontal structures and fed into the literature on teams and team
working (Stewart, 1992). However, as we have seen, when vertical structures are de-
emphasized it inevitably emphasizes co-operation and relationship building as a
basis for co-ordination, an approach supported by empirical work on the relationships between headquarters and their subsidiaries conducted by Roth and Nigh
(1992). This emphasis on informal relationships presents us with some familiar
themes. The global firm literature challenges the efficacy of the divisional structure
with its emphasis on the integration of sub-units and the sharing of their resources
(Ghoshal and Bartlett, 1995).

What so much of this literature reveals is that the traditional organization chart
is a poor representation of how many organizations really function. Informal structures are important, based on strong relationships – the word that appears again
and again. Networks are important – in one context and then in another – flexing
and changing over time. As soon as we identify one structure (and name it),

another appears, perhaps reflecting the rapidly changing environment in which organizations today operate. And processes are just as important as structure, processes that are 'continually shaped and reshaped by the actions of actors who are in turn constrained by the structural positions they find themselves' (Nohria, 1992). What this literature does not give us is any clear agreement on how to think about these new structures. As with many things in management, firms are continually experimenting, both intentionally and unintentionally, both formally and informally, trying to face up to the organizational challenges they face. And organization innovation often involves moving between extremes, yet maintaining business continuity as firms battle with the contradictions between hierarchies and networks, vertical and horizontal integration and sharing knowledge across units that both compete and collaborate and the dilemmas then posed in making decisions (Pettigrew, 1999).

CASE WITH QUESTIONS

Dell

Dell assembles computers. Originally assembled in the USA, they are now assembled also in Ireland, Malaysia, China and Brazil. However, from the start Michael Dell knew what the critical success factor for his business was. He used an expert to build prototype computers whilst he concentrated on finding cheap components. And the company still sources its components from around the world. Dell grew at an incredible pace, notching up sales of £3.7 million in the first nine months. The company pioneered direct marketing in the industry whereby systems are built to the customer's specifications after an order is placed, and then shipped directly to the customer. More lately, it has pioneered the development of integrated supply chain management, linking customers orders directly to its supply chain. At all times it has focused clearly on a low-cost/low-price marketing strategy.

> 'We built the company around a systematic process: give customers the high-quality computers they want at a competitive price as quickly as possible, backed by great service.'

Every division in Dell is tasked to continuously improve efficiency and reduce costs, and workers undertake extensive training through its team-based Business Process Improvement programme. This is aimed at reinforcing the importance of cost reduction, but also putting in place processes and procedures that allow efficiency savings to be made, giving the team control over implementing new ideas. As Dell says, 'Empower workers with the tools to make a difference and the innovation will follow.' Productivity at Dell, measured by the number of computers built per employee, has increased 240% in the last five years.

Dell was a pioneer of e-business. What makes Dell special today is its 'fully integrated value chain' – B2B2C. Suppliers, including many small firms, have real-time access to information about customer orders and deliveries via the company's extranet. They organize supplies of hard drives, motherboards, modems etc. on a 'just-in-time' basis so as to keep the production line moving smoothly. From the parts being delivered to the orders being shipped out takes just a few hours. Inventories are minimized and, what is more important, the cash is received from the customer before Dell pays its suppliers. These systems and processes are part of Dell's competitive advantage. They help keep Dell's costs low and allow it to build to order. In the 1990s, in order to protect this, the company started applying for patents, not for its products, but for different parts of its ordering, building and testing processes. It now holds over 80 such patents.

Dell has created a three-way 'information partnership' between itself and its customers and suppliers by treating them as collaborators who together find ways of improving efficiency:

> 'The best way I know to establish and maintain a healthy, competitive culture is to partner with your people – through shared objectives and common strategies ... Dell is very much a relationship orientated company ... how we communicate and partner with our employees and customers. But our commitment doesn't stop there. Our willingness and ability to partner to achieve our common goals is perhaps seen in its purest form in how we forge strong alliances with our suppliers ... Early in Dell's history we had more than 140 different suppliers providing us with component parts ... Today our rule is to keep it simple and have as few partners as possible. Fewer than 40 suppliers provide us with about 90 percent of our material needs. Closer partnerships with fewer suppliers is a great way to cut cost and further speed products to market.'

Dell's market place is highly competitive. Dell prides itself on good marketing of quality products but, most importantly, speedy delivery of customized products - factors it believes are reflected in the Dell brand.

> 'The idea of building a business solely on cost or price was not a sustainable advantage. There would always be someone with something that was lower in price or cheaper to produce. What was really important was sustaining loyalty among customers and employees, and that could be derived from having the highest level of service and very high performing products.'

Nevertheless, whilst Dell might not sell the cheapest computers in the market place, the price it asks must always be competitive and that means costs must still be kept as low as possible.

Up-to-date information on Dell can be found on their website: www.dell.com.

Questions

1. How much of a generic product is a Dell computer?
2. What do you think of Dell's marketing strategy?
3. From what you know about the company, is Dell's competitive advantage based solely on its external architecture? What else might contribute to this?

Strategic alliances

Strategic alliances have featured quite prominently in the literature on corporate entrepreneurship. They can take a number of different forms. A strategic alliance can be internal – between departments or other structures of the same organization – or external – between different organizations. It can encompass all of the functional areas of an organization or just a single function, such as R&D. It can straddle markets and hierarchies, providing a structure for co-operation. Parkhe (1993) defines strategic alliances as 'relatively enduring interfirm cooperative arrangements, involving flows and linkages that use resources and/or governance structures from autonomous organizations, for the joint accomplishment of individual goals linked to the corporate mission of each sponsoring firm.'

Strategic alliances can be an effective way of sustaining competitive advantage. They can be particularly important in relation to innovation and in that context. Aside from the explicit strategic and operational motives such as gaining access to new markets, acquiring new technologies, enhancing new product development capabilities or leveraging on economies of scale or scope (see the BBC/IBM, Sun Microsystems/Intel and KongZhong/DangDang/SouFun case insights), mutual learning is an important element in many alliances. Alliances facilitate organizational learning (Parkhe, *op. cit.*). Karthik (2002) states that 'alliances are pooling mechanisms comingling diverse unique skills and capabilities, and thus are able to create potentially powerful learning opportunities for firms. In fact, learning opportunities create "learning organizations" that are able to increase their absorptive capacities and to assimilate new ideas easily to remain competitive.' So, strategic alliances increase the learning community and the potential knowledge base of the organization. The risks involved in this are minimal but there are costs in finding a partner and maintaining the relationship.

Alliances evolve and change in nature over time. Firms involved in an alliance often have a mix of emotions, involving competition and collaboration in varying proportions, as the partnership evolves over time. Over time the partners build trust and mutual respect – essential in any relationship. Karthik (*op. cit.*) posited four distinct phases in the evolution of the relationship based on the work of Dwyer *et al.* (1987) and Wilson (1995):

1. *Awareness and partner selection*: In this phase the need for an alliance is recognized and the search for a suitable partner begins. Learning starts but it is largely unilateral as each organization finds out about the other and decide whether they can work with the other and also seeks to better understand the external market environment in which the alliance will work.
2. *Exploration*: In this phase partners begin interacting and set the ground rules for future interaction. Partners start to build trust and establish a common culture in order to build the social bonding process. Learning is still largely unilateral but there are elements of experimentation and mutual learning as a way of bridging the compatibility gap between partners.
3. *Expansion*: As trust builds, greater interaction takes place and partners grow closer. They stop probing each other and start working as a partnership. Learning is partly mutual as partners share common perceptions and goals and bridge expectation

gaps with a view to sustaining the relationship. Unilateral learning also takes place as partners attempt to internalize the other's embedded knowledge and skills.

4. *Commitment to the relationship*: This is the stage where 'significant economic, communication, and/or emotional resources may be exchanged' (Dwyer *et al.*, *op. cit.*) and boundaries between the partners have little significance. There is commonality of purpose, multiple levels of relationships and mutual learning processes. Learning at this stage is one of mutual capacity-building (Hamel, 1991) and both parties seek to maintain the relationship, building psychological contracts instead of legal ones.

CASE INSIGHT

In 2007 the **BBC** and **IBM** forged a strategic alliance following an agreement for a framework outlining several joint projects. One of the first was applying IBM image/video search technology to CBeebies and CBBC programmes. The IBM research system, called 'Marvel', has the ability to visually analyze images so as to categorize content based upon appearance. This allows images/videos to be more easily searched online for specific content. The project is the first of a number that will allow the BBC to unlock the commercial value of its massive TV and radio archive.

In 2007 Sun **Microsystems** and **Intel** announced a broad strategic alliance that centred on Intel's endorsement of Sun's Solaris operating system and Sun's commitment to deliver a comprehensive family of enterprise servers and workstations based on Intel's Xeon processors. The alliance also included joint engineering, design and marketing efforts as well as other Intel and Sun enterprise-class technologies. The alliance is expected to help with the widespread adoption of Sun's Solaris system but, perhaps more importantly, it is expected to move Intel's Xeon-based systems up the server value chain to datacentres and other high performance facilities. These environments are currently dominated by IBM and HP with a range of servers powered by an Itanium chip, which itself was co-developed with Intel.

In 2007 **KongZhong Corporation** announced a strategic partnership with **DangDang** and SouFun. KongZhong is China's leading provider of wireless value-added services and the operator of one of China's main wireless internet portals whilst DangDang is a leading e-commerce website specializing in books and consumer electronics and SouFun is one of the largest online real estate information providers. DangDang and SouFun will establish exclusive co-branded channels on KongZhong's wireless internet portal to provide wireless users with content and services.

Summary

Structures create order in an organization but there is no single 'best' solution. The most appropriate structure depends on the nature of the organization, the strategies it employs, the tasks it undertakes, the environment it operates in and its size.

Small organizational units are more responsive to the environment and large firms have responded to the entrepreneurial challenge by experimenting with different organizational forms. There is an accelerating trend to downsize and deconstruct large firms – breaking them down to smaller components so that even the core is better able to act entrepreneurially. More firms are outsourcing non-core activities, downscoping and using project forms of organization. They are developing strategic alliances with smaller firms and using them to 'outsource innovation'. They are flattening organizational structures, investing in information technology and new HRM techniques to make this happen.

Structures evolve as organizations grow and, as **Michael Dell** says, survival depends on swift adaptation. For larger firms, both hierarchical and matrix structures, or a combination, can be appropriate in different circumstances. However the traditional hierarchical structure is mechanistic, bureaucratic and rigid. It is most appropriate for simple tasks in stable environments. Entrepreneurial organizations typically face a high degree of environmental turbulence. If the tasks they need to undertake are complex, they are best served by an organic organization structure.

An organic structure has limited hierarchy and is highly flexible, decentralized with a minimum of levels within the structures. It is more horizontal than vertical. Authority is based on expertise not on role, and authority for decision making is delegated so that individuals are empowered to make decisions. It is informal rather than formal, with loose control but an emphasis on getting things done. Spans of control are likely to be broader. Team working is likely to be the norm. There are structures within structures that encourage smaller units to develop, each with considerable autonomy, but there are also structures in place that encourage rapid, open, effective communication between and across these units and through any hierarchy.

Richard Branson understands this, and his **Virgin** empire comprises some 270 separate, semi-independent companies, often set up in partnership with other individuals and organizations.

What so much of this literature on new forms of organizing reveals is that the traditional organization chart is a poor representation of how many organizations really function. Because of the increasing pace of change and increasing complexity in a global environment where knowledge is possibly the most important resource, formal structures struggle to cope. Informal structures are becoming increasingly important, based on strong relationships. Strong network connections are becoming vital – in one context and then in another – flexing and changing over time. Networks, virtual or real, encourage resource sharing and therefore can mitigate risk. **Dell** uses this as part of its B2B2C fully integrated supply chain that generates an information partnership between Dell, the customer and suppliers.

Strategic partnerships – like those between **BBC/IBM**, **Sun Microsystems/Intel** and **KongZhong/DangDang/SouFun** – are also important, particularly in the context of innovation, for both strategic and operational reasons but also as essential ways of transferring knowledge and increasing the size of the learning community.

Essays and discussion topics

1. Why does size matter for an organization?
2. Should large firms concentrate on projects with high cost and low uncertainty and leave those with low cost and high uncertainty to small firms? Will this happen?

3. Will small firms become more important in the twenty-first century?
4. Why do large firms deconstruct and downsize?
5. Consider Handy's 'shamrock organization'. What is in it for the company? What is in it for staff? What is in it for subcontractors?
6. Are 'shamrock organizations' becoming reality?
7. What are the implications for an appropriate organizational structure of a turbulent environment?
8. What is an organic structure? Can it be defined?
9. Do you agree that Virgin is just a 'branded venture capital company'? Why?
10. What are the advantages and disadvantages of the network structure – both real and virtual?
11. Why has globalization encouraged the growth of networks?
12. Why has IT encouraged the growth of networks?
13. Why has the increasing importance of knowledge encouraged the growth of networks?
14. How can networking encourage innovation?
15. Why are relationships important in networks?
16. What is meant by process being just as important as structure?
17. What are the prerequisites for an effective strategic partnership?
18. Is an organic structure just another way of describing a large network of small operating units such as strategic business units?
19. Is there such a thing as an ideal organization structure for an entrepreneurial firm? If so, outline what its elements should be.
20. Why should the entrepreneurial firm find developing the 'new forms of organizing' easy?

Exercises and assignments

1. Give some specific examples of an industry where a hierarchical, bureaucratic structure should be the best way to organize. Select three companies in this industry and investigate their organizational structure. Explain why their structure conforms or does not conform to your expectations, taking into account the success of the business in that industry.
2. List the type of organizations and market sectors or environments that face high degrees of turbulence. Select a particularly turbulent sector and research how the organizations within it are organized and the success, or otherwise, they have in dealing with it.
3. List and describe the different ways by which large organizations break themselves down into smaller sub-organizations. Under what circumstances are each of these approaches appropriate?
4. Select a large company that has deconstructed itself (e.g. Asea Brown Boveri, ABB). Research and write up its history and describe its success or failure. What lessons are to be learnt from this?
5. Provide three examples of strategic alliances and indicate why they are important.
6. Provide three examples of business networks and explain what use they serve.

References

Anderson, E. and Weitz, B. (1992) 'The Use of Pledges to Build and Sustain Commitment in Distribution Channels', *Journal of Marketing Research*, 29 (February).

Bhidé, A. (2000) *The Origin and Evolution of New Businesses*, Oxford: Oxford University Press.

Blau, P. M. (1970) 'A Formal Theory of Differentiation in Organizations', *American Sociological Review*, 35(2).

Burns, T. and Stalker, G. M. (1961) *The Management of Innovation*, London: Tavistock.

Chandler, A. D. (1962) *Strategy and Structure: Chapters in the History of the American Industrial Enterprise*, Cambridge, Mass: MIT Press.

Dubini, P. and Aldrich, H. (1991) 'Personal and Extended Networks are Central to the Entrepreneurial Process,' *Journal of Business Venturing*, 6.

Dwyer, R. F., Schurr, P. H. and Oh, S. (1987) 'Developing Buyer–Seller Relationships', *Journal of Marketing*, 51 (2).

Emery, F. E. and Trist, E. L. (1965) 'The Causal Texture of Organisational Environments', *Human Relations*, 18.

Fenton, E. and Pettigrew, A. (2000) 'Theoretical Perspectives', in A. Pettigrew and E. Fenton (eds), *The Innovating Organisation*, London: Sage.

Galbraith, J. R. (1973) *Designing Complex Organisations*, Reading, Mass: Addison-Wesley.

Galbraith J. R. (1995) *Designing Organizations: An Executive Briefing on Strategy Structure and Process*, San Francisco: Jossey-Bass.

Ghoshal, S. and Bartlett, C. A. (1995) 'Building the Entrepreneurial Corporation: New Organisation Processes, New Managerial Tasks', *European Management Journal*, 13(2), June.

Goldhar, J. D. and Lei, D. (1991) 'The Shape of Twenty-first Century Global Manufacturing', *Journal of Business Strategy*, 12(2).

Grant, R. M. (1996) 'Towards a Knowledge-based Theory of the Firm', *Strategic Management Journal*, 17 (Winter Special Issue).

Greiner, L. (1972) 'Revolution and Evolution as Organizations Grow', *Harvard Business Review*, 50 (July/August).

Haige, J. and Aiken, M. (1967) 'Relationship of Centralisation to other Structural Properties', *Administrative Science Quarterly*, 12.

Hamel, G. (1991) 'Competition for Competence and Inter-Partner Learning within International Strategic Alliances', *Strategic Management Journal*, 12 (Summer).

Handy, C. (1994), *The Empty Raincoat*, London: Hutchinson.

Handy, C. (1996) 'Rethinking Organisations' in T. Clark (ed.), *Advancement in Organisation Behaviour: Essays in Honour of Derek, S. Pugh*, Aldershot: Ashgate.

Johnson, J. E. (2004) 'Factors Influencing the Early Internationalisation of High Technology Start-ups: US and UK Evidence,' *Journal of International Entrepreneurship*, 2.

Karthik, N. S. (2002) 'Learning in Strategic alliances: An Evolutionary Perspective', *Academy of Marketing Science Review*, 10.

Konstadt, P. (1990) 'Into the Breach', *CIU*, 11 August.

Larson, A. (1992) 'Network Dyads in Entrepreneurial Settings: A Study of the Governance of Exchange Relationships,' *Administrative Science Quarterly*, 37.

Lawrence, P. R. and Lorsch, J. W. (1967) *Organisation and Environment: Managing Differentiation and Integration*, Boston, Mass: Division of Research, Graduate School of Business, Harvard University.

Lewis, J. D. (1990) *Partnerships for Profit: Structuring and Managing Strategic Alliances*, New York: Free Press.

Lorange, P. and Roos, J. (1992) *Strategic Alliances: Formation, Implementation and Evolution*, Oxford; Blackhills.

McDougall, P. P., Shane, S. and Oviatt, B. M. (1994) 'Explaining the Formation of International New Ventures: The Limits of Theories from International Business Research', *Journal of Business Venturing*, 9.

Miller, D. (1986) 'Configurations of Strategy and Structure: Towards a Synthesis', *Strategic Management Journal*, 7.

Morris, H. M. and Kuratko, D. F. (2002) *Corporate Entrepreneurship*, Fort Worth: Harcourt College Publishers.

Naisbitt, J. (1994) *Global Paradox*, London: Books Club Association.

Nahapiet, J. and Ghoshal, S. (1998) 'Social Capital, Intellectual Capital and the Creation of Value in Firms', *Academy of Management Best Paper Proceedings*.

Nohria, N. (1992) 'Introduction: Is a Networking Perspective a Useful Way of Studying Organizations?' in N. Nohria and R.G. Eccles (eds), *Networks and Organizations: Structure, Form and Action*, Boston, Mass: Harvard Business School Press.

Ohmae, K. (1989) 'The Global Logic of Strategic Alliances', *Harvard Business Review*, March/April.

Oviatt, B. M. and McDougall, P. P. (1995) 'Global Start-ups: Entrepreneurs on a Worldwide Stage', *Academy of Management Executive*, 9(2).

Parkhe, A. (1993) 'Strategic Alliance Structuring: A Game Theoretic and Transaction Cost Examination of Interfirm Cooperation', *Academy of Management Journal*, 36 (August).

Perrow, C. (1967) 'A Framework for the Comparative Analysis of Organizations', *American Sociological Review*, 32.

Pettigrew, A. M. (1999) 'Organising to Improve Company Performance', *Hot Topics, Warwick Business School*, 1(5).

Pettigrew, A. and Fenton, E. (2000) *The Innovating Organization*, London: Sage.

Pugh, D. S. and Hickson, D.J. (1976) *Organisational Structure in its Context: The Aston Programme 1*, Farnborough: Saxon House.

Pugh, D. S., Hickson, D. J. and Hinings, C. R. (1969) 'The Context of Organisation Structures', *Administrative Science Quarterly*, 13.

Roth, K. and Nigh, D. (1992) 'The Effectiveness of HQ–Subsidiary Relationships: The Role of Coordination, Control and Conflict', *Journal of Business Research*, 25.

Stewart, T. A. (1992) 'The Search for the Organisation of Tomorrow', Fortune, 125(10), 18 May.

Stinchcombe, A. L. (1959) 'Social Structure and Organization', in J. G. March (ed.), *Handbook of Organizations*, Chicago: Rand McNally.

Teece, D. J. (1992) 'Competition, Cooperation and Innovation: Organisational Arrangements for Regimes of Rapid Technological Progress', *Journal of Economic Behaviour and Organisation*, 18.

Thornhill, S. and Amit, R. (2001), 'A Dynamic Perspective of Internal Fit in Corporate Venturing', *Journal of Business Venturing*, 16(1).

Weber, M. (1947) *The Theory of Social and Economic Organisation*, Glencoe, Ill.: The Free Press.

Whittington, R., Mayer, M. and Curto, F. (1999) 'Chandlerism in post-war Europe: Strategic and Structural change in France, Germany and the United Kingdom, 1950–1993', *Industrial and Corporate Change*, 8(3).

Wilson, D. T. (1995) 'An Integrated Model of Buyer-Seller Relationships', *Journal of the Academy of Marketing Science*, 23(4).

Woodward, J. (1965) *Industrial Organisation: Behaviour and Control*, Oxford: Oxford University Press.

CHAPTER 9

Developing strategies for growth

CONTENTS

- Opportunities for growth
- Market penetration
- Market development
- Product/service development
- Diversification
- Mergers and acquisitions
- Sustainability and corporate social responsibility
- Sustaining growth
- Summary

LEARNING OUTCOMES

By the end of this chapter you should be able to:

- Describe the growth options facing an organization, the reasons for pursuing them and the advantages and risks associated with each;

- Explain the consequences of selecting particular strategies and the factors that are important in making each strategy work;

- Use Porter's Five Forces analysis to assess the competitiveness of an industry;

- Describe the different types of diversification and explain the degree of risk faced in pursuing each one;

- Describe the different types of mergers and acquisitions and explain the reasons for following this strategy and the risks involved;

- Explain the reasons why sustainability and corporate social responsibility must be at the heart of any growth strategy;

- Pick out the strategies that are most likely to lead to successful and sustained growth in an entrepreneurial organization.

Opportunities for growth

The dominant goal of the entrepreneurial firm is likely to be growth. As we have seen, understanding what has made the business successful in the past – in particular what makes it unique and what adds value for the customer – is a prerequisite for moving forward. In general terms, to achieve growth a company should:

- build on its strengths and core competencies;
- shore up its weaknesses;
- develop a marketing strategy for each product/market offering and the opportunity it presents that reflects the appropriate generic marketing strategy and the stage a product/market offering is at in its life cycle;

all placed in the context of its portfolio of product/market offerings.

Research tells us that the strategy with the best chance of generating the highest profits is to differentiate with the aim of dominating that market niche – and to do this effectively and quickly – and to continue to innovate based on that differential advantage. Although firms following other strategies do, of course, succeed, the importance of this research cannot be overemphasized. Business, like life, is about playing the odds. You ignore them at your peril.

The unique elements of the differentiation strategy are likely to be based on distinctive capabilities – like the entrepreneurial architecture – that, applied to a relevant market, becomes a competitive advantage. This will become the firm's core market, the one in which it has a distinct advantage by adding the greatest value for its customers. A focus on core business was emphasized in the 1980s (Abell, 1980) and popularized by Peters and Waterman (1982) as 'sticking to the knitting'. However, core competencies may be relevant to other markets and, even if they are not directly relevant, can often be leveraged by entering other markets in which, although the firm may not have the same distinctive competitive advantage, it can use economies of scale or its channels of distribution to gain market share.

Whilst the objective of entrepreneurial strategy is growth, its essence is that it is opportunity driven. Stevenson and Gumpert (1985) describe the entrepreneur as 'constantly attuned to the environmental changes that may suggest a favourable chance.' However, in order to start understanding the opportunities for growth, there is one further tool that helps analyze in a systematic fashion how growth can be achieved. It is called the Product/Market matrix, was originally devised by Igor Ansoff (1968) and shown in Figure 9.1. This simple conceptual framework uses existing/ new products on one axis and existing/new markets on the other. It then goes on to explore the options within the four quadrants of the matrix and how the options might be achieved.

Like all useful business frameworks it is attractively simple and intuitively logical. To achieve growth a company has four options:

1. Market penetration
2. Product development
3. Market development
4. Diversification.

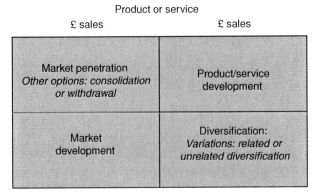

Figure 9.1   The product/market matrix

Market penetration (quadrant 1)

Market penetration involves selling more of the same product/service to the same market – just selling more to existing customers. If the firm has strong relationships with its existing customers this may be possible. It can also involve finding new customers from the same market segment. Cadbury Schweppes achieve this by constantly improving their channels of distribution and giving customers more 'indulgence opportunities' for their impulse-buy products. Using the Boston matrix, this is how you move from 'problem child' to 'star'. The best way of finding new customers is to understand existing customers – assuming that they are happy with the product/service offering – and try to find more of the same. This involves understanding why they buy and being able to describe the customers' common characteristics – effectively describing the market segment(s) buying the product or service. In a growth market there may be ample opportunity to achieve further growth in this way. The chapter underlined the importance of gaining market dominance as quickly as possible in these circumstances. However, the ease with which a business can pursue this policy will depend on the nature of the market and the position of competitors. In a static or declining market it is much more difficult to pursue this option, unless competitors are complacent or are leaving the market. To attract customers from an established competitor, they must be convinced that the alternative product or service offers greater value, and that might involve price reductions – not always an attractive strategy.

Market penetration is an essential part of gaining market dominance. However, once the market is mature there is unlikely to be significant sales growth. Consolidation should generate profit growth, but this strategy inherently starts to go against the entrepreneurial grain and is not one that an entrepreneurial firm is designed or inclined to follow. Inevitably the entrepreneurial firm will start to look at the other quadrants of the matrix to achieve its aims.

For the sake of completeness it is worth considering two other strategies associated with this quadrant:

1. *Consolidation* This involves keeping the products/services and markets the same, but changing the way the firm operates so as to generate more profit. For

example, niche markets are, by definition, limited in size and further expansion may threaten the niche. However, consolidation is often not a sensible option in a growing market as it leaves competitors free to take market share, which might then affect the firm's competitive cost base. In a mature market it is common for companies to place increasing emphasis on product quality, greater marketing activity such as further segmentation or reducing their cost base so as to create barriers to entry for new competitors. In a declining market, consolidation may involve cost reduction, volume reduction and ultimately selling off all or part of the business. An entrepreneurial firm is unlikely to favour a strategy of consolidation, except insofar as it forms part of a portfolio of strategies for different product/market opportunities.

2. *Withdrawal* An entrepreneurial firm might decide to withdraw from an area of activity if there are no further growth prospects, perhaps selling all or part of the business to capitalize on the growth so far. Richard Branson did this in 1982 when he sold his original business, Virgin Records, to concentrate on the airline business. It might also be just the right time to get a very good deal, for example because of consolidation in the industry. Withdrawal might be triggered, very simply, by the product or service offered by the firm coming to the end of its life cycle. In a declining market, when the firm has low market share and there is little chance of improvement, then a timely withdrawal may minimize future losses. Alternatively entry into the market might have been a mistake in the first place (using the Boston matrix terminology, the 'problem child' could not be turned into a 'star'), and the firm could not gain market share sufficiently quickly, so withdrawal is now the least worst option.

CASE INSIGHT

Standard Chartered operates in over 50 countries and has 29,000 employees. It was formed in 1969 from the merger of two banks. The Chartered Bank, was founded by a Scot, James Wilson, in 1853 to finance trade across the British Empire. The Standard Bank was also founded by a Scot, John Paterson, in Port Elizabeth, South Africa in 1863. But in November 2001 the Chief Executive, Rana Talwar, was ousted from office after a dispute with the Chairman based upon his failing strategy for expansion. This involved an aggressive acquisition strategy that required the bank to raise increasing amounts of money from investors to buy up banks that were still reeling from the effects of the Asian currency crisis and it was not yielding any profit growth. Indeed its share price was so low that there were rumours of take-over.

The new Chief Executive, **Mervyn Davies**, reversed this strategy, pulling out of planned acquisitions and paying back money to shareholders. He returned to the basics of good strategy for an established business. The new strategy is one of internal growth – expanding by offering consumer services in countries where people are getting richer such as India and China. At the same time he acknowledged that customers are very price-sensitive and he therefore streamlined the back-office operations and shifted them to Channai in India and Kuala Lumpur in Malaysia so as to minimize costs. In fact this has been so successful that these operations have become models for other banks thinking of transferring back-office operations offshore. The third leg of the strategy was to cut bad debts, although this was helped by the creation of credit-rating agencies in its major market of Hong Kong in the wake of a ballooning number of personal bankruptcies. Hong Kong remains the bank's biggest market, generating a third of its revenues. Other key areas include Singapore, Malaysia and Africa.

By 2003 Standard Chartered was generally thought to have turned the corner after a two-year period of extremely rapid change. It is listed on the Hong Kong stock exchange and in London, where it is in the top 25 firms measured by capitalization.

Market development (quadrant 2)

It is one thing to find new customers in a market that you are familiar with, but it is quite another to enter new markets, even when they are selling your existing products or services. Nevertheless, if a firm wants to grow it will have to seek out new markets at some stage. These might be new market segments or new geographical areas. In seeking new overseas markets the lowest-risk option is to seek out segments – or customers – that are similar to the ones the firm already sells to. Product *expansion* is essentially a strategy to seek out new markets for similar products, although it can also be a defensive strategy to counter competition.

One reason for finding new markets is to achieve economies of scale of production – particularly important if the product is perceived as a commodity and cost leadership is dependent upon achieving those economies. Another reason might also be that a company's key competency lies with the product, for example with capital goods like cars, and therefore the continued exploitation of the product by market development is the preferred route for expansion. Most capital goods companies follow this strategy – opening up new overseas markets as existing markets become saturated – because of the high cost of developing new products. By way of contrast, many service businesses such as accounting, insurance, advertising and banking have been pulled into overseas markets because their clients operate there. Finally, another reason to find new markets for a product or service might be simply that it is nearing the end of its life cycle in the existing market. This was the case with McDonald's and its entry into the East European markets.

Of vital importance in considering whether to enter a new market is its structure – the customers, suppliers, competitors – and the potential substitutes and barriers to entry. These determine the degree of competition and therefore the profitability likely to be achieved. Michael Porter (1985) developed a useful structural analysis of industries which he claims goes some way towards explaining the profitability of firms within it. He claims that five forces determine competitiveness in any industry. These are shown in Figure 9.2.

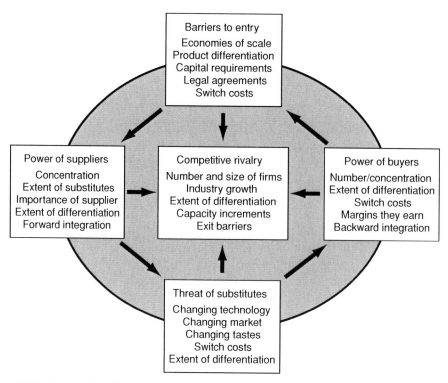

Figure 9.2 Porter's five forces

1. *The power of buyers.* This is determined by the relative size of buyers and their concentration. It is also influenced by the volumes they purchase, the information they have about competitors or substitutes, switch costs and their ability to backward integrate. Switch costs are the costs of switching to another product. The extent to which the product they are buying is differentiated in some way also affects relative buying power. The greater the power of the buyers, the weaker the bargaining position of the firm selling to them. So, for example, if buyers are large firms, in concentrated industries, buying large volumes with good price information about a relatively undifferentiated product with low switch costs they will be in a strong position to keep prices low.

2. *The power of suppliers.* This is also determined by the relative size of firms and the other factors mentioned above. So, for example, if suppliers are large firms in concentrated industries, with well-differentiated products that are relatively important to the small firms buying them, then those small firms are in a weak position to keep prices, and therefore their costs, low.

3. *The threat of new entrants.* Barriers to entry keep out new entrants to an industry. These can arise because of legal protection (patents and so on), economies of scale, proprietary product differences, brand identity, access to distribution, government policy, switch costs, capital costs and so forth. For example, a firm whose product is protected by patent or copyright may feel that it is relatively safe from competition. The greater the possible threat of new entry to a market, the lower the bargaining power and control over price of the firm within it.

4. *The threat of substitutes.* This revolves around their relative price performance, switch costs and the propensity of the customer to switch, for example because of changes in tastes or fashion. The greater the threat of substitutes, the less the ability of the firm to charge a high price. So, for example, a small firm selling a poorly-differentiated product in a price-sensitive, fashion market should find it difficult to charge a high price.

5. *Competitive rivalry in the industry.* The competitive rivalry of an industry will depend on the number and size of firms within it and their concentration, its newness and growth and therefore its attractiveness in terms of profit and value added together with intermittent overcapacity. Crucially important is the extent of product differentiation, brand identity and switch costs. The greater the competitive rivalry, the less the ability of the firm to charge a high price.

Porter claims that these five forces determine the strength of competition in the market – and therefore firm profitability. They are a function of industry structure – the underlying economic and technical characteristics of the industry. They can change over time but the analysis does emphasize the need to select industries carefully in the first place. The forces also provide a framework for predicting, a priori, the success or otherwise of the firm. For example, a small firm competing with many other small firms to sell a relatively undifferentiated product to a few large customers in an industry with few barriers to entry is unlikely to do well without some radical shifts in its marketing strategies.

Two further factors warrant consideration in deciding whether to enter a new market – entry and exit barriers. These are represented in the matrix in Figure 9.3. All things being equal, the most attractive market in terms of profitability is likely to be one with high entry barriers and low exit barriers – few firms can enter but poor performers can easily exit. With high entry barriers but high exit barriers, poor performers are forced to stay on, making the returns more risky as they fight for market share. Unfortunately, a firm seeking to enter these markets has to overcome the high entry barriers, whatever they be. For example, this could involve overcoming legal barriers or high investment costs. If entry barriers are low returns are likely to be low, but stable if exit barriers are low and unstable if exit barriers are high, and poor performers are forced to stay on if the market worsens.

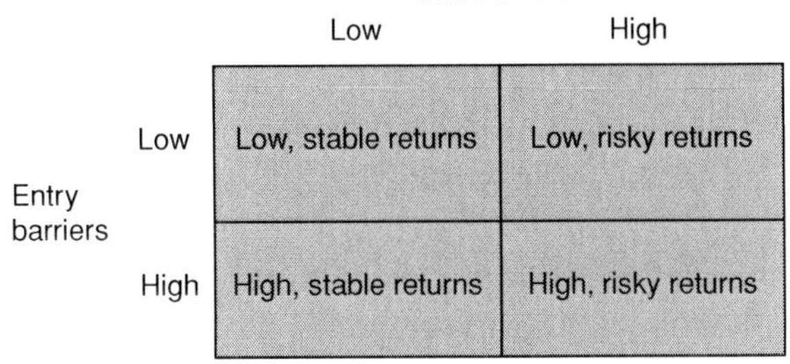

	Exit barriers	
	Low	High
Low	Low, stable returns	Low, risky returns
High	High, stable returns	High, risky returns

Entry barriers (row label)

Figure 9.3 Entry and exit barriers, profitability and risk

Source: Wilson, R. M. S. and Gilligan, C. (1997) *Strategic Marketing Management: Planning, Implementation and Control,* Oxford: Butterworth-Heinemann.

Exporting is a form of market development. For many firms the easiest way to export is to find a distributor in the selected country who understands the local distribution channels and variations in customer needs. The distributor might influence changes in the product or other elements of the marketing mix to suit local needs. The company might be expected to finance advertising and promotion itself and with no certainty of a profitable return. Finding a distributor can be difficult enough but if, for whatever reason, the distributor does not push the firm's products then there is little the firm can do other than change distributors, unless they are willing to take on the job of marketing in the country themselves – and that can be both expensive and risky. Cadbury Schweppes' problems with Pepsi stem from the compromises it made to distribute its drinks economically when it entered the US market. This situation was less than ideal, but it was a low-cost way of gaining entry to the market.

Another approach to penetrating an overseas market, particularly for a service, is to appoint a franchisee. Franchisees apply a fairly standard franchise format to the particular market in which they operate. Their market knowledge and dedication is vital if the market is to be effectively penetrated. If the franchise roll-out is successful they share in the success. To be effective, the firm and their franchisee or distributor must have a symbiotic relationship, one based upon mutual trust and with effective incentives to ensure success. Body Shop's rapid growth owes much to its successful global roll-out using a franchise format. In most countries a head franchisee was granted exclusive rights as user of the trade mark, distributor and, after an initial trial of running a few shops itself, the right to sub-franchise. In this way the firm built upon local market knowledge and minimized its risks. This model was not always followed because of the quality of the head franchisee. For example, the firm took back control of the franchise in France because the head franchisee was not delivering the volume of sales expected.

CASE WITH QUESTIONS

Royal Bank of Scotland

'Royal Bank of Scotland *are one of the top three banks in Europe. They are just very good at running businesses, with a high degree of entrepreneurial flair.'*
Anik Sen of Goldman Sachs (*The Times,* 21 July 2003)

Royal Bank of Scotland (RBS) is one of the oldest banks in the UK. It was founded in 1727 in Edinburgh, by Royal Charter, as the Royal Bank and opened its first branch in Glasgow in 1783. It developed a network of branches across Scotland in the nineteenth century but it was not until 1874 that it opened its first branch office in London. From the 1920s it grew by acquisition, swallowing Drummonds, William Deacon's Bank, Glyn, Mills and Co., and Child & Co., then merging with Edinburgh based National Commercial Bank of Scotland, which itself comprised the National Bank of Scotland and Commercial Bank of Scotland. At this stage it dominated 40% of Scotland's banking business.

In 1985 RBS merged with Williams & Glyn's to give it a presence in England and ownership of the banker to the Queen, Coutts. This was the first glimpse of the bank's entrepreneurial flair. It also set up Direct Line (the direct car insurance company) which went on quickly to become one of the dominant forces in direct insurance. Realizing it was very dependent on the UK market, RBS acquired Citizens Financial Group of Rhode Island, a small savings bank in the USA. It also started to refocus on its core business of retail banking and started on a round of cost cutting. It realized that retail banking was becoming a commodity and, to compete on price, it had to achieve economies of scale that were just not available to it on a conventional banking model. Its answer in 1997 was to set up the UK's first online banking service. Not content with this it realized that other organizations were probably better at marketing banking services than the banks themselves and joined forces with a number of well-known brands such as Tesco, the supermarket, and Virgin One to offer online banking. RBS did the 'back-office' operations, all the time driving down costs because of economies of scale. However, it also chose not to enter the high street price war being waged by its bigger rivals. In 2000 RBS bought its far bigger rival, NatWest (which included Ulster Bank), in what was the biggest take-over in British banking history. Whereas RBS had just 650 branches, NatWest had 1650 and Ulster Bank a further 228 branches. As a result RBS underwent a large round of redundancies to further cut back its cost base – a realization of what the core strategy was for this part of the business.

Since 2000 the bank has been continuing its policy of organic growth and opportunistic but tactical acquisitions. It has grown the wholesale side of its banking operations – corporate lending, derivatives, foreign exchange and leasing. It is now the biggest banker in the UK in small business and corporate banking. Its US bank, Citizens, has also acquired the Mellon Bank's regional retail franchise, Medford Bancorp and Commonwealth Bancorp, increasing its geographical coverage in New England and making it the twentieth largest US bank measured by deposits. It has also purchased Santander Direkt, a Frankfurt-based credit card company in what is thought to be its first steps into mainland Europe. More recently RBS purchased Churchill Insurance, a direct competitor to Direct Line, and now intends to merge it with Direct Line. It is also thought to be interested in taking over former building societies so as to give it more exposure to mortgage (house lending) business as well as a savings bank.

Today RBS is an international bank making profits of £5.1 billion in the first half of 2007 (up 11% on the same period in 2006). In 2002 RBS made pre-tax profits of £4.7 billion – five years earlier they had been just £1 billion. Its entrepreneurial executive Chairman is **Sir George Mathewson**. He joined the bank after being head of the Scottish Development Agency and has been accused of running the bank like a venture capital company. His Chief Executive, Fred Goodwin, is one of the youngest among the FTSE 100 and also came from outside the company.

Questions

1. What are the main elements of the Royal Bank of Scotland's strategy?
2. Why has it used acquisition so much?
3. Explain each acquisition and the reasons behind it.
4. Why is scale of operation so important to it? Has this driven some elements of strategy?

5. Compare and contrast the strategies of Royal Bank of Scotland with those of Standard and Chartered. Are there any market-based explanations for the different approaches?
6. In 2003 Standard Chartered became the only UK-listed bank to be part of the consortium that aims to help Iraq to rebuild. Why might the bank have entered this risky market?

Product/service development (quadrant 3)

Product/service innovation is one of the key characteristics of entrepreneurial companies. Ansoff's framework gets us to focus on the effect of product/service development in different markets, dealing first with the firm's existing market.

Product/service development can take a number of forms. Completely new products may be introduced into the portfolio because market opportunities are spotted. They might be completely new, innovative products to either replace or sell alongside the existing product range. Product replacement will be necessary when the product is nearing the end of its life cycle. Replacement may also be necessary if other firms produce a 'better' product and the firm is forced to react. Copied or 'me-too' products might be introduced where another firm has successfully pioneered the product in the market. At the other extreme small and evolutionary changes to existing products might be introduced. This may be necessary as competitors improve their products or when a product is nearing the end of its life cycle – a process called product *extension*.

Firms with a robust entrepreneurial architecture will be well placed to follow a strategy of innovation – rather than incremental change. The ability to innovate speedily is built into the architecture, as is a close relationship with customers – a customer focus. If there is a relationship of trust, customers are more likely to try the new product, provided of course they perceive a need for it and that means the company must also be good at communicating with customers in whatever way is most appropriate. In developing new products the customer-focused firm will have an advantage because, if it understands how its customers' needs are changing, it ought to be able to develop new products that meet them. The key to this strategy, therefore, is building good customer relationships, often associated with effective branding, and the ability to innovate quickly.

One advantage of this approach is that it is often far more cost effective to increase the volume of business with existing customers than it is to go out looking for new ones. What is more, good relationships often result in customers bringing in new customers through word of mouth or referral. However, developing new products, even for existing customers can be expensive and risky. Development must be grounded firmly in the needs of the existing market. And even then, if done too rapidly, it can mean resources are spread too thinly across an unbalanced portfolio.

Virgin is a good example of a brand that has been applied to a wide range of diverse products, mainly successfully, linking customers and their lifestyle aspirations. Virgin, however, rarely undertake 'production', relying instead on partners with developed expertise. On the other hand Mercedes Benz is a brand that has a strong association with quality and the company has capitalized on this by producing an ever-wider range of vehicles, always being able to charge a premium price for its product. This has allowed it to move into new and different segments of the vehicle market.

Diversification (quadrant 4)

Diversification involves selling new products into new markets. The rationale for this is normally one of 'balancing' the risk in a firm's business portfolio by going into new products and new markets and, ultimately, developing a business conglomerate. However, since this strategy involves unfamiliar products and unfamiliar markets it is normally seen as a high-risk strategy, with too many unknowns in the equation. Reflecting this, most conglomerates seem to be unattractive to stock markets, commanding a discount on their constituent parts.

Of course, market development and product development might go hand-in-hand, since the move into a new market segment may involve the development of variants to the existing product offering by altering the marketing mix or even changes to the product range. Product *extension* and *expansion* may similarly be viewed as incremental diversification, in that they involve elements of both new product development and seeking new market segments. However, the risk is mitigated because of the incremental movement in one or other element and it can be further mitigated if these developments are associated with a strong brand with values that are attractive to customers.

Risk is therefore dependent upon the extent of the diversification. The literature distinguishes between related and unrelated diversification and entrepreneurial firms face a distinct opportunity in the former.

Related diversification happens when development is beyond the present product and market, but within the confines of the 'industry' or 'sector' in which the firm operates. There are three variants:

- *Backward vertical integration* where the firm becomes its own supplier of some basic raw materials or services or provides transport or financing. When Anita Roddick first set up Body Shop it was purely as a retail business. In the 1980s it started its own warehousing and distribution network, based upon a sophisticated stock-control system, and built up a substantial fleet of lorries. Products could typically be delivered within 24 hours. It also started manufacturing its cosmetics mainly in the UK, although many of the ingredients came from overseas under its 'trade-not-aid' policy. These two elements of strategy initially worked well for it and generated substantial sales and profit growth but the manufacturing policy was reviewed in the late 1990s and Body Shop started to move away from manufacturing and concentrate on its core retailing activity.
- *Forward vertical integration*, where the firm becomes its own distributor or retailer or perhaps services its own products in some way. In this way Timberland, famous for its sturdy, waterproof boots, opened a number of prominently-sited retail outlets selling its boots and other Timberland-branded outdoor clothes and products.
- *Horizontal integration*, where there is development into activities which are either directly complementary or competitive with the firm's current activities; for

example, where a video rental shop starts to rent out video games. In this way Ford now earns more from financial services related to car purchase than from the manufacture of the vehicles themselves.

In an entrepreneurial firm the portfolio of core competencies can be combined in various ways to meet opportunities. So it can re-apply and reconfigure what it does best in a way best suited to meet the opportunities in new markets. In this way the entrepreneurial firm can have an advantage over others in applying this strategy. So, for example, Mercedes Benz uses new products to move incrementally into new markets and market segments, leveraging on its reputation for quality, for example with its small 100 Series. All of this has been within the industry it knows best. The primary competency lies in product development – it builds good quality cars which appeal in terms of aesthetics and emotions but are leveraged by an excellent brand. In this way it has a competitive advantage over other new entrants to the market, although not necessarily existing ones.

By way of contrast, unrelated diversification is a high-risk strategy for any firm. It happens where the firm develops beyond its present 'industry' or 'sector' into products/services and markets that, on the face of it, bear little relationship to the one it is in. The risks are high because the firm understands neither the product/service nor the market.

'Synergy' is often used as a justification for both related and unrelated diversification, particularly when it involves acquisition or merger. Synergy is concerned with assessing how much extra benefit can be obtained from providing linkages between activities or processes which have been previously unconnected, or where the connection has been of a different type, so that the combined effect is greater than the sum of the parts. It is often described as 'one plus one equals three'. Synergy in related diversification is mainly based upon core product or market characteristics or competencies – for example, Mercedes Benz leveraging on its reputation for quality of vehicles. The claimed synergy in unrelated diversification is normally based on financing – the positive cash flows in one business being used for the funding requirements of another. Another often-claimed synergy is based on the managerial skills of the head office.

Research indicates that most successful entrepreneurial firms follow a strategy of incremental, mainly internal, growth (Burns, 1994). They move carefully into new markets with existing products or sell new products to existing customers. Whilst Johnson and Scholes (2001) claim that attempts to demonstrate the effects of diversification on performance are inconclusive, they also admit that successful diversification is difficult to achieve in practice. However, many researchers have found that more focused firms perform better than diversified ones (Wernerfelt and Montgomery, 1986). This is reflected in their share price. What is more, it has been demonstrated that smaller firms that diversify by building on their core business – related diversification – do better than those that diversify in an unrelated way (Ansoff, *op. cit.*). This was established for a broader range of firms in the 1970s (Rumelt, 1974) and used as part of Porter's (1987) argument for firms that build on their core business doing better than those who diversify in an unrelated way.

The conclusion must be that diversification generally, but unrelated diversification in particular, is risky and therefore requires careful justification – although the pay-off can be large. Nevertheless one of the companies that has adopted a strategy of diversification most successfully is Lonrho, and its strategy has been one of unrelated diversification. Its interests range from hotels in Mexico to freight forwarders in Canada, from motor distribution in Africa to oil and gas production in the USA.

CASE INSIGHT

Crucial to success for dot.com firms is the 'business model' – how income will be generated. Arguably the most successful model is that of the online auctioneer **eBay**. eBay has 69 million registered users worldwide and hosts over 12 million items on its website. It is now the largest site for used car sales in the USA. Someone buys a computer game every 8 seconds. In 2002 it had sales of $1.2 billion. By 2005 sales were over $4 billion and it had over 5000 employees.

eBay's success comes from being nothing more than an intermediary – software running on a web server. Its customers, both buyers and sellers, do all the work. Sellers pay to set up their own auction, buyers use eBay's software to place their bids, shipping and payment are arranged between the seller and buyer and eBay takes 7–18% of the selling price as commission for letting them use its software. eBay is simply the trading platform. It holds no stocks and its involvement in the trade in minimal. After each transaction the buyer and seller rate the other. Next to each user's identification is a figure in brackets recording the number of positive comments – thus encouraging honesty and trust. It is a truly virtual business which also sells advertising space.

eBay developed a 'virtuous circle' in which more buyers attracted more sellers, who attracted yet more buyers and sellers – called 'network effects'. At the core of eBay's business is software rather than people. The company has bought software companies to gain exclusive use of their technologies and make the auction process more efficient. It therefore faces enormous economies of scale in attracting as many auction transactions as possible and, with that in mind, has moved into new areas such as used cars and even plans to host storefronts for small merchants. It has also started to sell private-label versions of its service to companies, for a fee.

In 2002 eBay purchased **PayPal**, the dominant provider of internet payments in the USA with over 12 million customers of whom 3.2 million are fee-paying business customers. The two companies are complementary but depend on each other. Indeed, auctions account for 61% of PayPal's business. PayPal allows customers to register details of their credit card or bank account with it so that when they buy something on the internet they just enter an e-mail account and an amount. Like eBay, it is fully automated, relying on software rather than people. Like eBay, Paypal also relies on the same 'network effects'. It initially paid users $10 to sign up their friends to enable it to reach its critical mass, but now the firm is signing up 28,000 new users a day without this incentive. The commercial synergy between eBay and PayPal is clear. Not only are the business models similar, but also the customers buying or selling on eBay can secure their payments by using PayPal. And now it is made more easily available to them more are using the service.

Mergers and acquisitions

Bowman and Faulkner (1997) add an extra dimension to the Ansoff matrix by considering core competency and method of implementation. They point out that any move into new markets or new products/services becomes riskier, the further the firm strays from its core competency. This is tantamount to a start-up. They also point out that the implementation becomes riskier as the firm moves from internal development through alliances into acquisition. The highest-risk strategy of all would therefore be to develop new competencies and their application into a new market with a new product/service, through an implementation policy involving acquisition. This brings us to the issue of mergers and acquisitions.

Mergers and acquisitions are frequently used by entrepreneurs as a tool for achieving rapid growth and also as a short cut to diversification. The compelling reason for this tactic is the speed with which it allows the entrepreneur to enter a new product/market area. Another reason might be that the firm lacks a resource, such as R&D or a customer base, to develop a strategy unaided. Often, particularly when a market is static, it is seen as the easiest way to enter a new market, for example overseas. Sometimes the reason for buying out a competitor is to buy their order book, perhaps related to shutting down their capacity, cutting costs and gaining economies of scale. Sometimes, as with Cadbury Schweppes and its purchase of Dr Pepper and 7UP, you are both buying a respected brand and a foothold in an overseas market and its channels of distribution to help market your existing products.

However, this tactic can be time-consuming, expensive and risky. By distracting management it can also damage short-term business performance. In fact there is no evidence that commercial acquisitions or take-overs – particularly in unrelated areas (other than in a distress sale) – add value to the firm. Many studies show that mergers and acquisitions suffer a higher failure rate than marriages and business history is littered with stories of failed mergers of titanic proportions such as AT&T's purchase of NCR in 1991, the second largest acquisition in the history of the computer industry. This failed largely because of the clash of cultures in the two companies. NCR was conservative, tightly controlled from the top whilst AT&T was 'politically correct', informal and decentralized. Within four years most of NCR's senior managers had left and the new company had become loss-making. In 1997 NCR was made independent again, having lost some 50% of its value.

The great conglomerate-merger wave of the 1960s did not generally lead to improvements in performance for those firms involved and was reversed by the large-scale selling of unrelated businesses in the 1980s. Porter (*op. cit.*), in his study of 33 major corporations between 1950 and 1986, concludes that more often acquisitions were subsequently sold off rather than retained, and the net result was dissipation of shareholder value. And yet companies of all sizes persist in following this strategy.

All too often acquisitions have too much corporate ego tied up in the deal and that can lead to a loss of business logic. It is important that there is a clear logic to any acquisition, related to the product/market strategy. For example:

- As a defensive acquisition to maintain market position, perhaps to gain economies of scale, or as a result of aggressive competitive reaction from rivals.

- As part of a strategy to develop new products related to the core products/markets of the firm when it does not have the capability to do so itself, for example because of R&D or technology.
- As part of a strategy to develop new markets, for example overseas.
- As part of a strategy of diversification designed to spread product/market risk, although this must be seen as the highest of high-risk growth strategies.

If a firm decides to undertake this high-risk strategy it first needs to decide on the industry into which it is to diversify. Related diversification will normally be into the same industry. If it is unrelated diversification then the industry should be one where the acquiring company has the key competencies required for success in the sector and, where there is a deficiency, they should be addressed by being present in the target company. The attractiveness of the industry will depend to some extent on the strategic direction of the company, informed by an analysis of the industry (perhaps using Porter's Five Forces and a SLEPT analysis). The acquisitions that are most likely to succeed are those for which an attractive market presents itself to a company with a good 'mesh' between the acquiring company's core competencies and the sector's required key competencies.

Of course, some acquisitions are simply opportunistic. For example, when a rival firm or a firm in a related area, goes into receivership the temptation to buy it out cheaply and quickly from the receiver might be irresistible and might also make sound commercial sense. Most acquisitions take three to nine months to complete but a sale from a receiver can be completed in as little as three weeks.

CASE INSIGHT

The **Reliance Group** is now the biggest business group in India with sales of over $12 billion and profits of over $950 million. It is a family-run conglomerate and was started by **Dhirubhai Ambani**, the son of a poor Gujarati school teacher who began work at a Shell petrol station in Aden. To make extra money he traded commodities and, at one time, even melted down Yemeni rial coins so as to sell the silver for more than the currency's face value. He returned to India and started a yarn trading company in 1959 which, by the end of the 1990s, had become an integrated textiles, petrochemicals and oil conglomerate that then diversified into telecommunications, power, biotechnology and even financial services. Initially the business grew primarily through exploiting contacts with Indian politicians and bureaucrats but, in the wake of the changes caused by economic liberalization in the early 1990s, it started to do things differently – it built production sites that were competitive in global markets. Dhirubhai also popularized share ownership in India – which is where financial services comes in – and the two holding companies now have over 3.5 million shareholders.

Dhirubhai died in 2002 and the business is now run by his two sons Mukesh and Anil. Both have MBAs from the USA and have been involved with the business for some 20 years, managing the company increasingly since their father had his first stroke in 1986 and having a strong role in forging it into the world-class company that it is today.

The major reason why mergers and acquisitions fail is because of failure of implementation. Claimed synergies may not be achieved, perhaps rationalization is insufficiently ruthless, possibly because clear management lines and responsibilities are not laid down. One of the major reasons for failure boils down to a clash of organizational cultures that does not get resolved. This can arise because of many factors, but it results in the merged organizations being unable to work together effectively. That was the major reason for the seemingly logical, but ultimately disastrous, takeover of NCR by AT&T in 1991, which nearly brought down both companies. For whatever reason, one common outcome of mergers or acquisitions is that many managers in the acquired company will leave within a short space of time. They may, of course, be 'pushed' rather than leave of their own volition, but nevertheless this means that the time scale for proactive management of change can be very short. Management of a merger or acquisition is therefore difficult.

CASE WITH QUESTIONS

Ineos Group

The Ineos Group was founded in 1998 when Jim Ratcliffe led a £91 million management buyout of Inspec's chemicals division. Jim is a qualified accountant who had previously worked for the US private equity house Advent. By 2007 Ineos had grown to become the world's third largest petrochemical company. Jim's strategy to achieve this was simple. He went out to buy undervalued subsidiaries from global oil and chemical giants, financed almost entirely by debt – high yield bonds and bank debt. The company has bought businesses from ICI, Dow Chemicals, Degussa, BASF, Cybec, BP and Norsk Hydro. It was Ineos' purchase of BP's petrochemical arm Innovene for £5.1 billion in 2006 that catapulted the company into the world rankings of the petrochemical industry. The deal quadrupled the company's turnover and signalled a move away from specialist compounds to the simpler chemicals from which they are made. Following a £1.6 billion bond issue in 2006 to refinance the purchase of Innovene, Ineos continued its acquisition strategy with the £76 million purchase of BP's German ethylene oxide business followed by the £460 million purchase of Norsk Hydro's polymers business in 2007.

Ineos sees itself as a leading global manufacturer of petrochemicals, speciality chemicals and oil products. It comprises 18 businesses with 68 manufacturing sites in 17 countries. It believes its strengths lie in its:

- High quality, low cost production facilities
- Well located, well invested, large plants that allow it to benefit from economies of scale
- Experienced management
- Leading market positions that allow it to be the supplier of choice for many large customers
- Operating diversity in products, customers, geographic regions, applications and end-user markets.

By 2007 the company had a turnover of some £18 billion and had some 15,000 employees. It was ranked the largest private company by the *Sunday Times* – with a turnover three times that of its nearest rival, the John Lewis Partnership. The company currently plans to build a £60 million biodiesel plant at the former BP site at Grangemouth and another at Antwerp as well as a £125 million phenol acetone plant in China. Jim Ratcliffe himself is a fairly low-profile entrepreneur, but he still owns about two-thirds of the business, giving him a paper fortune of some £3.3 billion and placing him in the top ten wealthiest people in Britain in 2007, according to the *Sunday Times* Rich List.

Up-to-date information on Ineos Group can be found on their website: www.ineos.com

Questions

1. What risks does Ineos face and how might they be reduced?
2. How secure is the personal fortune of Jim Ratcliffe and what steps might he take to secure it further?

Sustainability and corporate social responsibility

It is now widely accepted that many business practices have negative social and environmental side effects. Growing pressures are leading firms to give careful consideration to sustainable development and how it might contribute to the sustainability of competitive advantage and growth of the organization. These pressures come from:

- *Environmentalists* – who see companies rapidly using up the valuable but limited resources of the planet and at the same time contributing to global warming, which may ultimately cause the destruction of the planet. Green issues and the corporate 'carbon footprint' are rapidly becoming the most important issues facing business today.
- *Social reformers* – who see companies behaving in ways that they object to, for example by 'exploiting' cheap labour in developing countries, or providing poor working conditions. Trade unions and consumer groups have both focused on social issues in the past, often with the result that legislation limiting the activity of companies has been enacted (for example the minimum wage in Europe).
- *Social activists* – who see companies as having a broader social role in the community beyond the boundaries of the working environment. Corporate citizenship programmes, for example in which employees undertake charitable work in the community, have become a trendy outlet for many companies, whilst others like Body Shop and Timberland have practised this for years.
- *Ethical activists* – who see companies (such as Enron) behaving in unacceptable ethical ways usually by trying to mislead stakeholders. There is, of course, an overlap here with the agendas of the other groups. Nevertheless, business ethics has risen up the agendas of society as a whole and shareholders in particular, and companies are responding.

Often these issues are bundled together under the broad umbrella of corporate social responsibility (CSR). More and more companies are engaging seriously in CSR, and over 500 in the UK issue annual CSR reports on their performance. Much of the CSR literature is highly moralistic in nature, reflecting the idealism of scholars who question the profit maximization objective of companies (Wood, 2000). However, Burke and Logsdon (1996) argue that there are sound business reasons for following a strong CSR policy and organizations can expect five strategic outcomes:

- *Enhanced customer loyalty*: Certainly a strong CSR profile can reinforce and enhance brand image (e.g. Body Shop). Customers are increasingly drawn to brands with a strong CSR link and CSR has become an element in the continuous process of trying to differentiate one company from another. In 20 developed countries a survey of 20,000 people showed CSR-related factors collectively accounted for 49% of a company's image, compared to 35% for brand image and just 10% for financial management (Environics International, 2001).
- *Increased future purchases*: Whilst any product must first satisfy the customer's key buying criteria – quality, price etc. – a strong CSR brand can increase sales and customer loyalty by helping to differentiate it. On the other hand a bad CSR image can damage sales quite severely. The same Environics survey showed that 42% of consumers in North America would punish companies by not buying their product for being socially irresponsible. This fell to 25% in Europe but collapsed to 8% in Asia where CSR issues are seen as less important.
- *Reduced operating costs*: Many environmental initiatives can reduce costs (e.g. reducing waste and recycling, better control of building temperatures or reducing use of agrochemicals). Many social initiatives can increase employee motivation, cut absenteeism and cut staff turnover and an increasing number of graduates take CSR issues into consideration when making employment decisions.
- *Improved new product development*: Focus on CSR issues can lead to new product opportunities. For example, car manufacturers are striving to find alternatives to fossil fuels for their vehicles, whilst developing conventional engines that are more and more economical.
- *Access to new markets*: A strong CSR brand can create its own market niche for an organization. For example, the Co-operative Bank in the UK has a long history of CSR. It has set itself up as an ethical and ecological investor with an investment policy that is the most frequently cited reason why customers choose the bank. It also has been at the forefront of social auditing practices and has produced an independently audited 'Social Report' since 1997 that measures impact and identifies improvements the company could make in social responsibility areas.
- *Productivity gains*: Actions to improve working conditions, lessen environmental impact or increase employee involvement in decision making can improve productivity. For example, actions to improve work conditions in the supply chain have led to decreases in defect rates in merchandise.

Not surprisingly, therefore, strong CSR performance seems to be linked to financial performance. A 2002 study showed that the overall financial performance of the 2001 *Business Ethics* Best Citizen companies in the USA was significantly better than that of the remaining companies in the S&P 500 Index (Verschoor, 2002). There is growing awareness that incorporating CSR into mainstream corporate strategy translates into bottom line performance. In the short term it at least avoids negative consumer or activist publicity, in the medium term it delivers better performance for investors and the community and in the long term, by encouraging consideration of abiding social and environmental interests, it can give management a broader, long-term perspective on the sustainability of the company's performance.

Certainly companies like Body Shop have used CSR as a major plank in their branding since it was set up by Anita Roddick in 1976 – campaigning for many social, moral and environmental issues. But CSR predates Body Shop. In the UK Cadbury, Wilkin & Sons (maker of Tiptree Jams) and the Co-op are all early examples of businesses with a CSR dimension. Today many organizations, like the UK retailers Marks and Spencer (M&S) and John Lewis, and the US company IBM and outdoor-wear manufacturer Timberland, have extensive CSR programmes ranging from community involvement (staff working on community projects in company time) through to ethical sourcing (from humans and animals) and into environmental issues (such as M&S' objective to become completely carbon neutral). M&S' 100 point 'Plan A' is generally seen as a model for today's socially responsible companies.

There is also growing investor pressure to implement CSR. The Environics survey showed that over a quarter of US share owners bought or sold shares because of a company's social performance and a similar pattern emerged in Britain, Canada, Italy, and France (Environics International, *op. cit*). There are now stock market indices like the Dow Jones Sustainability Index and the FTSE4Good and, increasingly, mainstream investors see CSR as a strategic business issue and raise it in annual meetings. Activist groups also buy shares in targeted companies to give them access to these annual meetings so that they can raise CSR issues.

CSR can be integrated into the strategic planning process. Starting with external considerations in the *strategic analysis*, firms need to be aware of legislation and should compare themselves to competitors (Epstein and Roy, 2001) and find out about the expectations of external stakeholders (Smith, 2003). Similarly companies should investigate the expectations of its internal stakeholders (Smith, *op. cit.*) with a view to assessing the adequacy of its organizational capacity – its resources and processes (De Colle and Gonella, 2002; Epstein and Roy, *op. cit*). The firm should then be able to assess the fit between the CSR commitments it might aspire to and its central business objectives (Burke and Logsdon, *op. cit;* Smith, *op. cit*), which may or may not result in changing the *vision* and mission of the business. CSR *strategy formulation* follows, usually demonstrated as a list of commitments. According to Smith (*op. cit*), this should reflect 'an understanding of whether (and why) greater attention to CSR is warranted by that particular organisation.' *Strategy implementation* requires concrete actions to be undertaken but also it is important to publicize this to internal and external stakeholders to demonstrate commitment and attainment (Burke and Logsdon, *op. cit.*). These may have to be audited or evaluated (De Colle and Gonella, *op. cit*).

Sustainability and CSR can therefore be integrated into the strategic planning process. Indeed it should be at the heart of any growth strategy. It encourages the company to take a long-term view and reflects the concerns of the society in which it is embedded. However, it also makes good business sense, providing market and brand opportunities that translate into bottom line profits. CSR is set to become more important in the future and is likely to be an essential element of strategy for all companies.

M&S

M&S has always had an ethical dimension. It started offering staff welfare services that provided pensions, subsidized staff canteens, health and dental services, hairdressing, rest rooms and camping holidays back in the 1930s. In 1999 it published its own code of practice on Global Sourcing as a minimum standard for all suppliers in an effort to improve conditions for workers overseas. Since 2003 M&S has produced a Corporate Social Responsibility Report. In that year it was ranked top retailer and one of the top UK companies in Business and the Communities First Corporate Social Responsibility Index. Stuart Rose has taken this even further and started building it into the M&S brand identity. In 2006 the Look Behind the Label marketing campaign was introduced with the aim of highlighting the range of ethical and environmentally friendly policies M&S had.

These included:

- Fairtrade products – all coffee and tea sold by M&S is Fairtrade and it also offers clothing lines made from Fairtrade Cotton.
- Sustainable fishing – M&S sell only fish from sustainable sources.
- Healthy foods – M&S has removed 90% of its foods containing hydrogenated fats and oils and has cut salt across its food range.
- Support for charities – M&S supports a number of charities. For example at Christmas 2006 it introduced a range of products to support the housing charity Shelter predominantly in the food-to-go range including a range of seasonal Christmas sandwiches.
- Environment friendly – emphasizing the use of environmentally friendly textile dyes and use of environmentally friendly materials for store fit-outs such as flooring made from natural rubber as well as looking to source electricity from environmentally friendly sources.

However, in 2007 M&S went one very significant step further. It launched its 'Plan A', an ambitious 100-point plan to help combat climate change, reduce waste, safeguard natural resources, trade ethically and promote healthier lifestyles. The business-wide action plan will cost £200 million. By 2012, M&S aims to:

- Become carbon neutral – minimizing energy use, maximizing renewables and using offsets as a last resort.
- Send no waste to land fill sites – reducing packaging, recycling and reusing materials.
- Extend sustainable sourcing – using recycled materials, extending free range and organic food products, only selling fish from sustainable supplies.
- Set new standards in ethical trading – leading in labour standards and extending Fairtrade products.
- Help customers and employees live healthier lifestyles – through producing healthier foods and extending health and lifestyle support for employees.

The ambitious plan, which was widely welcomed by environmentalists, will transform the way M&S operates. M&S will set up a Supplier Exchange to share best practice and innovation. The economics of local and ethical sourcing are less straightforward than they might seem. A surprisingly high proportion of a product's vehicle miles come from shoppers driving to their local store. However, the move back to UK sourcing, at least for food, and the emphasis on identifiable, free range, often organic and fair trade produce undoubtedly hits a chord with many middle-class shoppers – M&S target market. And the M&S brand claims influence over 2000 factories, 10,000 farms and 250,000 workers, so if the initiative works its influence will be considerable, albeit tiny on a global scale. Becoming more sustainable is not just about philanthropy, it also make good competitive sense – at least for some businesses. Nevertheless the turnaround of M&S is far from complete.

Visit M&S's website, www.marksandspencer.com, to find out more about their CSR activities.

Questions

1. How embedded within M&S is CSR?
2. What is the role of CSR in the turn around of M&S?
3. Visit M&S's website to assess the progress of Plan A. How successful have they been?

Sustaining growth

Growth is a relative concept. Relative in terms of its measurement – over time – and relative in terms of its temporal context – compared to others in the same industry or sector. Sustaining growth over a prolonged period and compared to competitors is not easy. Many firms try and most flounder, at least at some points along the journey. That is partly because they do not control all the variables that affect them. The terrorist attack in the USA on 11 September 2001 and the recession it precipitated was not predictable and no firms had any plans in place to deal with its effects. However, all too often growth is not sustained because tiredness and complacency set in. Life cycles can be predicted and strategies put in place to counter them, particularly in the context of a portfolio of products or services. But it is people who neglect to do so. It is people that can both sustain and inhibit growth – not the nature of an individual product or service. And people need to be led and managed, but, more than all, motivated to achieve growth.

Beyond this, sustaining capability and distinctiveness is the key to sustaining growth. Using Kay's (1998) three capabilities, reputation, often communicated in a brand, is probably the easiest to sustain. Strategic assets can be defended over long periods but can disappear overnight – witness the events at Enron. But it is innovation that is probably the most difficult distinctive capability to sustain. And the entrepreneurial architecture needed for this can only endure in place and continue to be renewed and re-invigorated through effective leadership, structures, cultures and strategies.

Strategy is just a series of linked, logical actions. There are frameworks to help us develop it and research to underpin our judgement. But strategy is based upon the best judgements, at any one point of time, about imprecise factors and uncertain circumstances – playing the odds. A right decision today can so easily prove to be a wrong decision tomorrow and only a classroom case-study has the benefit of hindsight and 20:20 vision. The best you can expect is to make more right decisions than wrong decisions. And, if you are not making any wrong decisions, you are probably not making any decisions at all. Entrepreneurs keep moving – and not always in a straight line. So too should the entrepreneurial firm. The firm that endorses the status quo is no longer entrepreneurial.

Notwithstanding this, Porter (1991) noted five mistakes that organizations repeatedly make when implementing strategy:

1. *Misunderstanding industry attractiveness* – Attractiveness has little to do with growth, glamour or new technology but more to do with the Five Forces outlined earlier in this chapter.
2. *Not having real competitive advantage* – Organizations need to discover what makes them unique and different, to challenge the status quo and not just copy or incrementally change what competitors do.
3. *Pursuing an unsustainable competitive position* – Organizations need to decide on their core competencies and focus their attempts at exploiting competitive advantage on them rather than strategies that do not play to these strengths and therefore will be difficult to sustain.
4. *Compromising the strategy for growth with short-term goals* – Short-term growth targets can distract the organization from its long-term competitive strategy as it pursues short-term opportunities that are inconsistent with the core strategy.
5. *Failing to communicate strategy internally* – All employees need to know the organization's strategy and what it means for them. All too often they do not.

The entrepreneurial firm will constantly be attempting to develop new products or services and seek out new markets or segments. Judging what combination to pursue these in, at any point of time, is not easy. Pursuing too many at once normally involves extra risk. But pursuing them too late in the face of competition means losing out on what might be lucrative opportunities. This is the classic trade-off between risk and return – and no two people are the same in making this. The frameworks in this chapter can only help with the process of strategizing and inform the decision. They can never make the decision for you.

CASE WITH QUESTIONS

BAE Systems

BAE Systems is Britain's largest manufacturer, with sales of over £14 billion and some 88,000 staff based in over 100 countries world-wide. It is the largest defence company in Europe, and ranks seventh in the USA. Its size and growth have been largely due to mergers and acquisitions since its very inception.

Today's company began life as British Aerospace in 1977, a nationalized (government-owned) corporation formed from the merger of British Aircraft Corporation, Hawker Siddeley Aviation, Hawker Siddeley Dynamics and Scottish Aviation.

The company was privatized (sold off) in 1981. The 1980s saw a string of acqui-sitions, most with little obvious logic: Royal Ordnance in 1987 (munitions), Rover Group in 1988 (cars) and Arlington Securities in 1989 (financial). By 1992 the strat-egy of unrelated diversification was discredited and the company was on the verge of collapse. The chairman was forced to resign and the company reappraised its strategies, being forced to sell off Rover to BMW in 1993. Throughout the 1990s the company remained reliant upon a huge weapons contract with Saudi Arabia – a contract that would later prove controversial – but it also started increasingly turn-ing its focus to Europe. This time, rather than acquiring companies, it started form-ing alliances, doing deals with Dassault, Lagadere, Saab, Daimler Benz Aerospace, Siemens and others. The company also took part in the restructuring of Airbus and took a 20% stake.

However, its most important move was when it merged with GEC's defence business in 1999, giving it a far greater presence in the USA, and greater vertical integration of its activities. From here on the strategy shifted. Mergers and acquisi-tions were still very important, but the focus for this activity changed. Firstly the company focused very much on the defence business. It took a 33% stake in Euro-fighter, a 37.5% stake in MBDA, the world's leading missile systems builder, and a 20% stake in Saab AB, the aircraft manufacturer. In 2006 it sold its stake in Airbus, despite the success of the company.

Secondly, the focus shifted towards restructuring to give greater backward and forward vertical integration. In this way BAE could become one of the very few fully integrated suppliers of weapons for air, land and naval defence needs. It can supply the platform – for example, the ship or plane – and all the electronics, com-puters or missiles that go in it, which is where the real profit lies. This positions it with fewer direct competitors and providing the sort of turn-key service gov-ernments want. Where acquisitions were not possible, strategic partnerships were entered into.

Thirdly the focus shifted very much to the USA, the largest market for defence procurement in the world, and BAE started out on a strategy of buying its way into the US market. In 2000 it sealed its status as defence supplier to the Penta-gon by purchasing two electronics businesses from Lockheed Martin. By 2007 it had made 16 acquisitions in the USA at which point it made a $4.1 billion bid for Armor Holdings – the manufacturer of the famous Humvee armoured vehicles. Armor is a prime contractor in the Pentagon (this means taking overall respon-sibility for complete weapons systems), and its acquisition will seal BAE's status in the US market. However, continuing accusations about bribes being paid to a Saudi prince to obtain the huge contract on which it survived in the 1990s nearly resulted in the acquisition being blocked. Even before the Armor acquisition, the USA accounted for almost 30% of sales, with joint contracts such as the huge F-35 Joint Strike Fighter project. The UK now accounts for only about 25% of sales, with contracts such as the Eurofighter, the Astute-class submarine and Nimrod marine-surveillance aircraft projects.

The final aspect of BAE's strategy was that of attempting to reduce market risk in a cyclical, high-risk market by spreading its customer base across the world. There were also two reasons for wanting to move away from an over-reliance on the British market. Firstly, British defence procurement is now more open to competition than in any other Western country. Secondly, British defence contracts are normally fixed-price, unlike the USA where they are cost-plus with single figure mark-ups for the development of new products, and open competition, fixed-price for the production contracts. The British system has forced BAE to make some expensive writeoffs in the past.

Up-to-date information on BAE Systems can be found on their website: www. baesystems.com.

Questions

1. What do you think of BAE's logic for using acquisitions, mergers and strategic partnerships?
2. What are the dangers of using mergers and acquisitions as such a central part of any strategy?

Summary

To achieve growth a company should build on its strengths and core competencies, shore up its weaknesses and develop a marketing strategy for each product/market offering that reflects:

- The appropriate generic marketing strategy;
- The stage the product/market offering is at in its life cycle;
- All placed in the context of its portfolio of product/market offerings.

Research tells us that the strategy with the best chance of generating the highest profits is to differentiate with the aim of dominating that market and to do this effectively and quickly, and continue to innovate based on your differential advantage.

The unique elements of the differentiation strategy are likely to be based on distinctive capabilities that, applied to a relevant market, become a competitive advantage. This will become the firm's core market, the one in which it has a distinct advantage by adding the greatest value for its customers.

Growth through opportunity drives the strategy of an entrepreneurial firm. Ansoff highlighted four growth options:

1. Market penetration
2. Market development
3. Product development
4. Diversification

Any firm wishing to grow must follow a policy of market penetration (option 1) – selling more to existing customers and finding new customers in the market place – until that market is mature. The best way of finding new customers is to understand your existing ones and then try to find more of the same. Marketing mix can be altered to achieve higher sales but this can be difficult in a static or declining market.

Returning to the basics of business strategy helped turn around the fortunes of **Standard Chartered Bank**.

Market development is about finding new markets for existing products or services, thus benefiting from economies of scale or capitalizing on the firm's product-knowledge competency. In considering which markets to enter, consideration should be given to Porter's Five Forces and entry and exit barriers. Market development is most successful for companies whose core competencies lie in the efficiency of their existing production methods, for example in the capital goods industries, and are seeking economies of scale, or for firms adept at sales, marketing and developing close customer relationships. This has been a core part of **Royal Bank of Scotland's** strategy.

The classic example of market development is entry into overseas markets, either by opening overseas ventures or by exporting. Many exporters go through an agent who is able to distribute the product for them. Franchising is another approach, particularly for a service or retail business. To succeed there needs to be a symbiotic relationship, based on trust and effective incentives.

Product/service development involves developing new products or services and selling to your existing market. These can be completely new products or incremental changes to existing products. Product development is most successful for those companies whose competencies lie in building good customer relationships, often associated with effective branding. However, of equal importance could be the ability to innovate – both qualities of the entrepreneurial firm. Getting existing customers to buy more is also often very cost-effective.

Related diversification is about staying within the confines of the industry through either backward vertical integration (becoming your own supplier), forward vertical integration (becoming a distributor or retailer), or horizontal integration (moving into related activities). Related diversification is safest for companies who are adept at both innovation and developing close customer relations – key competencies of an entrepreneurial firm. In an entrepreneurial firm the portfolio of core competencies can be combined in various ways to meet opportunities. So it can re-apply and reconfigure what it does best in a way best suited to meet the opportunities in new markets. It therefore has a distinct advantage in related diversification. This is certainly the case in the **eBay** acquisition of **PayPal**, where there were also related marketing synergies.

Unrelated diversification is the riskiest strategy of all and involves developing beyond the firm's present industry, normally because of the claimed benefits of synergy.

Mergers and acquisitions are frequently used as means of achieving rapid expansion, gaining a foothold in new geographical markets or greater backward and forward vertical integration – as with both the **Reliance Group** and the **Ineos Group**. However, the tactic can be time-consuming, expensive and risky. There must be clear strategic reasons for a policy of merger or acquisition. The **Royal Bank of Scotland** has used opportunistic acquisition very successfully to grow the business and gain much needed economies of scale, at all times driving down its costs.

Most mergers and acquisitions fail because of failure of implementation and a clash of cultures. Claimed synergies may not be achieved, perhaps rationalization is insufficiently ruthless, possibly because clear management lines and responsibilities are not laid down.

Sustainability and CSR must be at the heart of any growth strategy. It encourages the long-term view and reflects the concerns of the society in which the company is embedded. It also makes good business sense, providing market and brand opportunities that translate into bottom line profits. **M&S's** 'Plan A' is generally seen as a model for today's socially responsible company.

Research indicates that most successful entrepreneurial firms follow a strategy of incremental, mainly internal, growth. **Standard Chartered** followed this strategy whilst at the same time addressing the realization that many consumer banking services are just commodities and are therefore price-sensitive. Related diversification only works when based on core competencies. The strategy of unrelated diversification is high-risk and only to be adopted after careful consideration. The further the firm moves away from its core competency, the higher the risk. Risk also increases as the firm moves from internal development through alliances to acquisitions.

BAE Systems has refocused on its defence business but has continued to use mergers and acquisitions as a way of gaining forward and backward integration – which is what the market requires of major defence contractors – and entry into its key market of the USA. It has also used it as a way of mitigating geographic market risk.

Essays and discussion topics

1. Penetrating the market is just about selling more. Discuss.
2. Penetrating the market is low-risk and therefore always the most attractive option. Discuss.
3. In what circumstances might product development be a lower-risk strategy than market development, and vice versa?
4. How might a firm go about exporting so as to minimize the risks that it faces?
5. Exporting is expensive and risky. It is therefore not an attractive growth option. Discuss.
6. How do you go about minimizing your exposure to currency fluctuations?
7. Diversification is the 'Wally Box' of the product/market matrix. Discuss.
8. Why might related diversification work best for entrepreneurial companies?
9. Under what circumstances might diversification be an attractive option?
10. Diversified companies underperform 'focused' companies. Discuss.
11. Why might a firm be looking for another to acquire?
12. Under what circumstances might an acquisition or merger be attractive?
13. What is synergy and how might it be achieved?
14. Why do so many mergers or acquisitions fail? Give examples.
15. What advice would you give to a company taking over another?
16. Why might a strategy of internal growth be less risky than one of acquisition?
17. In what circumstances might a strategy of internal growth be more risky than one of acquisition? Compare your answer to that of Question 18. Is there any such thing as an optimal strategy?
18. What are the problems of sustaining growth over a long period of time?
19. What CSR issues are important to you? Rank them in order of importance.

20. How important is CSR to a business and why?
21. Environmental sustainability should be a core requirement for all businesses. Discuss.
22. Why do you think Asian customers are less concerned about CSR issues than those in the USA?
23. CSR is something only big companies are able to address. Discuss.

Exercises and assignments

1. For your own Department in your University or College, use the Product/Market matrix to list the growth options that it faces for the courses on offer.
2. Select a country and find out what help is available in order to export to it.
3. Select a company that has grown rapidly over the last five years. Analyze the strategies it has followed to secure this growth.
4. Select a large, publicly quoted company and, using information from its website, write a report evaluating its CSR strategies.

References

Abell, D. F. (1980) *Defining the Business*, Hemel Hempstead: Prentice Hall.

Ansoff, H. I. (1968) *Corporate Strategy*, Harmondsworth: Penguin.

Bowman, C. and Faulkner, D. (1997) *Competitive and Corporate Strategy*, London: Irwin.

Burke, L. and Logsdon, J. M. (1996) 'How Corporate Social Responsibility Pays off', *Long Range Planning*, 29(4).

Burns, P. (1994) Winners and Losers in the 1990s, 3i European Enterprise Centre, Report 12, April.

De Colle, S. and Gonella, C. (2002) 'The Social and Ethical Alchemy: An Integrative Approach to Social and Ethical Accountability', *Business Ethics: A European Review*, 11(1).

Environics International (2001), *Corporate Social Responsibility Monitor 2001: Global Public Opinion on the Changing Role of Companies*, Toronto, Canada: Environics International (now Globescan).

Epstein, M. J. and Roy, M. J. (2001) 'Sustainability in Action: Identifying and Measuring the Key Performance Drivers', *Long Range Planning*, 34.

Johnson, G. and Scholes, K. (2001) *Exploring Corporate Strategy*, Harlow: Financial Times/Prentice Hall.

Kay, J. (1998) *Foundations of Corporate Success*, Oxford: Oxford University Press.

Peters, T. J. and Waterman, R. H. (1982) *In Search of Excellence*, London: Harper & Row.

Porter, M. E. (1985) *Competitive Advantage, Creating and Sustaining Superior Performance*, New York: The Free Press.

Porter, M. E. (1987) 'From Competitive Advantage to Competitive Strategy', *Harvard Business Review*, 65(3).

Porter, M. E. (1991) 'Knowing Your Place – How to Assess the Attractiveness of Your Industry and Your Company's Position in It', *Inc.*, 13(9), September.

Rumelt, R. P. (1974) *Strategy, Structure and Economic Performance*, Boston, Mass: Harvard University Press.

Smith, N. C. (2003) 'Corporate Social Responsibility: Whether or How?', *California Management Review*, 45(4).

Stevenson, H. H. and Gumpert, D. E. (1985) 'The Heart of Entrepreneurship', *Harvard Business Review*, March/April.

Verschoor, C. C. (2002) 'Best Corporate Citizens have Better Financial Performance', *Strategic Finance*, January.

Wernerfelt, B. and Montgomery, C. A. (1986) 'What is an Attractive Industry?, *Management Science*, 32.

Wood, D. (2000) 'Theory and Integrity in Business and Society.' *Business and Society*, 39(4).

CHAPTER 10
Business growth

CONTENTS

- Introduction
  - Why focus on growth?
- Looking at growth
  - The dimensions of growth
  - The components of growth
- Influences on business growth
  - The entrepreneur: motivation and aspiration
  - The business
  - The external environment
- Targeting growth
  - Arguments for targeting growth businesses
  - Arguments against targeting growth businesses
- Other phases — non-growth, decline and termination
  - Survival, consolidation, comfort and maturity
  - Decline
  - Termination
- Conclusions

KEY CONCEPTS

This chapter covers:
- The stages of business development after start-up.
- The reason why government policies have focused on growth businesses.
- How business growth can be interpreted.
- The internal and external influences on business growth.
- The arguments for and against targeting growth businesses.

- The issues arising in static, declining and terminating businesses, and how and why they might also be helped.

LEARNING OBJECTIVES

By the end of this chapter the reader should:

- Understand the possible stages of business development.
- Understand the rationale for a focus on growth.
- Appreciate what growth can mean.
- Understand the range of possible influences on growth.
- Appreciate why so few businesses grow to be large.
- Be aware of the case for and against a policy of 'picking winners'.
- Appreciate the main issues which can arise in the static, decline and termination stages also.

Introduction

Looked at aspects of the early stages in the life cycle of a business. It looked at idea development and start-up and considered a number of aspects of small business entrepreneurship. This chapter continues that sequence: looking first at business growth and then at maturity, decline and eventually termination.

Why focus on growth?

Of these stages, the one that gets most attention, encouragement and support is business growth. In the 1990s there was a substantial shift in focus and emphasis in the field of small business study towards the growing business. This shift in the UK and elsewhere was evident in policy-making, in the application of small business support, and in related research and commentaries. Fast-growing small firms have been described as 'gazelles', 'fliers', 'growers' and 'winners', and the targeting of effort towards them has been described as 'picking', 'stimulating' or 'backing' winners.

While more recently there has been a further shift back towards support for the start-up process, it is reasonable to ask why the interest in growth developed. It is likely that, just as the earlier emphasis on small businesses in general arose from a recognition of their contribution to the economy, this focus came from a similar desire to maximise that contribution. Birch's study, and other subsequent reviews, had claimed to show that the major proportion of net new jobs is created by small businesses. Governments and others saw that there could be economic benefit in supporting small businesses. More detailed analysis showed that many small businesses did not grow and therefore, once established, did not create more jobs. It was suggested that it was a relatively small proportion of small business starts that did subsequently show significant growth and were responsible for much of the main employment benefits over time. The argument, therefore, was that if small business support resources were limited, which was invariably the case, then the way to maximise results was to apply those resources where they would be most effective. The small business sector is huge and varied, and if support has to be rationed, and if growth businesses produce a disproportionately large share of the desired jobs, then the logical thing to do is to concentrate that support on growth businesses in order to secure the best return.

Associated with this line of argument have been other reasons to look favourably on growth businesses:

- There is a belief that to base support primarily on employment creation can be distorting. Instead, support should try to promote competitiveness in the economy, which should then in turn lead to jobs. Competitiveness embraces notions of innovation, dynamism, efficiency and the winning of greater market share, in particular in export markets. All these are associated with growth firms, which presumably grow because they are competitive. Promoting growth businesses therefore promotes competitiveness and ultimately wealth creation. According to the OECD, SMEs are directly producing about 26 per cent of OECD exports and about 35 per cent of Asia's exports.[1]
- There is a recognition that simply increasing numbers of small businesses may not increase total employment because of displacement effects. Those businesses that do survive may only do so at the expense of others. This is especially the case for businesses selling mainly to local markets and is one reason for the interest in hi-tech start-ups which are likely to have a much wider sales profile.
- Indigenous businesses are seen as crucial for regional development because they have the local roots that inward investments do not have. Moreover inward investment (which is also often referred to as foreign direct investment or FDI) often cannot provide the quick injection of jobs sometimes sought by regional development agencies. If a suitable indigenous business base does not exist then it has to be created from growing small firms, and there are considerable differences in the ability of certain regions to generate sufficient numbers of successful small firms.
- The UK economy is thought to suffer from the absence of a population of efficient and resilient medium-sized businesses that could provide a backbone in the manner of the German *Mittelstand* – globally competitive, usually family-owned, medium-sized businesses, often quoted as key to the success of the German economy. If such a 'backbone' is to emerge then it must come from small growth businesses. (Views on this vary, however. Levy notes that the 'distribution of manufacturing employees between small, medium and large firms' is not greatly different between the UK and Germany.[2] An alternative analysis contends that within the UK population of businesses there are more 'make-weights' and 'punchbags'. A 1995 study of 600 manufacturing companies in the UK, Germany, the Netherlands and Finland concluded that the UK had as many world-class firms as the other countries, but a significantly higher proportion of companies that lagged badly in many key aspects of performance.[3] It has also been claimed that 15,000 medium-sized businesses in the United States, while being only

1 per cent of all businesses, account for 25 per cent of all sales and 20 per cent of all private sector employment.[4])

- Growth businesses are inherently attractive to suppliers of funding and other business services, because the prospects for financial returns are greatest and because of the feeling of success through association.
- There is an increasing recognition that the proportions of established businesses which grow, and the rates at which they grow, vary much more across countries than do the rates of business start-up. That in turn suggests that there might be more potential to influence growth rates, and therefore that promoting business growth by established businesses might be a more cost-effective policy intervention than promoting business start-ups.

> We have also begun to recognise the importance of the 'gazelle' (rapidly growing businesses) phenomenon within the small business, as well as the middle size and large company universe. In fact, mobility across firm size is almost more interesting than firm size per se. I would say the number [of gazelles] is somewhere between 5 and 10 per cent. In my last look, 4 per cent of the firms were doing 70 per cent of the growth. So it's 4, 5, 6, 7 per cent. You can take it as far as you want. Rank all firms by the growth index we have developed and start peeling them off the top. Four per cent at 70; 5 per cent at 77; 10 per cent at 87.
>
> David Birch[5]

The trend towards concentrating support on growth businesses, pursued by the UK government among others, does not command universal support. Inevitably it results in relatively less support for small business creation. Many would see new businesses as potentially a vital element in a vibrant economy, even if they do not grow, since they produce a variety of products and services on which the economy and the growth businesses in it depend. It is also argued that new businesses are the seedbed for future growth businesses, and even if only a small proportion of the businesses in the seedbed do grow, the bigger the seedbed, the more seedlings that may grow. Indeed, a high level of volatility or business churn (the percentage of new firms born added to the percentage of older firms that die) is considered to be the rate at which an economy rejuvenates itself on a regular basis. Within the UK, for instance, there are examples of a high level of business churn in the more economically prosperous southeast of England and low levels of business churn in areas such as Northern Ireland. Moreover there is evidence that the size category of businesses in which net job creation is greatest, over a given period of time, is the up-to-20-employee category, because it contains the greatest number of businesses, including almost all new starts.

This debate, and its implications, is an important one for those who seek to enhance the small business contribution to economic development. It is therefore a key feature of this chapter.

Looking at growth

Overall, small businesses can be divided into three broad groupings. First, there is a high proportion of small businesses that have a short life. Then there is a second large group of businesses that, although surviving, remain small. The third group is by far the smallest: it consists of those businesses that achieve rapid growth. These groups have been referred to by Storey respectively as 'failures', 'trundlers' and 'fliers', and by Birch as 'failures', 'mice' and 'gazelles'. The following empirical data help to put the last, the fliers or gazelles, into context.

On the basis of a study of manufacturing firms in the UK, Storey claims that 'over a decade, 4 per cent of those businesses which start would be expected to create 50 per cent of employment generated'.[6] The Northern Ireland Economic Research Centre (NIERC) studied the performance of manufacturing firms from 1973 to 1986 and also found that almost 10 per cent of surviving firms created 43 per cent of employment.[7] (Applying Storey's assumption that 40 per cent of firms survive ten years, one can again conclude that 4 per cent of the original firms generated 43 per cent of employment.)

Other findings help to confirm the view that in the UK a small number of businesses have a disproportionate impact on job creation. The US experience is broadly similar. For example, a study of new firm growth in Minnesota found that 9 per cent of new firms formed in the 1980s provided over 50 per cent of employment after two to seven years.[8] While there are particular criticisms that can be made of these findings, the general picture is probably reasonably accurate: it is that a relatively small proportion of all small businesses account for the major part of the small business contribution to new jobs. In a follow-up study of all US establishments that started in the late 1990s, one of the principal findings was that employment growth was very sector-based, with growth occurring in the information, professional and business services, education and health services, and manufacturing.[9] The key employment determinant identified was sector survival rates in terms of the numbers employed per establishment that survived. Survival was therefore a crucial variable.

However it is important to note that demonstrating that, in any cohort of businesses, a few will create most jobs is not the same as demonstrating that, in any one year or combination of years, the greatest overall net job creation comes from the fastest-growing businesses. Indeed the up-to-20-employee size range appears to be the category that generates absolutely and relatively the greatest number of net new jobs.

The dimensions of growth

Before examining growth issues further it is logical to consider the possible dimensions, or meanings, of growth in the context of small businesses, and what observers or business owners interpret as the desirable aspects of growth. Storey, in presenting the statistics given above, makes it clear that, in common with others, he is using increases in employment as a measure of growth. Growth in a business can also be defined as greater turnover or increased profitability but, while these measures may all be seen as desirable, they may not even be positively correlated. As noted by

Smallbone and Wyer, 'a number of studies have demonstrated the close correlation that exists between employment growth and sales growth in small firms over a long period of time ... although increased employment is less clearly related to a growth in profitability'.[10] Some analysts may in addition interpret growth in the context of a broader product range, or an increased number of patents or of customers, none of which necessarily imply greater turnover, profitability or employment.

People with a financial interest in small businesses often want to increase the value of their investments by growth in shareholder value, which implies a growth in business earnings and net assets, which themselves may be achieved by growth in turnover and/or profitability (or the potential for it). Employment, therefore, is not necessarily a growth goal for them, but may be a by-product of it. For government support agencies straightforward growth in employment may however be the requirement, or at least an overall improvement in the economy, which is most likely to come from a growth in exports, or a replacement of imports, and which may lead to a growth in employment.

It is important therefore to realise that, while many people may want to see growth, it will mean different things to different people. For many people, growth in employment will generally be the primary goal. For those managing economies and balances of payments, growth in export turnover, or in import substitution, is critical. For shareholders, profitability as a means to enhance dividends and share value is likely to be predominant. The individual small business owner, however, as noted previously, may have one or more of a number of aspirations. These might include being a major local employer, creating wealth, building a large income, being seen as innovative or providing jobs for the family. Many of these will be derived from, or be facilitated by, growth in aspects of the business.

While researchers frequently measure growth in terms of employment, its potential to signify different things to different people means that care must be taken in describing it. Unless its meaning in a particular situation is clear, misunderstandings may arise. It may also be necessary sometimes to remember the distinction made between forms of growth. Some of the yardsticks used for measuring growth are indicated in Table 10.1.

The components of growth

Growing a business is not easy. The natural tendency of a business, like any other system subject to natural decay, is to regress. It takes energy and effort to prevent that and instead to grow. The easiest way to understand the effort needed is to look at the needs of a growing business and the things that must be done to address them.

Under almost every definition of growth, growing a small business needs resources, for which it needs money; it needs management delegation, co-ordination, systems and control; and it needs more sales, which may in turn come from new products or markets.

Understanding growth however requires a regard not just for these internal needs of a business, but also for the totality of the influences on it. Such influences can be external as well as internal and can hinder or help growth. They are illustrated in Figures 10.1 and 10.2 and see also Table 10.2.

Table 10.1 Yardsticks for business growth

Share value	Return on investment	Market share
Net worth	Size of premises	Exports/imports substitution
Profit	Standard of service	New products/services
Employment	Profile/image	Innovations, patents, etc.
Turnover	Number of customers	Added value

The natural trend:

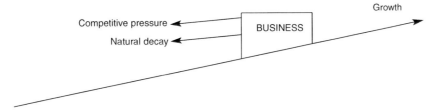

Positive influences:

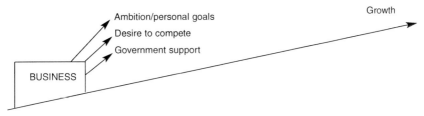

Influences, often overlooked, which tend to keep a business where it is:

Figure 10.1 Influences on a business

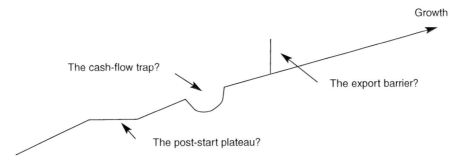

Figure 10.2 Nature of the path to growth

ILLUSTRATION 10.1

Previous academic approaches to understanding small business growth

---

There has been a considerable body of literature embracing very different approaches to understanding the growth process. This can be broadly divided into four categories as follows:

- Approaches exploring the impact of the entrepreneurial personality and capability on growth, including the owner-manager's personal goals and/or strategic vision.

- Approaches seeking to characterise the way the small organisation develops and influences, and is influenced by, the owner-manager. These approaches address issues of management style and stages of growth models.

- Approaches broadly embraced under the term 'business' which focus upon the importance of business skills and the role of functional management, planning, control and formal strategic orientations.

- Approaches which are more macro in scope and which usually have their academic base in industrial economics. These include sectoral approaches pertaining to regional development, a focus upon specific industry sectors or sub-sectors, for example, high-technology firms.[13]

There are obvious overlaps among these approaches. It is interesting to note however that recent economics literature on small firm growth has tended to focus on a combination of a life-cycle effect (young firms grow faster than older firms) and economic variables, especially financial variables, for an explanation of growth. Indeed in modern micro-economic theory there has been allegiance to a model of small firm growth which has led to the 'removal' of the 'human elements'.[14] Thus within economics there is a failing in empirical enquiry to address 'the key questions of entrepreneurial characteristics and motivations and how they may be translated into business strategy'.[15] Interesting studies by, for example, Barkham et al.[16] and Storey[17] have adopted a more comprehensive approach, seeking to bring together research in economics, geography, organisational studies and business strategy to examine the link between entrepreneurial characteristics, business strategy and small firm growth across a wide variety of types of small firm. Traditionally, however, the unit of study has often been the business, not the entrepreneur. The needs, aspirations and other characteristics of habitual entrepreneurs have been largely ignored by researchers, policy-makers and support agencies. 'The process of ownership diversification may shed new light on the way we can conceptualise start-up and growth dynamics.'[18]

One benefit of establishing the totality of influences on a business is that it helps to put any single influence in perspective. Without this there is a tendency to overestimate the effect of any particular influence. If, for instance, it is considered that R&D can help to build competitiveness and that a grant scheme would encourage R&D, then it might be thought that such a grant scheme would be a positive influence on a business. However, it is important to recognise the strength of the influences keeping the business where it is; they are likely to be much stronger than

Table 10.2 Some of the influences on a business

Type of influence	Internal	External
Positive	Owner's desire to increase profitability and/or to prove him or herself	Stimulus of competition Encouragement of others Favourable tax incentives
	Impetus of earlier growth	Encouragement and support from small business agencies
Negative	Bounce back from earlier uncontrolled growth Lack of ability of the owner and/or management team	Adverse tax, interest and exchange rates Improvements in the competition Product obsolescence
Those which can encourage a business not to change	Owner's lifestyle and the consequent need for the present level of return but not for more but not for more Inertia and the difficulty of mobilising the resources needed to do more Limits on internal capacity to plan, coordinate and supervise	Peer group pressure

the more dubious incentive of a grant. This has been likened to pushing a heavy object: friction tends to keep it where it is, unless the pushing force is sufficiently large, and attempts to reduce the frictional resistance might be more effective than attempts to increase the amount of external push.

Growth, or its absence, can however be attributable to a wide variety of factors. There is no comprehensive theory to explain which firms will grow or how they grow, but various explanatory approaches have been used. Of course, whatever approach or combination of approaches one favours, seeking to distinguish between what is necessary and what is sufficient for growth has been and is likely to remain an unattainable goal. Indeed most of the research work in this area 'fails to provide convincing evidence of the determinants of small firm growth as a basis for informing policymakers';[11] and again, 'Given the significance of employment created in rapidly growing small firms, it is surprising that theoretical and empirical understanding of the characteristics of these firms remains somewhat sketchy'.[12]

Influences on business growth

In the context of small businesses, what are the main influences on growth? Three types of influence in particular are examined below: first the influences of the entrepreneur, linked to his or her personality, behaviour, attitude and capability; then the influences due to the business itself, related to its structure and goals and to the performance of its management; and finally the influences of the external environment such as the business's sector, region and other strategic issues.

The entrepreneur: motivation and aspiration

The first approach focuses on the entrepreneur as a person. Personality and behaviour are believed to be causal factors for or against growth-orientated achievement. This is understandable. It is a characteristic of small business that powers of decision are centralised at the level of the owner-manager, so his or her personality, skills, responsibilities, attitude and behaviour will have a decisive influence on business strategy.

Typical of the analysts using this approach is Kirchhoff, who develops a 'dynamic capitalism typology' to explain the relationship between innovation and firm growth.[19] The typology divides firms into four categories: economic core, ambitious, glamorous and constrained growth. Each category has its own broad growth profile.

'Economic core' businesses are low on innovation and on growth. They are the largest single category, but fast-growing firms can leap out from the core; an example is Wal-Mart, the world's largest retailer, where the most significant growth came after over 30 years of operations. 'Ambitious' firms achieve high rates of growth with one, or a few, initial innovations. Growth comes from a gradual build up of market share. However, growth cannot be sustained without additional innovations (usually in the product or service or in its marketing). With additional innovations, firms become 'glamorous'. Microsoft is a good example. Glamorous businesses, according to Kirchhoff, can have experienced periods of 'constrained growth' for two broad reasons.[20] First, growth may be self-constrained owing to the owner's reluctance to relinquish ownership and control to generate the necessary resources for growth; and second, it may be constrained where businesses are genuinely limited by a lack of resources. They can often be highly innovative, but still unable to secure early stage capital.

Kirchhoff concludes that 'what is interesting about these four classes of firms is that they do not depend upon industrial sector, business size, age nor location.'[21] This typology, he continues, 'identifies the firms' behaviours that indicate the true ambitions and goals of the owners and defines their contribution to economic growth. Aspiring entrepreneurs need to realistically assess their personal ambitions and where they wish to be in this typology.'[22]

This is a clear attribution of business growth to entrepreneurial motivation and competency, as exhibited in a willingness to innovate. It is probably reasonable to assume that the motivation to grow is likely to be the *sine qua non* of growth. Yet for many business owners the growth of their businesses is not an objective. Growth is associated with many unattractive circumstances. These may include having to find work for others, loss of management control, reliance on others, sharing responsibilities and decision making, perhaps relinquishing some ownership stake, and unnecessary risk, although there is evidence from the UK and United States that survival and growth are positively correlated. (For US data see Knaup, 2005: note 9.)

A desire to spend more time with one's family or to engage in other forms of social and leisure activity are also valid reasons. Professional and social issues combine very often, as is noted in the significant amount of literature on the family business which recognises the influence of family in respect of growth and issues of ownership. Often growth is rejected where it might lead to a conflict of interests.

There are businesses that have a no-growth aspiration. As 'lifestyle' businesses, and in almost every case they are established solely to provide a satisfactory level of income. They are very often home-based, sole-trader operations employing no more than one additional person. Statistics reveal that well over half of all UK business owners in the late 1980s had no plans to grow. In addition there is a clear association between firm size and the desire to grow.[23]

Even among those entrepreneurs who seek growth, significant numbers would appear to seek only moderate or limited growth. They may reach a stage or plateau, described as a 'comfort zone', at which the owner is satisfied with his or her condition and the costs of pursuing continued growth exceed the expected benefits. These perceived costs will dominate over any material or psychological gains that might be expected from growth. As more than one owner has remarked, 'The problems grow geometrically while the firm grows arithmetically.'

> If growth of any kind is to be achieved it is important for the entrepreneur to be clear about their ambition for the business. Do they want to run a nice lifestyle business that could give them a good living for 20 years? Do they want to build the business up rapidly to sell it within five to ten years? Or do they want to build it piece by piece over time to pass it on? There is nothing wrong with any of these ambitions. They each can give the entrepreneur guidance on what risks they should be prepared to take and what they need to do to be successful in terms of the ambition they have for the business.
>
> Chris Gorman (Portfolio Entrepreneur)
>
> *Source*: Lecture to University of Stirling students, 2006.

With reference to the owner typologies, the 'lifestyle' owners would be classified as artisans/shopkeepers but some may grow sufficiently to assume the status of Hornaday's 'professional managers'. Carree et al. claim that their 'managerial' business owners are to be found in the majority of small firms.[24] They include many franchisees, shopkeepers and people in professional occupations belonging to Kirchhoff's economic core. Indeed they further note that Audretsch and Thurik, in their analysis of how and why entrepreneurship has contributed to economic and social development, assume that their two types have different economic roles in relation to unemployment.[25] They contend that the number of what they call 'shopkeepers' is likely to go up if the level of unemployment rises, but that that level is expected to go down if the number of Schum-peterians ('real' entrepreneurs) increases. In reality, of course, it can be difficult to distinguish one type of owner from another since most owners 'share attitudes associated with these extremes in a varying degree'.[26]

The motivation of the owner is undoubtedly a very important ingredient in the (no-)growth process and, of course, the motivation can change over time as the business develops and events external and internal to the business occur. It is a dynamic situation. Firms can appear to be in a steady state for many years and then begin to grow rapidly. Growth is not necessarily a continuous process for many firms, which is an important consideration for those who rely on recent past performance as a predictor of future performance. One possible reason is a need to establish the business – to build strong roots – before moving on and upwards. The majority of firms show no growth for their first six years, while more than 50 per cent of surviving firms show growth after six years. Indeed, rapid growth, when it happens, appears to begin after six to eight years of trading.[27]

It is also worth noting that a significant number of entrepreneurs, instead of managing their established businesses whether in a growth phase or not, may be much more stimulated by, or capable of, generating new business ideas and converting them into new ventures. The excitement and fulfilment for such people may be in creating something new, not in managing an existing operation. In fact while their businesses may essentially be in the early stages of business development, the entrepreneurs themselves can become obstacles to the further development of the business as neither their interest nor competency may be at the appropriate levels. Such people may favour multiple business ownership as habitual entrepreneurs.

The role of chance

The size distribution of a population of firms can be derived from a mechanical chance model. Thus, in aggregate, firm size follows a 'random walk'. This might suggest that there is some 'iron law' of firm growth which determines the size distribution. Indeed, studies suggest that there are many factors influencing firms' growth rates, and while two or three may exert a significant influence relative to the others, they still explain a relatively small proportion of any variance produced within a given sample of firms.

It is possible to conclude, therefore, that chance or luck plays a part in determining which firms grow. To suggest that all successful entrepreneurs were merely lucky is to overstate the situation, but as Reid and Jacobsen suggest, 'it is necessary to caution those who would ignore the role of chance in determining the fortunes of the small entrepreneurial firm.'[28] In addition, as Nelson and Winter note, 'luck is the principle factor that finally distinguishes winners from near winners – although vast differences of skills and competence may separate contenders from non-contenders.'[29]

The situation can be likened to one in which racing boats in a river may or may not catch the current. To be a winner may depend on luck as well as judgement – but if, due to a lack of skills or resources, one has been unable to get one's boat as far as the river, one will certainly not win.

There is certainly no lack of anecdotal evidence from successful entrepreneurs about the role of luck, and it is surely undeniable that 'in the presence of uncertainty and bounded rationality, fortune will play a significant if variable role.'[30]

Other entrepreneurial characteristics

It will also be apparent that the will or motivation to grow by no means guarantees growth. So a growth model that focuses on the individual entrepreneur as the key to the growth process must also take into account aspects of the individual other than motivation, such as traits, behaviour and resources. These factors will influence the entrepreneur's ability to achieve growth, as well as his or her will to do so.

Storey has reviewed a number of empirical studies that examine which characteristics of the entrepreneur, including motivation, are related to growth.[31] The conclusions drawn however do not permit the development of a profile or model of the growth-achieving entrepreneur in terms of the subsequent performance of the firm. There is some suggestion that the more significant variables, in addition to motivation, are education, age and management experience, all of which are positively correlated. (Motivation, however, in this instance refers only to why the business was established – not motivation to grow.) Barkham et al. found that the entrepreneurs associated with faster-growing manufacturing firms were relatively young and members of professional organisations, that they had worked as part of a larger entrepreneurial team, and that they had a network of other business interests which were mainly legally independent and separate small firms.[32] In some cases the existence of other businesses was advantageous; in others this was not so. Interestingly, there appears to be some evidence that businesses founded by groups are also likely to grow faster than those founded by single individuals, although no definite conclusions can yet be drawn. Indeed the focus on teams of enterprising persons rather than on individuals is commanding greater interest and research in recent times. It is becoming increasingly recognised that the 'lone wolf' entrepreneur, no matter how charismatic or how enterprising, limits the growth potential of the enterprise simply because of his or her personality and the physical limitations of individuality in practising entrepreneurial management.

Another characteristic of the entrepreneur that has also been studied is his or her willingness to accept external equity. As finance from an external source is usually needed to permit rapid business expansion, accepting equity involvement and sharing ownership removes a growth constraint (and of course equity is more likely to be available to growth businesses as they will be more attractive to investors). Alternative funding sources can be used, but usually not without increasing the business's gearing. It is reasonable to infer, therefore, that a willingness by the entrepreneur to share ownership, and therefore decision making and control, is key to the growth of some businesses. When the concept of the entrepreneur is extended to embrace his or her management style and strategic management practices, including the development and use of networks, conclusions are no simpler to reach. For example, there is an increasing tendency to link the business's growth with the quality and quantity of the personal and organisational networks that the entrepreneur develops.

Some studies support the contention that a greater use of external sources of information, advice and other resources results in faster growth, particularly for a high-technology business. It is logical to assume that, as the entrepreneur's resources are often limited and he or she has to gain some control over his or her socio-economic environment, networks play a more crucial role for the small business that seeks growth. Moreover the nature of networks appears to change as the business develops, which is also to be expected.

However, work on management style and networks is subject to criticisms which are frequently mentioned. To be useful, such studies need to distinguish cause and effect, and also to distinguish whether the factors being studied actually cause growth or merely facilitate (or hinder) processes determined by other influences.

Conclusion

The findings revealed by one Third World study are instructive.[33] It tested three groups of personal entrepreneurial competencies: first, those perceived to pertain to basic personality, such as assertiveness, determination and initiative; second, those relating to business management styles, such as efficiency orientation; third, those classified as business skill indicators, such as systematic planning. It was concluded from this however that personality variables are not useful predictors of business performance. The personality-orientated competency measures represented in the data did not relate consistently, it was claimed, to the various measures of business performance for the respondents.

It is reasonable to conclude, therefore, that what the entrepreneur 'is' (traits) is less important than what he or she 'does' (behaviour), because the latter effects change. The link between what one 'is' and what one 'does' is clearly largely undetermined. Moreover Gibb and Davies contend that 'Different types of entrepreneurial behaviour are required in different marketplaces to achieve growth and different traits, skills and competencies will be needed depending upon levels of uncertainty and complexity in the market.'[34]

In conclusion, it is reasonable to deduce that the entrepreneur's (or business leader's) ambition and desire to grow are critical. In addition, the skills of the entrepreneur are particularly important in the early stages of growth. The ability to broaden and adapt to changing circumstances is likely to be of major importance in removing obstacles to growth. Different types of behaviour may be required in different market situations and different personal competencies are likely to be needed to deal with the different levels of complexity and uncertainty in the business environment. It is important that entrepreneurs are willing to delegate and, by implication, that employees must be capable and willing to accept responsibility. It is also a truism to say that an inability to manage growth, despite a motivation to do so, will prevent growth. It is undoubtedly the case that many firms fail to grow because of a variety of barriers, including those of a technical, marketing and financial nature, but not least those which are managerial (which may in fact be at the root of most of the other barriers). How some management factors can help or hinder growth at different stages is captured in Figure 10.3.

Storey's research stresses the critical importance of the attitude and quality of the initial manager(s) whom the entrepreneur recruits. Such a finding would reinforce the importance of the management team to growth achievement and of the owner's ability to build such a team. These issues of management are explored further in the next section.

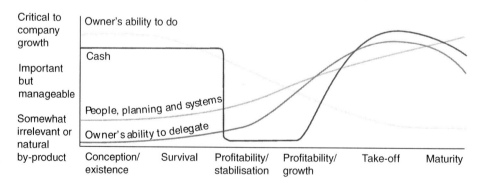

Figure 10.3 Management factors and stages

Source: N. C. Churchill, 'The Six Key Phases of Company Growth', 'Mastering Enterprise', *Financial Times* (1997), February, p.3.

The business

A second approach to explaining growth is to look at the characteristics of the business itself. These characteristics can be divided into two categories, chosen because they are firm specific:

- the firm's structure – ownership, legal form, age and size
- the firm's management skills and performance, including its access to resources.

Structure

Storey reviewed research from 11 studies on one or more of the elements in this category.[35] His conclusion was that little is known about the impact of ownership. It is not known, for example, whether a second or subsequent owner is more likely grow a business, nor is it known if an individual with more than one business is more likely to succeed in growing one or more of them, nor whether a business begun by a team is more likely to grow.

On the legal form of the business, it would appear that a limited company is more likely to grow as compared with a sole trader or partnership. This should not be surprising because most businesses convert to limited company status at some stage in their development and are frequently under various pressures to convert as they grow.

Most studies also conclude that younger and smaller firms grow more quickly than older and larger ones. It is important to note, however, that one reason for a correlation between size and growth is that it is easier to achieve a doubling in any growth parameter if the business is smaller to start with. Few large businesses would try a 100 per cent increase in employment at one stroke, but that is just what a previously one-person business does when it recruits its first employee. Additionally, many businesses will grow rapidly initially to reach the 'critical mass' needed to service their market efficiently, but subsequently 'plateau'.

In general findings about the firm's characteristics and growth are of very limited value for policy purposes. As with information about the entrepreneur, either the causal relationship is unclear or no meaningful basis for policy intervention has been identified. Indeed none of the structural factors identified indicates, with adequate clarity, anything about the ambitions or goals exhibited by a business's owners and managers.

Management

The second category of firm-specific characteristics relates to management performance. Many would argue that the motivation and ability of a firm to grow rests with the owner and his or her management team. Such an approach recognises that growth is related to a business's performance in the marketplace, and in particular to its ability to make rational (profitable) decisions about its products and/or services in the context of market development.

In short, a condition of growth is the ability of management to plan and implement the firm's growth in both strategic and operational terms. It is instructive to note that a European Observatory for SMEs annual report identifies four weaknesses of smaller businesses:[36]

- high mortality rates
- weak market orientation due to lack of strategic marketing approaches and to operating in small segmented markets
- low productivity of labour leading to high unit wage costs
- low equity–debt ratio and difficult and costly access to financial markets.

All of these weaknesses can be related to management inadequacy (as indeed can almost all aspects of small business performance). Even difficulty in raising finance can be attributed to a 'failure' of management adequately to search for sources, build networks, prepare suitable business plans or share ownership and control.

Evidence concerning the impact of a selection of firm-specific factors attributable to the performance of the management team is summarised by Storey.[37] These factors are: management recruitment and training, workforce training, technological sophistication, market positioning, market adjustments, planning, new product introduction, customer concentration, exporting (information and advice) and external equity. The list of factors reflects research that has been done, and is not necessarily an exhaustive list of management-related issues.

Unfortunately, as before, the findings are not conclusive. It seems to be counter-intuitive that proper practice in many of these factors, which conventionally constitute good management, are as yet not found to be correlated with growth in businesses. It is, however, suggested that three aspects of management do appear to be the most closely linked with growth, as opposed to size (an important distinction): these are market positioning, new products and management recruitment.

Market positioning

A key decision for any business is the definition of its market and where it perceives itself to be in relation to its competitors. While it is difficult to define precisely, market positioning has to do with notions of who the customers are, competitive advantage, product and service range and the role of quality, service and price. Illustration 10.2 discusses this in the context of ethnic business. These are important issues for management to clarify – otherwise, the business's ability to take corrective action if things go wrong will be limited. It would appear that the ability to know of and take advantage of market positioning (in other words, to determine one's niche) is related to growth success. Barkham et al. found that undertaking formal market research had strong associations with growth, while the use of agents (as opposed to in-house sales staff) to sell products had the reverse effect.[38]

New products

Related to market positioning is the development and introduction of new products. There is some evidence, but it is by no means conclusive, that new product introductions are associated with faster growth. Introducing new products is usually seen as part of the process of innovation, which is itself in much of the literature seen as the engine driving continued growth. Innovation is often limited however to development by absorption of new techniques. Indeed, definite conclusions in this area are difficult to draw from empirical studies, although the OECD expresses a commonplace view in suggesting that 'A businessman's attitude to using new technologies to ensure or increase competitiveness ... appears extremely significant. His attitude will be determined by his experience and training but also by those of his management team.'[39]

ILLUSTRATION 10.2
Breakout by ethnic entrepreneurs

It is contended that effective market definition and positioning and the appropriate introduction of new products can allow firms to grow, but this may not be so easy for ethnic businesses. These firms can benefit from a deep understanding of the needs of their co-ethnic clients and an ability to meet them, but Ram points out that many ethnic markets are static and fiercely competitive. Growth depends on breaking into non-ethnic markets but this is predicated on the development of an effective marketing strategy. Ram notes that not many ethnic firms are sophisticated marketers and that problems with underfunding, inadequate premises and equipment, labour-intensive production methods and inadequate insurance make breakout difficult. However, some firms with innovative products, differentiated market contacts and willpower do manage to enter new markets and achieve sustainable growth.

Source: M. Ram, 'Ethnic Minority Enterprise: An Overview and Research Agenda', *Journal of Entrepreneurial Behaviour and Research* (1997), 3, pp.145–56.

Management recruitment

Common sense dictates that as a firm grows it becomes more dependent on its management team. A CBI report revealed that there is a 'greater awareness of management weaknesses among growth firms', and that 'recruitment of outside managers also tends to increase with growth.' Table 10.3, taken from this report, highlights the perceived importance of management.[40] There is much other research evidence to show that not acquiring the right management expertise and not building the appropriate structure are amongst the main reasons why growth-orientated firms fail to achieve their objective of growth.

Other factors

Overall, one cannot deduce that other firm specific factors are not important for growth: there is merely an absence of strong evidence to demonstrate the causal relationship. Indeed, even for the factors highlighted in this section, the evidence presented remains open to challenge. Controversially, neither workforce nor management training is shown to be a causal factor influencing the growth of the business. Their association is with larger but not necessarily growing firms, and they are as likely to be a consequence as a cause.

What research there is confirms the importance of management development in a growing business, and demonstrates individual examples of its impact on

Table 10.3 Management weakness as a constraint on growth: internal barriers to growth (percentage of respondents citing factor as important)

Management team too small/too stretched	65
Reluctance to dilute ownership	57
Reluctance to take on new debt	55
Lack of successful innovation	40
Preference for maintaining the manageability of small size	40

Note: Respondents were 667 private companies with turnover between £2.5 and £25 m.
Source: Binder Hamlyn and London Business School (1994), 'The Quest for Growth', reprinted from *Managing to Grow* (London: CBI, 1995), p.11.

performance. It does not, however, isolate the impact of different approaches to management development (such as training, mentoring, counselling and the presence of non-executive directors) across a group of small businesses.

This emphasis on rational business management approaches to growth has led to an increasing flow of literature that attempts to link not only the personal characteristics of the entrepreneur but also those of the management team to planning and performance.

As with many factors studied, definitional problems make comparability of findings difficult, not least in the area of planning. Despite this, few studies demonstrate a convincing link between formalised planning and improved performance of the small firm. Planning seems to be related to size, not growth.

Many familiar with micro and small-firm behaviour will recognise that the 'informal and intuitive' dominates over formal planning procedures and is at least equally effective. Nor should the existence of a business plan be confused with planning! The OECD reports in its study on globalising SMEs that 'Successful small firms often do not rely on formal strategic planning although they are very conscious of what they want to achieve.'[41] Overall, however, it might be foolish to deny the significance of product and/or market-related decisions, cost/price decisions and constraint decisions (including time and finance) taken by a strategically aware management team as critical to business growth, despite the absence of conclusive evidence. Barkham et al. found that four business aims stated by owner-managers were significantly associated with growth: those of expansion of profits, improving margins, having a marketing strategy and improving the production process.[42] It is interesting to note that a study of 179 super-growth companies in the United States resulted in the identification of five factors leading to a 'winning performance'.[43] These were:

- competing on quality not prices
- domination of a market niche
- competing in an area of strength
- having tight financial and operating controls
- frequent product or service innovation (particularly important in manufacturing).

Barkham et al. reinforce this view in that their results reveal that it is the characteristics of the entrepreneur and the strategies he or she adopts which largely determine the growth of the small enterprise.[44] Company characteristics, including size, location and sector, appear to be influential but in a relatively minor way. To a large extent growth in small firms derives from the skills, values and motivations of the entrepreneur and the strategies adopted with regard to innovation, marketing and market research.

This approach to explaining small business growth reflects what Gibb and Davies described as a business or 'organisational' approach, emphasising the development sequence of a firm as it passes through a series of stages in its life cycle.[45] The different stages require different roles for the direction of the business, as suggested in Table 10.4, which also draws a parallel between the needs of a developing business and Maslow's hierarchy of needs.

The external environment

Yet another approach to understanding and explaining growth lies in examining the impact of factors or constraints external to the entrepreneur or the business. These include macro-economic variables such as aggregate demand, taxation, regulations, labour market skills and labour relations, but also embrace sector and region specific matters such as product/service and/or market, competition, government assistance, location and the availability (and use) of information.

Macro-economic variables

Looking first at macro-economic variables, it is clear that policies on demand, taxation, interest rates and public spending will affect the fortunes of small firms. Indeed government policies in these areas are intended to induce behavioural change by individuals and organisations. It is indisputable that these policies have a major impact on the trading performance of small firms.

Despite the continuing calls by small firm representative bodies for reduced regulations ('less red tape') it is not clear to what extent administrative and legislative burdens hinder business growth. It is reasonable to assume, however, that anything that absorbs time and resources that would otherwise be devoted to business development is likely to have a deleterious effect.

Studies in many OECD member countries, including the UK, highlight the constraining effect of small business being unable to obtain good quality or skilled labour even in a relatively slack overall labour market. At any given time, how much the problem is on the supply side (recruitment processes, remuneration, employment rights and conditions), as opposed to the demand side, is not clear.

Table 10.4 The different role needed for business development at different stages

Business stage	Related role	Maslow's hierarchy
Maturity	Leader	Self-actualisation
Expansion	↑	Recognition
Growth	Manager	Belonging
Survival	↑	Security
Start-up	Entrepreneur	Survival

In general, governments' macro-economic policies are geared to all enterprises and not just smaller businesses. Moreover, while the impact of governments' macro policies can fall unevenly on different sectors and/or markets (and labour markets are partially differentiated), the specific effect on the growth of an individual business is likely to be much less than the effect on business in general and not least on international competitive comparisons. It is unlikely, therefore, that macro-economic and national policies will explain differential growth rates within different sectors, whatever the effects across sectors.

Sector

A number of studies in recent years indicate that the average growth rate of firms is higher in some sectors than in others.[46] Particular attention has been paid in numerous studies to businesses in the high-tech sector where, for example, Westhead and Storey conclude that high-technology small firms in the UK not only have higher growth rates but also have lower failure rates than small businesses in other sectors.[47] Kirchhoff, examining US data, only partially agrees:

> The chances of achieving high growth are almost twice as great for high-tech firms as for low-tech firms. Still, among high-tech firms terminations take a greater toll as low-growth firms are unable to hang on for as long as low-tech firms.[48]

Kirchhoff attributes their superior growth performance to the high cost of innovation, which requires growth if the firm is to survive. However high-tech sectors can suffer reverses, as was shown in the 'winter of technology' in 2000 and subsequently when many ICT businesses collapsed.

Sectoral studies serve the purpose of highlighting the particular constraints and opportunities of sectors (such as financing problems for the high-tech sector). They do not typically offer a basis for predicting the extent to which growth businesses will emerge or in what conditions, however. They also encourage analysis of the structure of an industry, and especially the role of large firms and their interaction with smaller ones. Linkages between large and small firms may play an important role in influencing small firm growth. Growth can occur on the basis of servicing the needs of large firms; large firms can spin out numbers of small ones; strategic partnerships across a variety of functions can develop; large firms can provide management and technological support and advice. On the other hand, large firms through their power in the marketplace can hinder or eliminate small business growth through acquisition, control over intellectual property, slow payment and quasi-monopolistic practices.

It is misleading however to place too much reliance on sectoral performance from a policy perspective. As research has indicated, performance within sectors varies to a much greater extent than across them.[49]

Competition

It may appear prima facie that for a given market size, the smaller the number of competitors the greater the likelihood of any given business capturing a large share of the market. However, many influences may be operating, such as (dis)economies of scale, product or market differentiation, the relative importance of large and small firms in the market and transportation costs, which make it very difficult to define the 'competitiveness' of a market or sector. It is not surprising, therefore, that no correlation appears to exist between growth and competition. Porter argues however that greater competitiveness in an industry's home market can lead to stronger export performance and growth. (See 'The cluster effect' later in this section.)

Location

The concept of location is more complex than it first seems. Locational attributes such as those of being urban, rural, peripheral or central can mean differences in many of the other factors such as competition, labour market and government support. It then becomes difficult to determine which of the influences is at work.

However, it is safe to say, once again, that there is not yet enough evidence to suggest that growth is location-determined. Possible exceptions to this conclusion are businesses (usually service or service-related firms) serving local markets, because these are likely to be small, although the benefits of larger markets may well be offset by greater numbers of competitors. A review of lists of UK fast-growth firms (such as the Sunday Times/Virgin Fast-Track 100) suggests that they are disproportionately concentrated in the south of England. The changing composition of the Fast-Track 100 list of high growth firms for sales and profits also clearly illustrates the volatility of the performance of such firms.

Findings by Vaessen and Keeble in a recent analysis of small business by regional location, on the other hand, suggest a different link between growth and location.[50] Peripheral regions are found to contain proportionately more growing small businesses than what they call the 'core' region (southeast England). A partial explanation is that greater R&D and training inputs are generated in the peripheral locations. These findings can only be tentative however: their counterintuitive nature may suggest that differences in external environments are not sufficient to explain growth differentials. Indeed, to assume otherwise would be to suggest that the entrepreneur's and the business's behaviour are largely constrained by their location, an assumption that does not allow significant scope for variable responses. Either way, the policy implications are unclear.

Information and advice

The provision of information and advice by government agencies is itself a growth sector in many countries seeking to support their small businesses. This form of support can also come from private sector sources (such as bankers, accountants, non-executive directors and consultants); and the use made of accountants and bankers, at least in developed economies, would appear to be much higher than that made of public information and advice services. Indeed the uptake of public sector provision seems generally to be very low (less than 10 per cent of potential users). However, satisfaction with information and advice, from both public and private sources, appears generally to be high. Importantly, despite the significant investment being made in these services in the United States, the UK and the European Union generally, there appears to be no convincing evidence that their uptake improves business performance and growth, although growing businesses would appear to make greater use of information and advisory networks.

Government support

Government support can take a wide variety of forms, but usually consists of grant aid, subsidised loans and/or the provision of subsidised services such as consultancy, training and the provision of information and advice.

The impact of direct financial support from government or its agencies is the issue most often studied. Such support normally comes from local or regional agencies. The small business community generally expresses dissatisfaction with the grants regime, or at least with its administration. It is reported that it feels that grants go to large or foreign firms, that application procedures are too complicated and lengthy, and that not enough information is available on how to access grants.[51] Notwithstanding these views, significant sums across many regions have been provided to small business. Once again, research findings have been inconclusive in determining whether financial support generates further growth, improved profitability or less efficient performance.

The cluster effect

There is however one theory that links issues such as location, competition and government support to the competitiveness, and hence to the potential growth, of businesses. This theory is propounded by Porter who, following a four-year study of ten important trading nations, ultimately concluded that nations succeed in particular industries because their home environment is the most forward-looking, dynamic and challenging.[52] These conclusions, he suggests, contradict the conventional wisdom that labour costs, interest rates, exchange rates and economies of scale are the most potent determinants of competitiveness. It is too easy, he says, for governments to adopt policies, such as joint projects for R&D, that operate on the belief that independent research by domestic rivals is wasteful and duplicative, that collaborative efforts achieve economies of scale, and that individual companies are likely to under-invest in R&D because they cannot reap all the benefits. That view, he claims, is flawed and fundamentally misperceives the true sources of competitive advantage.

Porter argues that, while successful businesses will each employ their own strategy, they achieve competitive advantage through acts of innovation. Further, he believes that it is demanding buyers in the domestic market who pressure companies to innovate faster. Why is it, he asks, that certain companies based in certain countries are capable of consistent innovation? The answer lies in four broad attributes of a region. These are: factor conditions (labour force quality, infrastructure), demand conditions (the nature of home market demand), related and supporting industries (the presence of supplier industries and other related industries which are internationally competitive), and firm strategy, structure and rivalry (the conditions in the nation affecting how businesses are created, organised and managed and the nature of domestic competition). These four determinants form the points on Porter's 'diamond', and the diamond is itself a system. Together they affect the key elements that beget international competitiveness and, by implication, firm and industry growth.

How these determinants combine to produce a successful industry is complex, but Porter notes that internationally competitive businesses are usually found in geographically concentrated clusters of related businesses. 'Among all the points on the diamond, domestic rivalry is arguably the most important because of the powerfully stimulating effect it has on all the others,' asserts Porter, adding that 'Geographic concentration magnifies the power of domestic rivalry.'[53] One of the most commonly quoted examples is that of 'The Third Italy': a proliferation of concentrations of various industrial sectors benefiting from a variety of effects that include pools of skilled workers and technicians; related input from maintenance, service and design businesses; supporting companies that offer materials, supplies and other services, including subcontracting; and specialist businesses offering consultancy and advice on logistics, advertising, finance and general support. Support agency services develop that are geared to meet a cluster's needs in the form of education and training, research and development, and fiscal and legal advice. In Italy these interrelationships are reinforced by family connections and traditional links that significantly strengthen the power of the network. Such inbuilt cultural ties however complicate the situation for those who might otherwise think that they could merely 'import' the cluster effect. Despite this, efforts continue to create clusters of mainly high-technology companies. For example in the UK in 1999 a research team under Lord Sainsbury highlighted the importance of public sector encouragement of clustering, while a joint Department of Trade and Industry and Department for Education and Employment (both since renamed) White Paper *Opportunity for All in a World of Change* (February 2001) encouraged regional development agencies to continue developing existing and embryonic clusters.[54] On the wider front the OECD notes that smaller firms are increasingly going global, 'building on local networks and inter-firm clusters to derive scale economies in international markets'.[55]

General

This brief review covers only some of the factors that have been considered as possible influences on the growth performance of small businesses. This chapter has classified the range of factors into three broad categories: the entrepreneur, the firm and the external environment. Other classifications exist. The OECD, for instance, categorises the key factors in the competitiveness of SMEs as:[56]

- The owner's/manager's basic role (drive).
- Intangible investment ('intelligence management'), including:
  - the ability to obtain information through environmental scanning and search
  - at least an intermittent R&D capability
  - the quality of the firm's organisation
  - the quality of its training.
- Tangible investment (based on new management and production technologies).
- The business's strategic capabilities (innovation and flexibility).

However, as already noted, the research on these and other classifications and their components has produced no conclusive results and no firm evidence to support interventions, either to increase the pace of growth or to increase the number of growing businesses.

Nevertheless, it would be foolish to set aside a pragmatic approach to this problem, such as to note what businesses themselves have been saying. Table 10.5 shows the barriers to growth reported in a small firm survey of 2500 businesses in the UK in 1997[57] carried out by Cambridge University's Centre for Business Research, the results of whose 1990 study[58] are also shown for comparison. The top issues in both studies revolve around market demand and competition, the availability and cost of finance, and the firm's ability to deal with them, with the scores being sufficiently

Table 10.5 Constraints on small business growth

Constraint	Nature	Ranking	
		1997	*1990*
Increased competition	External	1	4
Availability and cost of finance for expansion	External	2	1
Marketing and sales skills	Internal	3	5
Availability and cost of overdraft finance	External	4	2
Growth of market demand	External	5	3
Management skills	Internal	6	6
Skilled labour	Internal	7	7
Acquisition of new technology	?	8	8
Difficulty of implementing new technology	Internal	9	9
Availability of appropriate premises	External	10	10
Access to overseas markets	?	11	11

Sources: 1997: adapted from A. Cosh and A. Hughes (eds), *Enterprising Britain; Growth, Innovation and Public Policy in the Small and Medium Sized Enterprise Sector 1994–1997* (Cambridge: ESRC Centre for Business Research, 1998) (revised in P. Burns, *Entrepreneurship and Small Business, Second Edition*: Palgrave Macmillan, 2007, p. 252; Table 9.1); ESRC Small Business Research Centre, *The State of British Enterprise: Growth, Innovation and Competitive Advantage in Small and Medium-Sized Firms* (Cambridge: ESRC Small Business Research Centre, 1992).

close together to highlight these issues as the key to growth. These are all primarily external factors. In addition, medium-sized firms reported inadequate management skills, and to a lesser extent marketing and sales skills, as greater constraints than did smaller firms. Younger and faster-growing firms stressed financial constraints, while faster-growing ones also placed management skills shortages higher. Manufacturing firms revealed generally more constraints than service firms, and innovating firms reported more than non-innovating ones.

It may be reasonable to accept these rather typical results (albeit no mention is made of administrative and regulatory burdens!) at face value, subject to two caveats: first, businesses may tend to blame external, and therefore uncontrollable, factors before internal, controllable, factors; and second, there is a tendency to confuse causes and effects. In the latter case, financial constraints may become apparent because of a lack of demand or, in the case of a growing business, because of a reluctance to dilute ownership or control or because of poor financial management skills.

A second common-sense approach is to recognise that growth is likely to be dependent upon the interaction of a number of influences, and that these influences may be important in different combinations for different businesses. This makes generalisations very imprecise and of limited use as guides to action. Growth is likely to occur when a number of the key factors in each category combine, although it is most unlikely that there is only one or a few successful combinations, and the combinations for success could change as the business develops and market circumstances alter. The dynamic process implied in this interpretation of how growth is generated through the interaction of the entrepreneur, the firm and its environment, local and regional as well as national and international, is at the heart of understanding the growth process itself. However, given the heterogeneity of entrepreneurs and of small businesses, and the complexity and diversity of the markets in which they operate, any attempt to produce a comprehensive the-ory or any meaningful analysis of growth may be unrealistic, at least in the short term. One may also add that there is no single correct management of a business for growth and that growth itself, as has been noted, is not a simple linear process: rather, businesses grow, contract and grow again several times and at different rates.

Targeting growth

As has been explained earlier in this chapter, much of the interest in growth busi-nesses arises because they represent employment potential and there is therefore a wish to target them for support to enhance that employment potential. Such a pol-icy of targeting growth has its proponents as well as its opponents. The arguments often used by each are set out below.

Arguments for targeting growth businesses

At least five arguments have been advanced for targeting growth businesses (and see also the list of reasons to look favourably on growth businesses at the beginning of this chapter):

1. Targeting increases the effectiveness of support measures. As explained earlier, statistical evidence has been presented that, over time, a proportionately small number of firms out of any cohort of businesses will create a large proportion of new jobs. It is consequently argued that targeted support for these 'growth' busi-nesses should be more effective in promoting jobs than more generalised sup-port, because it has a clear focus and concentrates resources where they are most needed and where they can produce the best results.
2. It minimises support requirements. By applying support only to growth busi-nesses, the total support requirement, and its cost, is reduced. Indeed with many hundreds of thousands of businesses starting each year, it is not feasible to deal with them all and make a sufficient impact with limited resources.
3. It encourages a clearer strategic focus on the needs of such businesses. Targeting growth businesses forces small business support organisations to identify more clearly how to support such businesses and to develop appropriate strategies for such support. It also helps agencies to develop a better understanding of the pro-cesses of growth in the target market and how best to assist such processes. High levels of expertise are thus more likely to be developed.
4. More business starts are not needed. There are situations, such as that pertaining in the UK in the 1970s and 1980s, where it has been argued that the rate of business starts was higher than that in some competitor economies. They had been devel-oped on the back of growth in the financial services sector but many were unsus-tainable. More business starts were not therefore needed and attention should instead have been focused on promoting business growth, which was needed.
5. Supporting start-ups distorts the market often as a result of the displacement effect. The market mechanism serves as the most efficient means of allocat-ing scarce resources and supporting start-up businesses will distort this. This

argument however only has validity if the assumptions underlying the neo-classical approach to economic theory always hold.

Arguments against targeting growth businesses

There are also at least four arguments against targeting growth businesses:

1. It is difficult. The process of picking winners has been likened to selecting a potentially good wine. It is viewed as more of an art than a science and is the preserve of a tiny group of cognoscenti with exceptional 'noses' and 'palates'; it is a skill that takes years of training and experience to acquire, and not everyone can do it even then. (Even the wine cognoscenti generally only make predictions for wines with a good pedigree, with the result that most of them missed the potential of the 'New World' wines.) It is not therefore something that can be systemised in business agencies.
2. It is not the same as providing venture capital. The venture capital industry would pride itself on picking winners, and needs to pick them to survive. However it only needs to select a few winners that would be enough for its own purposes, and it would acknowledge that it still selects a majority of 'dogs' that have to be compensated for by the occasional correctly chosen 'star'. Public support policy, in contrast, would seek to back all the winners and avoid any losers so as to avoid the charge of wasting or losing public money.
3. It is misguided. Those who regard targeting, or 'picking winners', as a misguided policy do so for the following reasons:
   - *The structure of business*: It is argued that the quality, volume and viability of new business starts can influence the strength and competitiveness of the small business sector. This in turn is at the root of the creation of an economy which not only generates jobs but also contributes to the achievement of wider economic and social goals, including productivity, living standards, price stability, diversity, choice and personal opportunity. It is suggested that three key questions need to be asked when considering the part that start-ups play in an economy:
     – Are there enough of them?
     – Is the quality of the stock of new and small businesses adequate?
     – Are start-up rates, and net additions to the business stock, rising or falling?
   Answers to these questions will help prioritise the importance of start-up support.
   - *The policy rationale for support of start-ups*: The key policy arguments for support are:
     – Start-ups are the seedbed for growth. This argument is summarised in the view that, without a healthy and quality stock of new businesses, the future supply of 'winners' or growth businesses will be curtailed. Not to support them, therefore, would be to reduce the pool of potential 'winners'.
     – Market failures constrain start-up rates. This argument seeks to highlight barriers to start-up which are attributable to organisational or institutional deficiencies. These 'market failures' are seen as impacting disproportionately

on new and small businesses, disadvantaging them. These barriers include cultural/social values, difficulties in financing, legislative and administrative burdens, including reporting requirements, and access to information.

- More employment creation. A 'picking winners' policy ignores the fact that most of the jobs in the small business sector still come from businesses with fewer than 20 employees; so not only are non-growth businesses and start-ups the source of future growth businesses, they provide employment now (between one-third and two-thirds of all new jobs in the UK). The assertion is not contrary to the findings that out of any group of existing firms measured over a discrete time period a small number will create a disproportionate number of jobs.

- Lower costs per job. Job creation costs are lower for start-ups than for many existing businesses. This argument is based on a perception that the costs associated with new jobs in start-ups are lower than for existing businesses including inward investment.

- The impact of start-up rates. High start-up rates have a positive impact on regional prosperity. There appears to be a positive relationship between start-up levels and regional prosperity-including a positive correlation between levels of new venture creation and employment generation.

4. What is needed is an enterprising culture. This set of arguments revolves around the view, that cultural values supportive of entrepreneurial activity and entrepreneurs can be considered a major influence on the level and success of start-up activity. In consequence it is argued that an investment needs to be made in building support and stakeholder networks positively disposed towards start-ups and growth rather than in direct intervention in growing businesses.

> I haven't figured out a way [to anticipate which firms will be the gazelles and which will end up the mice]. In fact, one of the fascinating things about the gazelles is that they sometimes appear to be mice for long periods of time.
>
> David Birch[59]

Other phases: non-growth, decline and termination

Birch's mice are businesses which stay small, but businesses of any size can remain static for periods either while they cope with issues such as survival or consolidation or because of reasons such as comfort or maturity. Such phases of business development are the reality for many businesses and therefore they are examined next along with other realities of business life such as decline and, if decline cannot be arrested, termination.

Survival, consolidation, comfort and maturity

A static stage in small business development may not sound very exciting, but it characterises the state of most small businesses. Once they have started their own business, many electricians, plumbers, chimney sweeps and consultants, for instance, rarely grow, and many other one-person businesses are the same: being static is the normal state for them.

Because, by definition, the static stage is not one that produces results in terms of more start-ups, jobs or other benefits, it is often ignored. Growth is a much more attractive stage in those terms, but in many cases it is in the static stage that the growth businesses of the future are to be found. Growth does not often follow immediately after start-up. But even if a static business is not a growth business of the future it can still perform a useful function. Together, static businesses provide significant employment. They also can be an essential part of the economic and social fabric, they can provide choice and diversity, they can provide the necessary infrastructure support for other growth businesses and they can be useful role models. They should not be ignored.

As with the separation of growth and expansion, it is possible to distinguish more than one type of stage during which a business does not grow. Survival has been the name given to that period following start-up during which a business may not grow but is nevertheless working hard to maintain its position and struggling to establish itself as a viable enterprise. Once established, a business may then have a period of building resources, of consolidation, before the next move. Just because a business shows few signs of growth for a relatively long period, this does not mean that it will never grow. In many cases the growth of a business has been likened to that of bamboo, which can lie dormant for many years before suddenly shooting up in a single season.

There is a large group of businesses whose growth is limited by their owners' ambitions or by their market niche. This stage has been labelled comfort or maturity. There may be many reasons why a business does not expand, such as the desired lifestyle of the owner-manager, the limits of his or her management capability, or even peer pressure not to get too far ahead. In general, however, this phase of development is characterised by a business which has taken up its share of the markets, has reached the limits of its capacity, or for any other managerial, political or social reason remains at the same size either in physical or economic terms.

A categorisation of static businesses can now be summarised:

- *Survival*: This is the stage which comes after start-up. Typically, a 'surviving' business has the potential to be a viable entity, but needs to work at it. It is probably a one-product or one-service business, but is concentrating on short-term issues of survival rather than the longer-term ones of future growth potential.
- *Consolidation*: After winning the struggle to survive or to grow, most businesses need a period of rest to build up the reserves they need to move forward. This may not be a conscious decision or a deliberate strategy. What was happening may only be obvious in retrospect, when subsequent growth can be seen to have been built on the contacts, the credibility and the expertise accumulated at this stage. A period of consolidation following a period of survival may be one during which even businesses that do eventually grow show few indications of their potential.

- *Comfort*: For a business that does not move on to growth, 'consolidation' can easily merge into 'comfort': the stage at which a business is doing enough to survive at least into the medium term and is providing enough profits to maintain the owner's desired standard of living. There may be little incentive to do anything different.
- *Maturity*: Maturity is generally seen as coming after some growth, and indeed there may still be slow continued growth. The businesses concerned, however, are no longer in the first stages of their existence. They may be passing the peak of their products' life cycles, or they may be on the verge of moving out of the definition of a small business because their management structure is facing a transition phase in which personal contact and word of mouth have to be replaced by more formal systems to cope with a larger organisation and more decentralisation. The onset of maturity may therefore be a transition, either onwards to bigger and better things, or sideways towards an eventual decline.

The issues

In general, the needs at this stage are for encouragement and incentive, either to prevent decline or to encourage expansion. The motivation of the owner is critical. A firm can be adapting and changing while staying still in terms of turnover or employment, but in the long term staying static is not a good strategy. It must always be presumed that competition will change or increase and in that case not to try to grow is to invite decline.

The needs of these businesses include:

- Needs of survival businesses
  - control of the business
  - generating revenues sufficient to cover all expenses
  - supervision of the work
  - both entrepreneurial and administrative management
  - simple structures, systems and controls
  - product and/or market research.
- Needs of mature businesses
  - expense control
  - increased productivity
  - niche marketing, especially if the industry is declining
  - watchdog top management, taking a leadership role
  - product innovation, to replace products towards the end of their life cycle
  - formal systems for objectives and budgets
  - further long-term debt or bridging finance
  - succession planning.

The succession planning issue possibly summarises one of the key dilemmas at this stage of the business. The entrepreneur behind the business has probably built it up from its inception, and has a keen sense of achievement and ownership. Now it is being suggested that he or she consider who should succeed to the management of the business. This might be advisable because the business needs it but for the owner concerned it means contemplating giving up the thing that may be the most important part of his or her life.

The longer term

As already explained, the static or survival stage can be seen as the norm for most small businesses. It is not therefore usually a stage on the way to something else, but an end in its own right. It can be preceded by start-up, growth or decline, and be succeeded eventually by growth, decline or termination. It is important to realise that, while this stage is described as static, it may only be so in the short term, and that often in the longer term not to move forward is to risk moving into decline when, because of a business's passivity, others take its market. Survival is not actually compulsory or automatic and there is a natural tendency towards regression. There is no superior power that will intervene to force all businesses to survive and so, ultimately, they must progress or die.

Decline

Decline is another of those stages of business development sometimes ignored by government agencies or support organisations when planning assistance. However, decline need not always lead to termination if the problems of the business can be addressed. Helping in the decline stage may therefore result in more surviving businesses or jobs than would otherwise be the case.

Definition

The business is losing its market share, profitability, management skills and the ability to sustain itself at a previous high level. You can often tell when a business is in trouble by looking at its staff turnover rate.

Where from and what next

Decline can come after any stage from start-up onwards. If nothing is done then it will in all probability be followed by termination. If it is arrested then it can be followed by a 'static' stage. If it is cured then a 'static' or even a 'growth' stage is possible.

The issues

The needs of the business are:

- confidence
- finance
- tolerance
- customers
- suppliers
- employees
- new management and leadership
- a strategic review and plan for a new direction, because the decline may be as a direct result of a market or other relevant business environmental change.

Termination

Businesses do terminate, as the figures in Table 10.6 indicate. In any healthy, living ecosystem there are both births and deaths. Individual business deaths may be

Table 10.6 Business survival rates: percentage of enterprises surviving after one, two and five years, by country

Country	Surviving after		
	One year	Two years	Five years
France	84	62	48
Germany	86	70	63
Ireland	91	70	57
Italy	87	66	54
Portugal	76	56	47
United Kingdom	87	62	47

Sources: France: INSEE and ANCE; Germany: IfM; Ireland: Department of Enterprise and Employment; Italy: INPS Data Bank; Portugal: MESS-Portuguese Enterprise's Demography; United Kingdom: Department of Trade and Industry. Reproduced from the *Third Annual Report of the European Observatory for SMEs* (Zoetermeer, The Netherlands: EIM Small Business Research and Consultancy, 1995), p.87.

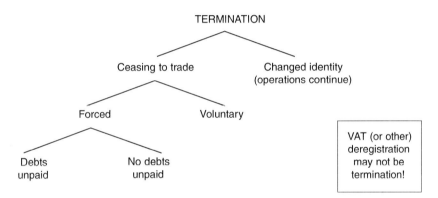

Figure 10.4 Types of business termination

deemed regrettable, but some are to be expected in the best of economies. It would be unhealthy to have none, and the policy should therefore to be to avoid the unnecessary ones but not to prevent terminations completely.

The terminology of termination requires care. The word 'failure' is often ascribed to the termination of a business. A business may cease to exist or otherwise change its identification for a number of reasons. A business can terminate if it is sold and its operations are absorbed into another: the operations of the business continue but its separate legal existence disappears. It can terminate when it chooses to cease to trade because those concerned see a better opportunity elsewhere, or it can terminate if it is closed when the owner retires. These are all terminations but they are not all failures. If VAT statistics are taken as guide, a business decline and subsequent VAT deregistration may be treated as a termination, and even as a failure, even if the business is actually still trading. Some of the varieties of termination are shown in Figure 10.4.

Definition

Termination can be any closure of a business, but the term 'closure' can be ambiguous. It might therefore be more accurate to define it as the ending of the separate legal identity of a business and its ceasing to trade as a separate entity. Perhaps a clearer definition of failure is when a business ceases to trade involuntarily.

The issues

The need is for excellent legal advice to indicate the best way to handle employees, customers, suppliers and finances.

Intervention

It is not necessarily a waste of resources to help a business to terminate. Compared with a bad termination, too late and with many debts, a properly conducted and orderly termination can save resources. It is important not to pour good money after bad, however difficult the entrepreneur finds it to call a halt to the operation of the business. Voluntary liquidation can also avoid unpaid creditors with the consequent risk to other businesses. This activity can be described as 'ethical entrepreneurship', where the entrepreneur accepts the responsibility of closure without damaging other businesses. This means closing the business while it can still pay its creditors and before it is closed by others. This can save ideas for adoption elsewhere. It can help people to learn and re-apply the valuable lessons they have learnt, instead of being put off ever running their own business again. Assistance, in the form of advice on how to do it well, can also be provided for this stage.

Conclusions

The two stages of business development of most interest to policy-makers have been start-up and growth, and of these it is growth that is thought to have the potential to deliver most benefit. To quote Storey again, 'It is the failure of UK small enterprises to grow into large enterprises that may be at the heart of the country's long-term poor economic performance.'[60] This chapter has therefore looked at business growth and at the arguments that have been advanced for and against targeting assistance to promote it more. A policy may have been decided on at present but the targeting debate is not over and the search for the Holy Grail, the formula for creating and/or picking winners, will no doubt continue. Growth businesses may still be desirable, even if they cannot be spotted in advance.

Growth is not however either an inevitable, or the final, stage of business development. Many businesses are static for much of their lives, and those lives end with periods of decline, followed by termination. Those stages should not be ignored by those interested in businesses. Businesses still have needs during them and, if something can be done to meet those needs, decline might be halted or an end prepared in an orderly fashion with the minimum of consequential damage to others.

THE KEY POINTS OF CHAPTER 10

- After start-up, survival, consolidation, growth, maturity, decline and eventually termination are all possible stages of business.

- The growth stage has however been of particular interest. Birch and others suggested that most net new jobs were created by small businesses but further analysis appears to have shown that it is a relatively small proportion of small businesses which grow and create most of those jobs. 'Over a decade, 4 per cent of those businesses which start would be expected to create 50 per cent of employment generated.'[61] However businesses with fewer than 20 employees still generate most employment.

- Because of their job creation potential, governments and others saw that there could be economic benefit in supporting small businesses. However, if small business support resources are limited, which is invariably the case, then it has been suggested that the way to maximise results is to apply those resources only to growth businesses. Therefore there has been considerable interest in learning what makes businesses grow and how such businesses can be spotted.

- It is important to realise that growth in a business context can have many meanings. For the investor it may be growth in shareholder value. For the business it may be growth in sales and in profits, and for government it may be growth in employment. These forms of growth may not all coincide.

- In the context of small businesses, there are a number of significant influences on growth including the entrepreneur's (or leader's) ambition and desire to grow, the skills of the entrepreneur, and the impact of factors or constraints external to the firm. None of these are useful as predictors, especially as chance also appears to be a key factor.

- In the context of the external environment, 'cluster' theory is of interest. It is based on research that shows that internationally successful businesses are often found in geographic clusters where the environment is most advantageous to them; that it is innovation that makes businesses competitive, and thus provides the potential for growth; and that it is demanding buyers in the domestic market that can pressure companies to innovate faster.

- Ultimately growth is likely to be dependent upon the interaction of a number of influences, each of which may be important in different combinations for different businesses.

- As for the issue of whether to target growth businesses or not, the debate is not over. The search for the Holy Grail, the formula for creating and/or picking winners, will no doubt continue. Growth businesses may still be desirable even if they can't be spotted in advance.

- There are other possible stages of business development after start-up that should not however be ignored. All businesses will have static periods and all are likely eventually to decline and to terminate. Understanding and assisting with these stages also could have economic benefits.

QUESTIONS, ESSAY AND DISCUSSION TOPICS

- How could more small business growth be encouraged?

- How might growth as an indicator of business success be measured?

- Is the natural tendency for a business to grow or decline? Explain your reasoning.

- Describe some broad academic approaches taken to analysing the influences on the growth of firms.

- Which of the following influences on the growth of a firm are likely to be the strongest in their impact: the entrepreneur(s), the firm's strategic positioning and operational procedures, or the external environment?

- The real barriers to growth are attributable only to managerial weaknesses; everything else is just an excuse. Discuss.

- What is the role of chance in the growth of small businesses?

- Trying to 'pick winners' is either like the search for the Holy Grail or is akin to looking for a needle in a haystack. It is, therefore, no basis for policy. Discuss.

- What are the arguments for and against implementing a business birth rate strategy in your region?

- What arguments would you advance for a government-funded scheme to help declining and/or terminating businesses? What assistance should such a scheme offer?

Suggestions for further reading

A. Atherton, A. Gibb and L. Sear, *Reviewing the Case for Supporting Business Start-Ups: A Policy Overview of Current Thinking on Business Start-Ups* (Durham: Durham University Business School, 1997).

R. Barkham, E. Hanvey and M. Hart, *The Role of the Entrepreneur in Small Firm Growth* (Belfast: NIERC, 1995).

P. Burns, *Entrepreneurship and Small Business*, 2nd edn (Palgrave Macmillan, 2007), Chapters 9,10 and 11.

D. F. Kuratko, J. S. Hornsby and D. W. Nattziger, 'An Examination of Owners' Goals in Sustaining Entrepreneurship', *Journal of Small Business Management*, 35(1) (1997), pp. 24–33.

M. E. Porter, 'From Competitive Advantage to Competitive Strategy', *Harvard Business Review*, 65(3) (1987), pp. 43–59.

D. Smallbone, R. Leigh and D. North, 'The Characteristics and Strategies of High Growth SMEs', *International Journal of Entrepreneurial Behaviour and Research*, 1(3) (1995), pp. 44–62.

D. J. Storey, 'Symposium on Harrison: Lean and Mean: A Job Generation Perspective', *Small Business Economics*, 7(5) (1995), pp. 337–40.

D. J. Storey, *Understanding the Small Business Sector* (London: Routledge, 1994), Chapter 5.

G. Timmons, *New Venture Creation: Entrepreneurship for the 21st Century*, 5th edn (Singapore: Irwin/ McGraw-Hill, 1999), Chapter 16.

References

1. OECD, *Globalisation and Small and Medium Enterprises (SMEs)*, Vol. 1, Synthesis Report (Paris: OECD, 1997), p. 7.

2. J. Levy, *Small and Medium Sized Enterprises: A Recipe for Success* (London: Institution of Electrical Engineers) as cited in D. J. Storey, *Understanding the Small Business Sector* (London: Routledge, 1994), p. 24.

3. DTI, *Competitiveness: Helping the Smaller Firm* (London: DTI, May 1995), p. 2.

4. OECD (1997), op. cit., p. 17.

5. Extract from an interview in: 'The Job Generation Process Revisited', *ICSB Bulletin,* Spring (1995).

6. D. J. Storey, *Understanding the Small Business Sector* (London: Routledge, 1994), p. 115.

7. NIERC, *Job Generation and Manufacturing Industry 1973 86* (Belfast: Northern Ireland Economic Research Centre, 1989).

8. E. Garnsey, 'A New Theory of the Growth of the Firm', in Proceedings of the 41st ICSB World Conference, Stockholm 1996, p. 126.

9. A. E. Knaup, 'Survival and Longevity in Business Employment Dynamics data', *US Monthly Labor Review,* May (2005), p. 50–6.

10. D. Smallbone and P. Wyer, 'Growth and Development in the Small Firm', in *Enterprise and Small Business: Principles, Practice and Policy,* edited by S. Carter and D. Jones-Evans (London: Financial Times/Prentice-Hall, 2000), p. 410.

11. A. Gibb and L. Davies, 'In Pursuit of Frameworks for the Development of Growth Models of the Small Business', *International Small Business Journal,* 9(1) (1990), p. 26.

12. Storey, op. cit., p. 121.

13. Gibb and Davies, op. cit., pp. 16–17.

14. H. Barreto, *Entrepreneurship in Micro-economic Theory* (London: Routledge, 1989).

15. R. Barkham, E. Hanvey and M. Hart, *The Role of the Entrepreneur in Small Firm Growth* (Belfast: NIERC, 1995), p. 2.

16. Barkham et al., op. cit., p. 2.

17. Storey, op. cit., pp. 137–43.

18. M. Scott and P. Rosa, 'Has Firm Level Analysis Reached its Limits? Time For a Rethink', *International Small Business Journal,* 14 (1996), pp. 81–9.

19. B Kirchhoff, personal communication.

20. Ibid.

21. Ibid.

22. Ibid.

23. C. Hakim, 'Identifying Fast Growth Small Firms', *Employment Gazette,* January (1989).

24. Quoted in M. Carree, A. van Stel, R. Thurik and S. Wennekers, *Business Ownership and Economic Growth: An Empirical Investigation,* Research Report 9809/E (Zoetermeer, the Netherlands: EIM Small Business Research and Consultancy, 1999), p. 11.

25. D. B. Audretsch and A. R. Thurik, *The Knowledge Society, Entrepreneurship and Unemployment,* Research Report 9801/E (Zoetermeer, the Netherlands: EIM Small Business Research and Consultancy, 1998), p. 11.

26. Carree et al., op. cit., p. 1.

27. B. Kirchhoff, 'Twenty Years of Job Creation Research: What have We Learned?', Proceedings of the 40th ICSB World Conference, Stockholm, 1995, pp. 195–219, at p. 210.

28. G. Reid and L. Jacobsen, *The Small Entrepreneurial Firm* (Aberdeen: Aberdeen University Press, 1988), p. 8.

29. Quoted in D. Deakins and M. Freel, *Entrepreneurship and the Small Firm* (London: McGraw-Hill, 2006), p. 162.

30. Ibid p. 162.

31. Storey, op. cit., pp. 126–37.

32. Barkham et al., op. cit., p. 15.

33. Gibb and Davies, op. cit., p. 18.

34. Ibid., p. 20.

35. Storey, op. cit., pp. 137–43.

36. European Network for SME Research, *The European Observatory for SMEs: First Annual Report* (Zoetermeer, the Netherlands: EIM Small Business Research and Consultancy, 1993), p. 24.

37. Storey, op. cit., pp. 144–54.

38. Barkham et al., op. cit., p. 16.

39. OECD, *Small and Medium Sized Enterprises: Technology and Competitiveness* (Paris: OECD, 1993), p. 21.

40. CBI, *Managing to Grow* (London: CBI, December 1995), p. 11.

41. OECD (1993), op. cit., p. 9.
42. Barkham et al., op. cit., pp. 16, 39.
43. Quoted in P. Burns, *Entrepreneurship and Small Business* (Basingstoke: Palgrave (now Palgrave Macmillan), 2001), p. 272.
44. Barkham et al., op. cit., pp. 15–18.
45. Gibb and Davies, op. cit., pp. 15–31.
46. Storey, op. cit., pp. 138–40.
47. P. Westhead and D. Storey, *An Assessment of Firms Located On and Off Science Parks in the UK* (London: HMSO, 1994).
48. B. Kirchhoff, personal communication.
49. D. Smallbone, R. Leigh and D. North, 'Characteristics and Strategies of High Growth SMEs', *International Journal of Entrepreneurial Behaviour and Research*, 1(3) (1995), pp. 44–62.
50. P. Vaessen and D. Keeble, *Growth Oriented SMEs in Unfavourable Regional Environments*, Working paper (Cambridge: ESRC Centre for Business Research, 1995).
51. Institute of Directors, *Your Business Matters: Report from the Regional Conference* (London: Institute of Directors, 1996), pp. 6–7.
52. M. E. Porter, 'The Competitive Advantage of Nations', *Harvard Business Review*, March-April (1990), pp. 73–93.
53. Ibid.: 82.
54. Quoted in Bank of England, *Finance for Small Firms: An Eighth Report* (London: Bank of England, March 2001), p. 60.
55. OECD, Directorate for Science, Technology and Industry, Industry Committee, *The Role of SMEs: Findings and Issues*, DSTI/IND(2000)15/REV1 (Paris: OECD, December 2000), p. 3.
56. OECD (1993), op.cit., p. 21.
57. A. Cosh and A. Hughes (eds), *Enterprising Britain: Growth, Innovation and Public Policy in the Small and Medium Sized Enterprise Sector 1994–1997* (Cambridge: ESRC Centre for Business Research, 1998).
58. Cambridge Small Business Research Centre, *The State of British Enterprise* (Cambridge: Department of Applied Economics, University of Cambridge, 1992).
59. Extract from an interview in 'The Job Generation Process Revisited', *ICSB Bulletin*, Spring (1995).
60. Storey, op. cit., p. 159.
61. Ibid., p. 115.

CHAPTER 11

Competitive advantage and strategy

LEARNING OBJECTIVES

After studying this chapter, you will be able to:

- describe the different schools of strategic thought relating to competitive advantage
- explain the concept of competitive advantage, and identify sources of competitive advantage
- describe and demonstrate the application of Porter's generic strategies
- explain low-cost, differentiation, focus and hybrid strategies
- define core competences and explain sources of competence

Introduction and chapter overview

The key challenge for any organization is the ability to gain and sustain a competitive advantage in the market or industry. This advantage can be based on alignment to environmental and industry structures, or by the continual adaptation, creativity and innovative use of organizational resources and networks. This chapter explores the means by which organizations can gain and sustain a competitive advantage through the use of positioning or the creative use of resources. The schools of strategic thought are examined before focusing on the identification of generic strategies as building blocks for the overall strategic direction of the organization. Once the generic strategies have been determined, the chapter explores the nature and role of competences and core competences. This sets up the alternative forms of strategic direction, strategic frameworks, and management of strategic risk.

Sources of competitive advantage

The main goal of strategic management is to produce sustainable competitive advantage for a business. Competitive advantage can arise from deliberate, planned strategies and emergent strategies, which arise from opportunistic moves by the business. Competitive advantage is not easy to achieve and is even more difficult to sustain. Superior performance is built and sustained through continuous organizational learning and results in a constant process of new strategy development and improvement in the way in which business activities are carried out.

The rapid pace of technological, political, economic and social change, the increasing turbulence of the business environment, the growing sophistication of customer needs and the drastic shortening of product life cycles that typifies 'hypercompetition' all mean that competitive advantage is often contestable rather than sustainable. In other words, the search for strategies that produce and sustain superior performance over a long period of time has become increasingly difficult. Competitive advantage can only be developed and sustained through the creation of new business knowledge based on continuous organizational learning and the deployment of dynamic capabilities (Teece, 2009).

The different strands of theory in strategic management offer several explanations and potential methods by which competitive advantage can be achieved.

The 'competitive positioning' theory is based on the structure-conduct-performance paradigm and is typified by Porter's five forces, generic strategy and value chain frameworks (Porter, 1980, 1985), which have subsequently been augmented by the concept of a hybrid strategy. While dated and arguably inflexible, Porter's work still forms an excellent platform for understanding the positioning school. For Porter, the first question to be answered was: 'in which industry should the business compete?' Potential industry profitability, and hence **industry attractiveness**, was established through five forces analysis. The factors that lead to industry attractiveness are:

- Industry's market size and growth potential
- The impact of environmental forces on the industry structure and dynamics
- Potential for entry and exit, and mobility in the industry
- Stability and dependability of demand
- Asset specificity, switching costs and capital costs
- Degree of risk and uncertainty in the industry's future
- Knowledge of the industry.

Industry attractiveness represents the potential to make a profit or gain strategic rent from a specific industry configuration.

Once the choice of industry was made, the organization had to determine which generic strategy to pursue, and then decide the optimum configuration of its value-adding activities to support the chosen generic strategy. The approach is essentially 'outside-in', with choices initially being concerned with which industry was likely to prove the most profitable. As such, the competitive dynamics revolved around the degree to which perfect information or knowledge could be achieved and how barriers to entry and mobility could be exploited.

As an alternative, the resource-based school (Prahalad and Hamel, 1990; Barney, 1991; Grant, 1991) emerged on the basis that competitive advantage results from the development and exploitation of core competences by individual businesses, whatever industry they are in. This theory is built on the notion that certain firms outperform their competitors in the same industry. If this is the case, competitive advantage cannot be explained entirely by different industry conditions. The explanation for competitive advantage must rest, at least in part, within the firm itself. For this reason, the approach to strategy is best regarded as 'inside-out', and explains why firms in the same industry experience different levels of success and performance.

The third, knowledge-based school (Sveiby, 1997, 2001) suggests that competitive advantage arises from the creation, development and exploitation of new knowledge through a process of organizational learning. Interestingly, the competitive positioning, core competence and knowledge-based approaches need not be viewed as mutually exclusive. Knowledge can be viewed as the basis of an organization's core competences and generic strategy, leading to innovation, the ability to adapt and adopt. Equally, a generic strategy can be viewed as being dependent on a particular set of core competences underpinned by an appropriate configuration of value-adding activities or dynamic capabilities (Teece, 2009).

GURU GUIDE

Karl-Erik Sveiby is a professor of knowledge management at the Hanken Business School in Helsinki, Finland. He is a subject expert in knowledge management and is often regarded as one of the founding fathers of knowledge management. He has considerable management experience, having worked with several international firms and was the proprietor of one of Scandinavia's leading publishing houses. Dr Sveiby has also extensive consultancy experience, and is the founder of Sveiby Knowledge Associates (www.sveiby.com), a consultancy firm specializing in providing knowledge management solutions to global firms.

His work in measuring the value of intangible assets has been extensively adapted by Swedish companies and has become part of a international standard in this field.

The development of a strategy will inevitably draw on some analysis of the business, its objectives, its resources, competences, activities and its competitive environment. Even in the context of an emergent approach to strategy, managers still require an understanding of the business and the consequences of alternative courses of action.

This chapter provides tools that can be employed in developing our understanding of current strategy and future strategic alternatives. The frameworks are first explored separately and then the linkages between them are developed. It is important to note that there is no universal prescription for building competitive advantage. Competitive advantage is, however, more likely to result from doing things differently from competitors and doing them better rather than from trying to emulate them. Hamel and Prahalad (1985) made a strong case that organizations should develop a 'strategic intent' to stretch their resources and competences to the limits in order to achieve superior performance. Similarly, superior performance is more likely to result from an informed approach to management based on an understanding of the firm, the environment in which it operates and the strategic alternatives available to it. This chapter provides the basis of an informed approach to the development of corporate strategies.

Competitive and collaborative advantage

Competitive advantage will depend on the ability of a firm to outperform its competitors. Sustainable competitive advantage requires that the firm outperforms its rivals over a long period of time. While there is no recipe or formula that can guarantee sustained superior performance, there are certain organizational behaviours that have been shown to make success more likely:

- *strategic intent:* constantly stretching the organization to its limits
- *continuous improvement and innovation:* continually trying to improve products and services, relationships with customers and suppliers, and the way that activities are organized and carried out
- *doing things differently from competitors:* devising ways of doing business that are different from and better than the approaches adopted by competitors
- *being customer oriented:* always seeking to meet customer needs
- *building knowledge-based core competences and distinctive capabilities*
- *developing clear and consistent strategies* that are understood by managers and customers
- *awareness of factors in the business environment,* potential changes and their likely implications for the business
- *collaborating with other businesses and customers* to improve agility and flexibility.

Any strategy ought to take these factors into account, as by doing so, it is more likely that the strategy will be more difficult for competitors to emulate. Collaboration with suppliers, distributors and customers can be particularly important for building competitive advantage that is sustainable, as collaboration can be particularly difficult for competitors to replicate. For example, the association of Ferrari's Formula One team with Shell has led the team to win a number of world titles. Ferrari engines are powered by high performance race fuels developed by Shell, and their partnership has been a crucial factor in Ferrari's successful campaign in winning constructor and driver titles at Formula One world championships.

Michael Porter's generic strategies

Perhaps the oldest and best-known explanation of competitive advantage is given by Porter in his generic strategy framework. Although this framework has increasingly been called into question in recent years, it still provides useful insights into competitive behaviour. The framework and its limitations are considered in this section.

According to Porter (1985), competitive advantage arises from the selection of the generic strategy that best fits the organization's competitive environment and then organizing value-adding activities to support the chosen strategy.

There are three main alternatives:

- *cost leadership:* being the lowest cost producer of a product so that above-average profits are earned even though the price charged is not above average
- *differentiation:* creating a customer perception that a product is superior to that of competitors' products so that a premium price can be charged
- *focus:* utilizing either a differentiation or cost leadership strategy in a narrow profile of market segments.

Porter argued that an organization must make two key decisions on its strategy:

1. Should the strategy be one of differentiation or cost leadership?
2. Should the scope of the strategy be broad or narrow?

In other words, the organization must decide whether to try to differentiate its products and sell them at a premium price, or whether to gain competitive advantage by producing at a lower cost than its competitors. Higher profits can be made by adopting either approach. Second, it must decide whether to target the whole market with its chosen strategy or whether to target a specific segment or niche of the market. Figure 13.1 shows cost focus and differentiation focus as two ends or extremes of a continuum. This is because actual strategies can exist at or anywhere in between the extremes. The same applies to the vertical direction. Broad and narrow are general extremes, where a broad strategy targets many markets and a disparate cross-section of customers, while a narrow or highly focused strategy may target a small number of segments (or possibly just one).

The point of Figure 13.1 is that it is best understood as a map. Companies in an industry can all be successful if they each choose different strategies. If, however, two or more competitors choose to compete in the same part of the map (that is, adopting the same or similar generic strategy), competition will become intensified among those pursuing the same strategy. By plotting competitors on the map, we can get an idea of where the most intense competition will occur. Sections containing only one competitor will experience the least competition.

Cost leadership strategy

A **cost leadership strategy** is based on a business organizing and managing its value-adding activities so as to be the lowest cost producer of a product (a good or service) within an industry.

A **cost leadership strategy** is based on a business organizing and managing its value-adding activities so as to be the lowest cost producer of a product (a good or service) within an industry.

There are several potential benefits of a cost leadership strategy:

- the business can earn higher profits by charging a price equal to, or even below, that of competitors because its unit costs are lower
- it allows the business the possibility to increase both sales and market share by reducing price below that charged by competitors (assuming that the product's demand is price elastic in nature)
- it allows the business the possibility of entering a new market by charging a lower price than competitors
- it can be particularly valuable in a market where consumers are price sensitive
- it creates an additional barrier to entry for organizations wishing to enter the industry.

A successful cost leadership strategy is likely to rest on a number of organizational features. Such features will relate to the means by which a cost advantage can be gained and maintained in the long run (although cost-based strategy tends to be difficult to sustain). As such, features such as lean supply chain, efficient production processes, aligned value systems, dedicated (tied in) supply, customer loyalty and price awareness of competitors are all critical.

Value chain analysis is central to identifying where cost savings can be made at various stages in the value chain and its internal and external linkages. Attainment of a position of cost leadership depends on the arrangement of value chain activities, so as to:

- reduce unit costs by copying rather than originating designs, using cheaper materials and other cheaper resources, producing products with 'no frills', reducing labour costs and increasing labour productivity
- achieving economies of scale by high-volume sales, perhaps based on advertising and promotion, allowing high fixed costs of investment in modern technology to be spread over a high volume of output
- using high-volume purchasing to obtain discounts for bulk buying of materials
- locating activities in areas where costs are low or government help, for example grant support, is available
- obtaining 'learning curve' economies.

A cost leadership strategy, coupled with low price, is best employed in a market or segment where **price elasticity of demand** exists, that is, where volume is relatively responsive to price. Under such circumstances, sales and market share are likely to increase significantly, thus increasing economies of scale, reducing unit costs further, so generating above-average profits. Alternatively, if a price similar to that of competitors is charged accompanied by advertising to boost sales, similar results will be obtained.

The term **price elasticity of demand** describes the extent to which the volume of demand for a product is dependent upon its price.

EXAMPLE Price elasticity of demand

The coefficient of elasticity is expressed in a simple equation:

PED = percentage change in quantity/percentage change in price.

The value of PED (price elasticity) tells us the price responsiveness of the product's demand. If, for any given price change, PED is more than –1, it means that the change in price has brought about a higher proportionate change in volume sold. This relationship between price change and quantity is referred to as 'price elastic demand'.

Demand is said to be 'price inelastic' if the quantity change is proportionately smaller than the change in price (resulting in a PED of less than –1). The larger the value of PED, the more price elastic the demand, and the nearer PED is to 0, the more price inelastic the demand.

The price elasticity of demand (the value of PED) depends on the market's perception of a product. Products tend to be price elastic if the market sees a product as unnecessary but desirable. Products will have a price inelastic demand if the customer perceives a *need* for a product rather than a *want* (such as the demand for most medicines, or tobacco).

org. design and structure

Burns + Stalker

A bigger to unit cost of production gets lower. As it gets lower the you can compete on price. Sell things in a mass level.

EXAMPLE   Ryanair: a cost leader

Ryanair has proved to be one of the most, if not the most, successful low-cost airlines. Despite the economic downturn of 2009, Ryanair maintained its performance and profitability. How it achieved this is well articulated in an interview by Tom Chesshyre (2002) of Michael O'Leary, chief executive of the Irish-based, low-cost airline Ryanair, which appeared in *The Times*.

In the article, Tom Chesshyre explains that *The Times* travel desk receives more complaints about Ryanair than any other airline and that complaints about delays, poor in-flight service, damaged luggage and lengthy check-in queues are common. Yet, O'Leary is quick to recognize that Ryanair rarely apologizes or offers compensation for these complaints.

When the interviewer questions this attitude, O'Leary responds: 'Our customer service is about the most well-defined in the world. We guarantee to give you the lowest airfare. You get a safe flight. You get a normally on-time flight. That's the package. We don't and won't give you anything more on top of that.' He adds: 'Listen, we care for our customers in the most fundamental way possible: we don't screw them every time we fly them. We care for our customers by giving them the cheapest airfares. I have no time for certain large airlines which say they care and then screw you for six or seven hundred quid almost every time you fly.'

However, the article states that many people are now tiring of this attitude and the Air Transport Users Council, which monitors airline complaints, testifies that Ryanair is one of the worst offenders. It explains that several of Ryanair's customers have complained about how difficult it is to talk to anyone when they have a problem, as they have to ring several times before eventually being put through to an operator. In response to this, O'Leary states that: 'Generally speaking, we won't take any phone calls ... because they keep you on the bloody phone all day. We employ four people in our customer care department. Every complaint must be put in writing and we undertake to respond to that complaint within 24 hours. Anyway, do you know what 70 per cent of our complaints are about? They're about people who want to make changes to what are clearly stated as being "non-changeable, non-transferable and non-refundable" tickets.'

Asked if he thinks people should be able to get refunds for his airline tickets, he replies: 'No ... because even if you can't change your ticket and you've got to buy a second one, you're still going to save money compared with buying a single ticket from the major airlines. Anyway, with our new system you can make some changes. If you pay 20 euros (at that time £12.30), you can change the time of your flight, but not the name on the ticket.'

Which, as the article correctly states, is a start.

Companies whose activities include high-volume standardized products are often cost leaders. The no-frills airlines are good examples. A basic product is offered and costs per sale are minimized by online booking, faster aircraft turnaround between flights, and no on-board free food.

Differentiation strategy

A **differentiation strategy** is based on persuading customers that a product is superior to that offered by competitors. This relies on creating added value for the consumer, be it real value or perceived. Value can be in terms of social, economic, political, belonging, emotional or situational, and is at the heart of understanding consumers reserved price for goods and services, or their willingness to pay a premium.

A **differentiation strategy** is based on persuading customers that a product is superior to that offered by competitors.

Differentiation can be based on premium product features or simply by creating consumer perceptions that a product is superior. The major benefits to a business of a successful differentiation strategy are:

- its products will command a premium price
- demand for its product will be less price elastic than that for competitors' products
- above-average profits can be earned
- it creates an additional barrier to entry to new businesses wishing to enter the industry.

A business seeking to differentiate itself will organize its value chain activities to help create differentiated products and to create a perception among customers that these offerings are worth a higher price.

Differentiation can be achieved in several ways:

- by creating products that are superior to competitors by virtue of design, technology, performance and so on
- by offering superior after-sales service
- by superior distribution channels, perhaps in prime locations, especially important in the retail sector
- by creating a strong brand name through design, innovation or advertising
- by distinctive or superior product packaging.

A differentiation strategy is likely to necessitate emphasis on innovation, design, R&D, awareness of particular customer needs and marketing. To say that differentiation is in the eyes of the customer is no exaggeration. It could be argued that it is often the brand name or logo that distinguishes a product rather than real product superiority. For example, men's shirts bearing the logo of Ralph Lauren, Calvin Klein or Yves St Laurent command a price well above that of arguably similar shirts that bear no logo. There is little empirical evidence of objectively better design or better quality materials. Differentiation appears merely to be based on the fact that the designer's name is fashionable and that their products bear the logo.

This strategy is employed in order to reduce price elasticity of demand for the product so that its price can be raised above that of competitors without reducing sales volume. This will, in turn, generate above-average profits when measured against sales (return on sales).

Figure 11.1 provides a simplified understanding of cost and differentiation strategies.

Focus strategy

A **focus strategy** is aimed at a segment of the market for a product rather than at the whole market or many markets. A particular group of customers is identified on the basis of age, income, lifestyle, sex, geographic location, some other distinguishing segmental characteristic or a combination of these. Within the segment, a business then employs either a cost leadership or a differentiation strategy.

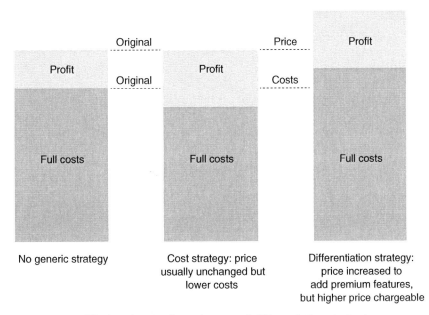

Figure 11.1 A simplified understanding of cost and differentiation strategies

Note: price = full costs plus profits

A **focus strategy** is aimed at a segment of the market for a product rather than at the whole market or many markets.

The major benefits of a focus strategy are:

- it requires a lower investment in resources compared to a strategy aimed at an entire market or many markets
- it allows specialization and greater knowledge of the segment being served
- it makes entry to a new market less costly and simpler.

A focus strategy will require:

- identification of a suitable target customer group, which forms a distinct market segment
- identification of the specific needs of that group
- establishing that the segment is sufficiently large to sustain the business
- establishing the extent of competition within the segment
- production of products to meet the specific needs of that group
- deciding whether to operate a differentiation or cost leadership strategy within the market segment.

An example of a business that pursues a focus strategy is Ferrari, which targets the market for high performance sports cars (a relatively small number of customers in relation to the total market for cars). Ferrari, unlike Toyota or Fiat, does not produce family saloons, minis, off-road vehicles or people carriers. It only produces high performance cars. Its strategy is clearly one of differentiation based on design, superior performance and its Grand Prix record, which allows it to charge a price well above that of its competitors.

Many businesses use a focus strategy to enter a market before broadening their activities into other related segments.

Porter's global generic strategies

A global context is important. In parallel, Porter (1980) has argued that competitive advantage rests on a business selecting and adopting one of the three generic strategies (differentiation, cost leadership or focus) to modify the five competitive forces in its favour so as to earn higher profits than the industry average. In this section, we look at how Porter extended the generic strategy framework to global business. The model suggests that a business operating in international markets has five strategy alternatives, which are defined according to their position in respect to two intersecting factors; the extent to which the industry is globalized or country-centred (horizontal axis) and the breadth of the segments served by competitors in an industry (vertical axis).

CASE STUDY   Mattel

If you are to stand the best possible chance of making and delivering products and services that your customers need and want from you, then you need to know what customers' needs and wants are.

However, knowing what your customers genuinely need and want from you, how much they are prepared to pay for this, and how often they are prepared to do business with you are the foundations of success, and, as such, distinguish the successful from the less so and the failures.

The Barbie organization was one of the first to recognize the importance of this, and, crucially, to take the next step and integrate the management of market and customer information into its product and brand development strategy. The Barbie organization was founded by Ruth Handler, who came across a German toy doll called Bild Lilli and reworked the design of the doll and named it after her own small daughter Barbara's family nickname – Barbie. The doll went into production and the company started operations in 1956.

The company set out to know everything that it possibly could about its customers – their buying habits, frequency of purchases, attitudes and values. They sought to understand the kinds of products that customers would and would not buy, and the life span of the dolls and their accessories. The result was akin to military intelligence gathering in its coverage and comprehensiveness, and both Ruth Handler and the Mattel organization (which took over the Barbie range of products in 1961) subsequently always boasted that they knew more about their customers than anyone else in the world.

The result was that when the first dolls arrived on the shelves of the world's toy shops in 1959, everyone was eagerly anticipating what they would look like and how the venture would go from a business point of view – quite literally: 'how it would play'. It became clear that there was a huge demand, not just for the dolls as they were, but also for products that would go with them – clothes, accessories and other add-ons.

From all of this grew what has come to be known as 'the eleven-inch doll market'. There was (and remains) a clear structure to this market:

- the products are bought by mothers and aunts for girls aged two and over
- the products are of value to girls aged two and over, as well as being acceptable and of value to those who buy them
- the products are played with and enjoyed by girls, and they also have to be acceptable to her friends and others whose opinions they value and respond to
- the products have a limited useful life, and the clothes, accessories and add-ons are a fundamental part of product effectiveness and value and brand development.

To remain successful, the company needed a regular flow of new products coming on stream all the time. It therefore needed to know and understand the kinds of products that would keep the customers coming back again and again. Part of the problem that had to be overcome was the availability of choices, both within the eleven-inch doll market, and also outside it (nobody likes to be limited to any one thing, and the buyers and consumers of Barbie dolls are no different). So the brand logo and distinctive colour scheme (a bright pink) were

developed so as to be capable of being attached to every product that came out. Also, the core range of products had to be universally available, and at prices that would allow for unconsidered, whim and largely cash purchases to be made. So the products were made available at all possible outlets, including supermarkets, department stores and independent corner shops. In the UK and many parts of the USA and the EU, the decline of independent toy shops made this range of outlets essential.

As the result, the product range now covers themed toys (castles, stables, cars, accessories for dolls' houses), films and video productions, cards and books, and other dolls (Barbie now has a large circle of friends and acquaintances, and a boyfriend Ken, who she separated from in 2004, but in 2006 they were hoping to rekindle their relationship, after Ken had a makeover). There is also a large range of accessories and add-ons for girls to use, including shoes, bracelets, bags, and hair and cosmetic products, which all carry the Barbie brand. There are limited editions, Christmas and seasonal specials, collectors' items and other exclusives. Barbie has had many careers, including surgeon, nanny, show jumper and schoolteacher, and each career has carried its own range of clothes and accessories. She has had over 40 pets and owned a wide range of vehicles. The first Barbie department store opened in Shanghai in 2009, and more are expected to follow.

The company carefully evaluates everything that carries the Barbie brand for compatibility as well as acceptability, and this remains a core priority of the market intelligence operation as well as product design. The fundamental wholesomeness of the products, and especially the images of girls and women that are portrayed, continues to be debated. Nevertheless, it is estimated that over a billion Barbie dolls have been sold worldwide in over 150 countries and the company states that it sells one Barbie product every seven seconds somewhere in the world. The overall strategic approach is structured so as to produce an income per customer in the UK of £80 per annum.

Case study questions

1. Where does the source of competitive advantage lie for products such as these?
2. Identify in detail the elements of strategy necessary to ensure that the product remains viable for the next two, five and ten years.
3. What are the main lessons for leaders and managers in all organizations to be learned from the experience and success of the Barbie product and the Mattel organization?

The five strategic positions are:

1. *Global cost leadership:* the business seeks to be the lowest cost producer of a product globally. Globalization provides the opportunity for high-volume sales and greater economies of scale and scope than domestic competitors.
2. *Global differentiation:* the business seeks to differentiate products and services globally, often on the basis of a global brand name.
3. *Global segmentation:* this is the global variant of a focus strategy, when a single market segment is targeted on a worldwide basis employing either cost leadership or differentiation.
4. *Protected markets:* a business that identifies national markets where its particular business is favoured or protected by the host government.
5. *National responsiveness:* the business adapts its strategy to meet the distinctive needs of local markets, that is, not a global strategy. Suitable for purely domestic businesses.

The model suffers from some flaws, in that a hybrid can be adopted rather than falling neatly into one of the areas. As in the case of the conventional understanding of generic strategy, it is possible for a business to pursue a hybrid international strategy. Nissan, for example, concentrates on cost control but also ensures that it differentiates its products on the basis of their reliability.

Configuration and coordination of internal activities

One of Porter's most important contributions to understanding global strategy is his work on the global value chain (1986, 1990). Porter makes the case that global competitive advantage depends on configuring and coordinating the activities of a business in a unique way on a worldwide basis. To put it another way, competitive advantage results from the global scope of an organization's activities and the effectiveness with which it coordinates them. Porter (1986, 1990) argues that global competitive advantage depends on two sets of decisions:

1. *Configuration of value-adding activities:* managers must decide in which nations they will carry out each of the activities in the value chain of their business. Configuration can be broad (involving many countries) or narrow (one country or just a few).
2. *Coordination of value-adding activities:* managers must decide the most effective way of coordinating the value-adding activities that are carried out in different parts of the world.

Coordination of value-adding activities: garment manufacturing abroad

Configuration and coordination present four broad alternatives. In the case of configuration, an organization can choose to disperse its activities to a range of locations around the world or it may choose to concentrate key activities in locations that present certain advantages. Many businesses concentrate the manufacture of their products in countries where costs are low but skill levels are good. Many clothing manufacturers manufacture their products in East Asia where labour costs are low but tailoring standards are high. An organization can decide to coordinate its worldwide activities or to mange them locally in each part of the world. The latter approach misses the opportunity for global management economies of scale. For Porter, the 'purest global strategy' is when an organization concentrates its key activities in locations giving competitive advantages and coordinates activities on a global basis. In the long term, according to Porter, organizations should move towards the 'purest global strategy' as far as is practicable.

Hybrid strategies

There is a body of evidence that suggests that successful strategy can be based on a hybrid (mixture) of differentiation, price and cost control. The hybrid strategy framework developed here is based on the following assumptions:

- strategy can employ a combination of differentiation, price and cost control
- differentiation can be used as the basis for charging a premium price or to increase sales and/or market share
- there are clear linkages between core competences, strategy and value-adding activities
- the framework is not intended as a recipe for competitive advantage, but rather as way of grouping different strategies.

The extent of differentiation, price and cost control will depend on the nature of the market in which the business is operating. In markets where consumers show a preference for quality, the emphasis will be less on price and costs, while in markets where demand is price sensitive, the emphasis will be on keeping both prices

Figure 11.2 Hybrid strategy

and costs as low as possible (Figure 11.2). Of course, organizations may also seek to shape customer attitudes by advertising and promotion so as to modify market conditions. Supermarkets like Tesco and Sainsbury's operate with a hybrid strategy; their product price range varies with quality and consumer choice. For example, Tesco has four cola varieties ranging from normal to diet to sugar-free versions. Each of them is priced differently, so Tesco fulfils the needs of both cost- and quality-conscious consumers.

Competence-based competitive strategy

The generic strategy model is not the only one that seeks to provide an explanation of the sources of competitive advantage. The competence or resource-based model emphasizes that competitive edge stems from the competences of an organization, which distinguish it from its competitors, allowing it to outperform them.

Part 2 of this book explained the ways in which internal analysis makes it possible to better understand core competences by a process of deconstructing them into the component resources and competences that act as their foundation. Here we build on this analysis to explore the ways in which existing competences can be extended and new ones cultivated, and examine how and where these core competences can be exploited so as to acquire and sustain competitive advantage. Much of the recent attention to the concept of core competence is based on the work of Prahalad and Hamel (1989, 1990) and Stalk et al. (1992), who advocated the idea of competing on the basis of capabilities. Similarly, Kay (1993) advanced the idea that competitive advantage is based on distinctive capability.

Perhaps the best-known explanation of core competence is that provided by Prahalad and Hamel (1990, p. 79):

Core competencies are the collective learning of the organization, especially how to co-ordinate diverse production skills and integrate multiple streams of technologies.

Prahalad and Hamel specified three tests to be applied in the identification and development of core competence. A core competence should:

- equip a business with the ability to enter and successfully compete in several markets
- add greater perceived customer value to the business's products than that perceived in competitor's products
- be difficult for competitors to imitate.

According to Prahalad and Hamel, there are many examples of core competence resulting in competitive advantage. Philips' development of optical media, including the laser disc, has led to a whole range of new hi-fi and IT products. Honda's engine technology has led to advantages in the car, motorcycle, lawn mower and generator businesses. Canon's expertise in optics, imaging and microprocessor controls has given it access to diverse markets including those for copiers, laser printers, cameras and image scanners.

Prahalad and Hamel argued that, in practice, competitive advantage is likely to be based on no more than five or six competences. These competences will allow management to produce new and unanticipated products, and to be responsive to changing opportunities because of production skills and the harnessing of technology. Given the turbulent business environment in many industries, this adaptability is essential if competitive advantage is to be built and sustained.

Kay (1993) took the concept of capability, initially identified by Stalk et al. (1992), to develop a framework that explains competitive advantage in terms of what he defines as 'distinctive capability'. This idea of distinctive capability has much in common with that of core competence, in that it views competitive advantage as being dependent on the unique attributes of a particular business and its products.

According to Kay (1993), distinctive capability results from one or more of the following sources:

- *Architecture:* the unique network of internal and external relationships of a business that produces superior performance. These can be unique relationships with suppliers, distributors or customers that competitors do not possess. Equally, the unique relationships may be internal to the business and based on the way that it organizes its activities in the value chain.
- *Reputation:* this stems from several sources, including superior product quality, characteristics, design, service and so on.
- *Innovation:* the ability of the business to get ahead and stay ahead of competitors depends on its success in researching, designing, developing and marketing new products. Equally, it depends on the ability of the business to improve the design and organization of its value-adding activities.
- *Strategic assets:* businesses can also obtain competitive advantage from assets such as natural monopoly, patents and copyrights, which restrict competition.

So what do the concepts of core competence and distinctive capability add to our understanding of competitive advantage? First, they provide us with insight into how a business can build attributes that can deliver superior performance. Second, they inform the process of determining where such competences and capabilities can be exploited.

The process of building new core competences or extending existing ones must take into account the following considerations:

- *Customer perceptions:* competences, capabilities and products must be perceived by customers as being better value for money than those of competitors. The business's reputation can be particularly important in this regard.
- *Uniqueness:* core competences must be unique to the business and must be difficult for competitors to emulate. Similarly, there must be no close substitutes for these competences.
- *Continuous improvement:* core competences, goods and services must be continuously upgraded to stay ahead of competitors. Product and process innovation are particularly important.
- *Collaboration:* competitive advantage can result from the business's unique network of relationships with suppliers, distributors, customers and even competitors. There is the potential for 'multiplier effects' resulting from the complementary core competences of separate businesses being combined.
- *Organizational knowledge:* competences must be based on organizational knowledge and learning. Managers must improve the processes by which the organization learns, builds and manages its knowledge. Today, knowledge is potentially the greatest source of added value.

Core competence, generic strategy and the value chain: a synthesis

It has been argued (see for example Heene and Sanchez, 1997) that the resource or competence-based approach is largely incompatible with the competitive positioning or generic strategy approach advocated by Porter (1980, 1985). Mintzberg et al. (1995), however, make the case that the two approaches are in many respects complementary rather than mutually contradictory. Perhaps the best way of illustrating the linkages between the approaches is through the value chain of the organization.

As competitive advantage is based on the unique approach of the individual business to its environment, it is not possible to identify a one-for-all prescription that will guarantee superior performance in all situations. Both the competitive positioning and the resource-based approach, however, provide frameworks that allow broad sources of competitive advantage to be categorized for the purposes of analysis and development of future strategy. A differentiation strategy, for example, will be likely to be dependent on core competences in areas of the value chain like design, marketing and service. Similarly, a cost or price-based strategy may well require core competences in value chain activities like operations (production), procurement and perhaps marketing. It is much less likely that a cost leader will have core competences based on design and service. The possible relationships between core competences, generic strategies and the value chain are shown in Table 11.1.

Where to exploit core competences and strategies

As core competences and business strategies are developed, it is necessary to decide where they should be exploited. Core competences and strategies can be targeted on existing customers in existing markets or it may be possible to target new customers in existing markets. Alternatively, it may be possible to target new customers in

Table 11.1 Core competences, generic strategies and the value chain

Value chain activity	Areas of competence associated with differentiation strategies	Areas of competence associated with cost/price-based strategies
Primary activities		
Inbound logistics	Control of quality of materials	Strict control of the cost of materials. Tendency to buy larger volumes of standard inputs
Operations	Control of quality of output, raising standards	Lowering production costs and achieving high-volume production
Marketing and sales	Sales (and customer relations) on the basis of quality technology, performance, reputation, outlets and so on	Achieving high-volume sales through advertising and promotion
Outbound logistics	Ensuring efficient distribution	Maintaining low distribution costs
Service	Adding to product value by high-quality and differentiated service	Minimal service to keep costs low
Support activities		
The business's infrastructure	Emphasis on quality	Emphasis on efficiency and cost reduction
Human resource development	Training to create a skills culture, which emphasizes quality, customer service, product development	Training to reduce costs
Technology development	Developing new products, improving product quality, product performance and customer service	Reducing production costs and increasing efficiency
Procurement	Obtaining high-quality resources and materials	Obtaining low-cost resources and materials

new markets. These markets may be related to markets currently served by the organization or they may be unrelated markets. The organization may also consider employing its competences in a new industry. These decisions are concerned with determining the 'strategic direction' of the business. Once this decision has been made, decisions must be made on the methods to be employed in following the chosen strategic direction.

The process of exploiting existing core competences in new markets is known as 'competence leveraging'. In order to enter new markets, it is often necessary for the organization to build new core competences, alongside the existing core competences that are being leveraged, so as to satisfy new customer needs. The identification of customer needs to be served by core competences is based on analysis of the organization's competitive environment using the resource-based framework. The alternative strategic directions an organization can pursue and the methods that can be employed in following these strategic directions.

Where to exploit core competences and strategies

As core competences and business strategies are developed, it is necessary to decide where they should be exploited. Core competences and strategies can be targeted on existing customers in existing markets or it may be possible to target new customers in existing markets. Alternatively, it may be possible to target new customers in new

GURU GUIDE

James Brian Quinn received a BSc from Yale University in 1949. Professor Quinn is currently the Emeritus Professor of Management at Amos Tuck School of Management at Dartmouth College, Hanover, New Hampshire. During his distinguished academic career, Professor Quinn has taught courses in technology management, entrepreneurship and business policy. He is a well-known authority in the fields of management of technological change, outsourcing and strategic planning. He is a respected lecturer and has acted as consultant for numerous leading US and foreign corporations, the US and foreign governments, and small enterprises. His work has been widely appreciated and has won several prizes, including the McKinsey prize for the most outstanding articles appearing in *Harvard Business Review* and the American Academy of Management's Book of the Year Award for Outstanding Contribution to Advancing Management Knowledge. In 1989, Professor Quinn was awarded the Outstanding Educator award by the Academy of Management, and in a rare gesture, his former students created the James Brian Quinn Chair in Technology and Strategy at Dartmouth College in 1999.

Professor Quinn has been a member of the board on Science and Technology for International Development for the National Academy of Sciences and served as the chairman of National Academy of Engineering committees on the Productivity of Information Technology in Services, Technology in the Services Sector, and Environmental Impacts of Services. He is also a visiting professor at various universities, including Monash University, Dalien University, University of Western Australia and the International University of Japan.

markets. These markets may be related to markets currently served by the organization or they may be unrelated markets. The organization may also consider employing its competences in a new industry. These decisions are concerned with determining the 'strategic direction' of the business. Once this decision has been made, decisions must be made on the methods to be employed in following the chosen strategic direction.

The process of exploiting existing core competences in new markets is known as 'competence leveraging'. In order to enter new markets, it is often necessary for the organization to build new core competences, alongside the existing core competences that are being leveraged, so as to satisfy new customer needs. The identification of customer needs to be served by core competences is based on analysis of the organization's competitive environment using the resource-based framework. The alternative strategic directions an organization can pursue and the methods that can be employed in following these strategic directions.

This is a helpful chapter to refer to when completing 1.1.3 Industry Life Cycle and

1.1.4 Porter's Five Forces within the External Analysis section and 1.2.2 Value Chain within the Internal Analysis section in Phase 1 of the **Strategic Planning Software** (www.planning-strategy.com). It would also be useful to recap the chapter before attempting to complete section 2.2 Competitive Strategy in Phase 2 of the **Strategic Planning Software** (www.planning-strategy.com).

For test questions, extra case studies, audio case studies, weblinks, videolinks and more to help you understand the topics covered in this chapter, visit our companion website at www.palgrave.com/business/campbell.

VOCAB CHECKLIST FOR ESL STUDENTS

Coefficient	Logistics	Outsourcing
Distribution channel	'No frills'	Procurement
Hypercompetition	Opportunistic	Synthesis
(see 'hypercompetitive')	Optical media	Unit cost
Infrastructure	(see 'optical' and 'media')	Whim

Definitions for these terms can be found in the 'Vocab Zone' of the companion website, which provides free access to the Macmillan English Dictionary online at www.palgrave.com/business/campbell.

REVIEW QUESTIONS

1. Explain what is meant by competitive advantage and where it comes from.
2. Describe how Porter's generic strategies can be used by an organization.
3. Explain what is meant by low-cost, differentiation, focus and hybrid strategies.
4. Define what a core competence is and how it can be used to gain competitive advantage.

DISCUSSION TOPIC

Porter's generic strategies related to the 1970s and 80s, and they are simply not applicable to 21st-century organizations. Discuss.

HOT TOPICS – Research project areas to investigate

For your research project, why not investigate …

- … which generic strategies are adopted by airlines operating in Continental Europe.
- … which core competences lead to the greatest cost focus advantage.
- … managers' attitudes to the applicability of hybrid strategies in music retail companies in your region.

Recommended reading

Grant, R.M. (1996) 'Prospering in dynamically-competitive environments: organizational capability as knowledge integration', *Organization Science*, 7(4): 375–87.

Kay, J. (1995) 'Learning to define the core business', *Financial Times*, 1 December.

McKiernan, P. (1997) 'Strategy past; strategy futures', *Long Range Planning*, 30(5): 790–8.

Newbert, S. (2005) 'New firm formation: a dynamic capability perspective', *Journal of Small Business Management*, **43**(1): 55–77.

Rumelt, R. (1991) 'How much does industry matter?', *Strategic Management Journal*, **12**(3): 167–85.

Teece, D.J., Pisano, G. and Shuen, A. (1998) 'Dynamic capabilities and strategic management', *Strategic Management Journal*, **18**(7): 509–33.

References

Barney, J.B. (1991) 'Firm resources and sustained competitive advantage', *Journal of Management*, **17**(1): 99–120.

Chesshyre, T. (2002) 'It's cheap but why not more cheerful?', *The Times*, 5 January.

Grant, R. (1991) 'The resource based theory of competitive advantage: implications for strategy formulation', *California Management Review*, **33**(3): 114–35.

Hamel, G. and Prahalad, C.K. (1985) 'Do you really have a global strategy?', *Harvard Business Review*, **63**(4): 139–48.

Heene, A. and Sanchez, R. (eds) (1997) *Competence-based Strategic Management*, London: John Wiley.

Kay, J. (1993) *Foundations of Corporate Success*, Oxford: Oxford University Press.

Mintzberg, H., Quinn, J.B. and Ghoshal, S. (1995) *The Strategy Process: Concepts, Contexts and Cases*, Englewood Cliffs, NJ: Prentice Hall.

Porter, M.E. (1980) *Competitive Strategy: Techniques for Analysing Industries and Competitors*, New York: Free Press.

Porter, M.E. (1985) *Competitive Advantage*, New York: Free Press.

Porter, M.E. (1986) 'What is strategy?', *Harvard Business Review*, **74**(6): 61–78.

Prahalad, C.K. and Hamel, G. (1990) 'The core competence of the corporation', *Harvard Business Review*, **68**(3): 79–91.

Stalk, G., Evans, P. and Shulmann, L.E. (1992) 'Competing on capabilities: the new rules of corporate strategy', *Harvard Business Review*, **70**(3): 57–69.

Sveiby, K.E. (1997) *The New Organizational Wealth: Managing and Measuring Knowledge-based Assets*, San Francisco, CA: Berrett-Koehler.

Sveiby, K.E. (2001) *What is Knowledge Management?*, www.sveiby.com.au/KnowledgeManagement.html.

Teece, D. (2009) *Dynamic Capabilities and Strategic Management: Organizing for Innovation and Growth*, Oxford: Oxford University Press.

CHAPTER 12

Small is beautiful: entrepreneurship in the bigger business

CONTENTS

KEY CONCEPTS

This chapter covers:

- Why corporate entrepreneurship and innovation are desirable in big businesses.

- Different approaches to the practice of corporate entrepreneurship.

- Why corporate entrepreneurship may need to be encouraged, the barriers to it and what can be done to promote its manifestation in strategic entrepreneurship, innovation and an entrepreneurial culture.

- Areas where there appear to be disadvantages of size and where being small can be an advantage.

- Some of the implications of ICT and e-business.

Introduction

The growth of small businesses because much small business policy and support have been focused on them in particular. However growth, or at least the maturity and size which come from growth, can be a disadvantage because it can be harder for the business to remain entrepreneurial. Even for big businesses, some aspects of 'small' can still seem to be 'beautiful'.

This chapter therefore looks at two aspects of 'small is beautiful' from the perspective of the bigger business. It looks at attempts by established businesses to continue to be entrepreneurial, a process which is often referred to as 'corporate entrepreneurship' or 'intrapreneurship', and it looks at situations where it really does seem to be an advantage to be small.

Entrepreneurship in bigger businesses

Growth in the early stages of a small business can be seen as a natural extension of its original formation, and at least to some extent it requires the same sense of adventure, of initiative and of opportunity. Many organisations have developmental stages and different priorities and practices prevail at different stages of development. For example, Greiner suggests that after the start-up or entrepreneurial phase, many organisations focus on the efficient division of labour and the elaboration of structure, which increases the need to formalize procedures and control behaviour.[1] Management effort focuses on efficiency and the maintenance of the status quo, and change becomes something to be resisted or avoided. Yet in a dynamic business environment, where competition is severe and where market developments present new opportunities, to stand still is to court regression.[2]

Standing still and maintaining order are appropriate reactions in a stable environment but the modern business environment is extremely dynamic, and standing still is not an advisable managerial option. A turbulent business environment is commonplace nowadays but it is worth emphasising why such a state of affairs exists.

Genus[3] and Jones-Evans[4] argue that many organisational contexts are now characterised by:

- a decline in stable mass consumer markets and an increase in fragmented markets in which product life cycles are much shorter than formerly
- a significant increase in the size of the service sector
- a marked reduction in labour market rigidities with major consequences for the employment patterns of individuals and the utilisation of labour by firms
- major technological and information revolutions which have transformed industries and organisations
- the deregulation of industrial sectors and the privatisation of nationalised industries
- intense international competition and the development of global production capabilities and markets
- the glorification of entrepreneurship and the enterprise culture.

Basically 'old certainties have been superseded by new and continuing uncertainties' and consequently organisations must innovate and differentiate products and services while improving quality.[5] They must do this by modifying their internal arrangements and their association with external parties.

Innovative responses to the modern organisational world are necessary for large and small firms but the approach is somewhat different in the more mature business. Business formation and early growth, which frequently depend on the ideas, drive and personality of the founder, are seen as the essence of entrepreneurship. Growth in a mature business also requires enterprise, ideas, drive and culture, but these must come at least in part from those working in the business as well as from an owner-manager.

> Today's businesses, especially the large ones, simply will not survive in this period of rapid change and innovation unless they acquire entrepreneurial competence.
>
> Peter Drucker[6]
>
> It is not the strongest of the species that survive, nor the most intelligent, but the ones most responsive to change.
>
> Charles Darwin

It was an American, Gifford Pinchot, who invented the word 'intrapreneurship' to describe the practice of entrepreneurship within mature businesses, a necessary practice if those organisations are to continue to develop indefinitely.[7] Organisational development implies change and improvement; it means doing new and more productive things that can sustain or enhance profit. This development requires the application of enterprise in the mature organisation: the process which has been described as intrapreneurship or, more recently, as corporate entrepreneurship.[8] Corporate entrepreneurship has been defined in a number of ways and some of the approaches used to develop it are considered in more detail later in this chapter. But before presenting them, the connection between entrepreneurship, innovation and enterprise is summarised in order to provide a context for corporate entrepreneurship.

Entrepreneurship

Entrepreneurship has been described in terms of:

> the ability to create something from practically nothing. It is initiating ... and building an enterprise rather than ... watching one. It is the knack for sensing opportunities where others see chaos, contradiction and confusion. It is the ability to build a 'founding team' to complement your own skills and talents. It is the know-how to find, marshal and control resources. Finally it is a willingness to take calculated risks.[9]

This definition is consistent with those used in Part I but it emphasises the range of activities that are needed to initiate and to launch the development of a new business venture. It does not dwell however on the nature of the business that is then created. A great deal of entrepreneurship or enterprise must still be exercised, even in a mundane small business, if that business is to survive. The interactions 'between smallness, exposure to the environment, ownership and personal control, condition the culture of the business'.[10] The task environment is complex and changeable, and the continuing exercise of enterprise is essential for success. Problems have to be solved for which there is little or no precedent.

Learning and problem solving are common activities in many working environments nowadays, but some people consider that true entrepreneurship occurs when individuals 'ignore the established ways of thinking and action' and seek novel ideas and solutions that can meet customer needs. Entrepreneurship is therefore:

> the innovatory process involved in the creation of an economic enterprise based on a new product or service which differs significantly from products or services offered by other suppliers in content or in the way its production is organised or in its marketing.[11]

In this approach entrepreneurship is therefore concerned with newness: new ideas, products, services or combinations of resources aimed at meeting the needs of consumers more efficiently.

Innovation

It has been described as the successful development of competitive advantage and, as such, it is the key to corporate entrepreneurship. For example, Pinchot, in his seminal work *Intrapreneuring*, argues that entrepreneurs in businesses are:

> the dreamers who do: those who take hands-on responsibility for creating innovation of any kind within an organisation. The intrapreneur may be a creator or inventor but is always a dreamer who figures out how to turn an idea into a profitable reality.[12]

More recently Kuratko and Hodgetts have argued that 'the major thrust of corporate entrepreneurship is to develop the entrepreneurial spirit within organisational boundaries, thus allowing an atmosphere of innovation to prosper';[13] the corporate entrepreneur therefore is an individual who initiates innovative change in mature firms.

It is also argued that it is the presence of innovation that distinguishes the entrepreneurial organisation from others. Covin and Miles go so far as to say that 'the label "entrepreneurial" should not be applied to firms that are not innovative.'[14] For them, innovation is necessary for corporate entrepreneurship and that means being innovative in relation to the competition. They suggest, for example, that firms which replace their basic technologies with new methods which are being disseminated throughout an industry can be regarded as innovative from an internal perspective but will hardly be considered innovative by outsiders. For Covin and Miles, innovation must 'increase competitiveness through efforts aimed at the rejuvenation, renewal, and redefinition of organisations, their markets or industries' if businesses are to be deemed entrepreneurial.[15]

Inventors are usually individuals, but corporate entrepreneurship is frequently carried out by groups or teams. Caird points out that there are leading innovators who are frequently the driving force behind innovations. They are 'the project champions', and the project 'has no chance of being realised without their belief and commitment'.[16] However, while the lead innovator may have inventing or managerial skill or both, many of Caird's innovators lacked marketing and general management skills, which were provided by members of the project team.

Innovation itself can take several forms, all relevant to corporate entrepreneurship:[17]

- Innovation in processes, including changes and improvements to methods. These contribute to increases in productivity, which lowers costs and helps to increase demand.
- Innovation in products, or services. While progressive innovation is predominant, radical innovation opens up new markets. These lead to increases in effective demand which encourage increases in investment and employment.
- Innovation in management and work organisation, and the exploitation of human resources, together with the capacity to anticipate techniques.

It is important in this context to recognise that innovation is not confined to the manufacturing sector.

Enterprise

If corporate entrepreneurship is the continuing generation of innovation by applying entrepreneurship within established businesses then it is, in turn, an example of the broad meaning of 'enterprise'. As a result the terms 'entrepreneurship', 'enterprise', 'innovation', 'change', 'intrapreneurship' and 'corporate entrepreneurship' are frequently used interchangeably and, while this is sometimes due to a looseness in writing style, it is clear that there are many similarities amongst the terms.

ILLUSTRATION 12.1
The Ten Commandments of innovation

---

1. Take risks – adopt a 'can do' philosophy.
2. Stimulate creativity and seek out new ideas.
3. Reward success and tolerate failure.
4. Set realistic targets and review.
5. Adopt an open management style.
6. Focus on the customer – cultivate partnerships.
7. Actively manage investors.
8. Know what your competition is up to.
9. Work with other companies and academics.
10. Patent/protect.

DTI presentation

Innovation and enterprise are known to be important in the private sector in most economies but Borins points out that they can also be commonplace in the public sector.[18] This occurs despite deterrents such as the close political management of the executive, aimed at securing a consistent implementation of policy, tight controls and checks aimed at preventing corruption, and the keenness of the media to expose any errors and mistakes that may be made. It is also part of the conventional wisdom that, because public services are generally not exposed to market forces, they are liable to operate inefficiently and that this will continue until they are forced by a public crisis to innovate. However Borins reveals that public servants often initiate external innovation to solve problems before they become crises, and that other innovations emerge in response to perceived opportunities, sometimes as a result of initiatives by politicians.

Corporate entrepreneurship

The importance of corporate entrepreneurship

Before discussing corporate entrepreneurship it may be helpful to establish the importance of this activity for business development. Management writers such as Peter Drucker have for a long time argued that entrepreneurial competency is essential for continued success. However Wiklund reviewed the literature on the connection between an entrepreneurial strategic orientation and business performance in established smaller companies and concluded that there is no simple link between them. He also raised a point about the timescale of any correlation and wondered if corporate entrepreneurship was a quick fix for firms in trouble or whether it did indeed produce long-term results.

It is recognised that size as well as maturity has an impact on corporate entrepreneurial activity, so Wiklund carried out research on Swedish businesses with between

10 and 50 employees. This is one of the few studies which utilises large longitudinal data sets in investigating the link between entrepreneurial orientation and business performance and therefore, although these were not large businesses, this research is relevant to the issues covered in this chapter.

Wiklund argues that, in the short run, proactive firms pay attention to environmental trends and can respond quickly to opportunities by introducing innovations. Their alertness allows them to target markets and charge premium prices. It also allows them to stay ahead of the competition and gain a competitive advantage. Wiklund believes that this alertness provides established smaller firms with a strategic advantage which compensates for their lack of resources. He also believes that firm-level entrepreneurship confers advantage in the longer term. Their early movement into markets allows entrepreneurial firms to dominate distribution channels and establish industry standards which consolidate their advantage.

There is some research support for the long-term benefit of entrepreneurship but, in view of the inconclusive evidence in support of the entrepreneurship–performance link, Wiklund carried out his longitudinal study to discover if performance was enhanced as a result of entrepreneurial strategy in both the short and long run. Results indicate that there is a positive association between entrepreneurship and performance in both the short and longer term, thus offering support for those who argue in favour of entrepreneurship.[19] However, it should be pointed out that the link is not a simple one. Wiklund found that availability of finance, which can be considered to be a 'pull' factor, had a stronger impact on performance than entrepreneurship, which is a 'push' factor. Having the money to complete requisite activities is very important. In another article Chandler et al. indicate that an innovation-supportive organisational culture does have a positive impact on revenue in many firms, but only under conditions of rapid environmental change.[20]

Defining corporate entrepreneurship

Corporate entrepreneurship may lead to superior performance but, as we have found with several of the issues raised in this book, there are various definitions of key concepts in this field. For example Miller, in the early 1980s, began to distinguish between conservatism and entrepreneurialism in established firms, and for him entrepreneurial businesses are proactive initiators who try to outdo the competition. They also have a proclivity for bold, risky acts and are highly innovative. In short they are innovative, proactive risk takers.[21] Recently Lumpkin and Dess have added autonomy and competitive aggressiveness to Miller's list of entrepreneurial attributes but it has been pointed out that Miller's instrument measures entrepreneurial disposition rather than entrepreneurial action.[22] Vesper has added to the debate on corporate entrepreneurship by suggesting that it is characterised by three activities:[23]

- the creation of a new business unit by an established firm
- the development and implementation of entrepreneurial strategic thrusts
- the emergence of new ideas from various levels within an organisation.

Vesper's last point is supported by Covin and Miles, who believe that in some businesses an entrepreneurial philosophy impregnates the entire organisation.[24] Zahra et al. suggest that there are many facets of firm-level entrepreneurship which reflect different combinations of:[25]

- the content of the entrepreneurship, which can be activities such as corporate venturing, innovation and proactivity
- the source of the entrepreneurship, which can be internal to the firm or external
- the focus of the entrepreneurship, which can be formal or informal.

These views cover a wide range of entrepreneurship, but from them three main ways can be identified in which larger and more mature businesses can seek to promote entrepreneurship within the business. These are the promotion of entrepreneurship through formal strategic decision making, which will sometimes require the creation of a separate corporate venture; the formal and informal development of innovative ideas by middle managers and professional staff, which often entails the creation of a new project; and the creation of an entrepreneurial philosophy throughout the organisation. Various terms have been used in the literature to describe these activities but in this chapter they are referred to as 'strategic entrepreneurship', 'developing innovation within organisations' and 'entrepreneurial culture' respectively.

Strategic entrepreneurship

In a start-up the entrepreneur is regarded as the key actor in developing a business idea, marshalling resources and creating an organisation to bring a new product or service to the market. In a competitive business environment it is clear that mature and larger organisations should continue to seek out new opportunities and make the necessary arrangements to convert them into new goods and services. At a strategic level this requires an effective plan and the proper positioning of the organisation to respond effectively to its environment.[26] Porter argues that strategic decision makers must appreciate the competitive dynamics of their chosen industry.[27] The current and predicted industrial structures strongly influence the rules of the competitive game and offer certain strategic choices for organisations. He suggests that strategic planners should analyse the current and expected state of competitive rivalry by paying attention to such matters as the threat from new entrants, the availability of substitutes and the power of suppliers and customers. Industries can be classified as attractive or unattractive, and Porter argues that the profit potential of an industry is a function of industry attractiveness coupled with an appropriate competitive strategy. He recognises that competitive forces within an industry can drive down profits but contends that organisations must position themselves properly in the industry. Strategic choice in pursuit of specific goals is more important than environment or structure in promoting innovation.

There are many criticisms of Porter's approach to strategic change but it is representative of a body of managerial thought which associates organisational development with rational, logical, strategic decision making by managerial elites in both the private and public sectors. In general this approach to corporate entrepreneurship is akin to what Heller calls strategic forcing.[28] The innovation is 'forcibly fitted into the resisting organisation [whilst] the "champion" project leader uses a mix of political power, organisational savvy, and technical powers to get the innovation past organisational roadblocks to implementation'.

That, however, might be considered to be a top-down approach to corporate entrepreneurship. Another view presents a model of corporate entrepreneurship which suggests that external variables such as market hostility, strategic variables such as competitive orientation, and internal variables such as internal competencies and resource availability all have a strong effect on the entrepreneurial orientation of an organisation.[29] Other environmental factors have also been suggested as drivers of corporate entrepreneurship, including growth markets and the demand for new products and services.[30] Either way corporate entrepreneurship is seen as having a strong influence on firm performance.

Influencing corporate entrepreneurship
Hornsby reviewed the literature on corporate entrepreneurship and identified five interrelated internal organisational conditions that influence corporate entrepreneurship.[31] These included:

- management support of entrepreneurial efforts
- work discretion and autonomy
- rewards and reinforcement
- time availability
- organisational boundaries.

The more that such conditions are in place, and seen to be in place, then the higher the probability of an employee deciding to behave in an entrepreneurial manner. Top managers may be strategically aware and see the need for change but they often forget that there are powerful individual, managerial, organisational and cultural reasons why innovative changes are resisted. Faced with resistance, managerial elites will attempt to overcome it at individual and organisational levels, so it seems sensible for powerful elites to understand how individuals react to change.

Resistance to change by individuals
Individuals in many organisations will resist change if they feel that their skills, status, power and relationships have to be altered significantly to meet the needs of the new order.[32] They will also want to understand why change is necessary. In this context it should be realised that people from different parts of an organisation interpret events in different ways and the need for change clearly perceived by senior managers may not be shared by other individuals and interest groups.[33] Sometimes they do not 'see' a problem, and therefore see no reason to change. Senior managers must also understand that individuals proceed through recognised phases, often typified by denial, resistance, exploration and commitment, as they experience a change in their situation, and that people therefore need time to digest changes.[34] Forcing change through is a dangerous approach; it must be managed effectively if people are to commit themselves to the new order.[35]

Independent versus corporate venturing
This view of strategic entrepreneurship in established firms indicates that new strategic directions may often require the creation of a separate corporate venture to deliver results. It might be argued that a separate corporate venture developed by an established business would bear a strong resemblance to other non-corporate

new business ventures. However, Jones-Evans points out that major differences exist between corporate and non-corporate ventures, not least in that with a new venture the ground rules for running it emerge as it develops, whereas the leaders of corporate ventures must conform to general corporate procedures from the start.[36] Such constraints may reduce flexibility in the corporate venture and inhibit development. Jones-Evans also argues that an existing firm will have an established product-market portfolio and the new corporate venture can expect to experience serious resistance if it attempts to compete in the same markets.

Another difference will be in financing. An independent new venture will have several potential sources of funding, and lenders will normally have considerable experience of assessing the potential of a new business. In contrast, new corporate ventures are likely to have only one source of funding, namely the corporate body; its financial custodians will seldom review more than a handful of corporate venture proposals per year and may not have the experience of evaluating emerging business proposals. In any event, evaluations will tend to be based on standard financial decision-making procedures and these may be inappropriate for evolving ventures. In addition, the initiators of rejected corporate venture proposals do not have alternative sources of funding to which they can go. In general non-corporate venture leaders are in control of financial and other decisions whilst corporate venture leaders must work within the constraints imposed by the established organisation.

Jones-Evans also points out that funding for a corporate venture will most likely be allocated at an early stage of a project's development. A return on investment will then be expected fairly quickly and if this fails to materialise all supplies of funds may dry up. In contrast the early funding of new independent ventures may be rather limited, and this may be quite appropriate. Even though new businesses tend to be under-capitalised they often obtain additional funding on a step-by-step basis. As new products or developments come on-line additional funding is sought, and this means that there may be no acquisition of major funding until it is warranted by developments.

As well as different sources of funding for new corporate and non-corporate ventures, there are also likely to be different sources of human resources. In a new venture, staff will be recruited in the labour market according to their skills and commitment to the entrepreneur's vision. In contrast corporate ventures may be staffed by existing corporate employees with more interest in developing their careers. They may see their transfer to a corporate venture as a promotion and a reward for their overall contribution to the firm. Further rewards for corporate venture staff will probably be in line with corporate remuneration procedures whereas staff in a non-corporate venture can more easily be rewarded in line with the profitability of the venture.

Jones-Evans considers that new ventures sometimes benefit substantially from having expert advice from a board of directors. Directors often have diverse backgrounds and can advise on financial, market and technical matters. Corporate ventures may not have this resource; indeed project leaders usually report to the board of the controlling firm and must compete with other shareholders to have their interests addressed.

In general there are significant differences in the strategic resource management and organisational processes in corporate as opposed to new ventures, and these differences will have an impact on the potential profitability of these dichotomous units. The differences will also impact on the likelihood of continued innovation.

Developing innovation within organisations

Aggressively and proactively seeking innovative opportunities outside the organisation is the essence of strategic entrepreneurship, but entrepreneurship is not the sole preserve of CEOs and managerial elites. Mintzberg contends that all managers, and many support staff and others, take on an entrepreneurial role as part of their work.[37] These individuals are in unique positions to understand what is happening within organisations and some of them are able to develop an interdepartmental perspective. Many will also be in touch with peers, customers, suppliers and others outside the organisation and can spot external opportunities. Many business founders are keen to retain strategic decision making themselves but as organisations grow they are rarely able to develop the skills and know-how, nor have access to all the resources needed, to continuously expand the business. Continued growth occurs when owners involve others, and not just those at the strategic apex of the business, in the entrepreneurial process. Indeed some people argue that strategy can emerge from various levels in the organisation; however the creation and development of innovatory strategic thrusts by people other than those in the top management group can only occur if appropriate managerial and organisational systems, structures, styles and cultures are in place. Not all management styles and organisational arrangements facilitate innovatory development and therefore organisational barriers to, and assistance for, innovation need to be considered.

Managerial barriers to entrepreneurship

Managers can and do act entrepreneurially as they proliferate in growing organisations and as they acquire more decision-making authority with the dispersal of company ownership amongst shareholders. It is incumbent on managers to look to the future but management is a multi-faceted job and attentions can focus on stewardship and control rather than on entrepreneurship. Stevenson and Gumpert argue that managers frequently regard themselves as trustees, and this engenders caution.[38] They are responsible for expensive human and material resources, and they feel duty-bound to use these resources wisely. They are concerned to earn an acceptable rate of return on their resources in the shorter term and to protect the lives and livelihoods of their employees.

Managers have numerous constituents who must be at least partially satisfied. Consequently, decision making and change entail a cautious process of negotiating with major players, and pursuing a less risky, middle-of-the-road strategy is preferred. Caution is also necessary, because larger organisations typically commit large amounts of resource to important projects at one time. A lot of analysis is usually done before a project is supported, but once the decision is made the organisation is committed. Entrepreneurs, on the other hand, evaluate many projects simultaneously and quickly drop those that do not look promising. Stevenson and Gumpert also point out that there is a connection between managerial power and the resources that managers control. This being so, they are reluctant to take risks and often therefore reinforce the status quo. Managers also tend to have a narrower focus than entrepreneurs and to be concerned with building the power and reputation of their departments. However the process of new product development should be holistic, and a narrow departmental focus can inhibit innovatory thinking.

Support staff are often technical experts who are keen to prove their worth to organisations by introducing as many innovative ideas as possible. By so doing they can increase the reliance of others on their expertise and consequently increase their power and status. While they are generally keen on newness and change, there are often conflicts between individual staff as they endeavour to extol to the organisation the virtues of their particular speciality. They are also likely to come into conflict with line managers who are keen to maintain the status quo as they seek efficiency gains.[39]

Barriers to innovation are commonplace in many organisations, but Borins shows that in public sector organisations there are additional obstacles.[40] His research reveals that many of the barriers emanate not only from the bureaucratic nature of public sector organisations but also from the inherent caution of various internal actors. The barriers to innovation come from 'attitudes within the bureaucracy itself, turf wars, difficulties in co-ordinating organisations, logistical problems, the difficulty of maintaining the enthusiasm of programme staff, difficulties in implementing a new technology, opposition by unions, opposition by middle management, and opposition to entrepreneurial action within the public sector'. In addition, many initiatives are opposed by politicians because they require additional resources, because of legislative constraints and because of direct political opposition. Furthermore, various external interest groups, including private sector organisations that would have to compete with the public sector, resist many innovations.

Organisational barriers

Managerial roles and responsibilities can induce caution but managers and professionals work in an organisational context and the realities of this environment can also encourage conservatism. This occurs because organisations as they grow and mature tend to install standard operating procedures and rules that constrain initiative. The first time a new job is tackled there is a time-consuming learning process, but after it has been repeated several times a satisfactory method will be identified, remembered and used again. If the task is done continuously then recommended methods will be written down and employees told to follow them as the correct procedures.[41] As the volume of output increases there is more division of labour and specialisation, which leads to the creation of functional departments. Behaviour of individuals must be predictable, and this is achieved by introducing standard work practices. To make sure that individual and group tasks coalesce, schedules, process plans and control mechanisms are introduced.

However, as the complexity of the task increases, people lose sight of the ends they are serving. 'Management must find the means to make behaviour lower down more predictable and so it turns to rules, procedures, job descriptions, and the like, all devices that formalise behaviour.'[42] Organisations, as they develop, introduce standard practices, but also develop less tangible but equally powerful cultures. They develop characteristic ways of doing things that are guided by a set of shared norms and values. Organisations are infused with values, and this culture transmits to people in the organisation what they should be doing, what they ought to believe in or what the organisation is really about. Standard procedures and culture are powerful controlling mechanisms, and can easily defeat innovatory initiatives.[43]

As mentioned above, strategic planning can assist entrepreneurship. Some writers suggest that, with sufficient will and skill, organisations can become almost anything they want to be. However, in practice this rarely happens. Organisations specialise, which can mean that a huge investment in plant, machinery and manpower may have to be written off if the specialisation changes.[44]

Drucker recognises that many of these factors affect organisations but considers that size, per se, is not 'an impediment to entrepreneurship and innovation; [the main impediment] is the existing operation itself and especially the existing successful operation'. Total commitment to the existing operation is needed to ensure continued success and to manage 'the daily crises' that normally occur. The current activity requires priority attention 'and deserves it'. Drucker goes on to argue that most successful firms of today will in ten years' time derive a significant proportion of their income from a similar product range to their present one, but for long-term survival they must also look for a new range. This is not easy. 'The temptation in the existing business is always to feed yesterday and starve tomorrow. The current business is not in trouble, and there does not seem to be any pressure to innovate.'[45] It is evident that even leading organisations such as IBM and Xerox, which have been very innovative businesses, can lose their competitive edge and be forced to withdraw from certain markets. Conditions change and the very procedures which proved very effective in one era are the source of disadvantage in another.[46]

Facilitating innovation

Porter has pointed out that continuous innovation is essential for organisational survival in competitive markets but, in view of the barriers, achieving it requires hard work, appropriate attitudes and proper structures. However, just as there is no single agreed route to developing enterprise, there are a number of suggestions as to what constitute the innovatory aspects of corporate entrepreneurship.

In considering policies, procedures, structures and cultures which help sustain corporate entrepreneurship it is possible to differentiate between, on the one hand, those activities which encourage the development of new thinking and new projects by decentralising innovation to middle managers and professional staff, and on the other those activities which extend the enterprising culture to every person in the organisation. In some cases it may prove difficult to locate a procedure in one or the other of these categories, but it seems that there are differences in the mindsets required for extending the formal and informal development of new projects to middle levels of an organisation and for creating a wider enterprise philosophy. Also, while the policies and procedures which support strategic entrepreneurship by top managers have already been discussed, some of the discussion which follows, especially that in connection with Lessem's work, is relevant to the encouragement of strategic entrepreneurship.

Roles

Lessem in particular has highlighted the importance of managerial roles and behaviour in supporting corporate entrepreneurship, although he uses the older term 'intrapreneur', which will therefore also be used here in discussing his work. He identifies the key to intrapreneurship as the intrapreneurs themselves and the roles they perform.[47] For him, the intrapreneur combines many of the qualities of the entrepreneur and the manager. The impatience of the entrepreneur with the constraints imposed by the organisation produces too much conflict with the desire of managers to control events. For Lessem, the concept of intrapreneur is important for two reasons. 'Firstly, it cuts across the division between management and enterprise. But secondly, it forms a bridge between enterprise and development.'[48]

For Lessem, there are several roles or archetypes that can elicit effective development in differing business contexts. Some support strategic entrepreneurship while others support innovation from below. In some situations rugged entrepreneurs are needed. They have an instinctive approach to opportunities and impatience when faced with obstacles. They seldom let a real or perceived lack of resources inhibit their search for new profitable opportunities. However, in a mature venture their impatience and aggression can create conflict.

It is recognised that large and mature companies may not be attractive to entrepreneurial types unless they can find opportunities in areas such as sales and new product development. The organisation should offer them the chance to take on risky projects, however. Their success should be rewarded, but failure must not lead to censure. Mature organisational entrepreneurs can develop the capacity to focus on business renewal as a goal.

In some instances entrepreneurial activity is not enough for development; what is needed is an adventurer. The latter is a major risk taker who enters uncharted waters in search of opportunity. There are difficulties in making huge changes in strategy, but in some instances this is required and the courage and forcefulness of the adventurer is indispensable. In an increasingly global economy, organisations need the drive and audaciousness of the adventurer to enter new and difficult markets.

Innovators are needed also. They are the first or early users of new ideas and are the essential link between research and accomplishment. They must create structures and a climate conducive to the generation of, experimentation with and realisation of new ideas. They encourage creativity, but they also have a strong commitment to the commercial exploitation of ideas. Innovators get their rewards from seeing the successful transformation of an idea into a successful good or service, but there can be a tendency to marginalise adventurers and innovators in successful businesses. Firms must find mechanisms to allow innovation to coexist with current product efficiency.

Exploring random innovative ideas may be exciting but firms also need a sense of direction and discipline. There must be some pattern in a firm's strategy and leaders need to ensure that new projects are aligned with their vision for the business. Leaders stand back from the intensive competition in firms and act as somewhat impartial arbitrators, co-ordinators and conflict handlers. The leader takes an overview, reconciles differing perspectives, and creates a climate of co-operation, but also exercises authority when necessary to keep the business on the rails. Like the leader of an orchestra, the business leader has concern for the final product and for the people, and uses a range of methods of influence to make sure that all play in tune.

In addition, the role of effective change agents can be crucial. They bring new products to market, implement new management systems and reorganise working arrangements. Change agents like freedom from controls and are not bound by convention, but they also possess the managerial and political skill to manage change programmes. They appreciate the importance of creating a general awareness that the status quo will not do in a turbulent era and in creating an image of the future and letting key players know what it will look like. Further, using change management theory, they can design and implement the practical first steps to bringing about change. They also recognise and can deal with resistance to change. Change agents are keen to do new things, and get their motivation from the mental excitement that accompanies change.

Change agents are important, but they cannot function on their own. Another key intrapreneurial type therefore is the enabler. Many authors point out the importance of creating a climate or culture for enterprise and innovation, and the lack of appropriate cultures in many organisations. Therefore a facilitator or enabler aims to:

> develop self-renewing, self-correcting systems of people who learn to organise themselves in a variety of ways according to the nature of their tasks, and who continue to expand the choice available to the organisation as it copes with the changing demands of a changing environment.[49]

Enablers use 'soft' behavioural skills to encourage people to question ideas, challenge conventions and seek, through collaboration with insiders and outsiders, to come up with forward-looking ideas.

Lessem also describes one more intrapreneurial type: the animateur. Organisations are technical and economic tools, but they are also living social systems, which need to be humanised and enlivened. An esprit de corps or sense of community is vital for a developing organisation, and this is where the animateur assists. The emphasis is on teams and on development through co-operation, problem solving and concern for the organisational community. Enablers and animators develop the supportive atmosphere and trust that is essential for individual and group risk taking in pursuit of better options.

Lessem's approach is useful in that it recognises the importance of numerous roles, from the aggressive and competitive adventurer and entrepreneur to the people-oriented enabler and animateur, in the continued development of mature organisations. Several of these intrapreneurial types can deliver innovation in appropriate situations, but others provide the change leadership skills to guide a project to fulfilment and create the flexible structures to sustain change.

Systems and structures that support innovation

Peter Drucker, in writing about innovation and entrepreneurship, like Lessem highlights the importance of managerial decision making but considers also that appropriate policies and procedures are needed. He considers that the essence of innovation and corporate entrepreneurship is the development of new or different processes, products or services that utilise resources more productively than before. He contends that innovators must systematically review the changes taking place in society to identify and exploit business opportunities. Entrepreneurial managers must also scan the environment to become aware of changes in those management principles and practices, production processes, and market structures and requirements that can conceivably have an impact on their organisations. They must also be aware of changes in knowledge, but are warned against an overemphasis on knowledge-based innovations. Some are spectacular and transform markets, but although the vast majority of innovations are more mundane they have a much greater cumulative impact on profits and employment.

ILLUSTRATION 12.2
Who is the intrapreneur?

Primary motives: the intrapreneur wants freedom and access to corporate resources and is self-motivated, but responds to corporate rewards.

Time orientation: the intrapreneur has end goals of three to 15 years, depending on the nature of the project, and strives to meet self-imposed and corporate time-tables.

Action: the intrapreneur does whatever is needed to accomplish tasks and is not interested in status.

Skills: the intrapreneur knows the business intimately, but recognises the importance of managerial and political skill.

Confidence: the intrapreneur is self-confident and courageous and, if necessary, will outwit the organisational system.

Focus: the intrapreneur focuses both inside and outside the business. The intrapreneur pays attention to customers and gets insiders to do the same.

Risk: the intrapreneur likes moderate risk and undertakes market research in order to understand the risks.

Failure and mistakes: the intrapreneur regards mistakes as a learning experience, but is sensitive to the needs of the organisation for stability and hence may hide risky projects from view.

Decisions: the intrapreneur is adept at communicating his or her own private vision to others and is willing to compromise to make progress with this vision.

Attitude towards the system: the intrapreneur dislikes the system, but learns to manipulate it.

Background: the intrapreneur is often from an entrepreneurial, small business, professional or farm background and is often middle class and highly educated, particularly in technical fields.

Source: 'Who Is the Intrapreneur?', adapted from G. Pinchot III, *Intrapreneuring* (New York: Harper & Row, 1985), pp. 54–6. Copyright © by Gifford Pinchot III. Reprinted by permission of the author.

It is important to emphasise the weight that Drucker attaches to solid, systematic investigation in the process of modernisation. This is seldom the result of genius or high-technology discoveries; more often it is the application of systematic search and logic to a host of organisational procedures and practices. Instalment credit or hire purchase, for instance, had a much greater impact on the business sector than more novel and spectacular changes. There are barriers to successful organisational innovation but, if the right managerial policies and practices are put in place, then innovation can become normal.

Many managers protect what they have currently, but if they are to change they must become aware that it is company policy systematically to give up those products and practices that are unproductive. They must therefore place all activities periodically 'on trial for their lives'. Managers should answer critical questions on the contribution products make to productivity and should be encouraged not to shore up the obsolete. Obsolete or declining products absorb scarce resources at the expense of the new. The best people tend to be charged with overcoming the problems associated with old products, whereas they should be encouraged to develop the new. Entrepreneurial business 'management must take the lead in making obsolete its own products and services rather than waiting for a competitor to do so'.[50]

Another approach is to use successful innovators as role models. They are asked to make presentations to their peers to explain their actions, to outline those factors that lead to success and those that cause difficulties. The fact that senior managers encourage this activity sends a clear message that innovative behaviour is appreciated. Then, if innovation is to become an important business function, mechanisms must be initiated to assess innovative performance. It is important to know what the expected outcomes of the innovation are likely to be, what resources are necessary and when results are to be achieved. Innovation concerns the new and largely unknown, but serious attempts must be made to gain feedback on progress to assess performance.

Policies, practices and appraisals assist innovation, but innovative ideas and their commercialisation are generated by people. Since behaviour is influenced by context, the organisational context must support innovative behaviour. Successful innovation emerges when organisations have appropriate personnel in post, when management systems support change and when a suitable climate obtains. The complexity of large organisations can stifle classic entrepreneurs, even if they are the company founders. Without appropriate policies the organisation is likely to become performance oriented rather than innovation oriented. 'Companies that have built entrepreneurial management into their structure ... continue to be innovators ... irrespective of changes in chief executives or economic conditions.'[51]

Just what is meant by entrepreneurial management and the creation of an appropriate climate? Jones-Evans argues that managers cannot tell people to engage in innovation: they self-select and will only continue to develop their ideas if appropriate organisational arrangements are in place.[52] An important requirement is to have clearly defined roles for those involved in the change process. In change management projects Jaffe argues that it is important to identify:[53]

- the top executive team of the whole organisation in which the innovation will develop
- the project sponsor – the person who makes the decision to make the change
- the project leader, who is often the person who has developed the new ideas
- the change navigator – the person with knowledge of and skill in implementing change programmes.

Innovatory change will not succeed unless the top management group supports it, and it will be problematic if there is not a skilled change agent in the entrepreneurial group. The leader has the detailed knowledge and enthusiasm to energise people but the sponsor must also be active in:

- overcoming the financial concerns of other managers regarding risky ventures, in both initial review and follow-up evaluations

- curing the need for resources by defending proposals in evaluation meetings, allocating initial exploration funding to new ideas and permitting flexibility in budgets in terms of money, people and equipment
- ensuring that corporate venturing develops quickly within an organisation by putting the rewards and initiatives in place for intrapreneurs
- fighting internal departmental issues, such as the hoarding of resources in one division, and empire-building.[54]

Jones-Evans also argues that it is important to retain those who initiate innovations in the corporate entrepreneurial team even if they lack managerial or organisational skill. If they are removed their strong motivational drive will be lost. Quite often the initial innovator does lack certain skills but this can be accommodated by creating a project team, which includes those with technical, economic, managerial and change management skills. It is also important for the project team to be kept intact even after the initial completion of the project. The team may have to respond to outsiders who develop new variants of the idea.

Corporate entrepreneurship is not easily confined within an organisational department. Bringing an idea to market will involve a great deal of knowledge which is located within functional departments. It is important therefore that corporate entrepreneurs and their associates have the power to make decisions and the political skill to obtain the level of co-operation they require. To avoid the damaging conflicts that can arise between departments, it may also be sensible to define innovation as a crucial business process and reorganise the business along business process lines (where a process is 'a specific ordering of work activities across time and place with a beginning, an end, and clearly identified inputs and outputs: a structure for action'[55]).

Corporate entrepreneurs have a strong proclivity for advancing risky projects, but as we have already seen, organisational policies and procedures often discourage managers and others from taking risks. Indeed failure is often seen as a barrier to career advancement. A mature business which wants to encourage corporate entrepreneurship must find ways of encouraging risky initiatives without damaging the careers of those individuals who lead these projects.

Resources must also be provided for corporate entrepreneurs. In the early stages of project development, time is a vital resource and those with an interest in developing new ideas must get away from regular duties. If a new idea looks promising then adequate funds must be made available. In general, there must be a degree of surplus or slack in organisations, which can be allocated to the generation and development of new business ideas.

If mature organisations are to continue to encourage entrepreneurship then corporate entrepreneurs must be appropriately rewarded. Organisations have been devising reward systems to motivate staff for a long time, but in view of the recent emergence of corporate entrepreneurship this presents a new challenge. Balkin and Logan have examined this issue and concluded that corporate entrepreneurs should be paid at or below market rate but that a significant bonus should be linked to the success of an innovative project.[56] In the short run, new venture personnel could be offered a profit-sharing option where profits from the new venture are paid to individuals in line with their current salaries. In the longer term, personnel could be offered shares in the new venture in proportion to their basic salaries.

CASE 7.1

New products at 3M

The Minnesota Mining Company (3M) has a reputation as one of the most innovative companies in the world. In the late 1980s it had developed more than 60,000 products, and almost a third of sales in 1988 came from products developed in the previous five years. Sales exceeded $10 billion in 1988 yet it was exceedingly entrepreneurial.

A major mistake by the founders around 1900 forced the company to innovate or go under and it has remained innovative for most of its subsequent existence. One early innovation was in the company's approach to selling. Rather than selling to purchasing officers, salesmen tried to meet their ultimate customers in the operating core of firms. They talked to production people and tailored their products to their needs.

These days 3M encourages innovative behaviour amongst all of its staff. It realises that many ideas will not reach fruition or become commercially successful but it works on the principle that the more attempts at innovation the more 'hits' there will be. Things that get in the way of innovation, like company politics or over-zealous planning, are stamped out. Co-operation, sharing information and informal communication are encouraged. Divisions are kept small – there were 42 in 1988 – and functional structures are discouraged. A product or process approach to departmental structures is favoured, individuals are multi-skilled and they are expected to accept responsibility. There is also a strong focus on teamwork. When an individual has a new idea he or she forms an action team drawn from manufacturing, technical and commercial staff. The team design and develop the idea and they are rewarded as the project passes important hurdles. Furthermore, the initiator of a successful development is given the chance to manage it as a founding entrepreneur. He or she runs a micro-company within 3M.

At 3M innovative thinking is encouraged and systems and structures are put in place to support it. However, resources are also made available. For example, there is a 15-per-cent rule which allows anyone to spend up to 15 per cent of their time on what they want to do so long as it is related to production. 'Genesis grants' of $50,000 are also available to allow people to progress projects beyond the ideas stage.

3M empowers its staff but there are guidelines and behavioural controls. The 25-per-cent rule is important and bonuses are based on achieving it. The rule states that 25 per cent of annual sales must emanate from products introduced during the previous five years. 3M is also keen on cost control. When Jake Jacobson became CEO in 1985 he said that manufacturing costs had to be reduced by 35 per cent by 1990 and the company initiated an innovative programme to achieve this goal. People are free to debate and discuss issues but they are subject to rigorous questioning by their peers. In effect individuals are controlled by means of peer review and feedback.

➡

3M has a focus on innovation, and the company philosophy and culture are instrumental in sustaining this. Innovation as a means of getting close to customers and their needs is the philosophical bedrock on which the company is built. Another basic belief is that managers must support and facilitate innovation and be constructive in their dealings with others. 3M's values seem to build loyalty. Staff turnover is low and the company seldom hires from outside.

Source: Based on R. Mitchell, 'Masters of Innovation: How 3M Keeps Its New Products Coming', *Business Week* (1989), 10 April, pp. 58–63.

Points raised

This is an example of the sort of deliberate steps taken by a company to ensure that innovation continues at a high level.

ILLUSTRATION 12.3

The reality?

Not all organisations are like 3M. For many the reality of attempts to be entrepreneurial in larger organisations are more likely to be one of unfriendly, protective secretaries and of unsympathetic bosses who are difficult to approach, and who are even more suspicious of ideas coming from the 'ranks'. Permission, support and resources are more likely to be refused and withheld rather than freely given. Modern bosses may have been taught to be more sensitive to employee ideas and be less prone to reject them openly, so instead they may listen politely and then quietly and slowly sabotage the project through inertia or a failure to deliver a vital resource.

How then can an intrapreneur go about succeeding in indifferent and even potentially hostile corporate environments? Part of the answer lies in becoming a 'guerrilla' working underground and unnoticed until success begins to speak for itself. Another aspect is resourcefulness, a dogged and creative ability to mobilise support. Finally there is courage and the determination to carry on despite all the odds.

Adhocracies

A theme of this chapter is that enterprise is both necessary and possible in organisations which, once established, need to continue to develop by introducing new products, processes or services while maintaining the efficiency of their existing portfolios.

There are organisations where innovation is the norm and which will continue to innovate boldly unless and until evidence emerges that there are dangers from excessive innovation. Miller and Friesen[57] point out that in these organisations the impetus for innovation comes primarily from the goals espoused by senior managers and associated strategies, but Covin and Slevin suggest that appropriate structural arrangements are also necessary.[58] Organisations in the computer, biomedical and film industries are constant innovators and require appropriate structures if they are to remain successful.

Mintzberg indicates that ad hoc flexibility is the key to this type of organisation.[59] This flexibility extends to the domain of strategy. Since these are innovative, problem-solving ventures, and individuals and teams are constantly working on new projects, no one can be sure how things will work out. So long as they fit in with the broad vision of the firm, successful projects which emerge from below will strongly influence strategy. Their structures are also highly flexible. There is no extensive division of labour or departmental specialisation, and little reliance on procedures, rules and plans. The reason is clear: as innovators they do not follow standard operating procedures and must devise new ways of tackling new jobs.

Because they are refined and complex innovators, these firms rely heavily on the knowledge of their expert staff, and quite often senior managers do not fully understand the intricate details of the work done by these staff. The power of knowledge becomes important and managers must delegate and have confidence in the ability of their experts. In addition, the experts will come together in ad hoc project teams to work on client problems. Teamwork is not easy, but the managers of project teams must be skilled in group dynamics, facilitation and motivation. The intrapreneurial roles of enabling and animation are vitally important and, because the work can only be done well in small groups, managerial spans of control are limited.

These structural arrangements are the antithesis of bureaucratic principles. Bureaucracies are control-oriented organisations, adhocracies are freedom seekers, and if both are housed in the same location then the culture of one will adversely impact on the effectiveness of the other. Drucker therefore argues for a physical separation of the innovative from the performance parts of businesses.

Coupling innovative projects and host organisations

Calls for the separation of innovative projects from mature organisations are common from popular management writers like Drucker, but Heller argues that two contrasting models of the link between host organisations and projects are common. In some cases an innovative project is developed by a 'product champion' who then, using his or her political skills, foists it upon and embeds it into a reluctant host organisation. Alternatively projects are 'imbued with the values and strategies of the firm and thereby channel their creations to be consistent with established consistencies'.[60] In this mode of development managerial elites monitor and encourage the alignment of new projects and corporate strategy. Heller believes, however, that it is more sensible to look at the link between host organisation and innovative project as a 'relationship of mutual influence between innovation and host organisational systems'. Loosening the link can allow the innovative unit to be creative in an atmosphere of psychological safety. It can also allow the innovators to deviate from the legitimate behaviour of the host organisation and can prevent problems in the innovative unit from percolating into the host organisation. Conversely, tight coupling can allow the innovative unit to benefit from the technical, human and financial expertise of the host organisation. Heller's research reveals that there are eight devices for coupling routine with innovating systems, as shown in Table 12.1.

It seems likely that in practice there will be less separation, forcing and assimilation of projects and hosts and more management of a dynamic interface between

Table 12.1   Categories of loosening and coupling mechanisms

There are three mechanisms which rely heavily on assumptions about what the organisation does with respect to:

• strategy	Projects which conform to the established
• existent technology	understandings are closely coupled with the host while
• and established markets	those which do not are unshackled.

and an additional five devices which connect projects by means of:

• funding	Decisions on these variables determine the extent
• senior management attention	of the coupling between host and project. Coupling
• structural location of the new product	brings advantages such as legitimacy and funding and
development activities	drawbacks such as interference and rejection.
• standard operating procedures	
• and human resources deployments[61]	

Source: Modified version of Table 1, p. 28 of T. Heller, 'Loosely Coupled Systems for Corporate Entrepreneurship: Imagining and Managing the Innovative Project/Host Organisation Interface', *Entrepreneurship: Theory and Practice* (1999), 24, p. 25–31. Reprinted by permission of Baylor University, publisher of *Entrepreneurship: Theory and Practice*.

the two through everyday decisions. There are some additional points of interest emerging from this research. Heller points out that coupling occurs at different levels and may lead to pseudo-looseness. This occurs when a project is given considerable flexibility at a total level but is expected to conform to senior management's decision-making parameters. She also argues that the oft-claimed motivational benefits of decentralisation may be more to do with changes in delegation than with an outcome of a particular structure. Tightly coupled projects which are set loose engender exhilaration. Nevertheless, while it might be attractive to separate innovative projects and host organisational systems completely, management of the interface is a more common occurrence.

Entrepreneurial competencies

It has been suggested that some business strategies, such as downsizing, have actually caused organisations to reduce their capacity to innovate and to identify and build on new opportunities. To offset such tendencies, and in recognition of their need to continue to develop opportunities, businesses are adopting specific strategies to build entrepreneurial competencies.

There are several strands to this approach in the strategic change literature but their primary focus is on the effective management of internal resources and the emergence of special competencies as a result of the intelligent utilisation of resources.[62] The creation of unique competencies allows organisations to rid themselves of outmoded procedures and develop new routines which allow the organisation to meet the changing needs of customers. Competencies also assist in altering the nature of competition in industries. Organisations redefine the nature of competition in a way which allows them to use their special combinations of production, service and information provision skills. Competent organisations provide customers with both tangible and intangible benefits. Some writers in this area concentrate on combining product and process technologies to afford competitive advantage, while others focus on the structural and cultural changes needed to create advantage.

A variant on this theme is provided by the 'capabilities school' promoted by authors such as Nonaka.[63] They take a more holistic approach to the effective leverage of resources and emphasise the importance of values in promoting special capacities. They recommend the use of language, metaphor and analogy in enhancing the creation of knowledge which can lead to improved customer-related capabilities.

Entrepreneurial culture

Mention of values leads into the final area for consideration in the corporate entrepreneurship debate. The ideology and values of senior managers are important determinants of entrepreneurialism in mature ventures but this must be supported by entrepreneurial management, organisational systems and structures.

Managers and professional staff at all levels will be expected to look to the future on occasions but there are those who argue that everyone in organisations must be entrepreneurial, including first-line supervisors, staff in the operating core, clerical workers and security personnel. Senior managers and others can create an environment which is conducive to entrepreneurship, but they cannot order it. If the dominant organisational form for most of the twentieth century was a bureaucracy which relied on standardisation, specialisation, rules and procedures, and obedient service by operators,[64] then the inculcation of an all-pervasive entrepreneurial orientation in bureaucratic businesses represents a huge shift in the organisational paradigm. It implies a shift in the culture and many of the elements of the cultural web that sustain the paradigm.

Table 12.2 illustrates some of the changes that emerged when the Baxi Heating company changed from a 'solid, slow manufacturing organisation to a more dynamic, market-focused organisation'. It can be seen that the structures, behaviours and assumptions needed to support the new paradigm are very different from those underpinning the old.

There are many contributors to the organisational culture debate but Peters and Waterman were early and influential protagonists. They believe that managers should not aim to control individual behaviour by issuing directives but should try to influence the way people think.[65] The goals are to win their hearts, to engender absolute commitment to the organisation, and to encourage them to challenge the status quo and try out new solutions to problems. This is a very different mindset from that which pertains in a bureaucratic organisation, and is brought about by various mechanisms, as shown in Table 12.3.

Genus argues that, while the proponents of the 'excellence school' are wary of concentrating too much on structural form, they believe that certain structures are crucial in promoting innovation and entrepreneurship.[66] To support an entrepreneurial culture it is essential that the structure be simple, non-hierarchical, decentralised, flat, team-oriented and flexible.

Managers, especially senior managers, play a key role in articulating and creating the culture of entrepreneurship, but they will only be successful to the extent that individuals identify with this ideology. Some individuals will identify naturally with managerial values, some will be selected to important teams because they so identify, many others will be successfully socialised and indoctrinated by management endeavour; but some will merely identify because they calculate that it is in their best interest to do so. Peters and Waterman give the impression that the modification of culture and its assimilation by all participants is a practical possibility for

Table 12.2 The old and new paradigms at Baxi Heating

Old	New
Solid	Dynamic and responsive
Stable/safe	Market-focused
Excellence	Continuous learning
Proud	Proud and profitable
Lifetime employment	Open communication and trust
Slow	Continuous improvement

Source: Based on J. Balogun and V. Hope-Hailey, *Exploring Strategic Change* (London: Prentice-Hall, 1999), pp. 50–1. Copyright © Prentice-Hall, 1999. Reprinted by permission of Pearson Education Ltd.

Table 12.3 A motivational framework

Feature	Remarks
Value-driven	It is vital that basic beliefs and values concerning what the organisation stands for should be communicated to all employees by managers who speak with one voice. Managers take the process of inculcating values seriously and preach it using analogy and metaphor rather than more direct methods.
Simultaneous loose-tight properties	Individuals are encouraged to challenge, debate and engage in innovation and entrepreneurship but these activities are the means. The ends are highly prescribed through adherence to basic beliefs, which are strongly reinforced by the cultural web. Workers are empowered but within tight confines.
People-orientated	People, who have the capacity to be extremely creative and flexible, are regarded as the greatest asset of excellent companies and a family atmosphere is frequently engendered. People are treated with respect and are well trained but are expected to perform.
Entrepreneurship	A critical feature of excellent companies is their ability to create an entrepreneurial orientation. This state of affairs is promoted by granting autonomy to the individual and 'product champions' are encouraged to run their own 'independent businesses' under the corporate umbrella. Entrepreneurship is also fostered by intense, open and informal communication facilitated by the provision of flip charts, whiteboards and tables in many locations throughout the organisation.
Customer and action-focused	Excellent organisations believe that the customer is king and that customers can be a fine source of new ideas. Excellent firms have a bias for action rather than analysis. Complex jobs are broken down into manageable bits and small is beautiful: it assists the management of units and creates a sense of ownership.
'Stick to the knitting'	Excellent firms stick to what they know well. They do not move readily into uncharted industrial sectors and, if they do, they first test the water adequately.

Source: Based on T. Peters and R. H. Waterman, *In Search of Excellence* (London: Harper and Row, 1982).

many organisations, but many other authors are less sure about the possibility of changing culture to order.[67] Even those authors who consider that cultural change is important and feasible believe that it is a long-term endeavour which requires leadership backed up by the other elements of the cultural web.

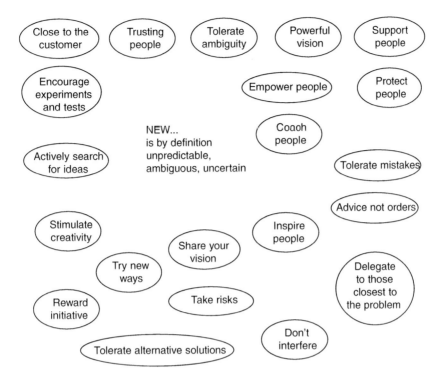

Figure 12.1 Manager mindset and behaviour for innovation

Source: Slightly modified from © The ForeSight Group Diagram, S Hamngatan 37, 41106 Göteborg, Sweden.

A new mindset

It is important for managers to set the tone and adopt a new mindset if they want all employees to act entrepreneurially, but as with culture, it is unlikely that they can produce innovation to order. In a real sense they must empower their innovative personnel rather than exercise power over them. Hales notes that much endeavour by managers is geared towards overcoming resistance to their authority and, in spite of a host of techniques such as participative management, quality circles and incentive schemes, many managers still exercise an autocratic form of power over others. However, he notes that many organisations are recognising that power in the sense of 'transformative capacity' or 'power to ...' now resides in the interdependence which is characteristic of work organisations.[68] For innovation and enterprise, 'power to ...' is more important than 'power over'.

Many of the attitudes, behaviours and organisational arrangements which support innovation are presented by Sven Atterhed and his colleagues, from the ForeSight Group, as in Figure 12.1.

Flexibility, experimentation, empowerment and risk taking are crucial in engendering an innovative spirit and capacity in mature organisations. Imported techniques can assist, but Atterhed argues that such mechanisms will achieve little if managers still try to reduce uncertainty and protect existing practices. He suggests that it is important to have a 'managerial mindset and behaviour that encourages enterprise and innovation and equips people to be open to the new'.[69] The new mindset 'requests and requires' that innovation be the responsibility of all. For Atterhed this will not happen unless management develops a new mindset.

A modern study of entrepreneurial culture

Hornsby et al. note the increasing interest in entrepreneurial culture in recent years but argue that very few studies have empirically tested the existence of factors thought to be important in creating such a culture.[70] They reviewed the literature on those factors in the corporate environment which are conducive to corporate entrepreneurship and conclude that five are important:

- management support
- work discretion
- rewards/reinforcement
- time availability
- permeable organisational boundaries.

In view of some claims in the literature that the managerial culture is different in Canadian and US firms, the authors looked at the initiatives coming from 353 mid-level managerial workers from 12 Canadian firms and from 174 managers from six US firms. They asked respondents to complete a Corporate Entrepreneurship Assessment Instrument to discover if the five supporting mechanisms were present in the two countries. They also asked six open-ended questions to assess the extent of entrepreneurial behaviour. The questions referred to:

- the number of ideas suggested in the last six months
- the number of ideas which were implemented
- the number of ideas implemented without official organisational approval
- the amount of time spent thinking about new work-related ideas
- the number of times managers talked outside their own departments about new ideas
- the number of times managers bypassed normal channels to pursue an innovative idea.

The results revealed that there were no differences between the perceived entrepreneurial cultures in US and Canadian firms. Furthermore, there were no significant differences between the reported entrepreneurial behaviours of the US and Canadian managers, although the former had greater absolute scores on all six indicators of behaviour. There was a positive connection between work discretion, managerial support, rewards and low organisational boundaries. Results also indicated that, while there was no difference in the overall level of innovative behaviour in US and Canadian firms, US managers were more likely to respond to an encouraging corporate culture than Canadians. The authors speculated that the more security-conscious Canadian managers did not respond very positively to expressions of support for innovation from senior managers. This study is useful for its timely review of the literature but even more so for its operationalisation of key variables and the introduction of a cross-cultural perspective on this subject.

A similar pattern to the Canadian results was also found among Japanese managers within a major multinational. In a study of a small sample of Japanese managers within NEC, the prime concerns of the managers were with the traditional Japanese lack of acceptance of failure and low tolerance of risk.[71] As Helms indicates:

> The traditional Japanese 'sarariman' or salary man takes great pride in his title and position within the [organisation] which provides him with status in society, security and a social life. To many, venturing outside the corporation with the knowledge of how difficult or impossible it would be to get back in, would be akin to the highest of gambles, with personal, family, social, and financial status at stake.[72]

Networks

So far, corporate entrepreneurship has been described as largely an intraorganisational process, as that is the original essence of the concept. However, there are situations where inter-firm contact and co-operation can help the process, especially in terms of innovation. Firms can search for opportunities and try to realise them by developing products to meet market needs. If, however, having seen an opportunity, a business does not have the wherewithal to address it, it may help if it collaborates with one that can supply the missing component(s). This can also bring benefits of shared knowledge, reduced development and process costs, reduced risks of failure and knowledge of key benchmarks. In some markets it is also common for customers to initiate innovations.[73] Users are often the first to recognise a need and may then pass such information on to manufacturers, or use it in co-operation with them to develop an appropriate new product.

A level of collaboration has long characterised innovation, but it has been argued that inter-organisational co-operation is much more common in today's world. One reason argued for by Alter and Hage is that, with the pace of change in technology and markets, the risks in carrying out innovation have increased considerably.[74] Innovators need time to recoup development costs but, in current conditions, product life cycles may be too short to guarantee recovery. They also argue that the state plays an increasing role in much industrial innovation. Often it encourages lots of players to get involved and promotes collaborative practices to let many of the players share in the benefits. Porter argues against encouraging joint ventures between domestic competitors, because this reduces the incentive to maintain a competitive advantage. However collaboration and the development of long-term relationships with customers and suppliers can help to reduce costs and enhance competitiveness.

Such inter-organisational relationships, however, are unlikely to develop instantaneously. Parties must be sensitive to one another and feel that the others have something of use to them. They must also communicate to explain their needs and examine possibilities for exchange. A degree of consensus is also important. They must have reasonably compatible values and be able to work problems through by means of 'adjustment and compromise: a process that entails negotiating and bargaining'.[75]

Market uncertainties, experience in developing long-term relationships, and the complexity of the innovation process have led many firms to form links with a number of outside organisations when generating ideas, developing prototypes and testing markets. As James notes, 'The significant change in the business environment ... has changed the focus of alliance strategies (for innovation) to the point where they are now becoming the rule rather than the exception.'[76]

When smaller is an advantage

Introducing corporate entrepreneurship into bigger businesses, and making them more entrepreneurial and innovative and thus more like small businesses in their market responses, is not always the best way to take advantage of new business opportunities, however. As Charles Handy argues, economic prosperity needs both

---

ILLUSTRATION 12.4

The rules of the new economy

The rules as applied to our economies by traditional economists have changed. In the old economies, convergence within and across countries was possible as, in the longer term, capital migrated to lower wage areas. But there is no such convergence in a knowledge economy. Knowledge doesn't spread so easily. It tends to stay 'regional', as evidenced by what some have alluded to as the knowledge 'black holes' of Silicon Valley, Route 128, Atlanta and Austin in the United States and of Cambridge in the UK. Knowledge develops within and through close personal networks which are facilitated by geographical proximity. Indeed it is also now well known that 'business angels', who are important to high-growth start-ups, concentrate their investments within easily accessible distances. It is an apparent paradox that in an era in which data and information can be transmitted globally in fractions of a second, knowledge is relatively immobile and still requires geographic proximity for its spread.

Factor	New economy	Old economy
Unit of analysis	The entrepreneur	The plant/business
Policy instrument	Knowledge infrastructure	Interest rates
Entry criteria	Knowledge (available to all)	Financial capital (available to a few)
Growth drivers	Entrepreneurs	Managers
Source of competitiveness	Knowledge and value added	Economies of scale and cost reduction
Infrastructure required	Knowledge infrastructure	Transport infrastructure Labour supply
Convergence	Knowledge stays regional	Capital moves to lower wage areas

It is interesting to note that in this context countries can be placed within one of three categories:

- Creators of knowledge: about 30 countries are, according to the number of patents filed, significant creators of knowledge.

- Users of knowledge: many countries, such as the former Soviet Bloc countries, use knowledge but do not appear to create it.

- Others: those countries which are neither creators nor users of knowledge, such as parts of Africa and Latin America.

To convert from a 'user' to a 'creator' it is necessary to have an infrastructure that both generates and applies knowledge. As well as universities and research institutes, that also requires, for example, market researchers and marketing organisations as well as knowledge-based businesses.

elephants and fleas.[77] Sometimes it is better to be a flea. Other examples of this can be found with high technology businesses and in the 'new economy' outlined in Illustration 12.4.

ICT and e-business

The 'new economy' has also been described as the knowledge economy. The term 'new economy' is used to encompass issues of the globalisation of business, the expansion of information and communication technology (ICT) and the increasing importance and pervasiveness of knowledge.[78] Indeed many now see the availability of appropriate knowledge as a key driver of competitiveness, superseding the availability of raw materials, energy or labour, which had been predominant. Information technologies, which facilitate the application of knowledge, promote new business methods and specialisations. The new economic conditions promote new opportunities for enterprise.

Knowledge, in comparison with other products of business, is also strange stuff. It can be sold, and yet still be retained by the seller after it has been sold. It can be shared indefinitely but not diluted. It can be valuable and, as intellectual property, its ownership can be protected, yet it is of most use when it is fresh, and it is hard to keep because if it is retained for too long it tends to leak out. It can belong to a company but it resides in the employees and, if they leave, it can go too.

The emergence of these new forms of economic activity creates new opportunities which are often taken up by small businesses, rather than through innovation in bigger businesses. As already noted, small businesses, especially at the time of their start-up, are often more flexible than big businesses and their speed of response is generally quicker. They can therefore occupy, and capitalise on, a niche opportunity more quickly than their bigger rivals. Their owner-managers do not have other operations to distract them and typically are fully committed to the new venture depending, as they often do, on it alone for their future. However it is not just small businesses which have made use of the Internet. Home shopping and airline booking are examples used by many people of bigger businesses using the technology to gain or maintain their market positions.

The introduction of ICT has been likened to the earlier introduction of the telephone or of the railways in the opportunities it offers and in its potential to change business. For other businesses the opportunities, Burns suggests, lie in the following areas:[79]

- The opportunity to establish the network through which other traders can gain access to the new marketplace. Businesses doing this can be likened to the railway companies which built and operated the early railways and may, like them, find that it is not in reality a source of long-term profit.
- The opportunity to use the technology to do business by becoming a trader in the e-marketplace, like the businesses which used the facilities provided by the railway companies to do their work better. These opportunities can in turn be of two sorts:
  - the opportunity to establish innovative trading businesses which exploit the unique characteristics of the Internet. These are businesses which could not exist without the Internet.

– the opportunity to use the Internet to reach a global market and to compete there on price, on the differentiated qualities of the product or service, or by focusing even more effectively on particular market segments. This is done by businesses which could probably operate without the Internet but which use it to reach a wider market.

It is the last of these areas of opportunity which will in particular have implications for businesses which are not themselves e-businesses. While they may not be using the Internet, many of their customers are, and by doing so they are finding other suppliers. Almost all businesses therefore need to see what ICT is doing to their market and to take appropriate steps to respond. Those steps may involve the businesses concerned using the Internet themselves, by becoming 'connected'. However in some cases it might be appropriate to change, or even end, the business. The growth of low-cost airlines with online direct booking of flights has taken business away from travel agents and they will not get it back just by using the Internet themselves.

The new economy is nevertheless an area in which it can help to be small and where there do appear to be disadvantages of scale, and there are other areas where this applies also. As a result some entrepreneurs prefer to grow the totality of their portfolio not by growing their existing business or businesses, but by forming new businesses. Richard Branson is an example of someone who has grown Virgin by new ventures, not by organisational control, but by his interest and the Virgin label. However not all of this 'growth' would be seen from a business-centred perspective because it arises not only from growth in the businesses themselves but from new business formations.

Conclusions

Innovation is at the heart of the spirit of enterprise. Practically all firms are born from a development which is innovative, at least in comparison with their existing competitors in the marketplace. If they are subsequently to survive and develop, however, firms must constantly innovate – even if only gradually. In this respect, technical advances are not themselves sufficient to ensure success. Innovation also means anticipating the needs of the market, offering additional quality or services, organising efficiently, mastering details and keeping costs under control.

EU Green Paper on innovation[80]

Small businesses are a reservoir, a source, both for the creation of jobs and for the development of diversity within economies. Capitalising on this reservoir means growing those small businesses and maintaining the attitudes of enterprise in the business upon which that growth will depend. That internal enterprise, in larger businesses, requires some different approaches from the enterprise which typically starts a small business. It has been called corporate entrepreneurship.

THE KEY POINTS OF CHAPTER 12

- Growth in the early stages of a small business can be seen as a natural extension of its original formation, but when a business reaches a steady state different attitudes can prevail and further change can be resisted. Maintaining growth in a more mature business can therefore require a different approach, a process of internal enterprise, which has been called 'intrapreneurship' or more recently 'corporate entrepreneurship'.

- Corporate entrepreneurship is therefore connected to the concepts of entrepreneurship, enterprise and innovation. Entrepreneurship has typically described the drive that starts a business, and a similar drive is needed to maintain its advance. Innovation is the successful development of competitive advantage and, as such, can be said to be the key to corporate entrepreneurship. That innovation can take several forms: innovation in processes and methods, innovation in products or services, and innovation in work organisation. Entrepreneurship and innovation, applied to the continued development of a business, are still enterprise even if the business is a larger one.

- There are however inherent difficulties in corporate entrepreneurship. These are such that some writers on corporate entrepreneurship, or formerly on intrapreneurship, have contended that many large corporations will in practice survive only by restructuring their businesses as confederations of small businesses. There are barriers of human resistance to change, barriers of management roles and motivation, and barriers of organisational structures and systems. Size, per se, is not an impediment to entrepreneurship and innovation, but the attitude and methods that size can bring are.

- The process of corporate entrepreneurship itself has been analysed in terms of the roles a corporate entrepreneur must play, including those of entrepreneur, adventurer, innovator, leader, change agent, animateur and enabler, many of which do not fit in easily with a large company ethos. The structures that best support the processes of corporate entrepreneurship have also been considered, with recommendations for solid systematic investigations into the relevance of current products and procedures and into the process of modernisation.

- Some organisations, in industries such as computers, biomedical products, and management consulting, are constant problem solvers and innovators. Flexibility is the key to their success. They are also frequently knowledge based and have structural arrangements that are the antithesis of bureaucracy. Empowerment is important, as well as having the right mindset.

- Corporate entrepreneurship can be seen as a response by bigger businesses to some of the perceived advantages of small businesses. However, despite this, there are areas of business, such as those in the 'new economy', where small businesses sometimes really do seem to have an advantage. In that situation some entrepreneurs, instead of trying to grow their existing businesses by making them behave like small ones, increase their portfolios by starting new separate small businesses.

QUESTIONS, ESSAY AND DISCUSSION TOPICS

- What can enterprise add to big business?
- What are the differences between the practices and processes of creating a new independent venture and the launching of a subsidiary venture by an established firm?
- How would you define the terms 'corporate entrepreneurship' and 'intrapreneurship'?
- Identify and describe three broad approaches which encourage the development of innovative projects within large organisations.
- Describe the types of managerial role which are conducive to innovation in an organisation.
- What might be done to create an entrepreneurial ethos throughout an established organisation?
- What are the principal determinants of business culture?
- Contrast this with your national business environment.
- Can you identify in business terms another example of the successful 'flea'?
- What is the future for e-businesses?

Suggestions for further reading and information

C. Handy, *The Elephant and the Flea* (London: Hutchinson, 2001).

P. Burns, *Corporate Entrepreneurship: Building the Entrepreneurial Organisation*, 2nd edn (Basingstoke: Palgrave, 2008).

P. Drucker, *Innovation and Entrepreneurship* (London: Heinemann, 1985).

T. Elfring (ed.), *Corporate Entrepreneurship and Venturing: International Studies in Entrepreneurship*, Vol. 10, 2005 (Springer).

D. F. Kuratko and R. M. Hodgetts, *Entrepreneurship: A Contemporary Approach* (Orlando, FLA: Harcourt College Publishers, 2001), Chapter 6.

References

1. L. E. Greiner, 'Evolution and Revolution as Organisations Grow', *Harvard Business Review*, July–August (1972), pp. 40–7.
2. P. Drucker, 'Our Entrepreneurial Economy', *Harvard Business Review*, January–February (1984), pp. 59–64.
3. A. Genus, *The Management of Change* (London: Thomson Business Press, 1998).
4. D. Jones-Evans, 'Intrapreneurship', in *Enterprise and Small Business*, edited by S. Carter and D. Jones-Evans (Harlow: Financial Times/Prentice-Hall, 2000).
5. Genus, op cit., p. 5.
6. P. Drucker, *Innovation and Entrepreneurship* (London: Heinemann, 1985), p. 132.
7. G. Pinchot III, *Intrapreneuring: Why You Don't Have to Leave the Organisation to Become an Entrepreneur* (New York: Harper & Row, 1985).
8. See for example S. A. Zahra and J. G. Covin, 'Contextual Influences On the Corporate Entrepreneurship-Performance Relationship', *Journal of Business Venturing*, 10 (1995), pp. 43–58.

9. J. A. Timmons, *The Entrepreneurial Mind* (Andover: Brick House, 1989), p. 1.
10. A. A. Gibb, 'The Enterprise Culture and Education', *International Small Business Journal,* 11 (1993), pp. 11–34, at 16.
11. J. Curran and R. Burroughs, 'The Sociology of Petit Capitalism: A Trend Report', *Sociology,* 20 (1986), pp. 265–79, at p. 269.
12. Pinchot, op. cit., p. 46.
13. D. F. Kuratko and R. M. Hodgetts, *Entrepreneurship* (Fort Worth: Dryden Press, 1995), p. 95.
14. J. G. Covin and M. P. Miles, 'Corporate Entrepreneurship and the Pursuit of Competitive Advantage', *Entrepreneurship. Theory and Practice,* 23 (1999), pp. 47–66, at p. 51.
15. Covin and Miles, op cit.: 52.
16. S. Caird, 'How Important Is the Innovator for the Commercial Success of Innovative Products in SMEs?', *Technovation,* 14 (1994), pp. 71–83, at p. 81.
17. 'Green Paper on Innovation', *Bulletin of the European Union,* Supplement 5/95 (Brussels: ECSC-EC-EAEC, 1996).
18. S. Borins, 'Loose Cannons and Rule Breakers, or Enterprising Leaders? Some Evidence About Innovative Public Managers', *Public Administration Review,* 60 (2000), pp. 498–507.
19. J Wiklund, 'The Sustainability of the Entrepreneurial Orientation–Performance Relationship', *Entrepreneurship: Theory and Practice,* 24 (1999), pp. 37–48, at p. 41.
20. G. N. Chandler, C. Keller and D. W. Lyon, 'Unravelling the Determinants and Consequences of an Innovation-Supportive Organisational Culture', *Entrepreneurship: Theory and Practice,* 24 (2000), pp. 59–76.
21. D. Miller and P. H. Friesen, 'Innovation In Conservative and Entrepreneurial Firms: Two Models of Strategic Momentum', *Strategic Management Journal,* 3 (1982), pp. 1–25.
22. G. T. Lumpkin and G. G. Dess, 'Clarifying the Entrepreneurial Orientation Construct and Linking It To Performance', *Academy of Management Review,* 21 (1996), pp. 135–72.
23. K. H. Vesper, 'The Three Faces of Corporate Entrepreneurship: A Pilot Study', in *Frontiers of Entrepreneurial Research,* edited by J. A. Hornaday et al. (Wellesley, Mass.: Babson Colleges, 1984), pp. 294–320.
24. Covin and Miles, op. cit., p. 52.
25. S. A. Zahra, D. F. Jennings and D. F. Kuratko, 'The Antecedents and Consequences of Firm Level Entrepreneurship: The State of the Field', *Entrepreneurship: Theory and Practice,* 24 (1999), pp. 45–63.
26. For a short critical review of the strategic planning approach to change see Genus, op cit., pp. 15–25.
27. M. Porter, *Competitive Strategy* (New York: Free Press, 1980).
28. T. Heller, 'Loosely Coupled Systems for Corporate Entrepreneurship: Imagining and Managing the Innovation Project/Host Organisation Interface', *Entrepreneurship: Theory and Practice,* 24 (1999), pp. 25–31, at pp. 25–6.
29. J. G. Covin and D. P. Slevin 'A Conceptual Model of Entrepreneurship as Firm Behaviour', *Entrepreneurship: Theory and Practice,* 16 (1991), pp. 7–25.
30. B. Antoncic and R. D. Hisrich 'Corporate Entrepreneurship Contingencies and Organisational Wealth Creation', *Journal of Management Development,* 23 (2004), pp. 518–550.
31. J. S. Hornsby, D. F. Kuratko, and S. A. Zahra 'Middle Managers' Perception of the Internal Environment for Corporate Entrepreneurship: Assessing a Measurement Scale', *Journal of Business Venturing,* 17 (2002), pp. 253–273.
32. L. Clarke, *The Essence of Change* (Hemel Hempstead: Prentice-Hall, 1994).
33. G. Zaltman and R. Duncan, *Strategies for Planned Change* (New York: Wiley, 1977).
34. D. Jaffe, *Leading Change* (Washington, DC: NTL Workshop, 1999).
35. C. Handy, *The Age of Unreason* (London: Arrow, 1990).
36. Jones-Evans, op. cit., pp. 244–6.
37. H. Mintzberg, *The Structuring of Organisations* (Englewood Cliffs, NJ: Prentice-Hall, 1979).
38. H. H. Stevenson and D. E. Gumpert, 'The Heart of Entrepreneurship', in *The Entrepreneurial Venture,* edited by W. A. Sahlman and H. H. Stevenson (Boston, Mass.: Harvard Business School Press, 1993), pp. 9–25.
39. H. Mintzberg, *Power in and Around Organisations* (Englewood Cliffs, NJ: Prentice-Hall, 1983).
40. Borins, op. cit: 504.
41. Mintzberg (1979), op. cit., p. 233.
42. Ibid., p. 233.

43. P. Selznick, *Leadership in Administration* (New York: Harper & Row, 1957).
44. W. Starbuck, *Organisational Growth and Development* (Harmondsworth: Penguin, 1971).
45. Drucker (1985), op. cit., p. 137.
46. D. Miller, *The Icarus Paradox* (New York: Harper Business, 1992).
47. R. Lessem, *Intrapreneurship* (Aldershot: Gower, 1987).
48. Ibid., p. 7.
49. J. Sherwood, 'An Introduction to Organisational Development', in *Sensitivity Training and the Laboratory Approach,* edited by R. T. Golembiewski and A. Blumberg (New York: Peacock, 1973), at p. 431.
50. Drucker (1985), op. cit., p. 142.
51. Ibid., p. 156.
52. Jones-Evans, op. cit., pp. 247–51.
53. Jaffe, op. cit.
54. Jones-Evans, op. cit., p. 247.
55. T. Davenport, *Process Innovations: Reengineering Work Through Information Technology* (Boston, Mass.: Harvard Business School Press, 1993), p. 5.
56. D. B. Balkin and J. W. Logan, 'Reward Policies That Support Entrepreneurship', *Compensation and Benefit Review,* 20 (1988), pp. 18–25.
57. Miller and Friesen, op. cit.
58. J. D. Covin and D. P. Slevin, 'The Influence of Organisational Structure In the Utility of an Entrepreneurial Top Management Style', *Journal of Management Studies,* 25 (1988), pp. 217–34, at p. 222.
59. Mintzberg (1979), op. cit., p. 433.
60. Heller, op. cit:. 26.
61. Ibid.: 28.
62. See Genus, op. cit., pp. 28–33, for a critique of the organisational capabilities school.
63. I. Nonaka, 'The Knowledge-Creating Company', Harvard Business Review, November–December) (1991), pp. 96–104.
64. See J. Balogun and V. Hope-Hailey, *Exploring Strategic Change* (London: Prentice-Hall, 1999), pp. 48–52 for a discussion of the paradigm.
65. T. Peters and R. H. Waterman, *In Search of Excellence* (London: Harper and Row, 1982).
66. Genus, op. cit., p. 35.
67. See Genus, op. cit., pp. 36–8; C. Mabey, G. Salaman and J. Storey, *Strategic Human Resource Management* (Oxford: Blackwell, 1998), Chapters 15 and 16 for a discussion of culture.
68. C. Hales, *Managing Through Organisation* (London: Routledge, 1993), p. 44.
69. G. Haskins, 'Entrepreneurship Inside Corporations', *efmd Forum,* 2 (1994), pp. 12–15. The ForeSight Group, 1990; diagram and quotation at p. 15.
70. J. S. Hornsby, D. F. Kuratko and R. V. Montagno, 'Perceptions of Internal Factors for Corporate Entrepreneurship: A Comparison of Canadian and US Managers', *Entrepreneurship: Theory and Practice,* 24 (1999), pp. 9–29.
71. M. Helms, 'Japanese managers: Their candid views on Entrepreneurship', *Competitiveness Review,* 13(1) (2003), pp. 24–34.
72. Helms, op. cit.
73. See W. G. Biemans, *Managing Innovation Within Networks* (London: Routledge, 1993) for a discussion of networks and innovation.
74. C. Alter and J. Hage, *Organisations Working Together* (Newbury Park, Calif.: Sage, 1993).
75. A. H. Van de Ven and D. Ferry, *Measuring and Assessing Organisations* (New York: Wiley, 1980), p. 312.
76. B. G. James, 'Alliance: The New Strategic Focus', *Long Range Planning,* 18 (1985), pp. 76–81, at p. 76.
77. C. Handy, *The Elephant and the Flea* (London: Hutchinson, 2001).
78. E. Garnsey, 'Knowledge-Based Enterprise In A New Economy', in *New Economy: New Entrepreneurs* (Zoetermeer, the Netherlands: EIM Business and Policy Research, January 2001), pp. 51–69, at pp. 51, 75.
79. Based on P. Burns, *Entrepreneurship and Small Business* (Basingstoke: Palgrave (now Palgrave Macmillan), 2001), pp. 177, 178.
80. 'Green Paper on Innovation', *Bulletin of the European Union,* op. cit., p. 19.

CHAPTER 13

The international and global context

LEARNING OBJECTIVES

After studying this chapter, you should be able to:

- define and distinguish between internationalization and globalization
- explain the factors that drive globalization
- describe and demonstrate the application of Yip's framework for analysing the extent of globalization in an industry and market
- explain the major global strategy alternatives
- describe the modes of international market entry

Introduction and chapter overview

With the advent of the internet and the ability of organizations to communicate and trade globally, independent of size, internationalization and the global context are central to many businesses. One of the most important considerations in the development and implementation of a strategy is the extent to which the organization's activities, products and markets are spread across geographical regions. While some businesses will be predominantly domestically based, others operate in many countries, and others still operate in almost all regions of the world. This chapter is concerned with a discussion of the key issues surrounding the *why* and *how* questions: why do organizations expand in this way and how do they go about it? The *why* questions are covered in a discussion of the factors that drive increased internationalization. The *how* questions are answered in a discussion of the market entry options.

Defining internationalization and globalization

Business has been international since the days of the ancient Egyptians, Phoenicians and Greeks. Merchants travelled the known world to sell products manufactured in their home country and to return with products from other countries. Initially, international business simply took the form of exporting and importing. The term 'international' describes any business that carries out some of its activities across national boundaries.

Globalization, on the other hand, is more than simply internationalization. A large multinational company is not necessarily a global business. In order for a business to become global in its operations, we would usually expect a number of important characteristics to be in place:

1. Global organizations take advantage of the increasing trend towards a convergence of customer needs and wants across international borders – fast foods, soft drinks or consumer electronics are good examples (see Levitt, 1983).
2. Global organizations compete in industries that are globalized. In some sectors, successful competition necessitates a presence in almost every part of the world in order to effectively compete in its global market.
3. Global organizations can – and do – locate their value-adding activities in those places in the world where the greatest competitive advantages can be made. This might mean, for example, shifting production to a low-cost region or moving design to a country with skilled labour in the key skill area.
4. Global organizations are able to integrate and coordinate their international activities between countries. The mentality of 'home base, foreign interests' that has been so prevalent among traditional multinational companies is eroded in the culture of global businesses. They have learned to effectively manage and control the various parts of the business across national borders and despite local cultural differences.

The development of an organization's global strategy, therefore, will be concerned with global competences, global marketing and global configuration and coordination of its value-adding activities.

Multinational and transnational companies are usually large and have direct investments in one or more foreign countries. The foreign investments may be part-shareholdings, but more usually are wholly owned subsidiaries. The difference is in the degree to which the foreign investments are coordinated.

KEY CONCEPTS

A **transnational company** has a high degree of coordination in its international interests. It usually has a strategic centre that manages the global operation such that all parts act in accordance with a centrally managed strategic purpose.

A **multinational company** is an international company whose foreign interests are not coordinated from a strategic centre.

Globalization of markets and industries

Levitt and market homogenization

It was Levitt (1983) who first argued that changes in technology, societies, economies and politics were producing a 'global village'. By this he meant that consumer needs in many previously separate national markets were becoming increasingly similar throughout the world. Developments in transport have not only made it easier to move products and materials between countries but they have also resulted in a huge increase in the amount that people travel around the world. This travel educates people to the products available in other countries and, on their return home, they often wish to have access to those products and services from overseas. This trend has been reinforced by changes in IT, particularly those related to cinema and television, which have been important in some aspects of cultural convergence. The development of the WTO (World Trade Organization), and its predecessor GATT (the General Agreement on Tariffs and Trade), has resulted in huge reductions in the trade barriers between countries since the Second World War. Rising income levels and cheaper travel throughout many parts of the world have also given economic impetus to the development of global markets.

It is not only markets that are, in many cases, becoming more global. Industries are also becoming more global. The value chains of businesses in many industries span the globe. In the case of the fashion house Yves Saint Laurent, for example, design and marketing are concentrated in France, while products are mainly manufactured in East Asia. Organizations concentrate some of their activities in locations where they hope to obtain cost, quality or other advantages. Other activities, like distribution, are also often dispersed around the world. The way a business configures its activities across national borders can be an important source of competitive advantage. The spread of an organization's value-adding activities around the world also means that there are important advantages to be gained from effective integration and coordination of activities.

GURU GUIDE

Theodore Levitt was born in 1925 in Vollmerz, Germany. He joined Harvard Business School in 1959.

His influential works were in marketing and his 1975 article 'Marketing myopia' is widely credited as marking the beginning of the modern marketing movement. He is the author of *The Marketing Imagination*, and is a bestselling author whose works have been translated into eleven languages. Professor Levitt is also credited for coining the term 'globalization', although it is more accurate to say he popularized an already existing term. He is the author of numerous articles on various subjects including economics, management, marketing and politics, and was the editor of the *Harvard Business Review* from 1985 to 1989. He won several honours and accolades, including the Academy of Management award for outstanding business book, the George Gallup Award for Marketing Excellence and the William M. McFeely Award of the International Management Council for major contributions to management. He was a four-time winner of the McKinsey award for best annual article in the *Harvard Business Review*. He died in 2006.

Levitt was the first management theorist to emphasize the importance of marketing at a time when budgetary control and productivity were the main factors. The argument that industry should be a customer-satisfying process and not a goods-producing process has changed the way business is conducted and emphasized the role of consumers in ensuring growth for organizations and economies.

Porter and multi-domestic markets

Porter (1990) argues that industries can be either global or multi-domestic. **Multi-domestic industries** are those where competition in each nation is essentially independent. He gives the example of consumer banking where a bank's domestic reputation and resources in one nation have tended to have little effect on its success in other countries. The international banking industry is, Porter agues, essentially a collection of domestic industries.

Multi-domestic industries are those where competition in each nation is essentially independent.

Global industries are those in which competition is global. The consumer electronics industry is a good example, where companies like Philips, Sony and Panasonic compete in almost all countries of the world. The implication would appear to be that businesses should adopt a global strategy in global industries and a multi-local strategy in multi-domestic markets. Yet the situation is not so simple as this. Even markets like consumer banking are becoming more global.

Global industries are those in which competition is global.

It is also the case that the degree of globalization of an industry or market may not be uniform. In other words, some aspects of an industry or market may be indicative of globalization, while others may be indicative of localization. The degree of globalization of an industry can be assessed using Yip's globalization driver framework (1992). This is a more useful framework than Porter's because it makes it possible to evaluate both the overall degree of globalization of an industry and which features of the industry are more or less global in nature.

Globalization drivers: Yip's framework

Yip (1992) argues that it is not simply the case that industries are 'global' or 'not global', rather that they can be global in some respects and not in others. Yip's globalization driver framework (Figure 13.1) makes it possible to identify which aspects of an industry are global and which aspects differ locally. Analysis using this framework can play an important role in shaping the global strategy of a business. A global strategy, according to Yip, will be global in many respects but may also include features that are locally oriented.

Yip (1992, p. 15) argues that 'To achieve the benefits of globalization, the managers of a worldwide business need to recognize when industry conditions provide the opportunity to use global strategy levers.' Table 13.1 shows a breakdown of the globalization drivers.

Yip's four drivers that determine the nature and extent of globalization in an industry are market drivers, cost drivers, government drivers and competitive drivers (Figure 13.1). We will consider each of these in turn.

Figure 13.1 Globalization driver framework

Source: Adapted from Yip, 1992

Table 13.1 A summary of the globalization drivers

Market globalization drivers	**Cost globalization drivers**
Common customer needs	Global scale economies
Global customers	Steep experience curve effect
Global distribution channels	Sourcing efficiencies
Transferable marketing techniques	Favourable logistics
Presence in lead countries	Differences in country costs (including exchange rates)
	High product development costs
	Fast-changing technology
Government globalization drivers	**Competitive globalization drivers**
Favourable trade policies	High exports and imports
Compatible technical standards	Competitors from different continents
Common marketing regulations	Interdependence of countries
Government-owned competitors and customers	Competitors globalized
Host government concerns	

Market globalization drivers

The degree of globalization of a market will depend on the extent to which there are common customer needs, global customers, global distribution channels, transferable marketing and lead countries. It is not simply a case of a market being global or not global. Managers must seek to establish which, if any, aspects of their market are global.

Common customer needs

Probably the single most important market globalization driver is the extent to which customers in different countries share the same need or want for a product. The extent of shared need will depend on cultural, economic, climatic, legal and other similarities and differences. There are numerous examples of markets where customer needs are becoming more similar, such as motor vehicles, soft drinks, fast foods, consumer electronics and computers.

The importance of McDonald's, Burger King and Pizza Hut in fast food, Coca-Cola and Pepsi in soft drinks and Sony and Panasonic in consumer electronics are all illustrative of converging customer needs in certain markets. Levitt (1983) refers to this similarity of tastes and preference as increasing 'market homogenization' – all

Common customer need: desktop PC

markets demanding the same products, regardless of their domestic culture and traditional preferences.

Global customers and channels

Global customers purchase products or services in a coordinated way from the best global sources. Yip identifies two types of global customers:

1. **national global customers** – customers who seek the best suppliers in the world and then use the product or service in one country, for example national defence purchasers who try to source the highest specification weapons and other military hardware from around the world for use by the domestic armed forces.
2. **multinational global customers** – they similarly seek the best suppliers in the world but then use the product or service obtained in many countries, for example transnational corporations source components for their products globally to ensure optimal quality standards.

National global customers seek the best suppliers in the world and then use the product or service in one country.

Multinational global customers seek the best suppliers in the world but then use the product or service obtained in many countries.

Examples of markets with global customers include automobile components, advertising (advertising agencies) and electronics. Nissan, for example, manufactures cars in a number of different locations around the world including Japan, the UK and Spain, but sources many components for all these locations globally. Businesses serving global customers must 'be present in all the customers' major markets' (Yip, 1992).

GURU GUIDE

George Yip was born in Hong Kong in 1948 and grew up in Burma and England. He was a professor of strategic and international management at London Business School and between 2003 to 2006 he was a senior fellow at the Advanced Institute of Management Research. He has also held professorial posts at Cambridge, UCLA and Harvard Business School. His business experience spans marketing and product management, consulting and innovation. He was the vice president and director of research and innovation at Capgemini Consulting and his business experience also includes management stints with Unilever and PricewaterhouseCoopers. He is currently the dean of the Rotterdam School of Management, Erasmus University, the Netherlands.

Professor Yip is a distinguished figure in global strategy and marketing management and his current research interests include internationalization, innovation and global customers. He is a fellow of the Academy of International Business and the International Academy of Management and *The Times Higher Education Supplement* ranked him among the 12 most successful academic consultants in the UK in any discipline (2006).

Alongside global customers, there are sometimes global, or more often regional, distribution channels which serve global customers. Global customers and channels will contribute towards the development of a global market.

Transferable marketing

Transferable marketing describes the extent to which elements of the marketing mix, like brand names and promotions, can be used globally without local adaptations. Clearly, when adaptation is not required, it is indicative of a global market. In this way, brands like McDonald's, Coca-Cola and Nike are used globally. Yet advertising for Nike can be both global and locally adapted, according the popularity of different sports in different parts of the world. If marketing is transferable, it will favour a global market.

Transferable marketing describes the extent to which elements of the marketing mix, like brand names and promotions, can be used globally without local adaptations.

Lead countries

When certain countries lead in particular industries, 'it becomes critical for global competitors to participate in these lead countries in order to be exposed to the sources of innovation' (Porter, 1990). Lead countries are those that are ahead in product and/or process innovation in their industry. These lead countries help to produce global standards and hence global industries and markets. Japan, for example, has leadership in the consumer electronics industry and leads developments within it, while the USA is the lead country in microcomputer and internet software.

Cost globalization drivers

The potential to reduce costs by global configuration of value-adding activities is an important spur towards the globalization of certain industries. If there are substantial cost advantages to be obtained, an industry will tend to be global.

Global scale economies

When an organization serves a global market, it is able to gain much greater economies of scale than if it serves only domestic or regional markets. Similarly, serving global markets also gives considerable potential for economies of scope. Thus businesses such as Procter & Gamble and Unilever, which produce household products like detergents, gain huge economies of scope in research, product development and marketing.

KEY CONCEPTS

Economies of scale describe the benefits that are gained when increasing volume results in lower unit costs. Although economies of scale can arise in all parts of the value chain, it is probably best understood by illustrating it using purchasing as an example. An individual purchasing one single item will pay more per item than a large company buying many of the same item. It is said that the purchaser who is able to purchase in bulk (because of the size and structure of the buyer) enjoys scale economies over smaller organizations who buy in at lower volumes.

Economy of scope describes the benefits that can arise in one product or market area as a result of activity in another. For example, research into material properties for the benefit of the NASA space programme (one area of scope) has resulted in advances in other areas such as fabrics, non-stick pans and coatings for aircraft. Organizations that invest heavily in R&D (such as pharmaceutical companies) are among those who are always seeking economies of scope – seeking to use breakthroughs in one area to benefit another.

Steep experience curve effect

When there is a steep learning curve in production and marketing, businesses serving global markets will tend to obtain the greatest benefits. In many high-tech and service industries, there are steep learning curves yielding the greatest benefits to global businesses.

The idea of the learning curve was first introduced in 1885 by Hermann Ebbinghaus, a German psychologist who pioneered the experimental study of memory. It has been used in many areas of life, not just in business, where it is often termed the 'experience curve'. The **learning curve** describes the rate at which an individual or an organization learns to perform a particular task. The gradient of the beginning of the curve is referred to as its 'steepness' and is the most important part. The steeper this first part, the quicker the task is being learned. The general shape of a learning curve is described as 'exponential' because the gradient usually decreases along its length as the time taken to perform the task decreases as those performing the task become more accomplished at it.

The **learning curve** describes the rate at which an individual or an organization learns to perform a particular task.

Let us take an example. When a lecturer sits down to mark a batch of exam papers, he must first familiarize himself with the questions and the answers that are expected. Having done that, the first paper will take the longest of all to mark. When the lecturer has internalized all the questions and answers, the time taken to mark each paper will reduce until the last few papers take the shortest time of all (Figures 13.2a, 13.2b).

Sourcing efficiencies

If there are efficiency gains to be made by centralized sourcing carried out globally, this will drive an industry towards globalization. Businesses like those in sports apparel and fashion clothing benefit from global sourcing to obtain the lowest prices and highest quality standards.

Favourable logistics

If transportation costs comprise a relatively high proportion of sales value, there will be every incentive to concentrate production in a few large facilities. If transport costs are relatively small, such as with consumer electronic goods, production can be located in several (or many) locations, which are chosen on the basis of other cost criteria such as land or labour costs.

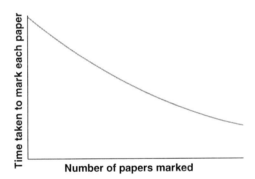

Figure 13.2a Shallow learning curve: a slow learner

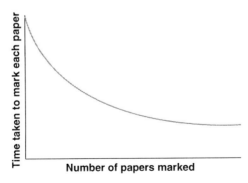

Figure 13.2b Steep learning curve: a fast learner

Differences in country costs

Production costs (raw materials and labour) vary from country to country, and, like favourable logistics, this can stimulate globalization. Thus, countries with lower production costs will tend to attract businesses to locate their activities in the country. Many Asian countries have been chosen as centres for production because of their favourable cost conditions. Although countries like Thailand suffered in some respects because of the devaluation of their currency in 1997–98, from the point of view of being chosen as centres for production, they have benefited. Currently, the value of the pound against the euro may have similar effects for Britain.

Fast-changing technology and high product development costs

Product life cycles are shortening as the pace of technological change increases. At the same time, R&D costs are increasing in many industries. These product development costs can only be recouped by high sales in global markets. Domestic markets simply do not yield the volumes of sales required to cover high R&D costs. Thus industries like pharmaceuticals and automobiles face rapidly changing technology and hypercompetition, together with high development costs. As a consequence, they must operate in global markets to ensure the volumes of sales necessary to recoup these costs.

Government globalization drivers

Since the Second World War, many governments have taken individual and collective action to reduce global trade barriers.

Favourable trade policies

The WTO, and its predecessor GATT, has done much to reduce trade barriers, which, in the past, hindered the globalization of many industries. Although there are still significant trade barriers in certain areas, the movement towards freedom of trade has been substantial, thus favouring globalization. The growth of customs unions and 'single markets' such as the European Union (EU) and the North American Free Trade Area (NAFTA) have also made an important contribution in this regard.

Compatible technical standards and common marketing regulations

Many of the differences in technical standards between countries that hindered globalization in the past have been reduced. For example, telecommunications standards, which have traditionally differed between countries, are increasingly being superseded by international standards. Similarly, standards are converging in the pharmaceutical, airline and computing industries, which makes it easier to produce globally accepted products.

There remain important differences in advertising regulations between countries, with UK regulations among the strictest. Generally, however, these differences are being eroded and this is expected to favour greater globalization.

Government-owned competitors and customers

Government-owned competitors, which often enjoy state subsidies, can act as a stimulus to globalization as they frequently compete with other global competitors, thus being forced to become more efficient and global market oriented. On the other hand, government-owned customers tend to favour domestic suppliers, which can act as a barrier to globalization. The privatization of many state-owned businesses in many European countries has reduced this barrier to globalization.

Host government concerns

The attitudes and policies of host government concerns can either hinder or favour globalization. In certain circumstances, host governments may favour the entry of global businesses into domestic industries and markets, which will assist globalization. For example, the UK government has, in recent years, done much to attract inward investment by Japanese and Korean companies. The more governments that espouse such policies, the greater the globalization of an industry. In other cases, host governments will seek to protect industries that they see as strategically important and will attempt to prevent the entry of foreign businesses.

Competitive globalization drivers

The greater the strength of the competitive drivers, the greater the tendency for an industry to globalize. Global competition in an industry will become more intense when:

- there is a high level of import and export activity between countries
- the competitors in the industry are widely spread (they will often be on different continents)
- the economies of the countries involved are interdependent
- competitors in the industry are already globalized.

High exports and imports

The higher the level of exports and imports of products and services, the greater the pressure for globalization of an industry.

Competitors from different continents

The more countries are represented in an industry and the more widely spread they are, the greater the likelihood of globalization.

Interdependence of countries

If national economies are already relatively interdependent, this will act as a stimulus for increased globalization. Such interdependence may arise through multiple trading links in other industries, being a part of a single market or being in a shared political alliance.

Competitors globalized

If a competitor is already globalized and employing a global strategy, there will be pressure on other businesses in the industry to globalize as well. Globalization in the automotive industry is high because of the pressure on organizations to compete globally. An automobile manufacturer will struggle to survive if it only serves domestic markets.

Yip's globalization driver framework provides an extremely useful tool for analysing the degree of globalization of an industry or market. Equally, it makes possible an understanding of which particular aspects of an industry or market are global and

CASE STUDY   Empire Supermarkets

Empire Supermarkets (ES) is one of the world's largest supermarket and department store chains, with activities in 11 countries. The company was founded by an agricultural cooperative as an independent outlet for its food products in Atlanta, Georgia, in the southern USA in 1950. ES found that there was a large, ready and more or less assured high-volume market for good food products at reasonable prices. By cutting out the middleman and wholesalers, ES was able to ensure speed of delivery, price advantages and quality assurance from an early stage of development. ES quickly expanded across the whole state of Georgia, and by the mid-1960s, it had stores in every state of the USA.

Now a major force in food retailing, ES started to expand its product range and its locations. The first out-of-country stores were opened in Canada in 1965 and Mexico in 1967. On 1 January 1970, ES opened its 10,000th outlet. Supported by a massive marketing campaign, ES expanded further. Over the next two decades, ES opened over 500 stores in Canada, and 200 in Mexico. ES also began to open town centre stores in the US, under the brand 'ES Central'. The company greatly expanded its product and service ranges, diversifying into clothes, household and garden goods, financial services and even car sales. This meant a major refurbishment of many hundreds of the company's existing stores. The refurbishments cost well over $4bn; however, subsequent results showed that the returns generated were in the order of ten times those that had been projected before the refurbishments went ahead.

However, this did not satisfy the growth demands from the company's major backers. So a new CEO was hired, Francis Belasco, a Canadian national who was recruited from Walmart, where he had made a name for himself as something of a retail guru. Under the leadership of Belasco, ES now looked towards the prosperous markets of Western Europe for further opportunities.

The initiative was given great publicity. The grand strategy was that there was to be a whole new retail world for the people of Europe – good quality food and goods at reasonable prices. This was based on ES's long-standing ability to command the supply side, and use its sheer volumes of demand to be able to guarantee steady long-term business to all its suppliers. It was the assurance of an effective supply side that had given ES its life, as the original cooperative had created it to ensure regular outlets and business volumes for its own produce.

The promise of quality food and a large and expanding range of other goods at affordable prices became the promise on which the customers of Western Europe would be lured away from Tesco and Asda in the UK, and Carrefour, Aldi and Lidl in Continental Europe. After all, all these goods were known to be much more expensive in Western Europe than in North America. ES began a programme of prime site acquisitions in France, Germany and Spain, and building work duly commenced. Belasco and everyone else involved looked forward to the same success that had been enjoyed in North America.

Exactly three years after the first announcement of the venture, ES opened its first 500 European stores on the same day. This was accompanied by a Europe-wide marketing, sales and promotional campaign, which generated major media and public interest. There was a huge, initially favourable response, and success appeared assured. Plans were drawn up for an expansion programme that would make ES a supermarket and department store giant in all the EU countries, and feasibility studies were commissioned for establishing a presence in Japan, Korea, China and India.

However, problems started to appear. ES struggled to gain the promised foothold in the UK and Europe. When they arrived to open their first stores, ES managers found that the main UK and European supermarkets and department store chains were already delivering many of the promises that ES were making. The European companies were themselves expanding all over the EU, establishing their own presence in the major locations of Central and Eastern Europe. Some were opening up new ventures in Asia, the Middle East and even North America. After all, the European companies had been given three years' notice of intent, and so they had plenty of time to prepare a response.

The goods and services on offer at the European supermarkets were also found to be substandard. The European giants had been given plenty of time to develop command of their own major existing and familiar suppliers. ES was therefore faced with having to find alternatives, and when it became apparent that ES was going to need them for a long time, supply side costs on the European venture rose sharply. Matters came to a serious pitch when one of ES's suppliers of plastic goods was caught dumping toxic effluent into the Danube, and another supplier of clothing and textiles was found to be using unpaid child labour. The resulting adverse publicity from both cases all but destroyed the venture.

So after the initial interest, customers and consumers went back to their own familiar outlets. The ES venture persisted for five years, but it never gained any commercially viable foothold, and earlier this year, it was closed down. The sites were sold off and ES returned to America. The European venture had cost a total of $38bn. Belasco was called before ES's major backers, who now demanded an explanation.

Case study questions

1. What has gone wrong with Empire Supermarkets' expansion plans and why? What are the main general lessons for any CEO, company or organization that seeks to become a global or international player?
2. What pressures demanded that ES went overseas? How do you assess and, where necessary, counter these pressures?
3. What other factors need to be taken into account when you do seek to drive into new markets and locations?

which aspects are localized. Each of the drivers must be analysed for the industry and market under consideration and the results of the analysis will play an important role in assisting managers to form the global strategy of their organization. The results will help to determine which features of the strategy are globally standardized and which features are locally adapted. Yip developed the concept of 'total global strategy' based on his globalization driver framework.

Yip's stages in a total global strategy

Yip (1992) argues that a successful global strategy must be based on a comprehensive globalization analysis of the drivers we encountered above. Managers of a global business must, he contends, evaluate the globalization drivers for their industry and market and formulate their global strategy on the basis of this analysis. If, for example, they find that customer demand is largely homogeneous for their product, they can produce a largely standardized product for sale throughout the world. If, on the other hand, they find that there are few cost advantages of global concentration of manufacturing because of unfavourable logistics or adverse economies of scale, they may choose to disperse their manufacturing activities around the world to be close to their customers in different parts of the world. Thus the 'total global strategy' of an organization can be a mix of standardization and local adaptation as market and industry conditions dictate.

Yip goes on to identify three stages in developing a 'total global strategy':

1. *Developing a core strategy:* this will, in effect, involve building core competences and a generic or hybrid strategy that can potentially give global competitive advantage.
2. *Internationalizing the core strategy:* this will be the stage at which the core competences and generic strategy are introduced to international markets and when the organization begins to locate its value-adding activities in locations where competitive advantages, such as low cost and access to materials or skills, are available. This will include the choice of which markets the business will enter and the means by which it will enter them.
3. *Globalizing the international strategy:* this stage is based on coordinating and integrating the core competences and strategy on a global basis. It will also include deciding which elements of the strategy are to be standardized and which are to be locally adapted on the basis of the strength of the globalization drivers in the industry and market.

Although we have used Levitt, Porter and Yip in this chapter, interested readers should consider reading the work of Bartlett and Ghoshal (1987, 1989), Hamel and Prahalad (1985) and Stonehouse et al. (2000).

Management across international boundaries

Coordination is of key importance when managing across international boundaries, especially for what are termed 'multinational enterprises' (MNEs). This coordination and control are often achieved through the management structure and aligned with the strategy and resources. Choosing between a multi-domestic strategy or a global orientation has always been a challenge. However, Bartlett and Ghoshal (1992) identify three possible strategic approaches, which are local responsiveness, the transfer of knowledge, and global efficiency. They argued that a focus on one strategy is no longer appropriate and that to succeed, organizations need to combine all three approaches. They termed this the 'transnational solution' (Bartlett and Ghoshal, 1992; Bartlett et al., 2008), an approach that addresses local and global issues as well as knowledge transfer.

Porter's diamond framework

Porter's 'diamond of national advantage' has become something of a classical theory of international trade. The framework provides a practical and systematic approach to understanding the competitive environments that nations create for their established industries and the conditions within which international competition occurs. The argument is that comparative advantage resides in the 'factor endowments' that a country may be fortunate enough to inherit. Factor endowments include land, natural resources, labour, and the size of the local population (see Figure 13.3). In addition to possessing these factor endowments, a nation can create new advanced factor endowments, such as skilled labour, a strong technology and knowledge base, government support, and culture.

The individual points on the diamond and the diamond as a whole affect four factors that lead to a national comparative advantage. These are:

- the pressure on companies to innovate and invest
- the availability of resources and skills
- the information that firms use to decide which opportunities to pursue
- the goals of individuals in companies.

The points of the diamond are described as follows:

- *Factor conditions:* A country possesses and creates its own key factor conditions such as skilled resources, infrastructure and technological base, and disadvantages in factor conditions will force innovation. Such innovation often leads to a national comparative advantage. Therefore understanding the factor conditions allows for an understanding of current and potential capability.

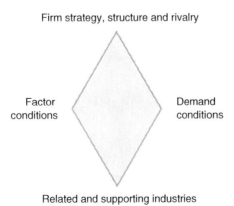

Figure 13.3 Porter's diamond
Source: Adapted from Porter, 1990

- *Firm strategy, structure and rivalry:* Local conditions affect firm strategy, with rivalry forcing firms to move beyond the basic advantages that the home country may enjoy, and seek to exploit other forms of advantage.
- *Demand conditions:* When the market for a particular product is larger locally than in foreign markets, local markets become more expert in production, expected standards and quality are higher, local consumers are more demanding and thus exports are more competitive.
- *Related and supporting industries:* When local supporting industries are competitive, firms enjoy more cost-effective and innovative inputs. The effect of this is strengthened when the suppliers themselves are strong global competitors.

So the diamond can be used to understand the balance and sources of a nation's competitive advantage, although one should consider that many of the elements are self-renewing and interdependent.

GURU GUIDE

Sumantra Ghoshal was born in 1948 in Calcutta, India. He graduated from Delhi University with an undergraduate degree in physics and has doctoral degrees from both MIT and Harvard Business School. His management stints include working for the Indian Oil Corporation and serving as the chairman of the supervisory board of Duncan Goenka. He had an academic spell with INSEAD business school, London Business School and Harvard Business School. He was also on the board of several companies including Mahindra British Telecom Ltd, the Lufthansa School of Business and Swiss Re. He was the founding dean of the Indian Business School in Hyderabad, and a fellow at the Academy of Management, the Academy of International Business and the World Economic Forum.

Professor Ghoshal is a management guru and has written influential articles focusing on the strategic, organizational and managerial issues confronting large and global companies. He has won several prizes, including the George R. Terry Book Award, the Igor Ansoff Award and Management Book of the Year award. He died in 2004.

Christopher Bartlett received an undergraduate degree in economics from University of Queensland in 1964. He graduated with a PhD in business administration from Harvard Business School in 1979 and joined the business faculty in the same year. Professor Bartlett worked as a management consultant with McKinsey's London office and a general manager at Baxter Laboratories in France. At Harvard he has held various distinguished positions including the faculty chair of International

Senior Management Program and chairman of Harvard Business School's international executive programme.

Professor Bartlett's interest focuses on managerial challenges in multinational firms and he has published influential books and texts in the areas of strategy, transformational change and leadership. His work is acknowledged internationally and he won the Igor Ansoff Award for best work in strategic management. He is also a fellow at the Academy of Management and the Academy of International Business.

The work of Bartlett and Ghoshal is fundamental in understanding the mindset needed of global matrix managers and the need for local, national and global knowledge and awareness in management.

Key strategic decisions

Once a business has developed core competences and strategies that can potentially be exploited globally, the decision must be made as to where and how to employ them. Initial moves into overseas markets will involve market development as these markets and segments can be regarded as new to the business. The initial market development may then be followed by product development and, perhaps, diversification.

When a business enters international and global markets, it will be necessary to build new competences, alongside those which have brought about domestic competitive advantage. These new competences could well be in the areas of global sourcing and logistics, and global management.

The globalization of a business does not happen overnight. It may well involve entry to key countries, with the largest markets first, followed by entry to less important countries later.

In the initial stages of globalization, the key decisions are usually:

- Which countries are to be entered first?
- In which countries are value-adding activities to be located?
- Which market development strategies are to be employed to gain entry to the chosen overseas markets?

Market entry decisions

The decision as to which countries and markets are to be entered first will be based on a number of important factors:

- *The potential size of the market:* is the market for the product likely to be significant? This will, in turn, be determined by the following factors.
- *Economic factors:* are income levels adequate to ensure that significant numbers of people are likely to be able to afford the product?
- *Cultural and linguistic factors:* is the culture of the country likely to favour acceptance of the product to be offered?
- *Political factors:* what are the factors that may limit entry to markets in the host country?

- *Technological factors:* are levels of technology adequate to support provision of the product in the host market and are technological standards compatible?

To begin with, a business will choose to enter markets in those countries where the above conditions are most favourable.

Location of value-adding activities

Managers must determine within which countries they will locate key value-adding activities of their business. They will seek to gain cost, skill and resource advantages. In other words, they will attempt to locate activities in countries where there are production advantages to be gained.

Such advantages depend on:

- *wage levels:* low wage levels will assist in low production costs
- *skill levels:* there must be suitably skilled labour available
- *availability of materials:* suitable materials must be accessible
- *infrastructure:* transport and communications must be favourable to the logistics of the business.

The existence of these conditions within a country will, in turn, depend on:

- *economic factors:* level of economic development, wage levels, exchange rate conditions
- *social factors:* attitudes to work, levels of education and training
- *political factors:* legislation favouring investment and so on
- *technological factors:* levels of technology and transport and communications infrastructure of the country.

Market development methods

Once decisions have been made as to which countries' markets are to be entered and where value-adding activities are to be located, the task for management becomes the determination of which method of development to employ to enter another country. Broadly speaking, a business can choose either internal or external methods for the development of overseas markets. Internal methods are usually slower, but tend to entail lower risk. External methods involve the business developing relationships with other businesses. The choice of method will depend on a number of factors:

- the size of the investment required or the amount of investment capital available
- knowledge of the country to be entered and potential risk involved (political instability)
- revenue and cash flow forecasts and expectations
- operating cost considerations
- control considerations (some investment options will have implications for the parent company to control activity in the host country).

Internal and external development methods are examined in more detail.

Internal development methods

Internal methods are based on the organization exploiting its own resources and competences and involve the organization carrying out some of its activities overseas. This may be exporting its products or setting up some form of production facilities abroad. The advantages of internal methods of development are that they maximize future revenue from sales abroad and they make possible a high degree of control over overseas activities. On the other hand, they can involve significant risk if knowledge of the host country and its markets are limited, and they may require considerable direct investment from the business. The major internal methods of development overseas are direct exporting, overseas production or assembly, and the development of an overseas facility.

Direct exporting

Direct exporting is the transfer of goods (or services) across national borders from the home production facility. Such exporting may simply be shipping a product, or, as sales increase, a sales offices may be set up overseas. Exporting, at its simplest, is the marketing abroad of a product made in an organization's home country. To avoid some of the pitfalls of direct exporting, such as a lack of local knowledge and access to distribution channels, many exporting businesses make use of local agents or distribute their products through locally based retailers, known as a 'piggyback' distribution arrangement.

Direct exporting is the transfer of goods (or services) across national borders from the home production facility.

Overseas production or assembly

Organizations may choose to manufacture or assemble their product overseas. There are a number of reasons for direct investment. Transport costs for the finished product may be so high as to discourage exporting or the business wishes to take advantage of local cost advantages. In some industries, direct investment may be an appropriate option to circumvent import restrictions put in place by host governments.

Development of an overseas facility

Establishing a foreign subsidiary of the business is an option when it is favourable for the parent company to have total control of its overseas operations, decision-making and profits. A subsidiary may carry out the full range of activities of the parent business or it may be only a manufacturing or marketing subsidiary.

External development methods

External methods of development involve the organization entering into relationships with businesses in a host country, which take the form of alliances or joint ventures, mergers and acquisitions (M&A), franchising and licensing. These methods often reflect 'offshoring' and have the advantages of providing local knowledge, potentially reducing risks, reducing operating costs, and reducing investment costs (except in the case of M&A). The major disadvantages (again except in the case of M&A) are reduced revenues and reduced control of activities as optimal income is traded off against the advantage of lower financial exposure.

International alliances and joint ventures

Alliances and joint ventures allow a business to draw on the skills, local knowledge, resources and competences of a locally based company. They reduce the risks of entry to overseas markets by providing local knowledge and they help reduce investment costs.

International mergers and acquisitions

A business may use M&A to enter overseas markets, which give a business access to the knowledge, resources and competences of a business based in the host country, thus reducing some of the risks of market entry.

International franchising

A **franchise** is an arrangement under which a franchisor supplies a franchisee with a tried-and-tested brand name, products and expertise in return for the payment of a proportion of profits or sales. The major advantage to the franchisor is that the risk, investment and operating costs of entering overseas markets are reduced considerably. At the same time, the franchisee can contribute their local knowledge while also benefiting from the lower risks associated with an established business idea. Much of Burger King's expansion overseas has come through franchise development.

A **franchise** is an arrangement under which a franchisor supplies a franchisee with a tried-and-tested brand name, products and expertise in return for the payment of a proportion of profits or sales.

International licensing

Licensing is similar to franchising but involves a producer transferring certain rights to a licensee for the sole use in a host country of its established brand, recipe, registered design or similar piece of intellectual property. The licensee pays the licensor a royalty for the use of the intellectual property and, as with franchising, gains from the established market position of the brand. Licensing is widely used in brewing and in some scientific industries.

Licensing involves a producer transferring certain rights to a licensee for the sole use in a host country of its established brand, recipe, registered design or similar piece of intellectual property.

STRATEGIC
PLANNING SOFTWARE

This is a helpful chapter to refer to when completing section 2.3 Development Strategy within Phase 2 of the **Strategic Planning Software** (www. planning-software.com).

For test questions, extra case studies, audio case studies, weblinks, videolinks and more to help you understand the topics covered in this chapter, visit our companion website at www.palgrave.com/business/campbell.

VOCAB CHECKLIST FOR ESL STUDENTS

Accolades	Gradient	Myopia
Advent	Heralded	Offshoring
Apparel	Hindered	Recouped
Exponential	Homogenization	Superseded
Franchiser, franchisee	Impetus	

Definitions for these terms can be found in the 'Vocab Zone' of the companion website, which provides free access to the Macmillan English Dictionary online at www.palgrave.com/business/campbell.

REVIEW QUESTIONS

1. Explain what we mean by internationalization and globalization, and highlight the differences.
2. Explain what factors drive globalization and suggest which are most dominant.
3. Explain how Yip's framework can be used to analyse the extent of globalization in an industry and/or market.
4. Explain the different modes of international market entry.

DISCUSSION TOPIC

It is better to grow and maintain market share in one country than to expand across national boundaries. Discuss.

HOT TOPICS – Research project areas to investigate

If you have a project to do, why not investigate …
- … approaches adopted by multinational organizations to meeting the legislation requirements in different countries.
- … the impact of currency fluctuations on financial institutions operating in the UK.
- … the competences required of a multinational manager.

Recommended reading

Arora, A., Jaju, A., Kefalas, A.G. and Perenich, T. (2004) 'An exploratory analysis of global managerial mindsets: a case of U.S. textile and apparel industry', *Journal of International Management*, **10**(3): 393–411.

Bartlett, C.A. and Ghoshal, S. (1989) *Managing Across Borders: The Transnational Solution*, Boston, MA: Harvard Business School Press.

Bitzenis, A. (2006) 'Decisive FDI barriers that affect multinationals' business in a transition country', *Global Business & Economics Review*, **8**(1/2): 87–118.

Buckley, P.J. and Casson, M.C. (1998) 'Models of the multinational enterprise', *Journal of International Business Studies*, **29**(1): 21–44.

Chakravarthy, B. and Perlmutter, H.V. (1985) 'Strategic planning for a global economy', *Columbia Journal of World Business*, **20**(3): 3–10.

Douglas, S.P. and Wind, Y. (1987) 'The myth of globalisation', *Columbia Journal of World Business*, **22**(4): 19–29.

Doz, Y. (1986) *Strategic Management in Multinational Companies*, Oxford: Pergamon Press.

Hamel, G. and Prahalad, C.K. (1985) 'Do you really have a global strategy', *Harvard Business Review*, **63**(4): 139–48.

Henzler, H. and Rall, W. (1986) 'Facing up to the globalisation challenge', *McKinsey Quarterly*, 4: 52–68.

Kedia, B.L. and Mukherji, A. (1999) 'Global managers: developing a mindset for global competitiveness', *Journal of World Business*, **34**(3): 230–51.

Porter, M.E. (1980) *Competitive Strategy: Techniques for Analysing Industries and Competitors*, New York: Free Press.

Prahalad, C.K. and Doz, Y.L. (1986) *The Multinational Mission: Balancing Local Demands and Global Vision*, New York: Free Press.

Prahalad, C.K. and Hamel, G. (1990) 'The core competence of the corporation', *Harvard Business Review*, **68**(3): 79–81.

References

Bartlett, C.A. and Ghoshal, S. (1987) 'Managing across borders: new organisational responses, *Sloan Management Review*, **29**(1): 45–53.

Bartlett, C.A. and Ghoshal, S. (1989) *Managing Across Borders: The Transnational Solution*, Boston, MA: Harvard Business School Press.

Bartlett, C.A. and Ghoshal, S. (1992) 'What is a global manager?', *Harvard Business Review*, **70**(5): 124–32.

Bartlett, C.A., Ghoshal, S. and Beamish, P. (2008) *Transnational Management: Text, Cases and Readings in Cross-border Management* (5th edn), Boston: McGraw-Hill/Irwin.

Hamel, G. and Prahalad, C.K. (1985) 'Do you really have a global strategy?', *Harvard Business Review*, **63**(4): 139–48.

Levitt, T. (1983) 'The globalisation of markets', *Harvard Business Review*, **61**(3): 92–102.

Porter, M.E. (1990) *The Competitive Advantage of Nations*, New York: Free Press.

Stonehouse, G., Hamill, J., Campbell, D.J. and Purdie, A. (2000) *Global and Transnational Business: Management and Strategy*, Chichester: John Wiley & Sons.

Yip, G.S. (1992) *Total Global Strategy: Managing for Worldwide Competitive Advantage*, Englewood Cliffs, NJ: Prentice Hall.

CHAPTER 14

The web, new technology and new organizational forms

Margaret McCann[1]

LEARNING OBJECTIVES

By the end of this chapter, you should be able to:

- explain the impact that the web has had on business
- describe related emerging web technologies including Web 2.0 and the mobile web and their business applications
- discuss various issues related to the digital age, including the digital divide, information overload and privacy of data
- understand management issues related to business use of the web and relevant management strategies that may be applied

---

Introduction and chapter overview

This chapter explores a key area for the future development of organizations and therefore business strategy, existing and emerging web technologies. The chapter starts by setting the context of web growth and the basic terminology needed to understand the technology. The impact of the web is then explored, in particular the influence it has had on business and industry, relationships and value-adding properties. The chapter then explores new and emerging technologies, including Web 2.0 and the mobile web, and ends by exploring issues associated with the digital economy, management issues and strategies relating to the use of the web.

The web

Although the terms are commonly used interchangeably, the internet and the World Wide Web (known as the 'web') are two different technologies. The **internet** is a global network comprising millions of computers, while the **web** is a way of accessing

---

[1] Caledonian Business School, Glasgow Caledonian University.

information via the internet, typically using browsers, such as Internet Explorer or Firefox, to access information on web pages. Other ways to access or transmit information on the internet include email, newsgroups and instant messaging.

The **internet** is a global network comprising millions of computers.

The **web** is a way of accessing information via the internet.

There are currently 1.9 billion internet users worldwide, which accounts for 28.7% of the world's population. The number of users has grown 444.8% from 2000 to 2010 (www.internetworldstats.com/stats.htm). Figure 14.1 demonstrates the rapid rise in internet users from 1995 to 2010.

The web first saw commercial use in the early 1990s. At that time, the web presence of a business mainly comprised a website in order to communicate and transmit information about its products and services. The web did not change the fundamental business model, as it did not provide new products and services but supported and extended processes, allowing access to a wider audience. Recently, the web has changed from the mainly read only medium, where businesses posted information on products and services, to one where users are encouraged to interact and contribute to web content. This is changing the way that businesses use the web, allowing them to interact openly and freely with customers, receive feedback on products and services, and collaborate with customers and suppliers.

Nowadays, the web is so fundamental to everyday life that no business can ignore the potential that it offers, and the way businesses adopt and exploit web technologies can determine their success or failure. Some businesses use the web to expand their business operations or change the way they operate and hence find new opportunities, while for others, it is fundamental to their very operation, for example Amazon, eBay, Google, Yahoo!. Without the web, these businesses could not and would not exist.

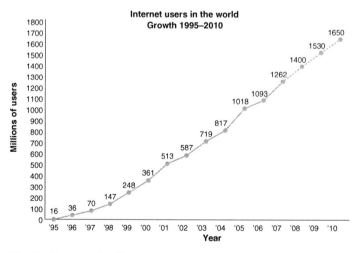

Figure 14.1   Worldwide growth of internet users, 1995–2010

Source: www.internetworldstats.com, copyright © Miniwatts Marketing Group

There are many different terminologies used when conducting business over the web. One of the most common is **e-commerce**, which can be defined as the buying or selling of goods or services via the internet. However, since the way business is conducted on the web is not restricted to the online transactions of buying and selling but also involves the important exchange of information between various parties, such as enquiries and feedback, a more accurate term to use is e-business. So we can define **e-business** as the use of technology throughout the supply chain of the business and the carrying out of business on the internet. It refers not only to buying and selling but also servicing customers and collaborating with business partners. This chapter discusses the web in the wider context of e-business.

E-commerce is the buying or selling of goods or services via the internet.

E-business is the use of technology throughout the supply chain of the business and the carrying out of business on the internet. It refers not only to buying and selling but also servicing customers and collaborating with business partners.

Such e-business between businesses and consumers or customers can be conducted in the following ways:

- *Business-to-business (B2B):* involves businesses transactions from one business to another in the supply chain (producer to wholesaler or wholesaler to retailer). Alibaba.com is a popular example of B2B in action. This site is a virtual marketplace linking exporters and importers, where buyers and sellers post leads on the products/services of interest. The site mainly caters to small and medium-sized businesses and has now morphed into a virtual monopoly for sourcing products from mainland China.

- *Business-to-customer/consumer (B2C):* the activities involved in the supply of products or services from a business to the end user. The most common and familiar facet of e-business is B2C. The electronics giant Apple not only sells its stylish, cutting-edge products through its B2C website, but also advises its customers to buy and download music from its popular iTunes music store.
- *Customer-to-customer/consumer-to-consumer (C2C):* the exchange of goods or services directly from consumer to consumer. This can typically involve auction sites such as eBay. Starting as a B2C site, Amazon's business model now allows the option to earn revenue through its C2C initiatives. Amazon's UK website allows individuals to sell/buy products from other individuals. Amazon benefits by charging a small referral fee for hosting and conducting the transaction.

The impact of the web on business

There are numerous ways that the web has impacted on business activities, ranging from small-scale efficiency gains to the transformation of an entire industry. In general, the web has been used to improve efficiency as it speeds up transactions and lowers the costs associated with business activities, such as the processing of enquiries and orders, and the creation, storage and distribution of information. It has increased flexibility and widened choice as customers can shop day or night, search for a range of suppliers regardless of location, shop in different ways (online store, auction site) and use comparison websites to compare prices, products and services.

We now cover some of the more important ways the web has impacted on business.

Transformation of industries

The web has changed the very way that business is conducted in some industries, such as the music and travel industries. The downloading of music from sites such as iTunes has changed the structure of the industry, forcing record companies and distributors to seek new business models. Artists can now publicize their own material through video-sharing sites such as YouTube (www.youtube.com) or social networking sites such as Facebook (www.facebook.com). Similarly, in the travel industry, high-street travel agents traditionally acted as intermediaries when customers were booking holidays. However, the web now allows customers to search for and book the various components associated with holidays directly, as well as read reviews and ratings from other travellers through sites such as Expedia (www.expedia.com) and TripAdvisor (www.tripadvisor.com), enabling them to make more informed decisions about their booking. This has forced some travel companies to change their business model to form strategic alliances with their competitors to offer a more cost-effective, extensive service (Deloitte, 2003). Others have remained competitive through improved customer relationship management or increased non-ticket revenue such as charging for baggage/check-in and so on (IBM, 2008).

Eliminate distance boundaries

Web technology can eliminate time and distance boundaries and offer flexibility in the location of work as there is no necessity for employees to be in the same location to work together. Employees may be able to access work systems remotely and so have the flexibility to work from home or any convenient location. Web or video-conferencing allows meetings to be conducted at any time of day or night without the need to travel. An international business can set up working practices so that different teams around the world share the workload. For example, one team can work during the day, while another team on the other side of world can take over at night. This allows the working day to be extended and does not involve pay for overtime or unsociable working hours.

Web technology also allows organizations to set up practices where better workforce skills are available or where the cost of work is cheaper. **Outsourcing** is the movement of a business process to another company with a more appropriate skills base, whereas **offshoring** is the movement of a business process from one location to another, usually another country, where the skills are cheaper. Outsourcing or offshoring can be set up for a range of manufacturing or support services. A good example of outsourcing is the call centre operations of UK insurance companies, the majority of which outsource their call centre operations to India with a view to reducing costs and a renewed focus on core competence. Typical conditions such as low-cost labour, time difference, and English-speaking professionals have contributed to this 'look east' policy of UK insurance majors.

Outsourcing is the movement of a business process to another company with a more appropriate skills base.

Offshoring is the movement of a business process from one location to another, usually another country, where the skills are cheaper.

Collaboration

Web technology can be used to encourage internal and external collaboration. Internally, employees can be encouraged to use technology to work together and share information and ideas with their colleagues. Businesses throughout the supply chain can use the web as a platform to work together by automating order processing between businesses, and the shipment and supply of goods or services.

Building alliances may lead to virtual/strategic alliances being formed between businesses. These alliances may exist as a virtual business, with no or limited physical premises and be composed of different geographically dispersed businesses such as developers, producers and suppliers working together.

Web 2.0 technology (see below) can also be used to find and build associations with other businesses. For example, social business networking sites such as LinkedIn (www.linkedin.com) and Ecademy (www.ecademy.com) can be used to find and build professional contacts, and there are a host of online forums and communities, which can be used to share knowledge and support.

Another interesting example of collaboration is the Open University's attempt to create virtual worlds for educational purposes. The OU owns six islands at Second Life, a multi-user virtual environment, home to more than 17 million users. 'Open Life', the name of one of the islands, is a virtual teaching environment where staff and students meet and participate in pedagogical activities. OU staff frequently use the environment to hold meetings, deliver lecturers and carry out the normal student-centred activities one would traditionally associate with the 'bricks and mortar' university learning environments.

For more information, go to http://www.open.ac.uk/cetl-workspace/cetlcontent/documents/496357225a459.pdf.

Customer relationships

The web allows businesses to build relationships with their customers as enquiries can be received directly and dealt with personally and more efficiently. Customers can be encouraged to offer feedback, either directly via email or comment forms or indirectly through electronic communities, providing a business with vital information on how customers perceive their goods or services. Argos, the catalogue retailer, allows its customers to write reviews on products sold at its website. Customers are free to write about their shopping experience, including product reviews and customer service, through online forms. This not only helps Argos to keep tabs on the performance of its products but also to improve customer relationships.

Improve marketing

Using a variety of means, such as previous sales data, registration information, or monitoring programs such as cookies stored on a customer's computer (see below), information can be gathered about a customer's profile and preferences. This then allows a business to segment customers and target marketing products according to information gathered on preferences. This may involve sending customers personalized adverts on special offers, promotions and other information relative to that customer. In the near future, the media company Sky hopes to be able to advertise directly to customers based on their preferences via their TV, using viewing information gained from their Sky+ boxes.

Personalization

Web technology can be used to offer personalized products/services. For example, the PC retailer Dell allows customers to place their order online, specifying details of the exact requirements of their system. The customer's computer is then built to order and shipped to them in a few days. Direct ordering reduces warehouse costs as the exact quantities are known. In addition, customers can track their order online.

Another business offering customized products is the sports retailer Nike. Its website (www.nikeid.nike.com) allows customers to personalize their own training shoes by choosing the colour, pattern, material and other design features.

The long tail

The 'long tail' is a term used to describe the way businesses have used the web to impact on the market. The **long tail** describes the strategy of selling a large number of niche products to a relatively small number of customers (Anderson, 2004). This is in contrast to 'traditional' retailers who tend to focus on selling a smaller range of popular items to the mass market. The total of the small volume of niche product sales can be larger than the high volume of sales of popular brands.

The **long tail** describes the strategy of selling a large number of niche products to a relatively small number of customers.

The online book retailer Amazon has been successful in selling a large range of books not available in traditional 'bricks and mortar' bookstores. In fact, many of the books that Amazon sell would be out of print if sold only through traditional methods. The web has allowed Amazon and other similar businesses to stock a wider choice of products, as they have used technology to ensure that their costs are low and to build alliances with other businesses. The use of technology to sell niche products can enable small businesses to compete against, and work with, larger enterprises.

The changing face of the web

The web was originally used in a rather passive way, as businesses created 'shop-front' websites to provide customers with up-to-date information on their products and services. Now the power of the web has shifted, as content is created and shared by many and customers are encouraged to use technology to interact and collaborate. This interactive web is termed **Web 2.0** – a term that is difficult to define precisely but is generally used for the content-sharing nature of today's web. It relates to the concept of social connections, participation and interaction, where businesses, customers, employees and partners connect with each other and generate content by sharing data, collaborating, socializing and contributing their own thoughts, ideas, experiences and knowledge. It allows businesses to communicate directly with their customers and understand their preferences and needs in detail and so target their specific requirements. Web 2.0 applications are easy to use and inexpensive, so offer tremendous potential for businesses of all sizes, even small businesses that may be unable to take advantage of more 'traditional' web technologies.

The term **Web 2.0** is commonly associated with web applications that facilitate interactive information sharing, interoperability, social networking, user-centred design and collaborative working.

As a marketing tool, Web 2.0 applications can enable businesses to engage with existing customers and to be proactive about finding new ones. Web 2.0 can change the type of marketing from general communications about products and services published on a website to community interaction through lots of conversations. Marketing professionals can use the wealth of information on these networks to better understand customers' needs or inform (push content to) existing customers.

The following are some Web 2.0 applications, with suggestions for their possible business application.

Blogs

Originating from the term 'web-log', **blogs** are websites that host frequently updated journals, which are used for writing short and typically informal communications. Corporate blogs are often used for internal and external communication as well as for marketing and promotion by providing information on the business and its market to local and global, existing and potential customers. Blogs can be used for knowledge transfer, to showcase and share expertise, to respond to frequently asked questions (FAQs), to present advice and solutions and, in so doing, retain customer loyalty. Customers can be invited to post comments to blog entries, so blogs can be used to interact and gain feedback or ideas from customers and help maintain close links. Blog posts may contain links to other related web pages, encouraging collaboration and joint ventures between businesses.

Blogs are websites that host frequently updated journals, which are used for writing short and typically informal communications.

Blogs can also be used internally within a company for information dissemination on recent business developments or even for staff feedback. Owner/manager blogging gives news straight from the decision maker. Infosys, the Indian software major, has another use for blogging; it uses blogs written by its employees to monitor views and opinions on job satisfaction, training needs, remuneration and so on. It encourages employees to write blogs on its intranet site to gather first-hand information on potential problems with a view to solving them at the earliest opportunity.

A recent blogging phenomenon is microblogging, which is blogging limited to shorter message length. Although microblogging has, to date, proved limited as a business tool (BBC, 2009), it may be useful for status updates for collaboration or for marketing of goods (Jin, 2009). The most popular microblogging tool is Twitter.

Wikis

The word 'wiki' is the Hawaiian word for quick, thus WikiWikiWeb was the first wiki software. A **wiki** is a web page that easily allows anyone to create, view and modify web content. The most well-known wiki is Wikipedia – the online encyclopedia written and policed by its users, who try to maintain quality of content. Wikis can be public (such as Wikipedia) or private, as security restrictions can be implemented which allow access only to certain users.

A **wiki** is a web page that easily allows anyone to create, view and modify web content.

Wikis enable users to communicate and work together on documents, empowering all to contribute and so promote knowledge transfer and collective intelligence. When a wiki is edited, version control means that all previous versions are saved and can be referred to or resurrected if required.

Wikis encourage internal or inter-company collaboration, as teams, especially if located in several locations, can work on documents and are good for project work, from the initial stages of brainstorming to organizing meetings and documentation. They are also ideal for centralizing company documents in one accessible location.

Social networking

The web can indeed be a powerful tool for interacting and expanding social relationships. This is especially evident in social networking sites, which allow users to build a personal web presence and connect with contacts (business or social) to communicate and share content. The membership of popular social networking sites such as MySpace and Facebook has expanded over the past few years and each now has millions of users. There are specific business social networking sites such as LinkedIn, which are commonly used to meet and communicate with business contacts and even hire staff. Although initially social networking sites attracted a younger audience, popularity among over 35s is growing (Cachia et al., 2007) and businesses are starting to exploit social networking to build business connections.

Within each site, users initially set up a profile of personal (or company) details, which will generally be visible to other users. B2B or B2C networks are built by searching profiles for communities of interest and requesting them to be 'friends'. In this way, potential customers can be targeted and views and content exchanged. Such networking can be viral as users pass content and information around. It has been found that marketers who can engage customers by interacting through social networking can form a closer bond (Vasquez, 2006).

Virtual worlds

The increasing power and sophistication of technology allows users to create an avatar, or virtual character, in a virtual world, such as Second Life. Avatars can communicate and interact in real-time emulating real-life business activities such as conducting meetings with new or existing customers, networking with other business users or buying and selling real or virtual products. Second Life even uses its own currency for trading, the Linden dollar.

Different business models exist within virtual worlds such as Second Life. Traditional businesses can set up a store for virtual trading or use the environment to experiment with new products and gain customer feedback, as Nike and IBM have done. On the other hand, many virtual businesses exist within Second Life, ranging from fashion retail to virtual wedding or party planning for avatars.

RSS

RSS (rich site summary or really simple syndication) is a technology that allows information to be sent to the user whenever a web page is updated. So rather than searching continuously for updates on an item of interest, the web page is sent as soon as new content is added. RSS can be used by businesses for keeping interested parties up to date with company news or for marketing to existing or potential customers or suppliers. The BBC provides RSS services for users to keep abreast with the latest and developing news stories. Users can subscribe to the BBC's service and can benefit from updated coverage on news items and reporting from their favourite correspondents.

RSS (rich site summary or really simple syndication) is a technology that allows information to be sent to the user whenever a web page is updated.

Podcasting and media sharing

Podcasting is the distribution of audio or video files that can be downloaded onto PCs or mobile devices such as MP3 players. Businesses can create and broadcast their own podcasts or subscribe to those produced by others. Podcasts can be used as a communication tool for marketing and showcasing of products or even for knowledge transfer in areas such as staff training. Regularly produced podcasts can be subscribed to using RSS, which informs the user when new podcasts are available and downloads them.

Podcasting is the distribution of audio or video files that can be downloaded onto PCs or mobile devices such as MP3 players.

Highly popular video-sharing sites such as YouTube or Google Video allow users to upload their own videos or view those produced by others. When content is added to these sites, tags are also incorporated, which are used to label, organize and identify content, allowing it to be found when searched by others. Video-sharing sites offer small businesses unique opportunities. For example, where TV advertising is prohibitive for small businesses, video-sharing sites can offer an ideal opportunity to showcase products.

Software as a service

The popularity of the web is changing the way that software can be purchased and used. Instead of businesses buying software as a package (product), software as a service is hosted by a service provider and made available to customers over the web. There is no need for customers to install the software on their own machine; instead, they can use the software via the web, from any location. There are many advantages to software as a service such as lower acquisition costs for businesses. Also, since the software is automatically updated, the latest version is always available and all users will use the same version. Some software as a service such as

Google Docs (http://docs.google.com) is free to use and designed for easy collaboration, as documents can be shared with different users, saved locally or to a Google file server, or published online for all users to access. Thus it is easy to access documents from any location with web access.

The mobile web

The web is increasingly becoming more than a PC-based phenomenon as the trend towards smaller technology enables access by a range of mobile devices such as smartphones, netbooks, personal digital assistants (PDAs), MP3 players and even games consoles. The **mobile web** refers to browser-based access to the internet from a mobile device, such as a smartphone or PDA, connected to a wireless network. The mobile web is quickly becoming a part of our day-to-day lives. These devices increase the overall audience and use of the web, allowing anytime, anywhere access, which has huge implications for business in terms of market size, mobility and flexibility. It is important that businesses realize the opportunities the mobile web can offer and adapt their web presence to optimize mobile business advantages.

The **mobile web** refers to browser-based access to the internet from a mobile device, such as a smartphone or PDA, connected to a wireless network.

Although mobile devices are extremely convenient, most have a small screen and limited keyboard for input. Accessing web pages can also be very slow, with limited scrolling and navigation. Therefore using web pages designed for PC viewing can be impractical and so businesses must specifically design a mobile version of their web presence, which takes into account the reduced screen size and limited typing ability of these devices. Typically, mobile websites will be simplified with less content but contextualized for the mobile business needs.

Mobile technology

To access the web wirelessly, users will typically use their mobile phone and/or Wi-Fi (wireless fidelity), using devices such as PCs, laptops, netbooks, PDAs or MP3 players. The convergence of technology means that mobile devices are becoming increasingly powerful, with smartphones now incorporating features previously found on PDAs.

The new generation of smartphones includes features such as large touch screens, while others incorporate pull-out keyboards. These devices allow users access to the web to send and receive emails, to social networking sites and satellite navigation. Many have one-button access to encourage users onto certain applications such as social networking sites, maps and mobile browsers, such as Google Mobile (www.google.com/mobile).

Wi-Fi-enabled equipment can connect to the web when it is within range of a wireless network. Any Wi-Fi-enabled device can be used to connect – including some mobile phones. Access to such networks can be free of charge or users can subscribe to private networks. For example, Wi-Fi is available in public hotspots, businesses, university campuses, trains, coaches, as well as in millions of homes. Hotels, bars, restaurants and airports often provide free access to wireless networks and many cities have announced plans to allow wireless access on a city-wide basis. Thanks to Wi-Fi, there is now a cybercafé at the base of Mount Everest.

Business opportunities

There are currently 3 billion subscriptions to mobile phones worldwide compared to 1 billion PCs (Ahonen, 2009). The global popularity of mobile phones, together with advances in mobile technology, offers new business and revenue opportunities to a wider market.

Businesses can use mobile technology to boost their productivity rate. The mobility and flexibility provided by mobile devices makes communication easier as employees can send and receive emails, create or edit documents or access company data from any location. Employees on the move can reach customers directly, at any time, regardless of geography, reducing response time, offering a more individualized and accurate service, and so improving customer relations. In addition, mobile devices can be more convenient as they are quicker to boot up than a PC or laptop. Speed of information access can be crucial for a business's competitive advantage.

This mobile web access can be combined with mobile marketing to great effect. Advertising can take the form of multimedia banners on the screen, email messages or advertising within mobile games or videos. Using global positioning systems (GPS), marketers can send targeted, location-sensitive adverts directly to mobile devices such as adverts for local restaurants or shops.

There is currently much research being conducted to enable mobile phones to be used as an electronic wallet, as an alternative to debit/credits cards. This is already popular in Japan, where mobile technology tends to be more advanced, and enables customers to make payments or purchases in stores using their phones (Sutter, 2009). Banks are also carrying out research to enable customers to use their mobile handsets to carry out banking services such as accessing account information, bill payments and money transfers (McGlasson, 2008). This means that mobile phones can be used not only to retrieve information quickly and efficiently, but also to compare prices and make payments from the one small device.

Other business examples of the mobile web include:

- estate agents have used mobile technology to display houses to potential buyers as they are travelling around viewing properties (Roberts, 2007)
- iPhone customers can upload airline tickets to their phone and scan the barcode directly rather than printing the ticket (Sutter, 2009)
- many restaurants now use mobile technology such as PDAs for wireless ordering so that a customer's order can immediately be sent and displayed on an electronic board in the kitchen. Such systems can also be connected to stock and ingredient ordering systems
- in storerooms, wireless inventory checking allows for speedy customer feedback and faster decision-making

CASE STUDY   Facebook

Facebook, founded in 2004, is a social networking website that allows interaction among people and helps them to connect with friends, relatives and co-workers. It offers a virtual space where members can chat, share photos, form groups, buy/sell products and play games. Mark Zuckerberg, one of the founders and a Harvard sophomore at that time, wrote codes for a website that allowed the posting of profiles of Harvard students, which was extended to include students from other universities and later went on to develop as Facebook.com.

Initial investments for the company came from venture capitalists and as the site developed, further finance was sourced externally. In its present form, the company regularly attracts investors and has its international offices in London, Dublin, Paris, Milan, Stockholm, Toronto and Sydney. Anyone over the age of 13 with an active email account can become a Facebook user. The website primarily targets adults and has a global reach in terms of its coverage. Recent estimates note that Facebook is typically active in western markets; it is the most popular social networking site with users in Europe, Canada and Australia and has a near monopoly in these markets. In the US market, it is fast catching up with MySpace and according to recent reports, it will overtake MySpace to become the most influential US social utility website by 2010.

The tag of the most dominant social networking website is backed up by some impressive figures:

- it has over 500 million active users – as of July 2010
- it adds approximately 200,000 users every week
- it accounts for 5.0% of all page views on the internet
- more than 30% of global internet users visit Facebook every day
- it is ranked second only to Google in overall website traffic statistics
- more than 700,000 websites link with Facebook
- approximately 4.1 billion photos have been uploaded since its inception
- it accounted for nearly 390 million unique users for the first three months of 2010
- site statistics indicate that, on average, a user spends about 30 minutes interacting with the website
- in English-speaking countries, Facebook is the market leader; its nearest rivals are MySpace, Bebo, LinkedIn, Hi5, Friendster and Open Social.

Facebook faces competition from regionally dominated social utility sites. Facebook lags behind companies in non-English speaking countries, which can offer social networking in native languages. For example, the Chinese language site qq.com is popular not only in China but also in Taiwan and other Southeast Asian countries. Similarly, the Arabic site Maktoob.com dominates the Middle Eastern market.

The domination of Facebook can be explored by examining the products and services it offers the market. Facebook's products can be broadly divided into two categories:

1. core site functions relating to products like inbox, profiles, networks, friends
2. applications like photos, notes, posted items and any other third party application a user decides to add to their profile account.

These work in tandem to offer a unique user experience that not only allows them to mimic real-world social interactions but also create newer ones that are exclusive to the online medium. For example, a user account has a fundamental profile page, which contains inbox, chat window, networks and pages. These features allow communication and information sharing between users and form the basis of the social networking platform. The applications are there to enhance user experience. Photo applications allow users to upload their pictures and another application allows them to be rotated, cut, edited and tagged. The group application allows users to create groups and invite other users who share similar ideas and viewpoints to join them. Yet another application allows users to sell/buy products through the online marketplace, while mobile applications allow interaction through mobile phones. This combination of core products and applications plays a major part in creating environments of extreme personalization and experiences that are distinctive and inimitable.

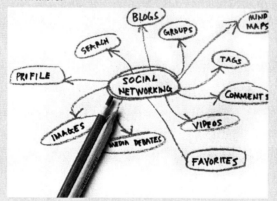

At the root of Facebook's success is technology, its own proprietary technology as well third party content developers. Facebook not only develops its own technology but also encourages third party participation in the development of applications through open source platforms and software. Overall, Facebook has agreements with more than 80,000 developers to come up with applications that are innovative, useful and can offer distinct user experiences. Facebook has its own custom-built search engine and an efficient remote procedure call framework. These technologies allow rapid information retrieval and a seamless integration of various subsystems written in a myriad of programming languages. Apart from its own technology, Facebook's strength lies in its ability to embrace open source software. Facebook was developed from open source software and the company actively encourages engineers and independent programmers to work with open source software and platforms. It provides opportunities for external companies and developers to produce applications that can be integrated and run from Facebook's platforms. This adoption of open source software has helped Facebook to come out with applications that not only provide a varied and a unique consumer experience but also a core competence against its rivals and competitors.

Facebook has 1,200+ employees and is privately owned – its founders still have control over the company and it is not listed in any of the world's stock markets. This means that very little information regarding its revenue and balance sheet information is available. Primarily, Facebook earns its revenues through onsite advertising and the sale of virtual goods; reports from popular research firms (TBI Research, Inside Facebook) indicate that the company earned about $640m (2009) in revenues from online advertising and a further $10m from the sale of virtual goods. According to Zuckerberg, in 2009, the company registered a cash flow positive for the first time and there is an expectation that it will reach the magical figure of $1bn in revenues by 2010. The private nature of the company and the inaccuracies with revenue information make it difficult to estimate the value of Facebook, but it is said to be worth around $10–15bn and there are talks of the company going public. Notwithstanding the huge valuation, it is expected to achieve operating profits in 2010 and with its significant user base, it may very well do so.

Case study questions

1. Do you think Facebook's sources of revenue are sustainable? Can online firms make a profit? What other opportunities are available for Facebook to increase its revenues?
2. As a technology-intensive organization, what are the pros and cons of Facebook's open source platform strategy?
3. It is said that Facebook benefits from network externalities and is highly dependent on huge user numbers. Do you agree with this?

- eBay mobile allows users of the auction site to keep in touch with their sales or bids and to be notified if they are outbid
- the sports website ESPN has, on occasion, had more fans check its mobile website for up-to-date scores than its PC site (Cuneo, 2007)
- tracking deliveries, such as pizza deliveries from Domino's or Papa John's.

Issues in the digital age

There are several important issues around the digital age, such as the digital divide and how to overcome it, information overload and the privacy of data, and these are discussed in some detail.

The digital divide

The web has the potential to improve lives through access to a greater amount of information than ever before, which, in turn, can lead to greater equity among society. However, it is recognized that not everyone has the same access to the technology required to retrieve the vast amount of information available, share global knowledge or compete through global markets. The **digital divide** refers to the gap between those who own, or have access to, technology and the web and those who do not. The divide not only refers to access to the physical equipment but also those who have limited skills to use the technology to access the associated information. Table 14.1 outlines some of the factors associated with the digital divide.

Table 14.1   Factors associated with the digital divide

Socioeconomic	Lack of computer ownership or access to web, which may be linked to income
Education	Lack of education and training leading to poor online skills
Employment	Those in professional occupations tend to have the skills and access to technology as part of their job, while manual workers or the unemployed do not
Generational	Older people who did not grow up with the technology may not be as at ease using it as younger people
Attitudinal	Willingness to use and learn new technology, which may be related to computer anxiety
Disabilities	Although the web may provide some people with disabilities access to facilities otherwise unavailable, it must be provided in a format that is accessible for different disabilities
Language	More than 50% of websites are written in English, therefore users require proficiency in the English language
Geographical	People who reside in rural areas or citizens of underdeveloped, poorer countries may not have broadband access
Security	Users may have various fears about the security of personal information or concerns by parents of children accessing unsuitable content

The **digital divide** refers to the gap between those who own, or have access to, technology and the web and those who do not.

The digital divide can exist both within and between countries but what may be the greatest divide is the gap between developed and underdeveloped countries (Cullen, 2001).

Bridging the global divide

one laptop per child

In the developed world, individual governments generally have policies in place to bridge the divide in their respective country, which can range from funding for community access to technology to telecommunications infrastructure to educational initiatives (Cullen, 2001) but these are not suitable for all countries. Although access to the web may be rare in some of the poorest parts of the world, there are currently some projects designed to help overcome this problem. The One Laptop per Child project (http://laptop.org/en/) aims to distribute inexpensive and robust laptops to schoolchildren in developing countries throughout the world. This project is described not as a technology project but as an educational project to provide skills and access to IT to empower children out of poverty and help the future economies of the countries involved.

Mobile phone technology is likely to improve web access in some rural communities and is already helping to bridge the divide in some areas. In Africa, the number of mobile phones subscriptions has risen from 16 million in 2000 to more than 280 million in 2009 (Rudebeck, 2009). This technology can help reduce isolation in some areas; for example, in Kenya, farmers can access prices from fruit and vegetable markets, and in Brazil, the unemployed are sent information on job opportunities by text. However, this, in itself, can lead to a further divide between those who own a mobile phone and those who do not (Rudebeck, 2009).

Information overload

The different technologies that can be used to access and communicate information, for example emails, mobile phones, blogs, social networks, together with the ease of publishing information on the internet, have led to a rapid increase in the amount of information available. When using a search engine to find information online, it is common to obtain results listing many thousands of websites. In addition, since these sites can be written and published by anyone, they may not provide information of any quality or accuracy. Users of the web must be aware of the issues involved in finding accurate and relevant information and be able to evaluate websites to differentiate between good and bad. There are no strict guidelines to evaluate the quality of websites but factors such as ensuring the website is up to date, author credentials, authority or publishing body and links to other quality sites can help to give an indication of quality.

Search engine features can be used to filter and so obtain fewer, more relevant results. Using the advanced search features to enter accurate search terms (and excluding other terms) can help to improve results. Search engines are becoming more sophisticated and increasingly more personalized and can now track a user's interests and previous searches to produce more relevant personalized results. Google takes into account a user's location through their computer's IP address to enable localized research results (Google, 2009). The latest metasearch engines, such as Yippy (http://search.yippy.com/), cluster results into subsets, and the search engine Mooter (www.mooter.com) can present these clusters visually (Mostafa, 2005).

Businesses can use search engine optimization strategies to help improve their ranking within search result listings. Although individual search engines will not disclose exactly how they calculate the ranking of individual websites, they include consideration of the number of occurrences of keywords within the page, number of previous hits and links to the site from other quality sites. It is also common to pay for sponsorship to enable a page to receive an enhanced place within the results list.

Privacy of data

The vast amount of data derived from global business activities, together with the increase in Web 2.0 applications designed to encourage sharing of information, has inevitably led to issues regarding the privacy and security of personal data.

The online activities of web users can be tracked through the use of cookies. **Cookies** are computer programs designed to collect information on a user's browsing activities, which provides important information on that person's interests, preferences and so on. Although users can block the use of cookies on their machine, the ethics of the use of such programs is debatable.

Cookies are computer programs designed to collect information on a user's browsing activities, which provides important information on that person's interests, preferences and so on.

Within the working environment, technology exists that can be used to monitor the online activity of a workforce such as keystroke tracking, web browsing or email monitoring. Although various countries' legal systems offer different guidelines on how such surveillance methods can or cannot be used – and an employer may argue that they are being utilized to provide a safe working environment or safeguard intellectual property – there are still ethical arguments over employees' rights to privacy.

When dealing with the privacy and security of personal data, it is important to distinguish between the data obtained through business transactions as opposed to the voluntary sharing of personal information on social networking sites. Members of such sites are often happy to disclose their activities, likes and dislikes, which can provide a wealth of useful information for marketers. On the other hand, businesses must protect any personal data obtained during business transactions to avoid adverse disclosure or threats from security misdemeanours, such as hacking or identity theft.

Despite attempts to standardize international guidelines on privacy, to date no uniform global regulation exists, with different countries offering different guidelines or legislation on data protection and privacy (Wafa, 2009). Therefore complex privacy issues exist for data that is sent from country to country and businesses cannot assume that the legislation of the country in which they primarily operate will satisfy the requirements in other countries that they may deal with.

In a high-profile case in 2000 involving Yahoo! Inc and LICRA, the main object of contention was whether the French judicial system had the power to address content on Yahoo!'s international American website. The French legal system wanted to block content relating to the sale of Nazi memorabilia to French visitors of the website, but Yahoo! argued that while it could block the content on the French version (Yahoo.fr) of the website, it could not do the same on its international site (Yahoo.com), which is governed by American law and jurisdiction. Since both the French and the American version were freely available to French consumers, the question was how to selectively block the objectionable content to the target audience. In the end, Yahoo! was forced to accept the French court's rulings.

Management issues and strategies for web activity

It is becoming increasingly difficult for businesses to gain competitive advantage through activities such as cost cutting or mergers and acquisitions (Robinson, 2008), therefore managers must consider more innovative ways to improve business performance. The web is now an integral part of everyday life and is increasingly central to business activities. This chapter has highlighted how the web can offer many innovative business opportunities, including how it can:

- Change the business model
- Provide a wealth of information – formal and informal

- Increase market for products and services
- Improve efficiency
- Improve flexibility
- Increase mobility of the workforce
- Improve customer relations
- Increase internal and external collaboration
- Provide information for direct marketing
- Personalization of products or services.

It is crucial that managers understand the potential and role that the web may play as well as the value, impact and competitive advantage that can be gained from its effective use. The strategy for web activity must fit with the overall business strategy, otherwise any investment in time and money may be more than the potential value gained, or even be detrimental to achieving overall business goals. Therefore anyone involved in designing or setting up web activities should be aware of the overall business objectives and priorities to ensure that all activities work towards achieving the same business goals.

When designing a strategy for web activity, management must first consider the extent of the web presence required. Questions to address must include:

- What does the web presence hope to achieve?
- What extent of business operations will be conducted via the web?
- Will the web be used to widen the market – to go global?
- Who are our customers?
- How are they likely to access the web (PC or mobile)?
- Will the web presence be a 'shop-front' website for product or service information? Or will it also be used to:
  - build alliances with other businesses?
  - accept customer queries, orders or payments?
  - incorporate Web 2.0 features such as blogs, wikis and social networking?

The following sections expand on the questions that management must address when designing the strategy for web activity.

Website design and content strategy

Any business website must work towards the overall business goals and ensure that the correct business image is portrayed. Therefore a content strategy should be in place to ensure that the website reflects businesses objectives, priorities and activities. Managers must define roles and responsibilities so that content is edited and presented in a uniform manner as well as ensuring that information on the website is well written, relevant, accurate, up to date, easy to navigate and optimizes the relationship with customers. There should also be mechanisms in place that consider:

- *Search engine optimization:* can customers find appropriate information about the business when using a search engine? If the business name is entered in a search engine, it should appear towards the top of the results listing. If not, keyword advertising and sponsorship may be considered.

- *Tracking statistics:* how many people, and who, is accessing the website?
- *Cross-linking:* what other websites does the site link to and vice versa?
- *Advertising:* should there be advertising on the business website? If so, it must be consistent with the purpose and image of the website.

Interaction with other businesses

The web can be used to build alliances with other businesses, making it easier to communicate, and buy and sell to others in the supply chain. The strategy for web activity must take into consideration if the web will be used to link with other businesses and, if so, which businesses; what links will be set up for (communicating, ordering, transfer of payment and so on); and who will be responsible for setting up the alliance and ensuring security.

Interaction with customers

There are many ways that the web can be used to interact with customers, therefore the strategy for web activity must also consider if the web will be used to interact with customers and how. This may be through the ordering of products or services, payment for products or services, and communication with customers. If setting up ordering and payment systems, security is paramount and customers must be confident that their details are protected.

Communication with customers can involve simple feedback through email or feedback forms, or wider communication using Web 2.0 applications. Web 2.0 applications such as blogs, wikis or social networking can be used to generate lots of valuable information but the strategy implemented must ensure that the information is used productively and that there is a return on investment. As part of the strategy, the following must be considered:

- What type of communication is being promoted?
- What is the most appropriate application for the purpose?
- What type of content should be included?
- Who will write content and keep it up to date?
- What writing style should be adopted?
- Who will manage comments and feedback?

Management must also understand that Web 2.0 can change the type of communication and how people express themselves to one that is more sociable, open and public and is only suitable for certain types of information. Communicating openly and promoting participation with customers can be used to gain valuable feedback as well as increase customer loyalty. However, it can also lead to negative feedback from them, so any strategy for the use of Web 2.0 must consider reputation monitoring. There must be procedures in place to regularly check the web for anything that might be negative to the business and to react quickly and effectively to such negativity. This may involve responding directly to negative feedback, making visible, positive statements to counteract customer complaints, and ensuring that positive (or even neutral) information is highly visible.

Businesses must also determine the most likely technologies that customers will use to access the web. Mobile web access is increasingly common, so part of the strategy for web activity may include a mobile strategy. The business may need a different web presence for mobile access, allowing customers with mobile devices to view the content more easily. Since mobile users may be accessing the website for only specific information or features, the content of the mobile web presence must be designed accordingly. Other factors to consider may include payment via mobile devices and using GPS to offer location-specific information.

Any web strategy should take into consideration issues associated with the digital age, as highlighted above. Understanding their customers in terms of social status, education, employment, age and so on will help a business to address issues associated with the digital divide. For example, there is little point in a business developing a complex web presence if their typical customers do not have access to web technology or have the skills or desire to use it. Understanding the geography of the customer base will determine if a global web presence is required and/or the language(s) required.

Global aspects

If the web is used as a tool to conduct business on a global scale, the strategy for the web presence must address international issues. Conducting business on a global scale requires cultural awareness – not only language translation but the business practice may have to be adopted to reflect the different cultures and take account of cultural differences. Pricing policies and shipping arrangements as well as contact information may also be required locally. In addition, the web presence must satisfy the legal and data protection requirements in all countries in which the business operates. This may involve designing a different web presence for all different countries and recruiting international lawyers to ensure they adhere to legal requirements of every country.

Privacy of data

The strategy must also include procedures that consider the privacy and security associated with the storage of customer data as well as any business transactions carried out over the web. Customers must be confident that the business has security procedures in place to protect customer data and ensure that the risk of security breaches is minimized. A visible privacy policy on a website is a way of communicating the importance of security and privacy of data to customers. This may include information such as what information the business collects, how it is collected, what it is used for, how customers can view and check their own information and how they can change it, if desired.

For test questions, extra case studies, audio case studies, weblinks, video-links and more to help you understand the topics covered in this chapter, visit our companion website at www.palgrave.com/business/campbell.

VOCAB CHECKLIST FOR ESL STUDENTS

Blogs	Externalities	Shop-front website
Cookies	Infrastructure	(see 'shop front')
Digital economy	Intellectual property	Social networking
(see 'digital cash')	Memorabilia	(see 'social networking site')
E-business	Pedagogical	Wikis
E-commerce		

Definitions for these terms can be found in the 'Vocab Zone' of the companion website, which provides free access to the Macmillan English Dictionary online at www.palgrave.com/business/campbell.

REVIEW QUESTIONS

1. Explain the impact the web has had on business.
2. Explain what we mean by the digital divide and how it can be resolved.
3. Evaluate the different web technologies and explain what Web 2.0 is.

DISCUSSION TOPIC

There is a popular belief that online networking sites like Facebook are detrimental to society – 'it further alienates people'. Discuss.

HOT TOPICS – Research project areas to investigate

For your research project, why not investigate ...

- ... how organizations use Web 2.0 technology to improve customer service.
- ... the extent to which the digital divide disadvantages users of government services.
- ... how mobile technologies could be used to improve efficiency of the supply chain of a ... organization.

Recommended reading

Fuller, A. W. and Thursby, M.C (2008) 'Technology commercialization: cooperative versus competitive strategies', *Advances in the Study of Entrepreneurship, Innovation & Economic Growth*, 18: 227–50.

O'Reilly, T. (2007) 'What is Web 2.0: design patterns and business models for the next generation of software', *Communications and Strategies*, 65(1): 17–38.

Shuen, A. (2008) *Web 2.0: A Strategy Guide: Business Thinking and Strategies behind Successful Web 2.0 Implementations*, Cambridge: O'Reilly Books.

Weitz, B. A. (2001) Electronic retailing: market dynamics and entrepreneurial opportunities, in G. D. Libecap (ed.) *Entrepreneurship and Economic Growth in the American Economy*, vol. 12, Elsevier Science.

References

Ahonen, T. (2009) *Tomi Ahonen Almanac 2009: Mobile Telecoms Industry Review*, eBook, http://www.tomiahonen.com/.

Anderson, C. (2004) 'The long tail', http://www.wired.com/wired/archive/12.10/tail.html.

BBC (2009) 'Twitter tweets are 40% babble', http://news.bbc.co.uk/1/hi/technology/8204842.stm.

Cachia, R., Compano, R. and Da Costa, O. (2007) 'Grasping the potential of online social networks for foresight', *Technological Forecasting and Social Change*, **74**(8): 1179–203.

Cullen, R. (2001) 'Addressing the digital divide', *Online Information Review*, **25**(5): 311–20.

Cuneo, A. (2008) 'More football fans hit ESPN's mobile site than its PC pages', *Advertising Age*, January, https://adage.com/.

Deloitte (2003) 'Online travel agents cast their web wide', http://www.htrends.com/researcharticle7447.html.

Google (2009) 'Google becomes more local', http://googleblog.blogspot.com/2009/04/google-becomes-more-local.html.

IBM (2008) 'The enterprise of the future ... in the travel industry', http://www-935.ibm.com/services/us/gbs/bus/pdf/gbe03111-usen-ceo-travel.pdf.

Jin, L. (2009) 'Businesses using Twitter, Facebook to market goods', http://www.post-gazette.com/pg/09172/978727-96.stm.

McGlasson, L. (2008) 'Emerging technologies: mobile banking, remote capture are key to attracting gen Y', http://www.bankinfosecurity.com/articles.php?art_id=897.

Mostafa, J. (2005) 'Seeking better web searches', *Scientific American*, **292**(2): 51–7.

Roberts, G. (2007) 'Trends in mobile technology, part 2: mobile matters in real estate', http://www.taggline.com/Mobile_Matters_Part2.pdf.

Robinson, R. (2008) 'Enterprise Web 2.0, Part 1: Web 2.0 – catching a wave of business innovation', http://www.ibm.com/developerworks/webservices/library/ws-enterprise1/.

Rudebeck, C. (2009) 'Closing the digital divide: how the spread of ICT is improving quality of life for millions in the third world', http://www.independent.co.uk/news/business/sustainit/closing-the-digital-divide-1640433.html.

Sutter, J.D. (2009) 'Wallet of the future? Your mobile phone', http://www.cnn.com/2009/TECH/08/13/cell.phone.wallet/index.html?eref=rss_tech.

Vasquez, D. (2006) 'Growing ad appeal of social networks: advertisers are beginning to overcome their fears', http://www.medialifemagazine.com/cgi-bin/artman/exec/view.cgi?archive=398&num=8514.

Wafa, T. (2009) 'Cyberspace law and internet regulation – global internet privacy rights: a pragmatic approach', *University of San Francisco Intellectual Property Law Bulletin*, **13**(2): 131–58.

CHAPTER 15
What is social enterprise?

CONTENTS

KEY TOPICS

- Definitions of a social enterprise
- Types of social enterprises
- Social enterprises and their contribution to the economy

LEARNING OBJECTIVES

- Understand the nature of the for profit element
- Be aware of the size of the voluntary sector and of the importance attached to it by the UK government
- Be aware of the variety of business formats within social enterprises
- Be able to define a social enterprise

Introduction

This chapter sets the scene for understanding social enterprises within the wider business community. It looks at how policymakers currently view the role of social enterprises in the economy. At this stage, we are looking at the larger and economic issues that drive and affect the formation and performance of social enterprises and why governments and others of influence seek to encourage the 'social economy'. To help understand policy, the former Department of Trade and Industry (DTI) publication entitled *Social Enterprise: A Strategy for Success* has been used as a central plank to define how most socially orientated firms see this issue. The role of the DTI and of the Department of Business, Enterprise and Regulatory Reform (BERR) is now subsumed into the new Department for Business, Industry and Skills (BIS).

From this we will seek to present an overview of the many operational models that could be used to set up and manage a social enterprise. We will also introduce one of the comparator themes within the book: the difference between the US approach to thinking about the overall social enterprise model and the perceived different approach adopted in Europe.

Finally, this chapter will look at the scale of the social enterprise sector in the United Kingdom to highlight the importance of this significant sector within the overall economy.

The aim of this chapter is not simply to define social enterprise but to discuss the changes that are taking place in this new and emerging business format.

The need

It is easy to start any textbook on social enterprise by looking at the definitions of a social enterprise and to list the many different forms that make up our understanding of the concept. Yet what we are really examining is quite often very simple: social entrepreneurs. These are people who are inspired to believe in a social cause and who decide to do something about it. *The classic bias for action.*

To explain, we start with the phrase: 'Poverty robs us of our dignity'. However it is not just poverty that robs people. It is also hunger, disease, and waste (a waste of human life). It is not just the poverty-stricken who are directly the victims of these conditions. Because these conditions are so widespread throughout the world, they undermine all societies. At a recent executive education programme held at Wharton University many problem areas were examined.[1] One of the presentations was based on the present economic conditions in Haiti. The country is described as one of the poorest countries in the Western Hemisphere with 80 per cent of Haiti's nine million citizens living below the poverty line. People in Haiti are so poor they sometimes stave off hunger pains by eating cookies made of mud.[2] Some Haitians do have work in the sweatshops of multinational companies, working all day in various garment-manufacturing factories for about $1 a day. The conditions in Haiti can rightly be considered to be less than humane. The Haitian government really does not look like it is capable of making a significant impact with respect to the plight of its citizens. So what next?

We can, in terms of Haiti, consider what it means to really live below the poverty line in that country. This is not easy. We can also point to an example of poverty robbing people of their dignity much closer to home. In Glasgow today, 35 per cent of children are in families who are on out-of-work benefit. In the UK as a whole this figure is 20 per cent. These children are considered to be living in poverty based on the criteria of the family being on out-of-work benefit (see www.ecpc.org.uk).

While the Haitian government is likely to be classed as a failed government, would we also classify the UK Government and the Scottish Executive as failed governments? Both Tony Blair and Gordon Brown, really, in this case, do seem to mean it when they set eradicating child poverty as a main goal of government. In June 2009 Prime Minister Gordon Brown introduced into parliament a Child Poverty Bill with the aim of taking 4 million children out of poverty by 2020. But fortunately (perhaps) the government does now seem to realize that it cannot solve things by itself and is actively embracing the idea of 'The Third Sector'.

Changes in society

Someone once said that the poor are always with us. The same could be said for hunger, disease, and waste. Today we are as a society much less likely to think that governments should and can solve these issues. We also have less confidence in institutions to solve these problems. To some extent in parallel with this view, there is more of a desire and belief that as individuals – social entrepreneurs, people within a social enterprise, people who care about others and about society – we can make a difference in what can be done. In the case of Haiti there is a clear need for alternative forms of enterprise based on improving the income and health not only of individuals but of whole communities.

In the case of OneWorld Health, $10 for a course of treatment can stop someone dying from the second most deadly parasitic disease in the world after malaria. The Aravind Eye Care system saves thousands of people from blindness for the cost of a few dollars.

Definitions of a social enterprise

Within the entrepreneurship and small firms' literature definitions are a thorny question. Those familiar with Winnie the Pooh might be familiar with the 'heffalump':

> [A] rather large and important animal. He has been hunted by many individuals using various trapping devices, but no-one so far has succeeded in capturing him. All who claim to have caught sight of him report he is enormous, but disagree on his particularities.
>
> (Kilby, 1979)[3]

The (social) entrepreneur 'heffalump', but the main focus throughout the book is less on the individual entrepreneur and more on the social enterprises that they form. The management question addressed is what would make these ventures succeed and how different are they from other forms of (small) business.

Within the UK there is a basic consensus on what constitutes a social enterprise. The most common definition that appears in texts written about social enterprise is

> [a] social enterprise is a business with primarily social objectives whose surpluses are reinvested for that purpose in the business or in the community, rather than being driven by the need to maximise profit for shareholders and owners.
>
> (DTI, 2002)[4]

This definition is derived from the DTI's *Social Enterprise: A Strategy for Success* published in July 2002. By this definition a social enterprise is a business that conducts trade in the market in order to fulfil its social aims. This means that it does not exist for the primary purpose of creating a profit for its owners in the way a conventional business would do. Instead it reinvests its surplus to achieve a specified social purpose.

> Simply put, a social enterprise is a business venture that brings people and communities together for economic development and social gain.

Because it is considered a business rather than a charity, the social enterprise is expected to generate a surplus and that surplus is to be used for the benefit of the community that it serves. There are however, many forms that social enterprises can adopt in order to define more clearly their purpose for various categories. These categories are as follows: community enterprises, cooperatives, development trusts, charities with trading arms, credit unions, social businesses, mutuals, fair trade organizations, and social firms. Social enterprises are part of the wider social economy. Pearce (2003) adopts a three-system framework to the economy. System 1 covers the private system; System 2 covers the public planned economy; and System 3 being the third system, covering self-help, mutual and social purpose organizations. There is some confusion here over what is meant by the social economy, social enterprises, and the third sector, as these terms are used interchangeably.

We prefer a four system model: government, the private sector, and the voluntary sector, with for-profit social enterprise straddling all the others, seeking at times to be independent through the build up of income streams from a mixture of grants and funding from the other three.

While we are dealing with the wider social enterprise model we are concerned to define one category in particular within social enterprise, namely the social firm. In part this is to prevent confusion between the two – the social enterprise and the social firm. Example 15.1 provides a fuller outline of the role of social firms.

EXAMPLE 15.1   The role of social firms

[A] social firm is a small business that provides employment opportunities for people who are disabled or disadvantaged in the labour market. Social firms have both commercial and social objectives. They operate in the market place generating income through sales of goods or services and they also employ a significant number of employees who have a disability who are fully integrated into the business. Social firms have a focus on developing a flexible, supportive working environment within a commercial operation. (Davister, Defourny & Gregoire, 2004)[5]

A good example of a for-profit social enterprise in action is to be found in the community-based operations of The McSence Group, provided as Minicase 15.1.

MINICASE 15.1 The McSence Group

It was back in 1984 that Brian Tannerhill, a local resident in Mayfield, Midlothian, first initiated the idea of forming a Community Business that would provide employment and services to his local community. This business was to be called Mayfield Community Self Employed Natural Collective Exercise or, more simply, McSence.

The support of local businesses was crucial to the early development of McSence. At the outset Brian Tannerhill persuaded local traders to commit £5 per week for the first year as a contribution to the start up costs of the community owned business on the condition that it did not compete with any of the contributors. This initiative raised £7500 and resulted in local business people being invited onto the Board to provide invaluable business experience.

Since those early days, McSence has grown into a group of companies that employs over 50 local people and generates an annual turnover of approximately £1.2 million. These companies include McSence Heatwise, McSence Limited, McSence Services, McSence Workspace and McSence CyberCycle that cover insulation, office cleaning, renting of workspaces to local community groups and local businesses and training and employment initiatives for local people.

Profits generated by the companies are ploughed back into the local community with recent examples being the provision of a youth centre and sports equipment for local youngsters.

Source: www.sensscot.net and www.mcsence.co.uk, accessed December 2008.

McSence was set up in response to the devastating effect of the 1984 coal miners' strike to create employment that would pay wages to local people. McSence was started entirely by private funding without any government grant or subsidy and continues to be a business run for the community by the community. Any profits made by the five operating companies are passed back to McSence Limited and this money is used to invest in new ventures for job creation for local people and in the form of community grants.

Chris Shaw, Chairman of the Board of McSence Limited

Question

1. To what extent is McSence the model of the ideal viable social enterprise?
2. What should be the future business development of McSence?

The characteristics of social enterprises

The DTI definition implies a series of characteristics that distinguish this form of enterprise. These characteristics have been referred to as 'triple bottom lines' – aims that have been adopted by the social enterprise community to distinguish them from for-profit small businesses (Social Enterprise London)[6] see Figure 15.1.

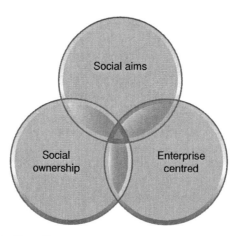

Figure 15.1 The triple bottom lines

Social aims

Social enterprises exist to serve a social purpose and in order to achieve this they conduct some form of trade. These social aims should be explicit and might include job creation, training or the provision of local services. Associated with the social aims social enterprises can be expected to have ethical values that might include local capacity building or addressing social disadvantage. They are accountable to their members and the wider community for their social, environmental and economic impact. They are also independent from public sector ownership and this makes them accountable to community stakeholders.

Social ownership

Unlike a conventional business social enterprises are not constituted to distribute profits to individuals but instead they hold their assets and income sources in trust for use by the community they serve. These are autonomous organizations that have governance and ownership structures based on participation by stakeholder groups (users or clients, and local community groups etc.). Profits are distributed for the benefit of the community or as profit sharing to stakeholders.

Enterprise centred

Social enterprises are directly involved in the production of goods or the provision of services to a market. They seek to be commercially viable trading concerns that make an operating surplus. While social enterprises may earn income from public service contracts and sales, they are not directly managed. It is the combination of these three factors: social aims, social ownership, and enterprise centred that defines the scope of their activities. Social enterprises are *hybrid* organizations that are expected to perform in the market like a small business but which retain the management ethos and values of locally defined charitable organizations. The tag 'triple bottom lines' may explain why this is an emerging term that is becoming used for a range of voluntary organizations that make the transition from a charitable to an enterprise orientation. In other words, a social enterprise does not just exist to create shareholder value through increased profitability, but encompasses a wider community stakeholder value of social awareness and environmental responsibility.

When putting together two words with meanings as broad as 'social' and 'enterprise', it generates confusion, especially at the international level.

This may in part explain the different approaches to supporting social enterprises in the US and Europe. This difference of approach will be referred to further in this chapter. It also points to a paradox. A social enterprise can be viewed as a new form of business organization but it is one that is derived from two existing forms of business: small business and not-for-profit organizations. Social enterprises are hybrids and as hybrids they can be expected to inherit both the good and the bad forms of their for-profit and not-for-profit business cousins. They can be seen as being halfway between the two since they have dual objectives: to make a profit for their stakeholders (in their community) and to contribute to the broader social good, while making a surplus.

Because of this paradox, social enterprises can be expected to play down their levels of profit-making in order to emphasize their social and environmental values. In terms of competitiveness, and unlike their small business counterparts, they can be expected to be more co-operative with other social enterprises – working to achieve specified social gains within the community. Given the limitations of access to support and funding, co-operation is often more of an ideal than a reality in the social enterprise economy.

Types of social enterprises

Social enterprises combine the need to be successful businesses with social aims. Unlike profit-orientated SMEs they, ideally, will emphasize the long-term benefits for employees, consumers, and the community. They come in a range of business formats but the most common factor is that they are mostly, but not exclusively, local and community-based organizations. Their format encompasses community enterprises and mutual organizations such as co-operatives, alongside non-governmental organizations. As yet the format does not facilitate working, or co-operating internationally. Even within the European Union levels and opportunities for multi-lateral co-operation between the 27 member countries, remain limited.

Types and terminology

Within the UK, there is no single legal model for social enterprise. Social enterprises can encompass companies limited by guarantee, industrial, and provident societies, and companies limited by shares; some organizations are unincorporated and others are registered charities (DTI, 2002).

The following list is taken from the Development Trusts Association and encompasses the types of firms and terminology often associated with the social economy.[7]

SEL 'social enterprise' definitions

(a) Community business

A trading organization which is set up, owned, and controlled by the local community and which aims to create ultimately self-supporting jobs for local people and to be a focus for local development. The term community business is normally used for social enterprises that have a strong geographical definition and focus on local markets and local services.

(b) Community Development Financial Institution (CDFI)

A financial services provider (possibly a community based bank, community loan fund or a community development venture fund) which has a mission to achieve social objectives. Some CDFI's will focus specifically on financial services for business and social economy organizations rather than on the needs of individuals. They may provide equity, quasi-equity or debt services. While some UK CDFI's are regulated as banks or building societies, most do not have deposit-taking status. The legal forms most often used are the Industrial and Provident Society (IPS) and, in association with charitable status, the company limited by guarantee.

(c) Co-operative

An autonomous association of persons united voluntarily to meet their common economic, social, and cultural needs and aspirations through a jointly owned and democratically controlled enterprise. An Industrial and Provident Society is a body incorporated under the Industrial and Provident Societies Acts, including most Co-operatives, quasi-charitable societies for the benefit of the community, and some development trusts.

(d) Micro-finance

Small savings and loans facilities with no (or very low) minimum deposit; and other financial services like insurance, money transfer or bill payment designed for people on low incomes.

(e) Mutuals

They take many forms: credit unions, co-operatives, building societies, and employee-owned businesses. They are organized by their members who band together with the common purpose of providing a shared service for which they all benefit.

(f) Non-profit or not-for-profit

These terms are commonly used to describe organizations which do not distribute profits, although they seek to make an operating surplus.

(g) Social business

A term sometimes used by social enterprises where there is a small core of members who act in a similar way to trustees. These social businesses often focus on providing an income or employment opportunity for disadvantaged groups, or providing a service to the community.

(h)   Social firm

A small business created to provide integrated employment and training to people with a disability or other disadvantage in the labour market. It is a business, which uses the market-orientated production of goods and services to pursue its social mission. A significant number of its employees will be people with a disability or other disadvantage in the labour market. Every worker is paid a market wage or salary appropriate to the job, whatever his/her productive capacity. Work opportunities are distributed equally between disadvantaged and non-disadvantaged employees. All employees have the same employment rights and obligations.

http://www.dta.org.uk/resources/glossary/selsocialenteprisedefinitions.htm (accessed in June 2009)

For the purposes of this book the working definition of a social enterprise is provided as Example 15.2

EXAMPLE 15.2   Definition of a social enterprise

A social enterprise is a business venture that brings people and communities together for economic development and social gain.
Because it is a business, it is expected to generate a surplus and that surplus is to be used for the benefit of the community that it serves.

The defining characteristics are provided as Example 15.3.

EXAMPLE 15.3   Social enterprise defining characteristics

Social aims
Social enterprises trade as a means of achieving these.

'Non-profit distributing'
Profits are reserved for reinvestment.
Social enterprise is not about amassing personal wealth.

Exercise some form of 'common ownership'
Usually owned in common by members and/or stakeholders.
Have some form of **democratic involvement** in management/decision making.

Exercise wider accountability
May be answerable to a 'constituency' of users, members, or stakeholders – sometimes a mixture of all three.
Tend to serve local communities.

Operational models in the US

Virtue Ventures, a US-based consulting firm specializing in social enterprise, have produced the following list of social enterprise operational business models:

- Entrepreneur support: The entrepreneur support model of social enterprise sells business support and financial services to its target population or 'clients', self-employed individuals or firms.
- Market intermediary: The market intermediary model of social enterprise provides services to its target population or 'clients', small producers (individuals, firm or cooperatives), to help them access markets.
- Employment: The employment model of social enterprise provides employment opportunities and job training to its target populations or 'clients', people with high barriers to employment such as disabled, homeless, at-risk youth, and ex-offenders.
- Fee-for-Service: The fee-for-service model of social enterprise commercializes its social services, and then sells them directly to the target populations or 'clients', individuals, firms, communities, or to a third party payer.
- Low-income client: The low-income client as Market model of social enterprise is a variation on the Fee-for-Service model, which recognizes the target population or 'clients' a market to sell goods or services.
- Cooperative: The cooperative model of social enterprise provides direct benefit to its target population or 'clients', cooperative members, through member services: market information, technical assistance/extension services, collective bargaining power, economies of bulk purchase, access to products and services, access to external markets for member-produced products and services, etc.
- Market linkage: The market linkage model of social enterprise facilitates trade relationships between the target population or 'clients', small producers, local firms and cooperatives, and the external market.
- Service subsidization: The service subsidization model of social enterprise sells products or services to an external market and uses the income it generates to fund its social programmes. The service subsidization model is usually integrated: business activities and social programmes overlap, sharing costs, assets, operations, income and often programme attributes.
- Organizational support: The organizational support model of social enterprise sells products and services to an external market, businesses or the general public.

Source: www.virtueventures/setypology (accessed in June 2009)

In addition, time and practice and the development of the social enterprise will mean that the very specific operational definitions given above will change and that we will see the combination of models to capture opportunities in both commercial markets and social sectors. Combining is a strategy to maximize social impact as well as diversify income by reaching new markets or creating new enterprises. In practice, most experienced social enterprises combine models, as few social enterprise operational models exist in their pure form. Operational models are like building blocks that can be arranged to best achieve an organization's financial and social objectives.

Model combinations occur within a social enterprise (complex model) or at the level of the parent organization (mixed model). An example of each of the model combinations is shown as Minicase 15.2 Cambiando Vidas (complex model) and Minicase 15.3 The Carvajal Foundation (mixed model).

MINICASE 15.2   Cambiando Vidas

Cambiando Vidas (an example of a Complex Model social enterprise)
In 1999 a new paved highway opened along Mexico's formally isolated coastal fishing villages in Nayarit State. This opened up the area to tourists, and consequently, to large developers. The result was a dramatic shift in the local economy from fishing and agriculture to tourism and infrastructure development. The shift displaced local residents, most of whom are poorly educated peasants who lacked the know-how and capital to capture the changing market. In response, Cambiando Vidas – 'Changing Lives', an educational organization – launched a comprehensive, multi-faceted rural development programme with complementary enterprise and social service components to preserve the local community and provide new livelihoods for its residents. Cambiando Vidas built a 'tool lending library' where residents could borrow hand and power tools and use them as implements in economic activities tied to tourism and construction. The second social component was a vocational training programme to teach construction skills – masonry, electrics, plumbing, and carpentry – to unemployed youth and adults in the community. On the enterprise side, Cambiando Vidas has initiated a B&B project and built (so far) six comfortable tourist rooms above residents' homes. Income from room rental is divided between owners as family income, and a revolving loan fund to build more B&B rooms. Apprentices from the vocational training programme provide the labour to build the B&Bs and gain work experience in the process. Cambiando Vidas plan to create local employment by launching a construction business and bidding directly on small building contracts, where it has identified a viable niche, as well as subcontracting to large developers. Profit from the construction business will be used to fund the secondary education and vocational training programme.

http:// www. virueventures.com/setypology/index,accessed in December 2008.

Question

1. Conduct a SWOT analysis on Cambiando Vidas. What does it tell you?

MINICASE 15.3   The Carvajal Foundation

Encouraging self-help in Colombia (mixed model)
The Carvajal Foundation, established in 1961, is one of the oldest and best examples of social enterprise in the Latin American region. The foundation was launched through a sizeable donation by the Carvajal Family, which donated 35.54 per cent

of its shares in its successful Colombian business operations. For more than four decades, the foundation has engaged in social development, mobilizing volunteers and large donations to catalyse change in the poorest communities across Cali. Carvajal's accomplishments include community-based programmes at the local level as well as national programmes, all of which have developed promising practices and economic development models that have been shared and replicated by other business and community groups in Colombia and elsewhere in Latin America.

As a social enterprise, the Carvajal Foundation has a firm commitment to its social mission to combat poverty on all fronts, and to deliver solutions that address community problems. The foundation's mission to realize the full development of individual potential is achieved mainly through education, entrepreneurial development, health care, housing, culture and arts, and environmental programmes, and incorporates business criteria into its activities, seeking to maximize operational efficiency and effectiveness.

Source: http://www.virtueventures.com/setypology/index, accessed in December 2008.

Question

1. Using the Internet to review the work of the Carvajal Foundation, compare and contrast it with the operation of Cambiando Vidas.
2. What are the similarities and differences between these two models of social enterprise?

Based on the cases above, it becomes evident that social enterprises:

1. Facilitate enterprise or social programme growth.
2. Increase revenues by entering new markets or businesses.
3. Augment breath or depth of social impact by reaching more people in need or new target populations.

In this sense a social enterprise is an amalgam of different types of not-for-profit organizations. Each of the formats listed have specific structural differences in how they are organized. But, it is not appropriate to classify them according to a legal definition, based on articles of associations or taxable status. It is the element of looking outside the legal status of a business, and the elements of community engagement and creating access for the disadvantaged that make the format distinct from those of smaller firms that trade for profit. Instead, the social enterprise can be seen as a value-based marketing organization that ethically addresses failures in the delivery of services to vulnerable groups within its communities. It does this by responding to a commercial imperative – setting up commercial trading operations that allow it to function independently.

For an example of the role of a social enterprise in helping a vulnerable group of people, in this case young Australians with mental health problems, please read Minicase 15.4 on The Inspire Foundation.

MINICASE 15.4   The Inspire Foundation

In late 1992, when a young man took his life on an Australian farm in north-eastern Victoria it had a huge impact on the young man's family and friends, – one of them was his cousin Jack Heath. At the time Jack was working in Parliament House Canberra as a Senior Adviser to Prime Minister Keating. In the prime minister's office, Jack was involved in the formulation of the multimedia initiatives detailed in the Government's major arts and communications policy statement, 'Creative Nation'. Daniel Petre, Michael Rennie and David Harrington played a key role with Jack in constructing those initiatives – Daniel was then head of Microsoft Australia and Michael and David were working for management consultants McKinsey & Company. In early 1995 Jack took leave from the Prime Minister's office. During that time he reflected on his own life and aspirations and the increasing number of youth suicides in Australia. When the Microsoft Network was first established, international figures participated in live chat sessions to encourage people to take up the new technology. From his home in Canberra, Jack joined people around the world in a chat session with American mind-body specialist Dr Deepak Chopra in San Francisco. Dr Chopra responded to a number of questions posed by Jack and, excited by the immediacy of the response and potential power of the technology, Jack called Daniel Petre. Familiar with Jack's concerns about the rising rates of youth suicide in Australia, Daniel suggested that Jack should consider doing something about this pressing social issue by harnessing the power of the Internet.

Microsoft then generously provided some seed funding that enabled the development of a prototype of the Reach Out service. In late 1996 Paul Gilding, who had recently returned to Australia after serving as Head of Greenpeace International, joined Jack, Michael and then Alexandra Yuille in formally establishing what is now the Inspire Foundation.

From this initiative, Reach Out was established to carry out the mission of helping young Australians lead happier lives through improved mental health. Reach Out is a web-based initiative to help the 480,000 Australians aged 18–24 living with an anxiety or substance abuse disorder. Funding for the work of Reach Out comes from public subscription and from community based fundraising.

Source: http://www.inspire.org.au and http://www.reachout.com.au, accessed June 2009.

Question

1. The Inspire Foundation has a national mission. Is there an essential difference in how a social enterprise with a national mission will seek to work as opposed to a more localized social enterprise?
2. What were the key building blocks in the creation of the Inspire Foundation?

The third sector and its contribution to the economy

Regardless of how social enterprises see themselves, government and policymakers see a different picture. The 'third sector' is increasingly referred to by politicians as *the* solution to engaging communities. Third sector organizations can be described as the organizations and groups that occupy the space between the state, the citizens and the private sphere, what is sometimes referred to as nongovernmental organizations, non-profit organizations or simply civil society (Cabinet Office, 2008).[8] Social enterprises are one of the key players within the third sector.

The following is extracted from an HM Treasury report from the United Kingdom *The Future Role of the Third Sector in Social and Economic Integration* (HM, July 2007).[9]

> The third sector is a vital component of a fair and enterprising society, where individuals and communities feel empowered and enabled to achieve change and to meet social and environmental needs. The Government recognizes the value of the diversity of organizations in the sector in providing a voice for under-represented groups, in campaigning for change, in creating strong, active and connected communities, in promoting enterprising solutions to social and environmental challenges and in transforming the delivery and design of public services. The third sector has always been at the heart of social and environmental change and the Government wants to continue to work to create the conditions where organizations can grow and achieve their aims.

The same report notes that

> the third sector makes an enormous contribution to our society, economy and environment. Hundreds of thousands of organizations and millions of volunteers make a practical difference in communities, from working with young people to developing new ways of recycling household waste.
>
> (1.10)

The third sector, sometimes referred to as not-for-profit organizations, is the term applied to the wider voluntary sector. It is noted that of the 166,000 registered charities in the UK there are *'around 55,000 social enterprises'*, according to the Annual Small Business Survey by the DTI (2005).[10] In essence the survey stated that what the UK government seeks is a partnership that ensures that *'public services are able to improve further by fully drawing on the understanding and experience of third sector in designing, developing and delivering services'*.

> [S]ocial enterprise offers radical new ways of operating for public benefit. By combining strong public service ethos with business acumen, we can open up the possibility of entrepreneurial organizations – highly responsive to customers and with the freedom of the private sector – but which are driven by a commitment to public benefit rather than purely maximising profits for shareholders.

From this discussion, it is apparent that the role of social enterprises within the UK economy is changing and changing quickly. The speed of this change may explain the interchangeability of the terminology that applies to social enterprises. With the rapid growth in the sector, it is inevitable that there would be concerns over assessing the impact of social enterprises.

The strategy for social enterprise within the United Kingdom

Within the Cabinet Office is the Office of the Third Sector. The Office of the Third Sector's responsibilities include national policy on social enterprise. The policy view from the Cabinet Office is based on the need to ensure that social enterprise activity is focused on working across government to create an environment in the UK for social enterprises to thrive. 'Our vision is of a dynamic and sustainable social enterprise sector contributing to a stronger economy and a fairer society.'

The government's commitments to supporting social enterprise are set out in the *Social Enterprise Action Plan*, which includes actions to raise awareness of social enterprise, ensure social enterprises have the right support, advice and finance, and enable them to work with government.

In 2007 The Office of the Third Sector commissioned a report into how the impact of the social enterprise sector could be assessed.

> It is the view of the report's authors that it is the very diversity of the sector that will make it difficult to assess its impact. Official research from the DTI (2005) shows that social enterprises employ more than 775,000 people in the UK and are operating in a diverse range of trades. The research also shows that UK social enterprises have an annual turnover of £18 billion. While they are found across the country, 22% are in London. Only half of all social enterprises operate in areas of high deprivation, with about 49% working in more affluent wards.
>
> (Hart and Houghton, 2007)

The question is whether the public-private partnership within a social economy is particular to the UK. Young (2000) identified five inter-related trends within the developed economies.[11]

Young argues that non-profit organizations are adjusting their business models to create earned income and developing their own commercial independence from traditional public sector funding sources. 'Within the US this is generally recognized as having given impetus to social purpose enterprises in which revenue generated businesses are owned and operated by non-profit organization's for the express purpose of employing at risk or disadvantaged individuals' (Young, 2000).

In this context please consider Minicase 15.2 Cambiando Vidas and Minicase 15.3 The Carvajal Foundation.

He also notes that that the relationship between profit and non-profit organization has become closer as they both collaborate in terms of social and environmental projects. In economic terms, the expectations for the social economy remain high. When the UK, the US and even the United Nations embrace the concept, it means that the changes can be expected to accelerate.

'[S]ocial enterprises' ... offer a solidarity-based model of organization to help their members achieve their socio-economic goals, through the creation of employment, provision of financial services, and promotion of social integration. These organizations also empower community members and encourage social change through responsible citizenship that exercises control over production, consumption, savings, investment, and exchange.

(Ocampo, 2007)[12]

What is not in doubt, it would seem, is the willingness of governments to support social enterprise, and the question to be addressed is about these support mechanisms. Should they be the same or should they be different to those available to small businesses as a whole?

Example 15.4 provides a summary of the issues covered in this chapter.

EXAMPLE 15.4   What is social enterprise?

There are a number of different definitions.

This is an emerging area of study. Definitions overlap.

Focus is on the business not the entrepreneurial individual as a means to success.

Triple bottom Line has been adapted to mean Social Aims, Social Ownership & Enterprise.

Paradoxically a social enterprise will play down profit-making to emphasize their social and environmental values.

Legal Models include amalgams of community businesses, co-operatives and social firms.

Government has its own perspective on the role and emphasizes support for disadvantaged groups, regeneration and 'public good'.

Revision questions

- Of the operational models listed in this chapter, can you identify a social enterprise to match each model?
- Which type of social enterprise is (a) McSence and (b) Inspire?
- What might a government hope to gain from a policy of actively supporting social enterprise?
- Is there an essential difference in how financial support should be assessed between small businesses and social enterprises?

Additional reading

Bridge, S., Murtagh, B. and O'Neill, K., *Understanding the Social Economy and the Third Sector* (Basingstoke: Palgrave Macmillan, 2009).

Dees, J., Emerson, J. and Economy, P., *Strategic Tools for Social Entrepreneurs* (New York: Wiley, 2002).

Hart, T. and Houghton, G., *Assessing the Economic and Social Impacts of Social Enterprise: Feasibility Report*, Office of the Third Sector, 2007. See www.cabinetoffice.gov.uk/third_sector and www. hull.ac.uk/ccrs.

Pearce, J., *Social Enterprise in Anytown* (London: Gulbenkian Foundation, 2003), p. 25. http://www. virtueventures.com/setypology/index.

References

1. Wharton Business School, University of Pennsylvania, *Eradicating Mud Cookies: Global Executives Try to Connect Profit to Social Good*. From http://knowledge.whartin.upenn.edu/article. cfm?articleid=2277, accessed in July 2009.
2. A video by CNN exists of this happening.
3. P. Kilby, *Entrepreneurship and Economic Development* (New York: Free Press, 1979), p. 40.
4. Department of Trade and Industry (DTI), *Social Enterprise: A Strategy for Success* (London: DTI, 2002).
5. C. Davister, J. Defourny & O. Gregoire (2004) 'Integration of Social enterprises in the European Union: An Overview of Existing Models', International Society for Third Sector Research, Toronto, Canada, 2004.
6. Social Enterprise London, available at http://www.sel.org.uk/knowledge.html, accessed in June 2009.
7. Development Trust Association, see http://www.dta.org.uk/, accessed in June 2009.
8. Cabinet Office, 'Better Together, Improving Consultation in the Third sector', 2008. Available as a download at http://www.cabinetoffice.gov.uk/media/99612/better%20together.pdf, accessed in June 2009.
9. HM Treasury, *The Future Role of the Third Sector in Social and Economic Regeneration*, July 2007, Cabinet Office Cm7189.
10. Annual Small Business Survey, 2005, DTI available, from http://www.berr.gov.uk/files/file38237. pdf, accessed in June 2009.
11. D. R. Young, *Alternative Models of Government-Nonprofit Relations. Nonprofit and Voluntary Sector Quarterly*, vol. 29 no.1 (2000), pp. 149–72.
12. Statement by Mr. José Antonio Ocampo, Under-Secretary-General for Economic and Social Affairs to the Civil Society Forum on 'Employment Working for All: Partners in Innovation', New York, 3 February 2007. Available at http://www.un.org/esa/desa/ousg/statements/2007/20070203_civil_society_forum.html.

Index